TRANSATLANTIC SUBJECTS

Transatlantic Subjects

Ideas, Institutions, and Social Experience in Post-Revolutionary British North America

EDITED BY NANCY CHRISTIE

McGill-Queen's University Press
Montreal & Kingston • London • Ithaca

ISBN 978-0-7735-3334-9 (cloth)
ISBN 978-0-7735-3388-2 (paper)

Legal deposit second quarter 2008
Bibliothèque nationale du Québec

Printed in Canada on acid-free paper that is 100% ancient forest
free (100% post-consumer recycled), processed chlorine free

This book has been published with the help of a grant from the
Canadian Federation for the Humanities and Social Sciences,
through the Aid to Scholarly Publications Programme, using funds
provided by the Social Sciences and Humanities Research Council
of Canada. Funding has also been received from the Department of
History, McMaster University.

McGill-Queen's University Press acknowledges the support of the
Canada Council for the Arts for our publishing program. We also
acknowledge the financial support of the Government of Canada
through the Book Publishing Industry Development Program
(BPIDP) for our publishing activities.

Library and Archives Canada Cataloguing in Publication

Transatlantic subjects : ideas, institutions, and social experience
in post-revolutionary British North America / edited by Nancy
Christie.

Includes bibliographical references.
ISBN 978-0-7735-3334-9 (bnd)
ISBN 978-0-7735-3388-2 (pbk)

1. Canada – History – 1763–1867. 2. Canada – Civilization – British
influences. 3. Canada – Relations – Great Britain. 4. Great Britain –
Relations – Canada. I. Christie, Nancy, 1958–

FC400.T73 2008   971.03   C2007-907087-6

Typeset by Jay Tee Graphics Ltd. in 10/12 Baskerville

Contents

J.G.A. POCOCK

Foreword

The invitation to write this preface has been not only an honour but an opportunity to enlarge my understanding of Canadian history. I am not Canadian and am a novice (till now a stranger) in the field of Canadian history; but I begin to see what it has been and what may be its place among the many histories, emerging, converging, and diverging, that go to make up British history as we are beginning to understand it. The premise and paradox of this historical field is that the term "British" is, and has always been, problematic; historians need to know what they mean by it, and the actors they study gave it more than one meaning and used it in more than one way. Yet its problematicity provides its continuity, and we need to avoid the assumptions that the problematic is necessarily fragile, and that the questionable is always about to run out of answers. If we ask what "British" has meant, we will be given many answers; that these answers cannot be reduced to singularity does not mean that they will cease to be given.

Upper and Lower Canada, Nova Scotia, and New Brunswick may not, in the period of this volume, have been collectively known as "Canada"; it is a question, to be answered by historians, when this entity began to be spoken of. The subtitle before us speaks of "British North America" – on the other coast of the American continent there began to be something that would be called "British Columbia" – and it is the adjective "British" that the following chapters explore. Its use denotes a continuity that was more than a survival. We conventionally speak of "the fall of the first British empire," "the loss of the American colonies," and so on; but in the Laurentian region (and, in another history, the Caribbean) there continues to be a British America, and we do not fully understand the history of the American Revolution unless we recognize that "Canada" was one of its outcomes. This is probably a commonplace to Canadian historians, but those of the United States are not the only community that needs to be reminded of it. The history of Quebec and the anglophone provinces can, of course, be narrated as that of a contested identity known as "Canada," but the present volume focuses on the history of "British North America" and explores the meanings and usabilities of the first adjective.

This is why *Transatlantic Subjects* is a contribution to "British history," and to the associated field known as "Atlantic history." Nancy Christie's introduction explores the several ways in which the collection acts upon both, but in this preface I should like to consider how each may be redrawn in the light of what this volume has achieved. Clearly the history of these colonies, particularly in the decade of the 1830s, was shaped by problems shared with, or exported from, the metropolitan state; this is why we are reading a "British history." How should, or must, the latter be presented in order to make intelligible what was happening in British North America? This volume reveals the extent to which these problems were confessional in character: problems of the relation between religious associations and civil or imperial authority. I do not need to affirm that these problems dominated Canadian history in order to recognize that they were present and important. The organization of British history for which they call is founded on the concept of a "long" – indeed a very long – "eighteenth century," defined, in terms for which we are indebted to J.C.D. Clark, as an age, beginning in and after 1660, when the historic constitution, including an institutionalized aristocracy and the parliamentary structure we whiggishly call "unreformed," was restored in conjunction with an episcopal and monarchical church, membership in which was a prerequisite to full membership in the English political order. Scotland achieved in 1689, and retained in 1707, a Presbyterian order in church and state of which similar things may be said. A reconquered Ireland remained largely Catholic, in a condition of latent ethnic and religious conflict which exploded briefly in 1798.

Transatlantic Subjects persuades me that Canadian history requires a framing of British history in which the "long eighteenth century" so defined must be carried down to the early middle of the nineteenth century and seen to conclude with a series of disruptions of the confessional state, beginning with Catholic emancipation in 1829 – itself a consequence of the union with Ireland in 1801 – and concluding with the Disruption of the Scottish kirk in 1843. The essays in this volume depict British settlers in what became Canada as responding in a variety of ways to these convulsions, not forgetting a transatlantic disruption in the Methodist connection as it moved away from John Wesley's high-church Toryism toward the culture of Nonconformity. That these disturbances in British North America were acute enough to entail actual rebellions, however, necessitates a further restatement of British history: the recognition that the last fifty or sixty years of the "long eighteenth century" were a period of counter-revolution, of reaction against perhaps the American and certainly the French Revolutions, in which the military, aristocratic, and ecclesiastical powers of the state were mobilized (not without elements of popular support) in defence of order, authority, and subordination. The fact that the history of British North America contains attempts to institutionalize a provincial aristocracy and established church, and radical opposition to both, has a significance independent of its weight in the formation of events. We are in a phase of "British history" in which these issues are living ones, and the journey from the Toryism and Loyalism of the 1790s to the relative liberalism of the 1840s is not predetermined.

To see the history of British North America as an extension of British history, so conceived, is to include both in an "Atlantic history," currently proposed and examined by David Armitage, Eliga H. Gould, and other historians; and here we must consider British history as the history of empire in many meanings of that word. The conventional transition from a "first British empire" to a "second" is the passage from an American empire to an Indian; but to understand "Atlantic history" we must attend rather to that maritime empire of naval bases, trading posts, and a few colonies, distributed across the planet by a British naval supremacy neither Revolution could shake. This global power is the occasion of the "second empire" studied by C.A. Bayly and others, and empire in India is a third entity interacting with it. Oceanic empire is a presence in the North Atlantic and ensures that the provinces of British North America are situated in a British history, an Atlantic history, and an American history, overlapping one another. Here, however, we must take account of a further element constituting "empire" of yet another kind: a flow of English, Scottish, and Irish (at this stage mainly Protestant) emigration, large and lasting enough to do much toward populating the expanding United States and establishing colonies of settlement at several points on the globe. If British Canada was settled in part by Loyalist and other emigrants from (or by way of) the United States, it was also populated by emigrants of this new kind, and it is they who do much to give it the character of a "British history." Indeed, the essays in this volume convey a dominant impression that the religious and political problems disturbing the colonies of Upper Canada were derived from those disturbing the British state at the end of the long eighteenth century, and very little from those of its independent and federal neighbour; it is British history that *Transatlantic Subjects* both obliges and encourages the reader to study.

There was once a convention of grouping categories of settlement that became Canada with those being contemporaneously established in the southern hemisphere, as constituting a field of study termed "Commonwealth history" or "the history of the white Dominions." I leave this volume, however, convinced that I have been reading a "British," "Atlantic," and "American" history, more closely tied to all these fields than were any of the colonies in the Southern Ocean (it was in this pelagic region, south of the two Capes, rather than in the Pacific basin, that these initially took shape). Perhaps the Pacific coast provinces that became Canadian are another story. Were not Victoria and Vancouver colonized by seaborne pakeha like those of Wellington or Melbourne? But New South Wales was only marginally a Georgian foundation, and post-1840 New Zealand was inescapably Victorian; it is hard to find in high southern latitudes the echoes of Paine and Cobbett that seem to make William Lyon Mackenzie a survivor from the world of E.P. Thompson. *Transatlantic Subjects* is a British history in an immediate and integral way that perhaps could not survive the voyage to the near-antipodes of Britain; the Britishness of the southern hemisphere was differently planted. Britain's maritime supremacy operated in more than one climate and more than one age; the long eighteenth century and its end are not the keys to its consequences everywhere.

These essays and the title under which they have been collected are much governed by the important but dangerous concept of "identity." In another place[1] I have argued that it is too easy to employ this concept in ways which overstress its contingency and presuppose its disappearance. I suggest that it is perhaps better – we are in an ideological debate – to have a history and be able to live in it. The peoples settling Upper Canada and the Maritimes in the third decade of the nineteenth century, I have learned from this volume, were in advance of me here; they defined their "Britishness" from their mixed origins in that union of multiple identities[2] and from their vigorous and articulate involvement in the religious and political contentions they had brought with them and continued to import. They did not regard either "identity" or its loss as imposed upon them by an alien and imperial Other; colonial they were, but post-colonial they were not. That is why this volume has something to teach the reader about Canadian history, British history, and history as experience.

NOTES

1 J.G.A. Pocock, *The Discovery of Islands: Essays in British History* (Cambridge: Cambridge University Press, 2005).

2 Laurence Brockliss and David Eastwood, eds, *A Union of Multiple Identities: The British Isles, c.1750–c.1850* (Manchester: Manchester University Press and St. Martin's Press, 1997).

Acknowledgments

This volume would not have seen the light of day without the collaboration and advice of of a number of individuals and agencies. *Transatlantic Subjects* was the fruit of a conference held at McMaster University in October 2004 which was funded by the Social Sciences and Humanities Research Council of Canada, the dean of Humanities at McMaster University, and the McMaster Department of History. Special thanks go to Professor Michael Gauvreau, my conference co-organizer, and to Wendy Benedetti for her timely administrative support both prior to and throughout the conference. To the invited participants I owe a great debt of thanks, not only for enthusiastically engaging with the transatlantic perspective of the conference but for their lively participation and spirit of fearless debate. As every author well knows, the publication process is often lengthy and tedious and I thank all the contributors for their great patience and support. In particular I wish to express my gratitude to Michael Gauvreau, Jack Little, Jeffrey McNairn, Bryan Palmer, and Brian Young for their acute reading of my introduction.

My initial idea to create a volume that explored the transatlantic connections between Britain and its British North American colonies in terms of social and cultural life was given strong encouragement from the outset by Don Akenson, senior editor at McGill-Queen's University Press, whose expertise in this domain was crucial in giving direction and shape to the project. As always, Roger Martin was instrumental in guiding the book through the labyrinthine Canadian scholarly publishing process and kept my spirits up at a particularly critical time. I would also like to thank the anonymous readers, including one individual who failed entirely to see the point of drawing a connection between Britain and Canada. One of the strengths of McGill-Queen's University Press is its outstanding editorial department led by the peerless Joan McGilvray. Thanks also to Susanne McAdam for ensuring a splendid production and cover.

Like many other scholars in the field of the "new British history" I have been greatly influenced and challenged by the many scholarly works of J.G.A. Pocock. That Professor Pocock agreed to write a preface for this volume was a great accolade. His intellectual generosity and his commitment to fostering a new understanding of overseas Britons was manifest throughout our correspondence. I am deeply appreciative of his continued support for the project, for his perceptive reading of my introduction, and most of all, for integrating the themes of *Transatlantic Subjects* into his keynote address at the British Worlds Conference in 2005 in Auckland, New Zealand, which canvassed the importance of British North America to an audience of historians of the British Empire.

This book is dedicated to John Kendle, professor of history, University of Manitoba, whose personal history and scholarly interests have always pointed to the continued historical interrelationship between Britain and Canada. I owe a profound debt to John, not only for giving me my first teaching position but for continuing to mentor me by encouraging me to pursue my own intellectual path (even when not fashionable) and, above all, for generously reading everything I wrote and providing trenchant commentary which greatly enriched the final product. It is with heartfelt gratitude that I dedicate *Transatlantic Subjects* to my friend and mentor, whose model of scholarship and ethics has greatly influenced me.

TRANSATLANTIC SUBJECTS

NANCY CHRISTIE

Introduction: Theorizing
a Colonial Past

Canada as a Society of British Settlement

The provinces in America may be looked upon as the last Stake that Great Britain has in America. The loss of them would totally extinguish her Empire in that quarter of the Globe and be attended with consequences more alarming perhaps than those of the late Revolt.

William Knox, "Proposals for Promoting
Religion and Literature," 3 April 1786[1]

William Knox's assessment flies in the face of the outlook, shared by a large number of historians of the British Empire, that the English polity's greatest rupture was the loss of her American colonies during the war of independence. David Armitage has, for example, concluded that Britain's Atlantic empire was destroyed by the American Revolution.[2] This perspective implicitly marginalizes Britain's West Indian possessions,[3] arguably the most economically important of her overseas territories in this period. More tellingly, the central role which Armitage and many other historians have assigned to the American Revolution as the decisive global event which separated the so-called First and Second British empires[4] notably obscures the importance of "the persistence of empire"[5] in the "other" provinces of North America, namely those regions of settlement which later became known as Canada.

Our title, "transatlantic subjects," is a phrase borrowed from an 1846 petition addressed to the British Parliament by Scottish agriculturalists and labourers from Upper Canada protesting the Corn Laws.[6] In borrowing this term, we present these essays as, in the first place, a recognition that the Atlantic world was bifurcated after 1776 between a new American nation and those societies which remained loyal to the crown. However, the contributions to this volume also work from the premise that, despite the political rupture of the rebellion of the Thirteen Colonies, the Atlantic world after the American Revolution continued to operate within a cultural system which incorporated the former American colonies, Britain, and the new immigrants to the British provinces of Nova Scotia, New Brunswick, Upper and Lower Canada. These new societies of British settlement participated in a realm of ideologies, institutions, and social practices that connected them with the imperial metropolis and the United States, as well as with the older settlers of the French empire who had become British subjects in 1760.

This book is the first Canadian response to the clarion call sounded by J.G.A. Pocock to broaden the meaning of "British history." In his 1982 article "The Limits and Divisions of British History: In Search of the Unknown Subject," Pocock enjoined British historians to reconceive the geographical and ideological parameters of their subject to include Britain's overseas possessions. In part to curb the incipient tendency to see Britain as part of Europe, Pocock redefined the study of British history as an "interaction of several peoples" within the British archipelago, a perspective which gave more equal weight to the Scottish and Irish experiences. However, he also reinterpreted Britain as a nation-state, an entity which might incorporate the white settlement colonies of Australia, Canada, South Africa, and New Zealand. And as part of this plea for a new conception of British history on a global scale, Pocock established new epistemological frameworks which connected the metropolis and the periphery, a practice now standard among practitioners of the New Imperial history. More importantly, from the perspective of this volume, Pocock has circumvented the theoretical straitjacket of orthodox nation-state-centred approaches which took the declaration of American independence as the benchmark to which all subsequent British provinces might aspire. In thus addressing the fault lines of whig history head-on, Pocock has been able to accept the logic of constitutional revision brought about by the American Revolution. At the same time, Pocock theorized a history whose *telos* was not necessarily the emergence of the nation-state. He did so by placing greater emphasis, in a Braudelian fashion, on the deeper pulses of cultural, economic, and social patterns which transcend orthodox political boundaries. In this way, he conferred renewed importance upon Britain's cultural provinces such as Canada, which he conceived as part of both the British Empire and the Atlantic world. Stating categorically that "the history of the [American] Revolution is incomplete without the history of Canada,"[7] Pocock has exhorted historians to read across traditional fault lines of the nation-state and empire and, in particular, to question the underlying assumption of a discontinuity between the First and Second British Empires. Pocock's argument has, thus, reaffirmed the revisionist historiographic concept of the "long eighteenth century."

Our focus on British North America as an important site for studying the evolution and translation of British cultures and social patterns outside the archipelago has been influenced by the important contributions of Linda Colley and Kathleen Wilson to the question of patriotic movements in Britain and the way in which these were explicitly shaped by expansion overseas.[8] More significantly, given this volume's emphasis on the various reconfigurations and redefinitions of the British nation-state after 1783, Dror Wahrman's recent recasting of the revolutionary experience as a largely cultural phenomenon is seen to reinforce Pocock's multi-contextual reading of the British experience as a transatlantic (and later a trans-Pacific) phenomenon. In his compendious volume, *The Making of the Modern Self*, Wahrman has analyzed the transformation from an *ancien régime* of identity, defined by unstable and malleable notions of gender, class, ethnic, racial, and political identities to a more modern and rigid, or essentialist, conception of the social order.[9] By reinterpreting the age of revolution – from the 1790s to the 1830s – in terms of cultural shifts rather than an abrupt political event, Wahrman has, like Pocock, created a theoretical perspective that allows for a flexible transnational perspective. Such an interpretive trajectory is not centred on the problematic of the formation of nation-states. It allows societies without a revolutionary experience and which did not become political nation-states – such as Britain's Canadian settlements – to be incorporated in a new way into a broadly British experience.[10] Having conceptualized his revolutionary project in terms of a "comparative triangulation"[11] between France, Britain, and its transatlantic extensions, Wahrman develops a culturalist model with direct implications for the way in which this broad transformation to "modernity" occurred in other "national" contexts. Indeed, Wahrman concludes with the question of how this transition to a new identity regime played out in other Western societies.[12] Because Wahrman has focused on the United States as a site which triggered this identity transformation, it follows that Canada, the newly created society of British settlement that was the direct creation of and consciously created as a foil to the new American republic, remains a crucial context in which to explore the ongoing reinterpretation of *ancien régime* culture and social relations within wider Britain.

Post-revolutionary British North America poses particular problems for the broad transition to modernity adumbrated by Wahrman. Like Kathleen Wilson,[13] Wahrman conflates modernity with empire – at

least with the emergence of Britain's eighteenth-century empire.
While it is important to demonstrate how new zones of cultural contact
destabilized and reformed British cultural assumptions, as Eliga Gould
and C.A. Bayly have affirmed,[14] the decades embraced by both the
American and French revolutions not only created a context for movements of cultural change and social reform but unleashed a counter-
revolutionary response, especially among political and social elites,
which was played out in a host of colonial sites. As Bayly has demonstrated in *Imperial Meridian: The British Empire and the World,
1780–1830*, the imposition of aristocratic values in church and state
abroad was absolutely crucial to a sense of social stability within the
archipelago proper. Indeed, one of the most important territorial sites
for this reassertion of agrarian patriotism was the Canadas, which were
consciously settled as a countervailing force of loyal conservatism to
offset the radicalism of the nation-state to the south. However, Bayly, as
a historian of East Asia, has followed the orthodoxy, established by historians of the Second British Empire from Vincent Harlow onward, of
envisioning the "swing to the East" as emblematic of British colonial
policy in the wake of the signal loss of its American colonies.[15]
Although, in *Imperial Meridian,* Bayly has theorized British expansion
in a global context, the conceptual core of his definition of empire
remains Britain's eastern possessions. This view has tended to margin-
alize the Canadian settlements and subsequent settler societies founded
between 1780 and 1830 and to over-emphasize the hegemony of autoc-
racy, military authority, and direct rule. In contrast, Eliga Gould has
offered a tamer view of the period of counter-revolution.[16] By continuing to give due prominence to the Atlantic sphere of overseas Britons,
she sees the turn to aristocratic assertiveness in the face of radical political alternatives as offset by new realities of a multicultural empire
which helped urge forward in indirect ways the forces of reform and
renovation, especially in terms of how Britishness was defined.[17] Like
Wahrman, Gould sees the American Revolution as a catalyst of change
but within a counter-revolutionary context.

The tensions between conservatism and change, between *ancien
régime* political and cultural forces and the forces of modernity, and
between the vision of conservative hegemony and the societal limitations for its imposition form the historiographical core of *Transatlantic
Subjects.* This volume of essays asks, how were British identities – read
class, political, ethnic, religious, familial – redefined in the wake of the
loss of the American colonies? How was the British transition toward a
more modern identity regime, defined by increasingly essentialist definitions of selfhood, overshadowed by the re-engagement with *ancien
régime* sensibilities in British North America? How did the contact in

the New World with an anti-revolutionary French cultural regime conflict with and redefine eighteenth-century notions of Britishness grounded, according to the celebrated account by Linda Colley, in reactions against French and Catholic Europe?[18] Were the forces of aristocratic, agrarian patriotism replicated in Britain's settlement colonies with the same self-willed hegemony as in India, or did the experience of pluralistic cultural and social immigration establish foci of competing hegemonic projects which resulted in a regime of destabilized and contingent identities? To what extent did ancient localism and customary mores reassert themselves in response to the attempt to reassert social authority in Britain's overseas possessions?[19] In this new multicultural society of variegated local and regional British fragments, were religious, class, ethnic, political and gender identities transformed in lock-step, as Wahrman contends, or was the cultural revolution toward modernity an interrupted and fractured process in the new settlement societies? To what extent did Britons conceive of their overseas possessions as loci of cultural experiment where reformist projects were inscribed?[20]

These questions afford us a vantage point from which to reassess the interaction of British society with its extensions overseas. Conventionally this relationship has been interpreted as a simple dichotomy between metropolitan core and the peripheries of colonies and dependencies.[21] Post-colonial theorists such as Catherine Hall and Kathleen Wilson have criticized the core-periphery interpretive framework because it erects hierarchies along racial lines by assigning greater historical significance to the experience of the white colonizer than to that of the subaltern peoples who were colonized. The work of an earlier generation of imperial historians privileged the metropolis by focusing more explicitly on the development of the state and its expansion overseas. Hall and Wilson have urged historians to take a more culturalist approach to the study of empire whereby Britain and her colonies are viewed as one coherent field of analysis, in which the experience of metropolis and periphery is treated as "mutually constitutive."[22] A similar view of Britain and her peripheries as a mutual "area of interaction" has been offered by David Fieldhouse, an economic historian of empire: "To understand the nature of imperialism we must study the colonies from within or, placing himself between core and periphery, look at both from the same distance simultaneously."[23] In certain respects, Fieldhouse's trajectory for explaining the dynamics of British expansion overseas was more radical than that posited by post-colonial theoreticians, not least because his interpretive bias lay much more explicitly with the colonies or peripheries. He believed they could be written about with little reference to the

metropolis. In this manner, Fieldhouse became the intellectual pro-
genitor of a host of important monographs, some of which took as
their starting point the comparative histories of the settlement colonies themselves. These histories focused primarily on the way in which
the societies of recent colonization, namely Australia, Canada, New
Zealand, and South Africa, were peopled by Britain for particular strategic and commercial purposes. Because these historians epistem-
ologically separated notions of nation and state,[24] they downplayed
the importance of the British metropolis by defining it in terms of its
constitutional connection, and interpreting its cultural influence
largely as a foil to explain the divergent social development of each of
her settlement offspring.[25] Nevertheless, despite the renewed emphasis which post-colonial historians of empire have placed on the
interpenetration of cultures around the empire and their claim to be
studying the metropolis and colonies as one analytic field, their real
historiographical interest lies with explaining "the impact of empire
on British social and cultural practices and identities," [26] a question
which overtly reaffirms the primacy of the metropolis in the imperial
relationship.[27] By contrast, this volume seeks to contribute to a
historiography which locates the central dynamic of empire in the
peripheries and, by so doing, elevates the historical experience of
white settlement colonies such as Canada.

In attempting to write a transnational history of post-revolutionary
British North America, this volume pursues the circum-Atlantic model
of cultural exchange furnished by David Armitage.[28] Although the
Scottish emigrants who coined the phrase "transatlantic subjects" used
a geographical idiom enunciated within a linear east-west axis, the theoretical perspective of this volume uses a tripartite interchange of cultural ideas and societal discourses among the nation-states and several
colonial provinces: the United States, Britain, and her British North
American colonies. Like Wahrman and Gould, Armitage has seen the
American Revolution as a catalyst for the creation of new definitions of
citizenship within the United States and Britain, and "[to] these two
political products of the war we might also add British North America,
later Canada, to make three states forged in the last quarter of the
eighteenth century."[29] Armitage's idea of a third "state"[30] must be
greatly qualified for, politically, Britain's North American provinces
remained colonial in terms of their constitutional relationship with
the English crown up until Confederation in 1867 and, arguably, they
retained a vestigially colonial status until the repatriation of the Canadian Constitution in 1982. For this reason it is crucially important for
historians to theorize a colonial past which avoids the distortions of
the nationalist narrative.[31] Those who have interpreted the historical

experience of new settler societies have done so mainly from the perspective that new settler societies are ineluctably ordained to replicate the destiny of the American Republic. Nationhood is affirmed through a rejection of, and ultimate independence from, the imperial power.[32] Although Canadian historians of recent years have vociferously debated the way in which we must recreate a national narrative which incorporates the revisionist perspectives offered by social history, it is just as important to position Canada within a broader transatlantic history which equally observes the two-state bifurcation of the Anglo-Atlantic world and the enduring ethnic, religious, economic, and institutional interconnections which persisted before and after the American Revolution.

This volume asks historians to read pre-Confederation Canadian history as an extension of British cultural, institutional, and social frameworks. Several generations of Canadian historians have recognized the myriad ways in which the Canadian Dominion was joined to Britain through its legal and constitutional edifices. The focus, however, was always the evolving Canadian nation in which the British metropolis progressively receded from view. Historians such as Donald Creighton, W.L. Morton, and Arthur Lower gravitated to the cosmology of social evolution – a reworking of the Victorian evolutionary frameworks which animated the disciplines of anthropology, sociology, and psychology – in order to demonstrate that Canada's progressive liberation from its colonialist and British cultural foundations was a natural (rational), linear, and positive process.[33] In his most famous work, *Colony to Nation* (1946), Lower narrated the maturation of a nation-state which moved ineluctably from dependent province of Britain to a North American society.[34] Lower's account is striking because of the extent to which he implicitly drew a correlation between the achievement of independent statehood for Canada and the growth of our cultural and economic dependency upon the United States, a view which has had a great currency among succeeding generations of historians. In narrating the loss of overt political ties with British imperialism we inadvertently wrote a history of covert subordination to American culture, which resulted in a deproblematizing of Britishness.

In the immediate postwar period, it was legitimate to view Britain as a declining and reactionary empire which could be contrasted with the democratic modernity of the United States.[35] Canadian history was left suspended between the history of two empires or two cultural monoliths: monarchical Britain and the republican United States, one declining and the other ascending. For the next generation of historians, who sought to jettison constitutional history and its associations with Britain in favour of social and cultural explanations of the Canadian past, the period immediately following the American Revolution appeared to be a portentous moment of cultural foundation. In rejecting a "colonialist" reading of the past, these historians sought an alternative unifying leitmotif and they discovered it in the Loyalists – Americans who rejected the republican experiment but who could "pass" as bearers of a separate history from that of Britain by virtue of their rootedness in the North American environment. By firmly attaching the politics of the counter-revolution to the Loyalists and their political progeny, historians in this mould conceived of the debates surrounding issues of loyalty, constitutionalism, and cultural foundations as a self-contained reflection of North America, with the British polity appearing as an occasional *deus ex machina* to intervene at critical junctures within a cross-border dynamic between the American Republic and the British North American colonies. When the British metropolis makes an appearance it is not in terms of its cultural influence or an ongoing political relationship, but as an intermittent constitutional factor. Thus there is no conception of British governance; there are merely moments in which imperial authority was imposed, encapsulated by the Constitutional Act of 1791 which created Upper and Lower Canada and established elected assemblies, the War of 1812, the suppression of the 1837–38 Rebellions, and Durham's constitutional reconstruction following the Rebellions.[36]

Within this framework, Loyalist ideology was the mirror of that of the American Patriots, the settlement process was one defined by Loyalist and late-Loyalist migrations, and the vigour of British North American religious sensibilities flowed from their kinship with American evangelicalism.[37] What this paradigm ignored was that republicanism was not simply an American manifestation, but was intrinsic to at least two centuries of political debate in England, Scotland, and Ireland and their transatlantic extensions. While the Loyalists may have founded New Brunswick and Upper Canada, societies which were not wholly defined by the Revolutionary moment existed prior to the American Revolution – Nova Scotia, Quebec, and Newfoundland (as well as well as the British West Indies). Finally, by constructing Methodism as a largely American import, this historiography ignored the other varieties of Protestantism, and excised from the canon the experience of British Protestants who emigrated in great numbers after 1815. Even historians of religion such as John Webster Grant, John Moir, and Goldwin French, who embraced the American experience to a much lesser degree than George Rawlyk, the pre-eminent interpreter of vitalist American religion in its Canadian guises, deployed a narrative structure that rested on a primary linear teleology in which the successive waves of British immigration after 1815 were subsumed by the larger process of becoming Canadian. Similarly, while John Moir acknowledged the Scottishness of the Presbyterian Church, its transatlantic roots were viewed largely as an antimodern "ethnic" fragment which impeded the proper emergence of a common Canadian sensibility.[38]

A similar nationalist optic pervaded the scholarly treatment of the period of British rule (1760–1840) in French Canada. Unlike their Anglo-Canadian contemporaries, the postwar generation of French-Canadian historians tended to downplay the centrality of the American Revolution. Abbé Groulx, Michel Brunet, and Guy Frégault emphasized the importance of the Conquest[39] while Fernand Ouellet focused on the economic transformations that occurred between 1800 and 1837[40] as critical to the formation of the idea of a French-Canadian nation-state. Within this interpretive rubric, Britain was seen merely as a political presence in its role as an occupying imperial power. More significantly, concepts of Britishness were reduced to considerations of the way English political power was exercised and how the English Anglican establishmentarian structures were in perpetual tension with a well-entrenched French-dominated Roman Catholicism. The pluralistic nature of Lower Canada was largely ignored despite the presence of sizable Scottish and Irish communities in both Quebec City and Montreal and the large number of English-speaking settlers throughout Lower Canada. Recent revisionist work by Allan Greer has situated the 1837–38 Rebellions in Lower Canada in a broader imperial framework which assumes multiple sources for the flow of radical ideas[41] and has thus questioned Lord Durham's dictum of "two nations warring in the bosom of a single state." A cluster of historians, principally Bruce Curtis,[42] Jean-Marie Fecteau,[43] Yvan Lamonde,[44] and Michel Ducharme,[45] in exploring the theme of governmentality, have been much more open to studying ongoing British influences within political discourse and various state structures. However, there remains a persistent desire to assimilate the Lower Canadian Patriots to American Republican ideas and values, thus giving the appearance of a vicarious Québécois participation in the American Revolutionary moment.[46] By expurgating the English and, especially, Irish influences on the thought of the Lower Canadian Patriots and thus imaginatively drawing the events in Lower Canada into the ambit of the American revolutionary experience, nationalist historians, such as Gérard Bouchard, can more easily suggest that Quebec's ultimate destiny is one of cataclysmic independence from the Canadian empire.[47] Though animated by a very different set of nationalist concerns, the historiographical trajectory in French Canada strangely echoes that of its English-Canadian counterpart in identifying Britain with the forces of anti-modernism and the United States as a progressive society which must be emulated.

The practice among many historians to overdetermine the impact of both the American Revolution and its North American limits, and the consequent impact of the United States on the formation of British North America, has recently been addressed in the work of Jack Little. In *Borderland Religion*, Little directly confronts the issue of American influence by studying the Eastern Townships, a part of Lower Canada which lay east of Montreal and bordered Upper Canada and northern New England. During a period when there were only pockets of small, American settlements in Upper Canada, the Eastern Townships formed the major site of American settlement. In this broad-ranging study of religious cultures, Little conclusively demonstrates that numbers carried little weight in shaping broader cultural identities in the face of well-funded British institutions – namely the Church of England and Wesleyan Methodism. Little argues that a common American culture with its republican and non-conformist values was quickly transformed by religious denominations amply supported by "the British colonial authority."[48] Aside from the problem of the degree to which specific forms of republicanism were co-extensive with a fixed notion of American identity in this period, Little's major historiographical breakthrough is to sever the equation between Methodism, Americanism, and radicalism. He attributes to the Wesleyan Methodists a much greater influence than has hitherto been accorded by historians such as William Westfall who, in writing a cultural history of Upper Canada, reaffirmed, through the lens of religion, the orthodox political polarities of American radicalism versus British conservatism.[49]

Because so much of our history has been written within the political terms and ideological constructions defined by issues of loyalty following the American Revolution and the War of 1812 and enunciated by the participants themselves, namely the liberal political economist Lord Durham, the Tory John Strachan, the radical William Lyon Mackenzie, and the Liberal-Tory Egerton Ryerson, historians have been unable to escape the polarities of American versus British identity which divided the Canadian community. Moreover, the period between 1791 and 1850 has been viewed principally as one leading up to Confederation in 1867 and it has thus functioned as a template of the nation. Consequently, this period has been seen as one in which those quintessential 'Canadian' values of political accommodation and social harmony were incorporated into the core of social life through what J.M.S. Careless and William Westfall have termed a political and Protestant consensus.[50]

This volume advances a very different interpretive framework. It aims to revise orthodoxies built around polarities of two monolithic cultures and widens the breach opened by Little by underscoring the varieties of British cultural streams and the power which British legal, religious, associational, and educational institutions wielded. As well, it gives considerable weight to British models of social hierarchy and the dynamic between the forces of reform and counter-revolution – both prior to and following the American Revolution – which were brought through mainly British avenues of social experience.[51] It views the period before 1850 as the working out of a series of British imperial experiments of both authoritarianism and ethnic pluralism. This gives priority to the variety of identities, institutions, and social dynamics which functioned both through and below the constitutional (legal) apparatus which has so dramatically figured in the history of this period. The approach is more sensitive to local variability, social and cultural conflict, and the importance of institutional frameworks. When discussions do touch on the question of 'national' identity, the purpose is not to celebrate but to deconstruct it into either its political or religio-ethnic references.

It is at this point that Pocock's notion of the three kingdoms may yield more positive interpretive results for the study of British North America. In illuminating the continued viability of ethno-political communities within the rubric of Britishness, Pocock has offered an intellectual paradigm which has direct application to the study of the pluralistic nature of British North American society.[52] He advances a multi-textual history which forefronts the variegations of social experience and cultural interaction and equally privileges all the British subcultures, and he avoids the teleology of the nation-state which informs even the most sophisticated theories of the transatlantic such as those of David Armitage. In this way, Pocock's reading of the British archipelago and its overseas expressions comes closer to that of H.V. Bowen, Ned Landsman, Nicholas Canny, J.M. Bumsted and Donald Akenson who have emphasized the "interprovincial" dialogue within the ostensible "nation."[53] Unlike some recent interpreters of the emergence of British patriotism, who see an increasing integration of ethnic regions within the British polity by the end of the eighteenth century,[54] Pocock's framework yields a notion of multiple monarchies and a multiplicity of ethno-political discourses which flow across the Atlantic where they in turn meet, interact, and co-mingle in such a way as to form new provincial identities, be they class, ethnic, religious, or political solidarities. As Pocock has written, "The premises must be that the various peoples and nations, ethnic cultures, social structures, and locally defined communities, which have from time to time

existed in the areas known as 'Great Britain and Ireland,' have not
only acted so as to create the conditions of their several existences but
have also interacted so as to modify the conditions of one another's
existence and that there are processes here whose history can and
should be studied."[55]

Here, then is a template by which to study the subcultures of the
British diaspora as they were recombined in British North America following the American Revolution. The formation of "transatlantic subjects" was thus a fluid, unstable process of competing national
traditions which had the potential for various outcomes: a reassertion
of older localisms or ethnic particularisms which had long disap-
peared in the metropolis; the direct transplantation of social norms
from the metropolis which remained either undiluted or modified by
the new world environment; or the creation, through contact, of a distinctly new cultural hybrid. And indeed, to Pocock's vision of a pluralistic Britishness defined by its three kingdoms, one might add a fourth
kingdom, that of France, when speaking of the "interaction of several
peoples"[56] in the settler societies of the New World.

In consciously conceiving Canada's past as a colonial past, this volume breaks new ground. It departs from the historiographical orthodoxy of the past four decades which has privileged a developmental
view of history organized around the emergence of a nation-state. As
Nicholas Canny and Anthony Pagden have rightly observed, all new
societies of settlement are trapped in a dialectic between finding themselves "to be at once the same, and yet not the same, as the country of
their origin."[57] In most historical treatments which have read the
nation in terms of the American Revolution, the very process of social
formation involves an implicit "retreat from empire."[58] If we are to
recapture the contingent and pluralistic aspects of these "emergent
cultures"[59] of Britain and recognize the ongoing process of reciprocal
cultural conversation between the various British metropoles and their
peripheries, it is crucial to conceive of the pre-1850 period of Canada's past as one which does not lead ineluctably toward the "modern"
nation-state defined by Confederation.[60]

Although a transnational history of Canada as a migratory space has
been conceptualized for later periods of colonization from Europe,[61]
the study of social formation by British peoples in terms of economic
development, the transplantation of legal and educational institutions, and the recreation of class, ethnic, religious, and other social
identities in the New World environment has been under-theorized.
Because they did not view the early period of Canadian history as one
of a distinctly colonial site, historians have not provided the
historiographical bridges necessary for defining Canada as a society of

recent settlement comparable with other colonial communities either in the Atlantic or Pacific. With a few important recent exceptions,[62] Canadian social and cultural history has worked from the premise that Canadian society was a self-sufficient entity. Its foundational context was thus eviscerated, and the analysis of the way in which English, Scottish, Irish, French, and American cultural mores and social folkways overlapped, recombined, and conflicted in the New World environment did not enter the mainstream of historical discussion and practice among Canadian historians.

The renewed call for the study of imperial history, fuelled by postcolonial studies and a greater interdisciplinary focus on issues of globalization and their impact on contemporary society, demands in turn that Canadian historians reconceptualize the nationalist frameworks fashioned by the nationalistic upsurge of the 1960s and 1970s into a broader transcultural perspective. Moreover, the reconfiguration of the study of the expansion of Europe away from the study of state politics toward a study of the informal empire of economic, social, and cultural exchange has provided theoretical pathways by which the localism of social history and community studies might be linked to the broader themes of colonial expansion. Among the many claimants to the new imperial history is Jack P. Greene. In his critique of the centralist and elitist assumptions of the study of imperial governance Greene has observed,

> Until recently, most historians of early modern empire used the coercive and centralized model of imperial organization derived from late-nineteenth- and early-twentieth-century empires. In this conception, empires were political entities in which colonies were presided over by powerful nation-states with vast administrative and coercive resources to enforce their claims to sovereignty. In these coherent entities, authority did not flow upward from colonial populations, most of which, even in colonies with substantial numbers of European settlers, were disenfranchised subject populations, but downward from distant centers."[63]

In her introduction to *The New Imperial History*,[64] Kathleen Wilson makes a similar claim in her more overt critique of the multi-volume *Oxford History of the British Empire*. In wishing to make the subalterns speak by focusing on the study of non-elites and in stressing the interconnectedness of metropole and periphery, Wilson's animadversions against orthodox imperialist histories as political history appear very close to the culturalist approach of Greene; Wilson, though, places far greater emphasis on the question of "difference" and the creation of racial "otherness." She has been severely criticized, however, for assuming a European hegemony of the colonizers over the non-white colonized peoples which fails to adequately disaggregate the pluralities within that assumed European core.[65]

Many facets of Wilson's approach to the writing of imperial history are essential to a richer understanding of the complexity of cultural encounters in Britain's overseas possessions, especially her observation that the drive to uphold European national identities, and the value systems which maintained them, was as important in forging unequal power relationships between reformers, planters, missionaries, merchants, and indigenous peoples as systems of legitimation affirmed through legal governance and outright territorial possession.[66] But her definition of "difference" as defined by race and her emphasis on social authority through cultural discourse makes her theoretical perspective less applicable to the study of the white settler societies where the civilizing process per se may not have been the central determinant of settlement and where notions of difference or "otherness" may have just as frequently functioned in non-racial contexts (McNairn this volume). For example, in British North America after 1763, the central issue of British patriotism did not revolve around the juxtaposition of European versus aborigine; British identity was maintained in contrast to the numerically dominant French-Canadian settlers. More problematically, as Donald Fyson demonstrates, the aim of the colonial legal system was not to exclude and turn the French-Canadian populace into "others" outside the liberties of British governance but rather to integrate them within the colonial system. And in yet another permutation on the theme of cultural dissonance and conformity, Brian Young not only sustains Fyson's revisionist analysis which shows the degree to which ordinary French-Canadians participated in and adapted to British institutions so as to empower themselves, but argues that French- Canadian Catholic elites in turn re-invented Britishness to create their own systems of class-based otherness which differentiated the patrician culture of seigneurialism from that of the emergent but subaltern middling sorts. (Fyson and Young this volume). Alternatively, although the Highlanders had already experienced a high degree of "colonial ambivalence" within the British archipelago, in the New World they were transformed from the colonized into the colonizers,[67] for in British North America the Highlanders formed the "shock-troops" of imperial defence where the wearing of plaid metamorphosed from a deviant act to a celebration of empire. Moreover, the very attempt to anglicize this Celtic fringe, which involved the writing down of Gaelic texts for translation, resulted in a renaissance of Gaelic identity which, in the New World, found new potential for expansion within the large number of Gaelic-speaking Presbyterian churches. As the work of Fyson and Young makes clear, the way in which one defines the colonizers and colonized is much more complex and mutable in different social milieux than has been assumed by post-colonial theorists.

If, as has been argued for Scotland, a form of cultural hybridization had taken place by the late eighteenth century, then this process of transplanting British culture overseas is surely a more variegated one than merely a simple division between white colonizer and racialized others. It is important, therefore, to underscore the way in which there were many colonialisms, some of which were defined, often obliquely, by race (Eamon and Vosburgh this volume) but that notions of class, ethnic, and religious subordination fractured what post-colonial theorists might postulate as one "hegemonic" act of colonization. Not only must historians disaggregate the different kinds of colonizers – the merchants, missionaries, settlers, government officials in Britain and those in the colonies[68] – but they must recognize that although the "colonizers" may have held some values in common, their aims were contingent upon their profession, gender, and place of origin and the degree to which these particular discourses became dominant was a function of both context and time. The outcomes of each of these imperial projects were divergent often conflicting with rather than reinforcing one another. And if agents of empires never formed as coherent a group, as Wilson and Hall have assumed, neither was there a coherent official imperial agenda, nor were these multitudinous "hegemonies" either consistent or always successful (Curtis, Gauvreau, and Webb this volume) in implanting themselves.[69] Many remained in the realm of imaginative construction. Moreover, it is important to deconstruct the very notion of the "civilizing process," for in the period covered by this volume, apart from the sporadic concentration of Methodist and Moravian evangelists among native groups, for the most part the central purpose of missionary activity in British North America was to bring white settlers within the embrace of the faithful. Moreover, as C.A. Bayly has so astutely argued, there was a set of aims and principles inherent in the aristocratic and agrarian phase of imperial expansion which diverged from the set of aims and their agents which later came to define what Ann Stoler has termed the "embourgeoisement" of imperialism after 1850.[70] These agrarian visions informed views of indigenous labour in ways that differed from post-1850 colonial practices. Adele Perry has demonstrated that colonial British Columbia took on a more acutely racialized and gendered complexion.[71] In British Columbia, in contrast to the peopling of post-revolutionary British North America, the reach of European authority was weaker and the demographic balance between indigene and white was tilted in favour of the former. Moreover, the aboriginal peoples had not been culturally constructed as "loyalists" vis-à-vis the American patriot "others" and the interconnected variables of scientific racism, demography, distance from the metropolis, and the importance of an indigenous labour force combined to form a colonialist regime in British Columbia which was significantly different from the process of British governance and social formation in eastern British North America a few decades earlier.[72]

Building on the work of Bailyn, Pocock, Greene, Armitage, and Braddick,[73] this volume steers clear of theories of empire which conceive of Britain as a single system; rather, the authors have cast their nets widely in analyzing the transference of various British cultures to the new social configurations of the New World, be those defined as Scottish and Irish, as mutable cultures of class, as political cultures in conflict, as debates by Christian political economists, as the promotion of reformist cultures, as religious cultures in their dissenting and establishment varieties, as scientific Enlightenment cultures, or as the culture of colonial administration. Following the lead of Frederick Cooper and Ann Laura Stoler,[74] the broader experience of social formation in new societies of British settlement is situated within an analytical framework which provides ample girth to interrogate both the politico-economic studies of the formal empire and the informal empire of cultural discourse and social praxis.

This book also aims to draw attention to the critical period in British history between the era of political and cultural revolution, its counter-revolutionary phase in which aristocratic, agrarian patriotism was reasserted, and the transition to the empire of free-trade liberalism. The work of C.A. Bayly has effectively rehabilitated this liminal era in British history and reinterpreted this critical period of intense political and social conflict, defined by the interplay of *ancien régime* politics and social values; the forces of religious dissent, political liberalism, and a widespread reformism; and a growing commercial ethos that served to pauperize increasing numbers of agricultural labourers and engender new radical movements and voluntaristic social institutions. All of these were exported to Britain's overseas extensions where the power of each constituent group was so tested as to recreate a novel set of social solidarities and cultural identities.[75] It is this recombined social matrix of British politics, society, and economy in flux, in which ideologies, practices, and identities were more sharply edged in the colonial setting than in the metropolis, which this volume aims to explore. The study of this alternative socio-politico framework of the British state writ large, which unfolded in a parallel universe to its metropolitan progenitor(s), is a response to the plea for a new British history, articulated by J.G.A. Pocock, as the study of the formation of British peoples overseas.

The first section of the volume is entitled "Agrarian Patriots," a phrase borrowed from C.A Bayly. The articles by Donald Fyson, Nancy Christie, and Brian Young examine the stream of social and cultural life which lay beneath the official voice of colonial imperium and advance a reconsideration of C.A. Bayly's dictum that the empire constructed in the wake of the American Revolution was autocratic, aristocratic, and agrarian. Although this period was defined by a more authoritarian, centralized system of colonial governance whose aim was to control marginal groups – in this case the French-Canadian populace of Lower Canada – through the extension of legal structures, it is important to explore the degree to which these idealized principles of imperial rule functioned in practice.[76] In his detailed examination of the civil courts in Lower Canada, Donald Fyson revises the impositional character of this authoritarian British imperial regime. In introducing their legal regime to Lower Canada, colonial officials hoped to use the law to create cultural uniformity in British North America, but as Fyson demonstrates, ordinary French Canadians did not simply resist British legal rule, as the orthodox interpretation of the period between the Conquest and the Rebellion of 1837 assumes, but pragmatically adapted and used British law to serve their own ends.[77] In essence, because of certain affinities between the French *coutume de Paris* and the British common law, the French Canadian populace did not perceive the British legal system as wholly alien and, through the daily practice of law, a legal hybrid was created in Lower Canada which smoothed the transition to British governance. Where nationalist Quebec historians have largely studied the implications of the Conquest by focusing on the access of French-Canadian political leaders to the assembly and the upper echelons of government and have thus argued that the exclusivity of British governmental institutions prompted French-Canadian patriot resistance, Fyson has studied the interstices of local governmental institutions to elaborate a revisionist narrative of the interaction between French-Canadian and British institutions which suggests that, in some aspects of contact, French Canadians were receptive to viewing themselves as British subjects in a constitutional sense while preserving through cultural institutions – namely the Roman Catholic Church – a continued sense of ethnic otherness. What is important is that the French-Canadian people themselves preserved this sense of separateness even as British officialdom aimed to include and thus assimilate French Canadians. In short, in view of Gould's emphasis on the new multicultural aspect of the Second British Empire after 1783,[78] Fyson's work, in showing how subaltern peoples exercised power, contributes to a more ambiguous reading of the impositional nature of legal structures,[79] and also reveals the large degree to which this altered British view of citizenship was shaped from below by the subject peoples themselves. Furthermore, Fyson shows that this transition toward a more culturally plural empire began in Lower Canada prior to the American Revolution and so was not simply dependent upon changing views of Britishness occasioned by that event.

Nancy Christie has plumbed the rich archival sources of letters and diaries in her study of elite and plebeian families during the process of migration in order to uncover the various ways in which the idiom of class was translated to the Canadas. Christie argues that although some migrants sought to transfer to British North America the structure of class relations which had existed in Britain, the New World society provided an economic and social environment which rendered social replication overseas an impossibility. In short, a monolithic England was never reproduced abroad despite an official discourse which stated otherwise. By looking beneath the rhetoric of aristocratic authority to the private world of social practice, Christie shows that historiographical interpretations which proclaim the hegemonic influence of counter-revolutionary forces in the empire after 1783 are untenable. There was no *ancien régime* tradition on which to build an authoritative gentry culture wherein the politics of deference between master and servant could be preserved. Therefore, the "pseudo-gentry" – those middling sorts who hoped to refashion their class identities anew – found the creation of an aristocratic culture undermined by the new economic conditions characterized by relatively cheap and widely available land. In new colonial sites, the process, begun in the English countryside, whereby deferential social relations were beginning to decline,[80] was accelerated, as the possession of even small farm lots transformed pauper immigrants into capitalists, thus rendering their own radicalism and the class idiom of patrician and plebeian redundant, at least during the optimistic first year of settlement.[81] By reading the class mores in immigrant labourers' own correspondence, Christie shows how customary rights were reinterpreted to mesh with the New World where no poor law, no tithes, lower taxes, high wages, and the availability of cheap land interrupted the politics of class transported from England. In addition, Christie has approached the study of the politics of class through the prism of labour relationships within the domestic sphere and has thus offered a new perspective on the gendered meaning of social conflict in which the very bodies of domestic servants were perceived to be as destabilizing to the preservation of the traditional social order as was the public sphere of political rebellion.[82]

Likewise, Brian Young has approached the problem of class relationships and the creation of patrician society in Lower Canada through the perspective of cultural and institutional arrangements. Indeed, in his revision of Marxisant interpretations of class, Young demonstrates how patrician or elite authority in French Canada was not upheld merely through the possession of wealth; the power to dominate as a social group was exercised through cultural means, through the creation and control of critical institutions, most notably the Catholic Church and the seigneurial system. By contrast with Upper Canada, where an aspiring cadre of patrician elites perceived their position to be weak and unstable, in Lower Canada viable ancien régime institutions flourished and provided a sense of history and tradition upon which patrician cultural power could be inscribed. Not only does Young's article provide an anti-materialist interpretation of class relations in the New World, but it also demonstrates how the Catholic Church and the seigneurial system, which were sanctioned by British politicians anxious to render French Canada loyal to the empire, were not instruments of elite collaboration, as the British had envisioned, and also the means by which Lower Canadian elites reinterpreted Britishness to include French and Catholic subjects. Like Fyson and Christie, Young has shown the degree to which the politics of the periphery reshaped the metropolitan centre, but read together these essays also caution historians to pay due attention to class in explaining the variants in social replication within New World settings.

The next section, entitled "Provincial Britons," investigates the ways in which particular ethnic, religious, and institutional ideas were consciously transplanted in the British North American colonies. Each article emphasizes the limitations which were placed upon various imperial projects by New World institutional and social conditions. Each in turn demonstrates the ongoing political interplay between the poles of reformism and counter-revolutionary social forces and, while these debates were re-enacted in the New World, they were distinctly informed by events in Britain. For example, the way in which Methodists on both sides of the Atlantic hoped to redefine themselves as true Britons was shaped by the fallout of the American and French revolutions. As Joanna Innes makes clear, dissenters suffered from Anglican portrayals of them as subversives, a construct which rendered them marginal and thus induced them to wrap themselves in the rhetoric of loyalty and conservatism. Todd Webb traces the emergent elaboration of Britishness among certain groups of Methodists in the Canadas to demonstrate how the vocabulary of patriotism was used as a strategy of legitimation, a view similar to that of Linda Colley who has argued that "[b]etween 1750 and 1830 a wide spectrum of aspiring social groups and sectional interests throughout Britain found patriotic and nationalist language invaluable."[83] And as Webb persuasively argues, because of the geographical proximity to a republican America, the construction of Methodists as political dissidents which unfolded in Britain in this period, when translated to the New World, cast them as even more subversive because radicalism was an ever-present political alternative which necessitated, in turn, an even more vociferous rebuttal and an even more extreme attachment to Britishness. In revising the orthodox nationalist framework for the study of religion in Canada, Webb deftly shows how Methodist leaders elaborated a sense of Britishness which was not modern, but which engraved into their thought a vision of colonial culture as a mirror of Britain, a view which had garnered widespread currency prior to the American Revolution, as Eliga Gould has contended.[84]

In a similar way, Michael Gauvreau shows the important role that religion played in the elaboration of Britishness outside of Britain. Like Webb, Gauvreau reveals the vast degree of divergence in the colonial setting for even those groups, such as the Anglicans, who sought to wholly replicate the English constitution of church and state in Britain's overseas extensions. They were forced, because of the peculiar social configuration of the Canadas, to drastically revise their initial idealization of the colonies as commensurate with Britain.[85] For each religious group, however, the outcomes of cultural transference elicited quite different results. Where the Methodists embraced the notion of an inclusive Britishness which eviscerated the other kingdoms of Scotland and Ireland, Anglicans and Scottish Presbyterians were impelled, because of the power of the laity within the local colonial church congregations, to retreat into an early modern accentuation of ethnic particularisms. Gauvreau thus questions the easy identification of empire and modernity and thereby reinforces the insight of Michael Zuckerman that "[f]orms that were fading in Britain were revived in the colonies";[86] in this case, an ethnic pluralism was reawakened by the destabilizing processes of immigration. Gauvreau's contribution to this volume thus calls into question Colley's paradigm of the ability of a capacious Britishness to absorb ethnic peculiarities and upholds John M. Mackenzie's recent suggestion that ethnicities may well have been strengthened in Britain's overseas peripheries.[87]

Not only did religious identities remain fluid in this era of societal transplantation, but as Bruce Curtis argues, in his investigation of the attempts to imbed new educational perspectives – in this case the

Anglican-inspired Lancasterian system of monitorial schooling – while the players in the debate remained the same on both sides of the Atlantic, the outcomes were radically different. Curtis draws attention to the importance of the particular religious configuration of Lower Canada. In contrast to the more pluralistic religious environment in Upper Canada studied by Webb and Gauvreau, where dissenting and establishment churches had to compete and had achieved a rough demographic balance, in Lower Canada the power of the Roman Catholic Church and the depth of *ancien régime* society spelled the death knell for movements of reform. As Curtis concludes, the failure to erect a monitorial school system which believed in the education of the lower orders resulted in a peculiar vacuum whereby confessional priorities remained the norm and ultimately came to dominate the structure of public education for the next 150 years.

Michael Eamon follows Curtis's trajectory in focusing on institutional failure. Eamon addresses a question central to cultural histories of the British transatlantic world, namely the issue of the degree to which Scottish Enlightenment ideas penetrated the New World. While scholars such as Ned Landsman and Mark Noll have stressed the importance of the Scottish Enlightenment in the grounding of American republican thought and for the institutional network of higher education,[88] for the most part Canadian historians have bemoaned the absence of the Scottish Enlightenment in Canada which resulted in the paucity of colleges and of social networks which might have anchored a culture of scientific improvement.[89] Eamon has presented a revisionist perspective on the problem of the missing Enlightenment by demonstrating, through a study of several medical and military amateur scientists and ethnographers, how Enlightenment ideas regarding medicine, conjectural history, and the taxonomy of plants and animals did indeed exist in the colonies.[90] But because these amateur scientists' sense of professional identity remained wedded to the Scottish metropolis, Canada remained a laboratory for Enlightenment pursuits and thus failed to develop its own distinct provincial institutional structure for its promulgation.

McNairn continues Eamon's theme of Canada as a laboratory for British intellectual debates; in this case books on travel and immigration became vehicles for the popularization of emerging ideas of liberal political economy in the British metropolis.[91] His article enters into a rich historiographical debate over the timing and manner in which Enlightenment ideas of civic virtue grounded in agrarian values evolved into a constellation of ideas embedded in the new science of political economy. The latter increasingly viewed political institutions as epiphenomena of economic forces and cast commercial improvement in a more positive light than had the previous generation of civic humanists. McNairn in fact offers an account of the slow erosion of the older Enlightenment vision of republican political virtue, and its replacement by a concept of the moral economic subject.[92] However, rather than merely interpreting travel literature as a "capitalist vanguard" which constructed non-economic racialist identities, McNairn instead provides a nuanced assessment of the particular forms of economic rationality which were incorporated into this literature of improvement. Building on the outstanding work of Boyd Hilton on the Christian political economic tradition in Britain,[93] McNairn deftly demonstrates the way in which the ideas of Thomas Malthus, who was one of the first theorists to argue for the benefits to the Mother Country of colonies and emigration, penetrated into the popular travel accounts. These were written largely by army and government officers and imagined the New World colonies as bastions of agricultural improvement for Britain's pauper population. Where historians have traditionally focused on the economic policies of the colonial office officials to argue for the emergence of liberal imperialism in this period,[94] the novelty of McNairn's approach is to show the widespread permeation of the new political economy into popular accounts in order to illuminate how the equation between virtue and progress – the hallmark of modern political economy – became the bedrock of an outlook which departed from the aristocratic agrarianism described by C.A. Bayly and which provided the intellectual roots for anti-mercantilist notions of economic growth. At the same time, however, this newer sensibility retained a distinct foothold in the past by continuing to interpret commercial progress as limited and by couching the positive attributes of improvement in the moral language of self-discipline and moral choice.

If, as McNairn argues, the model of society promoted by these traveller-Malthusians was one characterized by a capacious middle class, a similar implantation of this rural ideal of independent yeomen was put into practice by the largely Scottish land agents studied by Michelle Vosburgh. Like the travel writers analyzed by McNairn, Vosburgh's land agents borrowed extensively from a mixture of the Scottish conjectural histories which saw society in terms of the economic stages from barbarism to civilization and endorsed the views of the Scottish agricultural reformers in elevating the yeoman farmer, participating in the free market in land, as the ideal of the colonial social order.[95] Where colonial officials in the metropolis may have hoped to use land grants as a means to protect the frontier against the spread of American republicanism by establishing a landed gentry, Vosburgh demonstrates, through a detailed recovery of the day-to-day workings of the crown lands department, how the attitudes of the individual Scottish land agents forged a Malthusian policy of granting land to widows, small farmers, and native peoples as an alternative to the high official policy of genteel improvement. Thus the local "men on the spot" were important actors in creating a new social calculus, defined by individual economic independence, which might forestall the need to introduce the Poor Law system and would ideally hinder the development of the social inequalities, political unrest, and economic stagnation which had come to characterize the Britain of the 1830s. The land agents contributed in no small way to promoting a more modern notion of economic self-sufficiency differing from the pre-eminently political notion of independence promulgated by a patrician elite which defined virtuous citizenship in terms of being "independent from Courtly influence."[96] However, despite the fact that they subscribed to a broader concept of the middling sorts as the progenitors of social progress, as did the travel writers studied by McNairn, much of their economic outlook remained grounded in vestigial Enlightenment ideas, especially in the continued juxtaposition of agricultural and commercial progress, industry and luxury, and the adherence to an ideal of the public good against individual self-interest which formed the hallmarks of classical civic humanism.[97]

In the final analysis, the foundational supports of a colonial *ancien régime* were the established church, the state, the military, and landed agricultural patricians. If the rise to prominence of newer notions of the economic man paralleled the emergence of voluntary societies in the late eighteenth century, these were relative late-comers to the British North American settler societies largely, as Curtis and Young so well argue, because of the cultural entrenchment of institutions of gentry paternalism such as the Roman Catholic Church. In Upper Canada, because of its more pluralistic institutional environment, where the voices of religious dissent occupied a wider social terrain and where the power of the Anglican state remained embryonic, in part because of the peculiar mixture of emigrant cultures from both the United States and Britain, there was a greater cultural purchase for institutions of dissent compared with Lower Canada. Many of these pockets of political radicalism emerged out of Scottish Presbyterianism.[98] For example, the Seceder clergyman William Bell campaigned to establish voluntary societies such as temperance associations and mechanics' institutes in a conscious political effort to create alternate cultural spaces in which the aims of the middling and labouring citizenry might be joined to demolish the hegemony of gentry culture which he believed was rooted in the military, the judiciary, and the Anglican church. This emergent middling culture remained but a cultural critique of aristocratic values and was limited in its institutional power until the 1840s.[99] The creation of this competing institutional construction of the "middle-class subject"[100] forms the theme of Darren Ferry's exploration of the establishment of a network of Mechanics' Institutes in both Upper and Lower Canada. As Ferry contends, the central aim of these societies was to integrate working-class men (and some women) into a culture of self-improvement, defined through the rhetoric of inclusivity, in which the common good of economic improvement and upward social mobility was held up against the self-interestedness of political partisanship and sectarian conflict. Unlike England, where the Mechanics' Institutes were largely a failure, despite their bourgeois leadership, they flourished in Canada until the 1880s, when working-class members defected to newly created labour organizations such as the Knights of Labor. Until that time, however, the constructed notion of class harmony which they sought to promote did provide an alternative – albeit an unstable one – to the social and political dominance of the gentry-based polity. While these organizations may have provided alternate sites for the discussion of reformist social projects reaffirming liberal values of economic progress, individual self-sufficiency, and moral discipline, the Mechanics' Institutes never became forums for radical politics for, as Ferry argues, Chartists were firmly silenced.

Because these voluntary associations remained bastions of bourgeois ideology, political radicals in Upper Canada had no mainstream institutional platform and had to create their own sites of contestation in small, local newspapers. Although, as the article by Christie demonstrates, the class consciousness of pauper immigrants was at first tempered by the prospect of economic prosperity through the working of the market and the ideals of familial independence promulgated by the emigration and travel literature analyzed by McNairn, the Edenic colonial world of social equilibrium which these labourer-capitalists embraced remained but a chimera, and in the economic depression of the 1830s, this capitalist language of self-improvement became re-politicized into a discourse of political rebellion. Joyce Appleby, James Jacob, and Margaret Jacob have observed that "in colonial society far more than in England words were called upon to do the work of artifacts."[101] Although referring to revolutionary America, this insight holds true no less for colonial cultures without a revolutionary tradition, as the exploration by Bryan Palmer of the violent political disputation that pitted Tory against Radical makes clear. Although the harmonious and progressivist language of the Mechanics' Institutes represents one form of plebeian public identity, Palmer powerfully argues for a deeply entrenched fissure between patrician and plebeian which, by the 1820s, had become embedded across a wide geographical terrain. In investigating both the verbal and actual political violence which was sustained through Upper Canada across several decades, Palmer challenges the historical convention that the Rebellions of 1837–38 in Upper Canada were but shadows of their Lower Canadian counterparts. The latter have been elevated as real expressions of social breakdown characterized by class and ethnic hostility.[102] By exploring the persistent and pervasive nature of radical protest in both town and countryside, Palmer can more fully explain why Tory culture became unbound and was forced, through both the micropolitics of community censure and the pressure of the imperial state anxious to reconstruct authority on a broader social basis, to assume a more benign and inclusivist language and set of practices.[103] The movement was encapsulated by the Liberal-Toryism of the Ryersons and John A. Macdonald, the colonial avatars of the Christian political economy studied by Boyd Hilton in Britain and Jeffrey McNairn in Upper Canada.

The articles in this section, entitled "A Laboratory of Modernity," collectively elaborate the decline of the authoritarian, aristocratic imperial policies by demonstrating the multiple ways in which they were increasingly undermined and replaced by emergent liberal and "bourgeois" notions. These entered the social and cultural mainstream through local land policies which were more egalitarian than those adumbrated by the official mind of the imperial legislators; by theories of political economy which envisioned a society of independent farmers rather than the "aristocratic" social relations defined by gentry landowners and dependent tenants; by radical political movements; and by the increasing presence of voluntary societies devoted to self-improvement, diffusion of education for workers, and a "bourgeois" sensibility which believed in the unification of the middling and working peoples to offset the patrician-plebeian political accord of the *ancien régime* state. As each essay in this section demonstrates, the cultural and social spaces for promoting modern notions of the liberal market society were taking root by the 1830s, but older Enlightenment ideas of civic virtue, social deference, or Tory rule were not wholly thrown off until the 1840s. Thus, it was not until 1843 that the Reform and, later, Liberal-Tory politician Francis Hincks explicitly remarked upon the political and social ascension of "*the middle-classes* against the aristocracy,"[104] thus symbolically marking the end of a British empire defined by C.A. Bayly as autocratic, aristocratic, and agrarian. Indeed, the unfolding of the largely politically decentralized empire of local self-government, one at the same time underpinned by an increasingly jingoistic and culturally conformist view of the colonies as no longer

British but singularly "happy Englands," was anticipated by the young colonial secretary, William Ewart Gladstone, who outlined sometime during the 1840s his own civilizing mission of empire: "We cannot stamp the image of England on the Colonies like a coat of arms upon wax. For all true, genuine, wholesome, and permanent resemblance we must depend upon a law written not on stone but on the fleshy tables of the heart. It must be wrought wholly through the freewill and affections of the colonial community."[105]

This perspective on the "Englishness" of both the British archipelago and its overseas expressions has hitherto informed much of the historiography on empire and colonial nationalism. And it is the aim of *Transatlantic Subjects* to reveal the variety of social and cultural possibilities that preceded the closing of the settlement frontier in eastern British North America prior to the 1850s.[106] In tracing the way in which multiple ethnic, religious, class, and provincial social codes were transplanted to British North America following the American Revolution, this volume seeks to recover both the imperial and transatlantic context of Canada, thereby reconceptualizing what later became a new nation as provinces of British settlement. By analyzing the variable nature of British expansion to its northern Atlantic peripheries, *Transatlantic Subjects* aims to theorize a colonial past for Canada and to place at the centre of historical discussion a circum-Atlantic exchange of ideas and social forms, a perspective which has been largely eviscerated by the continued dominance of nationalist narratives of the Canadian polity.

NOTES

1 Quoted from Frederick Madden with David Fieldhouse, eds, *Imperial Reconstruction, 1763–1840: The Evolution of Alternative Systems of Colonial Government* (New York: Greenwood Press, 1987), 22–3.

2 David Armitage, *The Ideological Origins of the British Empire* (Cambridge: Cambridge University Press, 2000), 2. This periodization also informs the *Oxford History of the British Empire*. See P.J. Marshall, *The Oxford History of the British Empire, vol. 2, The Eighteenth-Century* (Oxford: Oxford University Press, 1998); Andrew Porter, *Oxford History of the British Empire, Vol 3, The Nineteenth-Century* (Oxford: Oxford University Press, 1999).

3 Catherine Hall's work has drawn attention to the West Indies in the nineteenth century as a field of colonization. See Catherine Hall, *Civilising Subjects: Colony and Metropole in the English Imagination, 1830–1867* (Chicago: Chicago University Press, 2002).

4 For the most recent reconsideration of the chronology of the disjuncture
   between the First and Second Empires, which locates it at the end of the
   Seven Years War (1763), see P.J. Marshall, *The Making of and Unmaking of
   Empires: Britain, India, and America, ca. 1750–1783* (Oxford: Oxford
   University Press, 2005). For the traditional statement of greater continuity
   between First and Second Empires, see Vincent T. Harlow, *The Founding
   of the Second British Empire, 1763–1793*, 2 vols. (London: Longman Green,
   1952–1964).

5 This phrase is borrowed from the title of Eliga H. Gould's compendious revi-
   sionist analysis of transatlantic British political debate during the American
   Revolution, *The Persistence of Empire: British Political Culture in the Age of the
   American Revolution* (Chapel Hill: University of North Carolina Press, 2000).

6 Library and Archives of Canada [LAC], McGillvray Papers, MG 24 I3, Petition
   1846.

7 J.G.A. Pocock, "The Limits and Divisions of British History: In Search of the
   Unknown Subject," *American Historical Review* 87, no. 2 (April 1982): 311–36.
   For a recent and more extended argument relating to this question, see
   J.G.A. Pocock, *The Discovery of Islands* (Cambridge: Cambridge University
   Press, 2005).

8 Linda Colley, *Britons: Forging the Nation, 1707–1837* (New Haven: Yale University Press, 1992); Kathleen Wilson, *The Sense of the People: Politics, Culture
   and Imperialism in England, 1715–1785* (Cambridge: Cambridge University
   Press, 1995).

9 Dror Wahrman, *The Making of the Modern Self: Identity and Culture in Eighteenth-
   Century England* (New Haven and London: Yale University Press, 2004). On
   the cultural definition of revolution, see Colin Jones and Dror Wahrman,
   eds, *The Age of Cultural Revolutions: Britain and France, 1750–1820* (Berkeley
   and London: University of California Press, 2002).

10 For a reassertion of the post-revolutionary Atlantic as an arena of
   nation-states, see Eliga H. Gould and Peter S. Onuf, "Introduction," in Gould
   and Onuf, *Empire and Nation: The American Revolution in the Atlantic World*
   (Baltimore and London: The Johns Hopkins University Press, 2005), 15.

11 Wahrman, *The Making of the Modern Self*, 313.

12 Ibid., 321.

13 Kathleen Wilson, "Introduction: Histories, Empires, Modernities," in
   Kathleen Wilson, ed., *A New Imperial History: Culture, Identity and Modernity in
   Britain and the Empire, 1660–1840* (Cambridge: Cambridge University Press,
   2004), 1–24.

14 C.A. Bayly, *Imperial Meridian: The British Empire and the World, 1780–1830*
   (London and New York: Longman, 1989); Eliga H. Gould, "Revolution and
   Counter-Revolution," in David Armitage and Michael Braddick, eds, *The Brit-
   ish Atlantic World* (Basingstoke: Palgrave, 2002), 210–13; Gould, "A Virtual

Nation: Greater Britain and the Imperial Legacy of the American Revolution," *American Historical Review* 87, no. 2 (1999): 476–89.

15 Harlow, *The Founding of the Second British Empire*, P.J. Marshall, "Introduction," in Marshall, ed., *Oxford History of the British Empire*, 15–16; H.V. Bowen, "Perceptions from the Periphery: Colonial American Views of Britain's Asiatic Empire, 1756–1783," in Christine Daniels and Michael V. Kennedy, eds, *Negotiated Empire: Centers and Peripheries in the America, 1500–1820* (New York: Routledge, 2002), 283.

16 Eliga H. Gould, "American Independence and Britain's Counter-Revolution," *Past and Present* 154 (Feb. 1997): 135.

17 Gould, "A Virtual Nation," 476–89.

18 Colley, *Britons*, passim.

19 On this important point, see Ned C. Landsman, *Scotland and Its First American Colony, 1683–1765* (Princeton: Princeton University Press, 1985), 225, 232.

20 Joanna Innes has suggested the need to study reformist movements in imperial settings. See Joanna Innes and Arthur Burns, "Introduction," in Arthur Burns and Joanna Innes, eds, *Rethinking the Age of Reform: Britain, 1780–1850* (Cambridge: Cambridge University Press, 2003).

21 See, for example, John Brewer, "The Eighteenth-Century British State: Contexts and Issues," in Lawrence Stone, ed., *An Imperial State at War: Britain from 1689 to 1815* (London and New York: Routledge, 1994), 66; Jack P. Greene, *Peripheries and Center: Constitutional Development in the Extended Politics of the British Empire and the United States, 1607–1788* (Athens: University of Georgia Press, 1986).

22 Catherine Hall, Keith McClelland, and Jane Rendall, "Introduction," in Hall et al., eds, *Defining the Victorian Nation: Class, Race and Gender and the British Reform Act of 1867* (Cambridge: Cambridge University Press, 2000), 56; Kathleen Wilson, "Introduction: Histories, Empires, Modernities," in Wilson ed., *A New Imperial History*, 3. For a discussion of the way in which American historians have conceived a more unified reading of British and American colonial history, see T.H. Breen, "Ideology and Nationalism on the Eve of the American Revolution," *Journal of American History* 84, no. 1 (June 1997): 14. For another important discussion on writing transnational history which provides greater emphasis on the British societies of settlement, see A.G. Hopkins, "Back to the Future: From National History to Imperial History," *Past and Present* 164 (Aug. 1999): 200, 205–6, 207–10, 216–18.

23 David Fieldhouse, "Can Humpty-Dumpty Be Put Together Again?: Imperial History in the 1980s," *Journal of Imperial and Commonwealth History* 12, no. 2 (Jan. 1984): 9–10, 17, 22. In this article Fieldhouse also noted the important role that the experience of empire played in altering domestic institutions and policies. For a similar critique of the new imperial history for "privileging the metropolitan gaze," see Richard Price, "One Big Thing: Britain, Its Empire, and Their Imperial Culture," *Journal of British Studies* 45, no. 3 (July

2006): 602–27. Price also upholds Pocock's view that historians must preserve a notion of the state and, while Price approves of the new culturalist approach to the empire, he exhorts historians to explore in greater detail the way in which the connections between metropolis and periphery actually function in practice. This has been the central aim of the contributions to this volume. For a similar argument that reads imperial history from the periphery, notably that of the white settlement colonies, see J.G.A. Pocock, "British History in a British World," keynote address to Fourth British World Conference, Auckland, 14 July 2005.

24 On this point, see Lawrence Stone, "Introduction," in Stone, ed., *An Imperial State at War*, 5; Pocock, "The Limits and Divisions of British History," 315.

25 See Donald Denoon, *Settler Capitalism: The Dynamics of Dependent Development in the Southern Hemisphere* (Oxford: Clarendon Press, 1983); Donald Denoon, "Understanding Settler Societies," *Historical Studies* 18 (1979); John Kendle, *The Colonial and Imperial Conferences, 1887–1911: A Study in Imperial Organization* (London: Longmans, 1967); John Kendle, *The Round Table Movement and Imperial Union* (Toronto: University of Toronto Press, 1975); Deryck Schreuder and John Eddy, eds, *The Rise of Colonial Nationalism: Australia, New Zealand, Canada and South Africa First Assert Their Nationalities, 1880–1914* (Sydney: Allen & Unwin, 1988); Carl Berger, *A Sense of Power: Studies in the Idea of Canadian Imperialism, 1867–1914* (Toronto: University of Toronto Press, 1970); James Belich, *Making Peoples: A History of the New Zealanders, from Polynesian Settlement to the End of the Nineteenth Century* (Honolulu: University of Hawai'i Press, 2001); Nancy J. Christie, "Prophecy and the 'Principles of Social Life': Historical Writing and the Making of New Societies in Canada and Australia, 1880–1920," PhD thesis, University of Sydney, 1986. More recently, see Susan Lawrence, ed., *Archeologies of the British: Explorations of Identity in Great Britain and Its Colonies 1600–1945* (London and New York: Routledge, 2003), 7; Lynette Russell, *Colonial Frontiers: Indigenous European Encounters in Settler Societies* (Manchester: University of Manchester Press, 2001); Andrew Hassam, *Through Australian Eyes: Colonial Perceptions of Imperial Britain* (Brighton: Sussex Academic Press, 2000); John Weaver, *The Great Land Rush and the Making of the Modern World, 1650–1900* (Montreal & Kingston: McGill-Queen's University Press, 2003); Peter Gray, ed., *Victoria's Ireland?: Irishness and Britishness, 1837–1901* (Dublin: Four Courts Press, 2004); Donald Akenson, *The Irish in Ontario: A Study in Rural History* (Montreal & Kingston: McGill-Queen's University Press, 1984); Akenson, *The Irish Diaspora: A Primer* (Toronto: P.D. Meaney, 1993).

26 Wilson, "Introduction," in Wilson, ed., *A New Imperial History*, 18, 20.

27 For reservations about the degree to which the empire affected British society, see Bernard Porter, "Empire, What Empire? Or, Why 80% of Early- and Mid-Victorians Were Deliberately Kept in Ignorance of It," *Victorian Studies* 46, no. 2 (2004): 256–63.

28 David Armitage, "Three Concepts of Atlantic History," in Armitage and
    Braddick, eds, *The British Atlantic World*, 17–20. For a recent discussion, see
    Carole Shammas, "Introduction," in Elizabeth Mancke and Carole Shammas,
    eds, *The Creation of the British Atlantic World* (Baltimore & London: Johns
    Hopkins University Press, 2005), 1–16. On a similar concept of the Atlantic
    as a cultural site and a view of empire which eschews the confines of a consti-
    tutional approach, see H.V. Bowen, *Elites, Enterprise and the Making of the Brit-
    ish Overseas Empire, 1688–1775* (London: Macmillan Press, 1996), ix, xiii.
    Bowen also rightly points out the difficulties of the core and periphery per-
    spective when one comes to situate Ireland. For a recent discussion that vali-
    dates the concept of the "Atlantic" as a necessary framework to break down
    essentialized national and imperial boundaries, but which is at the same time
    critical of the approach as too fixated on the West and America, see Peter A.
    Coclanis, "Atlantic World or Atlantic/World?," *William and Mary Quarterly*,
    3rd series, 63, no. 4 (Oct. 2006): 725–42. It is for this reason that I have pre-
    sented British North America both in terms of the culture of the "Atlantic"
    and the "British Empire."

29 Armitage, "Three Concepts of Atlantic History," 21.

30 Eliga Gould and Peter S. Onuf have recently conceptualized the Atlantic as
    "a system of independent states," a concept which does not do justice to the
    peculiarities of the settlement societies which later became Canada. See Eliga
    Gould and Peter S. Onuf, "Introduction," in Gould and Onuf, eds, *Empire
    and Nation*, 15.

31 For an important discussion of the deficiencies of nationalist narratives in
    American history, see Michael Warner, "What's Colonial about Colonial
    America," in Robert Blair St. George, ed., *Possible Pasts: Becoming Colonial in
    America* (Ithaca: Cornell University Press, 2000), 49–70.

32 For a recent example in Canadian historical writing, see Gérard Bouchard,
    Genèse des nations et cultures du Nouveau Monde (Montreal: Boreal, 2000).

33 Nancy Christie, "Nature's Design and the New Millenium: The Persistence of
    a Common Context for the Science of Man, 1920–1958," unpublished
    paper, 1988. This paper also studied the work of Australian historians of the
    period, most notably Keith Hancock, R.M Crawford, and G.V. Portus. On the
    impact of evolutionary thought on Victorian ideas of race, see Peter
    Mandler, "'Race' and 'Nation' in Mid-Victorian Thought," in Stefan Collini,
    Richard Whatmore, and Brian Young, eds, *History, Religion and Culture: British
    Intellectual History, 1750–1950* (Cambridge: Cambridge University Press,
    2000), 224–44. A recent generation of revisionist scholars, most notably Jane
    Errington and Jeffrey McNairn, while still concerned with interpreting
    Britishness in terms of constitutional/political debate, have broken free of
    the intellectual encumbrance of the nationalist paradigm which character-
    ized previous generations of scholars.

34 See Carl Berger, *The Writing of Canadian History: Aspects of English-Canadian Historical Writing: 1900–1970* (Toronto: Oxford University Press, 1976), 112–36; Arthur Lower, *Colony to Nation* (Toronto: Longmans, Green, 1946).

35 For a parallel historiographical movement in New Zealand, see J.G.A. Pocock, *The Discovery of Islands*, 3–23.

36 See G.M. Craig, *Upper Canada: The Formative Years, 1784–1841* (Toronto: McClelland and Stewart, 1963). For more recent revisionist perspectives, see Jane Errington, *The Lion, the Eagle and Upper Canada: A Developing Colonial Ideology* (Montreal & Kingston: McGill-Queen's University Press, 1987); David Mills, *The Idea of Loyalty in Upper Canada, 1784–1850* (Montreal & Kingston: McGill-Queen's University Press, 1988); S.J.R. Noel, *Patrons, Clients, Brokers: Ontario Society and Politics, 1791–1896* (Toronto: University of Toronto Press, 1990). For more recent literature which vastly broadens discussions of politics and the state beyond the Loyalist frame and which gives due regard to strains of British radicalism and reform ideas, see Carol Wilton, *Popular Politics and Political Culture in Upper Canada, 1800–1850* (Montreal & Kingston: McGill-Queen's University Press, 2000); Jeffrey L. McNairn, *The Capacity to Judge: Public Opinion and Deliberative Democracy in Upper Canada, 1791–1854* (Toronto: University of Toronto Press, 2000). On ethnic radicalism, see Michael Gauvreau, "Covenanter Democracy: Scottish Popular Religion, Ethnicity, and the Varieties of Politico-Religious Dissent in Upper Canada, 1815–1841," "The Intersections of Religious and Social History," ed. Nancy Christie and Michael Gauvreau in *Histoire Sociale/Social History* 36, no. 71 (May 2003): 55–84.

37 Janice Potter MacKinnon, *The Liberty We Seek: Loyalist Ideology in Colonial New York and Massachusetts* (Cambridge, MA.: Harvard University Press, 1983); D.G. Bell, *Early Loyalist Saint John: The Origin of New Brunswick Politics, 1783–1786* (Fredericton, NB: New Ireland Press, 1983); Ann Condon, *The Envy of the American States: The Loyalist Dream for New Brunswick* (Fredericton, NB: New Ireland Press, 1984). For a critique of this historiography and its emphasis on Loyalist influence, see Donald Akenson, *The Irish in Ontario.*

38 John S. Moir, *Enduring Witness: A History of the Presbyterian Church in Canada* (Toronto: Bryant Press, 1974); Moir, "American Influences on Canadian Protestant Churches before Confederation," *Church History* 36 (1967): 440–55; John Webster Grant, *A Profusion of Spires: Religion in Nineteenth-Century Ontario* (Toronto: University of Toronto Press, 1988); Goldwin French, *Parsons and Politics: The Role of the Wesleyan Methodists in Upper Canada and the Maritimes from 1780 to 1855* (Toronto: Ryerson Press, 1962); George Rawlyk, *The Canada Fire: Radical Evangelicalism in British North America, 1775–1812* (Montreal & Kingston: McGill-Queen's University Press, 1994).

39 Ronald Rudin, *Making History in Twentieth-Century Quebec* (Toronto: University of Toronto Press, 1997).

40 Fernand Ouellet, *Histoire économique et sociale du Québec, 1760–1850* (Ottawa: Fides, 1966).

41 Allan Greer, *The Patriots and the People: The Rebellion of 1837 in Rural Lower Canada* (Toronto: University of Toronto Press, 1993); Greer, "1837–8: Rebellion Reconsidered," *Canadian Historical Review* 76, no. 1 (March 1995). See also Allan Greer and Ian Radforth, *Colonial Leviathan* (Toronto: University of Toronto Press, 1992).

42 See Curtis's stimulating series of articles on "governmentality" and the transformations within the colonial government in Lower Canada in the 1830s, in particular, "Le redécoupage du Bas-Canada dans les années 1830: un essai sur la 'gouvernementalité' coloniale," *Revue d'histoire de l'Amérique française* 58, no. 1 (Summer 2004): 27–66; "State of the Nation or Community of Spirit?: Schooling for Civic and Ethnic-Religious Nationalism in Insurrectionary Lower Canada," *History of Education Quarterly* 43, no. 3 (2003): 325–49.

43 Jean-Marie Fecteau, *Un nouvel ordre des choses. La charité, le crime, l'État au Québec, de la fin du XVIIIe siècle à 1840* (Montreal: VLB, 1989); and *La liberté du pauvre: crime et pauvreté au XIXe siècle québécois* (Montreal: VLB, 2004).

44 Yvan Lamonde, *Histoire sociale des idées au Québec, 1760–1896* (Montreal: Fides, 2000), 222, in which he argues that the Lower Canadian Patriote discourse, despite influences from the revolutionary examples of the United States, Latin America, and Europe remained firmly moored in British legal and constitutional categories and, until 1836, valorized English models of government and the British Constitution while attempting to delegitimize colonial authority.

45 Michel Ducharme, "Penser le Canada: la mise en place des assises intellectuelles de l'État canadien moderne (1838–1840)," *Revue d'histoire de l'Amérique française* 56, no. 3 (Winter 2003): 357–86.

46 For the most thoroughgoing recent restatement of the predominance of American republican discourse in Quebec, see Louis-Georges Harvey, *Le printemps de l'Amérique française. Américanité, anticolonialisme, et républicanisme dans le discours politique québécois, 1805–1837* (Montreal: Boréal, 2005). See, however, the critical review by Yvan Lamonde in *Revue d'histoire de l'Amérique française* 59. no. 1–2 (Summer/Fall 2005): 155–8. He asserts the primacy of British references in the discourse of Lower Canadian Reformers.

47 Gérard Bouchard, *Genèse des nations et cultures du Nouveau Monde*.

48 J.I. Little, *Borderland Religion: The Emergence of an English-Canadian Identity, 1792–1852* (Toronto: University of Toronto Press, 2004), xiii.

49 William Westfall, *Two Worlds: The Protestant Culture of Nineteenth-Century Ontario* (Montreal & Kingston: McGill-Queen's University Press, 1989).

50 J.M.S. Careless, "Mid-Victorian Liberalism in Central Canadian Newspapers, 1850–67," *Canadian Historical Review* 31, no. 3 (Sept. 1950): 221–36; Careless, *Brown of the Globe, vol. 1, The Voice of Upper Canada, 1818–1859* (Toronto: Macmillan, 1959); Westfall, *Two Worlds*.

51 It is important to underscore the extent to which the dialectic between reform and conservatism was at work within Britain and cannot be reduced to an American versus a British inflection. See Arthur Burns and Joanna Innes, eds., *Rethinking the Age of Reform.*

52 J.G.A. Pocock, "Empire, State and Confederation: The War of American Independence as a Crisis in Multiple Monarchy," in John Robertson, ed., *A Union of Empire: Political Thought and the British Union of 1707* (Cambridge: Cambridge University Press, 1995), 319.

53 H.V. Bowen, "Perceptions from the Periphery, 284; Ned C. Landsman, *Scotland and Its First American Colony, 1683–1765*; Ned C. Landsman, *From Colonials to Provincials: American Thought and Culture, 1680–1760* (Ithaca and London: Cornell University Press, 1997); Nicholas Canny, *Kingdom and Colony: Ireland in the Atlantic World, 1560–1800* (Baltimore and London: The Johns Hopkins University Press, 1988); J.M. Bumsted, *The People's Clearance: Highland Emigration to British North America, 1770–1815* (Edinburgh: Edinburgh University Press, 1982); Donald Akenson, *The Irish in Ontario.* For an excellent discussion of the way in which Scottish nationalism is renegotiated through an overseas experience, see J.M. Mackenzie, "Empire and National Identities: The Case of Scotland," *Transactions of the Royal Historical Society,* 1998. On the study of the early modern empire as an extension of provincialisms within Britain, see David Armitage, *The Ideological Origin of the British Empire,* 9. Like Wilson and Hall, Armitage has conceived of reintegrating the history of the empire and British history by the study of intellectual history, in particular the political ideologies which sustained changing views of empire and state.

54 Colley, *Britons*; Wilson, *The Sense of the People.*

55 Pocock, "The Limits and Divisions of British History," 316.

56 Ibid., 313. This pluralistic cultural approach for studying the circum-Atlantic has the benefit of allowing Canadian historians to circumvent the Scylla and Charybdis of whether the dominant cultural influence on any given question is American or British.

57 Nicholas Canny and Anthony Pagden, eds, *Colonial Identity in the Atlantic World, 1500–1800* (Princeton: Princeton University Press, 1997), 9.

58 For this phrase, see Bernard Bailyn and Philip D. Morgan, "Introduction," in Bailyn and Morgan, eds, *Strangers within the Realm: Cultural Margins of the First British Empire* (Chapel Hill and London: University of North Carolina Press, 1991), 5. On the importance of studying Britain overseas after 1783 see Linda Colley, "The Politics of Eighteenth-Century British History," *Journal of British Studies* 25, no. 4 (1986): 375–6.

59 J.M. Bumsted, "The Cultural Landscape of Early Canada," in Bailyn and Morgan, *Strangers within the Realm,* 365.

60 This perspective runs counter to the conventional nationalist teleology which is evident in much Canadian scholarship dealing with the period. For major

examples, see Suzanne Zeller, *Inventing Canada: Early Victorian Science and the Idea of a Transcontinental Nation* (Toronto: University of Toronto Press, 1987); Carl Berger, *The Sense of Power;* J.S. Moir, *Church and State in Canada West: Three Studies in the Relation of Denominationalism and Nationalism, 1841–1867* (Toronto: University of Toronto Press, 1959); Goldwin French, *Parsons and Politics.*

61 Franca Iacovetta, *Such Hard-Working People: Italian Immigrants in Post-War Toronto* (Montreal & Kingston: McGill-Queen's University Press, 1992).

62 See, for example, Jack Little, *Crofters and Habitants: Settler Society, Economy and Culture in a Quebec Township, 1848–1881* (Montreal & Kingston: McGill-Queen's University Press, 1991), *Borderland Religion;* Margaret Conrad, ed., *Intimate Relations: Family and Community in Planter Nova Scotia, 1759–1800* (Fredericton, NB: Acadiensis Press, 1995). In a similar approach to the Planter project in Australia, see Patricia Grimshaw, Chris McConville, and Ellen McEwen, eds, *Families in Colonial Australia* (Sydney and London: George Allen and Unwin, 1985) which is explicitly written within a colonial framework.

63 Jack P. Greene, "Transatlantic Colonization and the Modern Redefinition of Empire in the Early Modern Era," in Daniels and Kennedy, *Negotiated Empires.*

64 Greene's theoretical critique derives from the analytical framework he established in *Pursuits of Happiness: The Social Development of Early Modern British Colonies and the Formation of American Culture* (Chapel Hill and London: University of North Carolina Press, 1988). Although it might be argued that Greene continued to write within a nationalist paradigm, he nevertheless created a model of social development which counterbalanced the powerful declension model of Puritan Massachussetts and which might be used for a range of settlement processes.

65 For critical assessments of Wilson and a post-colonial reading of the past, see Colin Kidd, "Ethnicity in the British Atlantic World, 1688–1830," in Wilson, *A New Imperial History,* 260–77; Stephen How, "The Slow Death and Strange Rebirths of Imperial History," *Journal of Imperial and Commonwealth History* 29, no. 2 (May 2000): 131–41; John Darwin, "Globalism and Imperialism: The Global Context of British Power, 1830–1960," in Shigeru Akita, ed., *Gentlemanly Capitalism, Imperialism and Global History* (Basingstoke: Macmillan/Palgrave, 2002), 43–64. For earlier practitioners of the new cultural and social history of empire, see Bailyn and Morgan, eds, *Strangers within the Realm;* Armitage and Braddick, eds, *The British Atlantic World;* Martin Daunton and Rich Halpern, eds, *Empire and Others: British Encounters with Indigenous Peoples, 1600–1850* (Philadelphia: University of Pennsylvania Press, 1999); J.G.A. Pocock, "The Limits and Divisions of British History"; P.J. Cain and A.G. Hopkins, "The Peculiarities of British Capitalism: Imperialism and World Development," in Akita, ed., *Gentlemanly Capitalism,* 207–55.

66 Wilson, "Introduction: Histories, Empires, Modernities," in Wilson, ed., *A New Imperial History*, 4–5, 11.

67 Janet Sorensen, *The Grammar of Empire in Eighteenth-Century British Writing* (Cambridge: Cambridge University Press, 2002), 38–9, 21.

68 John L. Comaroff, "Images of Empires, Contests of Conscience: Models of Colonial Domination in South Africa," in Frederick Cooper and Ann Laura Stoler, eds, *Tensions of Empire: Colonial Cultures in a Bourgeois World* (Berkeley: University of California Press, 1997), 163–97.

69 For the purposes of this volume, Ann Stoler's theories of empire, which conceive of a more contingent, destabilized process of colonial domination, better explain the particular imperial complexion of white settlement societies. See Ann Laura Stoler and Frederick Cooper, " Between Metropole and Colony: Rethinking a Racial Agenda," in Cooper and Stoler, eds, *Tensions of Empire*, 4, 7–12, 27.

70 Bayley, *Imperial Meridian*, in which he stresses the aristocratic nature of the 1780–1830 period of British settlement; Stoler and Cooper, "Between Metropole and Colony," 31, on the empire as a bourgeois project.

71 Adele Perry, *On the Edge of Empire: Gender, Race and the Making of British Columbia, 1849–71* (Toronto: University of Toronto Press, 2001). For an overview of Britons overseas which gives equal weight to the varieties of white settler "agrarian civility," its white supremacist proclivities, and its local variants, see John Darwin, "Civility and Empire," in Peter Burke, Brian Harrison, and Paul Slack, eds, *Civil Histories: Essays Presented to Sir Keith Thomas* (Oxford: Oxford University Press, 2000), 321–36.

72 On the greater affinities between British Columbia and the British Pacific settlements of Australia and New Zealand, rather than with the Atlantic world colonies which were more directly shaped by the experience of the Revolution, see Pocock, *The Discovery of Islands*, passim.

73 Bailyn and Morgan, *Strangers within the Realm*; J.G.A. Pocock, "The Limits and Divisions of British History"; Jack P. Greene, *The Pursuit of Happiness*; David Armitage and Michael Braddick, eds, *The British Atlantic World*.

74 Stoler and Cooper, "Between Metropole and Colony," 4.

75 On the complex historiography both in Britain and overseas, see, for example, Bayly, *Imperial Meridian*; P.J. Marshall, ed., *The Oxford History of the British Empire, vol. 2, The Eighteenth Century*; Peter Burroughs, "Imperial Institutions and the Government of Empire," in Andrew Porter, *Oxford History of the British Empire, vol. 3, The Nineteenth-Century*, 170–80; John P. Halstead, *The Second British Empire: Trade, Philanthropy and Good Government, 1820–1890* (Westport, CT and London: Greenwood Press, 1983); David Hancock, *Citizens of the World: London Merchants and the Integration of the British Atlantic Community, 1735–1785* (Cambridge: Cambridge University Press, 1995); Donald Winch, *Classical Political Economy and the Colonies* (Boston: Harvard University Press, 1965); John Gascoigne, *Joseph Banks and the English Enlightenment: Useful*

Knowledge and Polite Culture (Cambridge: Cambridge University Press, 1994); E.P. Thompson, *The Making of the English Working Class* (Harmondsworth: Penguin, 1963); K.D.M. Snell, *Annals of the Labouring Poor: Social Change and Agrarian England, 1660–1900* (Cambridge: Cambridge University Press, 1985); David Eastwood, "The Age of Uncertainty: Britain in the Early Nineteenth-Century," *Transactions of the Royal Historical Society*, sixth series, 8 (1998); Arthur Burns and Joanna Innes, eds, *Rethinking the Age of Reform*; Boyd Hilton, *The Age of Atonement: The Influence of Evangelicalism on Social and Economic Thought 1785–1865* (Oxford: Clarendon Press, 1988).

76 Bayly, *Imperial Meridian*, 6–9. On the turn toward authoritarian rule after the Seven Years War, see P.J. Marshall, "The British Empire in the Age of the American Revolution," in William M. Fowler, Jr. and Wallace Coyle, eds, *The American Revolution: Changing Perspectives* (Boston: Northeastern University Press, 1979), 194–6; Elizabeth Mancke, "Negotiating an Empire: Britain and Its Overseas Peripheries, c.1550–1780," in Daniels and Kennedy, eds, *Negotiated Empires*, 257–8.

77 For a more extended discussion of the function of criminal justice in the conquered colony of Quebec, see Donald Fyson, *Magistrates, Police, and People: Everyday Criminal Justice in Quebec and Lower Canada, 1764–1837* (Toronto: University of Toronto Press, 2006).

78 Gould, *The Persistence of Empire*; Gould, "A Virtual Nation," 210; Elizabeth Mancke, "Another British America: A Canadian Model for the Early Modern British Empire," *Journal of Imperial and Commonwealth History* 25, no. 1 (Jan. 1997): 20. On the theme of local collaboration in the empire, see P.J. Marshall, "Britain and the World in the Eighteenth Century: Reshaping the Empire," *Transactions of the Royal Historical Society* (1998): 1–18. On the way in which the Scots conceived themselves as politically British and culturally Scottish, which follows a similar accommodation with British rule by the French Canadians, see James Symonds, "An Imperial Rule?: Highland Scots, Emigration and the British Colonial World," in Susan Lawrence, ed., *Archeologies of the British*, 143.

79 On this point, see Christopher L. Tomlins and Bruce H. Mann, eds, *The Many Legalities of Early America* (Chapel Hill and London: University of North Carolina Press, 2001) where several essays demonstrate the way in which law can both uphold and undermine social norms.

80 See Ian Dyck, "'Rural War' and the Missing Revolution in Early Nineteenth-Century England," in Michael T. Davis, ed., *Radicalism and Revolution in Britain, 1775–1848: Essays in Honour of Malcolm I. Thomis* (Basingstoke: Macmillan, 2000), 183.

81 Due attention must be paid here to the observation of Keith Wrightson that languages of class obscure as much as they reveal about the actual structure of social inequality. See Keith Wrightson, "Class," in Armitage and Braddick, eds, *The British Atlantic World*, 147. Simply because pauper immigrants per-

ceived a less unequal society does not mean that this was so. Because the vastly important collection of pauper emigrant letters collated by Wendy Cameron, Sheila Haines, and Mary McDougall Maude does not follow the settlers beyond the first few years in Upper Canada, it is impossible to gauge the way in which the economic realities of the New World did not live up to the first flush of optimism which we read in these epistolary life narratives. See *English Immigrant Voices: Labourers' Letters from Upper Canada in the 1830s* (Montreal & Kingston: McGill-Queen's Press, 2000). On the persistence of radicalism, see the article by Bryan Palmer in this volume.

82 On this theme, see Philippa Levine, ed., *Gender and Empire*, Companion Series to the Oxford History of the British Empire (Oxford: Oxford University Press, 2004).

83 Linda Colley, "Whose Nation?: Class and National Consciousness in Britain, 1750–1830," *Past and Present* 113 (Nov. 1986): 117.

84 Gould, *The Persistence of Empire*, 181–214.

85 For a similar perspective which critiques the lack of attention to the role played by religion in the expansion of the British Empire, see John Gascoigne, "The Expanding Historiography of British Imperialism," *The Historical Journal* 49, no. 2 (2006): 586–7.

86 Michael Zuckerman, "Identity in British America: Unease in Eden," in Canny and Pagden, eds, *Colonial Identity in the Atlantic World*, 116; Colin Kidd, *British Identities before Nationalism: Ethnicity and Nationhood in the Atlantic World, 1600–1800* (Cambridge: Cambridge University Press, 1999).

87 John M. Mackenzie, "Empire and National Identities," 230–1.

88 Ned Landsman, *From Colonials to Provincials*; Mark A. Noll, "Common Sense Traditions and American Evangelical Thought," *American Quarterly* 37, no. 2 (Summer 1985).

89 See, for example, A.B. McKillop, *A Disciplined Intelligence: Critical Inquiry and Canadian Thought in the Victorian Era* (Montreal & Kingston: McGill-Queen's University Press, 1979); Michael Gauvreau, *The Evangelical Century: College and Creed in English-Canada from the Great Revival to the Great Depression* (Montreal & Kingston: McGill-Queen's University Press, 1991).

90 On the importance of Enlightenment ideas for the second British Empire, see Richard Drayton, "Knowledge and Empire," in Marshall, *Oxford History of the British Empire*, 250.

91 For a recent study of how travel writing was used in the metropolis, see Nigel Leask, *Curiosity and the Aesthetics of Travel-Writing, 1770–1840: "From an Antique Land"* (Oxford: Oxford University Press, 2002).

92 There is a vast literature on this intellectual transformation. See, for example, J.G.A. Pocock, *The Machiavellian Moment: Florentine Political Thought and the Atlantic Republican Tradition* (Princeton and Oxford: Princeton University Press, 1975); J.G.A. Pocock, "Cambridge paradigms and Scotch philosophers: a study of the relations between the civic humanist and the civil juris-

prudential interpretation of eighteenth-century social thought," in Istvan
Hont and Michael Ignatieff, eds, *Wealth and Virtue: The Shaping of Political
Economy in the Scottish Englightenment* (Cambridge: Cambridge University
Press, 1983), 237–43. On the substitution of political economic frameworks
for the language of republican politics, see Nicholas Phillipson, "Adam Smith
as Civic Moralist," in Hont and Ignatieff, eds, *Wealth and Virtue*, 179–202. On
the overlap of mercantilist and liberal imperialist ideas, see Sudipta Sen,
"Liberal empire and illiberal trade: the political economy of 'responsible government,'" in Wilson, ed., *A New Imperial History*, 137.

93 Hilton, *The Age of Atonement.*

94 See P.J. Cain and A.G. Hopkins, "Gentlemanly Capitalism and British Expansion Overseas, I: the Old Colonial System, 1688–1850," *Economic History
Review*, second series, 39, no. 4 (1986): 501–25. For the classic statement of
the emergence of the liberal empire, see Bernard Semmel, *The Rise of Free
Trade Imperialism: Classical Political Economy, the Empire of Free Trade and Imperialism, 1750–1850* (Cambridge: Cambridge University Press, 1970).

95 On this agrarian ideal as it was promoted around the empire, see C.A. Bayly,
Imperial Meridian, 157–9; Richard Drayton, *Nature's Government: Science, Impe-
rial Britain and the 'Improvement' of the World* (New Haven and London: Yale
University Press, 2000), chap. 3, "The Useful Garden: Agriculture and the
Science of Government."

96 On the healthy dependence of the labouring classes on the wealthy and
weakness of "colonial dependency" created when colonial governments
remained too "dependent" on courtly influence, see Lieut Col Walter
O'Hara Journal, LAC, MG 24 I 62, 28 Nov. 1837.

97 On this theme, see Lance Banning, "Some Second Thoughts on Virtue and
the Course of Revolutionary Thinking," in Terrence Ball and J.G.A. Pocock,
eds, *Conceptual Change and the Constitution* (Kansas: University Press of Kansas,
1988), 196–8.

98 For colonial Scottish religious institutions and culture as seed-beds of radical
and reformist political ideology, see Michael Gauvreau, "Covenanter Democracy: Scottish Popular Religion, Ethnicity, and the Varieties of Politico-religious Dissent in Upper Canada, 1815–1841," *Histoire sociale/Social History* 35,
no. 71 (Spring 2003): 55–83.

99 Nancy Christie, "'a witness against vice': Religious Dissent, Political Radicalism and the Moral Regulation of Aristocratic Culture in Upper Canada," in
Jean-Marie Fecteau and Janice Harvey, eds, *La régulation sociale entre l'acteur et
l'institution: pour une problématique historique de l'interaction/Agency and Institutions in Social Regulation: Towards a Historical Understanding of Their Interaction*
(Sainte-Foy: Les Presses de l'Université du Quebec, 2005), 420–34.

100 Caroll Smith-Rosenberg, "Black Culture: The Shadowy Origins of the American Bourgeoisie," in St. George, ed., *Possible Pasts: Becoming Colonial in America*, 243–4.

101 Joyce Appleby, James Jacob, and Margaret Jacob, "Introduction," in James Jacob and Margaret Jacob, eds, *The Origins of Anglo-American Radicalism* (London: George Allen & Unwin, 1984), 12.

102 This view of the Upper Canadian Rebellion remains the conventional wisdom of historians. See Colin Read and Ronald J. Stagg, "Introduction," in Colin Read and Ronald J. Stagg, eds, *The Rebellion of 1837 in Upper Canada: A Collection of Documents* (Toronto: Champlain Society, 1985). For the prominence of the Lower Canadian rebellion, see Allan Greer, *The Patriots and the People: The Rebellion of 1837 in Rural Lower Canada* (Toronto: University of Toronto Press, 1993).

103 For the transformation of both Reform and Tory political cultures in the years immediately following the Rebellion, see Carol Wilton, *Popular Politics and Political Culture in Upper Canada, 1800–1850.*

104 Toronto Reference Library, Robert Baldwin Papers, A51, Hincks to Baldwin, 15 June 1843.

105 Quoted in Paul Knaplund, *Gladstone and Britain's Imperial Policy* (London: Allen and Unwin, 1927), 61. For a characterization of this era as one defined by a "bleakly conservative modernity," see Cora Kaplan, "White, black and green: racialising Irishness in Victorian England," in Peter Gray, ed., *Victoria's Ireland?*, 68.

106 For the concept of the open and closed frontier as applied to new societies of settlement, see Howard Lamar and Leonard Thompson, *The Frontier in History: North America and Southern Africa Compared* (New Haven: Yale University Press, 1981).

PART ONE

Agrarian Patriots

DONALD FYSON

The Canadiens and British Institutions of Local Governance in Quebec from the Conquest to the Rebellions

In the greater part of the states to which I refer, the want of means at the disposal of the central executive is amply supplied by the efficiency of the municipal institutions; and even where these are wanting, or imperfect, the energy and self-governing habits of an Anglo-Saxon population enable it to combine whenever a necessity arises. But the French population of Lower Canada possesses neither such institutions nor such a character. Accustomed to rely entirely on the government, it has no power of doing anything for itself, much less of aiding the central authority. The utter want of municipal institutions giving the people any control over their local affairs, may indeed be considered as one of the main causes of the failure of representative government, and of the bad administration of the country ... The inhabitants of Lower Canada were unhappily initiated into self government at exactly the wrong end, and those who were not trusted with the management of a parish, were enabled, by their votes, to influence the destinies of a state ... There never has been, in fact, any institution in Lower Canada, in which any portion of the French population have been brought together for any administrative purpose.

Lord Durham, 1839[1]

With these trenchant comments, Lord Durham summed up his views on Canadien participation in the institutions of local governance that were so central to British conceptions of citizenship and politics. When it came to self-government following the English model, the Canadiens, the francophone Catholics of Quebec, badly needed education; compared to their Anglo-Saxon neighbours, for whom self-governance was inherent, they were quite simply culturally and historically unequipped. Durham thereby bundled race and governance together in a single package that helped explain the Rebellions and justify both Union and responsible government.

The reactions of conquered populations to the institutions imposed on them by the conquerors have long attracted the attention of historians of the British Empire. Quebec historiography has been no exception, and much of it has echoed Durham's observations, though often rejecting his conclusions. Mason Wade, for example, though sympathetic to the "French Canadians," nevertheless attributed what he called their "lack of civic consciousness" in part to their long history of exclusion from meaningful participation in local government, which he traced back to New France.[2] In the ample historiography concerning the effects of the Conquest, despite debates over matters such as the effects of regime change on the Canadien bourgeoisie, it is generally taken as a given that the Canadien population was excluded from power by the new institutional framework put in place from 1764. And in discussions of the lead-up to the Rebellions of 1837–38, institutional difficulties and, especially, Canadien alienation from power, are very often cited as being at the heart of deteriorating relations between the rulers and the ruled.[3]

On a more general level, in considering Canadien reactions to formal institutions in the period from the Conquest to the Rebellions, Quebec historians have concentrated on three main aspects. First, they have examined Canadien reactions to pre-Conquest institutions that were seen as key to preserving Canadien identity: the civil law, for example, including the law itself and the notarial system; the seigneurial regime; the Catholic church; and, stretching the definition of "institution" a little, the French language. Canadien attachment to these is often presented as a fundamental component of the constant battle against British assimilation.[4] There have also been studies of Canadien participation in democratic or quasi-democratic institutions that were British-inspired but Canadien-controlled due to the latter's demographic domination: for example, the House of Assembly from the 1790s, the parish school system from the late 1820s, the elected municipal governments of the 1830s or, once again stretching the definition, the political press. These are generally seen as relatively rapidly accepted by the Canadien population at large, in part as bulwarks against authoritarian encroachments by the British colonial administration or British culture, and allowing Canadiens to gain some measure of control over their destiny. Indeed, the abolition or suspension of many of these Canadien-controlled institutions in the mid–1830s, as part of broader political struggles, is seen as one of the key factors leading up to the Rebellions of 1837–8.[5] A very different conclusion has been drawn in the historiography with regard to Canadien reactions to other British-inspired institutions imposed on them by imperial or colonial administrations, and where Canadien control was contested or absent. Whether it be the unelected Legislative Council, seen as the instigator of many of the political confrontations of the 1820s and 1830s; the land registry system, perceived as a roundabout way of introducing key aspects of the English civil law; the criminal law, seen as fundamentally foreign; or the Royal Institution schools, snubbed by the Canadiens as blatant attempts at assimilation; all are portrayed as rejected by the Canadien population and indeed, in many instances, regarded as tyrannical, once again contributing to the confrontations that came to a head in the Rebellions.[6] Even hybrid institutions that drew on both French and British models, such as the militia or the roads repair system, are presented as accepted as long as they conformed to traditional norms, but opposed when changes were made.[7]

Not all of these assertions and assumptions have gone unquestioned in the historiography. As historians have long shown, Canadien attachment to pre-Conquest institutions such as the seigneurial system and the Church varied considerably according to social position, with both gaining far more elite than popular support; though it must not be forgotten that the failure of attempts to convert the Canadien population to Protestantism, and the relative unwillingness of Canadiens to settle outside the seigneurial zone, suggest at least passive acceptance of these institutions, and that even during the Rebellions, unlike revolutionary France, there was no desecration of churches or wholesale destruction of the symbols of seigneurialism.[8] The generalized assertion of Canadien attachment to and satisfaction with British-inspired but democratic institutions such as the House of Assembly has been less problematized, and indeed the system seems to have functioned relatively democratically; at the same time, work such as that on the exclusion of women from the vote has nuanced the direct equation too often made between electoral politics and democracy.[9] But what has largely remained unquestioned has been Canadien reaction to British-inspired institutions that were imposed from above. Even in much recent writing, the historiographical consensus has seemed clear, with the relationship presented as one of oppression, resistance, or avoidance.

This paper proposes a reconsideration of Canadien attitudes toward and participation in British-inspired and state-regulated institutions of local governance that were put in place in the decades between the Conquest and the Rebellions. In taking this local turn, it deliberately avoids the top-down institutions, such as the central administration or the parliamentary system, that have often been the focus of the historiography. The paper's local turn also explains the use of the broader term "governance" rather than the more restrictive "government," too

often associated with the central administration or with elected municipal bodies. The paper concentrates on examples drawn from two
areas of local governance largely inspired by British practices: local
criminal justice and local administration. In order to examine both
elite and popular-class Canadien reactions to and participation in
institutions associated with these fields of state power, the focus is on
two institutions that were of particular import for Canadien elites –
grand juries and the magistracy – and two that give some sense of how
ordinary Canadiens reacted to British-style institutions – locally
elected officials in the countryside (notably parish bailiffs) and local
criminal justice (notably recourse to it by the Canadien population in
general). The main argument is that, whatever their political and ideological take on these British institutions, which varied considerably,
the Canadien population as a whole, both elite and popular-class, recognized them as valid sources of power and participated in and used
them to an extent that belies the views both of Durham and of later
historians.

1. CANADIEN ELITES AND BRITISH INSTITUTIONS

The classic and still vibrant "decapitation thesis" suggests that the Conquest resulted in the wholesale replacement of a French and Canadien
elite by a new, British one.[10] British control of state institutions played
a key role in this exclusion. State officials made up a significant part of
the pre-Conquest elites; after the Conquest, the British colonial
administration attributed the lion's share of state positions to British
colonists, and even excluded the Catholic francophones altogether for
the first decade and a half of British rule. The Canadien elites were
thus forced to turn to other sources of political power, notably the
Assembly, from 1792, leaving the state to the British.

   This notion of Canadien exclusion has considerable truth to it at the
upper levels of the colonial state, among the senior administrators and
judges, for example. Thus, as Gilles Paquet and Jean-Pierre Wallot
showed, lucrative patronage positions were heavily weighted in favour
of British officials, with Canadien elites receiving a disproportionately
small share of the pickings.[11] But the notion of Canadien exclusion
from the institutions of power becomes less and less tenable the further one moves down the administrative hierarchy, and especially
within institutions of local governance. British administrators were in
fact quite happy to co-opt Canadien elites into local administration,
and Canadien elites were generally quite willing to be co-opted. The

participation of Canadien elites in two important institutions of local governance, the grand jury and the magistracy, is a case in point.

1.1 Canadien Elites and the Grand Jury[12]

In theory, the jury was one of the most significant innovations of the new post-Conquest legal system, in stark contrast with the pre-Conquest Continental model which vested judicial power in professional or semi-professional judges. In assessing the reaction of Canadien elites to this new system in the decades immediately following the Conquest, historians have generally asserted that the ideological significance of the jury, a fundamental component of British liberties, had no resonance for Canadiens in general and the elites in particular. They have pointed to negative comments such as the testimony of Quebec's Chief Justice, William Hey, who declared that "the higher part of the Canadians object to the institution itself, as humiliating and degrading"; or the views of the seigneur Michel Chartier de Lotbinière, who suggested that attachment to juries – which he sarcastically described as composed of "douze jurés que l'on nomme SES PAIRES" – was infantile, a product of "des préjugés de l'enfance." The introduction of juries in some civil matters in the 1780s also led to resistance among the Canadien members of the legislative council, who saw it as a backdoor attempt to introduce one of the fundamental elements of English civil law, contrary to the cherished provisions of the Quebec Act that guaranteed the continuance of French civil law. On the other hand, British officials also asserted that the Canadiens in general accepted juries in criminal matters, were most flattered to be asked to be jurors, and in fact made very good jurors, not least in that they listened attentively to the instructions of the judges.[13]

A closer examination of the functioning of the jury system reveals that Canadien elites at least were neither particularly opposed to participating in it nor particularly enthusiastic about it. Consider the example of grand juries, in the criminal justice system. Grand juries were especially important since they played both a judicial and a political role. Judicially, they made the first assessment of the weight of evidence against an accused and could stop a prosecution even before it went to trial. But they also had a significant role in politics and local governance. For example, as representatives of their judicial district, grand jurors were called on to make formal statements on matters of general public interest, their so-called representations. One of the first political controversies in post-Conquest Quebec, indeed, arose from the presentment of a Quebec City grand jury in 1764, which denounced Governor James Murray's administration and suggested a wide variety of political changes, including the calling of an assembly. The broader political controversy aside, the British members of the jury also represented that Catholic Canadiens, who were also on the jury with them, should be ineligible under the penal laws.

As this first jury presentment suggests, in Quebec, British administrators almost right from the start included Catholic Canadiens in juries, regardless of the English penal laws, though there was some uncertainty in the first couple of years. In making up grand juries throughout the period up to 1832, when a comprehensive jury law fundamentally changed (at least temporarily) the way juries were summoned, colonial officials generally applied the principal of the jury *de mediate*, summoning half anglophones, half francophones. This was a significant innovation from practices in other colonies with Anglo-Protestant minorities, such as Ireland or Maryland, where Catholics were excluded from juries.[14]

Of course, being summoned did not necessarily mean participating in and embracing; but if we can judge from participation, Canadien elites seem to have had no problem with sitting on grand juries. As table 1 shows, even while Chartier de Lotbinière and others were criticizing the institution of the jury, Canadiens did not boycott grand juries, and the composition of the juries that actually sat was almost exactly half anglophone, half francophone. And given the frequency of the criminal courts (six times a year, in two, then three different districts), even despite the practice of calling the same individuals to sit as grand jurors over and over again, jury service was still widely experienced by the Canadien elites: in the district of Montreal alone, between 1810 and 1832, some 500 different Canadiens sat as grand jurors.

Indeed, Canadien elites were somewhat more assiduous in their attention to this civic responsibility than their British counterparts. Already in 1774, Chief Justice Hey complained of the colony's British inhabitants, "They are wonderfully zealous for the trial by jury; and the misfortune is, they do not act up to it; for I can never get them to attend."[15] Fines were imposed for people who neglected jury duty; and among the grand jurors fined for non-attendance in Montreal's Quarter Sessions from the 1770s to the 1820s, two-thirds were anglophones. Canadiens seem thus to have been more intent on participating in this most potent symbol of British rights and liberties than were the British inhabitants of Quebec themselves.

At the same time, though, there is little indication that in the eighteenth century at least, Canadien elites particularly cherished the jury for its constitutional value. Observers like Governor Guy Carleton or

Table 1: Francophones as a proportion of grand jurors, district of Montreal, 1767–1833

	King's Bench (%)	Quarter Sessions (%)
1767–73	50	*not available*
1777–87	50	48
1787–1809	49	53
1810–29	49	50
1830–32*	53	61
1832–33	54	73

*before the jury reform law of 1832. SOURCE: Fyson, "Grands jurys," 99.

Francis Masères, the colony's attorney general, suggested that the Canadiens were relatively indifferent to juries, and indeed, juries were little mentioned in the discourse of the day, for example in the various petitions from Canadiens on constitutional issues. By the late 1820s, however, this had changed considerably, and the jury system was being defended by the *Patriote* party as a fundamental component of the constitutional birthright of Canadiens, under attack by administrators who sought to subvert this sacred institution by packing juries in order to ensure politically motivated convictions. The learned exposition on the history of the jury from its medieval origins to the present, establishing a direct path from Anglo-Saxon liberties to Lower Canadian reform, delivered by the moderate nationalist Joseph-Rémi Vallières de Saint-Réal before the House of Assembly in 1829 as part of a general attack on the Dalhousie administration, was a far cry from the sarcastic comments of Chartier de Lotbinière in the 1770s.

So why this Canadien acceptance and assiduity, when at first at least, the jury had no particular constitutional resonance for them? First, on a practical level, juries were perhaps not quite such an innovation as most contemporary observers and later historians have assumed, since Canadiens were not unused to being called on to participate in the civil justice system. As Hilda Neatby noted long ago, lay participation in judicial decision-making had in fact been an integral part of pre-Conquest French civil procedure, through the system whereby many civil disputes could be submitted to binding arbitration by arbitrators named by the parties. In France, the system in fact dated back to the middle ages, as did juries in England. As well, Canadiens in general, whether elite or popular-class, were well used to participating in the councils of relatives and friends who were legally summoned to give their advice on the disposition of property and dependents following the death of a family member, a practice which, like arbitration, continued unchanged across the Conquest.[16] The novelty of the jury system thus lay not in the judicial participation of or even judicial deci-

sions made by peers, but rather in the way of selecting the jury (by a
state official, the sheriff, rather than by the parties involved) and by its
use in criminal matters, where a jury might decide whether the
accused lost their liberty or even their lives. Public participation in
the justice system was less innovative than might be supposed from
a purely formalist interpretation of the apparently absolutist pre-
Conquest French state.

Second, in the cities at least, grand juries were an important source
of local power. Beyond the paternalistic power of judging one's fellow
citizens, grand juries were also one of the main avenues through which
local elites, both British and Canadien, could make their voices heard
in order to influence state decisions. In the absence of representative
municipal institutions before 1833, it was the justices of the peace who
administered Quebec's towns; and through their presentments in
Quarter Sessions, the grand jurors had a privileged access to the ear of
the justices on the bench. Though the justices often did no more than
listen, especially when grand juries criticized their administration, the
presentments often had more concrete effects. For example, grand
jury presentments in Montreal led directly to the justices framing new
municipal regulations to address grievances raised by the grand jurors
ranging from the burying of dead bodies within the city walls to the
impropriety of people swimming nude in the St Lawrence.

And finally, Canadiens came to recognize the jury in general as an
institution which, if properly used, could counter authoritarian tendencies of British administrators. Jury nullification in political prosecutions was an important factor in making the British criminal justice
system less tyrannical than it might have been had the governors been
given free rein, and was in fact frequently complained of by high
Tories in the 1830s, a complaint repeated by Durham in his report.[17]

1.2 Canadien Elites and the Magistracy[18]

In the magistracy as well, we find a British institution which Canadien
elites rapidly adapted to and indeed drew advantages from. In Quebec
from the Conquest to the Rebellions, following the model of local governance adopted in England and in the American colonies, justices of
the peace appointed directly by the colonial administration carried
out most of the business of criminal justice and a significant part of
local administration, including the administration of the cities of Quebec and Montreal up to their incorporation in 1832. As with juries,
these lay justices were a significant departure from the pre-Conquest
system, since the post-Conquest magistracy depended largely on the
voluntary activity of elites rather than on the payment of professional

magistrates, as was the case in the pre-Conquest royal and even seigneurial courts. Also, as with juries, the colonial administration attempted to co-opt Canadien elites by naming them to the magistracy. Indeed, as table 2 shows, francophones (almost entirely Canadiens) comprised significant and even overwhelming proportions of the magistrates appointed in the eighteenth and early nineteenth centuries. Overall, we can estimate that some 800 or more individual Canadiens were named to the various commissions of the peace in Quebec and Lower Canada between the Conquest and the Rebellions. As with juries, this was a far cry from the situation in other colonies such as Ireland, where Catholics were generally excluded from the magistracy.

The evident willingness of successive colonial administrations to appoint Canadiens as justices did begin to wane in the 1820s, as the Dahousie administration grew increasingly suspicious of Canadien elites and began removing them from the magistracy. By 1829, a committee of the House of Assembly declared that the number of Quebec-born justices in the district of Montreal, not "at all proportionate to the Canadian population," had "given birth to feelings of a most painful nature to the inhabitants of the Country."[19] Still, even then, apart from the district of Montreal, the proportion of Canadien magistrates increased again in the mid–1830s, just prior to the Rebellions, as later administrations adopted at least the facade of conciliation; although, by the middle of 1837, the Gosford administration once again took to wholesale dismissals of mainly Canadien magistrates whom it considered disloyal.

Appointment to the commission, however, did not necessarily mean activity as a magistrate; in England, for example, most appointed magistrates did not act. But as with grand juries, far from declining or neglecting to act as magistrates, many Canadien elites took their appointments seriously and were often as or more active than their British colleagues. Consider the magistracy of the district of Montreal. In the entire period from the Conquest to the Rebellions, the active magistracy was significantly or even predominantly francophone, as figures 1 and 2 suggest; even while, as table 1 showed, throughout the first third of the nineteenth century, francophones were in the minority on the commission. The exceptions were three brief periods: the 1760s, when the penal laws excluded Catholics from the magistracy (and even then, in the early 1770s, several particularly active Huguenot magistrates ensured that British justice had a francophone face); and the mid-1790s and late 1820s, where there was indeed a boycott of magisterial activities by Canadien elites, related to political tensions at the time (in the 1790s, the tensions over loyalty during the French revolutionary crisis, and in the 1820s, the crisis under Dalhousie).[20] The

Table 2: Proportion of francophone justices in selected general commissions of the peace, 1764–1837* (larger, bold type indicates half or more francophones)

			Districts of:		
Commission year	Montreal (%)	Quebec (%)	Trois-Rivières (%)	Gaspé (%)	Saint-Francis (%)
1764	10	15	–	–	–
1776	**58**	57	–	–	–
1785	**50**	44	–	–	–
1788/1790	**65**	56	**76**	41.	–
1794	**60**	64	**88**	19	–
1799	42	**55**	**79**	–	–
1810/1811	41	45	**50**	12	–
1815	–	**64**	48	–	–
1821/1823/1824	42	**61**	48	18	0
1828	32	49	35	14	–
1830	43	44	**64**	0	0
1833	32	45	**63**	–	0
1836/1837	43	63	**70**	36	0

* excludes ex officio justices. SOURCE: Fyson, *Magistrates, Police, and People*, 85.

proportion of francophone justices committing to the Montreal gaol in the 1830s is particularly striking. In the period leading up to the Rebellions, in the district most affected, the face of the British criminal law was as often as not a Canadien one.[21]

Nor were these Canadien magistrates all toadies of the administration, though there were a fair number of those. For example, those who essentially dominated the magistracy in the city of Montreal (and the bench of the Quarter and Special Sessions as well) in the first two decades of the nineteenth century were often moderate nationalists with links to the Canadien and, later, Patriote parties: men such as Jean-Marie Mondelet (a supporter of the Canadien party with strong ties to the Papineau and Viger families) or Pierre-Amable Boucher de Boucherville (arrested as a Patriote sympathizer following the Rebellions). And even in the 1830s, two of the most active Montreal magistrates were Denis-Benjamin Viger, the nationalist gadfly of both the administration and the Papineau wing of the Patriotes, and Pierre Lukin, one of only three magistrates who had opposed the use of the army in the infamous 1832 election riot in Montreal's West Ward which resulted in the death of several Canadiens after troops fired on the crowd.[22] Similarly, in 1808, during the crisis under Craig, Joseph Turgeon, a Terrebonne notary, longstanding magistrate, and supporter of the Canadien party, was denounced by David Ross, the King's Counsel in Montreal, for the electoral speech he gave which led to his defeating Ross's brother:

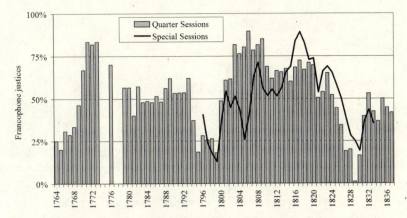

Figure 1: Francophone justices on the benches of the Montreal Quarter Sessions (criminal justice and local administration), 1764–1837, and Special Sessions (municipal administration), 1796–1833

SOURCE: Fyson, *Magistrates, Police, and People*, 115 (adjusted for 1771–73); Archives de la Ville de Montréal, VM35, Fonds des juges de paix de Montréal, Montreal Special Sessions registers.

[Turgeon] immediately addressed the people in the words "Mes amis, on nous forge des feres [sic], je vous ne dit pas plus long, mai m'effiez [sic] vous!!!". I suppose the annals of the late Revolution in France cannot furnish two speeches that had more diabolical effect upon the minds of the people than these above mentioned. It seemed to have electrified things and gained ground like wild fire, the people seemed perfectly convulsed and apparently seem'd to think that the two magistrates, in whom they were bound to have a certain confidence were informed of some black designs against them the inhabitants of this county that they dare not then develop, every man seemed to distrust his neighbor and a general wonder and movement took place, and I am informed, which by the bye I did not hear, a cry here and there, amongst the people, of point d'anglais, point d'anglais!! ... They are both justices of the peace and officers of the militia bearing the King's commission and how far they shew themselves deserving that honour and confidence their conduct on the 23 May last will shew ... When [party spirit] is roused ... and set in motion (when dormant) by the officers under government allows me to ask what is to become of us?[23]

But Turgeon was reappointed to the magistracy in 1810 nonetheless, as was the other magistrate mentioned in Ross's letter, Joseph-Édouard Faribault. More generally, of about 120 francophones elected to the

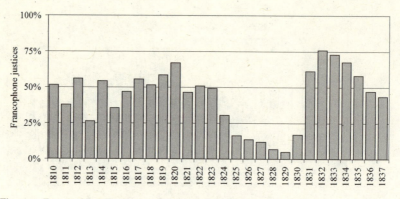

Figure 2: Francophone justices committing to the Montreal gaol, 1810–37

SOURCE: Fyson, *Magistrates, Police, and People*, 115, 1831–37

House of Assembly for the district of Montreal between 1791 and 1827, about 50 were or would become justices of the peace, many of whom were nationalists of one sort or another; and conversely, about a quarter of all francophone magistrates also served as MLAs. There was, of course, considerable political manipulation of the magistracy, even apart from the period under Dalhousie. Thus, while Turgeon may have avoided dismissal, Eustache-Ignace Trottier Desrivières Beaubien, the co-seigneur of Montarville, was summarily dismissed as a magistrate by Craig in 1810 because he had presented the Canadien leader Pierre-Stanislas Bédard at the hustings. But political manipulation did not automatically lead to Canadien exclusion.

There are several reasons for the strong presence of the conquered and the colonized in an institution of local governance essential to the preservation of British colonial rule. One was the necessity for the colonial administration to find representatives on the ground, especially in the Canadien parts of the countryside, but even in the cities, where many British merchants refused to serve actively in the magistracy because of the time it took. Further, there is no indication that Canadien elites found the magistracy overly challenging. Some did have initial reservations; for example, on learning of his appointment as a justice in 1776, Pierre Guy, a Montreal merchant, wrote to a friend,

Je tavous ingenument que mon premier mouvement a esté de remerciere, que la seul reflection d'indisposer son excellence contre moi est la seul raison qui mest arreté, que si je croioit sans lui deplaire pouvoire me demestre d'une emploie qui exige

beaucoup daplication je le feroit quand a letude en droit je nenait
jamais faite, juger sans lumière et connoissance nouvelle embaras
pour celui qui nen a pas de trop, estre asujetie au reflection
publique nes pas une encourgement pour moi.[24]

However, Guy soon became one of the leading magistrates of the city;
and overall, few Canadiens refused the administration's offer to join
the magistracy. Language was not the hindrance one might think:
though a handful Canadiens declined being appointed because they
could not speak English, many understood English, and at any rate,
until the mid–1820s at least, many of the justices' proceedings were in
large part in French.

But most importantly, even more than the grand jury, the magistracy
offered a way for Canadien elites to exercise political and social power
to a degree that was denied them at the upper levels of the state.
Beyond the possibilities for paternalistic control offered by judging
their social inferiors, Canadien elites could also use the magistracy's
power over local administration to advance local agendas. Thus, for
example, control over Montreal's Special Sessions gave Canadien
elites in the city a considerable say in the physical structuring of Montreal's road network; and using their power to pass municipal bylaws in
Quarter Sessions, Montreal's justices in the early nineteenth century
passed municipal regulations and made administrative decisions that
were both increasingly moralistic and increasingly free-market.[25]

2. ORDINARY CANADIENS AND BRITISH INSTITUTIONS

If Canadien elites thus seem to have adapted relatively well to these
British institutions, what of ordinary Canadiens? For British leaders
from Carleton to Durham, habitants in particular were simply ignorant peasants and, thus, incapable of any independant collective
action, political or otherwise. This view has had a persistent life in the
historiography. For example, in their examination of electoral politics
in Quebec since 1791, Jean and Marcel Hamelin consistently characterized the habitants in the period to 1840 as supremely ignorant, a
view encapsulated in their statement that "Baptiste n'avait rien
compris," which to them explained the failure of Lower-Canadian parliamentary democracy. And one recent survey of Quebec nationalism
asserts that in the eighteenth century, "Politics, apart from very sporadic disobedience, was beyond the ken of the habitant" and that
"Canadien society was not yet participant."[26] In much recent historiography, historians have sought to nuance this view of the habitants as
simply "potatoes in a sack," and show that they were, instead, capable

of self-governance, as evidenced in their participation in institutions such as the parish or the charivari; but still largely alienated from the British institutions imposed on them.[27] As we saw, with regard to institutions of local governance, the historiography generally postulates at the very least ignorance and avoidance, if not distrust and resistance. However, a closer examination shows a far more complex relationship between ordinary Canadiens and British-style institutions imposed from above, one that reveals the Canadiens' capacity both for adaptation and for collective action.

2.1 Rural Canadiens and Locally Elected Offices[28]

One way in which ordinary Canadiens participated in British-style institutions imposed on them was through locally elected officials in the countryside. Under the French regime, there were no such elected officials, at least in the eighteenth century. In form at least, all office-holders, from high colonial officials down to local bailiffs and militia officers, were directly appointed by the crown or the colonial administration, following the absolutist philosophy inherent in the governing of a French royal colony; though in practice, local recommendations and proposals, notably by local elites, probably played a significant role in apparently centralized decisions. This formal centralization was in sharp contrast to the American colonies, which had imported and expanded the English model of local office-holding, partly elective, partly appointive. In early modern England, indeed, local parish offices, both elected and unelected, have recently been characterized as the basis of a significant local democracy that contributed to the political education of at least the middling members of local rural society. Earlier historians of parish administration, such as the Webbs, had portrayed them as the purview of bumbling or malicious parish officials.[29]

In Quebec and Lower Canada, despite Durham's often-cited but erroneous assertion that "beyond the walls of Quebec, all regular administration of the country appeared to cease ... there are no county, no municipal, no parochial officers, either named by the Crown, or elected by the people,"[30] there were in fact a variety of locally elected officials. Several closely followed the English ideal of annually elected offices which in theory rotated through the male property-holders of each parish or other rural settlement: most notably, the parish bailiffs between 1765 and 1775, the sous-voyers (roads surveyors) from 1796 onward, and the fence and ditch inspectors from 1824. Others were elected less regularly or less generally: the police trustees elected in several rural villages from 1818; the trust-

ees for managing the commons of a dozen or so seigneuries in the
1820s; the school trustees elected in many parishes from the late
1820s; or the roads and bridges inspectors elected in most rural areas
in the mid–1830s.[31] Surveying all of these would evidently be impossible within the scope of this paper, especially since none, apart from
the school trustees, have been studied in any depth. Hence, to illus-
trate how these English institutions were imposed on and received by
the Canadiens, the remainder of this section concentrates on the
first, the system of parish bailiffs in the countryside in the 1760s and
1770s.

In the administrative system conceived in the aftermath of the Conquest and the restoration of civil government in Quebec, the lynchpins
in the connection between the central administration and the rural
Canadien population were to be the bailiffs elected in each parish of
the colony. These parish bailiffs performed a variety of functions. Judicially, they were to arrest offenders, transport prisoners, perform preliminary coroners' inquests, act as process-servers for the courts, and
even judge certain small civil disputes. They were also responsible for
supervising roadwork in their parishes. They had logistic duties, notably organizing the corvée in their parishes for providing firewood for
the British garrisons. And they were meant to serve as the conduit by
which official information flowed from the governors to the governed:
it was to them that the colonial administration sent copies of ordinances, proclamations, and the like for publication. In other words,
the bailiffs were intended to replace the militia captains of the French
regime and the military regime as the main agents of civil administration in the rural parishes of the colony, and to fill many of the same
roles as the English parish constable.[32]

Though the parish bailiffs' duties echoed the pre-existing French
administrative structures based on the militia captains, the mode of
selecting bailiffs was inspired instead by English ideals of local governance. Formally appointed by the central administration, the rural
parish bailiffs were nonetheless to be chosen from a list of six "good
and sufficient men" elected annually by parish assemblies and sent in
to the central administration, which then selected one head bailiff and
two sub-bailiffs and published their names in the *Quebec Gazette*. This
was a striking departure from the absolutist and centralizing spirit of
the French regime, where militia captains were commissioned directly
by the governor, with no democratic consultation. The filiations with
English concepts of civic duty and self-governance were also evident in
the provisions that no person was to be elected a second time until all
other eligible householders in the parish had served. Indeed, for
James Murray, the parallel with English constables was self-evident: his

comment on this provision of the ordinance, in his report to his superiors, was "We called them Bailiffs, because the word is better understood by the New Subjects than that of Constable."[33]

The parish bailiff system, like many of the administrative structures implanted at the beginning of British civil government, was only short-lived. The last bailiffs were named in 1773 and, though they were temporarily continued in office following the coming into effect of the Quebec Act in 1775, the restoration of the militia from later in the year and the administrative chaos engendered by the American invasion eventually put paid to the institution. Many were still in office in 1776, when government commissioners toured the countryside to investigate Canadien loyalty, but most were then formally dismissed, and in 1777 ordinances conferred most of the bailiffs' previous civil duties on the militia captains.[34]

Partly as a result of the brief existence of this experimental implant, the parish bailiffs have been largely dismissed in Quebec historiography. Most historians have been content with reproducing the few contemporary evaluations of bailiffs, such as those of Carleton and Hey, who described them as drawn from "the meanest and most illiterate of the Inhabitants," or those of Joseph Desrosiers, a former militia captain of Yamaska, who accused the bailiffs of acting as if they were superior to their fellow parishioners. These views were echoed by others in the colony, such as Pierre du Calvet, the irascible magistrate (and future political prisoner), who declared that "l'état de bailli devint le seminaire de la coquinerie, sous ce titre ils obtinrent le brevet d'être impuniement coquin ... le brigandage des baillifs appuïée de ces juges de paix, donnoit lieu à trop de plaintes multipliées." And the colony's English merchants denounced the bailiffs as well, as illiterate and prone to embezzlement.[35] Contemporaries, and historians after them, thus dismissed the bailiffs as neither good nor sufficient, in contrast with the militia officers, the "natural leaders" of the Canadiens whom the bailiffs only imperfectly replaced.[36]

But most of this anecdotal testimony is inherently flawed. Carleton was notoriously suspicious of anything that smacked of democratic institutions, whether it be assembly or elected bailiffs; Desrosiers was a former officer (and the seigneur of Rivière-David to boot) regretting his loss of prestige and power; Du Calvet was engaged in a feud with the other members of the magistracy and had every interest in portraying their actions, and those of their subordinates, in as black a light as possible; and the merchants who signed the petition were in fact protesting against Carleton's reform of civil justice, which they feared was to their disadvantage. Further, all these objections to the bailiffs resemble nothing more than the standard complaints levelled against the equivalent institution in England, the parish constables, complaints which have been shown to be largely exaggerated.[37]

An evaluation of the administrative efficiency of the system of parish bailiffs, compared to that of the militia captains who preceded and succeeded them, will have to await detailed studies of matters such as civil justice and the roads repair system. But we can make some preliminary observations on what this system meant for the adaptation of Canadiens to British institutions, and vice versa, based on a cursory examination of the surviving records relating to the appointment of bailiffs and a reconstruction of the lists of elected bailiffs for the district of Montreal.[38]

First, it is clear that parish elections were held regularly, with numerous surviving election returns and other documents; and this despite a tendency on the part of the colonial administration to weaken the initial democratic bent of the office. Thus, though the ordinance insisted on annual elections, there was no way for the colonial executive to enforce this and, by the late 1760s, if parishioners decided not to hold new elections, existing bailiffs were simply continued in office. Even more strikingly, in 1768, the executive, under Carleton, decided that all head bailiffs who wanted to serve, and against whom there was no complaint, should be continued in office.[39] Hence, had Canadiens wanted to avoid the electoral process, they could simply have ignored it. But although in the election in 1773 only about half of parishes sent in election returns, this was exceptional: in the two previous series of elections, in 1771 and 1772, about three quarters of parishes appear to have undertaken the necessary procedures, with a similar proportion in the elections of 1774 (which were abortive since the passing of the Quebec Act led the administration to suspend the nominations).

Overall, in the district of Montreal alone, some 1500 bailiffs and sub-bailiffs were named in rural parishes between 1765 and 1773, with these positions filled by roughly a thousand different individuals. In some parishes, the same bailiffs were named year after year, but in most the office rotated more regularly: of the thousand individuals named as bailiff or sub-bailiff, 70% were named only once, another 20% twice, and only 10% three times or more. Out of a population of perhaps 5000 to 6000 adult males, not all of whom would have been fit for office, this represented a very considerable degree of participation in local governance; and all, in theory at least, had been elected by their fellow parishioners.

The exact nature of the electoral process is less than clear. The ordinance gave virtually no guidance as to how the elections were to be organized, simply stating that the majority of householders in each parish were to hold the elections on 24 June of each year and the existing head bailiff was to return the list of those elected within fourteen days; but even with regard to these stipulations, practices varied considerably. Some parishes held their elections on 24 June as required, but many more did so in the days following, often timing their elections to church services. Similarly, most election returns were sent in directly by the head bailiff, but the hand of local elites is visible in some that were accompanied by letters from seigneurs, priests, notaries, and the like, or even prepared directly by them. As well, many lists purportedly prepared by the head bailiff were signed with a cross, and thus necessarily prepared by someone else. As a result, it is likely that some "elections" were no more than gatherings directed by the local priest or seigneur to validate their choices; but many more lists included the number of votes cast for each candidate and, in some cases, the names of the people who had voted for them, suggesting that true elections had been held.

There were many other irregularities in the process. Some election returns got lost on the way to Quebec City, with bailiffs complaining that they had been renamed despite having organized elections to replace themselves. Many parishes sent in the required list of six names, but others sent in only three. Further, most parishes did not follow the instructions laid down in the ordinance that head bailiffs be chosen among the previous year's sub-bailiffs, in order to ensure a degree of administrative continuity. In the district of Montreal, only 35 of the 335 men named head bailiffs had previously been sub-bailiffs. Some bailiffs also seem to have resisted replacement, in order to benefit from the power the office gave them. In 1771, for example, one Gauthier wrote the seigneur of Soulanges, Joseph de Longueuil:

> C'est avec un tres profond respect que je prends la liberté de vous écrire de la part des habitants de Soulange qui les deux années dernière ont nommé des nouveaux baillif au jour désigné et nos enciens baillif se plaisant en cette employ quoiquils nous fussent presque inutiles par l'incommodité de les avoir au besoins se sont gardé de produire les noms des nouveaux baillifs nommée crinte dettre relaxé pour éviter paréil abus les habitants de Soulange vous supplie tres humblement monsieur de vouloir bien vous interesser à faire recevoir Joseph Charlbonot et Jacob Chemitte quils ont nommée a cette effet le vingt quatre juin present mois conformement à lordonnance cest la grace que nous esperons de votre bonté et demeure avec tous le respect et la soumission possible.

De Longueuil forwarded the letter and asked that the two be nominated, which they were a couple of months later.[40] There were also regular complaints that bailiffs called assemblies irregularly, as in the 1770 complaint from L'Ange Gardien that "Ambroise Trudelle a fait la choix des baillis avec 5 aut habitans, il n'a point averti les autres." In a couple of cases, there were even rival nominations, with two distinct lists sent in for a single parish.[41]

But not all the complaints against the nomination of bailiffs should be taken at face value. In 1771, for example, a note purportedly from a number of Charlesbourg inhabitants complained bitterly that "on ne scai si c'est par dirision ou pastems que n'on les faits assemblé pour la nomination de nouveau Bailli puisqu'après les avoir denommé on lesse les susdit denommé pour en supstituer d'autre a leur place qui n'on été denomme d'aucun de la d. assemble Si cela arrive davantage les d. habitant se propose de ne pas se trouver dorenavant a aucun assemble qui ce pourrait faire dans la d. paroisse." This might appear to be an instance of the administration riding roughshod over local desires, but instead, the complaint seems to have been part of a local power struggle between two factions, one headed by the current bailiff and actual author of the note, Louis Paquet, and one supporting a rival, Nicolas-Charles Daunay, which accused Paquet of having rigged the elections from "lenvie ... de rester une troisième anné sans aucune approbation des dittes habitans a lexeption de huite dont quatre jeunesse."[42] Similarly, in 1770, Michel Chartier de Lotbinière, the seigneur of Vaudreuil, noted that "Noël Berthiaume de Kinchien qui s'en dit le baillif quoique personne n'avouë l'avoir nommé en cet effet, étend des commandement sur tous les districts de la seigneurie indifferemment, authorité qu'il s'est donné, qui répugne à tous également, personne ne le regardant d'aucun côté comme convenable a un pareil emploi."[43] This would have confirmed the oppressive nature of the British administrative system, a system which, as we saw, Chartier de Lotbinière denounced. In fact, however, Berthiaume had been named sub-bailiff of Kinchien in the official published lists in both 1768 and 1769; the only abuse was perhaps the overextension of his authority.

More fundamentally, through this whole rather messy process, parish assemblies preserved a good deal of autonomy. The administration under Carleton did make sporadic attempts to assert its control over the nominations, such as the 1768 decision to renew head bailiffs automatically. But overall, the administration seems usually to have respected the order proposed by the parish assemblies and named the first three men on the list, and when it did not, it was most often for particular circumstances such as one of the electees being unable to serve. And in at least one case, when inhabitants of a remote part of a seigneurie felt themselves ill-served by the bailiffs elected for the seigneurie at large and held elections for their own bailiffs, the administration obliged them by adding their choices to the list.[44]

As to the parish bailiffs themselves, the assertion that they were named from among the meanest of the habitants, as compared to the militia captains, is simply a fiction created by Carleton to justify his proposals to revive pre-Conquest authoritarian structures of governance. First, there was considerable continuity between the militia captains and the parish bailiffs, though the vastly greater number of the latter meant that many had never been and would never become militia officers. Thus, in the first elections in 1765, of 34 head bailiffs appointed in the district of Montreal only 5 had previously been militia officers, and in the district of Quebec, there are some indications that the administration deliberately avoided appointing former militia captains, even when they headed the lists sent in from the parishes.[45] However, of 93 immediately pre-Conquest militia captains in the district of Montreal who can be identified from various sources, 35 became bailiffs at some point. Likewise, of 65 head bailiffs appointed in the same district in 1773, only 4 became post–1775 militia captains; however, of 87 rural militia captains in a 1779 list, 33, or over a third, had previously acted as bailiffs.[46]

A limited prosopographical study of a random sample of 62 head bailiffs in the district of Montreal also suggests a quite different portrait. All but one were francophone, and indeed, there were only a handful of rural parish bailiffs who were not Canadiens. Of the 62, at least 51 were married; and as the others could not, for one reason or another, be identified in the sources used, the true proportion of married men was probably much higher. Their median age was 47, with three quarters being between 35 and 55; in other words, in the prime of life, with the authority that age brought. Most were born in or near the parish for which they had been named bailiff, and almost all died in that same parish. In other words, they appear to have been solid members of their local communities. In only one respect did they conform to the criticisms levelled at them. Twenty-eight of their marriage records give indications as to whether they could sign, and of these, only 3 declared that they could sign, while 25 declared that they could not. Their signature-based literacy rate of approximately 10% nevertheless corresponds almost exactly to what Michel Verrette found for Quebec's rural population as a whole in the 1760s and 1770s, using the same sources.[47]

Local parishioners thus elected parish bailiffs in great numbers; and regardless of the assertions of British officials and disgruntled former militia captains, they elected them from among their own. More generally, the bailiff elections were another example of a British colonial administration delegating the management of local affairs to local communities and, equally importantly, of local communities governing themselves. Certainly, the election process was far from smooth, and the degree to which it was fully "democratic" remains unclear. Local elites such as seigneurs and curés evidently influenced and manipulated the assemblies, and even when they did not, local factional disputes could impinge on the process. But taken as a whole, the process of electing and naming bailiffs suggests a form of grassroots participatory politics, at least partially democratic, in operation in the colony long before the creation of the House of Assembly. Indeed, at least one parish is reported to have expressed its regret at seeing the system of parish bailiffs replaced by the newly revived militia, since under the old system, the yearly elections prevented the office-holders from committing any abuses.[48]

Part of the reason that this elective system was surprisingly well accepted by the Canadien population was that, like the jury, though it was in some respects a British import, it was not entirely innovative. Though municipal institutions were indeed essentially absent from New France, especially in the eighteenth century, habitants were nonetheless used to making collective decisions in parish assemblies on some local matters, such as roads or vestry issues; and the practice continued across the Conquest, eventually leading, in the case of vestries, to conflicts between clergy and habitants in the 1820s and 1830s.[49] This meant that habitants had long been used to local political participation. As well, British administrators adapted the bailiff system to local structures. Apart from the use of the name "bailiff" rather than "constable," the system was also organized on the basis of pre-existing Catholic parishes, part of a more general trend whereby a nominally anti-Catholic British administration based itself for local administrative purposes on parishes erected by the Catholic Church.[50] And the day fixed for the elections, 24 June, was none other than that of Saint-Jean-Baptiste, an important feast day for the Canadiens; though as we saw, many elections were not in fact held on that day.

While the parish bailiffs represented the first introduction of the Canadien population to locally elected officials, they were not the last, though it would be more than twenty years before the creation of a new series of elected local officials, the sous-voyers, in 1796. Like the parish bailiffs, sous-voyers, fence and ditch inspectors, and the like have largely been ignored in the historiography. Historians have thus preferred Durham's declarations as to the absence of government outside the cities and the lack of Canadien administrative experience, thus ignoring the declaration of Durham's own commissioners on municipal government that "popularly elected officers now are, and have long been, depositaries of legislative, judicial and administrative powers for minor municipal purposes over the whole length and breadth of the province," referring to the sous-voyers and fence and ditch inspectors. As with the bailiffs, the elections of sous-voyers were, at least, regularly held, as is evidenced by the numerous election returns brought back by militia captains to the district Grand-Voyers; and though there was considerable opposition to the process at the very beginning, by the early nineteenth century most parishes were taking the necessary steps. The full scope, significance, and limitations of this further exercise of local democracy, however, remains almost entirely unexplored.[51]

2.2 Canadien Recourse to Local Criminal Justice[52]

If ordinary Canadiens were thus willing to participate in the very British exercise of electing parish officers from among themselves, even in the first decade of British rule, what of their reaction to British institutions of local governance that they did not control? Did they boycott them, or embrace them whole-heartedly? Examining Canadien recourse to British criminal justice provides one way of approaching this question.

From 1764, English criminal law and criminal procedure was taken to be in effect in the new colony of Quebec, definitively sweeping away the pre-Conquest French system. The view of administrators at the time, often repeated by historians up until the mid-twentieth century, was that the new subjects gladly accepted the manifestly superior British criminal justice system, happy to be rid of the oppressive French inquisitorial system.[53] More recent historiography, however, has postulated instead Canadien resistance to an alien legal system imposed by the conqueror, which had no ideological resonance for them, was based on laws and proceedings in a foreign language and staffed by foreigners, and which, as a result, they generally distrusted and avoided, especially in the eighteenth century but even, according to some, well into the nineteenth. As Louis Knafla asserted, "In Lower Canada, where the English criminal law was superimposed on a French-speaking society, the law was despised from the outset, and hostility increased from the 1790s down to the mid nineteenth century." This tied in to the broader debates on the effects of the Conquest and the causes of the Rebellions.[54]

As we saw in the preceding discussions of the grand jury and the magistracy, it is hard to discern any particular boycott of the English criminal justice system by the Canadien elites, at least insofar as their participation was concerned. But what of the Canadien population as a whole and, especially, the popular classes: the habitants, artisans, and labourers that made up the bulk of the population? How did they react

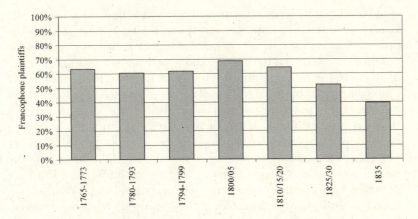

Figure 3: Francophone private plaintiffs before the justices of the peace, district of Montreal, 1765–1835

SOURCE: for 1765–73, BANQ-M TL32 S1 SS11 (Quarter Session registers); for 1780–1835, BANQ-M TL32 S1 SS1 (Quarter Sessions case files).

to this "alien" system? As there are virtually no sources that give direct access to popular Canadien perceptions of the criminal justice system, we can judge this mainly from their actions rather than their words.

First, we can readily dismiss the romantic notion of happy Canadien acceptance of a benevolent English criminal justice system. There were frequent episodes of resistance to the system: resistance to the application of militia, roads, and statutory labour laws in the late 1770s/early 1780s and in the 1790s; the persistence of illegal popular practices such as the charivari through to the 1820s and beyond; and direct challenges to the criminal justice system, ranging from the killing of bailiffs in the 1760s, through the rescue of a prisoner from the pillory by Montreal voyageurs in the 1790s, to examples of men defending their houses when bailiffs came to arrest their wives. It is hard to read anything but resistance into the 1820 assault by André-Auguste Mallard, of Montreal, against Emmanuel D'Aubreville, the city's watch quartermaster, in 1820, as Mallard purportedly declared that D'Aubreville was "un mouchard de la ville et des magistrats, un espion des Anglais et un traitre à sa patrie."[55]

But episodes of resistance do not mean the generalized rejection or boycott that many historians have implied. To gauge that, we must turn to actual Canadien recourse to the British criminal justice system. Here, the picture is much more complex. In the higher criminal courts, the proportion of non-francophones was often overwhelming, at two-thirds or even three-quarters of all parties. From this, it has been concluded that the criminal justice system was at best peripheral to the Canadien population. But the surest way to test popular reaction to the criminal justice system is not in the higher courts, where prosecutions were undertaken by the state and which heard a small proportion of all cases, but by examining voluntary recourse to the system by private plaintiffs (as opposed to official prosecutors such as police or judicial officers) in the justices' courts which heard most cases. As figure 3 shows, it is very difficult to talk of any particular Canadien boycott of the system, since Canadien plaintiffs made up about two-thirds of private plaintiffs from the beginning of British rule right through to the early 1820s. Since the vast majority of these plaintiffs were from the popular classes (farmers, artisans, labourers, and the like made up about 70% of plaintiffs in the district of Montreal from the 1780s to the 1820s), it seems that the Canadien population as a whole, voting with its feet, was not especially repulsed by this "alien" institution.

There are nevertheless some crucial nuances that have to be made regarding this overall portrait. For one thing, Canadien plaintiffs were still under-represented, since at most 5–10% of the colony's population in the later eighteenth century was British, and at most 20% in the first third of the nineteenth. As well, complaints from the rural areas where most Canadiens lived were far less frequent than their population warranted: in the district of Montreal, for example, about 60% of complaints came from inhabitants of Montreal itself, which comprised perhaps 10% of the district's population. Finally, there was also a noticeable decline in the proportion of francophones making complaints from the mid–1820s onward, which corresponded precisely to the decline in the presence and activity of francophone magistrates and the growing tensions between largely Canadien reformers and largely British Tories, beginning with the confrontations under Dalhousie. One might then be tempted to postulate the beginnings of a boycott of the system by the Canadien population.

Still, these nuances have themselves to be relativized. The urban-rural difference in recourse to criminal justice was a common feature in most early modern societies, regardless of their ethnic composition; indeed, in Quebec and Lower Canada, when this is combined with the fact that the British population lived disproportionately in the cities, it goes some way to explaining British over-representation among plaintiffs. Thus, if we consider only plaintiffs from the city of Montreal itself, in the late 1820s francophones made up about half of the city's population, and also comprised about half of all plaintiffs. More importantly, even the apparent continuing decline in Canadien recourse to the criminal courts in the 1830s was only a *relative* decline. Consider, for example, cases of less serious violence, where public order was not

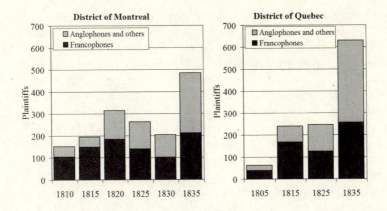

Figure 4: Plaintiffs in violence cases before the justices of the peace, districts of Montreal and Quebec, 1805–35

SOURCE: Fyson, *Magistrates, Police, and People,* 209.

seen as being at stake and which were thus left almost entirely to the initiative of the parties. As figure 4 shows, while the absolute number of Canadiens making such complaints did indeed decline in the mid-to-late 1820s, in both the main judicial districts of the colony, Montreal and Quebec, in Montreal so did the absolute number of anglophone plaintiffs, though not as much. Further, by the mid–1830s, the number of francophone plaintiffs had shot up again in both cities, though not as much as the number of anglophone plaintiffs. Thus, even at a time of heightened tension immediately preceding the Rebellions, and following incidents such as the Montreal West Ward election riots of 1832 which many have suggested discredited the magistracy, Canadiens continued to have recourse to the courts for these most personal of disputes.

There are also other indications that ordinary Canadiens, though perhaps not as enthusiastic as their British counterparts, were not particularly averse to using British criminal justice. For the eighteenth century, the impression is reinforced by the fact that the overall rate of criminal prosecution in the decades following the Conquest seems to have been significantly higher than that under the French regime.[56] Further, eighteenth-century Canadiens seem to have had little recourse to other forms of formal mediation: for example, unlike in some parts of France, the colony's notarial archives contain little evidence of infrajudicial arrangements between parties for any criminal or quasi-criminal affairs, including violence.[57] Likewise, while assault cases could be sued before the civil courts for damages, using French procedures, these suits were comparatively rare: even in the 1810s and 1820s, a few per year, compared to hundreds of assault cases before the justices, using British procedures.[58] Finally, we can also consider who was complaining against whom. If there was deep Canadien alienation from the criminal justice system, we would expect to see few cases of francophones complaining against each other. But throughout the period, cross-ethnic complaints were very much in the minority: even in interpersonal violence cases, and even in the late 1820s and early 1830s, about three-quarters of francophone plaintiffs were complaining against other francophones.

So why this Canadien recourse to a system that was so evidently English in inspiration, and for which there was almost certainly no generalized respect or deference? First, it was aided by the fact that the new justice system the Canadiens encountered was not, in practice, as different from the pre-Conquest French system as might appear in theory. Carleton himself noted this, when he testified that "The criminal law they [the Canadiens] have experienced is, in fact, not so extremely different. The mode of prosecution, the mode of deciding by the law, is very different; but the trial of great crimes, in nearly all civilized countries, is almost entirely the same."[59] And this also applied to crimes that were less "great." Assault cases, for example, were treated very similarly in both systems, with the initiative left up to the complainants and with many cases in both systems disposed of before reaching a formal trial.

Second was the question of language and ethnicity. On the one hand, procedures in the lower criminal courts, at least, were very often in French. Virtually all preliminary steps, such as the swearing out of depositions, the taking of bail-bonds and the like, were in the language of the party; there was most often a francophone justice available, and if there wasn't, at least a francophone or bilingual court clerk; and even the most formal of the justices' courts, the Quarter Sessions, operated in a mixture of French and English, depending on the parties of the case. But this linguistic and ethnic familiarity also extended to judicial personnel – the human face of the justice system. As we saw above, there was a very significant Canadien presence in the magistracy, which dealt with the bulk of criminal complaints, as also among jurymen. And this also applied to other judicial officers. Thus, a study of judicial auxiliaries across the Conquest shows a very significant continuity in the nature of the personnel of the courts, with bailiffs in particular continuing to be overwhelmingly francophone; the police in the late eighteenth and early nineteenth century were also largely francophone; and while the early criminal court clerks were all anglophones, they became increasingly francophone as time went on.[60] This did not mean that francophone plaintiffs and defendants came in contact with only francophone magistrates or officials, or that there were no problems around language, but even these were sometimes not what one might expect of a British system imposed on a francophone population. In the mid–1830s, for example, as a result of a temporary democratization of the jury selection process that obliged sheriffs to choose even grand jurymen from among property-holders at large, who were mostly Canadien farmers, several grand juries in the Montreal Quarter Sessions expressed their complete incapacity to proceed with their work as they neither read nor understood English.[61] But overall, the local criminal justice system that the Canadiens encountered could function very largely in their language. The alienation of ordinary Canadiens from the justice system was based far more on class and, in the case of women, on gender, as was the case in justice systems throughout the Western world.

Finally, Canadiens were not loath to have recourse to the local criminal justice system because it was a potential source of power not to be disregarded. For example, it was relatively easy and relatively cheap to make a complaint and have an opponent arrested and brought before a magistrate; and since in assault cases nothing would be done unless the plaintiff took the initiative, this gave plaintiffs quite a bit of discretion. Battered women, for example, and Canadiennes in particular, sought to use the justice system as some means of at least temporary protection from their abusive husbands, even though the system afforded them only limited protection.[62] Overall, from the Conquest to the mid-1820s, ordinary Canadiens, far from boycotting the local criminal justice system, were quite willing to use it when the occasion warranted.

CONCLUSION

Je viens de voir dans le Canada un million de Français braves, intelligents, faits pour former un jour une grande nation française en Amérique, qui vivent en quelque sorte en étrangers dans leur pays. Le peuple conquérant tient le commerce, les emplois, la richesse, le pouvoir. Il forme les hautes classes et domine la société entière. Le peuple conquis, partout où il n'a pas l'immense supériorité numérique, perd peu à peu ses mœurs, sa langue, son caractère national.

Alexis de Tocqueville to his brother, 1831[63]

During his brief visit to Lower Canada in 1831, Alexis de Tocqueville, just like Durham a few years later, was forcefully struck by the "two nations warring in the bosom of a single state." In contrast to Durham, however, he had an almost caricatural rosy view of the Canadien population, and of the habitants in particular, seeing them as the virtuous Frenchmen his fellow countrymen no longer were, and was highly critical of the "phlegmatic" British. But like Durham, he saw the Canadien population retreating behind and protected by its traditional French institutions: language, culture, and, especially, religion. In his words, "les Canadiens ont conservé tous les traits du caractère français." And, like Durham, he saw them as politically primitive: "Au total cette population nous a paru capable d'être dirigée quoique encore incapable de se diriger elle-même." The one notable exception was the Assembly, which Tocqueville saw as a Canadien institution sowing the seeds of the future survival of the race, notably through its support of education. And yet, he also criticized the office-holding elites as already well on the way to anglicization.[64]

Tocqueville's portrayal of the Canadien population in Lower Canada, though generating continued interest, has been less influential that that of Durham, not only because of its relative unimportance compared to *De la démocratie en Amérique* but also because much later francophone historiography of the period, from Garneau forward, was constructed against Durham's declarations.[65] And yet, Tocqueville's overly schematic and often erroneous characterizations of Lower-Canadian society find their echoes even today in popular perceptions of the period from the Conquest to the Rebellions, on matters ranging from exclusive British control of commerce to the exclusion of the Canadien population from power in general and the state in particular. As we saw, however, neither Durham, nor Tocqueville, nor many others have sufficiently appreciated the extent to which Canadiens, both elite and popular-class, were able to set aside their "national prejudices" and adapt themselves to the institutions of local governance imposed by the Conqueror, even those institutions which they manifestly did not control, such as the jury, the magistracy, or criminal justice. Taking the four examples discussed above, we can perhaps advance some general reasons which help us explain this.

First, and most evidently, we must not discount the British colonial emphasis on self-governance and on indirect rule. As long as the colonial administration could control the more important levers of power, it was content to leave much local administration to the Canadiens themselves. Thus, at the very beginning of British civil administration, the new British rulers delegated considerable local power to popularly elected officials, the parish bailiffs, who were guaranteed to be almost entirely drawn from the newly conquered Canadiens. The restoration of elected local officials in 1796, the sous-voyers, came at a time of considerable suspicion on the part of British officials toward the Canadien population and of democracy in general. And as for the magistracy, it was only in moments of extreme crisis, such as under Dalhousie or in the immediate lead-up to the Rebellions, that colonial administrations resorted to more systematic exclusion of Canadien elites from this source of power. The reproduction of this philosophy of local governance in Quebec and Lower Canada is particularly significant, since it created a political space which Canadiens were able to occupy, not only at the level of the Assembly, but in other institutions of governance as well.

A second factor was the similarity of many of these new systems to structures that had long been familiar to the Canadien population. Whether it be the jury, with its parallels in the participation of arbitrators and family members in the civil law; local participation and even local democracy in local administration at the parish level; or even the English criminal law, with its significant parallels to the French system, the new systems that the conquered encountered were often, in practice, far less different from those they replaced than might appear in theory. Even the participation of lay elites in the magistracy was not so far from some aspects of the French experience, where many notables also participated in civil administration through unpaid government commissions, though in the militia and in administrative positions rather than through the law.

And finally, and perhaps most importantly, there was the question of power. Canadiens had no particular love for British-inspired institutions of local governance; but neither did they avoid them. Instead, they engaged them as much as in any early modern society, primarily for reasons of pragmatism and power. As Tocqueville, Durham, and many after them have correctly pointed out, Canadiens from the Conquest to the Rebellions were indeed engaged in struggle for cultural survival, in the face of British assimilation, whether intended or not. These were not the only social tensions in Quebec and Lower Canada – as in all Western societies, struggles around issues of class, gender, and race also polarized the population. However, ethnic tensions cannot be swept under the carpet. That the Canadiens were able to adapt to the Conqueror's institutions and, often, turn them to their own advantage, not only at the level of the Assembly and the press, but also at the local level of juries, magistrates, local officials and even the criminal law, is a striking demonstration of their adaptability. And this extended to other fundamentally British institutions as well. For example, while collective petitioning was essentially banned in New France, Canadiens very quickly took to this new form of political activity in the years following the Conquest, and raised it to a high art in the early nineteenth century, rivalling their British and American counterparts.[66] In many respects, Canadien flexibility toward British institutions helped preserve them against assimilation, as much or more than die-hard attachment to institutions such as the seigneurial system and the Catholic Church, and is perhaps one of the reasons that colonial assimilationist policies, from the Royal Proclamation to the Union, were ultimately unsuccessful.

NOTES

1 Lord Durham, *Report on the Affairs of British North America* (London, 1839), 35–6.
2 Mason Wade, *The French Canadians, 1760–1967*, rev. ed. (Toronto: MacMillan, 1976 [1968]), 1: 48–9. For similar approaches in older Canadian historiography, emphasizing lack of Canadien participation in local government, see also John George Bourinot, *Local Government in Canada: An Historical Study* (Baltimore: N. Murray, 1887) and Kenneth Grant Crawford, *Canadian Municipal Government* (Toronto: University of Toronto Press): 20–1, 32–6.
3 On the Conquest, this is the position taken by historians with ideological perspectives ranging from Lionel Groulx, *Lendemains de conquête* (Montreal: Bibliothèque de l'Action française, 1920) and Michel Brunet, *Les Canadiens après la Conquête 1759–1775: de la révolution Canadienne à la révolution américaine* (Montreal: Fides, 1969) through Gilles Bourque, *Question nationale et classes sociales au Québec, 1760–1840* (Montreal: Parti Pris, 1970) to A.L. Burt, *The Old Province of Quebec* (Toronto: McClelland and Stewart, 1968 [1933]), vol. 1 and Hilda Neatby, *Quebec: The Revolutionary Age, 1760–1791* (Toronto: McClelland and Stewart). On the Rebellions, see, among others, Allan Greer, *The Patriots and the People: The Rebellion of 1837 in Rural Lower Canada* (Toronto: University of Toronto Press, 1993), chap. 5; Philip Buckner, *The Transition to Responsible Government: British Policy in British North America, 1815–1850* (Westport, CT: Greenwood Press, 1985), especially chap. 5; Fernand Ouellet, *Le Bas-Canada, 1791–1840: changements structuraux et crise* (Ottawa: Éditions de l'Université d'Ottawa, 1976), chaps 8–10; or Helen Taft Manning, *The Revolt of French Canada 1800–1835* (Toronto: MacMillan, 1962).
4 On the attachment of the Canadiens to the civil law and the seigneurial system, see Evelyn Kolish, *Nationalismes et conflits de droits: le débat du droit privé au Québec, 1760–1840* (LaSalle: Hurtubise HMH, 1994), and to the seigneurial system in particular, Jean-Pierre Wallot, "Le régime seigneurial et son abolition au Canada," *Canadian Historical Review* 50, no. 4 (1969): 367–93; to the notarial system, André Vachon, *Histoire du notariat Canadien, 1621–1960* (Québec: Presses de l'Université Laval, 1962): 53–76; to the Catholic church,

Lucien Lemieux, *Histoire du catholicisme québécois: Les XVIIIe et XIXe siècles,*
tome 1, *Les années difficiles (1760–1839)* (Montreal: Boréal Express, 1989), or
Serge Gagnon, *Plaisir d'amour et crainte de Dieu: sexualité et confession au
Bas-Canada* (Quebec: Presses de l'Université Laval, 1990); to the French lan-
guage, Danièle Noël, *Les questions de langue au Quebec, 1759–1850* (Quebec:
Conseil de la langue française, 1990), 59–251 and Michel Plourde, ed., *Le
français au Québec: 400 ans d'histoire et de vie* (Montreal: Fides/Publications du
Québec, 2000), 55–133.

5 On Canadien parliamentarism, Henri Brun, *La formation des institutions
parlementaires québécoises: 1791–1838* (Quebec: Presses de l'Université Laval,
1970), or John Hare, *Aux origines du parlementarisme québécois, 1791–1793:
etude et documents* (Sillery: Septentrion, 1993) as well as the standard political
histories; on parish schools, Louis-Philippe Audet, *Histoire de l'éducation au
Québec* (Montreal: Centre de psychologie et de pédagogie, association
coopérative, 1966), vol. 2 and Andrée Dufour, *Tous à l'école: État,
communautés rurales et scolarisation au Québec de 1826 à 1859* (Montréal:
Hurtubise HMH, 1996), 35–55; on municipal corporations, Lorne Joseph
Ste Croix, *The First Incorporation of the City of Montreal 1826–1836* (MA thesis,
McGill, 1972) and Marcel Plouffe, *Quelques particularités sociales et politiques de
la charte, du système administratif et du personnel politique de la cité de Québec,
1830–1867* (MA thesis, Université Laval, 1971); on the press, Gilles
Gallichan, *Livre et politique au Bas-Canada: 1791–1849* (Sillery: Septentrion,
1991), especially chap. 5 and Maurice Lemire et al., *La vie littéraire au Québec,*
vol. 2, *1806–1839. Le projet national des Canadiens* (Quebec: Presses de
l'Université Laval, 1992).

6 The clashes between the Legislative Council and the House of Assembly are
discussed in all the standard political histories, such as Ouellet, Buckner, or
Manning; on Canadien opposition to the registry offices, see Kolish,
Nationalismes et conflits de droits, 273–98; to the criminal law, see below, note
44; to the Royal Institution schools, Louis-Philippe Audet, *Le système scolaire de
la province de Québec* (Quebec: Presses universitaires Laval, 1952), vol. 3 or
Andrée Dufour, *Histoire de l'éducation au Québec* (Montreal: Boréal, 1997),
20–3.

7 Léon Robichaud, *Le pouvoir, les paysans et la voirie au Bas-Canada à la fin du
XVIIIe siècle* (MA thesis, McGill, 1989); Fernand Ouellet, "Officiers de milice
et structure sociale au Québec (1660–1815)," *Histoire sociale / Social History*
12, no. 23 (1979): 37–65; Greer, *The Patriots and the People,* 100–13; F.
Murray Greenwood, *Legacies of Fear. Law and Politics in Quebec in the Era of the
French Revolution* (Toronto: University of Toronto Press, 1993), 76–103.

8 Long ago, Jean-Pierre Wallot questioned Canadien attachment to the
Church, "Religion and French-Canadian Mores in the Early Nineteenth Century," *Canadian Historical Review* 52, no. 1 (1971): 51–94, though his reasons
for making this statement before a largely English-Canadian audience have

since been questioned (Gagnon, *Plaisir d'amour et crainte de Dieu*, 55). Allan
Greer also shows how, in the years leading up to and especially during the
Rebellions, both seigneurialism and the Church were increasingly contested
by the rural population; however, even though the rebels occupied several
seigneurial mansions, Greer cites only one instance of the burning of seigneurial registers, and even that was linked to a particular local dispute (*The
Patriots and the People*, 234–39, 287–88, 293, 345).

9   Nathalie Picard, *Les femmes et le vote au Bas-Canada de 1792 à 1849* (MA thesis,
Université de Montréal, 1992); Allan Greer, "La république des hommes: les
Patriotes de 1837 face aux femmes," *Revue d'histoire de l'Amérique française* 44,
no. 4 (1991): 507–28 and "Historical Roots of Canadian Democracy," *Journal
of Canadian Studies* 34, no. 1 (1999): 7–26.

10   The literature inspired by this perspective is vast, running from classics such
as François-Xavier Garneau, *Histoire du Canada depuis sa découverte jusqu'à nos
jours*, vol. 3 (Quebec: N. Aubin, 1848) and Lionel Groulx, *Lendemains de
conquête*, through Michel Brunet, *Les Canadiens après la Conquête*, to more
recent work such as David-Thierry Ruddel's *Québec City 1765–1832: The Evolution of a Colonial Town* (Ottawa: Canadian Museum of Civilization, 1987).
Note that for the purposes of simplicity, I use the term "British" to refer to
the colony's population of British descent, including those of American or
Canadian birth.

11   Gilles Paquet and Jean-Pierre Wallot, *Patronage et pouvoir dans le Bas-Canada
(1794–1812)* (Montreal: Presses de l'Université du Quebec, 1973).

12   This section is based in part on my article, "Jurys, participation civique et
représentation au Québec et au Bas-Canada: les grands jurys du district de
Montréal (1764–1832)," *Revue d'histoire de l'Amérique française* 55, no. 1
(2001): 85–120.

13   Hilda M. Neatby, *The Administration of Justice under the Quebec Act* (Minneapolis: Minnesota University Press, 1933); André Morel, "La réception du droit
criminel anglais au Québec (1760–1892)," *Revue juridique Thémis* 13, no. 2–3
(1978): 521–3; or Douglas Hay, "The Meanings of the Criminal Law in Quebec, 1764–1774," in Louis A. Knafla, ed., *Crime and Criminal Justice in Europe
and Canada* (Waterloo: Wilfrid Laurier University Press, 1981), 94–7. The
best condensed presentation of British officials' views on Canadien perceptions of the jury are in Sir Henry Cavendish, *Debates of the House of Commons in
the Year 1774, On the Bill for Making More Effectual Provision for the Government
of the Province of Quebec* (London: Ridgway, 1839), 100–61; Hey's comment is
on p. 151. Chartier de Lotbinière's comments are in Adam Shortt and
Arthur G. Doughty, *Documents Relating to the Constitutional History of Canada,
1759–1791* (Ottawa: Historical Documents Publication Board, 1918), 562–3.

14   Neal Garnham, *The Courts, Crime and the Criminal Law in Ireland, 1692–1760*
(Dublin: Irish Academic Press, 1996), 119–32; Beatriz Betancourt Hardy,

Papists in a Protestant Age: The Catholic Gentry and Community in Colonial Mary-land, 1689–1776 (PhD thesis, University of Maryland, 1993), 57.

15 Cavendish, *Debates*, 152.

16 Arbitration has yet to be studied in any depth in New France or post-Conquest Quebec; but see Neatby, *Administration of Justice*, 112, 210–11 (though she only begrudgingly admits the point). On France, see for example Jeremy David Hayhoe, *"Judge in their Own Cause": Seigneurial Justice in Northern Burgundy, 1750–1790* (PhD thesis, University of Maryland College Park, 2001), 485–98. On family assemblies, see Jean-Philippe Garneau, "Droit et 'affaires de famille' sur la Côte-de-Beaupré. Histoire d'une rencontre en amont et en aval de la Conquête," *Revue juridique Thémis* 34, no. 2 (2000): 515–61.

17 Durham, *Report*, 17–18.

18 This section is largely based on Donald Fyson, *Magistrates, Police, and People: Everyday Criminal Justice in Quebec and Lower Canada, 1764–1837* (Toronto: Osgoode Society / University of Toronto Press, 2006), especially 53–135, but also contains material not presented there.

19 *Journals of the House of Assembly at Lower Canada* 38 (1828–29), Appendix EE.

20 On the 1790s, see Greenwood, Legacies of Fear; on the 1820s, Manning, *The Revolt of French Canada*, and Ouellet, *Le Bas-Canada*; on the crisis under Craig, along with Manning and Ouellet, see Jean-Pierre Wallot, *Un Québec qui bougeait: trame socio-politique au tournant du XIXe siècle* (Montreal: Boréal, 1973). The decline in Canadien participation from 1824 partly reflected a change in the position of Police Magistrate and Chairman of the Quarter Sessions, the only paid position in the magistracy, which from its creation in 1810 through to 1824 had been shared between a Canadien, Jean-Marie Mondelet, and a British magistrate, Thomas McCord, but from 1824 through to the abolition of the position in 1830, was occupied only by British magistrates, Samuel Gale and David Ross. However, even if we consider only truly "voluntary" magistrates, the same basic pattern holds for the period 1810–30, though we can peg the francophone "boycott" more precisely, beginning in 1826 and becoming particularly acute in 1828–30.

21 The situation was a little different in the district of Quebec, with a similarly strong francophone presence through to the late 1820s, a corresponding decline in about the same years, but no recovery in the 1830s.

22 France Galarneau, "L'élection partielle du quartier-ouest de Montréal en 1832: analyse politico-sociale," *Revue d'histoire de l'Amérique française* 32, no. 4 (1979): 565–84.

23 Ross to Ogden, 11 June 1808, in Library and Archives Canada (henceforth LAC) RG4 A1 vol. 99, 31133–9. Note that since (as of the final revision of this paper) none of the LAC fonds and collections used have received their new archival designations, they are referred to here by their former archival reference numbers. Here, as elsewhere, capitalization has been modernized.

24 Guy to Baby, 9 Sept. 1776, LAC MG24 L3, Baby Collection, Letterbook of Pierre Guy 1767–82.

25 On the possibilities of power offered to elites through the control of municipal administration by the magistracy, see Ruddel, *Québec City 1765–1832*, 161–97 (though Ruddel argues, erroneously, that the magistracy in Quebec City was completely dominated by British merchants). Though a thorough study of municipal administration in Montreal before 1832 remains to be undertaken, see Donald Fyson, "Les structures étatiques locales à Montréal au début du XIXe siècle," *Les Cahiers d'histoire* 17, no. 1–2 (1997): 55–75 and "Local Judiciary, Local Power and the Local State: The Justices of the Peace in Montreal, 1764–1830," (unpublished paper at <http://www.hst.ulaval.ca/profs/dfyson/LocalJudiciary.htm>).

26 Jean et Marcel Hamelin, *Les moeurs électorales dans le Québec: de 1791 à nos jours* (Montreal: Éditions du Jour, 1962), 19; David Chennells, *The Politics of Nationalism in Canada: Cultural Conflict since 1760* (Toronto: University of Toronto Press, 2001), 58, 67.

27 For a forceful statement of this, see Greer, *The Patriots and the People*, chaps 3–4.

28 I have previously examined this question, much more summarily, in "La paroisse et l'administration étatique sous le Régime britannique (1764–1840)," in Serge Courville and Normand Séguin, eds, *Atlas historique du Québec: La paroisse* (Sainte-Foy: Presses de l'Université Laval, 2001), 25–37.

29 There has been no recent overall study of local administration in New France; the main references remain classics such as Gustave Lanctôt, *L'administration de la Nouvelle-France* (Montreal: Éditions du Jour, 1971 [1929]) and "Le régime municipal en Nouvelle-France," *Culture* 9, no. 3 (1948): 255–83, or André Vachon, "The Administration of New France," *Dictionary of Canadian Biography*, (Toronto: University of Toronto Press, 1969), 2: xv-xxv, along with a few more recent contributions, such as John Dickinson, "Réflexions sur la police en Nouvelle-France," *McGill Law Journal* 32, no. 3 (1987): 497–512, or André Lachance, *La vie urbaine en Nouvelle-France* (Montreal: Boréal, 1987), chaps 3 and 4. On the United States, see among others Bruce C. Daniels, *Town and Country: Essays on the Structure of Local Government in the American Colonies* (Middletown, CT: Wesleyan University Press, 1978) and *Power and Status: Officeholding in Colonial America* (Middletown, CT: Wesleyan University Press, 1986). On England, apart from the work of Sidney and Beatrice Webb, *English Local Government* (London: Longmans, 1906), examples include Joan R. Kent, *The English Village Constable, 1580–1642: A Social and Administrative Study* (Oxford: Clarendon Press, 1986) and "The Centre and the Localities: State Formation and Parish Government in England, circa 1640–1740," *Historical Journal* 38, no. 2 (1995): 363–404; Michael J. Braddick, State Formation in Early Modern England, c.1550–1700 (Cambridge: Cambridge University Press, 2000);

David Eastwood, Governing Rural England: Tradition and Transformation in Local Government, 1780–1840 (New York: Oxford University Press, 1994); or, for a forceful statement of the political importance of these offices, Mark Goldie, "The Unacknowledged Republic: Officeholding in Early Modern England," in Tim Harris, ed., The Politics of the Excluded, c.1500–1800 (New York and Basingstoke: Palgrave, 2001), 153–94.

30 Durham, Report, 36. This is cited among others at the beginning of the chapter on the state in Greer, The Patriots and the People (87), whose main argument is the anemic nature of the Lower-Canadian state.

31 The main acts and ordinances relevant to these offices are 4 George III 17 Sept. 1764 (bailiffs), 36 George III c.9 (1796) (sous-voyers); 58 George III c.16 (1818) and 4 George IV c.2 (1824) (police trustees); 4 George IV c.33 (1824) (fence and ditch inspectors). References to the commons can be found in Tables Relative to the Acts and Ordinances of Lower-Canada (Kingston: Derbishire & Desbarats, 1843), 135; the Tables also provide references to the various laws replacing or amending the previous laws.

32 Among others, see 4 George III "An Ordinance For regulating and establishing the Courts of Judicature ... " (1764); 6 George III "An Ordinance for repairing and amending the High-Ways ... " (1766); 10 George III "An Ordinance for the more Effectual Administration of Justice" (1770).

33 Shortt and Doughty, Documents Relating to the Constitutional History of Canada, 208n1.

34 Michael P. Gabriel, ed., Québec during the American Invasion, 1775–1776: The Journal of François Baby, Gabriel Taschereau, and Jenkin Williams (East Lansing: Michigan State University Press, 2005); Proclamation 27/4/1775; 17 George III c.5, 8 and 11 (1777).

35 W.P.M. Kennedy and Gustave Lanctôt, Reports on the Laws of Quebec, 1767–1770 (Ottawa: F.A. Acland, 1931), 65; Desrosiers to Carleton, 3 July 1769, in Carleton to Hillsborough, 28 March 1770, C.O. 42, vol. 30, f. 7–26; Du Calvet to Hillsborough, 28 Oct. 1770, C.O. 42, vol. 30, f. 168–199; petition of merchants and others of the city of Quebec, in Carleton to Hillsborough, 25 Apr. 1770, C.O. 42, vol. 30, f. 47–52. For historians' views of the bailiffs, see among others Seaman Morley Scott, "Chapters in the History of the Law of Quebec, 1764–1775" (PhD thesis, University of Michigan, 1933), 291–4.

36 The characterization of the militia captains as the "natural leaders of the people," drawn from classics such as Garneau or Groulx, has been repeated: Burt, The Old Province of Quebec, I: 81, Ouellet, "The British Army of Occupation in the Saint-Lawrence Valley, 1760–1764: The Conflict between Civil and Military Society," in Roy A. Prete and A. Hamish Ion, eds, Armies of Occupation (Waterloo: Wilfrid Laurier University Press, 1984, 26–8) and Philip Lawson, The Imperial Challenge: Quebec and Britain in the Age of the American Revolution (Montreal: McGill-Queen's University Press, 1989), 109.

37 See for example Kent, *The English Village Constable.*

38 The main sources are the published lists of appointed bailiffs in the *Quebec Gazette*, 23 Jan. 1765, 19 Aug. 1765, 24 Oct. 1766, 14 Sept. 1767, 31 Aug. 1768, 31 Aug. 1769, 28 Sept. 1770, 28 Sept. 1771, 22 Feb. 1773 and 1 Sept. 1773; these have also been republished (though with errors) by Denis Racine in *L'Ancêtre*, 4, no. 3 (1977) through 5, no. 3 (1978); LAC RG4 A3, vol. 1 (the letterbook kept by the civil secretary in his correspondance with the ' bailiffs) and LAC RG4 B22 (papers relating to bailiffs, including election returns).

39 Allsopp to Cuthbert and to Chartier de Lotbinière, 12 July 1770, Bibliothèque et Archives nationales du Québec, Centre d'archives de Québec, P313.

40 Gauthier to de Longueuil, 30 June 1771, and de Longueuil to Allsopp, 19 July 1771, LAC RG4 B22 vol. 1.

41 On L'Ange-Gardien, undated note c.1770, LAC RG4 B22 vol. 1; the rival nominations were in Varennes and in Pointe-Levy in 1772.

42 Paquet to Allsopp, 25 Aug. 1771, and petition from Charlesbourg inhabitants, 3 Sept. 1771, LAC RG4 B22 vol. 1.

43 Chartier de Lotbinière to Allsopp, 4 July 1770, LAC RG4 B22 vol. 1.

44 From Petite Rivière du Chêne in 1768: LAC RG4 B22 vol. 1.

45 This appears to have been done in about a half-dozen cases, perhaps on the theory that since these individuals had already filled local office, they should pass that responsibility on to others.

46 The identification of pre-Conquest militia captains was based on the lists provided in Marcel Trudel, *Histoire de la Nouvelle-France*, vol. 10, *Le régime militaire* (Montreal: Fides, 1999), 106–11 and on self-identification of militia captains in the Programme de recherche en démographie historique (Université de Montréal)'s database of parish records, <http://www.genealogie.umontreal.ca>; the 1779 list of militia captains is in LAC RG4 A1 vol. 23, 7746. In his study of Batiscan, Colin Coates also notes that the bailiffs and sub-bailiffs were members of the same families that had previously provided many of the local militia officers. *Les transformations du paysage et de la société au Québec sous le régime seigneurial* (Quebec: Septentrion, 2003), 114–15.

47 Michel Verrette, "L'alphabétisation au Québec 1660–1900" (PhD thesis, Université Laval, 1989), Appendix 4.1.

48 Gabriel, *Quebec during the American Invasion*, 52.

49 Lanctôt, *L'administration de la Nouvelle-France*, 145–6; Robichaud, *Le pouvoir, les paysans et la voirie;* Allan Greer, "L'habitant, la paroisse rurale et la politique locale au XVIIIe siècle: quelques cas dans la vallée du Richelieu," *Société Canadienne d'histoire de l'Église catholique, Sessions d'études* 47(1980): 28–30; Christian Dessureault and Christine Hudon, "Conflits sociaux et élites locales au Bas-Canada: le clergé, les notables, la paysannerie et le contrôle de la fabrique," *Canadian Historical Review* 80, no. 3 (1999): 413–39.

50 See Fyson, "La paroisse et l'administration étatique" for a fuller demonstration.

51 Durham, *Report*, Appendix C: 49. Election returns are found in the various papers of the Grands-Voyers at the ANQ, partially indexed in Pierre-Georges Roy, *Inventaire des procès-verbaux des grands voyers conservés aux archives de la province de Québec* (Beauceville: L'Éclaireur, 1923–32). Robichaud, *Le pouvoir, les paysans et la voirie* briefly discusses the election of sous-voyers but does not explore it in any detail. On the resistance of the 1790s, see among others Robichaud and Greenwood, *Legacies of Fear*, 76–103.

52 This section is largely based on Fyson, *Magistrates, Police, and People*, 184–309.

53 See for example Neatby, *The Administration of Justice under the Quebec Act*, chap. 12; for an overview of the administrators' views, see Morel, "La réception du droit criminel anglais au Québec."

54 Louis A. Knafla, "Aspects of the Criminal Law, Crime, Criminal Process and Punishment in Europe and Canada," in Knafla, ed., *Crime and Criminal Justice in Europe and Canada*, 7; also Knafla and Terry L. Chapman, "Criminal Justice in Canada: A Comparative Study of the Maritimes and Lower Canada, 1760–1812," *Osgoode Hall Law Journal* 21, no. 2 (1983): 245–74; for analogous though generally more nuanced views, see also Morel, "La réception du droit criminel anglais au Québec"; Hay, "The Meanings of the Criminal Law in Quebec," 84–5; Jean-Marie Fecteau, *Un nouvel ordre des choses: la pauvreté, le crime, l'Etat au Québec, de la fin du XVIIIe siècle à 1840* (Montreal: VLB, 1989), 128–9, "Between the Old Order and Modern Times: Poverty, Criminality, and Power in Quebec, 1791–1840," in Jim Phillips, Tina Loo, and Susan Lewthwaite, eds, *Essays in the History of Canadian Law*, vol. 5, *Crime and Criminal Justice* (Toronto: University of Toronto Press, 1994), 297 and (for a modified view) *La liberté du pauvre: sur la régulation du crime et de la pauvreté au XIXe siècle québécois* (Montreal: VLB, 2004): 97–9; Greer, *The Patriots and the People*, 91–100.

55 Bibliothèque et Archives nationales du Québec, Centre d'archives de Montréal (henceforth BANQ-M), TL32 S1 SS11, 27 Sept. 1820.

56 For an overview of changes in prosecution rates, see Donald Fyson, "The Judicial Prosecution of Crime in the Longue Durée: Quebec, 1712–1965," in Jean-Marie Fecteau and Janice Harvey, eds, *La régulation sociale entre l'acteur et l'institution: Pour une problématique historique de l'interaction* (Quebec: Presses de l'Université du Québec, 2005), 85–119.

57 In notarial archives from 1764 to 1783 (as indexed in the *Parchemin* database), the period when British criminal justice would have seemed the most alien, there are virtually no references to criminal matters. Of course, many minor disputes, potentially criminal (notably minor incidents of violence) were most likely dealt with entirely informally; but that was not a particularity of Canadien reactions to British justice, and is the case even today. On infrajustice and informal settlement in France, see notably Benoît Garnot, "Justice, infrajustice, parajustice et extrajustice dans la France d'ancien

régime," *Crime, Histoire & Sociétés* 4, no. 1 (2000): 103–20, as well Garnot, ed., *L'infrajudiciaire du Moyen Age à l'époque contemporaine* (Dijon: Éditions universitaires de Dijon, 1996). Much of the work on infrajustice in France has been based on notarized settlements of potentially criminal cases.

58 In BAnQ-M TL19 S4 SS1 (Montreal King's Bench, superior civil jurisdiction, case files) between 1795 and 1829, there are only about 160 cases of damages for interpersonal violence, compared to an estimated 5000 complaints before the justices.

59 Cavendish, *Debates*, 117.

60 Donald Fyson, "Judicial Auxiliaries across Legal Regimes: From New France to Lower Canada," in Claire Dolan, ed., *Entre justice et justiciables: les auxiliaires de la justice du Moyen Âge au XXᵉ siècle* (Quebec: Presses de l'Université Laval, 2005), 383–403; on the police, *Magistrates, Police, and People*, 136–83.

61 BANQ-M TL32 S1 SS11, Montreal Quarter Sessions register, 10–11 Jan. 1833, Sept. 1834, Jan. 1835, 21–22 Oct. 1836.

62 Ian C. Pilarczyk, "'Justice in the Premises': Family Violence and the Law in Montreal, 1825–1850," PhD thesis, McGill, 2003.

63 *Regards sur le Bas-Canada*, edited by Claude Corbo (Montreal: Éditions Typo, 2003), 43.

64 Ibid., passim.

65 On the affinities between Tocqueville and Durham, and the latter's probable intellectual debt to the former, see Janet Ajzenstat, *The Political Thought of Lord Durham* (Kingston: McGill-Queen's University Press, 1987), chap. 3. On Tocqueville's visit to Lower Canada more generally, Jean-Michel Leclercq, "Alexis de Tocqueville au Canada (du 24 août au 2 sept. 1831)," *Revue d'histoire de l'Amérique française* 22, no. 3 (1968): 353–64, Stéphane Dion, "La pensée de Tocqueville: L'épreuve du Canada-français," *Revue d'histoire de l'Amérique française* 41, no. 4 (1988): 537–52, Gérard Bergeron, *Quand Tocqueville et Siegfried nous observaient* (Sillery: Presses de l'Université du Québec, 1990), chaps 1–4 and Anne Trépanier, "Le voyage identitaire (et imaginaire) de Tocqueville au Bas-Canada: vieille France ou Nouvelle-France?," *Mens* 5, no. 1 (2004): 119–49. The continuing interest in Tocqueville is illustrated by the fact that his writings on Lower Canada have been reproduced at least three times – in Jacques Vallée, ed., *Tocqueville au Bas-Canada* (Montreal: Éditions du Jour, 1973), again by Vallée in the *Tocqueville Review* 12 (1990–91): 141–82, and in the edition by Corbo.

66 On petitioning in the nineteenth century, Steven Watt, "'Duty Bound and Ever Praying': Collective Petitioning to Governors and Legislatures in Selected Regions of Maine and Lower Canada, 1820–1838," PhD thesis, Université du Québec à Montréal, 2006.

NANCY CHRISTIE

"The Plague of Servants"[1]

Female Household Labour and the Making of Classes in Upper Canada

According to the writer Catherine Parr Traill, Upper Canada was a society characterized by sin and disorder, for it was "a country where old and young, the master and servant, are alike obliged to labour for a livelihood without respect to former situation or rank."[2] The confusion of class position and the absence of traditional markers of identity were major preoccupations for genteel immigrants like Traill. Throughout her literary works she returned again and again to the theme of the difficulties of planting British culture and institutions in a New World environment. In *The Young Emigrants,* Traill described the process of settlement in Canada as a fall from grace, a banishment from the Britannic Eden, in which sin became embodied in the persona of the female domestic servant whose "insolent freedom of manner"[3] had overturned customary relations of authority and class. Far from being passive and obedient, this servant knew her rights and well understood the laws of the market whereby the demand for labour surpassed the supply, which made her "less dependent on her mistress than her mistress on her."[4] What is significant is that social observers like Traill had a specifically gendered view of the cause of class inversion in Upper Canada, linking it with female domestics. But more importantly, they saw the household, and particularly the patriarchal family, as the formative realm for managing class relations in settler societies.[5]

STATUS IN THE NEW WORLD ENVIRONMENT

Like many other promoters of immigration, Traill wished to portray the New World environment as a field for upward mobility in which Britain's paupers could be lifted from "poverty to independence."[6] While genteel settlers may have shared a view of the benefits of a free trade empire, for they also aspired to upward social mobility, they imagined that the modern principles of political economy might be wedded to traditional notions of paternal social control.[7] The insolent female domestic servant, freely selling her labour in a buoyant market, was seen as the harbinger of unwelcome modern notions of contract; these disloyal women became the focus of patrician animosity because they undermined the traditional bonds of paternal interdependence. Genteel employers like Traill greatly feared that high wages and the availability of eligible young farmers would allow these women of "the working class"[8] to achieve a state of equality with married bourgeois women who, like her, were experiencing their own descent into poverty on unproductive farms. Far from reinforcing class lines, domestic service in Upper Canada was seen as a destabilizing force with real political consequences. In such an environment, the patrician class could no longer govern through a system of deference and consent. If one could not govern one's female labour force, how then could one exercise leadership in the wider political sphere? As Peter McGill so aptly observed in 1832, the year of the Reform Bill's passage in Britain, "one cannot always be *master* of one's actions" in these "melancholy times."[9] If the Canadian forest landscape has long been portrayed as one of darkness and foreboding, this literary trope embodied a particular class perspective, for it was originally the cultural construction of a fearful "pseudo-gentry" who saw in the farms that were carved out of the New World environment an unwelcome uniformity of work processes which undermined the natural class order.

One of the most striking aspects of Traill's portrait of social inversion in the New World is its almost total identification of the behaviour of female workers with the consequent destabilizing confusion of rank. This problem was most visibly manifested in the adornment of the female body. In *The Canadian Settler's Guide* Traill commented negatively on the habit of domestic servants dressing above their station in clothing that was of better quality than her own "homely apparel."[10] Why this obsession with dress? Traditionally, dress was seen as an outward symbol of rank and social hierarchy, but in the years following the American and French Revolutions this culture of "hierarchy of appearances"[11] was itself in flux, so that one's social station was no longer immediately readable from one's clothing. Thereafter the wearing of expensive clothing was seen as a form of class disobedience and as a democratic flouting of traditional social norms. With no sumptuary laws by which to reinstate the social hierarchy, the process of what Daniel Roche has termed "sartorial socialization"[12] remained unregulated. The European discourse on the instability of dress codes was amplified in the New World social environment because those commenting on dissident behaviour were themselves parvenus engaged in making their own fraudulent claims to superior status. With the perceived eradication of traditional identity markers, clothing became a particularly charged symbol of class instability. While labouring immigrants like John Barnes saw the removal of occupational markers, such as the round frock of the agricultural worker, as a sign of upward mobility, Dunbar Moodie, a landowner and half-pay officer, signified his poverty by remarking upon his inability to clothe his family "as well as respectable mechanics can do."[13] Alternatively, Sam Jarvis, one of the self-styled "little gentry" of Toronto, was engaged in the fraught competitiveness of social emulation; he deployed a farcical description of the vulgar apparel of Dr Widmer's wife, whose cambric pantaloons and chemise resembled male attire, to assert his own social superiority over a well-educated professional man.[14] Similarly, familial letters were replete with references to the charitable giving of clothing to poor women and servants as a means of expressing paternal *noblesse oblige*. This process was often reversed by servants who stole better clothing or who had such high wages that they could buy new rather than used clothing.[15] How unsettling to aspiring gentry women like Mary Jarvis, who often made her own clothes, or the cash-poor Mary O'Brien, a middling sort who achieved landed status by marrying a military officer and justice of the peace, but was forced to recycle her old clothing because the first call on their income was the payment of servants' wages.[16]

If the labour and income of the gentleman farmer was indistinguishable from that of the recently arrived British agricultural labourer, and if all were equally refashioning their class identity through emigration, then it followed that the making of class in new societies was an emphatically cultural process. For those aspirants to genteel station who often had less real economic power than the assisted immigrant and small farmer, one's occupation or income alone did not confer social rank; rather, one's position in the social hierarchy was a matter of appearances and manners, and depended primarily on the degree to which one could discipline labouring people within the household. The patriarchal family became the central institution that reinvested those reciprocal relations between patrician and plebeian with cultural power. Hence Catherine Parr Traill concluded her morality tale on how to subdue the working classes' desire for independence through participation in the market economy with a paean to the paternal ideal of "customs in common."[17] Writing as "a true friend of servants" Traill described the reciprocal "law of obligation" which was meant to harmoniously bind the classes together: "Were there more of that kindly feeling existing between the upper and lower classes both parties would be benefited, and a bond of union established which would extend beyond the duration of a few months or a few years, and be continued through life."[18]

Far from promoting the contractual relationships characteristic of the emerging capitalist cash nexus, as E.P. Thompson has maintained,[19] Upper Canadian gentry adhered to an older, patriarchal conception of social relations which they deployed in order to defuse the contract mentality of female domestic workers which they believed was instrumental in dismantling the distinction between patrician and plebeian. Where historians have seen these paternalistic social relationships as beneficial to the working classes, when seen from the point of view of the labourers themselves – a focus little pursued by historians of class – the cash nexus was considered a new "right" of Englishmen and a source of freedom and upward mobility in the New World environment. Domestic service stood at the crossroads of the assertion of two class identities: the gentry, whose status was defined largely by the ordering of female labour within the household, and the labourer immigrant cum capitalist farmer, whose patriarchal status hinged on sending his daughters out to service to earn wages in cash which were indispensable to buying out his government grant and thus lay at the heart of his sense of independence and social equality. In Upper Canada, the household work of young hired women was central to the emergence of modernity defined by the transition to the modern cash nexus.

E.P. Thompson's portrait of eighteenth-century England as a society characterized by increasing social distance between patrician and plebeian, caused by the penetration of capitalist economic relations within traditional aristocratic culture, has been steadily revised during the past two decades. Although J.C.D. Clark, a Tory historian, has criticized Thompson for seeing too great a contradiction between patriarchal social relations and the modern cash nexus, his own argument regarding an unreconstructed, dominant aristocratic culture served to uphold Thompson's view that the gentry had become more hegemonic by the end of the eighteenth century.[20] Many aspects of Thompson's paradigm have been refined, largely by the work of historians of the emerging middle classes such as Paul Langford, Jonathan Barry, Christopher Brooks, and by historians of gentry manners such as James Raven and Elizabeth Langland,[21] whose combined works have broadly confirmed two trajectories. First, the patrician class was much less hegemonic than previously thought and the problem of class, as interpreted both by the rising middle and established gentry groups, was largely a matter of culture and appearance, and cannot be approached merely from a numerical perspective of income or occupation. If gentry culture was much less monolithic in England and if power was highly decentralized and upheld largely through voluntary institutions rather than through a centralized state,[22] it is not illogical to demonstrate, as has Peter Linebaugh, that gentry hegemony was further diluted in the New World because of peculiar economic conditions such as the scarcity of labour, ethnic and religious diversity, and upward social mobility brought about by the cheapness of land.[23]

Second, although the new British historiography has amply demonstrated the vitality of an emerging middle-class authority by the eighteenth century, historians are still much undecided about how middle-class values altered the bipolar language of class posited by E.P. Thompson. If, as Paul Langford has argued, nothing "unified the middling orders" so much as aping the manners of the gentry, how does one distinguish between the cultures of the middling and the gentry? If gentry culture was expanding to include those who were not so identified by birth or land, to people who had the manners, education, and polish of a gentleman, it is possible to conclude, as James Raven and Dror Wahrman have, that middle-class emulation did little to revise the language of class based on a dual social system.[24]

Unlike most historians who have addressed the language of class in the public domain as part of the field of political argument, I aim to test the applicability of Thompson's model for Canada prior to 1850 by studying perceptions of class within the private realm of familial correspondence. This is not to say that this language is less political in its essence than the realm of public discourse, but that it was not activated merely for the purposes of political argumentation. Here, the language of rank or class functioned in a more variable and arguably more "neutral" context insofar as it was not merely imbricated with the categories of conservative, liberal, or radical. What is immediately striking about the use of language in family correspondence and social description in Upper Canada is the complete absence of any reference to the "middle" prior to 1832, even from critics of "aristocratic" culture such as William Bell, the radical Presbyterian clergyman. Despite the fact that Bell was, through his critique of duelling, gambling, drinking, and charivaris, carving out the principles of behaviour that would later be termed middle class, well into the 1840s his worldview continued to be defined by a binary struggle between the patricians and the people in which the "lower classes" included the middling sorts like himself.[25] While perceptions of society do not necessarily reflect the social structure in Upper Canada, what is significant is that the majority of immigrants, be they Scottish, Irish, or English, relied on the traditional hierarchy of ranks to imagine and describe the society they wished to create. Even working-class Scots, such as the Andersons who emigrated to Guelph, did not use the modern language of class, despite their awareness of the protests of handloom weavers but, rather, perceived society as a series of relative positions of high and low.[26]

If Bell, because of his political radicalism, identified with the lower classes, most immigrants of middling status by birth were intent on reinventing themselves as gentry in the New World. Indeed, the aspiration to become part of the landed class seemed within their reach because of the availability of land. However, because even pauper immigrants had the same access to land and often, through the use of the labour of their own children, improved their land faster, wealth alone did not serve as the barometer of class position. Even in England definitions of gentility were undergoing a transformation away from absolute categories defined by landowning or officeholding toward more nebulous constructions of "genteel," a definition which was dependent almost wholly upon what H.R. French has called a "very thin veneer" of cultural representation. For the most part, this 'pseudo-gentry'[27] refashioned themselves into patricians merely through the skilful deployment of language and a vigilant comparison with those about them.

Invariably, therefore, those who formed their social circle were always described as from the "highest and most fortunate ranks of life" or as "among the first in the place."[28] Anne Powell, prior to her marriage to the British-trained barrister William Powell, had been a milliner in Boston, which bestowed upon her a social status barely above the vulgar. However, in 1778, she fully embraced the language of social emulation when she stated that she could not bear the thought of "associating with People below what I had been used to" and that she intended, once in Upper Canada, to be visited only by the "genteelest people in the place."[29] Although Sam Jarvis, the Commissioner of Indian Lands, referred to "the lower class" when discussing the passing of the Alien Bill by the colonial legislature in 1827, he did not conceive of class in its modern socio-economic sense. Rather, he used this term much as he would have used the term "the People," a political category which included everyone outside the self-described gentry "now used, on all occasions and for all purposes."[30] Moreover, Jarvis and his circle of aspiring patricians conceived social identities in terms of a two-tiered model wherein the lower was juxtaposed against "the higher class." The "pseudo-gentry" regularly used a language of social description which was more akin to that current in early modern England, in which the social system was a stable, natural hierarchy of rank or station, and the boundaries between social groups remained fluid and indistinct.[31] Hence Jarvis remarked upon the "Old Feudal feeling of rank" which pervaded Upper Canada, and Robert Kerr, a fellow Tory, referred to those from "the highest and most fortunate ranks of life."[32] Even as struggles over the creation of modern socio-economic definitions of class were being waged in England, in Upper Canada the construction of the social order as a relativistic and complex layering of social groups was propounded by ambitious middling sorts because the cultural fluidity which so defined this altered construction of colonial "aristocracy" obviously served their interests. For as David Cannadine has maintained for the dominions of British settlement, "where such a feudal hierarchy did not exist the British were endlessly inventive in creating one."[33]

Often when the term "class" was used it could just as easily refer in a non-conflictual sense to a group of people, such as "a class of people called the Methodists,"[34] and was therefore empty of any specific socio-economic meaning. However, the more common distinction was made simply between the rich and poor, "the trade against the gentlemen," "the poorer Class" as against the "aristocracy," and more often when the phrase "lower classes" was employed it referred to the "distressed" poor rather than to a well-defined socio-economic category.[35] Even keen social observers like Mary O'Brien who was distinctly from the middling sort, having grown up with artisans and married a civil engineer who earned under £100 per annum,[36] rarely used the modern language of class. Rather, O'Brien gave the appearance of an even greater claim to gentility by deploying the two-model vocabulary of social identities of the "high and low."[37] Those middling sorts who wished to refashion themselves tended to deploy this two-class terminology; by contrast, middling farmers of a radical bent, such as John Grubb, though they also used traditional terms such as "station," embraced the three-stage model of society and saw their social identity as decidedly of "the middle condition" in the more modern economic sense of being of the "industrious" class between "poverty and riches."[38] Mrs O'Brien, and those who hoped to disguise their middling roots, clung tenaciously to the concept of a hierarchy of ranks as a means of proclaiming their status as one of the "gentlefolk"[39] of Upper Canada. She described Upper Canadian social structure in terms of organically connected, unchanging gradations defined as much by behaviour as by wealth: she referred to an Irish Leveller as being in "rank" below herself, to a youth in her employ as of "gentle degree," to those "within the pale of society," to the "lower orders" appealed to by the Methodists, to her servant George who "could not keep his station," to "various races" who owned "estates," to a "higher caste," and, more remarkable still, to her own "aristocratic prejudices as they relate to our inferiors in rank."[40] Interestingly, Mary O'Brien's conceptualization of social status within her hierarchy of degrees was never related to a person's wealth or occupation; rather, social differentiation was practised through the subtle use of dress, comportment, education, literacy, and manners.

Of course, this culture of appearances presented its own difficulties for parvenus, for if they were refashioning their social identity, other, less respectable immigrants could be engaged in the same counterfeiting of class. One needed to engage in more subtle fine-tuning of social distinctions apart from mere socio-economic condition. If one was a radical one was said to be distinctly beyond the reach of "the higher ranks of Society"[41] as Sam Jarvis made clear to his father-in-law in reference to Judge Willis. The latter's claim to genteel status was severely compromised by his association with "that class of people," namely radicals, tradesmen, and Irish. In Mary O'Brien's estimation, political radicals could never be true gentlemen; rather, they were but "greasy farmers" who gave "the appearance of gentlemen."[42] An ethnic tincture was likewise applied to the basic linguistic apparatus of social differentiation: references were made to "Yankee vulgarity"[43] while Mary O'Brien often used the term "class" as an ethnic rather than socio-economic reference. She remarked with dismay on an Irish family – "that class of people" – who were tenants but who had succeeded in posing as farmers who actually owned the land.[44] The culture of gentry emulation was indeed a tricky one, for while people like the O'Brien's masqueraded as "squires,"[45] it was often difficult to establish clear boundaries that excluded those whom the aspirant gentry wished to construct as their inferiors. Because of this fluidity of boundaries along the lines of wealth and occupation, the language of social description attached ethnic epithets to the often nebulous terrain of class gradations. Thus, references to "Yankee vulgarity" or the "Irish" were used to automatically denote those "uncivilized" "others" who were outside the framework of civil history and who were "never expected to be in the higher ranks of society." While everyone might appear to be a lady and gentleman, anyone who was Irish was thereby placed in a different category, for as Mary O'Brien so plainly stated, "an Irish country town lady is a very different thing from an English one."[46]

In Upper Canada the language of the "better sorts" was, for practical reasons, vague and somewhat inclusive. As Catherine Parr Traill herself observed, in the backwoods one was forced to rub shoulders with all kinds of people upon whom one might depend for help. One's conceptualization of social relations thus had to incorporate those "respectable" neighbours who might have "the appearance of gentlemen," resulting in a language of rank that remained broadly relative. Alternatively, the interests of the upwardly mobile middling sorts were better served by the emphasis on a more commodious definition of

gentility and an ideal of collective social identities marked by class fluidity rather than conflict. If in England, as Paul Langford has maintained, "nothing unified the middling orders so much as their passion
for aping the manners and morals of the gentry,"[47] in Upper Canada
the status seeking of the middling immigrant led to the almost wholesale evisceration of middle class consciousness. For the status conscious immigrant the bipolar model of society proved more
serviceable. In Upper Canada the modern language of class was distinctly absent from the vocabulary of the aspiring gentry, who preferred the traditional social description of ranks and orders. Those of
middle-class position in England did not imagine belonging to a new
rising middle class in the New World; rather, they pursued the status of
"gentleman," which consolidated the traditional vision of society as
divided between the higher and lower orders. In the private language
of family correspondence there is scant reference from any ethnic or
socio-economic group to a middle-class identity apart from that mentioned above from John Grubb, the Scottish radical, in the 1850s.

Dror Warhman has argued that the term "middle class" can be first
and foremost attributed to the language of political rhetoric. Indeed,
supporting his contention that the "middle class" was created by the
Reform Bill of 1832,[48] Mary O'Brien first mentions a tri-partite framework of social groups in reference to the reformed constitution which
she claimed created "the labouring class" and reconstituted a "second
class of aristocracy and mercantile people" out of the "very high aristocracy."[49] By 1835 this narrowly political connotation of the "middle"
was merging more distinctly into the modern socio-economic meaning of the term, as when O'Brien described the clerk in the local court
house as "a very respectable man, very poor with a large motherless
family of the middle rank between yeoman and gentleman."[50] However, the transformation in O'Brien's worldview was not wholly complete, for she still embraced the older concept of a continuous
hierarchy of groups defined by behaviour as much as by circumstance
by using the term rank and by referring to the clerk's behaviour and
his occupation. In this respect, the category of the "middle" was still
broadly inclusive of a wide range of occupations, thus serving as social
description bereft of the notion of conflictual social relations. The
concept of the middle was still articulated within the framework of traditional paternalism and social reciprocity and by a distinct minority
among a "pseudo-gentry" which preferred to embrace the social values
of the English upper classes.

If the ambitious middling sort of Upper Canada envisioned society as
a hierarchical structure defined by incremental degrees and relativistic
notions of higher and lower ranks rather than strictly delimited catego-

ries of collective identity, they did not conceive of status as connected in
any direct fashion to one's income. This is not surprising in a cash poor
society like Upper Canada, where servants often had more money on
hand than their masters. For the most part, middling immigrants such
as the O'Briens were keenly aware that, had they stayed in England, they
would not have had the means "to procure necessaries" but, at the same
time, despite rising expectations in Upper Canada, they struggled to
clear £40 per annum for several years as they cleared their land.[51] Their
experience was not qualitatively different from that of the pauper settler, for all remained relatively cash poor. Arguably, the aspiring gentry
who saw the ownership of labour as mandatory for status emulation
were even more cash poor insofar as wage contracts meant that servants
and agricultural labourers had the first call on their income.

While Mary O'Brien may have believed that, by acquiring substantial
land in Upper Canada, she had shed her modest beginnings – her relatives and friends were sailors and artisans – and could rightly claim a
new identity as one of the gentlefolk, she and her husband's actual
wealth placed them at the cusp between lower middling and the
skilled trades.[52] Likewise, Anne Powell experienced the rise and fall of
her class position. She began from "a rank of society" of milliners and
shopkeepers but rose quickly by marrying the young barrister William
Powell, who was, in her words, "of the highest of aristocracy" of
Boston.[53] William Powell rose high in colonial government service,
becoming first Solicitor General, then Attorney-General, and finally,
Chief Justice of Upper Canada. Once in Upper Canada, the Powells
were sufficiently wealthy to be able to consume luxury goods on their
travels to London – expensive linens, china, glassware, furniture, and
clothing[54] – which would allow them to keep up appearances as fashionable leaders of society. However, once widowed, Anne Powell constantly complained to her brother that "my Widow's Garb precludes
expense except in absolute necessities."[55] Indeed, once her own
income plummeted, Mrs Powell launched a moralistic critique of conspicuous consumption. While some historians have seen her denunciation as the benchmark of middle class values, far from embracing
modern notions of political economy or of virtues like self-control,
which were to become so emblematic of the Victorian middle class,
Mrs Powell's campaign against the vice of "unlimited indulgence"[56]
was merely a pragmatic response to the realities of downward mobility
faced by all social groups prior to 1850. Even though William Dummer
Powell could count himself among one of the governing elite of Upper
Canada, he (rightly) estimated that "[t]he family in its several
branches are not likely to rise in Situation here but if prudent they will
enjoy the Comforts of life."[57] By 1840 the Powell connection began its

slow decline in social prestige: Grant Powell was barely clinging to respectability, making only "a poor pittance" of £75 a year as a government clerk;[58] a female relative of Mrs Powell's had barely enough to "secure a competence for herself and two Daughters";[59] William's widowed sister-in-law was left sufficiently impoverished to force her to an economy "bordering upon privation of the comforts of life";[60] Mr Seymour, a clerk in a bank, had but "a poor subsistence";[61] their niece Charlotte Ridout began her marriage "in the enjoyment of easy circumstances" but within a few months was borrowing money from her brother and two years later she was "in straightened circumstances."[62] Most ignominous of all, John Powell, who had fallen into the vice of gambling, was financially ruined, had had his goods seized by the sheriff, and had sunk so deeply into debt as to have "forfeited his reputation as a man of honour or dignity;"[63] no one would give him money so that he could recoup his status as a gentleman.

While many of these protestations about privation do not entirely reflect the state of financial affairs within the extended Powell connection and must be read as a form of posturing, what they do reflect is the sense of unease experienced by this "imagined gentry" who presented as objective truth their ideal of society defined by providentially ordained and fixed "natural station[s]."[64] At the same time they all too keenly recognized that their status rquired daily vigilance since it depended on contingent comparisons with those about them. The culture of emulation was filled with constant anxiety as one was forced to witness the successes of others less genteel. Remembering the "humiliations and keen mortifications" of her humble youth, Anne Powell complained vehemently about the "improvidence" of her own male relatives as she watched vulgar men of business like William Allan surpass her in the pageantry of class emulation. Even the younger generation was trained in the culture of emulation. Hence Mary Powell caustically remarked to her grandfather, William Powell, that Allan's house was "quite a palace in appearance," putting the Powells "completely in the background."[65] On the day after the tragic death of the infant Agnes Strachan, Anne Powell's only observation was that Mrs Strachan was "surrounded by all the elegant comforts of an Episcopal Palace."[66] Of course, the Rt. Rev. John Strachan, the Anglican Lord Bishop of Toronto, was the greatest parvenu of them all. Born in Scotland, the son of a stonemason, Strachan managed to transform both his religion and his social station through immigration, and by a studious manipulation of the culture of appearances remade himself into one of the "aristocracy" of York, being the only gentleman other than the Lieutenant-Governor to have a complete retinue of liveried servants who rode in full spectacle beside his coach.

While Bishop Strachan was secure in his office and thus confident in participating in the theatre of patrician hegemony, others, such as the Jarvis-Powells and the O'Briens, had to work on a daily basis to shore up their claim to genteel status. The ideal of "independence," which they defined in terms of wealth that did not rely on officeholding,[67] remained beyond their grasp. As long as the family claim to respectability depended on government connections, their patrician status remained unstable and contingent. Government civil servants like Sam Jarvis had a salary "just sufficient to support their families."[68] But as Anne Powell observed in 1842, once the Reformers gained power under Baldwin and Lafontaine "no loyal subject can feel secure of his situation in the Queen's Government all are liable to be displaced to make way for a Rebel or Traitor successor."[69] Indeed, the Queen's own representatives had overturned the natural order of things by allowing traditional ceremonies of subordination to become props for alternative models of social relations. Thus the Powells castigated Lord Durham, one of the principal architects of the Reform Bill of 1832, and Governor of the Canadas in 1838, for permitting Methodist ministers and "*a colored Barber*" to present their cards and bow "with the other Gentlemen"[70] at official government receptions. Because of the confusion of ranks and the instability of wealth in the New World, commonplace English views of a providentially ordained hierarchy of social groups could not be automatically sustained and, to an even greater degree than in the Old World, neither land nor wealth was sufficient to ensure patrician authority. Hence, in Upper Canada, gentry dominance depended less on an economic base for its vitality than on the cultural promotion of a gentility of manners.

In the New World social environment, the theatre of patrician display was relied on to an even greater degree than in England, where it was presumed that people participated in the shared culture of a hierarchical social order. In settlement societies an uncongenial congeries of peoples, ethnicities, and religious traditions clung together to create a pluralistic environment in which the practices of social deference had to be redefined and reinforced. Even in England patrician culture had become less monolithic and the aristocratic code had been reconstructed. By the turn of the nineteenth century birth and land were deemed less important to the definition of gentlemanliness which, with the rise of large commercial interests, now included new notions of refinement. As never before, genteel culture was sustained by social performance. In the New World, notions of what was "ungenteel, unrefined and vulgar" were likewise reconstructed to include those who might attain only a "comfortable" existence in the New World.[71] Just as in England where a "bourgeois ideal of gentlemanliness"[72] was being carved out by new commercial interests, in Upper Canada genteel status began to include men of business under the rubric of the now more commodious definition of gentlemen.[73]

While one needed sufficient "Circumstances" to claim genteel status in Upper Canada, one's occupational identity counted for little in one's assumption of social superiority.[74] The commonplace triad that defined the language of gentrification was "character, fortune and influence."[75] The utilitarian language of the rising middle class was little in evidence. Virtues like hard work and application of skill were deemed less meaningful than one's comportment. Thus Anne Powell observed that while her son-in-law Sam Jarvis had talent, she had no doubt that his success must be attributed to his "urbanity of manners" and appearance.[76] Although one's work identity was not irrelevant, since officeholding was deemed one measure of gentlemanliness, work was not deemed a virtue in and of itself as it later would be within the system of middle-class values, but was firmly enhanced by one's outward display of character. While it might be important to know that Mary Powell's future husband earned £250 per annum, this was of less significance than that he had "goodly connexions."[77] Of William Powell's gaining a modest position as clerk in the probate office at Guelph, Anne Powell noted that "the emoluments are trifling" but "it gives a character."[78] William Jarvis was hailed as a paragon of gentlemanly masculinity because he had "by his own industry and good conduct obtained a high character throughout the country and his present office entitled him to a place in society which he holds with great credit to himself."[79] And as a suitor to Mary Powell he had the advantage over an Anglican clergyman with a steady income because he was superior in "appearance, manners and character." Conversely, one was deemed ruined not simply because of a "pecuniary situation" but because of the loss of one's credit or reputation in society.[80]

Faced constantly with the threat of downward mobility because of the instability of the fledgling colonial economy, aspiring gentry eschewed the English practice of integrating bourgeois values within a reconstructed aristocratic code, preferring to construct a colonial concept of gentility around less materialistic considerations. The true badge of a gentleman was character defined in terms of outward social behaviour and public deportment, rather than according to criteria of inner spirituality or morality, as a self-consciously middle-class observer might do. Thus Sam Jarvis esteemed Governor Maitland for his ceremonial display of appearing religious by kneeling on the bare floor of the church and was little interested in his actual beliefs.[81] In communicating to a plebeian sort, the vocabulary of success was quite different. When giving advice to a prospective immigrant, a family retainer in Ireland who was a druggist making only £32 per annum, Henry Gowan stressed the importance of talent and industry. By contrast, in recommending William Watson for the office of local magistrate, James Gowan stressed his attributes as "a man of Excellent character and good family."[82] The evisceration of work as a social identity became the benchmark of gentility. This resolutely uneconomic valuation of social position was aptly summed up by Anne Powell who maintained that "poverty and want are of minor consideration in comparison with Character."[83]

If middle-class values relating to virtues of hard work, creditworthiness, and economy were creeping into the vocabulary of the patrician code in England, as British historians have maintained,[84] in Upper Canada these more modern conceptions of society were firmly subordinated to gentry ideals of outward appearance and comportment. As Jean Mickle commented in a letter to her relatives in Guelph, in organizing her aunt's funeral "I endeavored not to be extravagant but genteel."[85] Moreover, at this time there was very little valuation placed on work as an emblem of manliness.[86] Indeed, one's occupational identity was more often remarked upon in order to distinguish imposters from those who had reached too far above themselves. While engaged in vigilant policing of her new social boundaries, Mary O'Brien, who was extremely sensitive about her own modest origins, was fond of exposing fraudulent parvenus. Hence she observed that the brother of Attorney General John Beverley Robinson was but "a storekeeper in New Market."[87] Later she gossiped about Mrs Ridout, portraying her as an obvious imposter because she had learned the accoutrements of politeness sufficiently well to make her manners appear natural and unaffected. After meeting Mrs Ridout in Toronto, Mary O'Brien recorded that Mrs Ridout, "formerly (by report) a cook but now the terror of York ... was very civil, talked sentiment which she does not understand & household affairs which she does very much like a cook & politics in which she is interested like the wife of a government officer."[88]

There were two tropes which characterized claims to genteel status. There was, first, a juxtaposition between those born to a particular station with its "purity of manners" and those who merely learned the artifice of gentility. Mrs O'Brien could thus caustically dismiss Mrs Yonge, a Scottish "good-tempered silly genteel enough young woman," ridiculing her for mistakenly attempting to equate being a lady with the ability to ride a horse.[89] When aspiring gentry like the Powells referred to "high breeding," they did not actually understand this to mean that there were fixed and irrevocable ranks in society. What they were referring to was the process which began in the late eighteenth

century in England where an increasing stress on the social category
"genteel" represented a lowering of social boundaries. Basically anyone who could read the vast array of advice literature produced in this
period could learn the proper manners which might distinguish one
from the "vulgar" commercial classes.

Anne Powell alluded to this increasing permeability of gentility
when she wrote to her uncle to say that she preferred her girls to
exhibit modesty rather than "the polished manners and the impudent
self possession which is now so prevalent even among vulgar and ignorant girls." Even as, or because, the concept of gentility was expanding
to include the wealthier manufacturing interests as well as those of
inherited rank, there was an even greater emphasis placed on appearing "naturally" born to high status. Since a growing proportion of
"pseudo-gentlemen" were self-consciously identifying themselves in
this way, it became increasingly incumbent to demonstrate time-hon-
oured possession of manners, dress, and polite conversation. Once the
somewhat dubious Mr O'Hara married into the Jarvis-Powell connection, he and his wife stopped being simply "queer" and indecent people and were touted by William Dummer Powell himself as among the
"first Classes of Society" because of their "unaffected simplicity and
tender elegance," knowing all the while that though displaying the
"Education and Manners" of a Gentleman, these pleasing attributes
had been recently acquired and "grafted" onto his unpromising Irish
ethnic culture.[90] In a similar vein, Mary O'Brien denigrated the cultural aspirations of the local Presbyterian clergyman (he being a
Scotchman) "as a man whose polish evidently arose not from the world
but from mental cultivation & Christian feeling & principle."[91] Basically he hadn't got it quite right. If one wished to pass as truly genteel
one had to acquire habits of "high breeding" very early on so as not to
appear too "fashionable" and sophisticated – code words for artifice
and hypocrisy – but to display "artless unsophisticated manners and
feelings."[92] Mary Jarvis was scandalized by William Jarvis's desire for an
evening wedding at home rather than a formal morning service in
church because this might make them objects of scorn within genteel
circles. The occasion compelled her to quip that "there is no teaching
some people *gentility*," a rather disingenuous comment given that all
the Powells recognized that they lived in an "artificial Society" where
the proper observances had to be studied carefully and that respectability was often but a thin veneer: on any given occasion one could
slip into the offence of keeping "vulgar" society, as Anne Powell once
did by being discovered in the pit of a theatre while in London.

In this climate of uncertainty and of counterfeit identities, distinctions of manners mattered a great deal and, without vigilant monitor-

ing of new forms of conduct, one could get it wrong. Such was the fate of Sam Jarvis, who attempted to publicly vindicate his honour by fighting a duel at a time when notions of genteel manliness founded on violence were becoming culturally outmoded.[93] Interestingly the origin of the Jarvis-Ridout duel was the perceived insult to Jarvis's social position from the Ridouts' claim that Jarvis's sister attended a school in Quebec "by the charity of Mr Ridout."[94] Those who lacked inherited rank, great wealth, or a firm position within the political hierarchy as bases for social status, had to properly educate themselves to carry off confident manners and appear to participate with ease and natural simplicity in the theatre of genteel sociability. To this end any number of etiquette manuals were available and in 1824 the *Upper Canada Gazette* announced the opening of a walking school to teach youth "genteel carriage of their bodies"[95] and proper speech so that one would not appear uncivil by making it look like "every word is studied."[96]

In Upper Canada one's claim to patrician status rested on not appearing too fashionable in one's dress; avoiding too conspicuous a display of luxury, redolent of commercial values; having a good education which avoided the now démodé practice of learning French (a particular problem in Upper Canada as it could lead to a desire for fripperies and conversations with Frenchmen!); and expressing fine feelings of sentiment.[97] These cultural ceremonies were important in establishing a self-conscious identity as a patrician elite. This identity comprised fine gradations of social status within a shared understanding of a hierarchical social structure with a broadly inclusive polite society.

However, the most critical social divide remained that between the higher and lower orders and here the traditional references of power and deference between patrician and plebeian had to be rigorously policed. There were two key means of establishing clear boundaries between the two classes: one was by dispensing charity, a role primarily ascribed to female gentlefolk;[98] the second and more efficacious exercise of authority among this self-made elite was through the control of the labour of others, namely of female domestic servants. Moreover, the control of familial dependents, including female servants, upheld patriarchal authority within the household and the society at large.[99]

THE "PERPLEXITY WITH SERVANTS"[100]

Historians who have focused on the statutes governing the master-servant relationship have concluded that the masters had all the power. Prior to the 1847 Act which formalized the power of masters to discipline their employees, the degree to which English common law applied to the Imperial provinces was as yet "ill defined."[101] When viewed from the perspective of aspiring patricians, analyzed within the wider problems of labour scarcity in Upper Canada, and seen from the perspective of plebeian family strategies, a different picture emerges regarding the viability of paternalistic control prior to 1850. The master-servant relationship in Upper Canada differed markedly from that in England largely because of the contours of the labour market which were in some respects peculiar to pre-industrial Canada. In settlement Australia, for example, where the supply of female labour outstripped demand, domestic servants, when compared to their Canadian counterparts, had less power to choose their workplace or negotiate for higher wages.[102] Colonial America in the eighteenth century was characterized by a context of high wages and scarcity of labour similar to Canada in the early nineteenth century, and the consequent need to control the supply of labour led to indentured servitude and later slavery. However, in the free trade empire of the post-revolutionary era where servants were not compelled to pay for their passage with their labour this solution was not available to the Upper Canadian elite.[103]

In England, the status of domestic servitude was more variable and dependent upon locality: hence the domestic servant who emigrated to London might suffer considerable downward mobility as she sold her labour in a highly competitive environment where employers had the upper hand in hiring and firing their household servants. Domestic servants in England also travelled much further from their families in search of work and, to some degree, experienced a greater sense of independence from parental authority, but at the same time would have been more vulnerable to the control of their employers.[104] In addition, because servants in England and France may have been compelled by law to fulfill their contracts, they lived for longer periods under one roof and were perhaps more exposed to the reforming influence of middle-class values.[105]

By contrast, in Upper Canada, domestic servants may have often been younger, but they lived in close contact with their own families and were thus less influenced by their masters, unless they were orphaned and formally apprenticed until the age of twenty-one. Because the labour of young women fell largely under the control of their own fathers, they were less willing to conform to the patrician conception of domestic servants as one of the family. Although the vast majority of single women below the upper middling rank were, at one time, domestic servants, they viewed this work as an aspect of their life-cycle, as a temporary means to save for marriage and to contribute to their own family economy. Because of the interim nature of life-cycle service there was a constant shortage of female labour, a condition which greatly profited the young women who were adept at negotiating higher wages for themselves, a situation that persisted at least until the late nineteenth century when the power relations between master and servant were altered.[106]

Nothing so evoked the instability of elite culture in Upper Canada as the persistent problem of the shortage of female servants. Mary O'Brien complained constantly about having to go on "begging expeditions"[107] in search of a servant, "begging" being an oblique reference to the class inversion that such a shortage involved. William Dummer Powell went as far as Kingston to hunt up a cook for his wife in York, "but I fear it will be hopeless," he informed her.[108] The lack of female servants compelled elite women to undertake more household work than they desired. Hence Mary O'Brien bewailed the fact that with only one servant she was up at dawn "to execute my various functions as cook, housemaid, dairy maid and nurse." On other occasions the servant shortage compelled Mary O'Brien to miss church service.[109] Similarly, Mary Jarvis protested vehemently about the crisis she faced when two servants departed after one was caught stealing and the other fell while skating.[110] And earlier Mary Jarvis's mother, Anne Powell, had written of the inconvenience of having no servants but one incompetent "Disbanded soldier."[111]

Early nineteenth-century familial correspondence is replete with this discourse of complaint with regard to the lack of female household labour. The burden of protest of elite women did not, however, fall on the practical inconveniences; rather, when these women talked of servants bringing "comfort" and order to their homes, they meant that their presence contributed to the idea of the natural government of patrician over plebeian for, even with servants, elite women milked cows, made candles, cooked, and cleaned.[112] For example, even with three servants, a kitchen helper, a housemaid, and a nurse, Mary Jarvis was "constantly employed" washing and sewing immediately following her confinement.[113] What was necessary was enough female labour to relieve the gentlewoman of sufficient burdens so that household chores did not lead to "the destruction of her taste or cultivation."[114] The constant complaints about the behaviour of servants that pervaded elite women's letters was at heart a fulmination about class inversion and a portrayal of a world turned upside down, where patrician mistresses were forced to be clients of their impudent and disloyal female servants who could leave at short notice. No wonder the Powells preferred to hire freed black slaves. This significant erosion of the distinction between free and coerced labour, in turn, defined much of their vehement reaction against the non-deferential attitudes they bemoaned among their servants, and accounts for the increasingly desperate statements in their correspondence about the need to establish control over servants. Indeed, it can be argued that much of the gentry discourse on the servant problem was founded on the overlap and coexistence of the coerced work of slaves and indentured servants and the world of the free labour market.[115]

In short, this was a discourse about the instability of class, expressing the fear that the power relations, inherent in the hierarchical social order, were being daily challenged at their foundation, on the terrain of household government, by independent girls who addressed "their masters in a tone of perfect equality."[116] More disturbingly, plebeian women constantly challenged traditional notions of paternalistic social relations by manipulating the market to their own advantage. Thus Mary O'Brien, who subscribed to this "moral economy of service,"[117] deeply resented the behaviour of young female labourers because, in regularly absconding back home to work for their fathers, they served the class interests of upwardly mobile labourer-farmers rather than the class ambitions of the aspiring gentry. The exercise of patrician patriarchy was also subverted when it became evident that plebeian fathers had greater control over the labour of their children than patrician employers could exert over their female household labourers. The intersection of class and gender (and ethnic) interests within the culture of paternalism was captured by Mary O'Brien who described how her husband had found "a promising young woman [from Scotland] who was well disposed to go to her but she and her sister were too dextrous in the use of the handspike with which he found them assisting their father & brother in extensive logging that she could on no account be spared."[118] In addition, it was clear that the way that class deference was affirmed had a specifically female complexion, for elite employers consistently preferred to hire young women and disdained the employment of men for fear that the dependent nature of service would undermine the ideal of manly independence.[119] It is to the ways in which female labour contributed to the making and unmaking of class patriarchy that I now turn.

It has become customary among historians of class to argue that having a servant was an immediate emblem of middle-class status. Indeed, the late nineteenth-century English social surveyor Seebohm Rowntree cited the keeping of a servant as marking the border between the working and middle classes, while William Booth proclaimed that more than one servant was mandatory for middle-class status. Modern historians have generally affirmed the social distinctions drawn by Rowntree and Booth. However, in Upper Canada, where the two-tier model of social relations persisted well into the nineteenth century, the keeping of servants was instrumental in reaffirming an upper rather than middle-class identity. That the public display of gentility rested on the hiring of servants was pungently evoked by Thomas Radcliffe who in 1833 objected that the "humbler Anglican clergy resembled Irish Methodist preachers" because "no one here is grand enough to have a servant riding after him."[120] Similarly, the wife of a "decent farmer" insisted on proclaiming her gentility by talking about "the badness of servants."[121] One suspects that her civil conversation on this theme was intended to make up for the "yeomanlike manner" of her husband.

For many this discourse of complaint about the scarcity of labour was the only means by which they could declare their status, for many of the aspiring elite often had merely one servant – which would have relegated them to middling status[122] – or none at all.[123] With her husband living in England Anne Powell was compelled to keep no servants. Her husband lived in similarly debased circumstances, with only one servant, but kept up appearances by choosing to make that one a groom who could accompany him in public.[124] As soon as Mary O'Brien's sister-in-law acquired a "good Gloucestershire girl" she could be once again identified as from "the rank of life from which we spring."[125] Likewise one's downward mobility was publicly affirmed when one became too poor to hire a servant. In such situations one had to rely on the labour of female relatives who were poorer than you. The appearance of keeping a servant was so instrumental in dictating one's "separation from the lower orders"[126] that Susanna Moodie had her daughter keep house for her. Although her decision prevented her daughter from earning wages in the household of others, she chose to secretly earn money by writing rather than publicly declare her descent into the lower orders by sending her daughter out to service.[127] Indeed, the reliance on the labour of relatives was deemed ungenteel and had to be disguised as much as possible. There is no clearer evidence that the keeping of female domestic servants was viewed as one of the principal means of reinforcing power relations of authority and deference between the classes than Mary O'Brien's reluctance to hire a *male* youth from her own class to clean house because she might have to treat him "as an equal."[128]

Where Mary O'Brien, like the status-conscious aspiring elite of Upper Canada, referred throughout her journal to the importance of servants in creating "aristocratic partition," and making much of the fact that "I must be genteel and take my servant with me,"[129] those middling sorts whose self-identity resided within the broad compass of "the people" rarely mentioned, let alone complained about, the behaviour of their servants. Indeed, William Bell, the radical critic of aristocratic culture, made only two references to servants in his lifetime: he remarked on the marriage of his servant Helen Christie as part of his larger record of marriages within his parish and he complained that two other servants had absconded.[130] Significantly this latter complaint focused on his loss of labour which forced him personally to bring in the hay and not on the imperiling of his class position. Similarly, the Scottish radical printer Marcus Gunn articulated a bourgeois view of service by casting the absence of servants in terms of lost work rather than a subversion of deferential relations. In middling families the hiring of servants was conceived in definitively contractual terms.[131] Moreover, middling families such as the Biggars, who were small shopkeepers, attached no shame to using relatives as servants.[132] Indeed, it appears that the keeping of servants of the same class was commonplace. For example, the Dougall family, who were artisan immigrants, regularly hired the daughters of their Scottish neighbours largely as a means to encourage intra-ethnic marriage.[133]

While both middling sorts and gentry families kept servants, the way in which they perceived the relationship between master and servant was qualitatively different. William Bell saw his servants not as members of his family but as commodities to be bought and sold in the free market. In fact, one of the principal ways in which he condemned aristocratic culture and articulated his own self-conscious middling identity was to constantly refer to the "unnatural" intimacy between master and servant upheld by the patriarchal ideal which led all too frequently to the "vice" of marriage between military officers and their young female servants. In 1824 he castigated an eighty-four-year-old Anglican clergyman (a former Roman Catholic priest) for marrying his thirteen-year-old servant girl and in 1827 told the moral tale of how a magistrate who had married his servant became a drunkard and died an early death.[134] Although Bell was generally opposed to charivaris, on these occasions he praised this customary form of plebeian protest because it served to solidify the middling farmers and poor artisans against the aristocratic pretensions of the professional elite. By defining such liaisons as vicious because they elided the work of the servant with the role of wife, Bell critiqued traditional notions of the patriarchal family, which he believed were destructive of evangelical-bourgeois ideas of marriage founded on a shared notion of Christian love.[135] Interestingly, Bell's critique of gentry attitudes toward women was similar to that offered by Leonore Davidoff;[136] but where modern historians have correlated the combining of roles of servant and wife with a middle-class value system, Bell believed this unseemly sexual intimacy between the classes was emblematic of traditional notions of the patriarchal family which he linked to the culture of gentility.[137]

Historians of nineteenth-century Britain and France have begun to consider the changing role of servants as a way to understand at what juncture the modern cash nexus achieved cultural dominance. Like E.P. Thompson, Cissie Fairchilds has argued that the late eighteenth century witnessed the demise of patriarchal notions of labour relations in which the ties between the classes were defined in intimate familial terms of loyalty and interdependence.[138] This chronology of the emergence of modern labour relations has been recently challenged by Sara Maza and most elaborately by Tim Meldrum,[139] who have argued that, when seen from the perspective of class-based femininities which operated within the culture of household labour, the traditional moral economy of service persisted well into the 1830s. In Upper Canada this patriarchal ideal was reinvigorated and dominated the culture until the 1870s and was only displaced by the growth of a powerful urban, commercial elite. In short, the study of domestic service is an essential component in understanding how a modern, liberal society emerged in Canada.

The self-made gentry of Upper Canada broadly subscribed to the notion of the patriarchal family; the household was viewed as a hierarchical and authoritarian structure in which the male head governed his dependents, which included his wife, children, apprentices, and domestic servants. While environmental factors on the expanding frontier and the availability of land have often been seen as creating more egalitarian social structures in the New World, such tendencies were checked by the upwardly mobile middling immigrant who consciously embraced hierarchical views because these were deemed instrumental to the process of gentrification. Indeed, one's domestic arrangements were believed to be a more reliable guide to class position than actual wealth or profession. These, I have argued, were disturbingly fluid in Upper Canada prior to the 1850s. While mistresses superintended the labour of servants on a daily basis, they did so on behalf of their husbands whose claim to masculine authority rested largely on their ability to control labour within the household. However, the patriarchal ideal also included servants as part of the family circle. Thus, when Mary O'Brien's brother Richard spoke of his family including nine persons, he referred to his wife, children, servants, and agricultural labourers, all of whom lived under his roof, ate at his table, accompanied him to church, and for whom he was obliged to care when ill.[140] Similarly, when Mary O'Brien alluded to "family discord" she was in fact referring to a spat between two servants; but, interestingly, while all her servants were treated as members of her family to whom she dispensed advice (on marriage), whom she tended in illness, and with whom she prayed, she did not include her black servants within this rubric of family but described them merely as "sable guests."[141] The patriarchal ideal which included servants within the embrace of family affections could be deployed to scold children, as when one patriarch upbraided his daughters for not writing by quipping that "even an old domestic that had been Faithful would deserve an acknowledgement."[142] What is clear, however, is that the modern nuclear family, with its attributes of affectionate relations and greater equality between the paterfamilias and his dependents, was not in the ascendant prior to 1850; rather, the family remained resolutely hierarchical and, despite the emergence of affectionate bonds, patrician masculinity rested on the control of domestic labour. Stated another way, the household remained one of the primary sites for disciplining labour and inculcating values of subordination and deference among (female) plebeian youth.

Clearly, though, these patricians were not simply mimicking their betters, for relations between mistresses and their servants were often intimate. Mary Jarvis told her mother that she trusted her black servant June as she would "one of the family."[143] Similarly, Sarah Hill poignantly marked the anniversary of the death of her beloved servant Jane because she had faithfully defended her mistress against her husband when Mr Hill exercised his patriarchal prerogative to beat both his wife and servant.[144] Mrs Cawthra not only gave gifts to her servants but she regularly acted *in loco parentis* by arranging the marriage contracts of her servants, just as she would have done for her children.[145] Moreover, masters often bequeathed substantial sums to faithful servants in their wills, made them coffin bearers at their funerals, invited servants to family prayers, and cared for elderly servants who were no longer able to work.[146] Indeed, the Ardagh family established the Home for the Reception of Indigent Women in Barrie with the sole aim of caring for one of their aged servants.[147] While such charitable acts bespoke a certain intimacy and cordiality between the classes, the giving of gifts, the instilling of religious views, care during sickness and old age were elite strategies to increase loyalty and to stabilize the social order by subduing class animosity through the creation of a common set of values between patricians and plebeians. Mary O'Brien's near obsession with refashioning the bodies of her female servants and her constant attention to their manners and state of cleanliness were oppressive forms of moral policing, just as the practice of renaming servants was meant to erase their identities and remake them into respectable respresentatives of the patrician family.[148] The idea that customs in common bound together the classes was but another form of class control, and all the more powerful since it was exercised in a manner that was both ubiquitous and invisible

because it was woven seamlessly into the web of everyday life. Thus
when the women who organized charities for ill and aged female servants stated that they did not aim to morally reform them, they were
not being disingenuous, for they shared an understanding of patriarchal social relations which presumed that class discipline was being
exercised within the personal realm of the productive household. It
was because of this broader cultural understanding about intersection
of work and moral reform that Bishop Strachan did not send Betsey
Garland, a fallen woman, to a charitable institution, but ensured that
she mend her character through "respectable service."[149]

If masters were to have certain duties to perform with regard to their
household dependents, it was hoped that servants would likewise
understand that they had certain obligations to fulfill within the web of
reciprocal social relations. That many female servants did not share
the same values as their employers is clear from the frequent outraged
comments about the disloyalty of servants. Having cared for her servants in times of sickness, Mary Jarvis excoriated even her former servants when they did not show up to pay their respects when a Jarvis was
ill: "you will be surprised to hear that neither Martha Bridgeland or
Mary Henley ever came to enquire after Mary as the former had some
excuse as her Mother was very ill at the same time: the other is a heartless bad minded girl."[150] It is apparent that the moral economy of service was a fragile entity and, therefore, the responsibilities of both
parties often had to be set out in formal contracts. The 1814 contract
between William Jarvis and Frederick Windermaker outlined the
reciprocal duties between master and servant: Windermaker must
"work and labour in the capacity of a Servant, in and about the Premises of the said William Jarvis, for the space of Six Calendar Months,
in consideration of the sum of fifteen pounds lawful money of Upper
Canada ... And the said William Jarvis doth further bind himself to provide for the said Frederick Windermaker sufficient Drink and lodging
for the support of the said Frederick ... "[151] When binding himself as
an apprentice David Paterson agreed to pay for his candles and clothing but he was allowed to keep a portion of the harvest for himself and
in exchange his master had to train him to weave, feed and lodge
him.[152] Even more evocative of patriarchal social relations, in which
concepts of household and family were elided and where contractual
and moral concerns were mixed, was the indenture of Catherine
Aiken which stressed how a "faithful apprentice" upheld the reputation of the family she served, for she was explicitly told that she must
not tell family secrets, she must not marry, play at cards or dice at the
master's loss, or haunt taverns or playhouses. In exchange for con-

forming to familial mores Catherine was to be taught household work, schooled, and provided with sufficient meat, lodging, clothing, and, at the age of twenty-one, with two cows and a featherbead.[153]

That the reciprocal bonds of paternalism were being "nibbled" away, not by the incipient economic rationalization of the gentry[154] but by the contractarian views of the female servants themselves, is evident from the protests of employers when their servants absconded without notice. When servants left abruptly they were never accused of breaking their contracts – even though it is clear that formal contracts were subscribed to by both parties. Rather, patrician employers deployed the language of paternalism to charge women with disloyalty and deceit, just as the ideal servant was praised for honesty, cleanliness, and manners rather than industry or usefulness.[155] Even servants who had worked for as little as a fortnight were expected to be loyal to the family. When their girl Christie left the household of the government clerk George Murray Jarvis in 1863, he angrily wrote his mother that Christie was "a heartless creature, and we are all glad she is gone."[156] Sarah Hill was similarly chagrined to find that her servant Maria departed "with the greatest indifference though she had lived so long with us."[157] Employers were particularly exercised when young women left to get married, since their departure was read as a means to thwart the presumed authority of masters to control the courtship of their dependents. We discover that Maria departed with "indifference" because she had her own life strategy, which involved getting married, and it is significant that when Maria agreed to return to Sarah Hill, she did so on her own terms and worked on a casual basis and not as a live-in servant. If, as E.P. Thompson has contended, the paternal attitudes of subordination and deference were being altered by the emerging commercial values of the expanding upper classes, there is little evidence of this among the Upper Canadian elite. Indeed, a rare reference to modern notions of political economy was mooted by a colleague of the wholesaler William Allan who, when apprenticing his son George, observed that "his time during office hours is my property." But, interestingly, this statement, though redolent of monetary association, was couched in the traditional vocabulary of patriarchal social relations, for he also pledged that, when hiring this young man, he would look after his welfare "as if he were my own son."[158]

If the mutuality of classes encompassed by the notion of paternalism was being eroded, we should focus on the attitudes and family strategies of the labouring immigrants themselves rather than on the impact of commercialism on gentry values, to understand the way in which the market society evolved in Upper Canada.

"WHERE A MAN CONSIDERS HIMSELF
AS GOOD AS HIS BOSS"[159]

Historians such as E.P. Thompson, E.J. Hobsbawm, and George Rudé,[160] who have written extensively about the breakdown of paternalistic social relations at the end of the eighteenth century, have extrapolated from the attitudes of radical leaders expressed in their political writings in order to understand the values and customs of ordinary working people. In the absence of adequate archival sources, the actual voices of workers could not be uncovered and, as a consequence, the views of leaders such as William Cobbett stood as a surrogate for the authentic beliefs of the agricultural labourers themselves.[161] Canadian historians now have the benefit of archives rich in family papers and the recent and remarkable collation of hundreds of pauper immigrants' letters edited by Wendy Cameron, Sheila Haines, and Mary McDougall.[162] Through these important letters historians are able to more accurately understand how labourers perceived paternalistic social relations, what customs they wished to have restored in the New World, and how the availability of "free land" and a fortuitous labour market enabled on these immigrants to refashion the balance between tradition and capitalism.

Extrapolating working-class behaviour from the pronouncements of the ruling elite has some obvious difficulties, for patricians deftly portrayed their society as one characterized by natural deference. For example, Lady David Smith deployed as a rhetorical device the image of hundreds of "respectable tradesmen" walking in the funeral procession of her husband to uphold the mutuality of classes.[163] In frustration, aspiring gentry occasionally admitted to "the spirit of equality and independence which subsists among the lower classes," but even this was a political device to alert erstwhile employers to greater vigilance in disciplining the behaviour of servants.[164] It is not unsurprising that labourer immigrants read their new social environment differently from the aspiring gentry. Like Catherine Parr Traill they drew contrasts between the Old World and the New, but where she interpreted the backwoods as a lost Eden, unemployed Scottish weavers like William Davies, who settled in Lanark township, told his sons and daughters back home that Upper Canada was "an asylum for those who cannot make a living at home" and that they now lived "in the greatest plenty" and owned three cows, largely because of the earnings of his daughters who were out to service at $2 and $4 per month.[165] Like the upper classes, however, immigrants envisioned Upper Canada in optimistic terms, as a safe-haven for those seeking upward mobility. As William Taylor Upton, an assisted immigrant, informed a neighbour back home, one can soon gain an "independency" and become a "man of property in 9 weeks."[166] The key to this new sense of independence, which implied both the ability to financially support one's family and a sense of individual rights free of paternal control, was the possession of land. Alexander Sinclair exclaimed to the Scottish radical settler Marcus Gunn, "Oh, what a nice thing it would be to have a piece of ground for one self to improve and work upon without being under the control of oppressors."[167]

Although settlers often farmed small lots and cleared unproductive land, and gradations of wealth permeated the rural frontier, emigrants, at least in the first few years after their arrival, believed that Upper Canada provided a fertile environment for the development of an alternative social model where distinctions of rank and the language of deference would eventually be eradicated. "Jack is as good as his master here. Masters are glad to get servants, and come to hire them: no running after masters," Henry Heaseman of Blandford, Upper Canada, informed his family in England in 1834. Even though still a servant, George Coleman experienced no conflictual relations with his master as he had in England. In Upper Canada he believed he could speak his mind, because with the scarcity of labour, he was not under the constant threat of "being discharged twice in a fortnight" and, in the absence of a formal Poor Law which reinforced social deference and inequality within the parish, he "now ha[d] not to meet the frowns of the overseer and be called a pauper."[168] George Carver likewise understood how the modern laws of political economy had produced a labour market where traditional paternalistic views of rank and deference could not flourish. Writing to his parents in 1833 he observed the very reversal of social relations that the patricians so feared in rural Upper Canada: "It is no use of high spirited farmers wishing to come out to this country, for they will not get their servants to wait upon them as at home, and to sit down at a second table to eat their crumbs. The servant is made equal with his master, on all respects of that kind, and not treated as a great many of the light headed farmers at home treat them, as dogs!" Indeed, in Upper Canada the laws of power and subordination seemed to have been drastically altered, for masters "are obliged to beg and pay to get a man for a few days."[169]

The frontier myth of social equality appears to have been first articulated by the labouring immigrants of Upper Canada. It was thus emblematic of a distinct class outlook rather than an actual social reality and was forged out of the radical doctrines of early nineteenth-century labour unrest. The contrast drawn constantly between the polarized society in England and the apparent social equality met with in Upper Canada demonstrates the degree to which social unrest and conflictual class attitudes had permeated far below the radical leadership and had become the vocabulary of the ordinary working man. What is striking, however, about the way in which these attitudes were transplanted to the New World is that they did not result immediately in a distinctive working-class language of opposition. Rather, the New World environment, with its scarcity of labour, high wages, and abundance of land, awakened the expectation of upward mobility which allowed these immigrants to imagine a one-class society, where "the working man is thought just as much of as his master"[170] and where the pretensions of the upper classes – "the gentlemen farmers, *as they call themselves*"[171] – were deemed no more than irrelevant posturing. The eradication of deference created a sense of equality, where manly men "scorned servitude"[172] and could freely express their rights.[173] But more, it appeared, from the perspective of the labouring immigrant, that the New World had produced a one-class society, a ubiquitous middle; "there are no beggers in this country, nor any carriages,"[174] but, as the Dundas bricklayer Richard Neal observed, evoking the traditional language of rank, "the people are all of one sort."[175]

Emigrant letters are also key sources in uncovering those customs or values which were held in common by patrician and plebeian. There were some aspects of paternalistic relations which emigrant labourers embraced. The reported references in their letters home to the freedom to hunt game and pasture their cattle in the open woods affirms E.P. Thompson's thesis that the tightening of the game laws in England was perceived by the labouring classes as an abridgement of their customary rights.[176] The right to hunt was seen as critical to labouring families; William Spencer remarked that "there is more privileges here, than is with you: we can fish and fowl as much as we please, and none to make us afraid. There is no gamekeepers, or waterkeepers."[177] Indeed, a large part of their transformed identity from poor labourer to middling farmer and their sense that they had achieved a "comfortable" existence rested on the ability of subsistence farmers to raise cattle on common pasture.[178] This custom assumed increased importance in the New World where there was no Poor Law system to relieve the impoverished and unemployed. K.D.M. Snell's contention that agricultural labourers saw state poor relief as an essential aspect of their customary rights is not, however, supported by evidence from emigrant letters. Indeed, this may have been one of the rights they jettisoned in the New World where they were transformed from paupers into free farmers, from receivers of relief to payers of taxes. In any case, the Poor Law seems to have been a hated system for, as Stephen Goatcher informed his wife in 1833, one of the benefits of living in the New World was that "I do not have overseers call on me for poor taxes as you have." Of course, this implies that he was not himself a pauper in England but earned a small income but sufficient to be taxed. In fact, the lack of taxes and the much hated church tithes were often discussed in emigrant letters. Their absence contributed to an altered perception of both the state and the church which contrasted to England where clergymen were automatically implicated in the oppression of the lower classes because they were implicated in the politics of subordination both as overseers of the poor and as the collectors of church tithes.[179]

There were other aspects of the shared culture of paternalism which were reinstituted and reinforced in the New World, namely, the personalist labour relations which had long been lost in England. By the time the pauper emigrants from southern England were making their way to Upper Canada, their work experience had changed drastically within their lifetime. As K.D.M. Snell has argued in his *Annals of the Labouring Poor*, the enclosure movement had hastened a decline in live-in service which in turn led to the decline in apprenticeship. Yearly contracts and apprenticeships were crucial to earning a settlement in a particular parish upon which depended one's right to poor relief. These changes had implications for family relations because labouring youth who were no long protected under their master's roof were likewise no longer taught to read and write. At the same time, male youth had to be fed by their own families, who then were forced to send their daughters out to service to earn wages. Economic change had important social consequences; with the breakdown of live-in service, with its constant contact between classes, more oppositional views of society emerged, and where previously economic relations had been softened by the moral overtones of familial concepts, labour was now rendered a sterile commodity of the market.[180]

Live-in service was freighted with symbolic significance for the agricultural labourer and seen as crucial to the preservation of the mutuality between the classes. The constant refrain in male emigrant letters was that they could dine at the same table as their masters rather than being given a hunk of cheese and bread in their pockets to be unceremoniously eaten under a hedgerow.[181] The customary culture which meant most to Henry Smart of Ancaster was that "[W]e don't do as you do in your country; wherever we work we live" and at high wages of $8–10 per month.[182] Isaac Wilson, a former husbandman in England and a radical thinker who saw the world as divided between the corrupt oligarchy of "placemen in extravagant salaries" and "the people," attributed his belief that rights rather than power was the principle in Upper Canada to the fact that capitalism had become combined with traditional customs in such as way that labourers could earn $20 per month and at the same time be "very kindly used," as he himself had been by his employers John Young and his wife, who "treat me with the kindness of a mother."[183] How ironic that Isaac Wilson died alone in the midst of the Rebellions because his mother was prevented from attending his deathbed for fear of travelling!

Emigrant labourers certainly believed that the customary rights of the people were being re-established in the New World. However, we should not immediately conclude that the resurrection of social practices such as live-in service or the apprenticeship of youth represented a conservative defence against the inroads of the capitalist cash nexus. It is clear that the older practice of sending one's children out to be apprenticed in other families had taken on a renewed vitality in Upper Canada, since almost all labouring emigrants from the south of England referred to apprenticing their children. Thomas Adsett in Waterloo told his former clergyman how he had "adopted" out all his children, "till they can do for themselves ... so that I shall have no more trouble."[184] This putting-out system seems at first sight to be a continuation of practices observed by Snell as a strategy of poor families burdened with too many mouths to feed,[185] but in fact it was an old practice adapted to new circumstances. For while children were sent out at a young age, boarded, clothed, and educated by their masters just as they had been prior to 1830 in England, the fact that one no longer had to pay for apprencticeships[186] and that the wages were higher because of the scarcity of labour, meant that this practice was no longer associated with a strategy of makeshifts characteristic of the poor. Rather, these older customs had been refurbished to serve the class ambitions of newly established farmer-capitalists who needed cash to pay for their land and thus become "independent yeomen."[187] To this end, many aspects of customary practices were jettisoned by labouring emigrants. Most notably, emigrants no longer wanted annual contracts (in part because the absence of a formal Poor Law system in Canada removed the need for a settlement) and preferred to hire by the month so that they could negotiate higher wages for themselves: "As I only agree by the month," noted Edward Longley from Guelph, "I am at liberty to better my condition should an opportunity appear."[188]

As to the preference for being paid in kind – a customary aspect of the moral economy much touted by William Cobbett – this seems to have been an aspect of the New World economy which labouring patriarchs particularly abjured. Joseph Brown, for example, was displeased to have been given thirteen bushels of wheat "on acct of Charlotte's wages."[189] In the numerous letters penned by assisted emigrants, each and every one itemized at length the cash wages of their daughters, and on only rare occasions were traditional perquisites such as clothing shown in a positive light.[190] In some instances, labouring families clearly bargained for payment in kind when it fit their own strategies for self-betterment: for example, George and Mary Hills negotiated terms such that Ellen's "mistress is learning her to write."[191] Above all, labourers who aspired to become independent farmers demanded cash. As the Dundas labourer Simeon Titmouse declared, "money or cash is very bad to catch," for with it the newly settled farmer could not only pay for his land but he could shop for "eatables or wearing apparel."[192] Following the lead of William Cobbett, historians of customary social relations have made much of the benefits of payment in kind, an interpretation of capitalist wage-labour not borne out by the attitudes of the labouring poor themselves. Writing from his new home in Ancaster, William Philips, a shoemaker, preferred the modern cash nexus to outmoded traditions: "They all hire work by the month: so much for a month and their board. They have not much money; so that you are obliged to take part in money, and part in goods, here being a great deal of barter amongst them. If you work a month, and can get all your wages in cash, it is thought much of."[193] If customs of barter persisted, this was because the gentry, who were also cash poor, preferred to pay in kind so as not to be compelled to part with the cash they also needed to pay for food and clothing at the local store. Mary Jarvis complained to her husband that she had to spend her last £10 on her cook who was "urgent for her wages," while Mary O'Brien was so cash poor that she often borrowed money from her female servants.[194]

Artisan-farmers in Upper Canada fully embraced the market economy and sought any means to trade in money rather than through barter.[195] Robert Forrest decided to make potash for the simple reason that it was "always paid in cash." His brother, however, discovered a more efficacious solution to the cash shortage, namely the hiring out of both his daughters at the ages of twelve and fifteen.[196] It is not surprising then, that in Upper Canada children were seen as "riches to parents" rather than as "harbingers of poverty," as they had been in England.[197] More significantly, the revived practice of sending daughters out to service was hailed by promoters of emigration and farmer patriarchs alike as a way to resurrect the power of the male head of household "to enforce obedience" among familial subordinates.[198] In short, female domestic service revived patriarchy in the New World. It not only allowed fathers to control the labour of their children, but the wages earned by daughters upheld the ideal of independent manliness by helping make labourers into freeholders. In this instance, the contribution of domestic servants was no longer a working-class strategy but served the needs of upward class mobility in that process of remaking "the English pauper" into a "good solid landowner," to quote the radical writer William Cobbett.[199]

The domestic service of females was a liminal experience, for their labour lay at the fulcrum of the making of two class identities: that of the aspiring gentry and their own upwardly mobile labouring-farmer families. However much patriarchal families may have desired that the mutuality of classes be preserved through the bonds of paternalistic labour relations, the servants and their families did not uphold this frame of social relations in the New World. However much patricians' attitudes toward their female hired help may have been imbued with a paternalistic ethos which viewed servants as family members and saw their labour in terms of a broader moral economy of obligations and duties, the pattern of a servant's labour between her own and her master's household remained largely under her father's control. Mary O'Brien articulated the sense of loss of power of masters to control their female labour: "I cannot get my little handmaid because her father wants her to pick up stones and the elder sister who is promised to me permanently cannot come for some days, so I must turn cook &c again for a little while."[200] On another occasion, Mary O'Brien was without a servant because Susan had been "recalled by her father" but, luckily, the economy of another rural family was such that because they were so "badly provisioned" they had to send their daughter out to service.[201] Girls left their jobs not because they were bad servants, as masters wished to imagine, but because their parents needed their labour or because they sought to "better themselves," as the Irish servant Bridget Lacy wrote her servant friend back home, by marrying farmers.[202]

Apart from those servants like Bridget Lacy who emigrated with their masters' families, the vast majority of female emigrants travelled with their own families, and their labour contracts were dictated by their parents. Until they became of marital age their wages were sent home, and even their courtship and marriage was determined by the consent of their parents.[203] Far from losing their identity in the values of their masters, as historians have concluded,[204] the life strategies of Upper Canadian female domestics remained firmly wedded to those of their own families. Gentry employers, resorting to the traditional vocabulary of the patriarchal ideal to state that servants "lived" with them rather than "worked" for them, defined work in the traditional context of the moral economy of paternalistic relations. As much as aspiring patricians might hope that such hierarchical views of society might be reinforced in the New World, they were daily subverted by the agency of female servants who saw the market in purely rationalistic terms, as a means to negotiate better wages. Female household labourers and their families were instrumental in forging a more modern view of labour relations as purely monetary, bereft of any moral overtones of obligation and mutuality between the classes. In the New World social environment, upwardly mobile labouring emigrants who hoped to embrace new identities as proto-capitalist farmers reinterpreted their understanding of the customary rights of labour and rendered them compatible with an emergent free market economy.[205] It was not a commercialized gentry who were the first to jettison the moral economy of service; rather the labouring Britons who emigrated to Upper Canada were less conservative in their defence of tradition. In the New World their incipient working-class consciousness, borne out of their experience in Britain as pauperized agricultural labourers, became a remembrance of things past when, in an environment of high wages, abundant land, and scarcity of labour, it was possible to reimagine themselves as upwardly mobile farmers in a one-class society.

In the final analysis, female domestic servants preferred to earn cash wages to buy their own fine apparel rather than to depend on the paternalistic hand-me-downs of their employers. And it was this power of female plebeians to subvert the transplantation of patrician hegemony to the New World, as much as the Rebellions themselves, that shaped the defensive social outlook of the pseudo-gentry of Upper Canada. The behaviour, dress, and labour strategies of female household servants were deemed to be as subversive as the behaviour of the Radicals and as instrumental to the making and unmaking of the lower and upper classes in Upper Canada. Writing in the midst of the Upper Canadian Rebellion, the Irish parvenu Lieutenant Colonel Walter O'Hara ranted about how his female domestic had robbed him of money and clothing: "it seems that the facility with which this class of people obtains a livelihood in this new country causes a scarcity of domestic servants. Any person of common energy and industry can easily raise himself above the necessity of being a servant."[206] Here surely was a world turned upside down, where lower-class heads of family could become "independent" yeoman patriarchs,[207] while the authority of aspiring gentlemen-patriarchs like Col O'Hara was being daily eroded and their masculinity impugned by having been rendered increasingly "dependent"[208] on the will of independent female domestics.

NOTES

1 Toronto Public Library (TPL), Baldwin Room, W.D. Powell Papers, Mary Jarvis to Mamma, 13 Sept. 1827.

2 Catherine Parr Traill, *The Backwoods of Canada* (Toronto: McLelland and Stewart, 1929), 24.

3 Catherine Parr Traill, "Female Servants in the Bush," in Michael Peterman and Carl Ballstadt, eds, *Forest and Other Gleanings: The Fugitive Writings of Catherine Parr Traill* (Ottawa: University of Ottawa Press, 1994), 169.

4 Traill, "Female Servants in the Bush," 169.

5 For the importance of women in consolidating class relations, see Elizabeth Langland, *Nobody's Angels: Middle-Class Women and Domestic Ideology in Victorian Culture* (London and Ithaca: Cornell University Press, 1995), 11.

6 Catherine Parr Traill, *The Canadian Settler's Guide* (Toronto: McLean, 1854), 5.

7 On the need to combine capitalism and tradition, see E.J. Hobsbawm and George Rude, *Captain Swing* (London: Lawrence and Wishart, 1969), 52.

8 Traill, *The Canadian Settler's Guide*, 10–11. Interestingly this is one of the few occasions when Traill used the term class in its modern economic sense.

9 TPL, Baldwin Room, William Allan Papers, Peter McGill to William Allan, 21 Aug. 1832.

10 Catherine Parr Traill, *The Young Emigrants or Pictures of Life in Canada, Calculated to Amuse and Instruct the Minds of Youth* (London: Harvey and Darton, 1826), 131; Traill, *The Canadian Settler's Guide*, 10–11. Traill's sister Susanna Moodie was also consumed with vestementary confusion. On this theme, see Cory Carole Silverstein, "Clothed Encounters: The Power of Dress in Relations between the Anishnaabe and British Peoples in the Great Lakes Region, 1760–2000," (PhD thesis, McMaster University, 2000), 60, 631.

11 Richard Wrigley, *The Politics of Appearances: Representations of Dress in Revolutionary France* (New York and Oxford: Berg Press, 2002), 230. On the emergence of female dress codes, see Paola Pugliatti, *Beggary and Theatre in Early Modern England* (Aldershot: Ashgate, 2003), 71.

12 Daniel Roche, *The Culture of Clothing: Dress and Fashion in the Ancien Régime*, trans. Jean Birrell, (Cambridge: Cambridge University Press, 1989), 102. See also Amy Wyngaard, "Switching Codes: Class, Clothing and Cultural Change in the Works of Manivaux and Watteau," *Eighteenth-Century Studies* 33, no. 4 (Summer, 2000): 533–42. On the theme of democratic dress and impersonation in the United States, see James H. Merrell, "The Cast of Countenance: Reading Andrew Montour," in Ronald Hoffman et al, eds, *Through a Glass Darkly: Reflections on Personal Identity in Early America* (Chapel Hill and London: University of North Carolina Press, 1997), 19; Michael Zuckerman, "Tocqueville, Turner, and Turds: Four Stories of Manners in Early America," *Journal of American History* 85, no. 1 (June 1998): 13–42; Jonathan Prude,

"'To Look Upon the Lower Sort': Runaway Ads and the Appearance of Unfree Laborers in America, 1750–1800," *Journal of American History* 78, no. 1 (June 1991): 124–59; David Waldstreicher, "Reading the Runaways: Self-Fashioning, Print Culture, and Confidence in Slavery in the Eighteenth-Century Mid-Atlantic," *William and Mary Quarterly*, 3rd series, 56, no. 2 (April 1999): 248, 252–4.

13 John Barnes to father, brothers, and sisters, 1 Jan. 1837, in Wendy Cameron, Sheila Haines, Mary McDougall Maude, eds, *English Immigrant Voices: Labourers' Letters from Upper Canada in the 1830s* (Montreal & Kingston: McGill-Queen's University Press, 2000), 250; Carl Ballstadt, Elizabeth Hopkins, Michael Peterman, eds, *Susanna Moodie: Letters of a Lifetime* (Toronto: University of Toronto Press, 1985), Dunbar Moodie to Robert Baldwin, 6 Feb. 1845.

14 Archives of Ontario (AO), Jarvis-Powell Papers, Sam Jarvis to Mary, 21 Nov. 1823.

15 TPL, Powell Papers, Mary Powell to Grandmamma, 5 Nov. 1827.

16 AO, Mary O'Brien Journal, 3 Feb. 1832; TPL, Powell Papers, Mary Jarvis to Mama, 29 May 1826.

17 On this theme, see E.P. Thompson, *Customs in Common* (London: Merlin Press, 1991).

18 Traill, *The Canadian Settler's Guide*, 6.

19 Thompson, *Customs in Common*, 39. Thompson has argued that economic rationalism nibbled away at the bonds of paternalism, and views the labourers as defending traditional paternal norms. Several historians have critiqued Thompson for idealizing the "golden age" of paternalistic customs. See Elizabeth Fox-Genovese, "The Many Faces of Moral Economy: a Contribution to the Debate," *Past and Present* 58 (Feb. 1973): 161–8; Roger Wells, "The Moral Economy of the English Countryside," in Adrian Randall and Andrew Charlesworth, eds, *Moral Economy and Popular Protest: Crowds, Conflicts and Authority* (London: Macmillan, 2000), 222–3; T.H. Breen, "'An Empire of Goods': The Anglicization of Colonial America, 1690–1776," *Journal of British Studies* 25 (Oct. 1986): 469–99. Breen is critical of historians who merely characterized the yeoman as anti-capitalist. For a discussion of the market economy literature and its applicability to Canada, see Nancy Christie, "Patriarchy and the Hidden Realms of Women's Agency," Conference on Feminism and the Making of Canada: Historical Reflections, McGill University, 7–9 May 2004. For a criticism of Marx for separating the "cash nexus" from social relations, see Craig Muldrew, "'Hard Foods for Midas': Cash and its Social Value in Early Modern England," *Past and Present* 170 (Feb. 2000): 78–80. For a more critical view of labour proletarianization within paternalistic social relations, see Nicola Verdon, *Rural Women Workers in Nineteenth-Century England: Gender, Work and Wages* (Suffolk: Boydell Press, 2002), 81.

20 J.C.D. Clark, *English Society, 1688–1832* (Cambridge: Cambridge University Press, 1985). For a pungent but apt critique of Clark, see Joanna Innes, "Jonathan Clark, Social History and England's 'Ancien Régime'," *Past and Present* 115: 165–200.

21 Thompson has been much criticized for ignoring the role of the middle classes. For a revisionist perspective on this score, see Paul Langford, *A Polite and Commercial People: England, 1727–1783* (Oxford: Clarendon Press, 1989); Jonathan Barry and Christopher Brooks, eds, *The Middling Sort of People: Culture, Society and Politics in England, 1550–1800* (London: Macmillan, 1994). For analyses of gentry culture which also incorporate the notion of the middle, see James Raven, *Judging New Wealth: Popular Publishing and Responses to Commerce in England, 1750–1800* (Oxford: Clarendon Press, 1992); Elizabeth Langland, *Nobody's Angels*. On the importance of using private family records to study class, see Pamela Sharpe, ed., *Women's Work: The English Experience, 1650–1914* (London: Arnold, 1998), 6; Michael Mascuch, "Social mobility and middling self-identity: the ethos of British autobiographers, 1600–1750," *Social History* 20, no. 1 (Jan. 1995): 45–61. For critiques of Thompson in the United States, see Barton J. Bledstein and Robert D. Johnston, eds, *The Middling Sorts: Explanations in the History of the American Middle Class* (New York: Routledge, 2001); Stuart Blumin, *The Emergence of the Middle Class: Social Experience in the American City, 1760–1900* (Cambridge: Cambridge University Press, 1989); Martin J. Burke, *The Conundrum of Class: Public Discourse on the Social Order in America* (Chicago: University of Chicago Press, 1995). For an insightful book which upholds Thompson's model, see Amy Dru Stanley, *From Bondage to Contract: Wage Labor, Marriage and the Market in the Age of Slave Emancipation* (Cambridge: Cambridge University Press, 1998).

22 Jeremy Black, *Eighteenth-Century Britain, 1688–1783* (New York and London: Palgrave, 2001), 184–5; Frank O'Gorman, *The Long Eighteenth-Century: British Political and Social History, 1688–1832* (London and New York: Arnold, 1997), 329.

23 Peter Linebaugh, "'All the Atlantic Mountains Shook,'" in Geoff Eley and William Hunt, eds, *Reviving the English Revolution: Reflections and Elaborations of the Work of Christopher Hill* (London and New York: Verso, 1988), 236.

24 Raven, *Judging New Wealth*, 18; Dror Wahrman, *Imagining the Middle Class: The Political Representation of Class in Britain, c.1780–1840* (Cambridge: Cambridge University Press, 1995).

25 On Bell's moral critique of aristocratic power, see Nancy Christie, "'A Witness Against Vice': Religious Dissent, Political Radicalism, and the Moral Regulation of Aristocratic Culture in Upper Canada," in Jean-Marie Fecteau and Janice Harvey, eds, *Agency and Institutions in Social Regulation: Towards a Historical Understanding of Their Interaction* (Sainte-Foy: Les Presses de l'Université du Québec, 2005), 420–34. For other Canadian historians who subscribe to this view, see J.I. Little, "Gender and Gentility: Lucy Peel's

Journal, 1833–36," in J.I. Little, *The Other Quebec: Micro-Historical Essays on Nineteenth-Century Religion and Society* (Toronto: University of Toronto Press, 2006), 74. See also Bryan Palmer's contribution to this volume. On this point for England, see Wahrman, *Imagining the Middle Class*, 210.

26 Guelph University Archives (GUA), Anderson Family Papers, John Kyd to John and Peggy Anderson, 12 Aug. 1836.

27 For the concept of the "pseudo-gentry" in England, see H.R. French, "Social Status, Localism and the Middle Sort of People in England, 1620–1750," *Past and Present* 166 (Feb. 2000): 66–99, esp. 97. See also H.R. French, "'Ingenious and learned gentlemen – social perceptions and self-fashioning among parish elites in Essex, 1680–1740," *Social History* 25, no. 1 (Jan. 2000): 44–66. French argues that middling emulation occurred only within the top 20% of ratepayers. Benoît Grenier has recently argued that a large proportion of the seigneurs of New France and Lower Canada came from very modest social origins. See his "'Gentilshommes campagnards': La présence seigneuriale dans la vallée du Saint-Laurent (XVIIe-XIXe siècle)," *Revue d'histoire de l'Amérique française* 59, no. 4 (Spring 2006): 409–49. I have not undertaken a quantitative analysis of this kind, but the smaller farmers and shopkeepers among the middling of Upper Canada did not participate in this tyoe of social emulation.

28 TPL, Powell Papers, Eliza Powell to dear Aunt, 26 Nov. n.d. This is a comment made about a wealthy woman who in widowhood lost her genteel position and had to take in boarders to support her seven children.

29 TPL, Powell Papers, A. Powell to William, 5 Feb. 1778; 26 Apr. 1778.

30 TPL, Powell Papers, Sam Jarvis to William Powell, 24 Dec. 1828, 28 Oct. 1825.

31 Keith Wrightson, "Estates, degrees, and sorts: changing perceptions of society in Tudor and Stuart England," in Penelope Corfield, eds, *Language, History and Class* (Oxford: Basil Blackwell, 1991), 101–30.

32 TPL, Powell Papers, Sam Jarvis to William Powell, 19 Dec. 1827; Robert Kerr to William Powell, 7 Apr. 1823.

33 David Cannadine, *The Rise and Fall of Class in Britain* (New York: Columbia University Press, 1999), 37–40, 127.

34 Thomas Adsett to friends, 4 Mar. 1833, quoted in Cameron et al., *English Immigrant Voices*.

35 NAC, Robert Bell Papers, 49, "William Bell Reminiscences," 28 June 1820; TPL, Powell Papers, Anne to brother, 29 Dec. 1840; Cornelius and Elizabeth Voice, to brother and sister, 20 Sept. 1835, in Cameron et al., *English Immigrant Voices*, 186–7; AO, Sarah Welch Hill Papers, n.d. Aug. 1832; NAC, McGillvray Papers, brother to John, 6 Sept. 1828; NAC, Marcus Gunn Papers, Marcus Gunn to John Bright, July 1869 in which he considers the church and the army to be "a gigantic system of out door relief for the Aristocracy." Gunn was a printer, journalist, and local businessman, with clear Liberal

political leanings, and thus the persistence of the older bipolar model of
society is even more remarkable.

36 An income of £100 per annum would place the O'Briens firmly in the middling rank; £50 per annum represented the bottom of middling and £200
the top. See Paul Langford, *A Polite and Commercial People*, 65; Penelope Corfield, "Class by name and number in eighteenth-century Britain," in
Penelope Corfield, ed., *Language, History, and Class*, 107.

37 AO, Mary O'Brien Journal, 8 Oct. n.d.

38 AO, MS 207, John Grubb Letterbook, John Grubb to brother, n.d. 1854. The
vocabulary of the middle-class idiom was likewise imbricated with the language
of morality. "The middle condition is the most eligible to the man who would
improve himself in virtue." There was an overlap during the 1850s in the two-
and three-tier models of society. Thus while seeking to adumbrate a concept of
the middle, Grubb at the same time continued to conceive of the world in
terms of the productive versus the idle class, of the "gold fingered gentry"
against the "industrious" middling and lower classes. On the overlap of class
description, see Cannadine, *The Rise and Fall of Class in Britain*, 59–106.

39 AO, O'Brien Journal, Feb. 1837.

40 AO, O'Brien Journal, 19 May 1829, 26 Feb. 1829, 20 Dec. 1829, 15 Feb.
1829, 8 Oct. n.d., 30 Apr. 1829.

41 TPL, Powell Papers, Sam Jarvis to William Powell, 13 May 1828.

42 AO, O'Brien Journal, 2 Feb. 1829.

43 TPL, Baldwin Room, William Allan Papers, J. Gamble to Mrs Allan, 11 Apr.
1844.

44 AO, O'Brien Journal, 30 Apr. 1829. In her 9 May 1829 entry Mary O'Brien
told of the disturbing ability of one Thomas Toppin, a cabinetmaker who
constantly reinvented himself .

45 AO, O'Brien Journal, 5 Dec. 1835.

46 AO, O'Brien Journal, 2 Aug. 1833. Mary O'Brien had herself married an
Irishman whose social origins were lower middling, having reached the mere
rank of midshipman in the navy. That his military service afforded him access
to land in Upper Canada was his only means of upward social mobility.

47 Langford, *A Polite and Commercial People*, 67.

48 Dror Wahrman, *Imagining the Middle Class*, 18. Wahrman argues that there
was no triumphant middle class by the 1780s and supports E.P. Thompson in
concluding that the binary struggle of patrician vs the people continued to
be the dominant view until the 1830s (199–236).

49 AO, O'Brien Journal, n.d. 1832.

50 AO, O'Brien Journal, 5 Dec. 1835. Even as late as 1900 Elizabeth Cawthra
mixed the older and newer languages of class in her reference to the
"women of the working poorer class." See TPL, Baldwin Room, Cawthra Family Papers, Elizabeth Cawthra Diary, 2 Nov. 1900.

51 AO, O'Brien Journal, 10 Feb. 1832. See also TPL, William Allan Papers, Margaret Johnston to William Allan, 28 Sept. 1836, on her decision to emigrate because of the depreciation of land in England. In Kingston she was a milliner and then a governess.

52 AO, O'Brien Journal, 2 Feb. 1829, 3 Apr. 1832 with references to shoemakers and sailors who were relatives.

53 AO, James-Powell Papers, Mrs Powell to Aunt Inman, 17 June 1775.

54 TPL, Powell Papers, W.D. Powell to George Murray, 10 1830, in which he quotes a salary of £1,000 as Chief justice and his pension of £200. In England he spent £400 on household goods and clothing. See Powell to Mrs Powell, 18 June 1816.

55 TPL, Powell Papers, Anne to brother, 5 Aug. 1844.

56 TPL, Powell Papers, Anne to brother, 16 June 1844.

57 TPL, Powell Papers, W.D. Powell to George Murray, 6 Apr. 1823.

58 TPL, Powell Papers, Anne to brother, 12 Jan. 1842.

59 TPL, Powell Papers, Anne to brother, 1 Oct. 1840.

60 TPL, Powell Papers, George Murray to Anne, 26 Nov. 1835.

61 TPL, Powell Papers, Anne to brother, 27 Oct. 1840.

62 TPL, Powell Papers, Anne to brother, 3 June 1840; Anne to brother, 28 Nov. 1839. Charlotte married Sam Ridout, the illegitimate son of the surveyor general who then became clerk to the Registry of the township earning £300 per annum. Sam Ridout's mother was said to be the illegitimate daughter of Mr Small, the clerk of the executive council. It was also said that Ridout earned £800 per annum. Historians should beware of taking at face value incomes itemized in familial correspondence as this was as much a part of self-promotion as was the systematic gossiping about one's tawdry origins.

63 TPL, Powell Papers, 3 June 1840, 28 May 1844.

64 TPL, William Allen Papers, W.A. Harvey to Isabella Allan, 21 Sept. 1846.

65 TPL, Powell Papers, Mary Powell to grandpapa, 5 Mar. 1828.

66 TPL, Powell Papers, Anne to brother, 20 Dec. 1839.

67 TPL, Powell Papers, Anne to brother, 24 Aug. 1840.

68 TPL, Powell Papers, Anne to brother, 15 Feb. 1841.

69 TPL, Powell Papers, Anne to brother, 5 Oct. 1842.

70 TPL, Powell Papers, Anne to brother, 28 Nov. 1839, 16 Mar. 1840.

71 TPL, F.F. Passmore Papers, Passmore to mother, 1 Jan. 1847. Passmore was an apprentice surveyor of middling status who hoped to rise sufficiently to attend theatres and ballrooms with the local elite and was very sensitive to how he dressed in public and who he associated with. Having his books about him was one of the ways he displayed his sense of "respectable" manhood while forced to board with working lads.

72 Raven, *Judging New Wealth*, 110.

73 TPL, Powell Papers, Anne to brother, 28 May 1844.

74 TPL, Powell Papers, Jane Warren to cousin, 14 Jan. 1807: "The Plowden family are truly respectable in every way, in Circumstances, in the estimation of the world, and in their Connections."

75 NAC, McGillvray Papers, James Harkness, St Andrew's Church, Quebec City, 3 Dec. 1822 used this language to describe his congregation and did not therefore have to specifically denote their wealth as culture alone was the code for patrician status.

76 TPL, Powell Papers, Anne to brother, 1 Oct. 1840, 12 Jan. 1842.

77 TPL, Powell Papers, Anne to brother, 19 Jan. 1843.

78 TPL, Powell Papers, Anne to brother, 29 July 1820.

79 TPL, Powell Papers, Mary Powell to grandmamma, 2 July 1828.

80 TPL, Powell Papers, Anne to brother, 27 Feb. 1840.

81 AO, Jarvis-Powell Papers, Sam Jarvis to Mary Powell, 30 Aug. 1818.

82 AO, Ardagh Family Papers, Henry Gowan to Samuel Whitney, 28 Feb. 1848.

83 TPL, Powell Papers, Anne to brother, n.d. See also, NAC, James Gowan Papers, Gowan to dear sir, 11 July 1846, recommending William Watson as a magistrate because he was a "man of Excellent character and good family."

84 See for example, Paul Langford, *A Polite and Commercial People*; Raven, *Judging New Wealth*. On the association of success with industry and creditworthiness as emblematic of middle-class culture, see Jonathan Barry and Christopher Brooks, "Introduction," in Jonathan Barry and Christopher Brooks, eds, *The Middling Sort of People*, 15. For the gentrification of middle-class culture, see Kathleen Wilson, "Citizenship, Empire and Modernity in the English Provinces, c. 1720–90," in C. Hall, ed., *Cultures of Empire: Colonizers in the Empire in the Nineteenth and Twentieth Centuries: A Reader* (New York: Routledge, 2000), 164; Pauline Maier, "The Transforming Impact of Independence Reaffirmed: 1776 and the Definition of American Social Structure," in James A. Henretta, Michael Kamen, and Stanley N. Katz, eds, *The Transformation of Early American History: Society, Authority, and Ideology* (New York: Alfred A. Knopf, 1991), 208; Amanda Vickery, *The Gentleman's Daughter: Women's Lives in Georgian England* (New Haven and London: Yale University Press, 1998), 13–38.

85 GUA, Mickle Family Papers, Jean to brothers and sisters, n.d. 1765. It is noteworthy that Jean was a milliner when writing this letter.

86 John Tosh, "The Old Adam and the New Man: Emerging Themes in the History of English Masculinities, 1750–1850," in Tim Hitchcock and Michelle Cohen, eds, *English Masculinities, 1660–1800* (New York and London: Longman, 1999), 220–2. Tosh has situated the transition from genteel to bourgeois culture in the 1840s, which reaffirms Wahrman's timeline and which dissents from much of the literature which sites the 1780s as the decisive decade of cultural change. Tosh draws a link between gentility and reputation and between bourgeois masculinity and work.

87 AO, Mary O'Brien Journal, 17 Feb. 1829. He did become a member of her book club despite his tawdry, commercial associations.

88 AO, Mary O'Brien Journal, 26 Jan. 1830. Posing as someone you were not often had dire consequences as in the case of an Englishman who set up shop in Hamilton and, having guaranteed several large loans by fashioning himself a successful man of business, absconded with the funds to Philadelphia, thus bankrupting Dr Moore, the local apothecary. TPL, Powell Papers, Sam Jarvis to W.D. Powell, 1 Apr. 1829. Inability to pay debts had a domino effect. On this theme, see Nancy Christie, "A 'Painful Dependence': Female Begging Letters and the Familial Economy of Obligation," in Nancy Christie and Michael Gauvreau, eds, *Mapping the Margins: The Family and Social Discipline in Canada, 1700–1975* (Montreal & Kingston: McGill-Queen's University Press, 2004), 69–102.

89 AO, Mary O'Brien Journal.

90 TPL, Powell Papers, Mary Jarvis to Eliza, 26 Nov. 1826, W.D. Powell to George Murray, 11 Mar. 1822.

91 AO, Mary O'Brien Journal, 14 Sept. 1834.

92 TPL, Powell Papers, Anna to Uncle George Murray, 5 Dec. 1818.

93 For the changing place of duelling in masculine culture, see Robert B. Shoemaker, "Public Spaces, Private Disputes?: Fights and Insults on London's Streets, 1660–1800," in Tim Hitchcock and Heather Shore, eds, *The Streets of London from the Great Fire to the Great Strike* (London & Sydney: Rivers Oram, 2003), 66. For Upper Canada, see Cecilia Morgan's article.

94 TPL, Powell Papers, file "Jarvis-Ridout Duel," n.d.

95 *Upper Canada Gazette*, 17 June 1824. On the importance of the body to the making of class see Ann Stoler, "Cultivating Bourgeois Bodies and Racial Selves," in Hall, ed., *Cultures of Empire*, 436.

96 The Grant Powells were thought by the rest of the family to be somewhat unrespectable and so Charlotte Powell was criticized for not appearing to be naturally genteel. TPL, Powell Papers, Eliza Powell to Ann Powell, n.d. On the emergence of new categories of gentility in this period in England, see Lawrence E. Klein, "The Polite Town: Shifting Possibilities of Urbanness, 1660–1715," in Tim Hitchcock and Heather Shore, eds, *The Streets of London*, 30, 36; Paul Langford, "The Use of Eighteenth-Century Politeness," *Transactions of the Royal Historical Society*, 12 (2002): 311–31; Anna Bryson, *From Courtesy to Civility: Changing Codes of Conduct in Early Modern England* (Oxford: Clarenden Press, 1998), 279, 287; C. Dallett Hemphill, *Bowing to Necessities: A History of Manners in America, 1620–1860* (New York and Oxford: Oxford University Press, 1999).

97 TPL, Powell Papers, Mary Jarvis to Mamma, 13 Sept. 1827, W.D. Powell to George Murray, 1 Nov. 1817, Anne Powell to George Murray, 5 Dec. 1818, Anne to brother, 8 Mar. 1837. It is apparent that conspicuous consumption did not become a barometer of gentility since many aspiring gentry had only the most basic domestic necessities. Thus Mary O'Brien's mother-in-law had only a "makeshift table, two chairs, a whisky and beer barrel, a few boks and a

drawing of Edward's" in her house. See AO, Mary O'Brien Journal, 20 May n.d. On the excesses of fashion and class attributes in England, see Vickery, *The Gentleman's Daughter*, 172–4.

98 Women commented more frequently than did men on the theme of poverty. See for example, AO, Mary O'Brien Journal, 18 Feb. 1829, 31 Dec. 1829; TPL, Powell Papers, Anne to brother, 19 May 1842; AO, Jarvis-Powell Papers, 21 Oct. 1820. Mary O'Brien dispensed charity personally to beggars at her door and recorded that Lady Colborne had organized a bazaar for collecting clothing for impoverished women. In addition, Lady Sarrah Maitland had organized a charity to relieve poor women in childbirth.

99 See Carole Shammas, *A History of Household Government in America* (Charlottesville and London: University of Virginia Press, 2002); Vickery, *The Gentleman's Daughter*. Vickery stresses the relationship between mistress and servant, 127–60; Christine Daniels, "'Liberty to Complaine': Servant Petitions in Maryland, 1652–1797," in Christopher Tomlins and Bruce H. Mann, eds, *The Many Legalities of Early America* (Chapel Hill and London: University of North Carolina Press, 2001), 224.

100 TPL, Powell Papers, George Murray to Anne Powell, n.d. On servant labour in Upper Canada, see Elizabeth Jane Errington, *Wives and Mothers, School Mistresses and Scullery Maids: Working Women in Upper Canada, 1790–1840* (Montreal & Kingston: McGill-Queen's University Press, 1995), 107–58.

101 NAC, Gowan Papers, James Gowan to Mr Shephard French, n.d. 1844. See also Jeremy Webber, "Labour and the Law," in Paul Craven, ed., *Labouring Lives: Work and Workers in Nineteenth-Century Ontario* (Toronto: University of Toronto Press, 1995), 136–9. For a more nuanced argument regarding the limitations as well as the ability to enforce the common law provisions, see Paul Craven, "Canada, 1670–1935: Symbolic and Instrumental Enforcement in Loyalist North America," in Douglas Hay and Paul Craven, eds, *Masters, Servants, and Magistrates in Britain and the Empire, 1562–1955* (Chapel Hill: University of North Carolina Press, 2004), 117–52.

102 Judy Collingwood, "Irish Workhouse Children in Australia," in John O'Brien and Dauric Travers, eds, *The Irish Experience in Australia* (Dublin: Poulbeg Press Ltd., 1991).

103 On indentured service in the United States, see most notably Sharon V. Salinger, *'To Serve Well and Faithfully': Labor and Indentured Servants in Pennsylvania, 1682–1899* (Cambridge: Cambridge University Press, 1987); David W. Galenson, *White Servitude in America: An Economic Analysis* (Cambridge: Cambridge University Press, 1981); Sharon V. Salinger, "Colonial Labor in Transition: The Decline of Indentured Servitude in Late Eighteenth-Century Philadelphia," *Labor History* 22, no. 2 (Spring, 1981); Sharon V. Salinger, "'Send No More Women': Female Servants in Eighteenth-Century Philadelphia," *Pennsylvania Magazine of History and Biography* 107 (Apr. 1983); Aaron S. Fogelman, "From Slaves, Convicts, and

Servants to Free Passengers: The Transformation in Immigration in the Era
of the American Revolution," *Journal of American History* 85, no. 1 (June
1998): 43–76. Fogelman attributes the end of indentured servitude to the
changing form of immigration and Salinger argues that it ended with labour
scarcity.

104 Jonathan Barry and Christopher Brooks, "Introduction," in Barry and
Brooks, *The Middling Sort of People,* 16. On the conventional view of life-cycle
service as a period of youthful independence, see I.K. Ben-Amos, *Adolescence
and Youth in Early Modern England* (New Haven: Yale University Press, 1994)
and P. Griffiths, *Youth and Authority: Formative Experiences in England,
1560–1640* (Oxford: Oxford University Press, 1996).

105 On the home as a primary site for class formation and for affirming hierarchical social relations, see Julie Hardwick, *The Practice of Patriarchy: Gender and
the Politics of Household Authority in Early Modern France* (University Park, PA:
University of Pennsylvania State Press, 1998); Sara C. Maza, *Servants and Masters in Eighteenth-Century France: The Uses of Loyalty* (Princeton: Princeton University Press, 1983); Cissie Fairchilds, *Domestic Enemies: Servants and Their
Masters in Old Regime France* (Baltimore and London: Johns Hopkins University Press, 1984); Theresa M. McBride, *The Domestic Revolution: The Modernization of Household Service, 1820–1920* (London: Croom Helm, 1976); Pamela
Horn, *Rise and Fall of the Victorian Servant* (New York: St. Martin's Press,
1975).

106 Magda Fahrni, "'Ruffled' Mistresses and 'Discontented' Maids: Respectability
and the Case of Domestic Service, 1880–1914," *Labour/Le Travail* 39 (Spring
1997); Lorna R. McLean and Marilyn Barber, "In Search of Comfort and
Independence: Irish Immigrant Domestic Servants Encounter the Courts,
Jails, and Asylums in Nineteenth-Century Ontario," in Marlene Epp, Franca
Iacovetta, Frances Swyripa, eds, *Sisters or Strangers?: Immigrant, Ethnic and
Racialized Women in Canadian History* (Toronto: University of Toronto Press,
2004), 133–60. Servants were sexually vulnerable and appear frequently in
church discipline records, although sexual relations were usually with men
from their own class. See Nancy Christie, "Carnal Connection and other Mis-
demeanours: Continuity and Change in Presbyterian Church Records,
1830–1890," in Michael Gauvreau and Ollivier Hubert, eds, *Churches and
Social Practice* (forthcoming McGill-Queen's University Press). On this theme
for England, see John R. Gillis, "Servants, Sexual Relations and the Risks of
Illegitimacy in London, 1801–1900," in Judith L. Newton, Mary P. Ryan, and
Judith R. Walkowitz, eds, *Sex and Class in Women's History* (London and
Boston: Routledge and Kegan Paul, 1983), 118–19, 139. Gillis argues that
working-class female servants had imbibed the mores of their middle-class
employers regarding marriage. On the propensity of middle-class women to
become servants for short periods prior to marriage, see Carolyn R. Maibor,
"Upstairs, Downstairs, and In-Between: Louisa May Alcott on Domestic

Service," *The New England Quarterly* 79, no. 1 (2006): 65–91; Faye Dudden, *Serving Women: Household Service in Nineteenth-Century America* (Middletown, CT: Wesleyan University Press, 1983). Dudden points out that, prior to 1850, many employers hired neighbours' daughters who were from a similar class as themselves.

107 AO, Mary O'Brien Journal, 3 Feb. 1834.

108 TPL, Powell Papers, W.D. Powell to Mrs Powell, n.d., Kingston.

109 AO, O'Brien Journal, 25 Dec. 1830.

110 AO, Jarvis-Powell Papers, Sam to Mary, 30 Dec. 1841.

111 TPL, Powell Papers, 11 July 1816, Mary Powell to Aunt.

112 See for example, AO, Mary O'Brien Journal, 4 Dec. 1828; TPL, Powell Papers, Mary Jarvis to Mamma, 22 May 1826. For a historian who emphasizes the contribution of servants to productive labour and dismisses class issues, see Edward Higgs, "Domestic Service and Household Production," in Angela John, ed., *Unequal Opportunities: Women's Employment in England, 1800–1918* (Oxford: Basil Blackwell, 1986), 136–7.

113 TPL, Mary Jarvis to Mamma, 30 July 1827.

114 AO, Mary O'Brien Journal, n.d.

115 David Eltis, "Free and Coerced Migrations from the Old World to the New," in David Eltis, ed., *Coerced and Free Migration: Global Perspectives* (Stanford, CA: Stanford University Press, 2002), 32–74.

116 AO, Mary O'Brien Journal, 17 Oct. 1829.

117 This phase is borrowed from Tim Meldrum. See his excellent monograph, *Domestic Service and Gender, 1660–1750: Life and Work in a London Household* (London: Longman, 2000), 196.

118 AO, Mary O'Brien Journal, 9 Nov. 1830.

119 On the discomfort of employing male youth in the home, see AO, Mary O'Brien Journal, 4 Dec. 1828, 27 May 1830, 4 June 1830, 18 Aug. 1829, 21 Aug. 1831; TPL, Powell Papers, Jane Powell to William, 20 May 1793. In the case of male slaves the question of manly independence was not an issue.

120 NAC, Stephen Radcliffe Papers, Thomas Radcliffe to father, n .d. Jan. 1833. See also AO, Daniel Fowler Diary, MS 199, n.d. who observed how a "gentlemanly" clergyman had no servants.

121 AO, Mary O'Brien Journal, 6 May 1829.

122 On this point, see Jonathan Barry, "Bourgeois Collective?: Urban Association and the Middling Sort," in Barry and Brooks, *Middling Sort of People*, 157.

123 AO, Ardagh Family Papers, Anna Ardagh Diary, 2 Oct. 1848, 23 May 1849.

124 TPL, Powell Papers, Mary to Eliza, 26 Nov. 1826; W.D. Powell to Grant Powell, 28 July 1828.

125 AO, Mary O'Brien Journal, 8 May 1830.

126 AO, Mary O'Brien Journal, 10 July 1830.

127 Peterman and Ballstadt, *Forest and Other Gleanings*, Susanna Moodie to Richard Bentley, 30 Dec. 1853. Susanna Moodie preferred to work herself as a writer than send her daughter out to service, which would have all too publicly displayed her downward mobility.

128 AO, Mary O'Brien Journal, 12 Aug. 1830. For a similar analysis of this event, see Errington, *Wives and Mothers*.

129 AO, Mary O'Brien Journal, 24 Apr. 1831, 17 Jan. 1831, 29 Jan. 1831.

130 NAC, Robert Bell Papers, William Bell Reminiscences, n.d. Aug. 1824, 18 Sept. 1840.

131 NAC, Marcus Gunn Papers, Alexander to Marcus, 8 Jan. 1842.

132 TPL, Baldwin Room, Biggar Family Correspondence, Isabella to John, 23 Feb. 1848, 31 Jan. 1849. Middling families were much more likely to hire widows from local workhouses because they were cheaper. On this see also AO, Sarah Hill Diary. Her middling family in Egbaston hired most of their girls from the workhouse.

133 GUA, Dougall Family Papers, Andrew Dougall to brother, 3 Feb. 1860, Margaret Fowlie to brother, 21 Aug. 1865. On the strategies of the lower middle, artisanal, and small farmers to hire household labour for reasons other than the upholding of class boundaries, see Geoffrey Crossick and Heinz-Gerhard Haupt, *The Petite Bourgeoisie in Europe, 1780–1914: Enterprise, Family and Independence* (London and New York: Routledge, 1995), 104; David Fitzpatrick, "The Modernization of the Irish Female," in Patrick O'Flanagan et al., eds, *Rural Ireland, 1600–1900: Modernisation and Change* (Cork: Cork University Press, 1987), 166. Fitzpatrick argued that in Ireland servants replaced child labour in farm families. By contrast, gentry families in the American south hired white servants in addition to black slaves for the purposes of social status. On this point, see Allen Kulikoff, *Tobacco and Slaves: The Development of Southern Culture in the Chesapeake, 1680–1800* (Chapel Hill and London: University of North Carolina Press, 1986), 276.

134 NAC, Robert Bell Papers, William Bell Reminiscences, 27 Mar. 1824.

135 On evangelical notions of marriage, see Nancy Christie, "On the Threshold of manhood: Working-Class Religion and Domesticity in Victorian Britain and Canada," *Histoire Sociale/Social History* 36, no. 71 (2003): 145–74.

136 Leonore Davidoff, "Mastered for Life: Servant and Wife in Victorian and Edwardian England," in Pat Thame and Anthony Sutcliffe, eds, *Essays in Social History* (Oxford: Clarendon Press, 1986), 2:132.

137 Anna Ardagh also believed that evangelicalism created a more equal relationship between the sexes; however, prior to 1850 such evangelical views were often still encompassed within patrician values. On the role religion played in early nineteenth-century feminism, see Nancy Christie, "Patriarchy and the Hidden Realms of Women's Agency."

138 Cissie Fairchilds, *Domestic Enemies*, 153. This accords with the timeline first established by Harriet Martineau. See Michael R. Hill and Susan

Hoecker-Drysdale, eds, *Harriet Martineau: Theoretical and Methodological Perspectives* (New York and London: Routledge, 2001), 42, 101.

139 Sara C. Maza, *Servants and Masters in Eighteenth-Century France*, 16, 198; Tim Meldrum, *Domestic Service and Gender*, 196.

140 AO, Mary O'Brien Journal, 19 Feb. 1830, 28 Oct. 1830, 24 May 1829, 12 May 1830.

141 AO, Mary O'Brien Journal, 7 July 1831, 3 Apr. 1832. In the ideal patriarchal family servants were cared for when ill. See for example, AO, Jarvis-Powell Papers, Anne Powell to Eliza, 20 Jan. 1821.

142 NAC, Fortune Family Papers, father to son and daughters, 25 Aug. 1817. The father wrote this while in prison for debt.

143 TPL, Powell Papers, Mary Jarvis to Mamma, 4 June 1824.

144 AO, Sarah Welch Hill Diary, 11 May 1844, 18 May 1844, 22 July 1844. The much-vaunted intimate relations between master and servant could also make servants vulnerable to sexual improprieties. See AO, Jarvis-Powell Papers, Mr O'Hara to Mr Jarvis, 4 June 1860, on his son's dalliance with his servant. By this date, interestingly, the servant was merely paid cash in order to disappear, thus marking the decline of the patriarchal ideal.

145 TPL, Cawthra Papers, Elizabeth Cawthra Diary, 1 Feb. 1896.

146 TPL, Cawthra Papers, 20 Nov. 1897; AO, Sarah Hill Diary, n.d., 1839; TPL, Powell Papers, Bishop Jacob Mountain to Powell, 8 Jan. 1822, regarding the placing of a servant under their "benevolent protection."

147 AO, Ardagh Papers, K. Ardagh to Ned, 20 July 1834. There were similar charities for aged and distressed housekeepers in England as early as the 1830s. See Sarah Hill Diary, 28 Sept. 1838.

148 AO, Mary O'Brien Journal, 1 Nov. 1828, 8 Oct. n.d., 15 June 1829, 26 Jan. 1829. So concerned was O'Brien with changing the names of her servants that she even stipulated this in formal labour agreements. See entry for 16 Sept. 1831. It was incumbent that servants behave in a way not to undermine the reputation of the family they worked for. See TPL, Powell Papers, Anne to brother, 11 July 1842.

149 AO, Mary O'Brien Journal, 17 Jan. 1829.

150 TPL, Powell Papers, Mary to Mamma, 13 Sept. 1827.

151 TPL, Powell Papers, Genealogical File, 29 Oct. 1814.

152 NAC, John Forrest Papers, apprenticeship agreement, 16 Apr. 1799.

153 TPL, Baldwin Room, Indenture of Catherine Aiken.

154 Thompson, *Customs in Common*, 39.

155 TPL, Willam Allan Papers, D. Botsford to Allan, 7 Mar. 1837, letter of recommendation for a servant; TPL, Powell Papers, Anne to Brother, 7 May 1841; AO, Mary O'Brien Journal, 30 Aug. 1832.

156 AO, Jarvis-Powell Papers, George Murray Jarvis to Mary Jarvis, 18 May 1863.

157 AO, Sarah Hill Diary, 16 June 1844.

158 TPL, William Allan Papers, C. Gamble to William Allan, 3 Nov. 1838.

159 NAC, John Hallas Papers, Hallas to dear friend, June 1842. Hallas was a
      bricklayer.
160 Thompson, *Customs in Common*; Hobsbawm and Rude, *Captain Swing*.
161 This is most evident in the work of the Hammonds. See J.L. Hammond and
      Barbara Hammond, *The Village Labourer* (London and New York: Longman,
      1978), 152–3, 182.
162 Wendy Cameron et al., *English Immigrant Voices*.
163 TPL, William Allan Papers, Sir David Smith to William Allan, 24 June 1837.
164 Traill, *The Young Emigrants*, 65.
165 NAC, John Forrest Papers, William Davies to sons and daughters, 25 Nov.
      1821. T.M. Devine has concluded that most Scottish emigrants were not
      unemployed when they departed but fled because of the fear of future down-
      ward mobility. See T.M. Devine, "Introduction," in T.M. Devine, ed., *Scottish
      Emigration and Scottish Society* (Edinburgh: John Donald Publishers, 1992), 23.
166 William Taylor Upton to George Warren, 16 Sept. 1832, quoted in Cameron
      et al., *English Immigrant Voices*, 52. The veracity of these published emigrant
      letters has been challenged. See Terry McDonald, "Come to Canada While
      You Have a Choice: A Cautionary Tale of English Emigrant Letters in Upper
      Canada," *Ontario History* 91, no. 2 (Autumn 1999): 111–16. The optimistic
      views expressed in the published letters of pauper emigrants accords with
      those expressed in private family letters of other working-class emigrants.
167 NAC, Marcus Gunn Papers, Alexander Sinclair to Gunn, n.d.
168 George Coleman to Mr J. Marten, 17 Dec. 1835, quoted in Cameron et al.,
      English Immigrant Voices, 189–90.
169 George Carver to father and mother, 18 Aug. 1833, 30 June 1834, quoted in
      Cameron et al., *English Immigrant Voices*, 148–9, 165.
170 Ann and Charles Cosens, to father, mother, and sister, 31 Mar. 1833, quoted
      in Cameron et al., *English Immigrant Voices*, 114.
171 Henry and Charlotte Tribe, to Noah Hill, 12 Feb. 1833, quoted in Cameron
      et al., *English Immigrant Voices*, 102.
172 AO, Mary O'Brien Journal, Sept. 1832.
173 Alexander Hilton to Uncle Henry, 16 Oct. 1836, quoted in Cameron et al.,
      English Immigrant Voices, 234.
174 George Hills, labourer, Ancaster, 5 Aug. 1832, quoted in Cameron, et al.,
      English Immigrant Voices, 34.
175 Richard Neal to friends and relatives, 20 July 1832, quoted in Cameron et al.,
      English Immigrant Voices, .
176 E.P. Thompson, *Whigs and Hunters: The Origins of the Black Act* (Toronto: Ran-
      dom House, 1975).
177 William Spencer, Bronte to father and mother, 10 Nov. 1836, quoted in
      Cameron et. al., *English Immigrant Voices*, 240. See also, James and William
      Goldring, York to Thomas Goldring, 9 Apr. 1833, quoted in Ibid., p. 115.
178 AO, John Wilson Papers, Isaac Wilson to brother Jonathon, 24 May 1812.

179 On the altered social relations between clergy and their congregations, see Michael Gauvreau, "The Dividends of Empire," in this volume.

180 This is a very brief encapsulation of K.D.M. Snell, *Annals of the Labouring Poor: Social Change and Agrarian England, 1660–1900* (Cambridge: Cambridge University Press, 1985), 100, 110–15, 215, 231–53, 321–8. On live-in service, see A. Kussmaul, *Servants in Husbandry in Early Modern England* (Cambridge: Cambridge University Press, 1981); Christopher Brooks, "Apprenticeship, Social Mobility, and the Middling Sort, 1550–1800," in Barry and Brooks, *The Middling Sort of People*, 69.

181 Thomas Adsett, Galt to father, 25 June 1833; Adsett to Rev. Ridsdale, 21 Dec. 1832, quoted in Cameron et al., *English Immigrant Voices*, 87, 123.

182 Henry Smart to James Napper, 1 March 1833, quoted in Cameron et al., *English Immigrant Voices*, 103.

183 AO, John Wilson Papers, Isaac Wilson to brother Jonathon, 19 Nov. 1811, 5 Mar. 1812, 2 Aug. 1828, 26 July 1830.

184 Thomas Adsett to Rev. Ridsdale, quoted in Cameron et al., *English Immigrant Voices*, 87.

185 See also Bridget Hill, *Women, Work and Sexual Politics in Eighteenth-Century England* (Oxford: Basil Blackwell, 1989), 142; Wally Seccombe, *Weathering the Storm: Working-Class Families from the Industrial Revolution to the Fertility Decline* (London and New York: Verso, 1993); Bettina Bradbury, *Working Families: Age, Gender and Daily Survival in Industrializing Montreal* (Toronto: McLelland and Stewart, 1993).

186 Edward and Hannah Bristow to brother, 20 July 1833, quoted in Cameron et al., *English Immigrant Voices*, 138–40.

187 William Cattermole, *Emigration: The Advantages of Emigration to* Canada (London: Simpkin and Marshall, 1831), 15 Aug., unsigned letter from Guelph; John and Ruth Waldon, St Catherines to Friends, 9 Jan. 1836, quoted in Cameron et al., *English Immigrant Voices*, 195.

188 Edward Longley to William Mitchell, 28 Sept. 1835, quoted in Cameron et. al., *English Immigrant Voices*, 200.

189 NAC, Joseph Brown Papers, 13 Apr. 1836.

190 For example, William and Sarah Jackman, Brantford, to son, 29 Oct. 1836, on how their daughter got some "very good presents from her mistress," quoted in Cameron et al., *English Immigrant Voices*, 236.

191 George and Mary Hills, West Flamborough, to John Drewitt, 18 Sept. 1836, quoted in Cameron et al., *English Immigrant Voices*, 228.

192 Simeon Titmouse, Dundas, to Jackson, 11 Sept. 1832, quoted in Cameron et al., *English Immigrant Voices*, 47–8.

193 William Philips, Ancaster, to Mrs Newall, 5 Aug. 1832, quoted in Cameron et al., *English Immigrant Voices*, 29.

194 AO, Jarvis-Powell Papers, Mary to Sam, 10 Apr., 1843; AO, Mary O'Brien Journal, 19 Aug. 1833.

195 For a detailed discussion of the historiography regarding the emergence of the market economy, see Nancy Christie, "Patriarchy and the Hidden Realms of Women's Agency."

196 NAC, John Forrest Papers, Robert Forrest to mother and father, 23 May 1824; William Forrest to John Forrest, 7 Sept. 1842. On the scarcity of money, see AO, John Wilson Papers, Isaac Wilson to Jonathon, 24 June 1821.

197 NAC, William Gibson Papers, William to brother and sisters in Scotland, 13 Mar. 1831.

198 Cattermole, *Emigration*, 15 Aug. unsigned letter from Guelph.

199 William Cobbett, *The Emigrant's Guide* (London: 1829), 44. The standard interpretation is that living out in other families allowed servants to escape family constraints. See for example, Michael Mitteraurer, "Servants and Youth," *Continuity and Change* 1 (1990): 11–38; John R. Gillis, *For Better, For Worse: British Marriages, 1600 to the Present* (Oxford: Oxford University Press, 1985), 173; Kerby A. Miller, with David N. Doyle and Patricia Kelleher, "For love and liberty: Irish women, migration and domesticity in Ireland and America, 1815–1920," in Patrick O'Sullivan, ed., *Irish Women and Irish Migration* (London and New York: Leicester University Press, 1995), 55. For an alternate interpretation, see Donald Akenson, *The Irish Diaspora* (Toronto: P. Meany Co. 1993), 117. For an excellent discussion of the familial wage model, see Yukari Takai, "Shared Earnings, Unequal Responsibilities: Single French-Canadian Wage-Earning Women in Lowell, Massachusetts, 1900–1920," *Labour/Le Travail* 47 (Spring 2001): 115–32.

200 AO, Mary O'Brien Journal, 9 Nov. 1830.

201 AO, Mary O'Brien Journal, 29 Apr. 1836.

202 NAC, Radcliffe Papers, Bridget Lacy to Mary Thompson, Dublin, Dec. 1832.

203 AO, John Wilson Papers, Isaac Wilson to Jonathon, 13 Dec. 1834, on how his brother-in-law protested his daughter's wages in court; AO, Mary O'Brien Journal, 17 Oct. 1833, 1 Nov. 1830, 29 Apr. 1836, on how mothers determined their daughters' contracts; AO, Sarah Hill Diary, 31 May 1843 on mothers demanding adequate wages for their daughters.

204 Maza, *Servants and Masters in Eighteenth-Century France*, 176.

205 On the ideal of combining tradition and capitalism, see Hobsbawm and Rude, *Captain Swing*, 52.

206 NAC, Walter O'Hara Journal, 12 Jan. 1837, 28 Nov. 1837.

207 GUA, Dougall Family Papers, Margaret Dougall to brother, n.d.: "Here a man can make himself independent of the world." AO, Jarvis-Powell Papers, Anne Powell to Aunt Inman, 16 Sept. 1824, on how the independence of her female servants was leading to their increased "dependence" on the lower classes. On the different class uses of the concept of independence, see

Patrick Joyce, *Democratic Subjects: The Self and the Social in Nineteenth-Century England* (Cambridge: Cambridge University Press, 1994), 88; Stephanie McCurrie, "The Politics of Yeoman Households in South Carolina," in Nina Silbert and Catherine Clinton, eds, *Divided Households: Gender and the Civil War* (Oxford and New York: Oxford Univesity Press, 1992), 27; John Smail, *The Origins of Middle-Class Culture: Halifax, Yorkshire, 1660–1780* (Ithaca and London: Cornell University Press, 1994), 33; John Belchem and James Epstein, "The Nineteenth-Century Gentleman Leader Revisited," *Social History* 22, no. 2 (May 1997): 190.

208 AO, Jarvis-Powell Papers, Anne Powell to Aunt Inman, 26 Mar. 1785: "The Pride of Independence is so prevalent here that the people had rather starve at home than live in my kitchen in plenty. Was I to take them to my table they would have no objection to *oblige* me. The want of good domestics is general, therefore I have less reason to complain but I wish a method could be found to render us less dependent on them." The method found to control the labour supply of women is part of a larger study I am presently undertaking. See Nancy Christie, "Strangers in the Family: Work, Gender and the Origins of Old Age Homes," *Journal of Family History* (forthcoming).

BRIAN YOUNG

Revisiting Feudal Vestiges in Urban Quebec

In the final analysis, you don't just belong to yourself alone.

Consul Buddenbrook[1]

In the course of running property for his own interests, safety and convenience he performed many of the functions of the state. He was a judge: he settled disputes among his followers. He was the police: he kept order among a
large number of people ... He was the Church: he named the chaplain ... He
was a welfare agency: he took care of the sick, the aged, the orphans. He was
the army ... Moreover, through what became an intricate system of marriages,
kinship, and sponsorship... [h]e could appeal for support if need be to a large
number of relatives in the country or in the towns who possessed property and
power similar to his own."

Alexander Marchant[2]

This chapter draws from my larger study of the place and authority of
two landed – and yet urban – families in Montreal and Quebec City,
the McCord and Taschereau families. I locate this study in the post-
revolutionary Atlantic world which in Canadian political chronology
covers the period from the Constitutional Act of 1791 to the Canadian
Confederation of 1867. Much of the recent historiography on the
intellectual foundations of Quebec takes root in liberalism, the
Enlightenment, modernism, and the French Revolution. Yet, the patrician society to which these two families belonged had unmistakable
conservative, monarchist, established church, and anti-modernist
characteristics.[3] These families, I suggest, were instrumental in framing local authority, institutions, cultures, and physical landscapes, and
in anchoring parallel hegemonies which evolved in both Protestant
and Catholic Quebec.

HISTORIOGRAPHICAL ISSUES

The reasons for the underestimation of patricians and their conservatism are complex. Horizons in Canadian historiography are still clouded by debate over conquest and national superiority. We also suffer from a lingering entrepreneurial historical tradition best summarized in Michael Bliss's *Northern Enterprise: Five Centuries of Canadian Business*.[4] In a country where beaver, cod, the Rocky Mountains, and an ubiquitous winter added romantic challenge and geographic determinism to the quotidian of the merchant capitalist, the staple theory, fur, and railway giants have dominated historical discourse, leaving patricians, with their concerns for landed wealth, family reproduction, and mediation of local conflict, as faceless and anachronistic pedants, useless in the modernist loop. If this seems exaggerated recall the long shadow of Donald Creighton whose 1937 classic, *Empire of the St Lawrence,* was republished by University of Toronto Press in 2002. Creighton, as every Canadian history student learns, made the British-Canadian merchant synonymous with Protestant virtue, elevating the St Lawrence and those who understood its mystical and economic significance into "the central truth of a religion."[5] Albeit with different methodologies, A.R.M. Lower, Fernand Ouellet, Gerald Tulchinsky, Doug McCalla, and multiple biographers in the *Dictionary of Canadian Biography* have reinforced the centrality in our historiography of the British merchant along the St Lawrence.[6] It is also important to note, as Catherine Hall and others have reminded us, the hairball entwinement in the British polity of the entrepreneur, Protestantism, imperialism, and racial concepts of national superiority.[7]

In Quebec, our social-history and class tradition is undoubtedly weaker than its European counterparts. Edward Thompson, for example, devotes a seventy-nine-page chapter to what he calls "Patricians and Plebs."[8] At the same time, strong Canadian writing in labour and feminist history, particularly treating the period after 1850, has pushed attention to factory, public, and home, resulting in panoramas remote from the authority sites of seminaries, seigneurial pews, parlours, robing chambers, and cemetery boardrooms. The best study of the urban family in Quebec, Bettina Bradbury's *Working Families: Age, Gender, and Daily Survival in Industrializing Montreal,* takes the working-class family as its frame.[9] Contrast that book's justifiable success with Pierre Petot's *La Famille,* which has never attracted a Quebec readership. A French legal historian, Petot looks to the past, emphasizing law, institutions, and structures and situating family relations in the context of custom, "ancienneté," "puissance paternelle," and "force obligatoire."[10] And where elite institutions *have* been studied it has often been in instrumentalist or social-control contexts.[11]

In the 1970s and 1980s, historians in French-speaking universities emphasized the modernity of Quebec, a full-fledged, progressive North American society liberated from a cleric-ridden ancien régime.[12] Among intellectual historians, Fernande Roy, her generation's most influential historian of Quebec ideology, is another who located the economic elite of French Montreal within a longstanding liberal ethic.[13] By the early1990s, social-science and intellectual history in a Quebec midway between two referendums on independence was lapped by identity histories inspired by the double prong of Benedict Anderson's *Imagined Communities* (1983) and Pierre Nora's *Lieux de la mémoire* (1985):

> L'imaginaire d'une société fonde son identité, the historian-curators of the Musée de la civilisation exhibition "Mémoire" wrote in 1992. Il lui assure cohérence, équilibre, cohésion et harmonisation. Il est créateur d'espaces de vie et de comportements acceptés.[14]

If those histories had little place for the aristocratic, the conservative, or the institutional, recent studies by Ronald Rudin and H.V. Nelles do chronicle elite culture, ideology, and influence but do so through an *événementiel* approach avoiding the pre-industrial context. For its part, the *Dictionary of Canadian Biography* painted the seigneurial class into a rural corner, placing seigneurs in the occupational group of agriculture, a group of "people known to have been engaged in the development of land."[15]

A generation of structuralist historians in Canada also contributed to keeping patricians in the shadows. Lunching, so to speak, at Maurice Dobb's table on the development of capitalist society, we learned that capitalism "as a mode of production did not grow to any stature until the disintegration of Feudalism had reached an advanced stage."[16] Since capitalism was clearly afoot along the St Lawrence, seigneurialism and its forms of authority and proprietorship were easily presumed to be marginal or the bailiwick of an effete French aristocracy. And when the two systems collided, the result was dramatic. H. Clare Pentland, for example, swept aside the significance of Upper Canada's "flirtation with patriarchy," describing what he called "the failure of hierarchical agriculture" in the face of a new "secular" "cosmic view": "the spirit of capitalism."[17] Marx himself, as noted by Hobsbawm and others, spoke in different tongues at different stages of his life, probably misunderstanding pre-capitalist society and its mechanisms.[18] Writing of the 'vol du bois' in the autumn of 1842, the young

Marx emphasized the role of law in mediating power relations between landed forest proprietors and peasantry. This conflict lost its centrality in the mature Marx of *Capital* and the *Communist Manifesto* where revolutionary production, commodities, the need for markets, and "naked, shameless, direct, brutal exploitation" swept away "all feudal, patriarchal, idyllic relations" drowning "religious fervour," "chivalrous enthusiasm," and "philistine sentimentalism."[19]

It fell, ironically, to Louise Dechêne, a specialist in the eighteenth century, and Paul-André Linteau and Jean-Claude Robert, two non-Marxist historians, to emphasize the role of patrician property in nineteenth-century urban Quebec. The former, in *Habitants et marchands de Montréal au XVIII siècle*, showed the centrality of feudal European institutions in Montreal and their "drag" in the face of frontier and new North American conditions. Her work implicitly challenged the fragment theory of Louis Hartz and Kenneth D. McRae's description of a society with "no despotism" and only a "moderate absolutism."[20] For their part, Linteau and Robert argued for the power of urban landed property, much of it held by francophone patricians. They did not, however, follow through on the feudal implications of their findings, framing land rather into the national question and French Canadian use of immoveable property for capitalist ends.[21]

This penury of works on power, ideology, sources of authority, old families, and the persistence of pre-industrial institutions has not gone entirely unnoticed. Allan Greer, for example, complained that a generation of historians "almost managed to write this class out of discussions of early Canadian society."[22] In the two decades since his lament, excellent studies have been published. Colin Coates wrote an innovative history of the Hale family as seigneurs in Sainte-Anne de la Pérade. He showed their broad influence on local life, particularly that of Elizabeth Amherst Hale who imported an "English noble aesthetic" to a French-Canadian community along the St Lawrence. Coates, however, places the Hales in a regime of declining seigneurial influence, describing their withdrawal from social relations as priests, militia officers, and local bourgeoisie rose to power.[23] This seigneurial effeteness found parallel in the Upper Richelieu Valley where Françoise Nöel describes the Christies, the region's dominant seigneurial family, as symbolically out of reproductive juice after 1845, a fate that coincided with absentee landlordship, long court battles among family members, and the "depersonalization" of seigneurial relationships as the Christies lost contact with the local community.[24] A more vigorous rural seigneurial tradition appears to have survived in nineteenth-century Saint-Hyacinthe. Here, both Christian Dessureault and Yvan Lamonde have demonstrated the ongoing political, social, and military significance of the seigneurs in a region critical to the history of nationalism, liberalism, and the rebellions of 1837-38. Jean Dessaulles, the most important of the county's three seigneurs, was a central figure in local institutions, commander of the Saint-Hyacinthe militia battalion, justice of the peace, church warden of his parish and, for several years late in life, legislative councillor.[25] Brother-in-law of patriote leader and fellow seigneur Louis-Joseph Papineau, his acceptance of a seat in the Legislative Council in 1832 was symptomatic of the deep divisions among patrician families over the reform cause. It is also clear that the Dessaulles' influence was not limited to smaller centres. Allied with the Montreal Papineaus by marriage and shared values, the Dessaulles also used their seigneurial-based power in Montreal. Louis-Antoine Dessaulles, son of Jean Dessaulles and co-seigneur of the Saint-Hyacinthe seigneury, mayor of Saint-Hyacinthe (1849-57), signator of the annexation manifesto of 1849, promoter of inventions and patents, and developer of a quarry for railway-bed stone, moved to Montreal in 1860. Here, he took on Bishop Ignace Bourget, editing *Le Pays* (1861-63), serving twice as president of the Institut Canadien, and witnessing at the Guibord trial (1870).[26] Commenting on Louis-Antoine and his son Georges-Casimir, two Dessaulles generations that "continuent à faire figure de seigneurs" after the official abolition of seigneurialism in 1859, Louise Dechêne speculates that it was the fact that " non contents de continuer de tirer du sol les honneurs et les rentes, ils investissent dans l'avenir de la région et pèsent sur l'orientation de son opinion."[27]

Bruce Curtis, in a section of *The Politics of Population* entitled "Feudal Science in the Nineteenth Century," gives another example of the ideological centrality of the seigneurial community, in this instance in the establishment of the Canadian census. Progeny of a prominent seigneurial family, Joseph-Charles Taché, in a rant against modernity, took a stab at Romanticism, Revolution, and urban life: "We were born, as a people, out of the Catholicism of the seventeenth century and out of our struggles with a wild and indomitable nature ... In no way are we sons of the Revolution and we do not need the expedients of modern romanticism to engage minds which believe and hearts which remain pure."[28] All the while, Curtis reminds us, Taché was promoting the use of statistics, "comprehensiveness," "management," "fitness," and "efficiency." Curtis provides clear evidence of the overlapping of modes and, whatever Taché's discourse, of the harmonization in practice of feudal and modern.

Historians, in fact, seem uncomfortable ceding place in the context of their social class to patricians like Taché. The biographies of seigneurs and other patricians flattened on the anvil of nineteenth-

century progress abound in the *Dictionary of Canadian Biography*, leaving
the strong impression that patrician families are somehow more fragile
and subject to dry rot than their industrial or commercial peers. For
example, Antoine Juchereau Duchesnay, related by marriage to the
Taschereau, whose Beauport manor featured black servants and foun-
tains, left "a huge fortune" that included five seigneuries and two fiefs;
within a generation, we are told, it was gone.[29] Fernand Ouellet has
also itemized the apparent decline of the French-Canadian seigneurial
elite in the late eighteenth century showing, with Annales-like fastidi-
ousness, their replacement by up-and- coming British merchants and
professionals. His anger at patrician conservatism, financial inepti-
tude, and dissoluteness is palpable: "À la fin du 18e siècle la décadence
des anciennes familles est suffisamment engageé pour que désormais
elles ne puissant aspirer – jouer un rôle déterminant dans les strutures
politiques et sociales. L'heure des commerçants et des professions
libérales est arrivée."[30]

Declining military significance has also been posted as a barometer
of patrician fatigue among French Canadians, particularly in comparison to a presumed colonial meritocracy and the dynamism of the sons
of Britain in the fur-trading and canal-building elites. The place of military tradition, male prowess, and the status of rank are not favoured
subjects in Canadian historiography. "Nostalgic", is the term that best
describes Roch Legault's image of the decline of the French military
elite as officers and sons melted in a British-dominated environment.
Families like the Duchesnay and St Ours, he argues, demonstrate, in
the words of one of his reviewers, "the downward course of French-
Canadian military life."[31]

In contrast to this vision of patrician marginality and meltdown in
nineteenth-century Quebec is a substantial international historiography that documents the persistence of patrician authority in urban
centres around the world. Madrid, for example, albeit admittedly an
imperial capital without water transportation, was a city where nobles,
ecclesiastics, and bureaucrats took precedence over merchants. Jesus
Cruz argues that Mexico City is a city whose "tone" was "set by its aristocracy, the colonial bureaucracy, and the Church" as well as by its
merchants.[32] Richard Rodger's *Transformation of Edinburgh* illustrates
how urban feudal forms of landholding and of institutional property
ownership determined land use, affected social relations, and contributed to perpetuating ecclesiastical and patrician power.[33] Using Paris,
David Harvey broadened his earlier focus on land rents and class structure into a larger culturalist and geopolitical interpretation, "a rich
experience" of urban power that encompasses art and literature and
extraordinary conservative "moments" like construction of the basilica

Sacre-Coeur as a place of "perpetual remembrance".[34] Similar German themes are discernible in David Blackbourn and Richard Evans' *The German Bourgeoisie.*[35]

LOCATING PATRICIANS

In the lee of this substantial scholarship, I want to resituate Lower Canadian patricians, locating them in Quebec's two most important cities, examining their ideology, their persistence over generations, their sense of place based on heritable estates, and emphasizing family strength rooted in what David Harvey calls "feudal residuals."[36] Patronage, birth, heritage, landed property, the convent, the elite professions, the established churches, and marriage stand tall here with power related to "authority" as much as "money." I want to give weight to feudal influences, to hierarchies, to cultural and ideological factors and, in political terms, to what Gordon Stewart calls a "century of authoritarian and non-representative rule."[37] In a sense, this represents an adjustment of my earlier work. Very much in the Dobbs-Thompson-Davidoff\Hall tradition, I over-emphasized the material, pockets, and wealth as the foundation of family, institutional, and class power. I emphasized "freedom of contract" in analyzing civil-law codification and seigneurial expropriation in a study of the Seminary of Montreal, underestimating the profound importance of custom in the former and the significance of moral authority in the latter.[38]

It is important to characterize the colonial particularity of the urban centres in which these two families flourished. Montreal and Quebec were unique venues within the empire – white, colonial, and violent places, formed from European cultures and Catholic majorities and strong Protestant minorities. In both these St Lawrence cities, language, thanks to important Irish immigration, cut across religious divisions, leaving Montreal, for example, with an English-speaking majority in 1851. In both cities, as will become apparent with the example of Ursuline schools, erection of Irish parishes was only part of the adjustment of Roman Catholic infrastructures to changing ethnic and material realities. Conquered in 1759-60, ceded in 1763, and thus walled off from the French Revolution, Napoleon, the Concordat, and Civil Code, French Canada inevitably accorded special place to memory, Catholicism, and *ancien-régime* institutions. The colony shared a long, porous border with the American republic, an indefatigable exporter of goods, people, and ideas. This served to increase the moral and political responsibility of the local elite, giving them what Pierre Bourdieu describes as "cultural capital" and "symbolic power."[39] Weber called this the difference between "naked money" and power nuanced by the social, legal, and the honorific.[40] The result was that, in both cities, egalitarian, liberal, and nationalist sentiments shared the sidewalks with strong hierarchical, conservative, and British-based monarchical and constitutional traditions. A vigorous North American capitalism, powered in part by non-conformism, had to negotiate with powerful, pre-capitalist forces for whom anti-usury, paternalism, seigneurialism, the Custom of Paris, and the established churches represented important principles. In Montreal, while canals, railways, manufactures, and the tearing down of the city's fortifications were physical manifestations of the marriage of capitalism and the city, some 20 per cent of its urban space, it is worth reminding ourselves, remained controlled by religious communities.[41]

TWO FAMILIES

One side of my family coin is represented by the McCords, Ulster provisioners who arrived in Quebec through the gateway of the British Conquest. Within a generation, one branch had moved upstream from Quebec to a shaky existence in Montreal. Unsuccessful in his distillery partnership, Thomas McCord found opportunity through the feudal door when, in 1793, he took ninety-nine year leases from the Grey Nuns and sisters of Hôtel Dieu on two of their estates, essentially lowlands southwest of the city walls. With the good fortune that alternated in McCord family history with bankruptcy and instability, Thomas McCord lived to see the Lachine Canal built nearby and the transformation of his pastures into an industrial suburb. His newfound seigneurial respectability and income facilitated his two sons' bicultural education at the Collège de Montréal and their accession to the law, judgeships, the established church, and wives of good family. Along the way, eldest son John Samuel McCord traded in Presbyterianism, drinking clubs, and the heritage of his Jewish mother for church synods, cemetery boards, and the more respectable Scot culture of his wife's family. Anne Ross was the daughter of former Attorney General David Ross who was listed in 1825 as the seventh largest property holder in Montreal (£880). Her family assets also included St Giles de Beaurivage, a seigneury listed as nineteenth in value in Quebec ($100,412) in 1863 and which, coincidentally, adjoined the much more important Ste Marie de Beauce seigneury of the Taschereau family.[42] On the McCord side, the Nazareth Fief was valued at £27,616 in 1840 with the two brothers sharing land rents from 247 individuals.

If seigneurial property and marriage gave the third generation of McCords in Canada a leg up to patrician status in nineteenth-century

English Montreal, the Taschereau had much deeper feudal tap-roots with concession of their first seigneury, Sainte-Marie in the Beauce, dating from 1736. Across the nineteenth century, a strong-backed peasantry on their seigneury; intermarriage with prominent families like the Panet, Duchesnay, Lindsay, or Desrivières; and careful attention to seminary and convent educations and to careers in the law, notariat, military, and clergy kept, not just one, but two branches of the Taschereau family at the pinnacle of the Canadian pecking order in the law, the church, and the state. For while the McCords' star rose in the 1790s and fell a century later with expiration of the leases on their two fiefs, the Taschereau have successfully passed their mantle from generation to generation over more than two centuries. Two Taschereau sat on the Supreme Court of Canada and another became Canada's first cardinal. Marie-Anne-Louise Taschereau served as superior of the Ursulines, Canada's most prestigious convent, while Louis-Alexandre Taschereau would accede to his province's highest elected post, becoming premier of Quebec in 1920.

It is clear that patrician wealth in its feudal form was steady, secure, and relatively stable, a sure source of local respectability and a reliable means to transmit family wealth. In open, river cities like Montreal and Quebec, destabilized by fevers, great fires, indiscriminate immigration, and raucous foreign ideas, the assurance of seigneurial anchor must have been grand: the best pews, schools, and clubs; the monopoly to grind the food and major cash crop of your peasants or, in the case of an urban fief, the right to collect land rents from both industrial proprietors and proletarians. Well-managed feudal, professional, or judicial incomes permitted a manor house, urban villa, or both, in which architecture, servants, and landscape might reflect profound cultural aspirations as well as provide a safe family haven for children and women. Merchants like Thomas McCord understood these truisms, filling up at the seigneurial pump when prices permitted. The Taschereau, too, moved in a complex family world in which education, careers, and, in the case of women, marriage, might take them to Quebec or further: what was constant, however, a virtual pole for christenings, widows, and a certain coherence in life, was Sainte-Marie de Beauce, its chapel and manor house. Was it just coincidental that both the McCord and Taschereau estates featured Greek columns? While annexed to their manor the Taschereau built a chapel dedicated to Ste Anne, the McCords developed their grounds around garden and vista, croquet and gazebo, leaving formal religious worship for Christ Church, their parish church. In both families, the honorific, the symbolic, and titles like "judge," "Sheriff," "Monsigneur," and "cardinal" wore well. Writing from vacation in India where his son-in-law was serving with the Royal Engineers, Supreme Court Justice Henri-Elzéar Taschereau led the campaign for titles for Supreme Court judges and, in 1903, he proudly accepted his knighthood.[43]

At the same time, feudalism was a social system that implied reciprocities and respect for customary norms: the hegemony enjoyed by the McCords and Taschereau brought corresponding responsibilities. All but the most decadent patrician would have agreed with Consul Buddenbrook's admonition to his layabout brother that "you don't just belong to yourself alone."[44] For while the merchant or manufacturer might presume to operate in a realm of individual interest, of freedom of contract, and of the autonomy of factory walls, patricians understood their complete interdependence with the local, the producer, the censitaire, the tenant. Their authority, be it as seigneur, judge, militia officer, or convent superior drew from customary usages and law and Christian tradition. Jean-Thomas Taschereau, seigneur and later judge of the Supreme Court of Canada, was suggesting much more than just seigneurial rights when he told an 1842 enquiry that "ours are vested rights" guaranteed to his family "by the public faith and by immemorial prescription."[45] Or, we can turn to the documents left by the eight Taschereau women who took the habit. Here the discourse is one of sacrifice, obedience, and resignation.

Marie-Célanire Taschereau, known religiously as Mère Saint-Elzéar, was a founder of Hôtel Dieu Hospital in Chicoutimi and second superior of the Monastère des Religieuses Hospitalières de la Miséricorde de Jésus. Her diary speaks of a "vocation au sacrifice": "c'est par l'obéissance et la résignation que Dieu m'appelle particulièrement – me sanctifier."[47] The same sense of authority and responsibility is evident in the McCords. For it was only with the strong wind of customary rights at his back that Judge John Samuel McCord could venture out on his rural Missisquoi circuit, send the hapless to the gallows, or allow his wife and children to summer among French-speaking peasants on the Beaurivage seigneury. German scholars of the bourgeoisie describe this as a sense of *Heimat*, an understanding of local connections, a perception of what it meant to be "bourgeois and German."[48]

These responsibilities took many forms. Leadership in a host of philanthropic organizations, in the military, legal, and religious professions, in the Masons and other associations, clubs, and societies only hint at their whirling dervish lives of service, occasions, and public activities. Synod, lodge, or burial ground were masculine poles: women served in church, female associations, classrooms, hospitals, philanthropies, and convent, the latter being the only "profession" open to elite women.

Women in the Taschereau Family who joined the Ursuline or Augustine Orders

---

Marie-Anne-Louise Taschereau dite de St-François Xavier (Ursuline)
b.1744 – Quebec
daughter of Thomas Taschereau and M-J Fleury de la Gorgendière
Profession: 1764

Marie-Célanire Taschereau dite de St-Elzéar (Augustine)
b. 1844 – Ste Marie de Beauce
Daughter of Thomas-Jacques Taschereau and Marie-Anna-Amable Fleury de
Gorgendière
Entered Hopital-Général de Québec as novice: 1874

Marie-Adélaide-Anne-Adine Angers dite de Sainte-Madeleine (Ursuline)
b. 1846
daughter of Albert Angers and Elmina Taschereau
Profession: 1869

Caroline Alexandrine-Amanda Taschereau dite St-Alexandre (Augustine)
b. 1847
daughter of Thomas-Jacques Taschereau and Marie Anna-Amable Fleury de
Gorgendière
Profession: 1876

Marie-Louise- Adèle Taschereau dite de Sainte-Monique (Ursuline)
b. 1872
Daughter of Jules-Jacques Taschereau and Hélène Nault
Profession: 1894
Clara Taschereau dite Marie-Jean (Ursuline)
b. 1888
daughter of Gustave-Olivier Taschereau and Clara Maguire (sister of Ursuline chaplain)
Profession: 1913

Caroline Taschereau dite Marie du Sacré-Coeur (Augustine)
b. 1871
Daughter of Dr Jules Taschereau and Hélène Nault
Profession: c 1890

Nor was moral and political leadership limited to responsibility for social lessers. Travelled, educated in English and French in seminary and convent schools, proprietors of libraries and borrowers of books, purveyors of the social arts and high culture, and regulars at the governor's ball, the officers' mess, and the bishop's parlour, patricians served as mediators with authority among both British and the ethnic other. Mediation might take practical form, like marriage between a Taschereau and Lindsay, law partnerships like McCord-Dorion, speeches, judgments, or treatises in the language of the other, or service at critical moments of ethnic brokering such as Thomas McCord's English-language secretaryship of the civil-code commission. Writing on 20 June 1867, just ten days before celebration of the Canadian Confederation, McCord prefaced *The Civil Code* with a declaration of ethnic unity and of the English community's support for the civil-law tradition: "The English speaking residents of Lower Canada, may now enjoy the satisfaction of at least possessing in their own language the laws by which they are governed, and the Province of Quebec will bring with her into the Confederation a system of Laws of which she may be justly proud; a system mainly founded on the steadfast, time-honored and equitable principles of the Civil Law, and which not only merits admiration and respect, but presents a worthy model for legislation elsewhere."[49]

If marriage alliances and law partners represented practical forms of mediation, oaths and the rituals and ceremonies surrounding them were symbolic manifestations: seigneurial fealty and military oaths of loyalty had religious counterpart in vows of celibacy and obedience. Through their vows in confrèries, children learned the significance of loyalty, faith, and respect. Montreal and Quebec were bitterly divided cities, unique in the magnitude of their turbulence, with their violence, it has been argued, having "no parallel anywhere else in the post 1783 British Empire."[50] In an urban, industrializing cauldron of conquered French and British authority, the Taschereau stand out as perennial proponents of collaboration, with all the ambiguities suggested by the term. Their oaths to the Crown symbolized their respect for Britain, its constitution and institutions and, by implication, their distaste for revolution and vulgar nationalism. At the Ursuline school they sponsored and frequented, graduation ceremonies included performances in English, and prizes might be distributed by Lady Aberdeen, the Governor General's wife; whatever the street growl, Ursuline graduations ended with "God Save the Queen" or "Dieu Sauve la Reine." Supporting the Crown during the American Revolution, despite the opposition of his peasants and the presence on his seigneury of Benedict Arnold's invading army, Gabriel-Elzéar Taschereau saw his manor sacked. Two generations later, and in the face of rising French-Canadian nationalism, Pierre-Elzéar Taschereau and Antoine-Charles Taschereau were elected to the Legislative Assembly in 1830 from the Beauce. Their victory procession along the Chaudière River was headed by flags proclaiming "Vive le roi!," "Vive la Constitution!," "Vive les représantants du people!," "Vive les Taschereau!"[51] This comportment had parallels easily discernible in other colonial elites. Writing of South Africa, with its profound racial and cultural crises, Robert Ross puts it this way: "through much of the

Benefactors of the Duchesnay-Juchereau Scholarship at the Séminaire de Nicolet, (1844-95)

	Age of entry; year	Home Town	Year of Graduation	Profession
Narcisse Duchesnay Juchereau	??	Beauport	1807	militaire
Charles Taschereau	15; 1812	Ste Marie de Beauce	1816	homme d'ètat
Alex-Juchereau Duchesnay	10: 1844	Quebec	1849	employé civil
Théod.-Juchereau Duchesnay	8: 1844	Quebec	1855	militaire
Alexandre Taschereau	?; 1870	Ste Marie de Beauce	1875	no profession given
Richard Taschereau	10: 1875	Ste Marie de Beauce	1880	pharmacien
Henri-Juchereau Duchesnay	11: ?	Quebec	1889	militaire
Auguste-Henri-Arthur Delisle	14: 1889	Cap Santé	1895	employé civil
Louis Taschereau	14: 1894	Ste Marie de Beauce	1895[55]	

nineteenth century, and indeed later, Englishness was the major symbol used to determine what was right and acceptable in the political life of the Cape Colony."[52]

RELIGION AND THE SCHOOL CONNECTION

Si l'archevêque de Québec montrait de la répugnance – voir partir au loin "ses" Ursulines, les deux fondations de la Pointe-Bleue (Roberval) et de Stanstead se présentaient davantage comme une affaire de famille.[53]

This use of the term "his Ursulines" by Monsignor Elzéar-Alexandre Taschereau and reference to their distancing from Quebec as a "matter of family" suggest the easy conjuncture between patrician families and the colony's most prestigious religious institutions. The latter represented sites of authority both male and female, of influential and socially useful careers, of a seminary or convent education, and had the added advantage of mortmain, a corporate status that suggested perpetuity to a patrician community consumed by feelings of fragility. Two examples – a family scholarship and the Taschereau connection to the Ursuline convent – make clear this relationship.

The Juchereau-Duchesnay, patricians and united by marriage with the Taschereau, established two scholarships, one for boys and one for girls. In 1837, Charles Maurice Juchereau-Duchesnay, imitating a common clerical practice of sponsoring seminarians, left £500 to the Séminaire de Nicolet. Of this sum, £300 was used to establish a scholarship for Duchesnay and Taschereau boys. Administered by the seminary, the scholarship was allocated by a "conseil de famille." As late as 1908, two destitute and orphaned Duchesnay brothers, lodged in the Quebec hospice of the Souers de la Charité. apparently benefited from the scholarship.[54] Also in the 1837 will was a smaller bequest of £350 for female family members to attend the Ursuline school in Quebec.

The Seminary acted as surrogate parent for Taschereau in residence and the school director reported regularly to the Bishop of Quebec, particularly on health matters: "Taschereau [Charles] ne va guère mieux, cependant je crois qu'on peut se rassurer à son sujet. Le docteur Cartier [G. Cartier] prétend que c'est un nerf tressailli, ou peut-être un abcès ... Je le crois vraiment malade et incapable de continuer ses études pour le moment, mais aussi le dégoût et l'ennui ont coopéré – le rendre encore plus incapable : la vertu lui plait un jour et le lendemain il n'en veut plus. Sa mère tout en voulant son plus grand bien le perdra si elle continue de le laisser maître de tous ses caprices."[56]

While the Séminaire de Nicolet was a regional institution junior to more reputed seminaries in Montreal and Quebec, the Ursulines had a reputation as the colony's pristine convent: their spirituality and intellectual life, their model of a celibate, selfless womanhood, their schools for girls, and their link to a mythic history of Quebec through their founder, Marie de l'Incarnation, assured them privileged place in French Canada. Their monastery, chapel, school, library, garden, and archives gave strong and complementary female presence to the equally gendered and nearby Séminaire de Québec. Strictly cloistered, the Ursuline's insistence on total female privacy contrasted with their very public place as land proprietors, educators, and cultural determinants, a paradox which only enhanced their mystique and authority.

Soon after their founding in Italy in 1534, the Ursulines, as part of the reforms of the Council of Trent, were cloistered, a practice maintained until Vatican II. A teaching order, they expanded in Italy, Switzerland, Germany, and particularly France where, by 1715, they had more than 350 monasteries.[57] The most important female teaching order in France, the Ursulines established hundreds of schools, essentially urban. In addition to oaths of chastity, poverty, and obedience, Ursulines in Paris took a fourth vow, to teach.[58] The order was introduced into Quebec by Marie de l'Incarnation. A mother at eighteen and a widow with an infant son a year later, she was irresistibly drawn to a religious vocation, taking a vow of chastity in her twenties, and, under the guidance of her spiritual director, humiliating and disciplining her flesh, improving her literary skills, and teaching. Despite the strong opposition of her family and in the presence of her eleven-year old son, himself later a priest, she took Ursuline vows in Tours in 1633: this, Nathalie Davis suggests, was not unusual after the Council of Trent when "innovative Catholic reformers thought that chaste widows were as capable as virgins of attaining the highest spirituality."[59] Familiar with the challenge of Canadian missions through reading the *Jesuit Relations*, Marie de l'Incarnation raised the necessary funds to establish the order in Quebec in 1639. Cloistered, but desirous of teaching Native girls, the Ursulines could not imitate the Jesuits' missions. Instead, and this ensured their long-term urban influence, they boarded and taught both Native and bourgeois girls at the convent itself. Despite fires, wars, and epidemics in seventeenth-century Quebec, the convent flourished. Marie de l'Incarnation herself learned three Native languages, preparing prayers and dictionaries in Algonquin, Huron, and Iroquois. By 1669, there were twenty-two sisters in the Quebec convent and some twenty-five boarders, mostly Native.[60] Alongside the training in household science, agriculture, and handicraft skills like birch-bark embroidery, the Ursulines, even among female orders, stood out as determined Marianists, emphasizing the Virgin's purity and her union of maternity and chastity. In the 1650s they participated in the founding of the Congrégation Enfants de Marie and the Congrégation de la Sainte Vierge en Amérique.

Unlike the Jesuits, the Ursulines were among the Roman Catholic institutions viewed favourably by British authorities after the Conquest. Use of the convent as a military hospital and their well-publicized care of the wounded became the stuff of legends of French nuns and British officers. Nor did loyalty and teaching skills represent their only assets in the new regime. Anxious to attract the French rump, those in the seigneurial elite who had remained in Canada, British authorities also recommended the Ursulines as a means of providing professions and fulfillment for their unmarried daughters. Attorney-General Alexander Wedderburn explained this role using the terms "honour," "accomodation," "spinsters," and "family": "Les couvents ... peuvent être nécessaires pendant un certain temps pour l'accomodation et l'honneur des familles. Il peut être expédient de conserver en permanence dans cette colonie quelques-unes des communautés pour servir de retraite honorable aux femmes célibataires."[61]

This Ursuline realpolitik, their property and constitutional independence from sister monasteries in France, their openness to biculturalism,

and their admission of Protestant pupils, was greatly accentuated with
the French Revolution and imprisonment and martyrdom of their
consoeurs. Into the nineteenth century, increasing numbers of English-speaking Catholics, including Mary McCord, daughter of the
codifier met above, were attracted to Ursuline vocations. The first
courses in astronomy in their school were given by Mère Dougherty de
St-Augustin while Mère Ste-Croix Holmes and Mère O'Conway de
l'Incarnation were prominent teachers of science. The English edition
of their 1847 prospectus promised Protestants and Irish Catholics an
"elevated and salubrious location" and courses in reading, writing, arithmetic, book-keeping, geometry, algebra, history, geography, botany and
foreign languages. Parents were assured that letters, incoming as well as
outgoing, would be censored and that student reading would be
restricted to the convent library.[62] As English became more prominent
at the school, mediation with the larger scientific and cultural communities came from English-language priests at the Séminaire de Québec
and the newly established St Patrick's Church. Father John Holmes gave
the convent its rock and mineral collection; their chaplain, Thomas
Maguire, helped acquire harps and an organ in Paris; and Father
Edward Horan, first principal of the Laval Normal School, purchased
American instruments for their physics laboratory. English-speaking laymen took increasing philanthropic interest in the alma mater of their
sisters and daughters. Well-travelled, wealthy, and collectors, they built
up the Ursuline museal, library, and laboratory collections. Dr
McLoughlin, brother of an Ursuline, offered globes; John Fraser presented shells, insects, and tropical plants; M. Cooper an insect collection; and George Forsyth added exotic plants, minerals, and insects
collected in Europe and the Far East.[63]

Ursuline leadership in intellectual life and high culture; their
impeccable standards, spirituality, and teaching reputations; their
association with female activities across Quebec's bicultural Catholic
elite, and their Marianism and moral fibre were attractive grist for generations of Taschereau and, across three centuries, the histories of
family and institution blend almost seamlessly. The scholarship for
Taschereau girls at the Ursuline school has been mentioned. Four
Taschereau women took perpetual vows at the Ursuline convent with
one, Marie-Anne-Louise Taschereau, becoming superior. As early as
age six, attendance by Taschereau girls at the Ursuline school was a rite
of passage. Most boarded, all participated in the pious associations
organized as after-school activities, and several, at the end of their
lives, lay as well as those in habit, were buried in the Ursuline crypt. For
generations, mothers, wives, aunts, and daughters shared a common
education, culture, and religious training. "À six ans, Marie-Célanire

[Taschereau] entrait au pensionnat des Révérendes Mère Ursulines de Québec, ou l'accueillit une autre tante maternelle. Le monastère antique avec ses grilles austères fit-il impression sur la bruyante espiègle? À l'école des filles de Sainte-Angèle, elle grandit en sagesse, en piété, en science aussi."[64]

Marie-Anne-Louise Taschereau (1743-1825), known as Mère Saint-François-Xavier, had impeccable seigneurial credentials. Her father, Thomas-Jacques Taschereau, was proprietor of Sainte-Marie while her mother, Marie-Claire Fleury de la Gorgendière, was raised in the neighbouring manor house of Saint-Joseph. At age ten, Marie-Anne-Louise was sent to the Ursuline boarding school. In 1764, aged twenty, she entered as one of the convent's first postulants since the Conquest and, two years later, she took perpetual vows.[65] First a teacher, her thirty-six year administrative career began in 1788 as bursar and culminated in three mandates as superior, 1793-99, 1808-11, 1815-18. These years were critical in Ursuline history, their finances, French connections, and stability profoundly threatened by the French Revolution. As part of a historic, patriarchical structure, the Ursulines sought spiritual advice from their chaplain and bishop, and business counsel from well-placed lay authorities. Mother Superior Taschereau was able to turn to men in her own family. "Frightened at the magnitude of the temporal responsibilities and at the requirements for good bookkeeping as well as for sound administration," we are told by her Ursuline biographer in the *Dictionary of Canadian Biography*, she turned to two of her brothers and her niece's husband. As well as being seigneur of Sainte-Marie, her brother Gabriel-Elzéar Taschereau was roads commissioner for the Quebec district and a member of the legislative assembly. He reorganized the convent's affairs and "kept an eye on the community's property" advising on issues of convent insurance, nuns' dowries, school repairs, and lawsuits on their Portneuf barony.[66] On his death in 1808, he was replaced as adviser by son-in-law Olivier Perrault, himself married to Marie-Louise Taschereau, virtual namesake of her aunt, Superior Marie-Anne-Louise Taschereau.[67] In regulating their temporal affairs in revolutionary France, another brother, Charles-Antoine Taschereau, lent important assistance. Captured at Montreal in 1760 and repatriated to France, he remained in correspondence with his sister and, from Paris, helped her recover Ursuline assets in France.

This relationship between the Ursulines and the Taschereau climaxed in the episcopacy of Elzéar-Alexandre Taschereau. An intimate part of his family and institutional world, the Ursulines received letters from the archbishop written with an intimacy which surprises. Bishop, archbishop, and later cardinal, his influence over the convent ranged from the banal, to the intimate, to matters concerning the institution's very future: the best fuel for altar lamps, Ursuline financial aid for the agricultural college at Ste-Anne de la Pocatière, the celebration of marriages in their chapel, and issues concerning land and other business. He wrote a particularly warm letter on receiving a package of plums: "Je vous remercie pour les belles prunes que vous m'avez envoyées ce matin. Vos missionaires feront bien d'en emporter au lac St-Jean pour civiliser cette population, car rien ne sert mieux à adoucir les caractères que les bons fruits.[68] He was frequently questioned about visits to the convent and the inviolability of the cloister. Should parents, for example, be allowed to visit a sick child in the Ursuline infirmary? Taschereau was particularly concerned with expansion of the community. The late nineteenth century witnessed tremendous pressure for expanded Catholic services, particularly in education. With its strong English-speaking membership, Ursulines were called on to establish schools, particularly in emigré communities in New England and Western Canada. Caught between their ferocious opposition to emigration and their mission to provide Catholic services, Quebec bishops frowned upon the establishment of infrastructures which might legitimize the phenomenon. Taschereau refused five requests to establish new Ursuline communities, reminding them that cloistering made them unsuited for service in rough conditions. Reluctantly, he did permit establishment of two communities, both in Quebec. In contrast to the bourgeois vocation of their school in Quebec, the girls' school established in the Lac Saint-Jean colonization town of Roberval (1881) emphasized domestic and farm skills.[69]

Named archbishop in 1870, Taschereau enthusiastically took up the beatification of Marie de l'Incarnation. An important part of the beatification process involved miracles and reputation. Here the letter of Supreme Court Judge Henri-Elzéar Taschereau figured prominently. Although Marie de l'Incarnation herself lived a century before the British Conquest, Judge Taschereau put her elevation to sainthood in the context of her Ursuline successors' tolerance and the respect they had won from Protestants: "Son oeuvre au Canada y est encore continuée par une communauté jouissant d'une confiance et d'un respect sans bornes, partagés non seulement par tout ce qui a le nom de Catholiques, mais même par les Protestants nombreux qui ne craignent pas de confier leurs enfants à celles qui ont succédé à la Mère de l'Incarnation."[70]

Like many in his generation, Taschereau was a passionate Marianist. As a student at the Séminaire de Québec years before the 1854 papal bull, *Ineffabilis Deus*, he joined the Congrégation de la Bienheureuse-Vierge-Marie-Immaculée. The cult of the Virgin was encouraged particularly among children and here the Ursulines, a teaching order, had an important role.[71] In 1845, the Jesuits established a confrérie, the Congrégation de Marie-Immaculée, apparently also known as the Congrégation Enfants de Marie, for Ursuline students in Quebec. In 1876, Archbishop Taschereau strengthened the confrérie, placing it under the direction of the Ursuline chaplain. This women's social group, which operated a workshop to make clothes for the poor, first held its meetings in the convent of the Soeurs de la Charité but by 1862 was meeting in the Ursuline parlour. Activities of the Congrégation – and at least a dozen Taschereau were members over the years – included pilgrimages and book borrowing from their library.[72] Two forms of promise were made:

> Moi _____ je vous choisis aujourd'hui pour ma mère, ma patronne et mon avocate; je prends la ferme résolution de ne jamais vous abandonner, de ne jamais rien dire ni faire contre vous, et de ne permettre jamais que par mes inférieurs il soit fiat quelque chose contre votre honneur. Je vous supplie donc de me recevoir pour votre perpétuelle servante; assistez-moi en toutes mes actions et ne m'abandonnez pas à l'heure de ma mort. Ainsi soit-il.

The second vow stated:

> Coeur Immaculé de Marie, Reine des anges et des saintes, auguste Mère de mon Dieu, me voici à vos pieds; je viens vous renouveler l'offrande de tout ce que je suis, voulant vous honorer, et vous faire honorer, autant qu'il dépendra de moi et que j'en serai capable. Que je suis heureuse ... Préservez-moi des illusions de la vie, protégez-moi contre les séductions, guidez-moi toujours dans les voies où me veut l'adorable Providence.[73]

At their Trois-Rivières convent, the Ursulines established five pious associations for girls in the 1860s.[74]

CONCLUSION

Marian devotion may seem a world away from the industrializing Quebec of the late nineteenth century, and very much on the periphery. The vows, however, recall the patrician society of Lower Canada. Elzéar-Alexandre Taschereau, who so energetically promoted the Congrégation, belonged to a family which, like the McCords, retained authority not only through the possession of wealth but through cultural means – the law, civil service, education, the Church. In Montreal,

Thomas McCord had built his family fortune on land leased from the Grey Nuns, land which was transformed into an industrial suburb. Later generations of McCords served as civil codifiers, judges, professed Ursulines. The Taschereau family in Quebec had much deeper seigneurial roots, their seigneury dating from 1736. Throughout the nineteenth century, the family's land-based wealth remained secure. With careful attention to seminary and convent education, family members moved into the highest offices – superior of the Ursulines, Supreme Court judges, cardinal, premier of the province of Quebec.

The vows, and the religious world to which they belong, express the values of interdependency, customary usage, law, and obedience, offering an alternative to individual interest, freedom of contract, and autonomy. Moreover, the persistence of patrician society through the institutions of seigneurialism and the Roman Catholic Church created conditions in which Britishness could be reinterpreted and adapted to include French and Catholic subjects.

NOTES

1 Thomas Mann, *Buddenbrooks. The Decline of a Family* (New York: Vintage, 1994), 314.

2 Alexander Marchant, "Colonial Brazil" in H.V. Livermore, ed., *Portugal and Brazil: An Introduction* (Oxford: 1953), cited in E.P. Thompson, *Customs in Common: Studies in Traditional Popular Culture* (New York: New Press, 1993), p.21.

3 See, for example, Jean-Marie Fecteau, *La liberté du pauvre : sur la régulation du crime et de la pauvreté au XIXe siècle québécois* (Montreal: VLB, 2004) and Michel Ducharme, *Aux fondements de l'État canadien. La liberté au Canada de 1776 à 1841* (PhD thesis, McGill University, 2005).

4 Michael Bliss, *Northern Empire: Five Centuries of Canadian Business* (Toronto: McLelland & Stewart, 1987).

5 Cited in *Canadian Historical Review*, 85, no.3 (Sept. 2004): 555.

6 Fernand Ouellet, *Histoire économique et sociale du Québec, 760–1850* (Montreal: Fides, 1971); A.R.M. Lower, *Great Britain's Woodyard: British America and the Timber Trade* (Montreal: McGill-Queen's Press, 1973); Gerald Tulschinsky, *The River Barons: Montreal Businessmen and the Growth of Industry and Transportation* (Toronto: University of Toronto Press, 1977).

7 Catherine Hall, *White, Male and Middle Class: Explorations in Feminism and History* (New York: Routledge, 1992) especially part 3, "Race, Ethnicity and Difference."

8 Thompson, *Customs in Common.*

9 Betting Bradbury, *Working Families: Age, Gender, and Daily Survival in Industri-alizing Montreal* (Toronto: McClelland & Stewart, 1993).

10 Pierre Petot, *Histoire du droit français. La Famille* (Paris: Éditions Loysel, 1992).

11 For example, Andrée Lévesque, "Deviant, Anonymous Single Mothers at the Hôpital de la Miséricorde in Montreal, 1929–39," *Historical Papers* (Ottawa: Canadian Historical Association Papers, 1984), 168–84 or Marta Danylewycz, *Taking the Veil: An Alternative to Marriage, Motherhood and Spinsterhood in Que-bec, 1840–1920* (Toronto: McClelland & Stewart, 1987); Allan Greer, "The Birth of the Police in Canada" in Greer and I. Radforth, *Colonial Leviathan: State Formation in Mid-Nineteenth-Century Canada* (Toronto: University of Toronto Press, 1992), 17–49; J-M Fecteau, J. Tremblay, and J. Trépanier, "La prison de Montréal de 1865–1913: évolution en longue période d'une popu-lation pénale," *Les cahiers de droit* 34, no. 1: 27–58; René Hardy, *Contrôle social et mutation de la culture religieuse au Québec, 1830–1930* (Montreal: Boréal, 1999).

12 The best example of modernist writing is Paul-André Linteau, René Durocher, Jean-Claude Robert, and François Ricard, *Histoire du Québec contemporain* (Montreal: Boréal, 1989).

13 Fernande Roy, *Histoire des ideologies au Québec aux XIXe et XXe siècles* (Montreal: Boréal, 1993).

14 Jacques Mathieu and Jacques Lacoursière, Les Mémoires Québécoises (Saint-Foy: Les Presses de l'Université Laval, 1991), 33.

15 Volume 5 for example, in its category of agriculture, places seigneurs along-side "improvers" and "settlers" although some seigneurs are double-listed under "business." Thirty-eight seigneurs were given biographies in the vol-ume compared to forty-four fur traders.

16 Maurice Dobb, *Studies in the Development of Capitalism* (New York: Interna-tional Publishers, 1947), 181.

17 H. Clare Pentland, *Labour and Capital in Canada 1650–1860* (Toronto: Lorimer, 1981), 57, 180.

18 See Hobsbawm's introduction to Marx, *Pre-Capitalist Economic Formations* (New York: International Publishers, 1965).

19 Marx and F. Engels, *The Communist Manifesto* (London: Penguin, 1967 [1872]), 82; for the young Marx see Pierre Lascoumes and Hartwig Zander, Marx: du "vol de bois" à la critque du droit (Paris: PUF, 1984); see also David Harvey, The Condition of Postmodernity (Cambridge, MA: Blackwell, 1990), 99–100.

20 Louise Dechêne, *Habitants et marchands de Montréal au XVII siècle* (Paris: Plon, 1974); Louis Hartz, *The Liberal Tradition in America* (New York: Harvest, 1955); Kenneth D. McRae, "The Structure of Canadian History," in Hartz, ed., *The Founding of New Societies* (New York: Harcourt Brace, 1964), 230.

21 Paul-André Linteau and Jean-Claude Robert, "Land Ownership and Society in Montreal: An Hypothesis," in G. Stelter and A. Artibise, *The Canadian City: Essays in Urban History* (Toronto: McClelland & Stewart, 1977), 17–36; Robert also studied a small-town seigneur, "Un seigneur entrepreneur, Barthélemy Joliette, et la fondation du village d'industrie (Joliette)", *Revue d'histoire de l'Amérique française* 26 (Dec. 1972).

22 Allan Greer, *Peasant, Lord, and Merchant: Rural Society in Three Quebec Parishes 1740–1840* (Toronto: University of Toronto Press, 1985), 104.

23 Colin Coates, *The Metamorphoses of Landscape and Community in Early Quebec* (Montreal & Kingston: McGill-Queen's University Press, 2000), 146, 99.

24 Françoise Noël, *The Christie Seigneuries: Estate Management and Settlement in the Upper Richelieu Valley* (Montreal & Kingston: McGill-Queen's University Press, 1992), 92.

25 Christian Dessureault and Yvan Lamonde, "L'élection de 1830 dans le comté de Saint-Hyacinthe: identités élitaires et solidarités paroissiales, sociales ou familiales," *Histoire sociale/Social History* 72 (Nov. 2003), 289.

26 Yvan Lamonde, *Louis-Antoine Dessaulles. Un seigneur libéral et anticlerical* (Montreal: Fides, 1994).

27 Louise Dechêne, ed., *Fadette: Journal d'Henriette Dessaulles* (Montreal: Hurtubise HMH, 1971), 15.

28 Bruce Curtis, *The Politics of Population: State Formation, Statistics, and the Census of Canada, 1840–1875* (Toronto: University of Toronto Press, 2001), 245.

29 Réal Bisson, *Dictionary of Canadian Biography*, 5: 464; In a second marriage (1789), Gabriel-Elzéar Taschereau married Louise-Françoise Juchereau Duchesnay.

30 Fernand Ouellet, *Éléments d'histoire sociale du Bas Canada* (Montreal: HMH, 1972), 101; see also Ouellet, *Le Bas Canada, 1791–1840. Changements structuraux et crise* (Ottawa: Les Éditions de l'Université d'Ottawa, 1976), 63.

31 Roch Legault, *Une élite en déroute: Les militaires canadiens après la Conquête* (Outremont: Athéna Éditions, 2002); see also Brett Rushforth's review in the *Canadian Historical Review* 85, no.3 (Sept.): 590–91. Greer flatly contradicts Legault, pointing out that, in inheriting his fief in 1834, François-Roch de St Ours was the first principal seigneur of St Ours in 162 years who was not a professional soldier and, although he was a colonel in the militia, who did not lead troops into combat. (*Peasant, Lord, and Merchant*, 109.)

32 Jesus Cruz, *Gentlemen, Bourgeois and Revolutionaries. Political Change and Cultural Persistence among the Spanish Dominant Groups 1750–1850* (Cambridge: Cambridge University Press, 1996), 16.

33 Richard Rodgers, *The Transformation of Edinburgh. Land, Property and Trust in the Nineteenth Century* (Cambridge: Cambridge University Press, 2001), especially 69–122.

34 David Harvey, *Paris, Capital of Modernity* (New York and London: Routledge, 2003), 340, 312; also useful for France are Éric Mension-Rigau, *Aristocrates et*

grand bourgeois. Éducation, traditions, valeurs (Paris: Perrin, 2007) and Guy Chaussinand-Nogaret, *Histoire des élites en France du XVIe au XXe siècle* (Paris: Hachette, 1994).

35 David Blackbourn and Richard Evans; eds., *The German Bourgeoisie: Essays on the Social History of the German Middle Class from the Late Eighteenth to the Early Twentieth Century* (London & New York: Routledge, 1991).

36 David Harvey, *The Urban Experience* (Baltimore: Johns Hopkins University Press, 1989), 91.

37 Gordon Stewart, *The Origins of Canadian Politics: A Comparative Approach* (Vancouver: University of British Coluimbia Press, 1986), 5.

38 Brian Young, *The Politics of Codification: The Lower Canadian Civil Code of 1866* (Montreal & Kingston: McGill-Queen's University Press, 1994); *In Its Corporate Capacity: The Seminary of Montreal as a Business Institution* (Montreal & Kingston: McGill-Queen's University Press, 1986).

39 Pierre Bourdieu, *Langage et pouvoir symbolique* (Paris: Seuil, 2001), 206.

40 H.H. Gerth and C. Wright Mills, *From Max Weber: Essays in Sociology* (New York: Oxford University Press, 1967), 180.

41 Jean-Claude Robert, *Atlas historique de Montréal* (Outremont: Libre Expression, 1994), 52.

42 Linteau and Robert, "Land Ownership and Society in Montreal," 29; Canada, *Cadastres abrégés des seigneuries du district de Québec* (Desbarats & Derbyshire, 1863) cited in Jean Benoit, "La Question Seigneuriale au Bas-Canada, 1850–1867," (MA thesis, Université Laval, 1978), 206.

43 James G. Snell and Frederick Vaughan, *The Supreme Court of Canada: A History of the Institution* (Toronto: Osgoode Society, 1983) 130.

44 Mann, *Buddenbrooks*, 314.

45 *Journals,* Legislative Assembly of Canada, vol. 3, Appendix F.

46 Archives du Monastère des Ursulines de Québec (AMUQ), " Fichers des Ancienne élèves des Ursulines de Québec" and Pierre-Georges Roy, *La famille Taschereau* (Levis: Imprimerie Mercantile, 1901).

47 AMUQ, Sr Ste-Marguerite-Marie, Supérieure, "Nécrologie de Mère Saint-Elzéar (Marie-Celanire Tashereau)," 1929, 9.

48 Celia Applegate, "Localism and the German bourgeoisie: the 'Heimat' movement in the Rhenish Palatinate before 1914," in Blackbourn and Evans, *The German Bourgeoisie,* 224–54.

49 McCord, *The Civil Code of Lower Canada* (Montreal: Dawson Brothers, 1873), x.

50 Stewart, *The Origins of Canadian Politics,* 5.

51 Roy, *La famille Taschereau,* 86.

52 Robert Ross, *Status and Respectability in the Cape Colony 1750–1870. A Tragedy of Manners* (Cambridge: Cambridge University Press, 1999), 43.

53 Dom Guy-Marie Oury, *Les Ursulines de Québec 1639–1953* (Sillery: Septentrion, 1999), 255.

54 Archives du Séminaire de Nicolet, F085/D44 Fonds Séminaire de Nicolet: Procure (Successions – pension Duchesnay) "Testament de Charles Maurice Juchereau-Duchesnay, 6 nov 1837." Soeur Agathe de Jésus to Rev. M. Proulx, Sup of Sem de Nicolet, 28 Aug. 1908. This was not an unusual bequest; in the 1820s, Charles de St Ours sponsored seminarians in the Richelieu Valley. (Greer, Peasant, Lord, and Merchant, 110).

55 J.-A I. Douville, *Histoire du Collège-Séminaire de Nicolet 1803–1903*, vol. 2 (Montreal, 1903).

56 Archives du Séminaire de Nicolet, Denis Fréchette, "Étude de la correspondance évêques de Québec/Séminaire de Nicolet 1804–1852," Abbé Paul Archambault à Mgr Joseph-Octave Plessis, 15 Nov. 1814, 8 Jan. 1815.

57 Jean Delameau, *Le Catholicisme entre Luther et Voltaire* (Paris: PUF, 1979), 89.

58 Ibid., 116.

59 Natalie Zemon Davis, *Women on the Margins: Three Seventeenth Century Lives* (Cambridge: Harvard University Press, 1995), 72, see also Marie-Emmanuel Chabot's biography, "Marie Guyart," *Dictionary of Canadian Biography* 1: 351–9.

60 Davis, *Women on the Margins*, 95.

61 Cited in Oury, *Les Ursulines de Québec*, 172.

62 AMUQ, Education, 'Prospectus,' 1847.

63 AMUQ, "Bienfaiteurs dans la cause de l'éducation (notes historiques)."

64 AUQ, Soeur Ste-Marguerite-Marie, 'Nécrologie,' Marie-Célanire Taschereau, nd.

65 Susanne Prince, "Marie-Anne-Louise Taschereau," *Dictionary of Canadian Biography*, 6: 751.

66 Ibid., 752.

67 Perrault served as Attorney-General in the highly unpopular Craig administration and in 1812 was given a judgeship.

68 AUQ, Correspondance et relations de Mgr Taschereau ... avec les Ursulines de Québec, Lettre à Mère Ste Catherine, supérieure des Ursulines de Québec, 1 Sept. 1881.

69 Oury, *Les Ursulines*, 255; Micheline Dumont and Nadia Eid, *Les Couventines. L'éducation des filles au Québec dans les congrégations religieuses enseignantes 1840–60* (Montreal: Boréal, 1986), 101.

70 Oury, *Les Ursulines*, 242.

71 M. Rappaport, ed., *Culture et religion. Europe – XIX siècle* (Paris: Atlande, 2004), 215.

72 AMUQ, "Congrégation des Enfants de Marie de l'extérieur."

73 AMUQ, "Congrégation des Enfants de Marie," Extraits de la promesse.

74 Dumont and Eid, *Les couventines*, 68.

PART TWO

Provincial Britons

TODD WEBB

How the Canadian Methodists Became British

Unity, Schism, and Transatlantic Identity, 1827–54

Historians examining the turbulent relationship between Canadian Methodism and British Wesleyanism between 1827 and 1854 have tended to focus on the British North American context alone. When they have looked at developments on the eastern side of the Atlantic, they have largely spoken in generalities. There is little sense in the work of Goldwin French or Neil Semple that there was something other than a monolithic British Wesleyanism with which the Canadian Methodists had to grapple during the negotiations around the unions of 1833 and 1847 and during the transatlantic battles that followed the collapse of the first union in 1840. They do not, for example, mention the connexional disputes that rocked the central governing body of British Wesleyanism – the Conference – in the 1830s.[1] John Moir quite rightly criticizes French for reducing the complex story of British Wesleyan and Canadian Methodist interaction to the view that "the clash between the Canadian party and the British party was evidence of a growing sense of Canadian self-awareness and identity by one side and an insensitivity to local issues and feelings on the other." Moir is somewhat more attuned than either French or Semple to the changing nature of British Wesleyanism during this period and to the critical and sometimes anomalous role that the British Wesleyan missionaries in Lower and Upper Canada played in the give-and-take world of colonial church governance. However, the picture that he presents does not probe either the wider British context or the process of cultural formation among the various groups involved in the conflicts that bedeviled Canadian Methodism during the second quarter of the nineteenth century.[2]

Since Goldwin French wrote in the 1960s, the history of Wesleyanism in Britain has been almost completely rewritten. The British Methodist scene, especially in the period between 1827 and 1852, is now best seen as one of violently clashing factions from the highest ministerial levels to the lowliest local Sunday school. All the groups caught up in the quarrels that divided the Wesleyan church had their own image of what it meant to be a Methodist. They also had a very good idea, in their own minds, of the way in which their opponents were threatening to destroy the heritage of John Wesley.[3] David Hempton, John Munsey Turner, and W.R. Ward also emphasize the impact that external actors and events had on the changing shape of British Wesleyanism, especially during the 1830s and 1840s. The Oxford Movement after 1833, the Disruption of the Church of Scotland in 1843, and Sir Robert Peel's Maynooth Grant in 1845 all found an echo within the Wesleyan connexion.[4] However, the place of the Wesleyans' overseas missions in the home connexion's "age of disunity" has never been addressed.[5] This is a surprising omission, given the strong missionary impulse that actuated the British Conference during much of the nineteenth century.[6]

This article is an attempt to place Canadian Methodism's period of upheaval between 1827 and 1854 in the wider context of British Wesleyanism's age of disunity and to analyze the impact of this relationship on questions of identity. This transatlantic perspective demonstrates the validity of Goldwin French's observation that the Canadian Methodists' post–1840 sense of self was sometimes expressed in terms of a British "outlook" or a British "spirit." However, French's overall argument, that the final product of union, disunion, and reunion was a more vigorous sense of Canadian nationality "freed ... from concern about metropolitan influences" needs to be rethought.[7] The outcome of that process was more complex. At one level, the battles fought between the British and Canada Conferences from 1827 to 1854 were about issues of church governance: who should lead and who should follow. They were also about who would define the meaning of Britishness and Wesleyanism in the north Atlantic world. The assumptions that, according to Eliga Gould, informed the first British Empire in America – British elites viewing the settler colonies as extensions of the home country and the settlers viewing their societies as so many replicas of Britain – did not cease to exist after 1783: they took on a new life among the Methodists of Britain and the Canadas. As was the case with the American revolutionaries and their British opponents and supporters, changing policies at the imperial centre gave rise to conflicting conceptions of British identity on both sides of the Atlantic.[8] For the British Wesleyans and the Canadian Methodists, however, the outcome of this conflict was the reconstitution of a mutually agreed upon definition of Britishness and Wesleyanism. Between 1847 and 1854, the leaders of both the British and Canada Conferences proceeded to impose that shared identity on all the colonial groups that fell under their purview. If there was a distinctly Canadian Methodist "self-awareness" by 1854, it was one cast in a British Wesleyan mould.

The attempt by the leadership of the Wesleyan Methodist Church in Britain to incorporate the Methodists of Upper Canada into their own connexion between 1828 and 1840 was part of a larger effort to stamp one particular vision of British and Wesleyan identity on both metropolitan and colonial Methodism. Drawn to Upper Canada by the sense that immigration was quickly turning that colony into an extension of the home country and connexion, the British Wesleyan leadership was troubled by the American and republican roots of many of the Canadian Methodist ministers and their often antagonistic relationship with the established Church of England. The leading British Wesleyans were determined to transform the Canadian preachers into what they considered proper Britons and Wesleyans – an identity based on a particularly conservative conception of both political loyalty and the doctrinal legacy of John Wesley. The Canadian Methodists, however, went into the union of 1833 with the belief that they already mirrored all that was good in British Wesleyanism: they were loyal subjects of the King and thoroughly orthodox followers of John Wesley, especially in terms of their opposition to church establishment. In August 1840 the union collapsed: a victim of one of the chief problems of transatlantic Britishness. A British and Wesleyan culture negotiated on the colonial periphery had rebounded on and now threatened to disrupt the connexional centre.[9]

What one British Wesleyan would eventually call "the wretched business of Canada" had its origins, then, in the internal conflicts of the home connexion.[10] Between 1827 and 1852 one group of ministers established a stranglehold over the governing machinery of the British Wesleyan church. They were the secretaries of the Wesleyan Methodist Missionary Society (the WMMS) and often either the president or secretary of the Conference.[11] At the centre of this clique stood Jabez Bunting, described by one of his critics as "great in mind, and great in influence – too great to be forgiven ... "[12] Between ten and twenty ministers followed Bunting's lead and made repeated efforts to elevate him into every available position of power within the connexion.[13] Chief among this "Buntingian Dynasty" were Robert Alder, John Beecham, Edmund Grindrod, John Hannah, Elijah Hoole, Thomas Jackson, George Marsden, Robert Newton, and Richard Watson.[14] Primarily, they were united not by what their detractors believed was a ravenous hunger for place and power, but by a view of what constituted or, at least, should constitute proper British Wesleyanism. As far as possible, a good British Wesleyan was supposed to be a Tory. Toryism, in this instance, was broadly defined as support for the established powers. In Buntingite eyes, there was little difference between campaigning for Conservative candidates in elections, celebrating the possible embarrassment or collapse of Whig and Liberal governments, supporting the exclusive privileges of the Church of England, and upholding the ministerial prerogative in the Wesleyan connexion itself.[15] In each case they believed that they were battling the forces of Jacobinical radicalism, first unleashed in the 1790s, and following the Biblical injunction to "fear ... the Lord and the king: and meddle not with them that are given to change."[16]

This is not to say that Bunting and his allies never saw a progressive idea that they did not hate. During their years of dominance in the connexion the Wesleyan Methodists were deeply involved in the antislavery movement and, in 1829, Bunting himself swung the church behind Catholic emancipation.[17] On some issues it was perfectly acceptable for both ministry and laity to agitate openly. For a sizable minority of preachers, however, those issues seemed far too few. There was little common ground between Joseph Beaumont, Joseph Fowler, Thomas Galland and other ministers on the liberal wing of the connexion and the Buntingites. During the second quarter of the century both the liberals and Tories in the ministry fought to make their respective candidates president of the Conference. Bunting and his supporters wanted to defend what they saw as the genuine heritage of John Wesley; Beaumont, Fowler, Galland, and the other connexional liberals were bent on reclaiming a Wesleyan heritage that they believed Buntingite centralization was destroying.[18] However, the most serious conflicts occurred between the Buntingian Dynasty and those connexional reformers who preferred to secede entirely rather than accept the implications of Wesleyan Toryism. These two groups – the Buntingites and the reformers – came to blows over one issue in particular in the 1830s: the former's support for the establishment principle.

Tensions within the British Wesleyan church flared up spectacularly in January 1832 when the minister Joseph Rayner Stephens began to call for the disestablishment of the Church of England.[19] In this he was one in a long line of preachers from John Wesley's day onward who wanted the Methodist connexion to take a more overtly dissenting position in regard to the church establishment. Wesley himself always resisted this trend among his coadjutors, seeking to find a comfortable if allusive *via media* between Church and nonconformity.[20] The Buntingites, therefore, felt themselves to be on firmly Wesleyan ground when they moved to silence Stephens. While never simply the slavish followers of Anglicanism, the Wesleyan Tories believed that the church establishment deserved their support: it was a means to a positive end. Ideally, it provided the basis for a national religion that shielded Britain from all the horrors of the "wide-spreading Atheism, Socialism, and Libertinism of the age."[21] Bunting thus contended that it was the duty of every Wesleyan Methodist "to maintain the most friendly feelings towards the Church, and to discountenance as far as we can ... that bitter and unchristian hostility" toward the establishment "which is now too much in fashion ... "[22]

Bunting went even further when the British Conference met in August 1834. Referring to Wesley's refusal to break with the Anglican communion, he asked rhetorically whether his fellow ministers ought to "arm themselves with pickaxes, and pull down the house in which our father [Wesley] was born, and in which he thought he died[?]" He categorically stated that "I will not mix with Methodism, unless the principle of maintaining our exact neutrality be this, not one inch nearer to, nor one inch further from the Church than we now are."[23] Despite receiving some support from Joseph Beaumont and other connexional liberals, Joseph Rayner Stephens was forced to resign from the ministry.[24] The WMMS's annual circular for 1834 summed up the Buntingite position on the whole affair. The Conference "could not consistently join in attempts to overthrow the National Establishment, considering that Mr Wesley to the end of his life avowed, and practically proved, his attachment to the Church of England." The Wesleyan connexion had to stop "the admission of the principles of Dissent among us."[25] This was a position that the Buntingian Dynasty intended not only to foster in the home connexion, but also to transplant to Methodist communities overseas.

Beginning in the late 1820s, Jabez Bunting and his supporters began to perceive a need to bring the American Methodists in Upper Canada under British Wesleyan suzerainty. In 1820, in order to avoid harmful collisions between the preachers of two Methodist connexions, the British Conference had agreed to confine its missionary operations in the Canadas to the lower province; the Methodist Episcopal Church in the United States had been given free rein in Upper Canada.[26] On a theoretical level, the British Wesleyans continued to regard themselves as "one" with their brethren in the American church. In actuality, however, the Buntingites were moving away from such transatlantic ecumenism. As Robert Alder made clear in his testimony before the House of Commons Select Committee on the Civil Government of Canada in 1828, the Wesleyan leadership did "not deem it right that the Methodists of Upper Canada should be under the jurisdiction of a foreign ecclesiastical body ... " A plan was in the works, Alder assured the committee, "by which the Methodists of

Upper Canada will be brought to act under the direction of the British Conference ... "[27] Alder himself had floated such a plan in the first weeks of 1828. His overall aim was to draw the Canadian Methodists away from their association with the American Methodist Episcopals or, indeed, from any thoughts of an independent existence. Instead, the Upper Canadians would be integrated into a greater British Wesleyan connexion on the same basis as the Irish Conference. Each year, a British preacher would be sent to Upper Canada to preside over the annual conference; the Canadian Methodists would advertise and sell British Wesleyan literature through their own magazine and Book Room; and the WMMS would grant a certain amount of money to the Canada Conference per annum for the support of its missions. This plan, Alder thought, would meet with the approval of all the Canadian Methodists in the province, except, of course, for those "incorrigible republicans" in their ranks.[28]

The Buntingites were entirely convinced that Methodism in Upper Canada needed to be grounded in Wesleyan Tory principles, which, to the Buntingites, were genuine British and Wesleyan principles. The WMMS felt sure that this was a course that would find favour with the "immense number of settlers which have gone out from Great Britain and Ireland, and are still flowing into the Province in large numbers every year ... "[29] These men and women were rapidly transforming Upper Canada into an extension of the home country and, having been British Wesleyans at home, "they naturally looked to the [Missionary] Committee to extend its care to them, and not leave them in destitution of the means of grace in a distant land ... "[30] The Buntingites also believed that these settlers and others were developing a keenly felt prejudice "against the acceptableness of the Canadian Brethren ... " This, Bunting and his supporters felt, was primarily the result of political attacks launched in the Canadian Methodists' official newspaper, the *Christian Guardian*, on the colonial government and the Church of England. Such partisan meddling in the civil affairs of Upper Canada "was not in the spirit or according to the practice of British Methodists; and contrary to the abstinence from such pursuits" which the WMMS required of its own agents overseas. It was also calculated to give offense to both the colonial and imperial governments.[31] To stop what they saw as the deterioration of Methodism in Upper Canada, doctrinally and politically, the Buntingites were willing to pour men and money into the colony. As one of secretaries of the WMMS, Richard Watson, put it in a letter to the imperial government, he and his fellow ministers would do their utmost both to "counteract anti-British feeling as it might rise up under the influence of a ministry foreign in its origin and too much impressed with the republican character" and to diffuse their own religious message throughout the province.[32]

The main obstacle to the unfolding of the Buntingite program in Upper Canada was the Canadian Methodist ministers themselves. In one area in particular, their image of John Wesley's heritage was markedly opposed to the Wesleyan Toryism of Bunting and his supporters. In 1826 and 1827 the Canadian Methodist preachers cut their teeth as a separate conference of the Methodist Episcopal Church in the United States in fierce combat with the colonial Church of England over what they perceived as the political illegitimacy and spiritual uselessness of a church establishment in Upper Canada.[33] By the early 1830s, now ministers of an entirely independent conference, the Canadian Methodists remained committed to opposing the establishment principle. This stance also shaped the Canadian preachers' opinion of the British Wesleyan connexion. When one of their number, George Ryerson, travelled overseas in 1831, he was unimpressed with the British Wesleyans' deference to Anglicanism. He was disgusted, he wrote, by "their servile & time serving clinging to the skirts of a corrupt, secularized & anti-Christian church." It was preferable, George Ryerson believed, "to bear the temporary censure of enemies in Canada, than the permanent evil & annoyance of having a Church & State" president of Conference from among the British Wesleyans.[34] Egerton Ryerson, George's younger brother, fervently believed that, in a colony where, he claimed, Methodists outnumbered Anglicans ten to one, the idea of erecting an established church was both inherently ridiculous and potentially divisive. The Canadian Methodists' ongoing battle with the Church of England, Ryerson argued in a letter to Richard Watson, was "a *necessary* act of defence for ourselves" and an important duty to the religious peace of the country.[35]

The Canadian Methodists also objected to any suggestion that they were somehow inherently less British than the Wesleyans in the home country. The sons of a United Empire Loyalist, the Ryerson brothers led the way. Testifying in 1828 before the House of Commons Select Committee on the Civil Government of Canada, George Ryerson specifically aimed to defend the British character of the Canada Conference. In an effort to sweep much of the connexion's American and often pro-republican past under the carpet, he noted that "all but four" of its ministers were "British subjects" either by birth or by naturalization.[36] The Canada connexion was also a body in which any British settler could and often did feel perfectly at home. According to Egerton Ryerson "[a]ll the [British Wesleyan] preachers in regular standing ... who have settled in this Province, have, on their arrival here, joined the Canada Connexion and have uniformly expressed their satisfactory conviction that Methodism is the same in U[pper] Canada as in Great Britain." The same remark could be made about the British Wesleyan laymen and women who had immigrated to the colony.[37] The conclusion was obvious: in July 1832 the leading ministers of the Canada connexion resolved that "as a large portion of the Canada Conference consists of Europeans, as the Methodist Societies from Great Britain, who have generally united with us, have uniformly expressed themselves satisfied with the economy of Methodism in Canada ... the influx of European emigration into this Province does not appear ... to render the organization of Methodist societies distinct from those already established expedient or advisable."[38] The only sure result of such an "appeal to *national* prejudices and feelings" would be the creation of divisions in the Methodist community in Upper Canada.[39]

Having to choose nevertheless between disruptions in their congregations and union with the British Wesleyans, the Canadian Methodist ministers decided to accept what they believed to be the lesser of two evils. In June 1832 four British Wesleyan missionaries arrived in York, the capital of Upper Canada, and were invited to meet with the Canadian preachers stationed in the city, including Egerton Ryerson and his brother John.[40] The *Christian Guardian* reported that "[t]he conversations which have taken place between members of the Methodist Conference and the Missionaries ... open up ... a cheering prospect to the interests of Wesleyan Methodism in Upper Canada": that prospect being "the incorporation of the whole into a common system of Christian conquest upon a common principle – and under a common management ... "[41] Egerton and John Ryerson were determined to avoid conflicts between the two conferences, even if that meant placing their connexion under the direction of the Wesleyans in Britain.[42] In the event, that is exactly what it did mean. Initially drawn up by the Canadian Methodists in consultation with Robert Alder and then revised by Jabez Bunting and Alder in Britain, the Articles of Union followed the general pattern that the latter had suggested in 1828.[43] They placed the Canadians in the same position vis-à-vis the British Wesleyans as the Irish Methodist connexion.[44] The Canadian Methodists would adopt "the Discipline, Economy, and Form of Church Government in general of the Wesleyan Methodists in England"; all new candidates for the itinerancy would be adopted according to British Wesleyan usage; all the Canadian Methodist ministers would be ordained by imposition of hands, as was done in the British Conference; the British Wesleyans reserved the right to send one of their own ministers to serve as the president of the Canada Conference; and in exchange for stable funding, all the missions to the Native Americans and "destitute settlers" were to fall under the WMMS's control.[45] The union of 1833 was more a matter of absorption than an agreement between equals.

Despite the fact that the terms of the union satisfied much of their agenda, the Buntingites quickly developed concerns over its actual operation. They realized that their attempt to incorporate the Canadians into a larger British Wesleyan world might well prove to be a double-edged sword. It threatened to bring Canadian Methodist ideas and practices into the British connexion. On 8 March 1834, Bunting wrote to the British-appointed president of the Canada Conference, Edmund Grindrod, noting that "[s]ome changes must be made in the plan of Union, or at least in the practical administration of it, in order to secure any decidedly beneficial result."[46] The president of the British Conference, George Marsden, agreed, noting that "the future prosperity of Methodism in British North America, depends much on the foundation being well laid."[47] Marsden met with Bunting, Grindrod, John Beecham, and Robert Alder in Sheffield in early April to discuss the alterations they felt were needed in the Articles of Union.[48] Above all else, the *Christian Guardian* had to become a wholly religious journal, avoiding all political controversy.[49] The cost to the British Wesleyan reputation at home would be too high if the Canadian Methodists continued on their anti-establishment course. As Bunting put it in late April 1834, "I own I do still fear that the political feelings of many of the Upper Canadian Methodists, unless it can be very greatly softened & neutralized, will make it impossible that *we* can long very satisfactorily identify our character with theirs."[50] After 1833, the Buntingite aim was to fix the Canada Conference firmly within a Wesleyan Tory framework as much to protect the interests and reputation of British Wesleyanism at home as to redeem Canadian Methodism itself.

Over the next six years, the Buntingian Dynasty's efforts to put their own stamp on Methodism in Upper Canada proved unsuccessful. Given the different positions of the British Wesleyans and the Canadian Methodists on church establishment, the Buntingites' lack of success was hardly surprising. The Canada Conference would not let the issue alone. In 1839 the Canadian ministry vowed to make the *Christian Guardian* into a purely "religious and literary Journal" but then defined church establishment as a matter of "religious politics."[51] The Canadian Methodists pledged loyalty to the forms of British Wesleyanism approved by the WMMS; they also, however, called for an end to what they saw as the anomalous position of the Church of England in Upper Canada: it had to be disestablished.[52]

The WMMS sent Robert Alder to Upper Canada in early 1839 in a final attempt to save the union from "the political and antichristian character" assumed by the Canadian connexional press toward the church establishment.[53] This stance was causing trouble in Britain. As the president of the British Conference put it in a letter to the secretary of the Canada Conference, "[t]he advocacy in the *Christian Guardian* ... of the principles of strict and systematic dissent, in opposition to all religious establishments, has given deep and just offence to many of our best friends in England ... " "If the *Guardian* persist in the course which it has sometime pursued," Thomas Jackson added, "the Union of the two Conferences can no longer be maintained."[54] Once in Upper Canada, Alder made it clear that, from a Buntingite point of view, the spirit of John Wesley still pervaded the British Conference "and that, in every sense compatible with the ecclesiastical independence of Methodism, the Wesleyan community stand in friendly relation to the established Church of England ... " This was a view "maintained by the Connexion during every period of its history" and especially since the withdrawal of Joseph Rayner Stephens. On behalf of Bunting and his allies, Alder demanded silence on the establishment issue in the *Christian Guardian* in order to "prevent that form of Methodism in Upper Canada with which, by the union, the character of the Methodism of Great Britain is identified from being involved '*in suspicion and contempt*' ... "[55] Canadian Methodism threatened to have more of an impact on British Wesleyan identity than the other way around.

In this respect, the course pursued by Egerton Ryerson between 1833 and 1839 almost seemed calculated to exacerbate British Wesleyan fears. During the first year of the union, Ryerson tried to transform the Buntingites into supporters of the Canadian Methodist campaign against the established church. He argued in 1833 that "[a]s to cordiality of feeling between Methodism and the Establishment, there is not much of it in general" in Britain. He repeated this wishful thought in 1838, stating that, though they were supportive of the establishment at home, the British Wesleyan leaders laughed "at the lofty and exclusive pretensions" of the Anglican church in Upper Canada. The fact that this was manifestly untrue caused Ryerson to change tack in mid-1838. He began to elaborate a British and Wesleyan identity independent of the Buntingian Dynasty. He seized what, for Methodists, was almost unassailable high ground, basing the Canadian Methodist opposition to colonial Anglicanism on a combination of the 1747 *Minutes* of the British Conference, John Wesley's own lack of support for national establishments in his published writings, and the works of William Blackstock and William Paley. He also bluntly stated that the Canadian Methodists' "loyalty is beyond impeachment – they love and honour their Sovereign – they revere and defend the British

Constitution." There was more than one way to be both a loyal Briton and a good Wesleyan. Ryerson stressed that his fellow Canadian Methodists had fought on the side of colonial government during the rebellions of 1837 and 1838 and yet still supported the position of the *Christian Guardian* on the establishment issue.[56]

When Ryerson appealed over the head of the British-appointed president of the Canada Conference to the Governor General for a solution to the establishment question, British Wesleyan patience reached its breaking point. In 1839, the British connexion drew up a series of charges denouncing Ryerson for his anti-establishment campaign.[57] The majority of the Canadian preachers repudiated those charges and dispatched Ryerson and his brother William to Britain to settle the outstanding issues between the two churches.[58] The Canadian troubles were quite literally coming home to roost.

It was unfortunate, then, for the future of the union that the Buntingian Dynasty's fears of transatlantic infection were progressively bolstered in the late 1830s by letters and reports from the British Wesleyan missionaries stationed in Lower and Upper Canada. Joseph Stinson, for one, was afraid that unless the provinces received a greater infusion of British Wesleyan preachers and influence, the union between the two connexions might degenerate into "a mere farce and greatly injure the British Conference and all lovers of British Methodism ... "[59] He was also alarmed at "the *bare possibility* of the British Conference being in the least degree identified" with the anti-establishmentarianism of the Canadian connexion. He strongly suspected that the Ryersons had entered the union with the ultimate aim of excluding "British influence" and using "the good name of the British conference to accomplish their own ambitions & selfish purposes."[60] Stinson was supported in such views by his fellow ministers.[61] Unity was what was needed, but unity on metropolitan terms; and if that could not be achieved, it would be better to cut the Canadian Methodists loose.[62] "[S]urely," Stinson stated to Thomas Jackson, "that policy which is right in one part of the Empire cannot be wrong in another part of the Empire ... " "[I]f the British Conference would maintain their own consistency & honour – they must either dissolve the *nominal* union which now exists or bring the Canadian Preachers as completely under their control" as the missionaries in Lower Canada, forcing them to accept church establishment.[63] Matthew Richey stated even more bluntly that "[t]he attempt to protract the union can only humiliate ourselves." "In the honour of true Methodism," he added, "& for the sake of the Cause of God, let something be done & done *quickly.*"[64]

None of the parties that converged on Newcastle-upon-Tyne for the British Conference of 1840 was in a mood to compromise. The British

Wesleyan leadership did not trust Egerton Ryerson, believing that
"[h]is teachings are in want of faith."[65] They felt that it would be a valuable exercise to preserve "sound Wesleyan Methodism" in Upper Canada, but not at the cost of abandoning the original Wesleyan Tory aims
of the union and allowing "Egerton Ryerson, or his family" to lord it
over the British connexion.[66] This position was reflected in the initial
treatment that Egerton and William Ryerson received when they
arrived in Newcastle: they were given what was, in Egerton Ryerson's
view, "a very cool reception from several of the preachers ... "[67]
Though the Canadian delegates pressed for an opportunity to address
the entire Conference on the union issue at once, they were ushered
into a special committee, dominated by the Buntingites and including
a recently arrived Joseph Stinson and Matthew Richey.[68] Behind
closed doors, the British ministers and missionaries determined that
the representatives of the Canada Conference had failed to establish
any justification for their connexion's continuing refusal to adopt British Wesleyan practices and policies. If the union was to continue, this
situation had to be rectified. As the official organ of Canadian Methodism, the *Christian Guardian* would have to "admit and maintain all the
acknowledged principles of the Wesleyan Methodist Connexion," by
which the members of the committee meant "that principle of our
Body, which asserts it to be the duty of the civil Government to employ
their influence ... for the support of Christian religion."[69]

The final act of the union was played out in front of the entire British Conference. It placed the transatlantic nature of the dispute
between the two connexions in stark relief. Egerton Ryerson made "a
speech enormously long" in defence of his own character and that of
the Canadian ministry.[70] After listening to this "strange medley" for
ten hours, Robert Alder noted that "[t]he Union is not yet dissolved
but it is passing away."[71] That was a very good thing from his point of
view; it would end all danger of British Wesleyanism being infected
with the anti-establishment tendencies of the Canada Conference.
"Unhappily," Alder said, "in this case it is our principles that are at
stake. With the prevailing party in Upper Canada, whose organ is the
Guardian, the mission of Methodism is not to cry 'Ye must be born
again'; but they think they are called to lay the foundations of political
government." Jabez Bunting responded with equal firmness to Egerton Ryerson's claim that the Canadian ministry should be allowed a
wide degree of local autonomy within the union. The thing was impossible: "[o]n great public matters we must merge our opinions. We cannot let the Connexion be committed to a violation of principles which
the Conference has affirmed." The Ryerson brothers, in turn, did not
believe that their fellow ministers in Upper Canada would accept a

Wesleyan Tory position on church establishment. As William Ryerson put it, "[i]n the Old Country an Established Church is good; it is not suitable to ours."[72] The union was dissolved by a vote of 38 to 13.[73]

That could have been the end of it. Before leaving Britain, however, the Ryerson brothers rushed into print with an excoriating pamphlet in defence of the Canada Conference.[74] A little under two weeks later, the WMMS, with the aid of Joseph Stinson, determined that "our ... operations in Upper Canada should be carried on for the future ... "[75] The stage was set for a major battle between the British and Canada Conferences.

Between 1840 and 1847 the Canadian Methodists further elaborated a British and Wesleyan identity in order to resist British Wesleyan hegemony.[76] This cultural development stemmed from the sheer ferocity of the conflict between the Canada Conference and the Buntingites and their agents in the colonies. That level of viciousness, in turn, was linked to the continuing transatlantic nature of the dispute: this was very much a civil war, splitting both connexions and compelling every party involved to further sharpen their own self-perception as loyal Britons and orthodox Wesleyans. In their efforts to ward off the charges of doctrinal apostasy and political disloyalty levelled against them by the British Wesleyan missionaries in the Canadas, the Canadian Methodists, like other settler groups in those colonies and across the British Empire, eventually found themselves claiming to be as British as the British themselves, if not more so.[77]

The Buntingite response to the Canada connexion between 1840 and 1845 was most notable for its intransigence. Short of unconditional surrender by the Canadian Methodists, the British Conference would not even consider making terms. In 1842, when the Canadian Methodists requested Joshua Soule, one of the bishops of the Methodist Episcopal Church in the United States, to act as an arbitrator between the estranged connexions, the British Wesleyan leadership refused the offer, judging it "inexpedient."[78] Two years later, the Buntingites declared that, while in theory they were always ready to consider reunification, they could not "entertain proposals for forming such a union as would identify us with them [the Canadian Methodists] until they are prepared to place themselves under the jurisdiction of this Conference, and so become, in truth and reality, one with us ... "[79] Such inflexibility was to be expected from the Buntingian Dynasty. Their vision of what constituted true British Wesleyanism came under increasingly heavy attack in the early 1840s. Between 1841 and 1843 alone, Bunting and his supporters came to blows with the liberals in the Conference over whether it was proper to wear the Geneva gown while preaching, over whether teetotal meetings should be allowed in Wesleyan chapels, and over the authorship and publication of the *Wesleyan Takings*, a series of anonymous, hostile pen portraits of Buntingite ministers. These disputes only increased the Buntingites' attachment to their own view of connexional identity. All "tattle about organic changes originates with the devil," Bunting declared. In 1842, the connexion suffered a decrease of 2,065 members and Bunting made "a most extraordinary speech on the importance of submission to Conference." The Buntingites also continued to speak in favour of the principle of church establishment. They refused to yield so much as an inch to any of their growing number of opponents.[80] The Canadian Methodists were included among this group.

It did not help that Canadian Methodism played a direct role in the British connexional warfare of the 1840s. The collapse of the union gave the liberals in the British Wesleyan ministry another stick with which to beat the Buntingian Dynasty. At the Conference of 1840, Joseph Fowler and Thomas Galland defended the Ryerson brothers from the "intemperance of language" of Bunting and his supporters.[81] Joseph Beaumont, in moving for dissolution, denounced Buntingite hegemony in the Canadas. He maintained that "there is just as much reason in the Canada Conference sending Presidents to us as for us to send Presidents to them; and they are just as competent to manage their own affairs, as we are to manage ours."[82] An older minister, Thomas Ludlam, took his opposition to Buntingism even further. He wrote a letter of support to the Canada Conference.[83] One of the few preachers at the Conference of 1834 who voted in support of Joseph Rayner Stephens, Ludlam accused the connexional leadership of acting in a thoroughly ungodly, unmethodistical way in supporting church establishment above transatlantic unity.[84] The liberals within the connexion were on the attack.

A hostile British press joined in the fray. This was especially so in the case of the London *Patriot*, which, as John Beecham put it, was soon "feasting away on Egerton [Ryerson]'s Pamphlet."[85] In response, the unofficial newspaper of the Buntingites, the *Watchman*, defended the connexion's history of arraying "itself against that party ... whose dearest object is to injure, and, if possible, to overthrow the National Church of this Realm, as an Establishment."[86] In three letters to the *Patriot*, Robert Alder fought back against "misstatements and misrepresentations designed to damage the character of the British Conference."[87] Things, however, only went from bad to worse. Copies of the *Christian Guardian* crossed the Atlantic. Pamphlets supporting the Canada Conference and violently assailing the Buntingites were published in London and circulated through the connexion. Egerton

Ryerson might argue that the Canadian Methodists could hardly be blamed if "some numbers" of their connexional newspaper had been sent to Britain, but, at the same time, he hoped that the circulation of newspapers and pamphlets from Upper Canada would "continue to increase until the removal of its causes shall supersede its necessity."[88] This direct intervention in the internal affairs of British Wesleyanism only increased the ire of Bunting and his supporters. Robert Alder condemned "the libelous attacks from the pen of Mr Egerton Ryerson ... and others – which are forwarded to this Country for the unworthy but vain purpose of promoting distrust and disunion in our connexion ... " Until they ended, there could be no talk of peace, much less of reunion.[89] War á outrance was the order of the day.

The British Wesleyan missionaries and laity in Lower and Upper Canada were the main players in the Buntingite campaign against the Canada Conference. Their approach to that role and the zeal with which they played it, however, were shaped by more than unconditional loyalty to the Buntingite vision of proper British Wesleyanism. After the dissolution of the union, they were also actuated by the fear that the wmms was on the verge of abandoning its congregations in the Canadas.[90] It was a reasonable apprehension: after all, the wmms had given up its missions in Upper Canada twenty years earlier when faced with competition from the American Methodists. The missionaries and their lay supporters responded to this perceived threat by emphasizing their own identity as Britons and Methodists. They deployed a rhetoric which was meant to position them as the one true offshoot of the home connexion in the Canadas, which the British Conference was obliged to aid and protect for the sake of God and empire. The laymen and women of Toronto and Kingston, for instance, pointed to the large numbers of British Wesleyan emigrants who had settled in Upper Canada and who wanted to continue under the home connexion's oversight. They stressed their "attachment to the Ministers, rules and doctrines" of British Wesleyanism and called for no compromise whatsoever with the Canada Conference.[91] The missionaries took up the same strain. "[T]he Loyal people of Canada," Thomas Fawcett stated, "do not wish to be separated from the Parent-Country either civilly or ecclesiastically."[92] The British Wesleyans in the Canadas were determined to prevent both those eventualities.

With that end in view, the missionaries openly attacked Canadian Methodism as a threat to British and Wesleyan identity in Upper Canada. The methods they used can best be gathered from the connexional newspaper that they established as the union began to shake itself to pieces in the summer of 1840. First published in Montreal, the *Wesleyan* had "upwards of 1100 subscribers" by October.[93] In the third issue, the editor, Robert Lusher, noted that though he and his fellow missionaries could not "recognize as truly Wesleyan, in every instance, the principles which have been adopted, and the policy which has been pursued by the [*Christian*] *Guardian*, especially during the last three years," they did not wish to be either its "Censor or Antagonist." They wanted to maintain the "friendly relation" with the Canada Conference that was supposed to exist between two branches of John Wesley's church. By its eighth issue, however, the *Wesleyan* was in full cry against Canadian Methodism, denouncing the "anti-British and anti-Wesleyan" Methodism of "at least the leaders of the Upper Canada Conference" and declaring their own "unqualified abhorrence of the course which the Rev. E[gerton] Ryerson, and those of his friends, who act with him, seem determined to pursue ... " In an attempt to widen the assault on the Canada connexion, Matthew Richey contributed an article describing the missionaries' "incipient struggles with those who are inveterately opposed to the existence in the Province of a British Wesleyan ministry" and noting that this "opposition is shrewdly suspected ... to be rather intimately allied to a sensitive dislike of every thing British ... "[94] The Canadian Methodists were opposed to true British Wesleyanism and therefore to all things British.

This discursive strategy continued to be the stock-in-trade of the *Wesleyan* after it moved to Toronto in mid–1841. In the prospectus for the second volume, the new editors, Matthew Richey and John G. Manly, adopted a more blatantly political line, promising to "teach and enforce the principles of sound and scriptural loyalty to the noblest of earthly Governments – the Government of Great Britain." In this, the *Wesleyan* would be conforming to the practice of the "venerated Parent Connexion, and be, therefore, at once *British* and *Wesleyan*," two things, the editors implied, that the Canada Conference was not. Like the Buntingites at home, the missionaries and their lay supporters venerated the "Glorious Constitution both in Church and State, under which as Britons we have the happiness to live – and our constant aim ... is, to maintain inviolable, and support to the utmost of our power, the Altar and the Throne." Here was the very stuff of Wesleyan Toryism. It would be "one of the heaviest calamities with which this magnificent country could be visited," an article in a later issue noted, if it were deprived "of the ministrations and institutions of pure, primitive, loyal, uncorrupted, British Methodism. The hearts of the people are at all points prepared to hail its approach, and rejoice in its light."[95] The implication here, of course, was that, while the people in the colony were redeemable, the Canada Conference itself was hopelessly impure, worldly, disloyal, and corrupt. The heavy brigades of

British Wesleyanism were well and truly in the field. The difficulty the Buntingites would face, by the late 1840s, would be reining them in.

In the meantime, the reaction of the Buntingites and their missionary allies to the dissolution of the union created a genuine crisis for Canadian Methodism. In Britain, Wesleyan ministers were not above poaching ministers from competing Methodist denominations.[96] Those concerned with the Canadas took active steps to draw preachers away from the Canada connexion, arguing that it would "greatly weaken the Ryerson influence & in promoting this we are doing service to the cause of religion" in the colonies.[97] By the time the Canadian ministers met at their annual Conference in June 1841, fifteen of their fellows had deserted the church and joined a newly constituted British Wesleyan missionary district for Upper Canada.[98] Most of these preachers needed no urging from the WMMS to make the move. They departed the Conference pledging friendship, but also publicly complaining about "pledges broken by Mr [Egerton] Ryerson" and expressing dissatisfaction with the proceedings of the Canada connexion.[99] They took their twin messages of discontent and purified Britishness and Wesleyanism to the major centres of both British settlement and Methodist strength in the province, including Hamilton, London, and Toronto.[100] The results were unhappy ones, as far as the remaining Canadian Methodist ministers were concerned. By mid-1841, they recorded the loss of approximately 525 members to the British Wesleyan missionaries spread across ten circuits.[101] Though not crippling, such losses were extremely vexing for a church that measured gospel success almost entirely in terms of membership. At the Conference of 1842, the Canadian ministers denounced the "schisms and divisions" being created in their societies by the agents of British Wesleyanism as "causeless, unmethodistic and unjustifiable" and completely at variance with the ideal of Methodist "oneness" that the WMMS had embraced in 1820.[102] This reaction to missionary activity in Upper Canada was characteristic of the Canada connexion's overall response to the crisis that it faced in the early 1840s.

Under the pressure of events, the Canadian Methodists fervently argued that it was the British Wesleyans, both in Upper Canada and on the other side of the Atlantic, who were betraying the heritage of John Wesley. The Canada Conference, they stated, was more purely Wesleyan than either the Buntingites or the missionaries in the colonies. In October 1840 the Canadian ministers accused the British Wesleyan leadership of unilaterally wrecking the union and so violating those "Wesleyan and Scriptural principles" still upheld by the Canada connexion.[103] They also staked a claim to being as orthodox as the British connexion in terms of their regular doctrine and discipline, both of which, they pointed out, had been recognized as "truly Wesleyan" by their fathers and brethren in the home country while the union lasted. On the issue of church establishment, the Canadian Methodist position was equally clear and, to their minds, uncompromisingly Wesleyan. The ministers would not be advocates for the establishment principle in Upper Canada, "especially," they resolved, "as Mr Wesley himself and his Conference regarded a National Church as having no ground in the New Testament, but as being 'a merely political Institution.'"[104]

By June 1841 the Canadian Methodists were even more keen on defending their identity as unsullied Methodists. Meeting in Conference, the preachers denounced both the Buntingian Dynasty and their missionary agents in Upper Canada for contravening John Wesley's strictures against schism and his idea of worldwide Methodist "oneness." The missionaries, in particular, were performing "*un*-missionary work" and creating all the "evils of schism, strife, and division" among the Canadian Methodist congregations. A year later the Canada Conference levelled its guns at the WMMS, declaring that it was a violator of "the sacred principles of Methodist unity."[105] The Canada connexion, in contrast, refrained from invading the missionary congregations in Lower Canada from 1841 onward.[106] The not so subtle subtext here was that, if anyone was falling into worldly declension, it was the British Wesleyans and not the Canadian Methodists. Despite being buffeted from all sides by those who ought to have been their allies, the latter were remaining true to the old gospel paths first blazed by John and Charles Wesley. They were uncorrupted Wesleyans transplanted in Upper Canada.

The Canadian Methodists were also New World Britons. In October 1840 they revived and elaborated on a claim they had first made in the early 1830s, stating that their connexion was "as much a British Wesleyan Conference as the Conference held in England."[107] The ministry expanded on this point in an attempt to minimize the inroads that the British Wesleyan missionaries were making in the church's membership. The Ryerson brothers were the first into the breach, arguing, as they had ten years before, that British immigrants were perfectly at home in the Canada connexion. In their *Report* on their mission to Britain, Egerton and William Ryerson stated that "the *Old Country* part of the members of our Church were the most forward and ardent" in their support of the editorial policies of the *Christian Guardian*. That newspaper, they claimed, had received memorials denouncing the interference of the WMMS in Canadian Methodist affairs from areas where "the official members of our church were almost entirely emigrants from Great Britain and Ireland." These men and women, free-born Britons one and all, knew "how to appreciate their rights and privileges on the Western, as well as on the Eastern side of the Atlantic ... "[108] This was more than desperate propaganda. Henry Mayle, a British emigrant settled near Brantford, denounced the British Wesleyans' failure to understand that Upper Canadians would never accept "a dominant Church party nor Tory ascendancy." By trying to foist both church establishment and Conservative hegemony on the colony, the British Conference was engaged in "nothing less than a factious opposition to the liberal views about to be carried out in Canada by Her Majesty's Government ... "[109] The Canadian Methodists, in contrast, were paragons of British loyalty.

The Canadian Methodists' adoption of a self-consciously British identity found its most forceful expression in two articles – "A Voice from Canada" and "A Second Voice from Canada" – that appeared in the *Christian Guardian* in December 1840 and February 1841. They were written by George Playter, a minister who grew up among the Wesleyans in Britain, emigrated to Lower Canada in 1832, joined the itinerancy in Upper Canada two years later, and who, when the union between the British Wesleyan and Canada connexions collapsed in 1840, decided to side with the latter.[110] In these articles Playter addressed the Buntingites as both a "countryman" and as "a Wesleyan Minister." From the vantage point of this dual identity he attacked the missionaries' attempts to identify themselves as Britons to the exclusion of all others: "'*British, British, British*,'" the missionaries said, "and their tongues never tire in uttering, nor their ears of hearing, nor their pens in writing '*British, British, British*.'" To state that a person was British because he or she was connected with the British Conference was no more than a sophistic sleight of hand. "The name," Playter argued, "does not bestow the attributes of character, but the attributes of character the name." Addressing the wmms directly, he continued, "Monopolizing the name to your party, is insinuating a denial of it to ours. However, while we are more careful about the character than the term, we are consoled with the fact, that as your agents did not bestow, neither can they remove, that 'good name which is rather to be chosen than great riches.'" The Canadian Methodists, in Playter's view, had proven their British identity through their actions. The Wesleyans in the colony and in the home country, in contrast, were undeserving of the designation British; they only used it in an "insinuating" and "mean" way to attack those who ought to have been their gospel co-workers in the Canadian ministry.[111]

This self-image was adopted by the Canada connexion as a whole. At their 1841 Conference, the ministry offered Playter its "cordial thanks" for his "able and admirable papers in defense" of their church.[112] Indeed, even before the publication of the second "Voice from Canada," Canadian Methodists began to argue that, when it came to the meaning of Britishness, they had nothing to learn from either the Buntingites or the missionaries in Lower and Upper Canada. They firmly believed that the laity's "British affection is beyond a just impeachment" and that they themselves were "more ... British at the present time than the leading members of the British Conference and the Missionary Committee are." The laymen and women on the Barrie Mission came at the same point from the opposite angle, arguing that "the conduct of those calling themselves British Missionaries" was both "[a]nti-British" and "without principle ... " A year later, one self-declared member of the Canada Conference combined these two statements of British identity: "one of the greatest obstacles to the civil and religious prosperity of our country is the unholy strife occasioned by our British [Wesleyan] brethren. Canada might now have been something beside a British Province, if native Canadians had not spilt so much blood in its defence."[113] Unlike the missionaries or their Buntingite leaders, Canadian Methodists were staunch supporters of a united and peaceful British Empire. In effect, they had transformed themselves into greater Britons, superior in their cultural purity to the British Wesleyans in the Canadas and across the sea.

There were, then, several competing and antithetical British and Wesleyan identities in existence among the Buntingites, the Canadian Methodists, and the British missionaries and their lay supporters in Lower and Upper Canada by the early 1840s. Yet, in 1846–47, the Canada and British Wesleyan connexions agreed to reunite. And, strange to say, the terms of the union of 1847 were almost exactly the same as those of 1833 – granting overall authority to the British Conference.[114] There was one important departure from the terms of 1833; even this, however, was no triumph for Canadian Methodist autonomy. The new Articles of Union created the post of co-delegate: a minister who would take charge of the administrative affairs of the Canada connexion if the British-appointed president was unable to spend a whole year in the colony. This vice president could be either a Canadian or British Wesleyan preacher, though the final say on the appointment rested, as always, with the British connexion.[115] According to John Carroll, Canadian Methodism's most gifted nineteenth-century historian, the explanation for the union of 1847 lay in changes in British Wesleyanism itself. Carroll described Jabez Bunting admitting to Egerton Ryerson that "in some respects, with regard to public questions, the Canadians had been 'right,' and they [the British Wesleyans] had been 'wrong.'"[116] In contrast, in 1847, Robert Alder told his fellow British Wesleyan ministers that he had found "a total change in the

Canadian Conference since 1839."[117] There was some truth behind each of these quotations. Cultural and structural changes in both British Wesleyanism and Canadian Methodism created the conditions necessary for the union of 1847. The leading figures in the two connexions came together around a broader, more inclusive British and Wesleyan identity and, in the seven years after the reunion, attempted to tame the more militant identity that had taken shape among the British missionaries and their lay supporters.

The period between 1840 and 1847 witnessed the collapse of Wesleyan Tory exclusiveness among the Buntingites. The Disruption of the Church of Scotland in 1843 forced Jabez Bunting and his supporters to rethink their overall position on church establishments. In May 1843, Thomas Chalmers led 454 of his fellow evangelical ministers out of the General Assembly of the Church of Scotland and founded the Free Kirk. The issue at stake here was the right of the state to intrude in the internal affairs of the church, especially around the question of whether lay patrons should have the ability to force ministers on certain parishes. In 1834, the Scottish courts ruled that wealthy laymen did possess that right, much to the dismay of Chalmers and his fellow non-intrusionists. When the civil courts began to interfere with the Church's own courts in 1842, the breaking point was reached; the Free Kirkers determined to forge a national religion outside the pale of the Scottish church establishment.[118] The Buntingites supported the Scottish evangelicals even before the Disruption occurred, joining with others in 1843 to invite Chalmers to London to give a series of lectures discussing "whether it is *practicable* to carry out the *principle* of a Church Establishment without destroying the *spiritual* independence of the Church."[119] Bunting answered the question himself at that year's British Conference, stating, in the wake of the schism, that he had once hoped that "such a thing was possible as a Established Church without State interference. But now I see it to be impossible. I wish two thousand clergymen would leave the English Church in the same way" that the Free Kirkers had.[120] Though the Buntingites were unwilling to join with militant Dissent in an anti-establishmentarian assault on the Church of England, they readily attacked the practice of church establishment while still paying lip service to the principle.[121] The *Watchman* summed up the new position of the Buntingian Dynasty early in 1844, stating that "there is no Established Church in existence on behalf of which, as it now stands, we could conscientiously contend."[122]

The Buntingite view of the Church of England itself also underwent a major shift in the 1840s. Bunting and his supporters were reacting to the rise and progress of the Oxford Movement. The Movement began

in 1833 when, in response to the Irish Church Temporalities Bill of
Lord Grey's Whig government, the Anglican minister John Keble
preached a sermon in St Mary's Church, Oxford, on "national apostasy," denouncing the erastianism of the Church of England. Keble was
soon joined in his campaign for Church independence by three other
Oxford men: Richard Hurrell Froude, Edward Pusey, and John Henry
Newman. In the fall of 1833, they began to publish a series of *Tracts for
the Times*, aimed at reforming what they saw as the corruption of Anglicanism at the hands of English politicians and evangelical ministers
and bishops. In these essays, Keble and his fellows emphasized the writings of the Church Fathers against the usual Protestant and evangelical
reliance on the Scriptures alone. To most evangelicals the Tractarians
seemed to be drifting in the direction of Popery by the early 1840s.[123]
Methodism itself came in for direct attack by the Tractarians in Edward
Pusey's 1842 *Letter to the Archbishop of Canterbury*. Pusey denounced the
Wesleyans for making justification by faith into a heretical justification
by feelings. According to this Oxford don, the Wesleyans substituted
class meetings and love feasts for the genuine sacraments. Pusey
argued that, for Methodists, the state of one's feelings had become
more important than following the Ten Commandments.[124] That such
an attack should come from within the ranks of the established church
was particularly shocking to Buntingite sensibilities.

The Buntingian Dynasty turned on the Church of England with all
the zeal that it had once used in its defence. In 1841, the same year
that Newman wrote *Tract* 90, demonstrating that Anglicanism's Thirty-
Nine Articles were not inconsistent with Roman Catholic doctrine,
Bunting made the extraordinary statement that "[n]o person on earth
or in heaven ... can reconcile Methodism with High Churchism."
"Unless the Church of England will protest against Puseyism in some
intelligible form," he continued, "it will be the duty of Methodism to
protest against the Church of England."[125] That is exactly what the
British Wesleyan Conference set out to do. In 1842 the Buntingite
Thomas Jackson wrote a pamphlet in reply to Pusey's *Letter to the Archbishop of Canterbury*. Jackson assailed High Churchmen for their love of
an effete religion "adorned with gold lace and ostrich feathers" and
accused Pusey himself of seeking a union between the Church of England and Roman Catholicism.[126] Wesleyans, the *Watchman* stated in
November 1842, refused to trifle with an Anglican revival of Popish
superstition.[127] They preferred to align themselves with other strictly
evangelical churches to combat resurgent Roman Catholicism in organizations like the British and Foreign School Society or the violently
anti-Catholic Evangelical Alliance.[128] Under such circumstances,
co-operation with the Canadian Methodists could hardly be refused.

The preface to the new Articles of Union, written in Britain by a committee of the WMMS, made that clear. In a period "when Evangelical Denominations are exemplifying a pervading and earnest desire to manifest their oneness in Christ, and thus will away the reproach which for so many ages has attached to the division and mutual acrimony of the Protestant Church, it is extremely desirable that the unseemly differences which ... have unhappily existed between the two Branches of the Wesleyan Methodists in Western Canada ... should terminate ... "[129] Among the British Wesleyan leadership, support for both the Church of England and the establishment principle had been effectively eliminated as components of proper Britishness and Wesleyanism by 1846. Under such circumstances, reunion became a viable alternative to continuing factiousness.

The British Wesleyan missionary Joseph Stinson shared this outlook. A change of opinion in regard to both the politics of the Canada Conference and the establishment principle in the late 1830s and 1840s allowed him to become the chief advocate of reunion in Britain. Observing the progress of several prominent connexional reformers through Sheffield in 1846, Stinson could not understand why "we should be so distant with the poor sinners" in Upper Canada when "*greater sinners* amongst us at Home are cherished and allowed to occupy the high places of our connexion." "We have been too thin skinned about Canadian whiggism," Stinson told Robert Alder, "we have to endure plenty of it in England – lank, straight haired whiggery."[130] A mild form of political liberalism should not disbar the Canadian Methodists from membership in the British Wesleyan family. Neither should their approach to church establishment. Stinson began to turn on the idea of unconditional support for the Church of England in 1838 while still in Upper Canada. He complained of the unwillingness of Anglican ministers to do Wesleyanism "*common justice*" in the colony and how, in his estimation "they patronize *Popery* ... at the expense of Methodism ... " Methodism, Stinson now believed, should be put on an equal footing with the Church of England and become in "all intents & purposes an *Establishment* ... "[131] By May 1842 Stinson was even more convinced that the Anglicans cared "just as little about us [the British Wesleyans] as they do about the Canadian Methodists & if they could sweep us all out of the Province they would do so with a good will."[132] This was very vexing after all the support that the British Wesleyans had given the establishment principle down the years. In Sheffield, in 1844, Stinson explicitly tied his new view of the Church of England to the issue of reunion, arguing that "[t]he aspects of the times at home and abroad surely are plainly indicating that our very existence as a church depends in no small degree upon our unity, particularly in Canada where Popery & Puseyism are likely to attain Gigantic Power."[133]

A wing of the Canada connexion was also progressively more open to the idea of co-operation with the British Wesleyans on British Wesleyan terms after 1840. As he had in 1832 when the missionaries were threatening to break up the Canadian Methodist congregations in Upper Canada, John Ryerson took a leading role in this movement. Egerton Ryerson once described his brother as "a life-long Conservative" and John did work hard among the Methodists in the Bay of Quinte in the elections of 1836 to keep the Reformers out.[134] Yet, he was no doctrinaire Wesleyan Tory of the Buntingite school. John Ryerson was prepared to denounce the British Wesleyans in the colony when he thought they were overstepping their authority or taking the connexion in a harmful direction, especially around the issue of church establishment. In 1838 he pilloried the British-appointed president of the Canada Conference, William Martin Harvard, for "running about the city [Toronto], fawning, bowing, smiling, eulogizing, flattering etc. etc. etc.; to make proselytes to himself ... " and the then editor of the *Christian Guardian*, Ephraim Evans, for his support for the British missionaries and their "*dear Church* [of England]."[135] In general, however, John Ryerson believed that the future of Methodism in Canada lay within a wider British Wesleyan world. He struggled to preserve the union at the Canada Conference of 1839, at one point playing an instrumental role in defeating his brothers Egerton and William's efforts to end it then and there.[136] He threw himself into the effort to rebuild the union with equal verve after its collapse.

In April 1841 John Ryerson approached Joseph Stinson and "expressed in the strongest terms his regret" at the two Conferences being "arrayed against each other." John agreed that his brother, Egerton, had done wrong in making the *Christian Guardian* into a political journal and suggested that the majority of his fellow preachers "would gladly become bona fide members of the British Conference" as missionaries. By the next month, John Ryerson was proposing that, if they became agents of the WMMS, the Canadian ministers would place their church property under the control of the home connexion. According to Ryerson himself, this idea was supported by "the best men" in the Canadian ministry at their Conference in 1841.[137] In November 1843, John told Stinson that he had "done all in my power to induce the [Canadian] preachers to an arrangement as much in accordance with your views as possible ... " He had successfully prevented references in the *Christian Guardian* "offensive to the British Conference, and indeed I have been trying all in my power, both with preachers and people, to bring about a settlement and restore peace to our Zion ... "[138]

He convinced Robert Alder of his sincerity.[139] By 1846 he had also convinced the majority of his fellow ministers of the wisdom of the course he had plotted out over the previous six years. The Conference that year appointed John Ryerson and the equally conservative Anson Green as representatives to the British connexion to negotiate a reunion.[140] This may have been an immediate reaction to falling membership: in 1845 and 1846 the Canada connexion lost 2,200 members to the British Wesleyan missionaries in Upper Canada and to other denominations.[141] It was also, however, the culmination of a new willingness among the Canadian Methodist ministry to rejoin a wider British Wesleyan world under changed Buntingite leadership.

In cultural terms, the new union that was created in 1847 came to rest on the basis of a commonly agreed upon sense of British and Wesleyan identity among the leading elements of both Conferences. The Canadian Methodists freely accepted a subordinate position within a larger British connexional organization. Between 1847 and 1862, only British Wesleyans served as president of the Canada Conference.[142] When, in 1855 and 1856, several Canadian ministers floated the idea that one of their own should be made president of the connexion, the suggestion was greeted with "amusement" by their fellow preachers. Asahel Hurlburt, who had been one of the chief opponents of the reunion, "deprecated any alteration, from the fact of our present success, and which had marked the history of the past years."[143] When Anson Green became the first Canadian preacher to fill the presidential chair in 1863, he declared that "[t]he ice is now broken, and the way prepared for other Canadian ministers to fill our Conferential chair ... "[144] Evidently, this was a minority opinion. Over the next eleven years, only three more native-born Canadians served as president.[145]

It helped that the British Wesleyans who were appointed to the presidency of Canada Conference after 1847 said what their colony colleagues wanted to hear. The days of a Buntingite minister travelling across the Atlantic in order to charge the Canadian Methodists with political disloyalty and flagrant breaches of faith and doctrine were over. The post-reunion British Wesleyan presidents gave new life to a tempered sense of British and Wesleyan identity among the Canadian Methodists. They described the Canadian Methodists as "our children; and, in all future time and contingencies, they will be our brethren. They will carry out and perpetuate all that is valuable in our system, and, planting old England on a new soil, will reproduce our nation on a gigantic scale."[146] Speaking on behalf of their Canadian Methodist charges, they noted that the British Wesleyans had "a great deal of the beautiful, and the wealthy, and the wise, and the morally and materially powerful ... which now we cannot compare with; but we have them all in Embryo ... "[147] They even went one step further, arguing that, in some ways, the Canada Conference had already exceeded the home connexion: by the 1870s it had become the real religious establishment of the colony.[148]

Having established an identity that was acceptable on either side of the Atlantic, the connexional leadership in Canada and Britain spent the next seven years attempting to contain the more militant notions of Britishness and Wesleyanism that had been set loose after the dissolution of the first union in 1840. The task was most pressing among the British missionaries and their lay supporters in Upper Canada. Their fear of abandonment rekindled by the Canadian Methodist deputation to the British Conference of 1846, the missionaries turned their self-identification as guardians of pure Britishness and Wesleyanism against the home connexion. It would be disastrous, they argued, to withdraw an official British Wesleyan presence from provinces that, in terms of population alone, were becoming increasingly British every year.[149] Even an alliance with the Canadian Methodists threatened to "*prove most fatal to British Methodism in this country.*"[150] The British Wesleyan laity in Upper Canada also reacted badly to the idea of reunion. The laymen of Kingston refused outright to contemplate any union with the Canada Conference that did not secure absolute British Wesleyan hegemony in Upper Canada.[151] The same tune was sounded by the laity of Toronto, Hamilton, and London.[152] One Toronto layman put the matter squarely: "I have been a British Methodist all my days and intend to be a British Methodist. No power on earth shall ever make me a Ryerson Methodist," including, apparently, the WMMS.[153] These missionaries and their lay supporters had become quintessential loyalists: men and women who asserted "a British identity for reasons not always apparent or agreeable to the makers of policy and opinion in the United Kingdom."[154]

The British Wesleyan leadership and several of their missionaries in Upper Canada moved quickly to suppress this revolt against connexional authority. Matthew Richey, who, like Joseph Stinson, had become a convert to reunion, took the lead in the colony. Faced with irate memorials from Toronto, Bytown, and Kingston, he attempted to calm the anger, but looked to Robert Alder's coming for a definitive settlement of the issues at hand.[155] As early as September 1846, the WMMS had determined to send Alder to Upper Canada to meet with its agents "for the purpose of effectually carrying out the object contemplated" in the new Articles of Union.[156] Once in the province, Alder told the assembled missionaries that "with regard to the printing of resolutions, and exciting the people to disaffection by conversation, it is much to be deplored; they would have done better to have been praying." Having given the missionaries that tongue lashing, Alder declared that there was no going back on the union now that it had been established. In an effort to put a damper on their fears, however, he pointed out that the British Conference did retain a veto power over the actions of the Canada connexion.[157]

This had the desired effect. The missionaries passed a resolution stating that, having spoken to Alder and attended "the interesting deliberations of the Canada Conference on the momentous subject," they were "constrained" to recognize in the reunion "the special guidance of Providence and Spirit of God ... " They also noted that, since the union with the Canadian Methodists "will not separate us from our esteemed and endeared brethren of the British Conference," they trusted that their attachment to British and Wesleyan ways would "increase rather than diminish by these arrangements."[158] The Britishness and Wesleyanism of the missionaries in Upper Canada had been successfully directed into safer channels. The operation was less successful with the laity. In 1861 a visiting British Wesleyan minister, William Boyce, found that many of the English immigrants in Upper Canada still bore no love for the Canadian Methodists "except so far as they abide by English usages ... "[159] After 1846, however, the missionaries were no longer willing to follow any lay secessionists into the spiritual wilderness. They had found a comfortable home within the reconstituted union.

There still remained the problem of dealing with the British Wesleyan community in Lower Canada. By 1852 the WMMS was well advanced in a plan to unite the missionary district in that province with the Canada connexion.[160] The British-appointed president of the Canada Conference, Enoch Wood, was afraid, however, that "the old leaven will be a formidable barrier against the tendencies of the brethren [in Lower Canada] moving in the right direction, notwithstanding the practical evidence of the good of the Union in all Canada West."[161] Wood's fears were justified. William Squire, one of the leading missionaries in Lower Canada, stated that his District would be more willing to contemplate union with the Canadian Methodists "were the whole work in this country purely British." Since Methodism was most certainly not "purely British" in Upper Canada, "it will be difficult to assimilate the work, and bring it to a necessary unity."[162] Within a year, however, Wood was able to convince the majority of the missionaries to consent provisionally to the new arrangement, despite the efforts of some of them to stave off all consideration of the plan.[163] It probably helped that the WMMS had previously chastised the missionaries for daring to assume that they were "especially set for the defence of Methodism in British America, and possess such an independence of action as cannot in the nature of things belong to any District ... "[164] For their part, the Canadian Methodists strove to put the missionaries' worries about the nature of their connexion at ease. They stressed that the entire discipline of their church would be extended to Lower Canada, "including the articles of union between the British and Canada Conference ... "[165] In other words, like their counterparts in Upper Canada, these missionaries would not be entirely cut adrift from British Wesleyanism; instead, they would become part of an even larger British and Wesleyan family. When the final version of the plan was accepted by the missionaries in May 1854, it stated, once again, that they would be governed under the complete Articles of Union.[166] A militant British and Wesleyan identity among the missionaries in the Canadas was dead: killed by a kinder, gentler version embraced by both their leaders overseas and the Canadian Methodists.

The interaction of the British Wesleyan Conference, the British missionaries and their lay supporters in the Canadas, and the Canadian Methodists between 1827 and 1854 demonstrates the complexity of British and Wesleyan identity in the north Atlantic world. At the beginning of the period, the differing Buntingite and Canadian Methodist visions of Britishness and Wesleyanism became a source of almost continuous conflict between the two connexions. When the first union between those churches collapsed in 1840, the British missionaries' fear of abandonment by the home connexion helped strengthen their perception of themselves as the guardians of a pure British and Wesleyan identity in the Canadas. That self-image was turned on the Canada Conference as the Buntingites strove to protect their own vision of British Wesleyanism from what they regarded as the insidious tactics of Canadian Methodism. In response, the Canada connexion was forced to further elaborate its own claim to an unsullied British and Wesleyan identity. By the mid-1840s, then, there were several conceptions of Britishness and Wesleyanism in play across the north Atlantic, clashing with and reinforcing one another. Cultural and structural change among both the British Wesleyans and Canadian Methodists beginning in the early 1840s ended this situation. The impact of the Oxford Movement and the Disruption of the Church of Scotland on British Wesleyanism effectively undermined the Buntingite vision of an identity based on Wesleyan Tory principles. Among the Canadian Methodists, the majority of the ministry accepted the leadership of John Ryerson and his belief that the future of the connexion lay within a wider British Wesleyan connexional structure. By 1847 the two groups had achieved reunion based, in large part, on a shared concept of British and Wesleyan identity that gave the home connexion a position of leadership and that acknowledged and even encouraged the aspirations of the Canadian Methodists. Over the next seven years, the leading elements in the newly united Conferences worked together to impose this new sense of self-awareness on the still recalcitrant British missionaries and laity in the colonies. By 1854 there was a cultural unity among the Methodists in the Canadas that would have been almost inconceivable twenty-one years earlier. In the end, however, it was a thoroughly British Wesleyan culture.

The story of conflicting British identities was not unique to Methodism in Canada. In several ways, the long and tortuous story of the winning of responsible government in Upper Canada paralleled the developments outlined in this article. The supporters and opponents of parliamentary reform were divided along the same cultural lines as the Canadian Methodists and British Wesleyan missionaries of the mid 1840s. The moderate Reformers William Warren Baldwin and his son Robert argued that, by implementing executive responsibility to the Legislative Assembly, they would be transplanting a pure version of the British constitution to the colony.[167] Opposed to this view of the future of Upper Canada was another elaborated by the province's Tory leadership. They were equally sure that they were the true Britons, preserving the inherently stable, tripartite division of the British constitution in the colonial government.[168] However, like the British Wesleyan missionaries in the Canadas, the Tories were never entirely comfortable in their reliance on the goodwill and consistency of British politicians. They had learned that lesson early on. In 1815 and 1816 the imperial authorities in London put forward a plan to move the capital of Upper Canada from York to Kingston. This idea was vehemently opposed by Tories throughout the colony. They were afraid that the Americans would read the relocation of the capital as a sign of an impending British abandonment of the colony. In opposing this plan, the colonial Tories openly declared that the British government had an obligation to support and protect their fellow, transplanted Britons. Even more importantly, from a cultural point of view, this opposition was based on the belief that transplanted Britons had a right and a duty to hold the home country to its obligations. Changes in imperial policy in London would not be permitted to upset an established British colonial culture.[169] That was wishful thinking. Convinced by Baldwinite arguments from abroad and by political changes at home, the Colonial Secretary Lord Grey granted the Canadas responsible government in 1848. Like the British Wesleyan leadership during the same period, Grey was motivated, in large part, by the aim of creating the conditions necessary for the formation of a new and stronger British society on the other side of the Atlantic.[170]

By examining the shifting relationship among the Wesleyans in Britain, their missionaries and lay supporters in the colonies, and the

Canadian Methodists themselves, we have seen how important it is to view church governance and cultural change within the widest possible transatlantic perspective. Only by adopting such a framework can we understand the often complex interrelationships that gave rise to a unified culture among the Methodists of central Canada by the 1850s. A transoceanic point of view also demonstrates that, while that cultural unity, in a Canadian context alone, may seem like an example of a unique Canadian Methodist self-awareness, forged primarily by events internal to the colony and eventually free from the influence of the home country, it is actually best understood as the product of a series of heated debates over the meaning of Britishness and Wesleyanism that divided the Methodist communities of both metropole and colony in the 1830s and 1840s. By the 1850s this was a self-image, however, that was supported by both Canadian Methodists and British Wesleyans in the home country. The cultural assumptions that underpinned the first British Empire in America did indeed have a long and complex existence after 1783; they would continue to shape Canadian Methodism and its relationship with the British Wesleyan connexion until the two churches finally and amicably went their separate ways in 1874.

NOTES

1 Goldwin French, *Parsons and Politics: The role of the Wesleyan Methodists in Upper Canada and the Maritimes from 1780 to 1855* (Toronto: Ryerson Press, 1962), 134–64, 171–91, 217–42, 248–53; Neil Semple, *The Lord's Dominion: The History of Canadian Methodism* (Montreal & Kingston: McGill-Queen's University Press, 1996), 76–86, 92–9.

2 John Moir, "Notes of Discord, Strains of Harmony: The Separation and Reunion of the Canadian and British Wesleyan Methodists, 1840–1847," *Canadian Methodist Historical Society Papers* 4 (1984): 2, 10, 12–13.

3 David Hempton, *Methodism and Politics in British Society, 1750–1850* (London: Century Hutchinson Ltd., 1987), 179–216; W.R. Ward, *Religion and Society in England, 1790–1850* (London: B.T. Batsford Ltd., 1972), 135–76, 236–47, 251–77; Michael R. Watts, *The Dissenters: The Expansion of Evangelical Nonconformity* (Oxford: Oxford University Press, 1995), 458–69, 614–25.

4 Hempton, *Methodism and Politics*, 188–9, 191–4; John Munsey Turner, *Conflict and Reconciliation: Studies in Methodism and Ecumenism in England, 1740–1982* (London: Epworth Press, 1985), 146–72; Ward, *Religion and Society*, 216–17, 241–4.

5 The quotation is from John Kent, *The Age of Disunity* (London: Epworth Press, 1966).

6 The best general history of the Methodist mission effort between 1786 and
   1885 is N. Allen Birtwhistle, "Methodist Missions," in Rupert Davies et al.,
   eds, *A History of the Methodist Church in Great Britain* (London: Epworth Press,
   1965–88), 3:1–71.
7 French, *Parsons and Politics*, 188–9, 271, 286–7.
8 Eliga H. Gould, "A Virtual Nation: Greater Britain and the Imperial Legacy of
   the American Revolution," *American Historical Review* 104, no. 2 (April 1999):
   481, 484; *The Persistence of Empire: British Political Culture in the Age of American
   Revolution* (Chapel Hill: University of North Carolina Press, 2000), 181–214.
9 This problem of "Britishness" is touched on in Carl Bridge and Karl
   Fedorowich, "Mapping the British World," *Journal of Imperial and Commonwealth History* 31, no. 2 (May 2003): 5–6.
10 John Rylands University Library of Manchester (hereafter JRULM), Methodist
   Archives and Research Centre (hereafter MARC), Joseph Taylor papers, MAM
   PLP 105.6.37, Joseph Taylor to Joseph Entwisle, 1 Sept. 1840.
11 G.G. Findlay and W.W. Holdsworth, *The History of the Wesleyan Methodist Missionary Society* (London: Epworth Press, 1921–4), 1:107–8; George Smith, *History of Wesleyan Methodism*, 3rd. ed. (London: Longman, Green, Longman,
   and Roberts, 1862), 3:585–6.
12 [James Everett], *Wesleyan Takings: or Centenary Sketches of Ministerial Character*,
   3rd ed. (London: Hamilton, Adams, and Co., 1841–51), 1:6.
13 JRULM, MARC, Edmund Grindrod papers, MAM PLP 47.16.21, Edmund
   Grindrod to Jabez Bunting, 11 Mar. 1820; ibid., MAM PLP 47.16.22, Edmund
   Grindrod to Jabez Bunting, 12 Jan. 1824; Kent, *Age of Disunity*, 65.
14 The phrase "Buntingian Dynasty" comes from [James Everett], *All the Numbers of the 'Fly Sheets' Now First Reprinted in One Pamphlet* (Birmingham: William
   Cornish, 1850), 34.
15 Watts, *Dissenters*, 411–12, 460, 541–2; JRULM, MARC, John Beecham papers,
   MAM PLP 7.2.33, John Beecham to Jabez Bunting, 28 Feb. 1838; JRULM,
   MARC, Robert Alder papers, MAM PLP 1.36.7, Robert Alder to Jabez Bunting,
   11 Jan. 1839. For an overview of Wesleyan Toryism see Hempton, *Methodism
   and Politics*, 181–6.
16 For the response of the Wesleyan Methodist leadership and the British elite
   in general to the "wreck of nations" in the 1790s and afterward see C.A.
   Bayly, *Imperial Meridian: The British Empire and the World, 1780–1830* (London: Longman Group UK Ltd., 1989), 100–2, 195, 251; Ward, *Religion and
   Society*, 21–104. The quotation is from Proverbs 24:21.
17 Alex Tyrrell, *A Sphere of Benevolence: The Life of Joseph Orton, Wesleyan Methodist
   Missionary (1795–1842)* (Melbourne: State Library of Victoria, 1993), 67;
   Hempton, *Methodism and Politics*, 208–9; Watts, *Dissenters*, 425.
18 D.A. Gowland, *Methodist Secessions: The Origins of Free Methodism in Three
   Lancashire Towns: Manchester, Rochdale, Liverpool* (Manchester: Manchester
   University Press, 1979), 16.

19 On Joseph Rayner Stephens see Michael S. Edwards, *Purge This Realm: A Life of Joseph Rayner Stephens* (London: Epworth Press, 1994), 2–14.

20 Turner, *Conflict and Reconciliation*, 9–29.

21 *Watchman*, 12 Dec. 1838 quoted in Hempton, *Methodism and Politics*, 185.

22 Jabez Bunting to James Kendall, 24 April 1834 in W.R. Ward, ed., *Early Victorian Methodism: The Correspondence of Jabez Bunting, 1830–1858* (Oxford: Oxford University Press, 1976), 59–60.

23 Benjamin Gregory, *Side Lights on the Conflicts of Methodism during the Second Quarter of the Nineteenth Century, 1827–1852* (London: Cassell and Company Ltd., 1898), 155, 161.

24 JRULM, MARC, John Rattenbury papers, MAM PLP 86.28.76, John Rattenbury to Mary Rattenbury, 6 Aug. 1834; Edwards, *Purge This Realm*, 15–16; Gregory, *Side Lights*, 161–4.

25 School of Oriental and African Studies (hereafter SOAS), Methodist Missionary Society Archives (hereafter MMSA), Wesleyan Methodist Missionary Society (hereafter WMMS), Home and General, Circulars, Fiche #1988, 30 Aug. 1834.

26 On this point see French, *Parsons and Politics*, 73–4; Semple, *Lord's Dominion*, 51–2.

27 *Report from the Select Committee on the Civil Government of Canada. Ordered by the House of Commons, to be Printed, 22 July 1828* (S.I.: s.n., 1828), 295.

28 SOAS, MMSA, WMMS, Home and General, Home Correspondence, Fiche #148, Robert Alder to George Morley, 7 Jan. 1828.

29 UCA, WMMS-C, Minutes of the General Committee of the WMMS, Reel 1, 15 Feb. 1832.

30 SOAS, MMSA, WMMS, Home and General, Circulars, Fiche #1988, 9 Sept. 1833.

31 UCA, WMMS-C, Minutes of the General Committee of the WMMS, Reel 1, 15 Feb. 1832; Semple, *Lord's Dominion*, 79–80.

32 UCA, WMMS-C, Box 16, File 105, #17, Richard Watson to Lord Goderich, 22 Nov. 1832.

33 William Westfall, *Two Worlds: The Protestant Culture of Nineteenth-Century Ontario* (Montreal & Kingston: McGill-Queen's University Press, 1989), 24–7.

34 UCA, Egerton Ryerson papers, Box 1, File 8, George Ryerson to Egerton Ryerson, 6 Aug. 1831.

35 UCA, WMMS-C, Box 15, File 94, #26, Egerton Ryerson to Richard Watson, 19 Oct. 1831. Emphasis in original. See also French, *Parsons and Politics*, 136.

36 *Report from the Select Committee on the Civil Government of Canada*, 219. For the American Methodist presence in Upper Canada up to 1815 see Nancy Christie, "'In These Times of Democratic Rage and Delusion': Popular Religion and the Challenge to the Established Order, 1760–1815," in George A. Rawlyk, ed., *The Canadian Protestant Experience, 1760–1990* (Burlington: Welch Publishing Company Inc., 1990), 22–3, 28, 41–2.

37 UCA, WMMS-C, Box 15, File 94, #26, Egerton Ryerson to Richard Watson, 19
   Oct. 1831.

38 Ibid., Box 16, File 100, #27, Extracts from the proceedings of the Board of
   Managers of the Missionary Society of the Methodist Church in Canada, [2
   July 1832].

39 Ibid., Box 15, File 94, #26, Egerton Ryerson to Richard Watson, 19 Oct.
   1831. Emphasis in original.

40 Egerton Ryerson, *Canadian Methodism: Its Epochs and Characteristics* (Toronto:
   William Briggs, 1882), 309–10.

41 *Christian Guardian* (hereafter *CG*), 27 June 1832, 130.

42 R.D. Gidney, "Egerton Ryerson," in *Dictionary of Canadian Biography* (hereafter *DCB*) (Toronto: University of Toronto Press, 1967-), 11:785.

43 UCA, WMMS-C, Box 16, File 100, #30, James Richardson to James Townley,
   John Beecham and John James, 16 Aug. 1832; UCA, WMMS-C, Minutes of the
   General Committee of the WMMS, Reel 1, 10 June 1833.

44 UCA, WMMS-C, Outgoing Correspondence, John Beecham to the General
   Superintendent and Conference of the Methodist Episcopal Church in
   Upper Canada, Aug. 1833; *CG*, 16 Oct. 1833, 193. For an overview of the
   connexional relationship between the British and Irish conferences see
   Dudley Levistone Cooney, *The Methodists in Ireland: A Short History* (Blackrock:
   Columba Press, 2001), 127–8.

45 *The Minutes of the Annual Conference of the Wesleyan-Methodist Church in Canada,
   from 1824 to 1845, inclusive* (Toronto: Anson Green, 1846), 63–5.

46 JRULM, MARC, Jabez Bunting papers, MAM PLP 19.2.3, Jabez Bunting to
   Edmund Grindrod, 8 Mar. 1834.

47 JRULM, MARC, George Marsden papers, MAM PLP 73.17.39, George Marsden
   to the General Secretaries of the WMMS, 28 Mar. 1834.

48 JRULM, MARC, Jabez Bunting papers, MAM PLP 19.2.6, Jabez Bunting to John
   Beecham, 29 Mar. 1834; ibid., MAM PLP 19.2.6a: Jabez Bunting to John
   Beecham, 31 Mar. 1834.

49 From Robert Alder's point of view, the Canada Conference of 1834 promised to avoid all political campaigning in the pages of the *Christian Guardian*:
   CG, 12 June 1839, 129. See also *Minutes of the Annual Conference … from 1824
   to 1845*, 84.

50 JRULM, MARC, Jabez Bunting papers, MAM PLP 19.2.10, Jabez Bunting to
   Edmund Grindrod, 25 Apr. 1834. Emphasis in original.

51 *Minutes of the Annual Conference … from 1824 to 1845*, 214–15, 233–4; Anson
   Green, *The Life and Times of Anson Green, D.D.* (Toronto: Methodist Book
   Room, 1877), 183–4.

52 *Minutes of the Annual Conference … from 1824 to 1845*, 141, 166–7, 183–4.

53 UCA, WMMS-C, Minutes of the General Committee of the WMMS, Reel 1, 30
   Jan. 1839.

54 Thomas Jackson to the Secretary of the Canada Conference, 23 Mar. 1839 quoted in Egerton Ryerson and William Ryerson, *Report of their Mission to England, by the Representatives of the Canada Conference* (S.I.: s.n., 1840), 5.

55 *CG*, 29 May 1839, 121; ibid., 12 June 1839, 129. Emphasis in original.

56 Ibid., 25 Dec. 1833, 25; ibid., 5 Sept. 1838, 174; ibid., May 16, 1838, 109; ibid., 12 June 1839, 130; ibid., 12 Dec. 1838, 21; ibid., 12 June 1839, 130.

57 JRULM, MARC, Wesleyan Methodist Church, Conference Journal, NUG Shelf 364a, 1840, 166; UCA, John Douse papers, Box 1, File 3, John Douse to Eliza Douse, 13 June 1840.

58 UCA, Minutes of the Annual Conference of the Wesleyan Methodist Church in Canada (hereafter WMC-C), Reel 1, 10–19 June 1840.

59 SOAS, MMSA, WMMS, Home and General, Home Correspondence, Fiche #213, Joseph Stinson to William Lunn, 28 July 1837.

60 UCA, WMMS-C, Box 23, File 159, #6, Joseph Stinson to Robert Alder, 23 May 1839. Emphasis in original.

61 See for example ibid., Box 23, File 159, #1, Ephraim Evans to Joseph Stinson, 8 Jan. 1839.

62 An argument that had a long history in conservative thought in Britain. See J.G.A. Pocock, "Josiah Tucker on Burke, Locke, and Price: A study in the varieties of eighteenth-century conservatism," in *Virtue, Commerce and History: Essays on Political Thought and History, Chiefly in the Eighteenth Century* (Cambridge: Cambridge University Press, 1985), 159–62.

63 UCA, WMMS-C, Box 23, File 159, #26, Joseph Stinson to Thomas Jackson, 9 Dec. 1839. Emphasis in original.

64 Ibid., Box 23, File 159, #10, Joseph Stinson and Matthew Richey to Robert Alder, 9 Nov. 1839. Emphasis in original.

65 Ibid., Box 24, File 168, #29, Elijah Hoole to Robert Alder, July 1840.

66 UCA, Church Album Collection, Portraits and Letters of the Presidents of the British Conference, Reel 1, Album 4, George Marsden to Jabez Bunting, 1840.

67 Egerton Ryerson, *The Story of My Life: Being Reminiscences of Sixty Years' Public Service in Canada,* J. George Hodgins, ed. (Toronto: William Briggs, 1883), 273.

68 UCA, Church Album Collection, Portraits and Letters of the Presidents of the Canada Conference, Egerton Ryerson to Jabez Bunting, 7 Aug. 1840; Ryerson and Ryerson, *Report of their Mission to England,* 12; C.B. Sissons, *Egerton Ryerson: His Life and Letters* (Toronto: Clarke, Irwin and Company Ltd., 1937–47), 1:557–8.

69 JRULM, MARC, Wesleyan Methodist Church, Conference Journal, NUG Shelf 364a, 1840, 166–9.

70 SOAS, MMSA, WMMS, Home and General, Home Correspondence, Fiche #233, John Scott to an unknown correspondent, 10 Aug. 1840; Ryerson and Ryerson, *Report of their Mission to England,* 14–18.

71 SOAS, MMSA, WMMS, Home and General, Home Correspondence, Fiche #229, Robert Alder to Elijah Hoole, 13 Aug. 1840.

72 The above quotations are from Gregory, *Side Lights*, 292, 293–4.

73 Ibid., 294.

74 JRULM, MARC, Elijah Hoole papers, MAM PLP 55.32.34, Elijah Hoole to Jabez Bunting, 28 Aug. 1840; Ryerson and Ryerson, *Report of their Mission to England*, 19.

75 UCA, WMMS-C, Minutes of the General Committee of the WMMS, Reel 1, 9 Sept. 1840.

76 Much like the American colonists of the first British Empire according to Kathleen Wilson, *The Sense of the People: Politics, Culture and Imperialism in England, 1715–1785* (Cambridge: Cambridge University Press, 1998), 282–3.

77 For examples of this process at work in Upper Canada and other parts of "greater" Britain see Allan Smith, "Old Ontario and the Emergence of a National Frame of Mind," in F.H. Armstrong, et al., eds., *Aspects of Nineteenth-Century Ontario: Essays Presented to James J. Talman* (Toronto: University of Toronto Press, 1974), 205–7, 209; J.G.A. Pocock, "Contingency, identity, sovereignty," in Alexander Grant and Keith J. Stringer, eds, *Uniting the Kingdom? The Making of British History* (London: Routledge, 1995), 301.

78 UCA, Minutes of the Annual Conference of the WMC-C, Reel 1, 8 June 1842; JRULM, MARC, Joshua Soule papers, MAM PLP 98.6.18, Joshua Soule to Jabez Bunting, 3 Aug. 1842; JRULM, MARC, Wesleyan Methodist Church, Conference Journal, NUG Shelf 364a, 1843, 449.

79 Ibid., 1845, 634. Emphasis in original.

80 Gregory, *Side Lights*, 304–7, 308, 321, 331, 338–9, 341, 350–1, 361; Ward, *Religion and Society*, 254–5.

81 Gregory, *Side Lights*, 291.

82 Sissons, *Egerton Ryerson*, 1:558. Bunting agreed with Beaumont's motion for dissolution, but for different reasons. He believed that the union was "a perfect *ignis fatuus*" – a perfect illusion. Gregory, *Side Lights*, 294.

83 UCA, Minutes of the Annual Conference of the WMC-C, Reel 1, 26 Oct. 1840; UCA, WMMS-C, Box 24, File 168, #12, Joseph Stinson to Robert Alder, 2 Nov. 1840.

84 JRULM, MARC, John Rattenbury papers, MAM PLP 86.28.76, John Rattenbury to Mary Rattenbury, 6 Aug. 1834; *CG*, 18 Nov. 1840, 13.

85 JRULM, MARC, John Beecham papers, MAM PLP 7.3.3, John Beecham to Jabez Bunting, 6 Oct. 1840.

86 *Watchman*, 7 Oct. 1840, 325.

87 The quotation is from ibid., 14 Oct. 1840, 334. See also ibid., 21 Oct. 1840, 343; ibid., 11 Nov. 1840, 366. Alder wrote these responses under the pseudonym "Observer." See JRULM, MARC, John Beecham papers, MAM PLP 7.3.3, John Beecham to Jabez Bunting, 6 Oct. 1840.

88 *CG*, May 5, 1841, 110; UCA, WMMS-C, Box 29, File 201, #21, William Martin Harvard to Robert Alder, 13 Sept. 1845; *Reply of the Canada Wesleyan Conference, June 1841, to the Proceedings of the English Wesleyan Conference and its Committees, August and September 1840* (London: Thomas Tegg, 1841), 40–1.

89 UCA, WMMS-C, Box 25, File 176, #16, Robert Alder to Joseph Stinson, 4 Oct. 1841.

90 See for example ibid., Box 24, File 168, #15, Joseph Stinson to Robert Alder, 30 Nov. 1840; UCA, WMMS-C, District Minutes, Canada/Upper Canada, Reel 5, 4 June 1841.

91 The quotation is from UCA, WMMS-C, Box 25, File 169, #35, Leaders and Stewards of Kingston to the General Secretaries of the WMMS, 17 May 1841. See also ibid., Box 25, File 169, #11, Official Members of the Toronto Circuit to Robert Alder, Mar. 1841; ibid., Box 25, File 169, #23, Thomas Fawcett and Hugh Shaw to the General Secretaries of the WMMS, 26 Apr. 1841 written on behalf of the Stewards and Leaders of the Goderich Circuit.

92 Ibid., Box 25, File 169, #22, Thomas Fawcett to the General Secretaries of the WMMS, 14 July 1841.

93 UCA, WMMS-C, Box 24, File 161, #19, William Lunn to Robert Alder, 12 Oct. 1840.

94 *Wesleyan*, 3 Sept. 1840, 22; ibid., 15 Oct. 1840, 49; ibid., 12 Nov. 1840, 65; ibid., 21 Jan. 1841, 105.

95 Ibid., 24 June 1841, 196; ibid., 9 Feb. 1842, 86; ibid., 8 Feb. 1843, 84. Emphasis in original.

96 JRULM, MARC, James Dixon papers, MAM PLP 34.17.20, James Dixon to Jabez Bunting, 3 Mar. 1842. Dixon noted that it would give him great pleasure to steal away a minister from the New Connexion and so "weaken an antagonist body, founded as it is on a wrong basis ... "

97 JRULM, MARC, William Lord papers, MAM PLP 70.33.26, William Lord to Jabez Bunting, 11 Mar. 1842. The British Wesleyans succeeded in suborning J.C. Davidson, though it helped that he was already leaning in that direction. See UCA, WMMS-C, Box 26, File 177, #25, J.C. Davidson to Joseph Stinson, 5 Jan. 1842; UCA, Minutes of the Annual Conference of the WMC-C, Reel 1, 8 June 1842.

98 *Minutes of the Annual Conference ... from 1824 to 1845*, 262; UCA, WMMS-C, Box 24, File 168, #12, Joseph Stinson to Robert Alder, 2 Nov. 1840; UCA, WMMS-C, District Minutes, Canada/Upper Canada, Reel 5, 28 Oct. 1840; ibid., Reel 5, 4 June 1841.

99 *CG*, 4 Nov. 1840, 5; *Wesleyan*, 12 Nov. 1840, 64–5.

100 UCA, WMMS-C, District Minutes, Canada/Upper Canada, Reel 5, 28 Oct. 1840; UCA, WMMS-C, Box 24, File 168, #15, Joseph Stinson to Robert Alder, 30 Nov. 1840.

101 *Reply of the Canada Wesleyan Conference*, 34–5.

102 UCA, Minutes of the Annual Conference of the WMC-C, Reel 1, 8 June 1842.

103 *Minutes of the Annual Conference ... from 1824 to 1845*, 257. See also *CG*, 30
     Dec. 1840, 38.
104 UCA, Minutes of the Annual Conference of the WMC-C, Reel 1, 27 Oct. 1840;
     Minutes of the Annual Conference ... from 1824 to 1845, 251, 258.
105 Ibid., 281–2, 293, 324. Emphasis in original.
106 Though they did threaten to do so on several occasions: *CG*, 9 Dec. 1840, 25;
     ibid., 30 Dec. 1840, 38; ibid., 13 Apr. 1842, 98. For the Canada Conference's
     official policy see *Minutes of the Annual Conference ... from 1824 to 1845*, 283–4.
107 UCA, Minutes of the Annual Conference of the WMC-C, Reel 1, 28 Oct. 1840.
108 Ryerson and Ryerson, *Report of their Mission to England*, 7. Emphasis in original.
109 UCA, Egerton Ryerson papers, Box 2, File 44, Henry Mayle to Egerton
     Ryerson, 16 Nov. 1840.
110 Goldwin French, "George Frederick Playter" in *DCB*, 9:634–5.
111 *CG*, 9 Dec. 1840, 25; ibid., 10 Feb. 1841, 61.
112 *Minutes of the Annual Conference ... from 1824 to 1845*, 269.
113 *CG*, 30 Dec. 1840, 38; ibid., 6 Jan. 1841, 41–2; ibid., 19 Jan. 1842, 50.
114 Moir, "Notes of Discord, Strains of Harmony," 12.
115 *Minutes of Twelve Annual Conferences of the Wesleyan Methodist Church in Canada,*
     from 1846 to 1857 inclusive (Toronto: Anson Green, 1863), 35–8.
116 John Carroll, *Case and His Contemporaries; or, the Canadian Itinerants' Memorial*
     (Toronto: Samuel Rose, 1867–77), 4:432.
117 Gregory, *Side Lights*, 420.
118 Stewart J. Brown, *The National Churches of England, Ireland, and Scotland,*
     1801–1846 (Oxford: Oxford University Press, 2001), 292–312, 348–62.
119 JRULM, MARC, John Beecham papers, MAM PLP 7.3.13, John Beecham to Jabez
     Bunting, 12 Jan. 1843. Emphasis in original. See also John Beecham to Jabez
     Bunting, 14 Jan. 1843 in Ward, ed., *Early Victorian Methodism*, 280–1.
120 Gregory, *Side Lights*, 348; Ward, *Religion and Society*, 242–3
121 Gregory, *Side Lights*, 350–1; Hempton, *Methodism and Politics*, 189–90.
122 *Watchman*, 31 Jan. 1844 quoted in ibid., 190.
123 C. Brad Faught, *The Oxford Movement: A Thematic History of the Tractarians and*
     Their Times (University Park: Pennsylvania State University Press, 2003), 5,
     69–70.
124 Hempton, *Methodism and Politics*, 165; Turner, *Conflict and Reconciliation*,
     162–3.
125 Gregory, *Side Lights*, 317.
126 Thomas Jackson, *A Letter to the Rev. Edward B. Pusey, D.D.* (London, 1842), 99
     quoted in Hempton, *Methodism and Politics*, 166. See also Watts, *Dissenters*,
     544.
127 *Watchman*, 9 Nov. 1842, 356.
128 Edward Jones to Jabez Bunting, 15 Nov. 1844 in Ward, ed., *Early Victorian*
     Methodism, 308 and n2. On Wesleyan Tory support for the Evangelical Alli-
     ance see Ward, *Religion and Society*, 218–19.

129 UCA, WMMS-C, Minutes of the General Committee of the WMMS, Reel 1, 14 Sept. 1846.

130 UCA, WMMS-C, Box 30, File 216, #11, Joseph Stinson to Robert Alder, 2 Mar. 1846. Emphasis in original.

131 SOAS, MMSA, WMMS, Home and General, Home Correspondence, Fiche #214, Joseph Stinson to Robert Alder, 29 May 1838. Emphasis in original.

132 UCA, WMMS-C, Box 26, File 177, #7, Joseph Stinson to Robert Alder, 9 May 1842.

133 UCA, Egerton Ryerson papers, Box 3, File 68, Joseph Stinson to Egerton Ryerson, 18 Nov. 1844.

134 Thomas H.B. Symons, "John Ryerson," in *DCB* 10:639; Sissons, *Egerton Ryerson*, 1:348–9.

135 UCA, Egerton Ryerson papers, Box 2, File 35, John Ryerson to Egerton Ryerson, 22 May 1838. Emphasis in original.

136 JRULM, MARC, John P. Lockwood collection, Matthew Richey to Jabez Bunting, 3 July 1839.

137 UCA, WMMS-C, Box 25, File 169, #12, Joseph Stinson to Robert Alder, 16 Apr. 1841; ibid., Box 25, File 169, #13, Joseph Stinson to Robert Alder, 20 Apr. 1841; ibid., Box 25, File 169, #18, Joseph Stinson to Robert Alder, 3 May 1841; ibid., Box 25, File 169, #19, Joseph Stinson to Robert Alder, 16 June 1841.

138 UCA, Matthew Richey papers, Box 1, File 2, John Ryerson to Joseph Stinson, 7 Nov. 1843.

139 UCA, WMMS-C, Box 30, File 216, #10, Robert Alder to Joseph Stinson, 4 Mar. 1846.

140 Ibid., Box 30, File 216, #9, Joseph Stinson to Robert Alder, 30 June 1846; UCA, Minutes of the Annual Conference of the WMC-C, Reel 1, 3 June 1846; Green, *Life of Anson Green*, 290–1.

141 French, *Parsons and Politics*, 248–9; Moir, "Notes of Discord," 11.

142 George Cornish, *Cyclopaedia of Methodism in Canada* (Toronto: Methodist Book and Publishing House, 1881), 30.

143 UCA, WMMS-C, Box 40, File 291, #[?], Enoch Wood to Elijah Hoole, William Arthur and George Osborn, [1856].

144 Green, *Life of Anson Green*, 389.

145 Cornish, *Cyclopaedia of Methodism in Canada*, 30. The Canadian Presidents of Conference were Richard Jones (1865), James Elliott (1867), and Samuel D. Rice (1873 and 1874).

146 James Dixon, *Personal Narrative of a Tour through a part of the United States and Canada*, 2nd ed. (New York: Lane and Scott, 1849), 158.

147 UCA, WMMS-C, Box 43, File 316, #7, Enoch Wood to Elijah Hoole, 2 July 1863.

148 William Morley Punshon, *An Address delivered in the Free-Trade Hall, Manchester, at the Open Session of the Wesleyan Methodist Conference* (S.l.: s.n., 1871), 6; Westfall, *Two Worlds*, 52.

149 UCA, WMMS-C, District Minutes, Canada/Upper Canada, Reel 5, 20 June 1846.

150 UCA, WMMS-C, Box 30, File 209, #4, William Case to Matthew Richey, 24 June 1846. Emphasis in original. See also ibid., Box 26, File 178, #14, William Martin Harvard to Robert Alder, 11 June 1842; ibid., Box 29, File 201, #25, William Martin Harvard to Robert Alder, 6 Dec. 1845.

151 UCA, WMMS-C, Box 30, File 209, #12, Resolutions of the Leaders Meeting of Kingston to William Martin Harvard, Matthew Richey, and Robert Alder, 10 Nov. 1846.

152 Ibid., Box 30, File 209, #10, Resolutions of the Toronto Stewards and Leaders, 23 Nov. 1846; ibid., Box 30, File 209, #9, Memorial from the Hamilton Circuit, 7 Dec. 1846; ibid., Box 31, File 224, #31, Official Members of the London Circuit to the Chairman and Ministers of the Western Canada in special District Meeting assembled, 6 Feb. 1847.

153 Ibid., Box 31, File 224, #34, William Martin Harvard to Robert Alder, 17 Feb. 1847.

154 J.G.A. Pocock, "Commentary," in Prosser Gifford, ed., *The Treaty of Paris (1783) in a Changing States System* (Lanham: University Press of America, 1985), 205.

155 UCA, WMMS-C, Box 29, File 210, #19, Matthew Richey to Robert Alder, 25 Nov. 1846; ibid., Box 29, File 210, #20, Matthew Richey to Robert Alder, 12 Dec. 1846.

156 UCA, WMMS-C, Minutes of the General Committee of the WMMS, Reel 1, 14 Sept. 1846.

157 UCA, WMMS-C, Box 31, File 224, #[?], Summary of the discussions between Robert Alder and the members of the Canada West District, 26 May 1847.

158 Ibid., Box 31, File 224, #6, William Martin Harvard and William Scott to the President and Members of the Wesleyan Conference, England, 17 June 1847.

159 National Archives of Canada, William Billington Boyce papers, Journal, 6 Aug. 1861, 318.

160 UCA, WMMS-C, Outgoing Correspondence, John Beecham to Enoch Wood, 7 Apr. 1853.

161 UCA, WMMS-C, Box 26, File 267, #13, Enoch Wood to Elijah Hoole, 14 May 1852.

162 Ibid., Box 36, File 260, #13, William Squire to George Osborn, 18 June 1852.

163 Ibid., Box 37, File 268, #2, Enoch Wood to John Beecham, 21 May 1853.

164 UCA, WMMS-C, Outgoing Correspondence, John Beecham, Elijah Hoole, George Osborn, and William Arthur to the Missionaries in the Eastern Canada District, 30 Mar. 1853.

165 UCA, WMMS-C, Box 37, File 268, #[?], Resolutions adopted by the Wesleyan Conference in Hamilton City, Canada West, 6 June 1853.

166 Ibid., Box 38, File 281, #21, Enoch Wood to John Beecham, 22 May 1854.
167 Jeffrey L. McNairn, *The Capacity to Judge: Public Opinion and Deliberative Democracy in Upper Canada, 1791–1854* (Toronto: University of Toronto Press, 2000), 43–7.
168 David Mills, *The Idea of Loyalty in Upper Canada, 1784–1850* (Montreal & Kingston: McGill-Queen's University Press, 1988), 18–19.
169 Jane Errington, *The Lion, the Eagle, and Upper Canada: A Developing Colonial Ideology* (Montreal & Kingston: McGill-Queen's University Press, 1987), 137–8, 144–7.
170 John Manning Ward, *Colonial Self-Government: The British Experience, 1759–1856* (Toronto: University of Toronto Press, 1976), 211, 235–6, 240–1, 269, 287, 290.

MICHAEL GAUVREAU

The Dividends of Empire

Church Establishments and Contested British Identities in the Canadas and the Maritimes, 1780–1850

Between 1822 and 1824, a bitter dispute between Rev. Henry Hayden and a group of his parishioners agitated the Anglican parish of Rawdon, Nova Scotia. In late 1822, the churchwardens of the parish informed the Society for the Propagation of the Gospel in Foreign Parts (SPG), the Church of England body that recruited and paid the salaries of missionaries in the colonies, that a person purporting to be an SPG missionary had arrived in the parish demanding control of the church property. However, in the eyes of the suspicious parish laity, "he appears to be too flighty and unsteady in his mind and actions, for to be fit for the Government of a Flock, or the management of the Glebe." Relations between Hayden and the lay managers of the church rapidly deteriorated, the major problem centring on Hayden's performance of the public duties of a clergyman. A year later, in a formal petition to the SPG, the churchwardens alleged that their clergyman's performance of divine service was "so irreverent as to grieve the Soberminded." Of even greater concern to a small rural congregation where money for church purposes was in short supply, Hayden interpreted the Anglican liturgy in a way that had alienated "Serious People," – in effect, the most active and committed church members – from the parish. Further, the churchwardens charged, "with regard to his Respectability the indecent manner in which he appears at home at times and also abroad ... in Respect of Apparel, Excite ... Laughter and Ridicule."[1]

However, although some claimed that Hayden had publicly abused his detractors from the pulpit, and had even entered the houses of his opponents to harangue them "in a violent manner and used very profane Language," the minister was not without his supporters in the Rawdon parish. At the beginning of 1824, a counterpetition from a group of "Episcopalians and Dissenters" praised their clergyman for his faithful discharge of duty, stating "his example has been in unison with his doctrine which we consider in every respect unexceptionable."[2] Despite these endorsements and the fact that in terms of social status and educational attainments, Hayden's MA from Trinity College Dublin – a badge of membership in the Protestant gentry of Ireland – placed him far above the average of Church of England clergy in British North America, both the SPG and Bishop John Inglis took the extreme step and agreed to his absolute removal from the Diocese of Nova Scotia in 1824. What is significant here is that authority within the colonial church was nebulous because of divided jurisdictions between the local bishop, congregations, and the SPG. The SPG recruited and paid the colonial clergy, local congregations provided and maintained the church buildings and accommodation for the clergyman, and the bishop on the spot inducted and supervised local ministers. Thus, the usual pattern of discipline in cases of clerical misconduct was one of delicate negotiation. It frequently involved a series of ongoing admonitions or, in more serious cases, personal intervention by the bishop to resolve tensions, or an agreement to transfer the minister to another mission. Outright dismissal was an exceptional solution, one that led a clearly irate Hayden to expostulate to his employers that "I never wd. have purchased either land or stock had I not considered my situation absolutely as permanent as a Benefice in England."[3]

Hayden's parting shot affords us a point of entry into the interplay between religious institutions and the ambiguous and contested meanings of "Britishness" in the post-Revolutionary colonies of the Canadas and the Maritimes. In the aftermath of the American Revolution, the United Church of England and Ireland (otherwise known as the Anglican Church) was deliberately designated the established church of the colonies and was assigned a mission of maintaining and extending British authority.[4] Read at the level of religious discourse on both sides of the Atlantic, Anglican apologists for the idea of establishment advanced the argument that identity of religious institutions in the British Isles and British North America would create an overarching and homogeneous "British" patriotism; cultural and, ultimately, political unity between the imperial centre and the colonies would flow from the close similarity of institutional structures of church government. Later, the Church of Scotland, after 1820, proffered a claim to co-establishment on the grounds that it alone could ensure the participation of Scottish immigrants in a unifying "British" imperial project. Such a strategy would, in the setting of the New World, continue a politico-cultural process that had enlisted the enthusiastic energy of the Church of Scotland at home: that of softening and ultimately obliterating early-modern ethnic differences and perceptions of the past that had prevailed in the British Isles before the mid-eighteenth century. For promoters of the Church of Scotland, these older identities would be replaced by the benefits of an Anglo-Britishness anchored in constitutional liberty and commercial progress.[5]

However, Hayden's protest against his removal, and especially his disillusioned realization that religious authority and the status of a clergyman in Nova Scotia bore no relationship to what prevailed in England, suggests that, in the colonial setting, "Britishness" was far more about conflict, fragmentation, and the elaboration of strategies of cultural separation than about unity, homogeneity, and integration. His initial assumption, that the supposedly seamless identity between structures of church government and religious practice gave him nearly absolute security of tenure in his parish, when coupled with the financial inducement of a yearly salary of £150 from the SPG, was sufficient to lure this native of County Kilkenny, Ireland, to serve in the colonial church establishment in Nova Scotia. An additional incentive was the disadvantage of competing for what would in all likelihood be an ill-paid situation in the supposedly privileged Church of Ireland.[6]

However, if religious conditions in Ireland impelled Hayden's migration, they also formed the backdrop of his acrimonious relations with his congregation and Bishop John Inglis. Although his detractors cast many aspersions against his "respectability," the source of Hayden's troubles lay not in any personal misconduct or low social station, but in the differing theological emphases which demarcated ethnic divisions within the Anglican establishment. The Irish Church in which Hayden had received his education formed a governing structure separate from the Church of England, with which it was nominally united, and was characterized by a prevalent Calvinism that Irish clergy proudly asserted as a badge of historic difference between their institution's expression of "Britishness" and the dominant "High Church" temper that prevailed in England.[7] By the 1820s, this "Calvinism" had become a conduit for a rising tide of Evangelicalism which, according to Donald Akenson, had a powerful animating effect on the Church of Ireland.[8] The evangelical temper almost certainly influenced Hayden's approach to the Anglican liturgy, as his home in Kilkenny was part of the Diocese of Ossory, a major nucleus of Evangelicalism in Ireland.[9] It should be stated in this context that Hayden's supporters in the parish included "Episcopalians and Dissenters" – read Anglicans sympathetic to Evangelicalism, and non- Anglican Evangelicals. Seen in this light, Hayden's error, apparent in dropping distinctive Anglican Church vestments and adopting a more effusive manner of expression, lay in introducing "evangelical" practices into church services; in modern parlance this would be called a form of outreach to non-Anglicans. Unlike the Church of Ireland, which was

hospitable toward evangelical practices, the colonial diocese of Nova
Scotia, like its counterpart in Quebec, was firmly in the grip of a High
Church bishop whose authority was buttressed by the resolutely orthodox Society for the Propagation of the Gospel.[10] Indeed, Bishop John
Inglis displayed so firm an animus against any evidence of "Calvinism"
or evangelical tendencies in his clergy that, in 1826, he went so far
as to admonish his episcopal counterparts in England to exercise
extreme caution in ordaining clergymen suspected of evangelical tendencies for colonial service. His removal of the well-educated, and
arguably quite popular, Hayden was clearly designed to prevent the
emergence of an Evangelical "party"[11] in his diocese that might contest his authority.

Here, in the local politics of a colonial church congregation, lies the
theme that is central to this paper, the way in which religious institutions in British North America, especially those closely connected to
the political state, defined and balanced the tensions that existed
within the term "British." In recent years, historians of Upper Canada
like Jeffrey McNairn and Carol Wilton have drawn attention to the varied and contested nature of "Britishness" at the level of political ideology and practice.[12] However, historians who have examined religious
institutions have too frequently rested content with viewing the established churches, and particularly Anglicanism, as social and cultural
monoliths, as expressions of a conservative imperative and a High
Churchism,[13] and have neglected one pivotal characteristic of both
the Anglican Church and the Church of Scotland: their primary role
in the Canadas and the Maritimes was to transplant and express,
through religion, "British" values and institutions. Indeed, as Alexander Murdoch has recently argued for the British Isles, "Britishness,"
because it was primarily about state-building, was first and foremost a
system of institutional, rather than cultural identities.[14]

But what did "Britishness" mean in the late eighteenth and early
nineteenth centuries, when interpreted through the lens of the major
institutions designed for its expression and promotion? Was it monolithic and integrative, or was it a force for conflict and fragmentation?
During the past fifteen years, historians of the British Isles have elaborated a definition of British nationalism that stresses, above all, its unifying and homogenizing features. According to Linda Colley, British
nationalism was a particularly "modern" construct, resting on the twin
pillars of Protestant identity and an expansive sense of commercial
hegemony, both of which were affirmed during a long series of wars
with Catholic, absolutist, "backward" European countries like France.
Although Colley admits the persistence of older and "local" ethnic
identities within the British Isles, particularly among lower socio-

economic strata, these were, by the early nineteenth century, relegated to a decidedly marginal status, tributary to a dominant patriotic culture that had adopted a set of common symbols, rhetoric, and practices.[15] In the context of the evolving British Empire, particularly in the reconstruction that occurred after the American Revolution, the Anglican Church, as the dominant state church of the British Isles, had the principal role of grafting this "modern," unifying British identity onto colonial society. However, in the cultural conditions of British North America, characterized by a high degree of religious and ethnic pluralism, church authorities found themselves financially and socially dependent upon lay people, and the clergy far reduced in social position and status. These conditions occasioned a nearly constant level of conflict between clergy and congregations in which the Anglican establishment found its position contested and negotiated at every turn. And out of this series of struggles there resulted an inversion of the process described by Colley, in which "Britishness" became synonymous with modernity as a unifying and homogenizing identity: in the British North American colonies, "Britishness," as expressed in religious terms, emerged as a terrain of fragmentation and as a series of contested discourses and practices in which early-modern ethnic identities were vigorously reasserted and defended.

From the sixteenth century onward, the Church of England, as the church of the English monarchy, had been one of the primary instruments of British state-building, imperial expansion within the British archipelago, and the forging of an overarching "British" national identity. Eighteenth-century England, as the work of J.C.D. Clark has underscored, was a "confessional state," in which membership in the political community was coextensive with belonging to the Church of England. The Anglican Church was, through its system of parishes, the effective agency of local government and authority, and was integral to an understanding of that talismanic entity, the "British Constitution."[16] According to Eliga Gould, at the conclusion of the American Revolution in 1783, Britain was left with an empire that appeared to be far more culturally diverse than it had in the 1760s.[17] This lack of cultural homogeneity, in turn, accentuated the importance of church institutions. The whole basis of British control in the Canadas and the Maritimes rested less on political structures, economic ties, or military power, than on the promotion of a culturally uniform British identity expressed first and foremost by the provision of the full apparatus of Church of England religious institutions. Political allegiance, and the colonial connection itself, was equated with the constitutional establishment of the Church of England. "Can anything," proclaimed Rev. John Strachan, the Anglican Archdeacon of York (Toronto) in 1828, "attach the colonies to the Parent State so strongly as a community of religious feeling?" In his estimation, the Anglican Church was "the only effectual barrier to separation from the Parent State."[18] Here, the explicit similarity between the institutions of a colonial religious establishment and those of England replicated the process adopted by England to incorporate the peripheral societies of Ireland and Scotland. However, unlike these countries, or indeed even the Thirteen Colonies, post-Revolutionary British North America seemed to offer a kind of blank slate, an experimental laboratory where it would be possible to found the colonial tie upon a new imperial vision in which a purely "English" cultural homogeneity would encompass a unitary (and morally superior) British identity created without the encumbrances of an ascendancy or penal laws, one which would rest on the sole criterion of the spiritual efficacy of the Church of England polity.

Anglican clergy founded their claims to social authority on the idea that, because the hierarchical type of church government in the colonial church exactly mirrored that of the Church of England at home, membership in their institution incarnated a unitary "Britishness" that could be transferred back and forth across the Atlantic. They thus adamantly asserted that the established church in the colonies was an extension of, and no different from, that of England, and that as a social group, they enjoyed the same rights, status, and privileges as their counterparts at home. This notion of equivalency was expressed in 1826 by several senior clergy in the Diocese of Quebec, who informed Bishop Charles James Stewart that the diocese formed "a regular portion of the English Establishment" and was connected with the Archbishopric of Canterbury "'in the same manner' as any Bishopric within the Province of Canterbury in England."[19] These clergymen were, of course, well aware that this lofty claim bore no relation to the reality of their working conditions, for the same memorandum complained that "our Clergy ... with very few exceptions, are merely upon the footing of Missionaries chargeable upon the bounty of a benevolent Society at Home ... "[20] Anglican ministers in the colonies, instead of holding an independent status at the head of a legally constituted parish which gave them security of tenure, revenue from tithes and fees, and membership in the local landed elite,[21] found themselves severely reduced in status, mere contract employees of the Society for the Propagation of the Gospel. Furthermore, a good deal of financial, social, and even religious authority rested in the hands of lay members of their congregations.

The central difficulty in the Anglican Church's attempt to articulate a unitary transatlantic "Britishness" based on institutional commonality and the authority of its own clergy lay in the lack of legal equivalency between the English parish and its counterpart in British North America. In England, the parish was the basic unit of local government, with a system of enforceable tithes and obligations encompassing education, social order, and social welfare which, in effect, fully integrated the Anglican clergy into the state. No matter what privileged status the colonial constitutions accorded to the Church of England in terms of political recognition or revenue from public lands,[22] the Anglican clergy could not get around the basic reality that the colonial parish was not an institution of civil government; their position gave them no claim to admission to local structures of authority; and relations with their congregations were, from the first, established not upon the old regime basis of law and obligation, but within a far more voluntaristic framework.[23]

The ambiguities inherent in this situation were aptly expressed in a 1792 petition from the congregation of the Anglican parish of Christ Church, Montreal, which requested the Lieutenant-Governor to constitute it as "a Parsonage or Rectory, according to the establishment of the Church of England." Although, at one level, this might be read as an affirmation by Anglican laity of the exact transplantation of English institutions, the parish of Christ Church was equally adamant that they wanted all the advantages of parish status "but without subjecting them, by such establishment, to the payment either of Tithes or Parish rates, they being too few in number to be able to support these charges, even if other circumstances rendered the collection thereof practicable and legal."[24] Ironically, although the 1791 constitution of the Canadas authorized both the imperial and colonial governments to erect parsonages and rectories "according to the Establishment of the Church of England" and to present Anglican clergymen to these livings,[25] both the Upper Canadian assembly explicitly and the British Government itself implicitly, by instituting the system of Clergy Reserves designed to give the Church a permanent revenue, also barred the collection of tithes for the support of the church. Here, clearly, lay a stumbling block to the clergy's argument that close similarity of religious institutions expressed a unitary, or transferable, "Britishness."

In 1804, Rev. John Stuart, the Anglican minister at Kingston, pointed out one of the central inconsistencies in the colonial constitution's assumption that royal power could exactly replicate English religious institutions in Upper Canada. After a lengthy negotiation with the provincial authorities over the title to some lands near the church, he informed Bishop Jacob Mountain that the government believed that the colonial clergy could never be placed on the same footing as the English clergy, because "we could never be *inducted*; for that would

intitle us to Tithes &c ... we must content ourselves with being dependent on Government for our support, and might expect every reasonable Indulgence, *we behaving as becometh.*"[26] Rev. John Beardsley, who
had accompanied a group of Loyalist refugees to New Brunswick,
sought to convince the SPG of the need for some alternative to the
institutional parish. "I could render myself more useful," he declared,
"in the character of an Itinerant Missionary in this part of the province, than any clergyman could settled in any one Town, or plantation
on the Rivers."[27]

Others were far less sanguine about this far more distant, client-like
relationship between church and state that confronted Anglicanism in
the Canadas and the Maritimes. Missionaries like Rev. William Ellis of
Windsor, Nova Scotia, complained that they could not count on the
assistance of local authorities to promote the church's interests. In
1776, he denounced the magistrates as a set of "labourers and
mechanics, many of them are poachers and all are given to class
hatred."[28] In the latter turn of phrase, Ellis implicitly pointed to the
fact that none of the colonial "British" constitutions, unlike those prevailing in England, rested on an exact correspondence between membership in the established church and office-holding. Irrespective of
Anglicanism's privileged status in each of the colonies, Dissenters and
Catholics in British North America were part of the political nation.
What Ellis in fact meant was that many of the Windsor magistrates were
Congregationalist or Baptist dissenters who had no intention of prop-
ping up or extending Anglican authority. Even at the highest levels of
the colonial state structure, Anglican clergy could rely on only rather
tepid support. One anonymous complaint to the SPG regarding the
irreverent conduct of the provincial Lieutenant-Governor put the matter this way: "the Bell which on the Sunday afternoon gives the Sum-
mons for others more devoutly affected to attend Evening Service is
the signal for his Excellency's Dinner, the Bottle, and the Toast."[29] The
lack of integration between church and state, and the absent legal
structure of Anglican parishes induced Rev. Peter de la Roche of
Lunenburg to expostulate in 1775 that "Christianity in America is a
Spectre void of all Substance."[30] Colonial clergymen were well aware
that their social authority was seriously compromised by a double
dependency: because they were "missionaries," they were first subjected to the rather uncertain backing of government officials of the
colonial and imperial state which employed and paid them; second
they were dependent on their congregations, whom they had to assiduously cultivate in order to avoid being transferred or removed, and
whose financial contributions would ultimately have to form the basis
of their incomes.

"Religion in this country," lamented Rev. George Best, Anglican missionary at Granville, Nova Scotia, "is generally speaking, one of convenience we are everything by turns, but nothing for a constancy – we have a great many of those kinds of people, who profess to *wish* well to all denominations, but do not good to any."[31] Significantly, Best's comment on the nature of religion in colonial society centred not on the actual state of belief, but on the general reluctance of the colonial governments and local congregations to commit themselves to anything that smacked of consistent financial support for the Anglican clergy. The main source of clerical income was the British Government's temporary financial commitment to create an Anglican primacy in the colonies, which between 1816 and 1833 afforded Anglican ministers a basic stipend of £150. With the shift by the reformist Whigs toward a more "pluralist" ecclesiastical policy, these amounts were reduced by 30 per cent in 1833, and a further 20 per cent in 1834. This, according to Rev. William Abbott, missionary at St Andrews', Lower Canada, was insufficient "to enable the Clergy to maintain their families without being too much involved in temporal affairs."[32] Reporting on the state of the Diocese of Nova Scotia in 1827, Bishop John Inglis reported that contributions from the people toward support of clergy and church were "always uncertain and generally of small amount ... They seldom extend beyond procuring a residence for the Clergyman, and in some cases amount to nothing."[33] Colonial church leaders like Bishop George Mountain of Quebec argued vociferously, and sought through a combination of means – revenue from the Clergy Reserves, glebe lands, and the voluntary support of congregations – to maintain £150 as the minimum standard of clerical income. Otherwise, Mountain argued, the "poverty of our Missionaries" would impair the respectability of the Anglican clergy, whom he described as already "fast sinking below those of the Wesleyan connection."[34] Although diatribes against the wealth and privilege of the Church of England formed a powerful trope in the discourse and identity-formation of a number of religious denominations and political groups in British North America, and despite the prospect of revenues from government payments and lands to which clergymen of other denominations had no access, the reality of life for the vast majority of colonial Anglican clergymen prior to 1850 was poverty, a poverty that was frequently rendered more unbearable when juxtaposed against the expectation, held by many, that service in the colonial church constituted an opportunity of enhanced status and upward mobility.

Lack of local financial provision and loss of personal income formed the standard refrain of the Anglican clergy's comments on relations with their congregations. From Rev. Peter de la Roche's experience at

Lunenburg in 1779 where, he declared, the congregation did not subscribe, and even on Communion days gave little more than a dollar,
and where, he charged, the parishioners were despoiling the Glebe,[35]
to that of Rev. John Wenham of Fort Erie, Upper Canada who, on his
arrival, found "the house which was promised for my reception in
every respect wholly unfit even by the confession of the Trustees it was
indeed a wretched tenement perfectly uninhabitable,"[36] Anglican
clergy were concerned to expose what they considered their own poverty, and the financially unco-operative character of the people whom
they served. This led clergymen to an extreme punctiliousness in collecting those revenues to which they considered themselves legally
entitled. Rev. James Reid, who succeeded the wealthy aristocrat
Charles James Stewart in the parish of St Armand, Lower Canada,
engaged in an unseemly scrabbling with his parish clerk over fees.
Reid protested to Archdeacon George Mountain that Stewart had
relinquished to his parish clerk half the fee of ten shillings the clergyman collected for performing marriages, although Stewart had
advised Reid that this precedent was not binding on his successor. "I
found it difficult," Reid reported to the Archdeacon, "to make an alteration, though I think it both a hardship, and an act of injustice, thus to
give up the one half of the only perquisite I have in the place. I beg
therefore you will have the goodness to inform me for my future government, what the legal ecclesiastical fee of a Clerk is, who has hardly
any duty to perform except that of making the responses in Church on
Sundays."[37] More genially, the veteran minister John Stuart of
Kingston, who, unlike his more recently arrived colleagues, was a
native of North America, and more familiar with the hard bargaining
that characterized the relationship between clergymen and their congregations under the voluntary system, described in 1794 the compromise he reached with the churchwardens in order to pay off the
church's debt, in which Stuart "voluntarily relinquished any claim" to
control of the pew rents. "Indeed," he sardonically concluded, "the
sacrifice was not great on my Part, for I well know, no Part of it was
intended for me."[38]

This discourse both indicated and reinforced a kind of clerical class
consciousness among the colonial Anglican clergy,[39] one that firmly
established the connection between colonial congregations' inability
or unwillingness to provide support, the Anglican ministers as an
embattled, isolated group of gentry vertiginously poised on the
knife-edge of poverty,[40] and the need to maintain, at all costs, what
appeared to be the only certain source of potential revenue for the
clergy: the economic support from the imperial state which, in the

Canadas, took the form of Clergy Reserves to which the Anglicans made exclusive claims. While clerical leaders like Bishop Mountain opposed religious voluntarism on political grounds, dwelling on the necessity of a church establishment[41] – meaning the British state's financial support of the Anglican Church – the local clergy's opposition to voluntarism derived from other sources. For Rev. John Wenham, the central meaning of church establishment the establishing of a clear social and cultural distinction between the Anglican clergy as a class and the clergy of other denominations. In his estimation, government stipends and the Clergy Reserves gave Anglican ministers no real economic advantage because the real incomes of those of other denominations "if their previous habits of life and the requirements of their offices are taken into account, are to all intents and purposes much greater."[42] However, payments from the state were essential to enhancing the Anglican clergy's corporate sense of itself as a class of gentlemen who were connected with government, and the basis of a transatlantic equivalency which would place "a Country Clergyman upon a similar footing with their Brethren in England."[43] This sense of distinction and participation in a wider British citizenship would, they believed, simply disappear under a voluntary system. Rev. James Magrath, an Anglican missionary at Toronto, even noted the *disadvantages* of the Clergy Reserves because, in his estimation, these constituted an obstacle to greater financial commitment from congregations, which used the existence of the Reserves as an argument to avoid making voluntary payments to clerical salaries. However, Magrath preferred the establishment system because it seemed premised on the independence of the clergy as a class. "In short," he informed the SPG,

> When I consider the difficulty of collecting the scattered dollars, the many & long rides which they will require frequently without success ... the unpleasant feelings which might arise in cases of non payment, the loss of that independence which the Church now possesses; the reduction of its ministers to the level of sectarian preacher, who are feeling sensible of the unpleasantness & precariousness of voluntary contributions; & of which they are so anxious to make us participators ... I should prefer endeavouring to support my large family, consisting of nine individuals, on my small, diminished fixed stipend to any application to the purses of my flock.[44]

Magrath's conclusion, that "We must have an Established Church or no Church at all,"[45] was less an expression of political and constitutional reality, than the forceful enunciation of the social aspirations of a group of men who had left Britain seeking in the transatlantic unity of Anglican institutions an opportunity for accession into the ranks of the gentry.

In great part, this defence of personal and corporate gentry status reflected the social origins of the colonial Anglican clergy as a group. With the exception of King's College in Windsor, Nova Scotia, the Anglican Church in British North America, until the 1840s, lacked a network of educational institutions that would assure a regular supply of clergymen. Compelled to rely on overseas sources of recruitment, colonial church leaders and officials of the SPG from an early stage expressed considerable dismay at what they considered the marked inferior social status and commitment of those British clergy who sought positions in the colonial church. Dr Morrice, the pertinacious secretary of the SPG, averred to Bishop Mountain that his organization had no remedy for its inability to "prevail with any Clergyman of Character, however bad his situation may be, or however confined by his prospects, to exchange it for what he considers little better than a Banishment for life."[46] Simply put, until the 1830s, when the British government reforms of the finances and administration of the Church of Ireland, curtailing the prospects of employment and promotion within that institution, brought a steady stream of well-educated young clergymen to British North America, the colonial church had to depend on what Archdeacon G.J. Mountain in 1821 termed "irregular persons"[47] to staff its missions and parishes. Despite the severe shortage of clergy for the Diocese of Quebec, Mountain advised the SPG that the Bishop would not ordain or employ any candidate whose previous background had been in the military, and would actually give more favourable priority to clergy from other denominations who wished to convert to Anglicanism.[48] However, this could hardly be considered a permanent solution to the manpower problems, which threw the colonial church back on men from the British Isles.

In the case of the Diocese of Nova Scotia after 1815, most of these British recruits, according to Judith Fingard, were generally young men with some ministerial experience as underpaid curates at the bottom of the ecclesiastical ladder, often employed in the poor backwaters of Welsh dioceses, frequently with large families, who sought relief from debt in British North America.[49] The potential for difficulties with the appointment of such young men in quest of upward mobility was illustrated by the case of Rev. Richard Knagg, whose four-year career in the Diocese of Quebec involved transfers to three missions, including a final one to the backwater of Gaspé, at the request of outraged congregations. Bishop Mountain was prepared to be rather tolerant of Knagg, considering him "a worthy, & a pious man, & well versed in the Scriptures, but he has so great a want of respectability of appearance, such a clownish simplicity of manners, & so total an ignorance of the world, that it can be only among people all of whom are of the lower order that there can be any probability of his success in his Ministry." The Bishop was eventually forced to return Knagg to England because he had allegedly "threatened to blow out the brains" of a member of his congregation.[50] Other acceptable sources of recruitment included the Scottish Episcopal Church which, as a non-established church, would have afforded its ministers little in the way of financial security in Britain. One such clergyman was Rev Roger Aitken, pastor of an episcopal congregation in Aberdeen which "from the smallness of its number, the poverty of its people, and the enormous price of all the necessities of life, is no longer able to affford a suitable allowance to its clergyman." In pressing the SPG to employ him as a colonial missionary, Aitken referred to the fact that he had "no fixed stipend, but must depend on the voluntary offerings of my people and nothing can be more precarious. Having a family to provide for, I consider it my duty to embrace any favourable opportunity that may occur for that purpose, consistent with the character of a clergyman."[51]

If men like Aitken believed that they were escaping poverty and barriers to preferment at home, and were entering a colonial setting where they would enjoy the deference and legal perquisites of an English-style parish, they were sorely disappointed by their experience. Parishes and missions in the British North American colonies were not institutions of civil government, and what authority the institutional church enjoyed was divided and contested between government, the ecclesiastical hierarchy, and the local congregation. In Nova Scotia, after the American Revolution, the British government, in a gesture of accommodation with North American religious sensibilities, deliberately instituted a kind of tripartite religious authority. While the bishop licensed clergy and instituted them to benefices, the Lieutentant-Governor had the right to present clergy to benefices, grant them marriage licenses and probate of wills, jurisdictions which in England devolved upon bishops. More significantly, the British government recognized a kind of democratic congregationalism; local congregations had the right to be consulted about the appointment of new ministers and would in fact nominate a ministerial candidate for presentation by the governor[52] – a situation in certain cases leading to competition between ministers, each vying to secure the approbation of the "voice of the people."[53] Clergymen like Rev. Roger Aitken learned to their great chagrin and personal cost that they could not ride roughshod over local rights, as Aitken attempted to do in his station at St John's, Lunenburg, in 1822, where he engaged in a lengthy dispute with his congregation over their alleged failure to complete his parsonage. When he attempted to gain his point by encroaching on the congregation's "previously enjoyed exclusive right of choosing their own churchwardens," the Anglican laity circulated a petition for his removal. Rev. John Inglis, the Ecclesiastical Commissary acting in the absence of Bishop Stanser, was anxious to support Aitken's authority and unwilling to indulge local assertion. However, Inglis realized that Aitken's conduct had so thoroughly alienated the congregation from the church that the only solution was to "delicately as I could, urge ... it upon him to apply for the Society's permission to remove."[54]

Although in the Diocese of Quebec there was no explicitly legal basis for the clergy sharing authority with their congregations, the nature of the relationship between the SPG and the colonial church imposed from the first a dependence on local wishes and needs. It is necessary to underscore in this context that the SPG was not an "evangelical" body; that is, its policy was not to send missionaries to gather new congregations but to provide religious services where congregations and institutional support were already constituted. Thus, for Bishop Mountain, if he was going to recommend that a particular locality be provided with a clergyman, the people of the area had to fulfill a number of conditions in advance. These involved building a church, erecting a suitable parsonage, and contributing, as far as possible, toward the clergyman's support. Mountain also explicitly prohibited local Anglican congregations from entering into agreements with dissenters to build what were in effect "shared-access" churches which would impose limits on the authority of the local Anglican minister and bishop.[55] In practice, however, Mountain was frequently forced to modify these conditions and arrange for government grants to build churches, or allow local congregations to provide rental accommodation for the clergy rather than building a parsonage. Some congregations, as Dr Morrice, the SPG secretary lamented, made lavish promises of support in order to secure a minister, but then evinced "little concern to fulfil their engagements."[56] In other parts of the Diocese, such as the Eastern Townships, the factor of opposition from Dissent and the desire of the Anglican authorities to compete for popular adherence introduced greater flexibility into what were considered the financial obligations of local congregations.[57]

Whatever the legalities of the Anglican position, this constant need for negotiation indicated that social and religious authority in British North America did not reside exclusively in the clergy, but was diffused and shared with the laity of their congregations, whose religious sensitivities always had to be taken into account. Even in the area of control of public worship and definitions of what constituted "correct" sacramental practice, where it might have been expected that Anglican clergymen, like their Catholic counterparts, would be accorded a privileged status as controlling access to church rituals,[58] Anglican clergy were constantly faced with local demands to modify ritual prescriptions. Thus, Rev. William Ellis of Windsor, Nova Scotia, informed the SPG that in order to please a congregation largely composed of former Dissenters, he was in the habit of omitting the sign of the cross during baptism,[59] a demand also faced five decades later in Upper Canada by the Irishman Rev. B.C. Hill, who discovered that a number of Presbyterians in his congregation "seemed to depreciate it as earnestly as if [they] thought it was the peculiar Mark of the Beast."[60] Even that central religious ritual of the imperial connection, the prayers for the Monarch and royal family, was a contested terrain. As Rev. Joseph Abbott declared in 1819, his mission of St Andrews, Lower Canada, was an American settlement, and "those very people that profess to be real Churchmen have requested me to dispense with reading the Liturgy the Lords prayer the prayer for the King & royal family & to model the Liturgy after their own fancy." High Churchmen like Abbott and his counterpart, Rev. John Langhorn, missionary at Ernesttown, Upper Canada refused to comply with these requests,[61] but more evangelically minded clergymen, like Rev. B.C. Hill, were quite prepared to temporize and negotiate. Hill recounted that on the question of prayers for the King, his congregation at Glanford forced him into an elaborate rationalization that "we did so pray not as believing that their Souls were more precious in the sight of God, than that of the poorest person in the land, but that while praying for them in particular we were in fact praying for all over whom their wide extended influence wd. operate either for good or for evil."[62] This re-presentation of Anglican ritual in a more democratic form served, in effect, as a metaphor for the clergy's own compromised authority in British North America, where one's position in an institutional hierarchy, even one backed by the imperial state, did not confer social authority. Significantly, in the case of clergy like Hill, their hold on the allegiances of their congregations depended not upon an externally imposed authority, but upon their own abilities to successfully navigate and negotiate between the frequently conflicting demands of their ethnically and religiously pluralist congregations and their ecclesiastical superiors.

If the inability to transplant the legal and political institutions of the English parish to the colonial setting proved a barrier to Anglicanism's attempt to enunciate a unitary, transatlantic British identity, this induced the Church, between 1815 and the mid–1830s, to found their claim to authority more fully in the realm of culture rather than simple institutional equivalency. More particularly, Anglican clergymen had to connect the church institution and the political order in such a way as to conveniently silence references to the English parish as a legal entity. In their attempt to build colonial congregations, Anglican clergymen were constantly made aware that any hint that their ministrations were directed toward setting up a legal parish system on the English model was, quite literally, the kiss of death. In Upper Canada, an Irish clergyman, Rev. Bold Cudmore Hill, a graduate of Trinity College, Dublin and a paragon of evangelical activism, recounted that on visiting a house in Canborough, south of Hamilton, he asked a Presbyterian woman about the reluctance of the people of the locality to listen to his preaching. She informed him that

> "there was a general agreement among the people here not to receive you at all or give you any encouragement to preach, as 'twas commonly reported among them that the Government was determined to enforce tithes – that you were one of the Clergymen sent out first to make the trial whether the people wd. consent or not." This reminded me of the 'Tea' that was sent out to Boston in the year '75 & I felt thankful that I escaped a similar fate with the obnoxious 'Tea.'[63]

In this case, long-established memories that the Church was, in England and Ireland, enmeshed in a system of compulsory legal exactions seriously compromised the religious effectiveness of the institution.

In order to avoid such associations, church leaders and local clergy played up the sense that "Britishness" was an inclusive, integrative set of discourses and social practices which brought together, conflated, and softened both ethnic differences and religious pluralism. The clergy hoped to forge a politically reliable basis of colonial opinion and political participation – encompassed under the rubric of "loyalty" – and, more tellingly, to create in each locality an effective and united basis of voluntary financial support for the Anglican Church by which to "top up" salaries from the government, SPG,[64] and the revenue from the clergy reserves, thus giving the clergy the social status of old-country "parsons" and "rectors," if not the full legal powers, and giving Anglicanism a decided pre-eminence over its religious rivals.

"Loyalty," declared Rt. Rev. George Mountain, the Bishop of Quebec in 1843, "is another conspicuous fruit of Church-principles in a Colony." He reiterated that "the Bishops and Clergy ... will never fail to inculcate a deep and dutiful attachment to the Monarchy of England," and underscored the close connection between political allegiance and religion, by concluding that "these feelings and principles are vitally interwoven with the system of the Church."[65] Mountain's priority on the institution of the Church of England, rather than the structure of the British Constitution, as the source of political authority and belonging, bears some further analysis. High Churchmen like Mountain were firm monarchists, speaking of the institution in quasi-mystical, some might say traditionalist terms, but they exhibited a far more modern sensibility in vigorously rejecting utilitarian notions of an "alliance" between church and state that might place religion at the mercy of the civil power. In their lexicon, "loyalty" meant a link of conscience and feeling between church and state, which they argued depended on the sacred qualities they assigned to the form of church government. They argued that it was the Church of England's faithfulness to its primitive, apostolic constitution that in fact sanctified the British monarchy and state.[66] Viewed from this perspective, the Anglican attempt to foster "Britishness" in the colonies did not rest on the transplantation of the structures of mixed monarchy, or the exact political balance of King, Lord, and Commons. Indeed, Anglican clergymen spent very little time in elaborating the technicalities of the British Constitution.[67] For them, the affirmation of an inclusive, unitary British identity was the direct consequence of a divinely commissioned, visible hierarchy of bishops and clergy whose system of religious education, supported by the imperial and colonial state, could alone create a reliable and loyal public opinion. For Rev. John Strachan, the extension of the talismanic constitutional "birthright" of Englishmen to the colonies was less a function of the transplantation of the structures of the civil polity than of the structures of Anglican church government.[68] In other words, the tenor of this discourse elevated clergy and church as the operative parts of the British Constitution in the colony.

However, if "Britishness" was going to hinge on the nature of church government, the obvious problem for Anglican clergy in British North America was that their church was, after all, the church of the English state, and not the state church of the entire United Kingdom. How could its structure and system of worship appeal to the majority of colonial Protestants who were not English in origin, but were Scotch, Irish, and American? Anglican clergy were aware that the colonies were the scene, not only of a bewildering religious pluralism, in which their church stood in a minority position to a well-rooted Roman Catholicism and to many types of evangelical dissent, but more significantly of an ethnic pluralism that cracked and fissured the public face of Britishness in North America. As early as 1783, one Loyalist clergyman described his charges as being "mostly poor" and "of very various

Churches, Dispositions, & religious Sentiments," and concluded that
"to systematize them under the national Church" would prove an
extremely arduous task.[69] The fragmenting potential of competing
British ethnicities was apparent even at the highest levels of the colonial state, since a large proportion of imperial civil servants and military officers were, after 1760, recruited from the non-English
peripheries of Great Britain.[70] In 1820, Bishop Jacob Mountain complained about the conduct of the Scottish nobleman Lord Dalhousie,
the Governor of Lower Canada. "Our present Governor," he stated, "is
a Member of the Church of Scotland ... He attends our Church &
receives the Sacraments there: but, on every third Sunday, he goes to
the Kirk." What roused Mountain's ire was the fact that instead of wor-
shipping in a private chapel, Dalhousie chose to make his religious
allegiance to the United Kingdom's "other" national church a matter
of public display. Mountain observed that in the capital, "a great part
of our Congregation consists of persons originally Presbyterians who
have conformed to our Establishment." He feared that "his Lordship's
example will tend to weaken their attachment to us."[71]

In their attempt to build congregations, local clergymen were
acutely aware of the diverse ethnicities that prevailed among immigrants from Britain, often noting not only their national, but regional
origins. Rev. George Spratt, the Anglican missionary in Yonge and Bastard Townships, Upper Canada, declared that the bulk of his church
was made up of Irish immigrants.[72] Anglican churches and Angli-
can-managed schools were, these clergymen believed, the key to fusing
this congeries of ethnicity into a British identity in which a common
religion would provide the key integrating dynamic. Rev. Micajiah
Townsend, who served in the Eastern Townships of Lower Canada,
reported optimistically on his efforts to visit a settlement of Protestant
Irish in Sherrington Township and a Scotch settlement in Beauharnois
that "the prospect is favourable for the erection at no very distant
period, of a Church, and a School in connection with the Royal Institution," the school in particular serving, in his estimation, as a "bond of
union, to strengthen their attachment to our church."[73] Clergymen
like Rev. Caleb Cotton of Dunham, Lower Canada, were always intent
on reminding their superiors that they were making serious efforts to
win English and Irish immigrants away from Methodism, often including in their reports to the Bishop and the SPG the fact that a number of
Methodists were attending their services, although they were quick to
exonerate themselves from any "liberality of opinion" or suggestion
that these new adherents had been won over through any compromis-
ing alteration to Anglican understandings of the liturgy, sacraments,
or government of the church. [74] However, ethnic diversity, and espe-

cially persistent Scottish allegiance to rival national religious institutions, frequently bedevilled Anglican institution-building. One clergyman, Rev Edward Parkin, ruefully declared that while he had been successful in securing monetary contributions for building an Anglican church at Chambly, an area where there was a predominant population of Scottish Presbyterians, "the wealthy amongst the Scotch would have contributed more liberally to the Church, if it had been that of Scotland."[75] Negotiating British "national" religious sensibilties could be a particularly daunting task. Such a disagreement brought to nought the mission of Rev John Suddard at Gaspé in the early 1820s. At New Carlisle, although he had the backing of a prominent local magistrate, Suddard was constrained to admit failure to complete his church, failure caused by a "misunderstanding among the committee for building, together with a general inclination towards Presbyterianism, the settlers being chiefly of Scottish descent."[76]

In overcoming the centrifugal pull of this ethnic pluralism, colonial Church of England clergymen adopted what were, in effect, two interlocking strategies that emphasized the appeal of the inclusive and integrative character of the British identity promoted by their church. The first, analyzed by Nancy Christie over a decade ago, was a "harder" approach of polarizing religious differences by equating religious dissent with political radicalism and American republicanism.[77] While, on the one hand, this might be dismissed as a knee-jerk anti-democratic response on the part of rather panicky conservatives, it could also be read as a very cunning strategy to overcome the extreme religious pluralism of colonial society by luring under the Anglican umbrella all those British North Americans who, for whatever reason, rejected the American label and distrusted the American associations of Baptist, Methodist, and Presbyterian preachers. The second, or "soft" strategy was the often deliberate softening, in both discourse and practice, of apparent dissonances between "English" and "British," and a deliberate attempt to negotiate and compromise with other Protestant ethnic communities through provision of the Anglican liturgy in languages other than English, or, through monetary and other inducements, recruitment of Protestant clergy of other national or dissenting churches.

Writing in 1819, Rev. B.B. Stevens of Chambly described the efforts of "the British Residents at Chambly ... assembled for the purpose of considering the Expediency and Practicality of erecting an English Episcopal Church within the said Parish."[78] Here lay the core of the Anglican institution-building project, and ultimately the key to the process of imperial state-building: the continuing ability to assert that there was no opposition between "English" and "British." Recent studies of identity and national consciousness in the British Isles have emphasized the lack of a distinctively "English" nationalism before the late nineteenth century. The key to this conundrum lies, according to these historians, in the fact that English identity was largely subsumed under the internal process of empire-building within the British Isles and the external process of projecting British power in the overseas colonies. The unifying element in this enterprise was an Anglo-British patriotism, founded on a common bond of Protestantism, in which the English element was primary but, as an ethnicity, deliberately downplayed in order to highlight an overarching political, cultural, and religious mission that would enlist the participation of other ethnic groups.[79]

The discourse of colonial Anglican clergy was insistent on the ability of its liturgy and ritual to provide the very kind of common Protestantism that affirmed a political loyalty to the British monarchy and state but could also transcend and reconcile ethnic differences.[80] Church leaders were intent on presenting their institution as incarnating a kind of inclusive "Britishness" that rested not upon the English language, but upon the accommodating character of the Anglican services and ritual forms. Bishops like John Inglis and Jacob Mountain listened sympathetically to the petitions of local congregations such as that of the "Germans of the Lutheran Church" of Montreal who asked the SPG to send them a German-speaking clergyman, especially when this group held out the prospect that they might eventually be persuaded to adhere to Anglicanism.[81] However much they might have believed that Protestant differences could be submerged in a common "Britishness," their commitment to inclusivity would certainly have been tested by the Lunenburg Germans who not only insisted that the clergyman be allowed to preach one sermon in German on Sunday, but also engaged in a kind of religious syncretism by incorporating into public worship prayers from the Lutheran rubric that had been used "for private purposes." As well, the Germans demanded that they "not ... be under the control, direction, and management of the Rector of St John's at Lunenburg."[82]

The very composition of the colonial clergy itself stood as a persuasive illustration of the fact that, when transplanted to the colonial setting, a typically "English" institution could actually encapsulate a larger "Britishness" by recruiting and providing career opportunities for ethnic "others." In this respect, the Anglican Church overseas closely resembled, in its ethnic composition, the British military and civilian office-holders in the colonies. At the very highest levels of the colonial church, prior to 1850, the leadership was anything but "English." The first bishop of Nova Scotia, Charles Inglis, was an Irish immigrant to the Thirteen Colonies. Although Inglis was succeeded in 1817 by Robert Stanser, a Cambridge-educated Yorkshireman, the latter was only in Nova Scotia for one year, retiring for health reasons to London and leaving the management of the diocese in the hands of Inglis's son John, who became Bishop of Nova Scotia in his own right in 1824.[83] In the Diocese of Quebec which, until 1839, encompassed both Lower and Upper Canada, Jacob Mountain, while possessing all the trappings of an English gentleman's education at Cambridge, came from a family of Huguenot converts.[84] Mountain was succeeded in his episcopal charge, first by the Hon. Charles James Stewart, the son of a Scottish peer, and then by his son George. Even adult conversion to Anglicanism was no barrier to promotion or success in the colonial church, as illustrated by the career of Rev. John Strachan. Educated as a minister of the Church of Scotland, Strachan took orders in the Church of England shortly after his arrival in Upper Canada, and he rose to prominence, becoming first Archdeacon, and then Bishop of Toronto in 1839. Although Bishop Mountain looked disparagingly on the Aberdeen-educated Strachan's non-English educational credentials, and chided him for his defective mastery of English prose,[85] Strachan himself stridently asserted his "Britishness," referring admiringly to the capaciousness and inclusiveness of the Anglican church polity, placing himself within a long line of Scottish worthies, former adherents of Presbyterianism who became convinced of the spiritual authenticity of episcopal government. "I need not," he remarked, "be ashamed of doing what Archbishops Tillotson and Secker, and Bishop Butler have done before me." [86] Indeed, it was not until 1845 that a diocese in Canada or the Maritimes received its first authentic "English" bishop in the person of Rev. John Medley, a High Churchman appointed to the see of Fredericton, a precedent followed by the appointment of Rev. Francis Fulford in 1850 to the new diocese of Montreal. The episcopal presence of Englishmen was, however, effectively counterbalanced by the appointment of Rev. Benjamin Cronyn and Rev. John Travers Lewis, both Irish graduates of Trinity College, Dublin, respectively to the new dioceses of Huron (1857) and Ontario (1862).[87]

If the peripheral nationalities within the United Kingdom were disproportionately represented among the Anglican upper clergy in British North America, the lower ranks were even more a pastiche of ethnicities and religious persuasions. In 1841, the ninety-one clergy serving in Upper Canada comprised thirty-two men of English birth, thirty-one of Irish birth, three born in Scotland, fifteen born in Upper Canada, and ten born elsewhere.[88] Indeed, as Donald Akenson observed over twenty years ago, the largest single source of Anglican recruitment for Upper Canada was Trinity College, Dublin.[89] The colonial Church of England was most affirmedly not a bastion of English ethnicity. These non-English clergy ranged from the more exotic like Rev. V.P. Mayerhoffer, a Hungarian Roman Catholic priest whose conversion "brought him out of the hidden darkness of the Roman Superstition" and secured him employment ministering to a group of German Protestant settlers at Markham, Upper Canada,[90] to downwardly mobile Irish gentry like Rev. Samuel Bealey Ardagh, who chose to abandon his benefice in Ireland and become an SPG missionary at Barrie, Upper Canada. Ardagh's decision to accept what seemed at first sight the more uncertain prospects of the colonial mission field was motivated by the fact that an Irish property that had been bequeathed to him and his sisters was "burdened with a pauper population of one family to every 4 or 5 acres." Although Ardagh placed a high value on the agricultural potential of his Irish estate, he was driven to Upper Canada by the increasingly violent nature of the relations between the Protestant gentry and their Catholic tenants. "About five years since," he informed Bishop G.J. Mountain, "the tenants ceased paying any rent & refused to surrender ... About 2 years since the Government sent down a Stipendiary Magistrate ... whom they shot." The constant threat of violence, which rendered the revenues of the estate entirely uncertain, and the fact that he had assumed both the debts and the responsibility for his sister's family upon the death of her husband,[91] compelled Ardagh to give up his permanent situation in Ireland and take a better paid post in the colonial church.

Although historians have become increasingly conscious of the ways in which the presence of a large and self-conscious group of Irish-born and educated clergy powerfully influenced the theology and internal politics of colonial Anglicanism,[92] further research on the social composition and patterns of recruitment of the colonial clergy would undoubtedly reveal even greater ethnic diversity. Scattered references throughout the SPG correspondence reveal that some local Anglican ministers, like Rev. Daniel Falloon, who served in the Eastern Townships in the 1840s, and Rev. George Spratt, who served at Yonge in Upper Canada, had originally been Methodist preachers.[93] The lists of SPG clergy also reveal a large number of Scottish names, clergymen whose origins, like those of Rev. Roger Aitken, missionary at Lunenburg, were either Scottish, drawn from the non-established Scottish Episcopal Church,[94] or, in the case of Rev. James Stuart and his son George, pillars of the Kingston church, American. Bishops frequently reported on their success in luring clergymen like Rev. James Reid, a former Scottish Congregationalist, or Presbyterian ministers like Thomas Creen, Thomas Campbell, and John Grier into Anglican orders.[95] The "adoption" of Scottish Presbyterians was highly regarded as a sign of Anglican vitality because the Church of Scotland was, after all, a rival establishment within the United Kingdom and, after 1815, stridently pressed its claims to be co-established in the British North American colonies.

Thus, Bishop Charles Stewart in 1826 was eager to close with the offer of Rev. John MacLaurin, the Church of Scotland minister of Lochiel, Upper Canada, who sought Anglican orders and promised to bring his several congregations into the Church of England fold. MacLaurin was well educated, having attended the University of Edinburgh and St Andrews, and arrived in Upper Canada after a term as a private tutor in the Duke of Buccleuch's family. In Stewart's eyes, these impressive connections and credentials were buttressed by the fact that MacLaurin declared in his letter that while a student, he had frequently attended the Scottish Episcopal Chapel in Edinburgh and was already quite sympathetic to the more hierarchical structure of the Anglican Church.[96] In setting forth his reasons for seeking Anglican orders, MacLaurin stressed that money was not the issue, declaring that his income was as much as he could expect as an SPG missionary. Rather, he stated to Stewart that he, and many of his congregation, "consider that much less essential difference exists between the Church of England and the Church of Scotland, than there is between different ministers of either Church." What was ultimately persuasive in his decision was "a strong conviction that my life would be more usefully and happily spent in the Communion of the Church of England ... I am convinced that the Church of Scotland will not permanently be established in the Canadas." Here, the principle of establishment, and the status that it conferred upon the clergy, was enough to turn MacLaurin from his national allegiance. Although Stewart admonished him that there were, indeed, great and meaningful doctrinal differences between episcopacy and presbytery, he was ultimately prepared to ordain MacLaurin and recommend adding him to the SPG missionary rolls,[97] that is, until a year later, when Stewart received information "of his being open to the charge of intemperance." Although MacLaurin was able to dispose of this canard, the Bishop was then apprised of the fact that there were also "matters of a pecuniary nature" that blemished MacLaurin's character, and these were substantiated,[98] compelling Stewart to abandon the process of ordination. Two key considerations are underscored by this abortive negotiation. On the one hand, the desire of men like MacLaurin to make the switch to Anglicanism seemed to validate the idea that membership in the Anglican communion was, indeed, the primary attribute of "British" identity. On the other hand, MacLaurin was quite specific that "establishment" – the political connection with the state – was, in terms of his own sense of status, Anglicanism's principal attraction. It was precisely this element that, by the 1830s, was proving to be the most contested, and the weakest link in Anglicanism's ongoing attempt to posit a uniform religious identity as the determinant of a transatlantic British citizenship.

"It gives me great pleasure," wrote Rev. John Sprott of Musquodoboit, Nova Scotia in 1826, "to hear that the waste places of our Transatlantic Zion are to be enclosed and cultivated by labourers from the North British Church." Sprott, a Church of Scotland missionary employed by the Glasgow Colonial Society, used the phrase "North British Church" to express his pride in what had become a key feature of Scotland's social, political, and cultural life since Union with England in 1707: his country's entry into the modern world by participation in the making of a greater "Britain."[99] A year later, Sprott waxed eloquent about the people in his community, declaring that they were "strongly predisposed in favour of Scotland and Scottish men. We look to it with a hallowed feeling of tenderness and veneration as the land of our fathers the birth place of a Knox and a Melville, a Blair and a Robertson. The Repository of religious principles and practical wisdom."[100] Sprott's attempt to define a place for Scotland in the British North American colonies fused two discrete, and at times contradictory, elements: a claim to participate in the emerging "modern" cultural and political attributes that demarcated "Britishness," and a much older ethnic national consciousness, encapsulated in references to Scotland's early-modern religious history. Clergymen like Sprott sought to carve out a place for the Church of Scotland in colonial society by stressing the ways in which, as an established church, the institution articulated an inclusive "Britishness" that buttressed colonial political and cultural allegiance. But two key factors ensured that the other element of the equation, the early-modern ethno-religious identity that asserted that Scotland's historic independence was a function of the preservation of distinct religious rituals and institutions, actually became more dominant in the Canadas and the Maritimes. First, the colonial constitutions themselves stood as obstacles to a vision of inclusivity that would admit the Church of Scotland to equal religious privileges as an establishment; second, because, like their Anglican counterparts, Church of Scotland clergy in the colonies were far more subject to their congregations than their colleagues at home, they were pushed by the more aggressively popular, ethno-religious sensibilties of ordinary emigrant believers to a more hard-edged defence of national religious particularism that, in fact, subverted and seriously fragmented "Britishness" as an overarching colonial identity. A "modern" Anglo-

Britishness was compromised by a reinvigorated "traditionalist" early-modern theological language of cultural separation and independence, one that emphasized the morally and spiritually superior church polity of Scotland's national church over that of England. In the process, Scottish Presbyterianism in British North America developed a powerful "ethnic," rather than simply an overarchingly "British," inflection. Here, Scotland's national religious institutions stood as an effective strategy of resistance to Anglican attempts to define a single transatlantic citizenship around a uniform religious allegiance.

"Britishness" emerged as a contested terrain in the late 1820s and 1830s less as a result of pressures from "dissenters" like the Methodists, who have occupied a disproportionate place in the historiography of colonial Canada,[101] than of the activities of what at first sight might appear an impeccably "conservative" institution, the Church of Scotland. As the established church of Scotland, this institution had a recognized legal and constitutional position within the United Kingdom itself. More tellingly, during the eighteenth century, the Church of Scotland clergy had been at the forefront of an attempt by Scottish elites to, in essence, discipline and "subvert" older ethno-religious discourses that from the sixteenth century onward underwrote a sense of independent Scottish nationhood, and to project a new Anglo-Britishness based on English models of constitutional liberty and commercial prosperity.[102] This, its proponents believed, would both assure Scotland's political and cultural assimilation into the "internal" empire of the United Kingdom, and allow Scotchmen, as "North Britons," a participation as equals in the development of the "external" or colonial empire.[103] With the foundation of the Glasgow Colonial Society in 1825, the Church of Scotland acquired a missionary arm by which to systematize the national church's commitment to Britain's overseas imperial enterprise. It should be observed in this context that Presbyterian congregations and clergy had long been active in British North America as a focal point of Scottish ethnic identity,[104] but the GCS defined its particular mission in terms of a synthesis of a national church connected to the imperial state, British allegiance, and a Scottish ethnic religious hegemony over other Presbyterian groups in the colonies. Indeed, the GCS was aware that colonial Presbyterians were a rather diverse lot; ethnically comprising Americans, as well as immigrants from Scotland and Northern Ireland; religiously, with groups of Secessionists and those wedded to the establishment principle divided into a number of competing congregations and synods; and linguistically, divided into English-speaking "Lowland" immigrants and Gaelic-speaking Highlanders. However, they maintained that their efforts would "consolidate the Church of Scotland in America and ... to give

here a weight sufficient to carry along with her the other lesser Presbyterian sects."[105] Thomas McCulloch, a leading Nova Scotia Seceder
Presbyterian, devoted a good deal of effort to keeping the Church of
Scotland off what he considered his "turf," warning in 1826 that Scottish emigration was small, scattered among many other ethnic groups,
and that the clergy of the established church, expecting steady financial support from local congregations, consequently had the least
chance of success. The clergy of the Scottish Establishment,
McCulloch contended, were mentally out of step with the "American"
character of the local population, which was already well-served by
native clergy. As if this was not enough, McCulloch declared that the
introduction of the Church of Scotland would result in factions and
distinctions among colonial Presbyterians that had not previously
existed.[106]

As Scottish immigration to all parts of British North America
increased dramatically after 1815, promoters of the Church of Scotland deployed two effective arguments to counter opponents like
McCulloch, one pan-British, and the other more narrowly "ethnic."
First, they could point to the obvious political connection with the
British state itself. The formation of Church of Scotland congregations
presided over by clergy recruited in Scotland would provide nuclei
around which could coalesce "good and loyal subjects of our King ...
and to our inestimable constitution, the birthright, boast, and pride of
every true Briton."[107] The national church, as a number of its proponents were quick to point out, if backed by the British state, would
check "Sectarianism," meaning the American-style welter of Presbyterian groups, and by having congregations managed by clergy explicitly
connected to the British state, would furnish colonial Presbyterians
with a principle of unity and loyalty. For this reason, Church of Scotland clergy welcomed an ad hoc policy developed by the imperial government in the early 1830s of giving them regular grants on condition
that they formed a duly constituted local synod linked to the Scottish
Establishment, thus checking the ever-present centrifugal tendencies
within Presbyterianism that conferred too much authority on laypeople and congregations.[108] As Rev. Kenneth McKenzie emphatically
stated in refuting the voluntarist arguments of Seceder Presbyterians
like Thomas McCulloch, "the government of the country ought to
look after them; and ought to support & encourage Clergymen in the
colonies who by their very connection with establishments are pledged
and in principle bound to promote the spread and growth of loyalty
and attachment to the Constitution."[109]

Like their Anglican counterparts, Church of Scotland clergy viewed
the connection with the British state through some system of endow-

ment as essential to maintaining the corporate status of the clergy as a group. The missionaries recruited by the Glasgow Colonial Society were generally men who, though well-educated in Scottish universities, were unable, because of lack of connections, to secure a permanent call to a parish at home. One minister, Rev Mark Young Stark, despite glowing references from Dugald Stewart, found little in the way of career prospects at home because of the prevailing system of patronage within the Church of Scotland, in which lay aristocrats imposed their own nominees on parishes, a situation which tended to discriminate against candidates with more "evangelical" religious convictions. Stark stood firm against family pressures to take Anglican orders, citing his allegiance to Scotland's historic national faith,[110] and preferred emigration to Dundas, Upper Canada in 1833. Upon his arrival there, he wrote enthusiastically that he now had a permanent situation as a "*real minister*" and further, he had been able to purchase land, making him "a *Laird* although somewhat on a Lilliputian scale."[111] However, ministers like Stark were also confronted with the fact that congregational support was at best small-scale, and at worst, entirely irregular,[112] and for this reason they vociferously rejected the notion that support for religion should be a voluntary matter. "If we had £100 a year from Govt.," he informed his mother in 1837, "we might manage to get on. ... I have not so much reason to complain as many others but the voluntary system altogether is a most complete delusion."[113]

However, in contrast to their Anglican counterparts, Presbyterian ministers had to navigate a more careful course in pressing their claims for state salaries. Scotland's national church, being presbyterian in its structure, had a formal commitment to the independence and autonomy of local congregations which, if they selected and called the minister, were expected to assume a major role in paying his salary. Most Church of Scotland missionaries were adherents, at least nominally, of the "evangelical" party within the church which defended the rights of congregations over those of lay aristocratic patrons, and thus, in urging state endowments, cited these as necessary in order to maintain their status as educated professional clergy who held the respect of their congregations. Rev. Alexander Ross stated in 1830 that he did not think that he and his colleagues would be successful "if they were known to be poor and dependent in a country where every industrious man can make himself independent."[114] John Burns, a lay promoter of the Scottish establishment, similarly indicated the necessity of a link between a state-endowed clergy and "British" identity, as opposed to the "American" or voluntary system. "The people," he declared, "generally despise what is so easily obtained & regard such Preachers as vagrants. They have been too much accustomed to strolling Preachers from the United States & Ireland which has given them a very unfavourable idea of all those who come along in this manner."[115] What they envisioned was not a complete endowment by the state, which might compromise Presbyterianism's ideal of spiritual independence, but a harnessing of government support and the voluntary principle, in which payments by the state to the clergy would act as inducements to greater contribution by local congregations. The Glasgow Colonial Society itself carefully balanced the fact that a settled ministry, in which the social and cultural arrangements of the Scottish parish could be transplanted, would be difficult to achieve among colonial congregations whose means could not support such a system, with the Presbyterian commitment to a high level of local autonomy. "It would not be desirable," concluded the GCS, "that clergymen proceeding to the Colonies should be made altogether independent of the people to whom they preach,"[116] an injunction reinforced in 1838 by Hon. William Morris, one of the key lay advocates of the Church of Scotland's claim to a share of the Clergy Reserves. Morris was careful to emphasize that a limited state financial support was designed only to "secure the decent and permanent support of public worship," which in no way absolved local congregations from a high level of voluntary financial contribution. "The congregation," he stipulated, "must be required to contribute a portion of the minister's stipend ... else a state of indolent indifference may arise."[117]

If the introduction of the Scottish establishment was viewed as essential to unifying all Presbyterians in an expansive, transatlantic, pan-British, politico-cultural unity, the arguments used by its proponents frequently sounded a far less "modern" note. Both Scottish clergy and laity evoked a much older sense of national consciousness centred on the forceful equation of ethnic character and the preservation of Presbyterian religious institutions. The managers of the Dalhousie Public Library, who had been so quick to come forth with their allegiance to the "British" monarchy and constitution could, in the same breath, affirm a vigorous "attachment to our uncorrupted creed."[118] Indeed, for many of these immigrant Scots, the transplantation of a British identity was dependent on "the force of those religious impressions and habits, which they received and formed in their native land."[119] "We still retain," proclaimed one Glasgow Colonial Society report, "an ardent love for our national church. We look upon our connection with it, as a link, and a powerful one, in the mighty chain of affection which unites us to the beloved land we have left." Significantly, religious institutions and rituals – "the solemn stillness of the Scottish Sabbath," "the Scottish worship," and, especially, the impressiveness of "the Sacrament of the Supper," the ancient rite of communion[120] –

were identified as the key "bonds" of affection between the homeland and Scottish communities overseas.

Indeed, Scottish communities in British North America took shape not so much around the "modern" language of British constitutionalism and commercial prosperity as around the implantation of early-modern religious institutions and practices. Although the Church of Scotland clergy, much like their Anglican counterparts, viewed themselves as a social group whose education and ministerial position gave them a superior and independent status in colonial society, and campaigned vigorously for state support in order to secure this "independence," the very modest financial support given by the Glasgow Colonial Society made them even more dependent than the Church of England clergy on their congregations. What should be emphasized is that the Glasgow Colonial Society, in contrast to the SPG, was a purely private philanthropic body and did not receive public financing from the British state to make grants to the colonial clergy. This dictated a much lower level of ministerial stipend, £30 for Church of Scotland clergy as opposed to the £150 enjoyed by Anglican missionaries, a monetary constraint that forced the promoters of the GCS to adopt the firm policy that they would only commit to sending clergy to British North America if local communities submitted a "bond" or "engagement" whereby they promised, for a certain number of years, to pay an adequate clerical salary.[121] Here was a situation rife with hard bargaining between local congregations desiring the service of a minister and the expansionist religious imperialism of the GCS. Unlike the hierarchical structure of the Anglican Church, Church of Scotland Presbyterians prided themselves on a more "democratic" church polity in which laity would receive clergymen "on trial," and reserved the final decision as to whether to give them a lifetime call. In 1831, Rev. Mr Dunlop, the GCS missionary, found himself in the unpleasant situation of negotiating with a recalcitrant congregation at Guelph. Jealous of their local autonomy, this group of Presbyterians refused to enter into a firm engagement with any minister they had not seen and heard, and went so far as to reject one candidate on the grounds that they found his sermons "prelatical."[122] Two years later, Rev. F. McNaughton attempted to secure a permanent call from the Scottish settlers at Thorah Township, Upper Canada, urging that it was only proper that they receive him "on the same terms on which ministers are received in Scotland." He was "sneeringly" informed by congregational elders and church members that "they would receive no minister during his life, and that if they paid him they would retain the power of removing him when he ceased to please them." The matter

ended well for McNaughton, but only because, unlike many other
Scottish clergymen, he had a sound working knowledge of Gaelic. In
the neighbouring settlement of Vaughan, a group of Highlanders
entered the bidding war for his services, but they would only pledge
themselves for six years, declaring that even this was too much of an
abridgment of their local autonomy, "that they had never heard of any
people in Canada who bound themselves so long."[123]

Two major consequences flowed from the clash between the colo-
nizing imperatives of the leaders of the Scottish establishment and the
long-standing tradition of local autonomy. Because they, and not the
church at home, would ultimately assume sole financial responsibility
for paying the clergyman, congregations were able, in advance, to
essentially "negotiate" the credentials and qualities of a minister, and
in so doing, they were emphatic that what they wanted were "evangelical" clergy whose views of doctrine, ritual, church polity, and religious
practice would closely coincide with their own. Declared Rev. James
Hannay of New Brunswick in 1834, "In a Missionary, *popular gifts* are
indispensable,"[124] a term that emphatically directed immigrant clergymen to eviscerate any attachment to the values or practices of the
"moderate," or anti-evangelical, party within the national church that
identified with maintaining aristocratic leadership, and adopt the
more demotic expression of the "popular" or evangelical party.[125] For
example, in 1824, James Thomson of Miramichi, New Brunswick
wrote to Dr Burns that any minister sent out by the GCS "ought to be a
good Preacher, not a reader, Evangelical, Pious, intelligent, well-
grounded in Presbyterian principles, Liberal with regard to other
denominations."[126] Here, evangelicalism denoted a commitment to a
transatlantic populist egalitarianism and a willingness to co-operate
with other religious groups in interdenominational philanthropic
endeavours, but it also stressed a firm maintenance of "traditional"
Scottish religious forms and practices – in other words, a strategy of
boundary-making for an ethnic community. In criticizing a number of
his fellow-clergy in Lower Canada, Rev. Archibald Colquhoun of
Chateauguay lamented that they had "been so remiss in the dispensa-
tion of the ordinances ... baptism and the communion of the Lord's
supper, without asking one question of the applicants respecting their
knowledge, or requiring a certificate of good character" that they
would be better to "join the Moderate Party."[127] Even the well-estab-
lished Presbyterian community of urban Montreal was quick to stipu-
late that what they required in a clergyman was "unreserved piety in
visiting statedly or accidentally the sick or the well," a practice which,
they informed the GCS, was "absolutely necessary to give force to the
labours of the pulpit ... On this continent a liberal equality is visible,

and when a Minister of Christ acts with it, and in character, it highly exalts him."[128]

Two ministerial practices, "visiting" and the matter of reading sermons, were particular yardsticks by which congregations could measure the "evangelical" character of their minister and, at the same time, deploy presbyterianism in the defence of ethnic particularism. The matter of "visiting" was one in which the more egalitarian or "liberal" spirit of North American congregations' aspirations to lower the social barriers between clergy and laity at times clashed with the more genteel proclivities of Scottish-born and educated clergy. In 1830, Rev. George Struthers of Horton, Nova Scotia, scathingly denounced "visiting" in a letter to the Glasgow Colonial Society as a particularly objectionable form of pandering to congregational scrutiny. While not opposed to visiting parishioners for religious purposes, Struthers declared that these clerical visits were in fact not the ones that were desired by the congregation: "They expect that he should spend a great part of his time in going from house to house talking of the news of the day, and attending parties, and some Clergymen gratify their humors and imagine they are benefiting the interests of religion by doing so." Struthers dismissed this as "degrading to the clerical character."[129] So objectionable did he find this kind of social levelling that, in 1832, he took "French leave" of the Horton Presbyterians, and found a more congenial situation in Bermuda.[130] A stronger note of ethno-religious particularism was sounded by the emphatic prohibition against the reading of sermons. Indeed, the opposition of "preacher" and "reader" was a constant feature of the correspondence between Scottish emigrant congregations and the Glasgow Colonial Society. As Rev. Kenneth McKenzie bluntly put the matter, "the Society must lay an *absolute interdict* on one and all of their Missionaries ... against reading their discourses. The practice is especially abhorred by the people. However able a Preacher is otherwise, let him be a reader and he is not acceptable. The people think every Sermon read is a borrowed one and consequently they will not entertain for any length of time a high opinion of such as use their papers."[131] Here, McKenzie was referring particularly to the fact that among Scottish Presbyterians of more humble social ranks, "reading" a sermon was frowned upon as a particularly aristocratic vice and was regarded as a dangerously "English" liturgical innovation that would corrupt and compromise the distinctiveness and independence of Scottish religious institutions.[132] So seriously did the GCS take this assertion of ethnic religious values that, in 1830, they actually refused to send out Rev. Mr Aitken, an extremely well-qualified clergyman whose literary attainments would have pleased the urban congregation of Quebec City, for balking at their demand that he stop reading his sermons.[133]

Among the small farmers, tenants, labourers, rural clergy, and minor professionals who formed the backbone of Scottish emigration to the Canadas and the Maritimes, a common sense of "Britishness" was frequently qualified by, and subordinated to, older patriotisms and a sense of ethnic difference that centred particularly on the distinctions of church polity between Presbyterian and Anglican. By the 1830s a firm connection had been forged among Scottish Presbyterian immigrant communities in British North America between an evangelicalism that promoted the "modern" values of self-improvement, moral rectitude, and self-discipline and the aggressive assertion of elements of an early-modern ethnic patriotism that looked to the history of seventeenth-century religious struggles around the preservation of traditions of religious ritual and church government.[134] This connection illustrates the force of the historian John MacKenzie's recent observation that British imperial expansion, rather than serving as the vehicle for an overarching national identity, actually enabled the sub-nationalisms of the United Kingdom to survive and flourish.[135] Indeed, although historians like Linda Colley have stressed the integrating power of a "British" patriotism in the early nineteenth century, she has also cautioned that these values and practices carried far more weight among the aristocracy and commercially successful elements of English and Scottish society.[136] And because the vast majority of immigrant Scots were not drawn from these classes, the arrival of numerous Scottish clergy after the late 1820s resulted in the vigorous reactivation, on the part of both clergy and laypeople connected with the Church of Scotland, of features of the early-modern Scottish "parish state" that had largely fallen into disuse in Scotland as a result of expanding urbanization, commercial capitalism, and a more competitive religious pluralism. In addition to insisting on the solemnity of the communion sacrament which symbolically and emotionally bound immigrant Scotchmen in the New World to the religious history of their homeland,[137] there was a largely successful attempt among local congregations in Upper Canada and the Maritimes to institute the disciplinary church courts that had, in sixteenth- and seventeenth-century Scotland, provided the national church with a powerful basis of community cohesion and control.[138]

In the colonial setting, the reactivation of such structures was a deliberate choice by both clergy and laity, as both were interested in indicating that "Scottishness" was affirmed as primarily religious and institutional in character. Among both *Transatlantic clergymen* and immigrant laypeople, the transplanting of "orthodoxy" – meaning the historic structures of Scottish church government – was of central significance in reconstituting and asserting ethnicity in the colonial setting.[139] In an atmosphere where clergymen were frequently at odds with their congregations over finances, these older models of church government, like the church disciplinary tribunals, in which both clergy and lay elders had a voice, could uphold community solidarity around a shared set of religious practices.[140] As well, for immigrant Scots, they served the function of forging a Scottish hegemony within the wider culture of British North American Presbyterianism. "In Scotland," declared Rev. Monson of Dartmouth, Nova Scotia in 1829, "the people within the limits of a country parish are taught one catechism, sit under one Minister, are accustomed to hear one doctrine preached & have one mode of church discipline practised."[141] American and Northern Irish Presbyterians, in particular, were viewed as somewhat theologically suspect because their churches, unlike the Scots', did not possess strong disciplinary machinery.[142] A rallying around this visible institutional machinery underwrote the conviction of Scottish leaders that their particular imperial task was the incorporation, through the machinery of church government, of Presbyterian co-religionists under their leadership.

Among both Church of Scotland clergy and local congregations in the Canadas and the Maritimes, there was a distinct accentuation of the institutional components of presbyterianism as transplanting and preserving Scottish ethnicity. And it was these peculiarly "early-modern" expressions of identity, rather than a common political language of "Britishness," that in the 1830s dictated the way in which Scotland's national church in the colonies sought to articulate a relationship with the British state. The catalyst in this colonial inversion was the vexed question of church-state relations and, in particular, the issue of which churches should share in the revenues of the Clergy Reserves. In Great Britain itself, the 1707 Anglo-Scottish Treaty of Union had confirmed both the independence and the established status of the Church of Scotland as enjoying an exclusive link, within Scotland, with the British monarchy. However, in British North America, colonial constitutions privileged only the Church of England, a view concurred in even by colonial governors like Lord Dalhousie who were themselves members of the Church of Scotland.[143] With increasing outrage, Church of Scotland ministers in the colonies pointed to the obvious injustice of a permanent parliamentary grant to the Anglican SPG totalling £16,000 a year for the payment of clergy in the Canadas and the Maritimes, contrasted with a niggardly ad hoc annual grant of £750 for Church of Scotland clergy. And this despite the fact that in their estimation, Presbyterians far outnumbered the Anglicans! As well, in both Upper and Lower Canada, the Church of Scotland was confronted with the fact that the provincial legislatures "appear to have proceeded upon the false, unfounded assumption, that the Church of England is the Established Church in all the British Dominions, Scotland alone excepted."[144]

In seeking equal access to government in the form of co-establishment, the Church of Scotland clergy's initial strategy was to draw on its eighteenth-century heritage as a promoter of an inclusive, Anglo-Britishness that rested on notions of constitutional right. An undated letter in the *Kingston Chronicle* proclaimed that "the National Church of North Britain is in right and justice entitled to be put on a footing of equality with that of England in these provinces." Citing the 1707 Treaty of Union as overriding the colonial constitutions, the author claimed that because the Canadas had been conquered by "the United arms of Scotland and England," Scotland's national church was entitled to an equal participation in all state provisions for the clergy.[145] The Church of Scotland's claim to equality with the Church of England was at first pressed through Britishness as inclusion, with the 1707 Union held up as the Scotsman's passport into the full possession of imperial citizenship.[146] In fact, this is what the Scottish establishment had been saying since the early eighteenth century: that although Scotland had an independent religious polity, Britishness implied a unitary, universal political identity. However, in nineteenth-century British North America, this "modern" language was rendered largely inoperable, and was replaced, among the local clergy and their lay supporters, by a more jarring, older language of ethno-religious patriotism that in Scotland had been relegated to the realm of historical curiosity in the novels of Sir Walter Scott, or banished to margins of Seceder theological polemic.[147] In the Canadas and the Maritimes a much older form of Scottish ethnic patriotism was fuelled by annoyance that the promise of Anglo-British integration was not being fulfilled. Scottish particularism, as Colin Kidd has observed, was much stronger as an expression of presbyterian sensibility, and as a defence of Scotland's distinctive religious institutions.[148] Among colonial Scots, this annoyance grew to the point where ethnic particularism overbore integration, as clergy and congregations became increasingly frustrated with the local legislatures' failure to enact measures granting the colonial church of Scotland access to endowments, and with the reluctance of a more "liberal" British government to interfere in colonial ecclesiastical arrangements.

Significantly, in 1828, when Presbyterian clergy connected with the Church of Scotland drew up the first collective statement of their claim to co-establishment in the colonies, although they evoked the more assimilationist language of British constitutionalism and the Treaty of Union, the main grounds of their critique of Anglican exclusivism and British colonial religious policy did not turn on these arguments. They meaningfully advised the imperial authorities to endeavour "to give full scope to the diffusion of British (i.e. English, Scotch, and Irish) feelings and influences, and not to obstruct any of those channels by which they may be communicated."[149] Because, for them, "Scottishness" was precisely equated with a well-defined presbyterian institutional church polity, the articulation of "Britishness" in the colonial setting shifted from integration to ethnic fragmentation. "We are unable to perceive," concluded the Pastoral Letter, "why it might not be as wise and liberal a policy to cherish and promote Scottish feelings and habits, since the Scottish people form a much greater proportion of the population."[150]

Here, the terms of engagement had undergone a seismic shift. It was no longer a question of claiming a place in an Anglo-British state as junior partners escaping a less than desirable feudal past, but of asserting a superiority on the grounds that Scotland's early-modern presbyterian church polity was somehow more closely attuned to the emerging "modern" liberal society in the colonies. This was exactly the argument pressed by a Church of Scotland layman, John Rae of Hamilton, Upper Canada, who advanced the notion that Britain's post-Revolutionary empire was not maintained by force, but by culture, the "manners, feelings, and habits"[151] of emigrant Britons. Anglicanism, resting upon an episcopal polity, could not succeed in forging this cultural unity because its hierarchical, aristocratic government was out of step with more egalitarian British North American social structures. Presbyterianism, and, in particular, its expression in the Church of Scotland, was the only church of the British Isles fully congruent with colonial values. "Its doctrines," declared Rae, "have been characterised as calvinistical, austere, puritanical; these terms seem to imply that it is the religion of the people. ... Its original form, giving the election to the congregation, suits our liberal nation."[152] Rae's vision effectively presaged the outlines, not of a universal Anglo-Britishness whose countenance radiated the rational politeness of the Enlightenment in which older religious differences had been submerged in a common patriotism, but of a "British Canadian" identity which bore many uncanny resemblances to the Scottish character, so deeply etched by the politico-religious structures of the Presbyterian Reformation. Scotland's national church, which in Scotland was a primary institution promoting integration in a common imperial identity, had emerged by the 1830s in British North America as the key to upholding not only a Scottish ethnic separateness, but an empire fragmented by Atlantic difference and nourished by local pre-modern patriotisms fuelled by the rivalry of competitive Protestant churches.

Following the colonial rebellions of 1837–38, both the Church of England and the Church of Scotland moved further away from a commitment to an overarching Britishness as the foundation of a common imperial citizenship and authority. In the short term, the Church of Scotland gained access to the "dividends of empire" – a formal relationship with the colonial state and a share of the Clergy Reserves in Upper and Lower Canada – but this did not bring either clergy or congregations into an "Anglo-British" consensus. Rather, the presence of the imperial state, read as an "anglicizing" entity, was the source of further conflict and fragmentation within Presbyterianism, because the nature of the link between clergy and their congregations rested, in the final analysis, not on a transatlantic British patriotism, but on an effort to protect the "purity" and "independence" of Scotland's ethnic religious institutions from outside regulation and interference. In 1844, the secession of clergy and congregations who adopted the banner of the Free Church shifted the balance within British North America in favour of religious voluntarism. Early-modern ethno-religious patriotism, the basis of colonial Scots' sense of "Britishness," emerged as an important component of the Reform party's reconstitution around the rapid and complete disengagement of church and state.[153]

Of perhaps greater significance, however, the Church of England, which arguably had the strongest stake in promoting a common Britishness as the basis of a politically and culturally uniform empire, also consciously participated in an early-modern ethnic inversion after the 1840s. In part, this was dictated by the fact that Anglicans had, during the Rebellions, looked into the abyss and realized that the close identification of the church with extreme political conservatism was corrosive of its religious character. Anglican churches, like that of Rev. Mayerhoffer in Markham, Upper Canada, were targets of rebel disaffection,[154] a realization that led more "evangelical" local clergy such as Rev. F.L. Osler to vociferously declaim against political preaching.[155] This, in turn, implied a retreat from one of colonial Anglicanism's major strategic positions: that the Established Church was the institution that best promoted an inclusivity in a common British imperial order. What, then, was the Church's role? Unlike those who have viewed the 1840s and 1850s as inaugurating a period of Anglican retreat from the public sphere and the shift to a "Protestant consensus,"[156] this paper contends that Anglican leaders in fact adopted a course similar to that of the Church of Scotland, insisting on the "English" ethnic character that differentiated and erected boundaries between their church and others. But what constituted "Englishness" in the colonial setting? Like its Scottish counterpart, "Englishness" was an evocation of the pre-modern, but here, one in which the political-governmental in the narrow sense would be replaced by a cultural aesthetic as the ultimate source of transatlantic unity: resplendent ritual that would harmonize social differences, theological polemics that emphasized the continuities and apostolic character of the hierarchical episcopal government, and the way in which these structures would preserve among immigrants "those recollections of the land of their fathers."[157] However, the Anglican inversion served only to produce greater internal ethnic tension between "English" and "Irish" identities, as the latter's identification with the Church of England had always firmly resisted "High Church" tendencies.

The colonial experiences of the "national" churches of England and Scotland in British North America between 1780 and 1850 began with the premise that these institutions would incarnate and articulate an inclusive "British" imperial citizenship. By 1840, however, any sense of "Britishness" as an integrative political identity, much as it might characterize the emerging national consciousness in the British Isles, had largely receded in the Canadas and the Maritimes, contested and undermined by the aggressive reassertion of early-modern ethnic identities anchored in competing and ultimately hostile institutional church polities. The strange death of a common imperial "Britishness" in the largest settlement colonies urgently calls historians to reconsider, for both the British homeland and the empire, the supposed integrative, "modernizing" features of Protestantism as a common source of identity and symbols of belonging.[158] And for Canadian historians, it suggests the need to reintegrate struggles over "Britishness" into our history, particularly to appreciate the ways in which the formation of the institutions and cultural values of "liberal" society was a complicated and ambiguous process that owed far more to the religious features of a pre-modern past than has hitherto been acknowledged.

NOTES

1 National Archives of Canada [NAC], Society for the Propagation of the Gospel in Foreign Parts [henceforth cited SPG], C Mss. Canada, Dio Nova Scotia, 1792–1850, Reel A–172, Churchwardens of Rawdon to John Nova Scotia (Rt. Rev. John Inglis, Lord Bishop of Nova Scotia), 13 Dec. 1823. The National Archives of Canada holds the microfilmed collection of SPG material related to Canada. The originals of this collection are held in the Library of Rhodes House, Oxford University, United Kingdom.

2 NAC, SPG, C Mss. Canada, Dio Nova Scotia, 1792–1850, Reel A–172, "Memorial from Episcopalians and dissenters of Rawdon," 20 Jan. 1824; Ibid., Churchwardens of Rawdon to John Nova Scotia, 13 Dec. 1823.

3 Ibid., Rev. Henry Hayden to SPG, 10 June 1824.

4 Scholars who have examined the process of building the "Second British Empire" after 1783 have concluded that the Established Church came to be regarded as a key resource for state and empire building and, consequently, there was a more forceful projection abroad of the Anglican Church, particularly in colonies where there were substantial communities of people of British descent, or where the majority of the people were Christians. See C.A. Bayly, *Imperial Meridian: The British Empire and the World, 1780–1830* (London and New York: Longman, 1989), 108–9; and, on the main outlines of British imperial religious policy in the nineteenth century, Andrew Porter, "Religion, Missionary Enthusiasm, and Empire," in Andrew Porter, ed., *The Oxford History of the British Empire*, Vol. 3: *The Nineteenth Century* (Oxford: Oxford University Press, 1999), 222–46.

5 For a stimulating analysis of the components of the "Anglo-British" patriotism promoted by the established Church of Scotland in the eighteenth century, see Colin Kidd, "North Britishness and the Nature of Eighteenth-Century British Patriotism," *Historical Journal,* 39, no. 2 (1996): 361–82.

6 Historians of the Church of Ireland in the eighteenth and early nineteenth century have highlighed the discrepancy between the legally privileged position of the Church, and its rather modest clerical revenues. S.J. Connolly, for example, has noted that in the 1720s, only 1/3 of the beneficed clergy enjoyed incomes in excess of £100, and that plural office-holding was one of the few ways of making an adequate income. See Connolly, *Religion, Law, and Power: The Making of Protestant Ireland, 1660–1760* (Oxford: Clarendon Press, 1992), 180–3. For the early nineteenth century, Donald Akenson's *The Church of Ireland: Ecclesiastical Reform and Revolution, 1800–1885* (New Haven: Yale University Press, 1971) has observed that a process of internal reform within the Church of Ireland not only would have restricted this source of clerical income, but in the 1830s, the reforms of the Irish Establishment launched by the Whig government in London would have provided serious financial disincentives for young clergymen seeking a career in the Church of Ireland. For Hayden's Irish origins, see *Classified Digest of the Records of the Society for the Propagation of the Gospel in Foreign Parts, 1701–1892* (London: SPG, 1895), 862, 865.

7 For the uses of Calvinism by Irish Church leaders like Archbishop Ussher since the seventeenth century as indicating a separate, and more ancient, historical origin from its English counterpart, see Colin Kidd, *British Identities before Nationalism: Ethnicity and Nationhood in the Atlantic World, 1600–1800* (Cambridge: Cambridge University Press, 1999).

8 Akenson, *Church of Ireland,* 132.

9 For evangelicalism in the Diocese of Ossory, see Richard W. Vaudry, *Anglicans and the Atlantic World: High Churchmen, Evangelicals, and the Quebec*

Connection (Montreal & Kingston: McGill-Queen's University Press, 2004), 142–3.

10 The "High Church" and anti-Evangelical character of both colonial bishops and the SPG have been noted by historians. For the Diocese of Quebec, see the recent treatment by Vaudry, *Anglicans and the Atlantic World*; and for Nova Scotia, see Judith Fingard, *The Anglican Design in Loyalist Nova Scotia, 1783–1816* (London: SPCK, 1972).

11 NAC, SPG, C Mss. Canada, Dio Nova Scotia, 1792–1850, Reel A–172, John Nova Scotia to SPG, 27 Aug. 1829; Ibid., John Nova Scotia to SPG, 10 Mar. 1826; Ibid., C Mss. Canada, Dio Nova Scotia, Bishop John Inglis, 1833–41, Box 1/3b, John Nova Scotia, "Circular Letter to Colonial Clergy re Colonial Church Society," 15 Apr. 1841.

12 For this approach from the perspective of political ideology and intellectual history, see Jeffrey McNairn, *The Capacity to Judge: Public Opinion and Deliberative Democracy in Upper Canada, 1791–1854* (Toronto: University of Toronto Press, 2000); and for an informative treatment of popular political radicalism, see Carol Wilton, *Popular Politics and Political Culture in Upper Canada, 1800–1850* (Montreal & Kingston: McGill-Queen's University Press, 2001).

13 Major statements of this line of interpretation include William Westfall, *Two Worlds: The Protestant Culture of Nineteenth-Century Ontario* (Montreal & Kingston: McGill-Queen's University Press, 1989); Curtis Fahey, *In His Name: The Anglican Experience in Upper Canada, 1791–1854 (Ottawa: Carleton University Press,* 1991); Peter A. Russell, "Church of Scotland Clergy in Upper Canada: Culture Shock and Conservatism on the Frontier," *Ontario History*, 73, no. 2 (June 1981): 88–111.

14 Alexander Murdoch, *British History, 1660–1832: National Identity and Local Culture* (New York: St Martin's Press, 1998), 69, 151.

15 Linda Colley, *Britons: Forging the Nation, 1707–1837* (London: Pimlico, 1992).

16 For eighteenth-century England as a "confessional state," see the key work by J.C.D. Clark, *English Society, 1688–1832: Ideology, Social Structure, and Political Practice during the Ancien Régime* (Cambridge: Cambridge University Press, 1985). For the development of the parish-based system of local government as a key element of early-modern English state-building, see Steve Hindle, *The State and Social Change in Early Modern England, c. 1550–1640* (Houndmills: Palgrave Press, 2000), 205–6, 229. Church establishment was also a key factor in the extension of English authority in Ireland from the early seventeenth century onward. See Nicholas Canny, *Making Ireland British, 1580–1650* (Oxford: Oxford University Press, 2001); and Connolly, *Religion, Law, and Power*.

17 Eliga Gould, *The Persistence of Empire: British Political Culture in the Age of the American Revolution* (Chapel Hill and London: University of North Carolina Press, 2000), 210–11.

18 Archives of Ontario [AO], John Strachan Papers, Reel 3, Strachan to Sir Rob-
    ert Peel, 15 Feb. 1843; "Extract of Dr Strachan's Sermon, on the Death of
    the Lord Bishop of Quebec," in *Claims of the Churchmen and Dissenters of Upper
    Canada Brought to the Test: in a Controversy between Several Members of the Church
    of England and a Methodist Preacher* (Kingston, U.C.: Herald Office, 1828), 19.
    See also Lambeth Palace Library, Archbishop Howley Papers, Strachan to
    Howley, 7 June 1826.

19 Anglican Diocese of Montreal [ADM], RG 1.4, Bishop C.J. Stewart, "C.J. Stew-
    art Correspondence 1826," G.J. Mountain, Archeacon of Quebec, Rector of
    the Parish of Quebec, J.L. Mills, Chaplain to H.M. Forces at Quebec, Evening
    Lecturer at the Cathedral Church; George Archbold, Assistant Minister at
    Quebec, preacher to Protestant settlers in parts adjacent, Edmund Wil-
    loughby, Sewell Minister to the Chapel of the Holy Trinity at Quebec, R.R.
    Burrage, Missionary in charge of Pointe Levi and Beauport, to C.J. Quebec,
    11 Jan. 1826.

20 ADM, Ibid., 11 Jan. 1826.

21 For the close relationship between Church of England clergy and the landed
    elite of eighteenth century England, see Jeremy Black, *Eighteenth-Century Brit-
    ain, 1688–1783* (Houndmills: Palgrave, 2001), 130.

22 The colonial constitutions of both the Canadas and the Maritime provinces
    contained various provisions that gave the Anglican Church a privileged
    status. Historians have debated whether this amounted to a full-fledged
    status of "establishment." Certainly these privileges constituted a political
    flashpoint, and opponents of Anglicanism at times charged that they were an
    "establishment." For Anglican status in Upper Canada, see Fahey, *In His
    Name*, xv-xvi, 1–11, and for the rather different provisions made for
    Anglicanism in colonial Nova Scotia, see Fingard, *The Anglican Design in
    Loyalist Nova Scotia*, 26.

23 In a recent study of Anglicanism in the Eastern Townships of Lower Canada
    prior to 1850, Jack Little has suggested the adaptability, in a number of
    respects, of the institutional church to local demands, in which the Church
    paid generous salaries to its missionaries, and largely funded the building of
    churches, alleviating local congregations of the burden of initially establish-
    ing the institution. See "'In the Desert Places of the Wilderness': The Fron-
    tier Thesis and the Anglican Church in the Eastern Townships, 1799–1831,"
    Histoire sociale/Social History, 36, no. 71 (May 2003): 31–53. Little has fol-
    lowed up these insights at greater length in *Borderland Religion: The Emergence
    of an English-Canadian Identity, 1792–1852* (Toronto: University of Toronto
    Press, 2004), which provides substantial evidence that "British" churches
    such as Anglicanism and Wesleyan Methodism were institutionally far more
    effective than American Protestant groups.

24 ADM, RG 1.2, Bishop Charles Inglis, "Petition from the Parish of Montreal,
    1792."

25 Adam Shortt and A.G. Doughty, eds, *Documents Relating to the Constitutional History of Canada, 1759–1791* (Ottawa: King's Printer, 1918), Constitutional Act, sections XXXVIII, XXXIX, XLI, and XLII.

26 Quebec Diocesan Archives [QDA], Jacob Mountain Papers, C4, Rev. John Stuart, Kingston, to Mountain, 22 Sept. 1804; Ibid., C5, Herman W. Ryland, "Observations relative to the Protestant Church Establishment in Upper and Lower Canada," ca. 1806–07. British legal opinion appeared to uphold the view that by establishing the clergy reserves, the Constitutional Act had explicitly barred the Church of England from collecting tithes, a view hotly contested by Bishop Mountain. See QDA, Jacob Mountain Papers, C1b, Jacob Quebec to General Prescott, 1 Mar. 1797.

27 NAC, SPG, C Mss. Montreal and Sorel, 1778–1793, Reel A–170, Rev. John Beardsley, St John's River, NB to SPG, 26 Apr. 1784.

28 NAC, B Mss. Nova Scotia, 1760–86, Reel A–166, Rev. William Ellis, Windsor, NS, to SPG, 14 Sept. 1776.

29 NAC, SPG, B Mss. Nova Scotia, 1760–86, Reel A–166, Anonymous to SPG, n.d.

30 NAC, SPG, B Mss. Nova Scotia, 1760–86, Reel A–166, Rev. Peter de la Roche, Lunenburg, to SPG, 15 Aug. 1775.

31 NAC, SPG, C Mss. Canada, Dio Nova Scotia, 1814–44, Reel A–172, Best to SPG, 1 Feb. 1822.

32 NAC, SPG, Rev. William Abbott to SPG, 30 Jan. 1835; Ibid., C Mss. Canada, Dio Lower Canada & Upper Canada, Miscellaneous Lower Canada & Upper Canada, 1822–49, Box IVb/42, Reel A–210, "Memorial of the Undersigned Ministers of the Church of England in the Canadas ... to the Right Honorable E.G. Stanley, His Majesty's Principal Secretary of State for the Colonies." On the shift in policy regarding "exclusive" colonial establishments and the financing of the colonial church, see Richard Brent, *Liberal Anglican Politics: Whiggery, Religion, and Reform, 1830–1841* (Oxford: Clarendon Press, 1987).

33 NAC, SPG, C Mss. Canada, Dio Nova Scotia, 1792–1850, Reel A–172, John Nova Scotia, "Report of Diocese, 1827."

34 NAC, SPG, C Mss. Canada, Dio Quebec, 1819–45, Box IV/31, Reel A–200, G.J. Montreal to SPG, 14 Feb. 1840.

35 NAC, SPG, B Mss. Nova Scotia, 1760–86, Reel A–166, Rev. Peter de la Roche to SPG, 2 Aug. 1779. For similar accusations, see Ibid., Reel A–166, Rev. John Eagleson, Cumberland, NS, to SPG, 16 Jan. 1775; Ibid., Reel A–166, Rev. William Ellis, Windsor, NS, to SPG, 14 Sept. 1776; NAC, SPG, C Mss. Canada (Pre-Diocesan), 1752–93, Reel A–170, Rev. John Sayre, Halifax, to SPG, 2 Oct. 1783.

36 NAC, SPG, C Mss. Canada, Dio Quebec, Upper Canada, 1824–42, Box IVa/40, Reel A–207, Rev. John Wenham, Fort Erie, to SPG, 15 June 1824.

37 ADM, RG 1.5, Bishop George Mountain, "G.J. Mountain, Archdeacon, Correpondence 1823," Rev. James Reid, St Armand, to G.J. Mountain, 11 Apr. 1823.

38 NAC, SPG, C Mss. Canada, Dio Quebec, 1788–1837, Nova Scotia, Upper Canada, Quebec, Box IVa/38, Reel A–207, Rev. John Stuart to SPG, 15 Mar. 1794; Ibid., Rev. John Langhorn, Ernesttown, U.C., to SPG, 15 May, 1806, in which he reported that he excused two families of communicants from paying fees for the upkeep of the church on the grounds of their poverty.

39 For the class consciousness, rather than actual class status, of Anglican clergy in Upper Canada, see Fahey, *In His Name*, 222.

40 For an analysis, in a broader framework, of the gentry discourse of downward mobility in Upper Canada, see Nancy Christie, "'The Plague of Servants,'" in this volume.

41 NAC, SPG, C Mss Canada, Dio Quebec, 1819–45, Reel A–200, G.J. Montreal, "Extract from a Letter of the Bishop of Montreal to His Excellency Sir George Arthur, Lt. Governor of Upper Canada," 20 Aug. 1838.

42 NAC, SPG, C Mss. Canada, Dio Quebec, Upper Canada, 1824–42, Box IVa/40, Reel A–207, Rev. John Wenham to SPG, 29 Jan. 1830.

43 ADM, RG 1.3, Bishop Jacob Mountain, "Jacob Mountain Correspondence, 1819," Rev. Joseph Abbott, St Andrews, Lower Canada, to Mountain, 12 Sept. 1819.

44 NAC, SPG, C Mss. Canada, Dio Quebec, Upper Canada, 1824–42, Box IVa/40, Reel A–207, Rev. James Magrath, Erindale on the Credit, to SPG, 25 June 1834.

45 Ibid., Magrath to SPG, 25 June 1834.

46 ADM, RG 1.3, Bishop Jacob Mountain, "Jacob Mountain Correspondence 1805," Dr Morrice, secretary, SPG, to Mountain, 5 Mar. 1805. Morrice had expressed similar sentiments ten years earlier to Bishop Charles Inglis of Nova Scotia, stating that it was "difficult to prevail with any decent Clergyman, tho' in poor circumstances here, to abandon his home & country." Morrice further disdainfully stated that "Those who are most ready to leave it are unfit to remain in it, or to go to any other." Morice to Inglis, 27 Oct. 1795, quoted in Fingard, *The Anglican Design in Loyalist Nova Scotia*, 95.

47 NAC, SPG, C Mss. Canada, Dio Quebec, 1819–45, Box IV/30, Reel A–200, Rev. G.J. Mountain to SPG, 15 June 1821.

48 Ibid., G.J. Mountain to SPG, 15 June 1821.

49 Fingard, *The Anglican Design in Loyalist Nova Scotia*, 55.

50 NAC, SPG, C Mss. Dio Quebec, 1795–1848, Box IV/29, Reel A–199, J. Quebec to SPG, 26 Dec. 1820; Ibid., G.J. Mountain to Rev. Mr Knagg, 1 May 1824.

51 NAC, SPG, C Mss. Canada, Dio Nova Scotia, 1790–1850, Reel A–171, Rev. Roger Aitken to SPG, 23 Aug. 1813.

52 Fingard, *The Anglican Design in Loyalist Nova Scotia*, 19–24, 155.

53 For examples, see SPG, C Mss Canada (Pre-Diocesan), 1752–91, Reel A–170, Rev. Weeks to SPG, 1 Sept. 1779; Ibid., Reel 166, Rev. Dr Mather Byles, Halifax, to SPG, 7 May 1782; Ibid., Reel A–171, Rev. Walter, Shelburne, NS to

spg, 4 Feb. 1785; Walter to spg, 31 Aug. 1785. Panton-Walter affair at Shelburne over erection of parish.

54 For the Aitken affair, see nac, spg, C Mss. Canada, Dio Nova Scotia, 1790–1850, Reel A–171, "Vestry & Churchwardens of St John's Parish, Lunenburg, to Rt. Rev. Robert Stanser, Lord Bishop of Nova Scotia, 1822"; Ibid., Rev. John Inglis to Bishop Stanser, 8 June 1822; Inglis to Stanser, 3 Aug. 1822; Aitken to spg, 4 Sept. 1822.

55 For Mountain's conditions, see spg, rg 1.3, Bishop Jacob Mountain, "Jacob Mountain Correspondence, 1815," J. Quebec to Rev. Micajiah Townsend, 10 Oct. 1815.

56 adm, rg 1.3, Bishop Jacob Mountain, "Jacob Mountain Correspondence, 1804," Dr Morrice to Mountain, 22 Mar. 1804.

57 See spg, C Mss. Canada, Dio Quebec, 1795–1848, Reel A–199, Rev. Micajiah Townsend, Christie-Caldwell Manor to spg, 26 Nov. 1818; Ibid., Rev. Caleb Cotton, Dunham, Lower Canada to spg, 1 Nov. 1818; adm, rg 1.3, Bishop Jacob Mountain, "Petition from St Armand, 1826"; Ibid., "Jacob Mountain Correspondence, 1825," Rev. G.J. Mountain, St John's, to Bishop Mountain, Easter Monday, 1825.

58 For a perspective that argues for the social and cultural authority of Quebec's Catholic clergy that flowed from their exclusive control of access to ritual, see Ollivier Hubert, *Sur la terre comme au ciel: la gestion des rites par l'Église catholique du Québec (fin XVIIe – mi XIXe siècle)* (Sainte-Foy: Les Presses de l'Université Laval, 2000).

59 nac, spg, B Mss. Nova Scotia, 1760–86, Reel A–166, Rev. William Ellis, Windsor, NS, to spg, 14 Sept. 1776.

60 nac, spg, C Mss. Canada, Dio Quebec, Misc. Upper Canada, Box IVb/42, Reel A–210, Rev. B.C. Hill, "Report to the Upper Canada Clergy Society."

61 nac, spg, C Mss. Canada, Dio Quebec, 1795–1848, Reel A–199, Rev. Joseph Abbott to spg, 26 Apr. 1819; Ibid., 1788–1837; Dio Nova Scotia, Upper Canada & Dio Quebec, Box Iva/38, Reel A–207, Rev. John Langhorn to spg, 19 Apr. 1804; Ibid., Langhorn to spg, 10 Oct. 1806.

62 nac, spg, C Mss. Canada, Dio L.C., Dio U.C., Box IVb/42, Reel A–210, Misc. Upper Canada, Rev. B.C. Hill, Report to Upper Canada Clergy Society.

63 nac, spg, C Mss. Canada, Dio L.C., Dio U.C, Box IVb/42, Misc. Upper Canada, Reel A–200, Rev. B.C. Hill, "Report to the Upper Canada Clergy Society."

64 It should be noted in this context that the bulk of the salaries of the colonial clergy were paid by the spg through an annual parliamentary grant to the society that amounted, after 1816, to £16,000 for the British North American colonies. However, the Society operated on the liberal principle that such grants were intended to be temporary rather than permanent, and that the colonial churches should, as rapidly as possible, become financially self-supporting.

65 NAC, SPG, C Mss. Canada, Dio Quebec, 1819–45, Box IV/31, Reel A–200,
    G.J. Mountain, "Journal of Episcopal Visitation," 23 May 1843. See also Ibid.,
    C Mss. Canada, Dio Nova Scotia, 1792–1850, Reel A–172, John Nova Scotia
    to Spg, 28 Mar. 1828.

66 For this newer, and less state-centred strand of thinking within eighteenth
    century Anglican high-churchmanship, see Peter B. Nockles, *The Oxford
    Movement in Context: Anglican High Churchmanship, 1760–1857* (Cambridge:
    Cambridge University Press, 1994), 47–63.

67 In a somewhat different context, McNairn, *The Capacity to Judge*, has also
    noted the decline of the notion of constitutional mixed monarchy as a conse-
    quence of the rise of public opinion.

68 John Strachan, *Canada Church Establishment: A Copy of a Letter Addressed to R.J.
    Wilmot Horton, Esq.* (London, 1827); Strachan, "Church Establishment," ca.
    1827, in G.W. Spragge, ed., *The John Strachan Letter-Book, 1812–1834*
    (Toronto: Ontario Historical Society, 1946). See also AO, Strachan Papers,
    Reel 3, John Toronto, "Circular to the Clergy and Laity of the Bishopric and
    See of Toronto," 15 Jan. 1840.

69 NAC, SPG, C Mss. Canada (Pre-Diocesan), 1752–93, Reel A–170, Rev. W.
    Walter, Shelburne, NS, to SPG, July 1783.

70 For the prominence of Scottish and Irish elements in the management of the
    British Empire, see Colley, *Britons*, 117–32.

71 NAC, SPG, C Mss. Canada, Dio Quebec, 1795–1848, Box IV/29, Reel A–199,
    J. Quebec to SPG, 26 Dec. 1820.

72 NAC, SPG, C Mss. Canada, Dio Quebec, 1788–1837, Box IVa/38, Reel A–207,
    Rev. George Spratt to SPG, 5 Nov. 1828. See also Ibid., Dio Quebec, 1819–45,
    Box IV/32, Reel A–200, "Statement of the Rev. A.W. Mountain, late Chap-
    lain at the Quarantine Station, respecting the Emigrants," n.d., ca. 1845;
    Ibid., Dio Quebec, 1795–1848, Box IV/29, Reel A–199, Rev. Jehosaphat
    Mountain, Trois-Rivières to SPG, 25 Feb. 1796.

73 NAC, SPG, C Mss. Canada, Dio Quebec, 1795–1848, Reel A–199, Rev. Micajiah
    Townsend to SPG, 1 May 1827; Ibid., Townsend to SPG, 1 Nov. 1827.

74 NAC, SPG, C Mss. Canada, Dio Quebec, 1795–1848, Reel A–199, Rev. Caleb
    Cotton to SPG, 1 Feb. 1822; Ibid., Cotton to SPG, 1 Feb. 1821.

75 ADM, RG 1.3, Bishop Jacob Mountain Correspondence, Rev. E. Parkin,
    Chambly, to Mountain, 25 Nov. 1819.

76 NAC, SPG, C Mss. Canada, Dio Quebec, 1819–45, Box IV/30, Reel A–200,
    Rev. J. Suddard, Gaspé, to SPG, 23 Oct. 1820.

77 See Nancy Christie, "'In these Times of Democratic Rage and Delusion': Pop-
    ular Religion and the Challenge to the Established Order, 1760–1812," in
    G.A. Rawlyk, ed., *The Canadian Protestant Experience, 1760–1990* (Montreal &
    Kingston: McGill-Queen's University Press, 1990), 9–47.

78 ADM, RG 1.3, Bishop Jacob Mountain Correspondence, 1819, Rev. B.B.
    Stevens, Secretary, Chambly, to Mountain, 17 Aug. 1819.

79 On the ambiguities of "nation" and "empire" for the English, see the illuminat-
ing study by Krishan Kumar, *The Making of English National Identity* (Cambridge:
Cambridge University Press, 2003), ix-x, 155–8,178–9. Paul Langford,
Englishness Identified: Manners and Character, 1650–1850 (Oxford: Oxford
University Press, 2000) has stated that "It is difficult to discover any alleged
British characteristic that does not in practice coincide with an alleged English
characteristic … English character, so to speak, was the dynamic force,
squeezing out Celtic claims to determine what made Britain British." (14)

80 NAC, SPG, B Mss. Nova Scotia, 1760–86, Reel A–166, Rev. John Breynton,
Rector of Halifax to SPG, 24 June 1760; NAC, SPG, C Mss. Canada, Dio Nova
Scotia, 1792–1850, Reel A–172, Rev. John Bumgent, visiting missionary,
"Report on Truro," July 1820; Ibid., Dio Quebec, 1795–1848, Reel A–199,
Rev. Caleb Cotton, Dunham, to SPG, 20 Apr. 1810; Ibid. Dio Quebec,
1788–1837, Box IVa/38, Reel A–203, Rev. John Strachan, York, to SPG, 18
Nov. 1832.

81 ADM, RG 1.3, Jacob Mountain Correspondence, 1820–22, "Parish of Montreal
– Petition from "Germans of the Lutheran Church," ca. 1821. See also NAC,
SPG, C Mss. Canada, Dio Nova Scotia, 1792–1853, Reel A–172, "Proposal
from the Lutheran Congregation at Lunenburg, NS, concerning joining the
Communion of the Church of England, 1821."

82 NAC, SPG, C Mss. Canada, Dio Nova Scotia, 1792–1853, "Proposal from the
Lutheran Congregation at Lunenburg." On Anglican attempts to accommodate the linguistic sensibilities of non-English speakers, see ADM, RG 1.5,
Bishop G.J. Mountain, G.J. Mountain, Archdeacon, W.P. Christie Papers,
1825–35, Christie to Mountain, 2 Dec. 1829, Christie to Mountain, 29 May
1830, on the subject of securing French-speaking Protestant clergy.

83 For Stanser's background, see Judith Fingard, "Robert Stanser," *Dictionary of
Canadian Biography*, Vol. 6 (Toronto and Quebec: University of Toronto
Press/Les Presses de l'Université Laval, web-based version, 2000).

84 T.R. Millman, *Jacob Mountain, First Lord Bishop of Quebec: A Study in Church and
State.* (Toronto: University of Toronto Press, 1947).

85 Archives of Ontario [AO], John Strachan Papers, Reel 1, Jacob Quebec to
Strachan, 25 Sept. 1809. This was occasioned by the visit of Bishop Mountain
to Strachan's academy at Cornwall. Unimpressed by the prosody of Strachan's
pupils, Mountain, a staunch Cambridge man, tartly informed him that "This
defect is very general among scholars from your part of the Island."

86 Strachan, *A Speech, in the Legislative Council, Thursday Sixth March 1828; on the
Subject of the Clergy Reserves, Published by Request* (York, U.C.: Robert Stanton,
1828), 25–6.

87 For the Irish backgrounds and ethnic connections that secured the episcopal
elections of Cronyn and Lewis, see James J. Tallman, "Benjamin Cronyn,"
Dictionary of Canadian Biography, Vol. 10 (Toronto and Quebec: University of
Toronto Press/Les Presses de l'Université Laval, web-based version, 2000);

D.M. Schurman, "John Travers Lewis," *Dictionary of Canadian Biography*, Vol. 13 (Toronto and Quebec: University of Toronto Press/Les Presses de l'Université Laval, web-based version, 2000).

88 J.J. Talman, "Some Notes on the Clergy of the Church of England in Upper Canada prior to 1840," *Transactions of the Royal Society of Canada*, Third Series, section 2, 32 (1938).

89 Donald Harman Akenson, *The Irish in Ontario: A Study in Rural History* (Montreal & Kingston: McGill-Queen's University Press, 1984), 265.

90 NAC, SPG, C Mss. Canada, Dio Quebec, 1824–42, Box IVa/42, Reel A–207, Rev. V.P. Mayerhoffer, "Memorial to SPG, 1831."

91 NAC, SPG, C Mss. Canada, Dio Quebec, 1819–45, Box IV/32, Reel A–207, Rev. S.B. Ardagh (Barrie) to G.J. Montreal, 12 Apr. 1848. The more usual channel for Church of Ireland recruits was that young men unable to secure permanent benefices in Ireland would be recommended for colonial service. This was the case of Rev. Edward James Burton, a Prebendary of Donoughmore and magistrate of the County of Galway who, despite these lofty titles, was only curate of a parish in the Diocese of Meath. Burton was appointed SPG missionary at Terrebonne in 1822. See NAC, SPG, C Mss. Canada, Dio Quebec, 1790–1856, Box IV/34, Reel A–204; ADM, Jacob Mountain Correspondence, 1820, Richard Graves, DD, Professor of Divinity in Trinity College, Dublin to J. Quebec, 4 Nov. 1820. Both Burton and Ardagh fit the description of "evangelical."

92 It has been estimated that in 1857 in the new diocese of Huron, 15 of 42 clergy were either educated at Trinity College, Dublin, or born in Ireland. See Tallman, "Benjamin Cronyn." For Eastern Upper Canada, see Donald Akenson, *The Irish in Ontario* (Montreal & Kingston: McGill-Queen's University Press, 1984). If anything, one suspects that the statistics are under-estimated. Studies of evangelical theological tendencies within Anglicanism have been reluctant to give these an ethnic dimension. See, however, Vaudry, *Anglicans in the Atlantic World*, who assigns some importance to Irish immigrant clergy in establishing and fostering evangelical networks in Upper and Lower Canada. Further research is required on the ethnic divisions within colonial Anglicanism, including comparable statistical work for Lower Canada and the Maritimes, the tracing of ethnic networks of ecclesiastical placement and promotion and, on a local level, an exploration of the way in which the ethnicity of ministers related to the ethnic composition and ambitions of their congregations.

93 For Falloon, see NAC, SPG, C Mss. Canada, Dio Quebec, 1790–1856, Box IV/34, Reel A–204, "Rev. Daniel Falloon, 1826–46."

94 NAC, SPG, C Mss Canada, Dio Nova Scotia, 1790–1850, Reel A–171, Aitken to SPG, 23 Aug. 1813.

95 Writing to the SPG in 1826, Bishop Charles Stewart of Quebec, who had been instrumental in turning his fellow-Scot, James Reid, from evangelical dissent

to Anglicanism, reviewed several cases of "adoption" of ministers from other communions, claiming particular success with Campbell, Grier, and Creen from Presbyterianism. However, in the case of George Spratt, "a remarkable disappointment ensued," which Stewart attributed to "mental derangement." See NAC, SPG, C Mss. Canada, Dio Quebec, Letters of Bishop Stewart, 1821–39, Box IV/33, C.J. Quebec to SPG, 28 Dec. 1826.

96 NAC, SPG, C Mss Canada, Dio Quebec, Upper Canada, 1824–42, Box IVa/40, Reel A–207, John MacLaurin to C.J. Quebec, 3 Nov. 1826; ibid., MacLaurin to C.J. Quebec, 26 Sept. 1826.

97 NAC, SPG, C Mss Canada, Dio Quebec, Letters of Bishop Stewart, 1821–39, Box IV/33, Reel A–203, C.J. Quebec to Rev. John MacLaurin, 18 Nov. 1826; Ibid., C.J. Quebec to SPG, 28 Dec. 1826.

98 NAC, SPG, Dio Quebec, 1821–39, Bishop Stewart Letters, Box IV/33, Reel A–203, C.J. Quebec to SPG, 7 Nov. 1828.

99 For a general analysis of Scotland's contribution to empire-building, and the effects of empire on Scottish society, see T.M. Devine, *Scotland's Empire, 1600–1815* (London: Allen Lane, 2003). It should be noted that Devine's work stresses the commercial and economic aspects of this process.

100 United Church Archives [UCA], Records of the Glasgow Colonial Society [GCS], Vol. 1, Reel 1, Rev. John Sprott, Musquodoboit, NS to Rev. Dr Burns, May 1827; Ibid., Sprott to Burns, 12 Jan. 1826.

101 Historians of Upper Canada in particular have suffered from an over-fascination with the commanding personalities of John Strachan and the Methodist leader, Egerton Ryerson. See William Westfall, *Two Worlds: The Protestant Culture of Nineteenth-Century Ontario* (Montreal & Kingston: McGill-Queen's University Press, 1989); David Mills, *The Idea of Loyalty in Upper Canada, 1784–1850* (Montreal & Kingston: McGill-Queen's University Press, 1988).

102 For the role of leaders of the Church of Scotland in this process, see Colin Kidd, *Subverting Scotland's Past: Scottish Whig Historians and the Creation of an Anglo-British Identity, c. 1689- c. 1830* (Cambridge: Cambridge University Press, 1993).

103 For the view that Scotland's "North Britishness" constituted a "provincial" English identity, see Kidd, "North Britishness and the Nature of Eighteenth-Century British Patriotism."

104 For a stimulating treatment of how Presbyterianism and its distinctive religious institutions and practices came to define Scottish ethnicity in the American colonial setting, see Ned C. Landsman, *Scotland and its First American Colony, 1683–1765* Princeton: Princeton University Press, 1985), 255.

105 UCA, GCS, Vol. 2, Reel 1, Rev. D. McFarlan, Ewing Place to Dr Burns, 1 June 1830. From an early stage, the GCS made concerted attempts to secure Gaelic-speaking ministers to serve the religious needs of Highland Scots emigrant communities. See UCA GCS, Vol. 1, Reel 1, Rev. Alexander MacLean, St

Andrews, NB to Dr Burns, 26 Sept. 1825; Ibid., Reel 6, *Seventh Annual Report of the Glasgow Society* (Glasgow, 1833), 14. For the more politically radical and voluntarist attitude of Scottish Seceder clergy toward the imperial state, see Michael Gauvreau, "Covenanter Democracy: Scottish Popular Religion, Ethnicity, and the Varieties of Politico-religious Dissent in Upper Canada, 1815–1841," *Histoire sociale/Social History* 36, no. 71 (May 2003): 55–83.

106 Thomas McCulloch, DD, *Memorial from the Committee of Mission of the Presbyterian Church of Nova Scotia to the Glasgow Society ...* (Edinburgh: Oliver & Boyd, 1826), 30, 13.

107 UCA, Scottish Record Office, Collection 45, Dalhousie Muniments, Thomas Scott, John McIntyre, Charles Baillie, William Lambie, James Muir, James Robertson, Managers of the Dalhousie Public Library to Lord Dalhousie, 1 Sept. 1828.

108 UCA, GCS, Vol. 2, Reel 2, Rev. Alexander Ross, Aldborough, U.C. to Rev. David Welsh, 16 Mar. 1831; Ibid., Rev. William Singer (Kirkpatrick by Moffatt) to Dr Burns, 15 Jan. 1831; Ibid., William Morris, Perth, U.C. to Dr Welsh, 10 Dec. 1830; "Abstract of the Minutes of the Synod of the Presbyterian Church, held at Kingston, June 8TH to 13TH ... " *Sixth Annual Report of the Glasgow Society, 1832* (Glasgow, 1832), 30.

109 UCA, GCS, Vol. 1, Reel 1, Rev. Kenneth McKenzie, Pictou, NS to Dr Burns, 27 June 1828; Ibid., Rev. Alexander MacLean, St Andrews, NB to Dr Burns, 26 Sept. 1825.

110 UCA, Mark Young Stark Fonds, 86.202, Rev. Mark Young Stark to Sir George Napier, 4 Apr. 1833: "I confess that my own feelings are in favour of the Church of Scotland, in ... what I conceive to be not unimportant respects that while any hope remains of making myself useful in it, I should be unwilling to change merely because a living presents itself in the other."

111 UCA, Mark Young Stark Fonds, 86.202, Rev. Mark Young Stark, Dundas, U.C. to My Dear Mother and all friends at home, 10 Dec. 1833.

112 On the state of the incomes of New Brunswick Presbyterian clergy connected with the Church of Scotland in 1843, see UCA, GCS, Reel 7, "Letter from Rev. James Hannay, Moderator of the Synod of New Brunswick, to the Rev. David Welsh, D.D., regarding the state of the Presbyterian Church," 12 May 1843. See also UCA, GCS, Vol. 2, Reel 3, Rev. George Romanes, Smith's Falls, U.C. to Dr Burns, 16 Oct. 1834; UCA, GCS, Vol. 2, Reel 1, Rev. Alexander Ross, Aldborough, U.C. to Dr Burns, 25 May 1830.

113 UCA, Mark Young Stark Fonds, Mark Young Stark, Kirkhill Cottage, Dundas to My Dear Mother, 10 Jan. 1837.

114 UCA, GCS, Vol. 2, Reel 1, Rev. Alexander Ross, Aldborough, U.C. to Dr Burns, 25 May 1830.

115 UCA, GCS, Vol. 1, Reel 1, John Burns, Montreal, to Rev. Dr Burns. See also Ibid., Vol. 1, Reel 1, Rev. James Archer, Annapolis Royal, NS to Dr Burns, 6 Sept. 1824.

116 UCA, GCS, Reel 6, *Fourth Annual Report of the Glasgow Society* (Glasgow, 1830); Ibid., *Sixth Annual Report of the Glasgow Society* (Glasgow, 1832), 19–20.

117 William Morris, *A Letter on the Subject of the Clergy Reserves, Addressed to the Very Rev. Principal McFarlan, and the Rev. Robert Burns, D.D. by William Morris, of Perth, Upper Canada, 1838* (Toronto: British Colonist, 1838), 24.

118 UCA, Dalhousie Muniments, Thomas Scott et al. To Lord Dalhousie, 1 Sept. 1828.

119 UCA, GCS, Reel 7, "Letter from James Fleming, George Todd, Arch'd Ferguson, Robert Tait, James Ferrier, and Henry Walker, Montreal to Rev. Dr Scott, Greenock," 25 Oct. 1825.

120 *The Fourth Annual Report of the Glasgow Society* ... (Glasgow: Printed for the Society, 1830), 20–1; UCA, GCS, Vol. 1, Reel 1, James Brown, George Eaton, John McIntyre, Elders of the Presbyterian Congregation, Dalhousie Settlement, U.C. to Dr Burns, 5 Sept. 1825.

121 UCA, GCS, Reel 6, *The First Annual Report of the Glasgow Society (In connection with the Established Church of Scotland) for Promoting the Religious Interests of the Scottish Settlers in British North America* (Glasgow: William Collins & Co., 1826), 9. One typical bond was that of the people of Tabutinsac, NB, who collaborated in sharing a minister's salary with the neighbouring communities of Bay de Vin and Black River. Each of these settlements would have been too small to meet the financial exigencies of the GCS on their own. The bond stipulated that the people of Tabutinsac would guarantee £60 for five years, entitling them to one-half the minister's services. The communities of Bay de Vin and Black River agreed to guarantee another £60, on condition that the minister perform the services at Black River in Gaelic. They also requested the GCS to provide a further £50 for five years. See UCA, GCS, Vol. 2, Reel 2, Rev. James Souter, Newcastle, Miramichi, NB to Dr Burns, 5 Apr. 1832

122 UCA, GCS, Vol. 2, Reel 2, Rev. Mr Dunlop, York, U.C. to Rev. David Welsh, 15 Jan. 1831. A similar reluctance to enter into an engagement with a minister "whom they had not heard" was evinced by the settlers of Lanark, U.C. See UCA, GCS, Vol. 2, Reel 1, Matthew Leech, President, Robert Mason, Secretary, Lanark, U.C. to Dr Burns, 25 Nov. 1829.

123 UCA, GCS, Vol. 2, Reel 2, Rev. F. McNaughton, Vaughan, U.C. to Dr Burns, 21 Aug. 1833.

124 UCA, GCS, Vol. 6, "Extract of a Letter from Rev. Mr Hannay of Richibucto, NB, Dated February 1834," *Ninth Annual Report of the Glasgow Society* (Glasgow, 1835), 40.

125 For these divisions within the national church, which revolved around the rights of aristocratic patrons or local congregations to "present" ministers, see for the social, religious, and political views of the "moderate" leadership the fine study by Richard B. Sher, *Church and University in the Scottish Enlightenment: The Moderate Literati of Edinburgh* (Princeton: Princeton University Press, 1985); and for the "popular" party, Ned C. Landsman, "Presbyterians

and Provincial Society: The Evangelical Enlightenment in the West of Scotland, 1740–1775," in John Dwyer and Richard B. Sher, eds, *Sociability and Society in Eighteenth-Century Scotland* (Edinburgh: The Mercat Press, 1993), 194–209.

126 UCA, GCS, Vol. 1, Reel 1, James Thomson, Miramichi, NB to Dr Burns, 29 June 1824. See also: Ibid., John Burns, Montreal to Dr Burns, 23 May 1825; Ibid., Vol. 2, Reel 1, "Letter from the Rev. K.J. Mackenzie, Pictou, on the state of various settlements in Nova Scotia, 19 Nov. 1829"; Alexander Davidson, John Fraser, James Gilmour, et al., Trustees of St James' Church, Newcastle, Miramichi, NB to Dr Burns, 16 Jan. 1830.

127 UCA, GCS, Vol. 2, Reel 2, Rev. Archibald Colquhoun, Georgetown, Chateauguay, L.C. to Rev. John Geddes, Feb. 1833.

128 UCA, GCS, Vol. 1, Reel 1, James Fleming, George Todd, Archibald Ferguson, Robert Tait, Montreal to Dr Burns, 25 Oct. 1825.

129 UCA, GCS, Vol. 2, Reel 1, Rev. George Struthers, Horton, NS to Dr Burns, 23 June 1830.

130 UCA, GCS, Vol. 3, Reel 2, Mr G. Woodsworth, Horton, NS to Rev. John Martin, Halifax, 18 June 1832.

131 UCA, GCS, "Letter from the Rev. K.J. Mackenzie, Pictou, on the state of various settlements in Nova Scotia, 19 Nov. 1829."

132 Ibid. "Letter from the Rev. K.J. Mackenzie." Similar opinions that the extemporaneous sermon was a mark of superior spiritual commitment and a statement of national resistance to a creeping anglicization were also evident in Scottish communities of Upper Canada. See AO, Bell Family Papers, Rev. Andrew Bell to Rev. William Bell, 26 Sept. 1825.

133 UCA, GCS, Vol. 2, Reel 1, John Stewart (Lorn of Machline) to Dr Burns, 15 Feb. 1830.

134 Mark Noll has emphasized the survival of a "people's Calvinism" among the lower socio-economic strata of Scottish society. See "Revival, Enlightenment, Civic Humanism and the Evolution of Calvinism in Scotland and America, 1735–1843," in George A. Rawlyk and Mark A. Noll, eds, *Amazing Grace: Evangelicalism in Australia, Britain, Canada and the United States* (Montreal & Kingston: McGill-Queen's University Press, 1994), 75, 95, 101.

135 John M. MacKenzie, "Empire and National Identities: The Case of Scotland," *Transactions of the Royal Historical Society*, 1998, 230.

136 Colley, *Britons*, 193.

137 For the cultural meanings of the communion sacrament in both early-modern Scotland and America, see Leigh Eric Schmidt, *Holy Fairs: Scottish Communions and American Revivals in the Early Modern Period* (Princeton: Princeton University Press, 1989).

138 For an assessment of the religious and cultural implications of the reassertion of this early-modern religious structure in colonial Canada, see Nancy Christie, "Carnal Connection and Other Misdemeanours: Continuity and

Change in Presbyterian Church Courts, 1830–1890," in Michael Gauvreau and Ollivier Hubert, eds, *The Churches and Social Order in Nineteenth- and Twentieth- entury Canada* (Montreal & Kingston: McGill-Queen's University Press, 2006), 66–108. For the key features of the Scottish "parish state" and an analysis of its decline, see T.M. Devine, *The Scottish Nation, 1700–2000* (Harmondsworth: Penguin Books, 1999), 84–102.

139 UCA, GCS, Reel 5, Rev. Robert Archibald, Chatham, NB to Dr Burns, 7 Mar. 1837; Ibid., Vol. 2, Reel 1, Rev. Alexander Ross, Aldborough, U.C. to Dr Burns, 4 Mar. 1830; Ibid., Vol. 2, Reel 1, Rev. Gavin Lang, Shelburne, NS to Dr Burns, 24 Dec. 1829; Ibid., Vol. 1, Reel 1, Anonymous Correspondent to Dr Burns, 12 Feb. 1828.

140 Although Christie notes that the church disciplinary tribunals at times involved conflict between clergy and laity, it was not a case of one-way imposition. Laity frequently used this machinery to scrutinize and control the behaviour of clergy and, more importantly, the institution expressed a broader consensus between clergy and lay congregational leaders.

141 UCA, GCS, Vol. 2, Reel 1, Rev. Mr Monson, Dartmouth, NS to Dr Burns, 28 Apr. 1829; Ibid., Reel 5, Rev. Robert Archibald, Chatham, NB to Dr Burns, 7 Mar. 1832.

142 Presbyterians from Northern Ireland, unlike their co-religionists from Scotland were, of course, a religious minority in what was an Anglican state and, after the early eighteenth century, experienced enormous difficulty in maintaining congregational disciplinary machinery, particularly in the face of the demands of "New Light" clergy and lay leaders to give greater priority to the rights of conscience. On the religious situation of Presbyterians in eighteenth century Northern Ireland, see the key study by Patrick Griffin, *The People with No Name: Ireland's Ulster Scots, America's Scots Irish, and the Creation of a British Atlantic World, 1689–1764* (Princeton: Princeton University Press, 2001), 37–8. Scottish Presbyterian ministers in Upper Canada, like Rev. William Fraser, frequently commented that "the Presbyterian people of this place are almost all Irish and I know that these people are by no means so well enlightened in the doctrines of the Gospel as the Scotch inhabitants. They truly need line upon line – precept upon precept." See UCA, William Fraser Papers, 86.109/TR, Diary, 14 Dec. 1834, 18 Nov. 1834.

143 See UCA, Dalhousie Muniments, Lord Dalhousie to Lord Bishop of Quebec, 15 Dec. 1827.

144 UCA, GCS, Reel 7, "Report of a Committee of the Gl. Assembly of the Scottish Church, on application from the members of that Church in Canada & approved in the Assembly, 30 May 1835"; Ibid., Vol. 2, Reel 1, Rev. John Martin, Halifax to Dr Burns, 25 Dec. 1829; Ibid., Rev. Robert McGill, Niagara, U.C. to Dr Burns, 16 Aug. 1830; Ibid., Dr Lee (Edinburgh) to Dr Burns, 5 Apr. 1832.

145 UCA, GCS, Reel 7, "The Church of Scotland in Canada," from a letter in the *Kingston Chronicle*, n.d.

146 UCA, GCS, Reel 7, Rev. George Romanes, Smith's Falls to Dr Burns, Apr. 1837.

147 Kidd, *Subverting Scotland's Past*, 250.

148 Kidd, "North Britishness and the Nature of Eighteenth-Century Patriotism," 365–6.

149 UCA, GCS, Reel 6, "A Pastoral Letter from the Clergy of the Church of Scotland in the Canadas, to their Presbyterian Brethren," printed in *The Canadian Miscellany: or the Religious, Literary & Statistical Intelligencer*, 1, no. 1, (April 1828): 12.

150 Ibid., 12.

151 John Rae, *A Letter to the Honourable E.G. Stanley, M.P., on the Comparative Claims of the English and Scotch Churches in Canada, to the Protection of the British Government, and on the Propriety of Establishing a Fund for the Support, that it may be Deemed Expedient to Give to them, from a Revenue Arising from the Rent of Land* (Montreal: Montreal Herald, 1828), 6.

152 Ibid., 17–18.

153 For the importance of this traditional Presbyterian patriotism to the politics of George Brown and the Upper Canadian radical reformers, see Michael Gauvreau, "Reluctant Voluntaries: Peter and George Brown, the Scottish Disruption, and the Politics of Church and State in Canada," *Journal of Religious History*, 25, no. 2 (June 2001): 134–57.

154 NAC, SPG, C Mss. Canada, Dio Quebec, 1824–42, Box IVa/42, Reel A–207, Rev. V.P. Mayerhoffer to Lord Bishop of Montreal, 8 Jan. 1838.

155 Ibid., Dio L.C./Dio U.C., Box IVb/42, Misc. Upper Canada, Reel A–211, Rev. F.L. Osler, 1839–1846, "Journal," 17 Nov. 1839.

156 Westfall, *Two Worlds*.

157 G.J. Mountain, *The Responsibilities of Englishmen in the Colonies of the British Empire. A Sermon Preached in the Cathedral Church of Quebec, before the St George's Society of that City, on the 23d April, 1847* (Quebec: J.C. Fisher, 1847), 5. See also AO, Strachan Papers, Reel 3, Strachan to Rev. John Henry Newman, 15 Aug. 1839.

158 Possession of a common Protestantism forms the central pillar of Linda Colley's definition of an emerging "British" sense of nationhood in the early eighteenth century. The existence of such a unified Protestantism has been recently questioned. See the essays in Tony Claydon and Ian McBride, eds, *Protestantism and National Identity, Britain and Ireland, c. 1650-c. 1850* (Cambridge: Cambridge University Press, 1998), which take Colley to task for ignoring the extent to which Protestantism remained fragmented, both nationally and denominationally; there was little common consensus, even on the issue of anti-Catholicism.

BRUCE CURTIS

Monitorial Schooling, "Common Christianity," and Politics

A Transatlantic Controversy[1]

In the first two decades of the nineteenth century in England, the rapid spread of elementary schooling on the monitorial model elaborated by Joseph Lancaster was the source of intense and heated debate. The expansion had been spurred on by the necessity of educating a developing working class. The debate followed Lancaster's system across the Atlantic. This chapter reviews the debate, with particular attention to the fate in England and Lower Canada of Lancaster's claims to offer "education without proselytism," that is, to separate out sectarian religious instruction from what became, in consequence, "civil education."

Drawing on and extending teaching methods used by the Anglican Dr Andrew Bell in the early 1790s at the Madras Asylum, an institution for the orphaned children of English soldiers, Lancaster applied features of the industrial division of labour, military discipline, and rational accounting to charity schooling. Wealthy Dissenters, utilitarians, and liberal Whigs, including Patrick Colquhoun, William Allen, Francis Place, Joseph Fox, Jeremy Bentham, Henry Brougham, and the senior Mill were partisans of the Lancasterian system. The system and its founder were praised lavishly in the pages of the *Edinburgh Review* by Sydney Smith and Brougham, among others, as well as in the *Monthly Review*, the liberal press, and in a large pamphlet literature. Attempts were made in the first decade of the nineteenth century both in Parliament and out to place Lancasterian schools in every parish in conjunction with the Poor Law. Lancaster himself attracted royal patronage in 1805.

While Lancaster's model of schooling was rejected by the utopian socialists for its mechanical discipline and failure to develop the sensibilities and rational capacities of students,[2] it was partisans of the Church of England, somewhat later supported by the hierarchy, who mounted the most systematic attacks on it, eventually succeeding in removing the royal patronage. The charity school author, Sarah Trimmer, wrote an early pamphlet in opposition to Lancaster, and various Anglican priests and bishops fulminated against his schools from the pulpit, their views then circulating in the sermon literature. Trimmer convinced Andrew Bell to enter the conflict. In the pages of the *Quarterly Review* and in longer published pieces, Lancaster's model was denounced repeatedly by Robert Southey. At times, Samuel Taylor Coleridge was effective in attacking it in the press and in public speeches.

The attempts of Lancaster's supporters to organize schooling at the national level moved the Anglicans in 1811 to form a National Society to promote their own monitorial schools, on the model elaborated by Bell, in parishes throughout England and Wales. Lancaster's partisans riposted by forming the British and Foreign School Society, but the superior resources of the Church left them in a minority position in the field. As a result of the school controversy, in England – the first industrial capitalist nation – direct control of the elementary education of the population by the state bureaucracy did not develop until the end of the nineteenth century.

Though they were largely triumphant in England, in the 1810s Bell's partisans considered that the British and Foreign School Society might well have greater success abroad.[3] Lancaster's innovations crossed the Atlantic within a very few years of the 1805 publication of his detailed description of the system in *Improvements in Education*.[4] In the British North American colony of Lower Canada, an account of Lancasterian schooling appeared in the press as early as 1808, and 1500 copies of a Lancasterian manual were printed by the Legislative Assembly in 1815 for general distribution. Several attempts were made in the 1810s and 1820s by the Assembly to pass legislation, or to achieve royal sanction for legislation, establishing a colony-wide Lancasterian school system. The colonial Anglican Church responded in part by organizing monitorial schools of its own on the model elaborated by Andrew Bell. Parts of the Catholic hierarchy initially offered lukewarm support for monitorial schooling through the Société d'Éducation de Québec. However, the Montreal bishops were strenuously opposed to Lancaster's system, and priests did little to promote schooling at the parish level. Still, by the mid 1820s, there were large, competing monitorial schools in operation in the colonial cities and Lancaster's school manual had been translated into French. In the following decade, the Lancasterian British and Canadian Schools in Quebec and Montreal began to offer free teacher training, and leaders of the colony's liberal and increasingly nationalist Patriote party, which dominated the colonial Legislative Assembly, embraced monitorial schooling as the best means to promote literacy in the countryside. Lancaster himself was in Montreal for the years 1829–33.

With Lancaster's system came the English political controversy, inflected by the particular conditions of colonial social relations. The English debate itself was multifaceted, and tactics shifted over the course of the first two decades of the nineteenth century, both with the relative strength of the parties involved and with the shifting realities of working-class schooling and of class and international politics. My focus on the issue of "education without proselytism," according to which the tenets of a common Christianity would provide the moral element of a secular education, stems from an interest in projects for the creation of liberal self-government and representative democracy. I am concerned both with plans for the organization of political spaces in which liberal rationalities would prevail against the logic of mercantilism, against the dogma of state religion, and against the projects of socialism, and with practices aimed at the construction of forms of rational individuality, or liberal political subjectivities. After examining the English debate from this viewpoint, the chapter considers how the liberal, Lancasterian project for a common Christianity fared in Lower Canada in the period leading up to the political and military struggles of 1837–38.

THE MONITORIAL SYSTEM

Monitorial schooling has been discussed exhaustively over the last two decades, especially because it was an exemplary "perfect machine of power" for Foucauldian studies of discipline. Nonetheless, a brief preliminary account of versions of the method may prove helpful. Joseph Lancaster was the master of a charity school in Southwark, London in the 1790s when he came across Andrew Bell's description of the school he had conducted at the Madras Asylum.[5] Bell employed some of his own students as assistants, taught beginning writers to trace out their letters in sand, and adopted what was seen as a very innovative phonic method of teaching to read. The students were grouped in achievement classes, where taking places was encouraged; regular records were kept of the comportment of individual students; and misconduct was dealt with weekly by a jury composed of the school as a whole. Bell eliminated corporal punishment. He suggested that his method could usefully be applied to the schooling of the poor, although he suggested in passing that the poor might not be taught to write.

Bell and Lancaster had a lengthy and relatively friendly interview at Christmas, 1804, but the evangelical Sarah Trimmer soon convinced

Bell that Lancaster's non-sectarian approach to religious instruction threatened the existence of the Church of England. Anglicans began organizing their own schools in which the catechism was taught and church attendance required.[6] Although the question of who invented what and who borrowed what from whom remained contentious for much of the Bell-Lancaster controversy, the core of both versions of the system was essentially the same. As the English debate matured, Lancaster's partisans among the political economists accepted this similarity, and claimed that the best measure of any productive process was its cheapness, trying to demonstrate that Lancaster's system was best in this regard.

Lancaster proposed that one master could teach several hundred students by dividing them into achievement classes under the supervision of student monitors. He reduced the necessary material supplies for the schoolroom dramatically and displaced most administrative labour onto monitors as well. Lancaster adopted, invented, or extended methods for teaching reading, writing, and arithmetic cheaply and efficiently. Books, paper, pens, and ink were eliminated for all but the most advanced students. Beginners learned to write their letters in sand, later moving on to writing on slates. Lancaster adopted Bell's phonic method of teaching to read but also based instruction in arithmetic on the reading and copying of problems and solutions, in contrast to the prevailing method of teaching by rules. Any student able to read, it was claimed, could teach arithmetic without knowing anything about it, and could learn arithmetic by teaching it. Moreover, students learned to write as soon as – if not before – they learned to read, and they learned to read in the vernacular before encountering Latin (if they encountered it at all). Writing was by dictation; there was no place for composition, at least for the great majority of students.

Although there was to be a school library, all but the most advanced classes used reading lessons printed on large cards posted along the walls of the schoolroom. Classes under the supervision of a monitor regularly moved from their seats in rows facing the front of the schoolroom, where collective work was done, to teaching circles arranged facing the walls of the schoolroom. Elaborate systems of signalling and signage were used to coordinate movement. Lancaster promoted individual achievement by encouraging "emulation" through the taking of places in the monitorial groups, each student wearing a number attesting to his/her standing. An elaborate system of accounting, worked by specialized monitors and based on the distribution of tickets and emblems, and on regular recording, made it possible for promotion and demotion to be both individual and frequent. Lancaster encouraged students individually to accumulate tokens, which could be exchanged for prizes, and to compete for achievement medals. Achieving students wore tickets in the schoolroom, inscribed with such messages as "Merit in Spelling" or "Merit in Reading" and pasteboard prints were also worn. The best students were distinguished by different grades of medals. Classes in the school were encouraged to compete among themselves for pride of place, and misbehaviour was dealt with by the distribution and recording of demerit tickets as well. But Lancaster's punishments included many other practices regarded as controversial, ranging from the attaching of weights and shackles to the bodies of delinquents, punishment parades before the whole school, in which offenders wore demeaning costumes, and cross-gender public humiliations. Students were not beaten.[7]

THE ENGLISH CONTROVERSY

The Bell-Lancaster controversy sprawled over a number of issues. Who could claim to have invented the system was debated fiercely for more than a decade, until most participants concluded that virtually all the pedagogical practices in question had existed somewhere before Bell and Lancaster. Many participants argued that there were fundamental differences between the two versions, but after two decades monitorialism increasingly came to be seen as a technical process that could be mobilized for quite different purposes. The virtues and dangers of teaching to small or large groups of poor children were canvassed and alarm was expressed early in the debate by such writers as Sarah Trimmer, both that the poor were encouraged to associate in large groups, and that military discipline in charity schools would produce revolutionary citizen armies.[8]

Mercantilist and anti-mercantilist themes were also evident in the debate, provoked by Bell's published observation that the poor might not need to be taught to write, and also by Tory reaction to Samuel Whitbread's 1807 parliamentary speech calling for national schooling on Lancaster's model. In response to the latter, Davies Giddy famously stated in the Commons what was perhaps already seen as quaint mercantilist opposition to educating the poor; it would promote social mobility and cause insubordination and discontent. Schooling would make workers "factious and refractory, as was evident in the manufacturing counties; it would enable them to read seditious pamphlets, vicious books, and publications against Christianity; it would render them insolent to their superiors; and, in a few years, the result would be, that the legislature would find it necessary to direct the strong arm of power towards them."[9] Henry Brougham took apart these arguments for the Lancasterians, tracing them to Mandeville's *Fable of the Bees*, and attempting to demonstrate their spuriousness. By the second decade of the nineteenth century, when it was increasingly clear in England that the issue was no longer whether, but rather how and by whom the working class should be educated, Bell's apologists were excusing the opposition to the teaching of reading as a momentary lapse caused by outdated fears provoked by the French revolution.[10]

The extent to which social mobility ought to be encouraged was a matter of contention among Lancasterians themselves, and there were detailed discussions of the political and moral tendencies of most of the technical devices employed in monitorial schools. Nonetheless, considering matters more abstractly, the English debate took place in an important moment of cultural and political transition. The mercantilist logic of governing the poor through their ignorance had been undermined by a complex of forces, including the impact of ideas of enlightenment and revolution, changes in class and domestic relations provoked by the wartime capitalist boom, the emergence of working-class political consciousness, and the rise of religious dissent. Some workers were educating themselves; the ignorance of others was seen by ruling groups increasingly as a threat to, rather than as a guarantee of, social stability, and the Established Church seemed incapable of defining the common basis of a new political education. The shift to projects for governing the poor and workers through a secularized intelligence, rather than through ignorance and religious superstition, was far from automatic. Tory administrations in the late 1810s and 1820s continued to prefer policies of ideological repression to those of managed enlightenment.[11]

Still, for the dominant groups, the prospect of generalized schooling raised the issue of the form and the content of the intelligence appropriate for workers and the "lower orders." As older forms of paternalist and household supervision were undermined by the growth of market and wage relations, the site and methods of moralization and enlightenment became political concerns. While Lancaster's supporters and opponents had both come to accept that the school would be the site of education, his opponents in the Established Church argued that direct doctrinal religious instruction, preferably in small schools, was the safest means. Lancaster's partisans sought rather to shape character through practices of habituation, in which doing rather than doctrine was paramount, and in large schools where economies of scale were possible. Neither party seems to have argued that educated workers would be equipped actively to participate in politics and to have opinions worth expressing, or needed outlets for creativity. Rather, both accepted some version of the position that schooling was necessary to make workers loyal, moral, and obedient. Nonetheless, the schooling project implicitly raised the question of the space or forum, the discursive and political framework, in which such developed rational capacities would be operative.

GOVERNING THROUGH INTELLIGENCE

I am particularly concerned with the debates that surrounded Lancaster's promotion of what I have called a common Christianity. In North America at least, a generic New Testament Christianity provided much of the moral and ethical ground upon which liberal representative government was to stand. "Above all things," Lancaster wrote in the introduction to his *Improvements*, "education ought not to be subservient to the propagation of the peculiar tenets of any sect." Education need not be subservient to sectarian differences, for beneath them lay a common ground that consisted of "a reverence for the sacred name of God and the Scriptures of Truth; a detestation of vice; a love of veracity; a due attention to duties to parents, relations, and to society; carefulness to avoid bad company; civility without flattery; and a peaceable demeanor."[12] A non-sectarian Christian education could be scriptural, so long as the scriptures were read "without note or comment"; moral duties were common to all. As David Hogan has argued, what distinguished Lancaster's schooling from the charity schooling of his epoch and from Bell's model of instruction was not its break with Christian religion, but rather with established conceptions of Protestant piety, deference, renunciation, and regeneration. This was an educational model in which individual achievement and advancement through accumulation and competition reigned, despite Lancaster's concerns with engineering social stability and hierarchy, and despite his frequent invocation of religious language. In Hogan's terms, it was a theatre of market discipline.[13] "Literary" was to be separated clearly from "religious" instruction.

Again, while conservative critics continued to claim that schooling would cause the poor "to get above themselves" while calling established authority structures into question, it would be both naïve and wrong to see in Lancaster's conceptions an education aimed at producing critical individual self-reflection or at attacking relations of class or political authority directly. Lancasterian schooling sought to produce a literate, disciplined, moral, orderly population, able to understand its obligations both civil and religious, but saved from extreme material and moral deprivation. His was a highly mechanized system that allowed little space for autonomous activity on the part of anyone – master, monitors, or students.[14] Mobility was limited, as it had been under Church education, to the most talented boys (there is no mention of mobility for girls) who would receive a more extensive education and who might aspire to a clerkship or to one of the lesser professions. Some versions of monitorial schooling were paired with craft training.

On the other hand, Lancaster's partisans among the political economists and Philosophic Radicals included his project in their critique of aristocratic privilege and mercantilist policy. James Mill's analysis of the role of popular education in the ideal liberal democracy, where the political interests of all would be enfolded by those of men of large property and middle rank, was particularly influential. "Two things are absolutely certain," he wrote, "that without the bodily labour of the great bulk of mankind the well-being of the species cannot be obtained; and that if the bodily labour of the bulk of mankind is carried beyond a certain extent, neither intellect, virtue, nor happiness can flourish upon the earth." Society depended on the exploitation of the working class, but the progress of capitalist civilization depended upon the working class acquiring a degree of material and, more particularly, of intellectual comfort. In Mill's liberalism, the greatest good of the greatest number was the object and measure of social arrangements. "As the happiness, which is the end of education, depends upon the actions of the individual, and as all the actions of man are produced by his feelings or thoughts," Mill proposed that "the business of education is, to make certain feelings or thoughts take place instead of others." Fellow-feeling, produced by attendance at common school, had the potential to quell social antagonism. Given a minimum necessary level of material comfort, schooling could produce happy, moral, industrious individuals. Of course, not all members of society could receive all levels of education, for the higher levels demanded freedom from labour and the existence of society depended on the labour of the bulk of the population. Education would necessarily be unequal. Still, under the guidance of men of property, workers could occupy a place in a common intellectual culture, and must be educated for their own good and for that of society as a whole. Their education was, first and foremost, to be practical.[15] Thus, Lancaster's partisans saw popular education as an intelligent guarantee for society, one clearly more productive of order and peace than was continued ignorance.

"What is the dreadful secret the poor are to find out when they have learned to read and write?" asked Sydney Smith in his response to Sarah Trimmer's attacks on Lancaster. The "guzzling, semi-inebriated country gentlemen" who winked and nodded among themselves when Samuel Whitbread's scheme for national education was discussed in Parliament might better learn to read themselves. Smith claimed that at least a million people in England had learned to do so since the French revolution, and society was more tranquil as a result. The Tory fear that educated workers would read seditious pamphlets was spurious: such pamphlets would always circulate, but an educated population would be able to form correct estimations of their worth, and the standard of popular literature in general would improve. Popular education would not cause the poor to refuse to work: they could not eat books and ink. Instead, it would lead to a better use of the products of labour, with reading in the domestic circle displacing the alehouse as the scene of recreation.[16]

THE CONSERVATIVE REACTION

Social stability depended on an intelligent working class; the mercantilist position had lost all credible support by the first decades of the nineteenth century. Conservative educational critics accepted this reality, while offering a three-pronged attack on the Lancasterian scheme. The scheme was said to undermine the unity of state and church, thereby threatening the existence of both. The instruction of youth had been a legal obligation and right of the Established Church since the Reformation, and while some neglect of education was evident, the reinvigoration of existing provisions would lead to an adequate supply of parish schools. There was no cause to delegate education to such private bodies as the Royal Lancasterian Association. Second, the project of a common Christianity was effectively a campaign for the dominance of dissent. Such was the case because the beliefs Christians held in common across their differences were not essentially Christian, but rather deist. Hence, social stability depended on doctrinal instruction. Finally, the methods employed and doctrines promoted in the Lancasterian system produced demoralized individuals, unfit for their duties to themselves and others. The system encouraged social mobility and spread dangerous political capacities without providing for their effective regulation.

From the evangelical Sarah Trimmer to the poet laureate Robert Southey, the existence of a state church and its need to command schooling to produce uniformity of belief was a basic presupposition. As Trimmer put it, "The history of mankind in all civilized nations may be referred to, in order to prove the necessity of having a religion of some kind connected with the state, and it has ever been thought essential that children should be educated in the doctrines and tenets of the *national religion*, so as to preserve a general uniformity throughout the nation; though licence might be granted to individuals and communities, for deviations from the establishment for *conscience sake.*"[17] Samuel Taylor Coleridge adopted the same line, writing that "national conformity is as necessary as family conformity to public happiness." While some toleration of dissent in religious matters was perhaps wise, "certainly it is criminal in the Government to encourage dissention."[18] And Southey echoed that "a state is secure in proportion as the subjects are attached to the laws and institutions of their country; it ought, therefore, to be the first and paramount business of the state to provide that the subjects shall be educated conformably to those institutions."[19]

Lancaster's partisans attacked the proposition that the security of the state depended on religious conformity. Henry Brougham sought to demonstrate that a policy of preventing instruction or of limiting it to a narrow set of uniform doctrines would be fruitless. It was practically impossible to prevent some of the poor from learning to read something, and once one person could read, he or she would inevitably read to others. The poor would necessarily be exposed to seditious pamphlets and books and immoral images; only if they were thoroughly educated would they be able to evaluate these properly and doctrinal instruction was inadequate to the task. Sydney Smith argued that since the English in fact enjoyed the best government in the world, there was absolutely nothing for the state to fear in allowing the poor to learn about political matters. The liberals chided the partisans of the Church for believing their own institution so weak as to be seriously threatened by the spread of reading and writing among the poor.[20] Doctrinal instruction in the schoolroom was also presented as an obstacle to the efficient teaching of reading and writing. The Church had nothing more to fear from such teaching in Lancasterian schools than it had in the past when such teaching was the responsibility of parents at home.[21]

For Lancaster's opponents, however, one implication of the necessary connection between church and state was that religious instruction could not be left to the Sabbath, as Lancaster and his supporters proposed. The Act of Uniformity accorded the Established Church the obligation to instruct youth throughout the realm in the state religion. Lancasterians countered that this obligation was limited to the teaching of the Church catechism on Sundays. However, as Trimmer put it, "religious education is an EVERY DAY BUSINESS," and must be at the core of instruction.[22] While everyday religious education was certainly a matter of doctrine, it was also a tactical matter in the schoolroom that concerned the methods that should be employed to produce good members of society. Thus the conservative commentators denounced Lancaster's encouragement of his students to accumulate merit points that could be exchanged for prizes. Such methods would produce men and women who would only do what was right if it held out the promise of material reward. The security of the state and of the social order depended on people doing what was right for its own sake, and this was a doctrinal matter. People should be taught to behave out of love and fear of God, not from the kinds of earthly reward promoted by Lancaster.[23]

Southey, who attributed much of the early success of Lancaster in promoting his schools to his lower middle-class willingness to make a spectacle of himself, was particularly articulate in the matter of rewards. Rewards should not be the motive that governed behaviour, but things that came to those who deserved them. The utilitarian spirit in Lancaster's system, which the political economists so admired, was denounced by Southey as "the system of those base-minded sophists who make selfishness the spring of all our actions." The spread of Lancaster's schools would actually validate utilitarian claims about human selfishness "by the deterioration of feeling which it must necessarily produce."[24] Again, because Lancaster refused doctrinal instruction in the schoolroom in favour of general or abstract moral principles, his conservative critics claimed that his students would end up with no fixed principles of any kind. Churchmen were certainly not about to "walk in any new road traced out by the restless spirit of modern innovation."[25]

Lancaster's supporters in turn were scornful of these arguments, which, for them, amounted to excluding self-interest as an educational principle. It was all very well to say that reward should be for reward's sake, and that one should do one's duty because it was right. But all love and fear of God, they claimed, originated in the love and fear of man; it was the desire to please and the fear of displeasing parents and teachers that first inspired respect and reverence for Testament or catechism. Only after the child had mastered the skills of literacy could it appreciate the sense of doctrine. Moreover, the doxa of reward for reward's sake was ineffective for educating the poor, but a good defence of oligarchy. Why should a poor child exert itself on the vague promise of rewards that might someday come to the worthy when "mature, bearded men, who fall into this cant, require the immediate stimulus of a guinea; or, at least, a return for their labour in a month or a year" before they would do anything, demanded Sydney Smith? Everywhere in England men anxiously awaited honours: "Nothing, in our opinion, can be so preposterous as the objections made to an order of merit in a school."[26]

Lancaster's conservative critics strongly rejected the notion that there existed a common Christianity in principle, as well as the notion that Lancaster, in fact, could instruct students in such a common body

of belief. The essence of the Established Church was its Catechism and
Articles; any system of schooling that excluded them could not be supported by Churchmen. In fact, said his opponents, Lancaster's argument that all Christians could be educated together was a propagation
of the doctrine of dissent, as congenial to Quakers; it was certain to
undermine faith in the established religion. It did not, in truth, even
include everyone; as Southey pointed out, it excluded Jews and deists
of various stripes from the outset.[27] It was spurious to argue that Christians differed only in inessentials. There were sharp differences in
church discipline: members of the Established Church had an obligation to attend church on Sundays, while Dissenters did not.[28] Moreover, as John Bowles argued in a pamphlet published in response to
Whitbread's plan for a national Lancasterian school system, different
Christian sects took views on fundamental matters that were completely incompatible: one need only compare the positions of
Socinians and Trinitarians on the nature and character of Christ. What
would remain after doctrinal differences were removed "will certainly
not be Christianity. It will be scarcely any thing else than DEISM." The
consequences of such teaching were especially dangerous:

> the influence of such a system upon those who are educated in it,
> must, in after-life, be of the most pernicious kind. The best that can
> be expected of such persons is, that they will not "hold fast" to any
> form of doctrine – that they will never be firm, or steady, or long
> consistent in any system of faith; and that through life they will be
> wavering and inconstant, and "blown about by every wind of doc-
> trine." But the danger, nay the probability is, that, after many fluctua-
> tions, they will become sceptics, and, perhaps, complete infidels ...[29]

Trimmer argued that Lancaster's plan to teach the scriptures without
offering any comment or explanation that might offend sectarian sensibilities was practically impossible. As soon as a teacher was asked any
question about a scriptural passage, an explanation would be offered,
and doctrinal issues would immediately be present – as they should be,
for "these texts have a meaning, and it should be explained to young
people, or they gain no instructions from them." Henry Brougham
argued that in this matter, Lancaster's opponents "have not blushed to
use the very worst arguments of the Romish bigots, and to proclaim
the dangers of entrusting an unprepared multitude with the free use
of *the Scriptures*." In so doing, they effectively lent "a kind of sanction to
this worst of Popish abominations."[30]
    While Anglicans gestured to the rights of Dissenters to enjoy free-
dom of religion, and presented their opposition to Lancaster's com-

mon Christianity as a defensive stance, from the outset of the debate there were clear indications that the Church had a proselytizing mission. Sarah Trimmer suggested as much in 1806, citing the Book of Daniel,[31] which she claimed Lancaster did not understand. After the organization, in 1811, of the National Society for promoting the Education of the Poor in England and Wales in the Principles of the Established Church, it became quite clear that conversion was at the heart of the Church's project. The National Society program included the teaching of the Church of England Catechism and obligatory attendance at services on Sunday. The Society claimed it had every right to demand that children admitted to its schools attend its church services. This would be no obstacle to Methodists, the largest body of Dissenters, for they were said to agree with the Church in matters of doctrine and even discipline; Presbyterians and Independents as well differed in discipline, not doctrine, and hence could comfortably send their children to Sunday service. The Quakers and Socinians might object, but they were small and wealthy sects capable of maintaining their own schools, while Baptists had an established missionary society. Children would not become members of the Established Church by reading its catechism at school "unless they are likewise accustomed to attend *divine service* at church. It is the *place of worship*, which they frequent on a Sunday, which will make them churchmen, or dissenters."[32]

The Lancasterians' loss of royal patronage and reorganization as the British and Foreign School Society, combined with the formation of the National Society, shifted the nature of the debate dramatically from 1812. The Lancasterians were thrown onto the defensive and now adopted or re-emphasized two lines of argument. First, a uniform system of schooling alone could effectively educate the poor and, since Lancaster's model was by far the cheapest and most efficient, it should be the one adopted. Again, and perhaps more significantly, the threat from the greater resources of the Established Church caused the liberals to overcome their scruples against state intervention in the educational field.

Following the first line, Lancaster's supporters argued that most neighbourhoods were far too poor to support two schools. The introduction of competing Church schools was thus tantamount to a continuing promotion of ignorance for the poor. Members of the Established Church could freely send their children to Lancasterian schools, because these offered no interference with religious doctrines, but Dissenters would be unable to send their children to schools where the established catechism was taught and where church attendance was required. Moreover, it was possible to demonstrate in pounds, shillings, and pence that Lancaster offered instruction every bit as good as Bell and more cheaply. Those who sought the education of the poor would thus prefer "schools which reduce expence to its lowest possible amount; and which, by training together the different religious denominations of the people from their infancy, will tend to unite them in sympathy and affection, even when they differ in religious belief and observances."[33]

Again, the intervention of the Church effectively shut down the liberal project of a national educational system under the direction of a private association enjoying royal patronage. Liberals were forced to appeal for a national system under state auspices, and to overcome their scruples about state intervention to do so. Sydney Smith did much of the necessary ideological work on this matter in the *Edinburgh Review*. While affirming his commitment to the "maxim of politics, which philosophy has extracted from experience," that things were best done by private interests wherever possible, the education of the poor was a partial exception. The state would have to set things in motion "when it unfortunately happens that the mass of a people are exceedingly ignorant, and at the same time too poor to pay for instruction." True, there might be a "danger of training the people to habits of servility and toleration of arbitrary power, if their education be entrusted to Government, or persons patronized by the Government," but the possible benefits of having "the faculty of reading and writing widely diffused through the whole body of the people" were so great that it was worth the experiment. "Grant, in any quarter of the globe, a reading people and a free press," Smith concluded, "and the prejudices on which misrule supports itself will gradually and silently disappear."[34]

LOWER CANADA

The legally recognized presence of the Catholic Church, the predominantly peasant character of the French-Canadian rural population, and rising anti-colonial initiatives shaped educational projects and conflicts in colonial Lower Canada. The colonial debate over monitorial schooling rehearsed parts of the English literature, and colonial and imperial intellectuals, politicians, and administrators tried to promote a non-sectarian Christianity as the moral basis of secular education in the colony both before and after the rebellion of 1837. The Catholic and Anglican churches shared much common ground in their opposition to Lancasterian schooling. However, colonial educational politics were marked by the failure of the Catholic Church to organize its own elementary schools, even while it was able to block most attempts of the Anglican Church at spreading schools, and even while it worked to co-opt or to undermine lay projects for schooling the countryside. The pressures in England to deal with an increasingly independent industrial working class by educational means were not present in the colony; governing through ignorance remained a viable tactic.

Monitorial schooling expanded rapidly in the two Lower Canadian cities, in towns, and in some villages as a means of dealing with pauper children. By the mid–1820s, large Lancasterian schools were run by the British and Canadian School Society in Quebec, Montreal, and Trois Rivières. National Schools on the Bell plan were present at least in Quebec and Montreal, and the Catholic Société d'Éducation de Québec also offered monitorial schooling for pauper children, initially with the endorsement of Bishop Plessis. In the 1820s and early 1830s, the colonial Assembly moved to spread monitorial schooling throughout the countryside. As school visitor for the District of Quebec, John Neilson, chair of the Assembly's Permanent Committee on Education, defined school districts so that they would include enough children (a hundred) for instruction by women teachers using the monitorial method.[35] Joseph Lancaster was himself in Montreal from 1829 to1833, where he received a parliamentary subsidy for educational "experiments,' and corresponded with Neilson and the Patriote political leader Louis-Joseph Papineau about plans for modifying the monitorial method for use in rural schools. In the mid–1830s, the Assembly began to fund free training for a number of candidate teachers in the British and Canadian schools. Moreover, the state-funded Royal Institution for the Promotion of Learning, active after 1818 and managed largely by the Quebec diocesan association of the Society for the Propagation of the Gospel, required that its schoolmasters be trained in Bell's system. There were about eighty Royal Institution schools at the end of the 1820s. [36]

The Catholic Church laid claim to the right to control the education of Catholics, insisting that this right had been recognized by the 1774 Quebec Act.[37] This claim was guarded jealously against the incursions both of the Anglican and other Protestant churches, and against the projects of secularizing liberals. Monitorial schooling, in its Bell and Lancaster versions, was anathema to the Catholic hierarchy. The promotion of Bell's system was menacing, but at least it was the work of a familiar devil – the Anglican Church. If that church attempted to use state power to further its proselytizing mission, under the guise of the common education of members of all denominations, at least it was an episcopal church. Lancaster's version, by contrast, was championed by the laity and by secularizing liberals. Its success would lead to the effective separation of church and state and the complete transformation of the role of education in the social order.

As Bishop Lartigue wrote to Bishop Plessis in 1825, while the Lower Canadian Assembly was debating a bill to create parish elementary schools using Lancaster's system, "Ceci est une affaire majeure où tous les vrais Canadiens et les catholiques doivent se réunir pour faire tomber à plat un projet aussi désastreux pour ce pays. C'en est fait de l'éducation chrétienne dans notre patrie et par conséquent de la religion des générations futures, si on laisse introduire ce système biblique gazé sous le nom de Lancastre."[38] Lancaster's system was objectionable to the Church's conception of a Christian education in virtually all its details. With the Anglicans, the Catholic hierarchy objected in principle to the proposition that children should read the Bible "without note or comment" and, indeed, commonly maintained that many parts of the Bible were not fit to be read by lay people at all. In addition to this doctrinal position, the proposition that scholars should draw their own conclusions from the Bible was individualizing. It abstracted the individual from the spiritual and moral authority of the clergy and encouraged that individual to make his/her own moral judgments. Individualism and skepticism were closely linked and thus threatened the communal basis of ecclesiastical authority. Again, the "système biblique gazé" implied that a generalized biblical morality would be the backdrop to an education that was effectively secular or secularizing. Even though Lancaster's students did not actually get their hands on books until they made it to his sixth class, well past the age at which most young people would have left school, those who did make it were exposed to reading that was not in a narrowly religious idiom.[39]

Any member of the Catholic hierarchy reading Lancaster's own account of his system, which the Legislative Assembly had reprinted and distributed widely in 1815, would find two other objectionable characteristics in it. First, in the nature of the case, the students instructed themselves. A teacher-priest would be able to supervise only from a distance, and hence an important form of popular association beyond clerical control would be created. The monitorial school was the educational counterpart of the tavern. Again, the schools were coeducational, at least potentially, and Lancaster's punishment practices included cross-gender humiliations, such as having a girl wash a boy's dirty face in view of the assembled school, that deeply offended both Anglican and Catholic sensibilities.[40]

The substance of these Catholic objections to Lancasterian schools was very close to the objections voiced by Anglicans in the English debate. There were three peculiarities to the situation in Lower Canada. First, by the time the debate became particularly intense, it was archaic in England. With Brougham's 1820 Education Bill, English Whigs had largely conceded the field to the Established Church. By 1836, when Canadian politicians were thinking of hiring monitorial teachers for their new normal schools, the method had largely fallen out of favour in Europe and parts of America. A second peculiarity was that proponents of monitorial schooling in Canada saw a potential for the schooling of peasants in a pedagogical method that was tailored for an urban proletarian population. But what differed especially in the colony was the Catholic Church's educational strategy toward the threat of secular monitorial schooling.

Faced with the initiatives of supporters of the Lancasterian schools, who controlled the Assembly from the late 1820s, and with the proselytizing initiatives of the Anglican Church through the Royal Institution, the Catholic Church ultimately adopted a reactionary position. Such a position was not predetermined: the Church had at least three tactical choices from the 1820s in an overall strategy of preventing the separation of church and state while preserving its monopoly over the education of Catholics. It could attempt to organize its own educational system in both city and countryside using its considerable financial and logistical resources. It could make common cause, either with other denominations, or across the lay/clerical divide, to pursue some version of a public educational system in which it would be able to exercise leadership, educating its own flock and fending off the incursions of others. Finally, it could attempt to block the extension of public educational projects, especially to the countryside, maintaining some version of the eighteenth-century educational pattern, in which the peasantry would receive catechetical instruction, while promising students could be recruited for religious vocations.

These tactical options were not mutually exclusive; the hierarchy, parish priests, and lay Catholics were not always united in their initiatives; and the Church faced a variety of constraints, both material and political, that limited its room for manoeuvre. The possibilities for collaborating with other groups in schooling diminished in the wake of the Spanish War of Succession and the Papal Encyclical against liberalism of the middle 1830s. The vagaries of imperial Canadian policy and the low level of attention paid to colonial matters also shaped educational politics. Thus the Catholic Bishops were twice prepared to accept the organization of separate confessional committees within the framework of the Royal Institution in the 1820s, but oligarchic opposition in the colony or hesitation in the Colonial Office blocked both initiatives. This was just the period in which the Irish Bishops accepted a notion of "common Christianity" as the basis of a national educational system.[41]

At the level of the colony as a whole, two attempts by the Church to organize its own elementary school system failed miserably. Under the Vestry School Act of 1824, the parish vestries (*les fabriques*) were authorized to hold property for school purposes as a corporation and to devote up to a quarter of the vestries' revenues for the provision and maintenance of elementary schools for boys and girls. Yet, as Richard Chabot has shown, most curés were far more interested in using parish funds to build ostentatious churches and presbyteries and to furnish them lavishly than they were in building schools. Many priests accumulated considerable personal fortunes, which sometimes endowed local vestry schools at their death, but most were themselves little educated and were suspicious of plans for educating their parishioners. Schooling beyond the catechism was seen to be damaging economically and dangerous socially and morally, because it encouraged social mobility and skepticism.[42] Despite exhortations from the bishops, very few parishes paid any attention to the Vestry Act, and a second attempt by Bishop Lartigue of Montreal to make the government convert all elementary schools into *fabrique* schools came to naught. Again, after the failure of the Assembly's 1836 School Bill, Bishops Lartigue and Signäy urged parish priests to take over the existing elementary schools under the provisions of the 1824 Vestry Act, which remained in effect. An inquiry two years later showed that very few had done so: in the Quebec archdiocese, for instance, nineteen of twenty-six parishes had no *fabrique*-sponsored schooling of any kind, three of the remaining seven parishes offered rudimentary instruction paid for out of the legacies of deceased priests, and the others made small donations for the private schooling of pauper children.[43]

Indifference to the organization of parish schools was matched by attempts to prevent the organization of schools by others, although there was a good deal of local variation in such matters. One priest bragged to a French correspondent in 1817 that when a Lancasterian teacher had come to start a school in his parish, he had driven him out by buying the lot of ground on which his school stood and by opening a vestry school of his own. Other priests acted against attempts by residents to accept a Royal Institution school, or to organize a Trustees school. At Cap St Ignace in 1829, for instance, residents complained that the curé Parent used the pretext that their French immigrant teacher did not possess a certificate of qualifications from France to demand that the Royal Institution school be closed. On an earlier occasion, it was said Parent had also blocked the opening of such a school "sous le faux prétexte que les Écoles Établies Sur les bâses actuelles, Sont des institutions contraire à la religion." It was said to be well known that the real cause of Parent's opposition was "L'antipathie qu'il Eprouve pour un Etablissement qui tend à répandre l'instruction et les lumières parmi le peuple."[44] Again, in some parishes the church-wardens attempted to claim that they, and not the trustees elected under the 1829 School Act, were entitled to the school grant. In a few parishes, the curé welcomed a Royal Institution school, against the wishes of his bishop, seeing in the £100 subsidy a way to provide a parish school at no expense to the vestry. The Anglican Church was certainly not above such kinds of initiatives in its own right, and there were claims of the Royal Institution attempting to block the formation of trustee schools in the period between 1829 and 1832 where their schools were still being subsidized by the Assembly.[45] Finally, after clergy were allowed to serve as school visitors and trustees under amendments to the 1829 Trustees School Act, the clergy gained a strong measure of control over most rural schools. Parish school districts accepted the school grant, but under clerical supervision, and little in the way of instruction was actually delivered in many parishes.

For much of the first half of the nineteenth century, then, the Lower Canadian Catholic Church continued to play the role and to adopt the mercantilist stance with regard to rural elementary education that was characteristic of the period following the Reformation. Education was first and foremost about ensuring religion and morality by containing such learning as was dispensed within a Catholic religious framework. The moral character of the flock was also dependent on the prevention of sexual misconduct through the rigid separation of the sexes at school, a dangerous place of association beyond the supervision of the paterfamilias. Learning for the great mass of the population was restricted to learning to read in order to be able to read the catechism, and perhaps to write in order to write one's name. Reading instruction in eighteenth-century France, and perhaps also still in nineteenth-century Lower Canada, began for the French reader by learning the Latin alphabet and parts of the liturgy.[46] In this way, the Church sought to recruit cantors. Moreover, supervision by the parish priest was intended to prevent the unbridled growth of learning that might easily lead to skepticism. As late as the mid–1830s, we can see from reports filed by schools funded under the 1829 Trustees School Act that a great many, perhaps the majority, of Lower Canadian French-language elementary schools contained no non-religious books of any sort. Insofar as the schools cultivated or stimulated the imagination of students, they did so entirely within the confines of a doctrinal religious idiom.[47]

In contrast to the condition of elementary schooling, Catholic collegiate education was much more highly developed. With a priesthood that was declining in size relative to the colonial population and facing political difficulties in recruiting abroad, the hierarchy was eager to train its own clerics. In the early nineteenth century, it began to support the organization of classical colleges under clerical supervision, in addition to the seminaries in Quebec and Montreal. Beginning with Nicolet in 1803, and ending with L'Assomption in 1836, six colleges were eventually incorporated by the legislature. These provided classical instruction to the sons of the dominant class, but also increasingly to the sons of wealthy peasants. In the absence of an effective system of parish elementary schools, colleges were constrained to offer some instruction in the basics. These institutions were certainly not imposed on local communities; a college was an important economic and symbolic addition to a village economy and many people supported collegiate education from motives of piety. An 1835 petition for legislative support for the completion of the Collège de L'Assomption, for instance, bore the signatures of thirteen men and the crosses of over eight hundred others, close to the entire adult male population of the parish. In this case, illiterate men wanted a college neither they nor the vast majority of their sons would ever attend.[48]

While the colleges generated candidates for the priesthood, they also instructed a considerable number of men who subsequently became doctors, notaries, and lawyers. By the late 1820s, the developed literary skills of the professional middle classes contrasted sharply with the illiteracy of the mass of the peasant population. The elitist Catholic educational economy contrasted with that which developed in English-speaking areas. In the former, most educational resources were devoted to the higher branches of instruction; in the latter, to the elementary branches. These differences reverberated through ethnic cultures. Moreover, in the advanced college classes in Rhetoric, students practised mock parliamentary debates and, at least before the 1830s reaction, teachers in some institutions took markedly liberal stances on some political questions, such as the separation of church and state. The Church thus, ironically, produced its own would-be gravediggers, in the class of secularizing liberal professionals who came to form the leadership of the Patriote party and who came to promote Lancasterian monitorial schooling as the basis for a colonial system. The multiplication of classical colleges also created recruitment problems for these institutions and caused some college principals to agitate for systematic elementary education in order to increase the pool of potential classical scholars. While many, if not most, parish priests continued to prefer an ignorant and docile rural population to a literate one, there was pressure from within the Church as well as from without to raise the general educational level of the population as a whole. Containing the heightened level of instruction within a religious idiom was a challenge the Church would face after 1841 especially.

Finally, in the towns and cities, and in contrast to the Anglican Church's activities on both sides of the Atlantic, the Catholic hierarchy made no serious effort to compete with monitorial schools on either the Bell or Lancaster model with institutions of its own. With the exceptions of several urban convent schools, which drew a relatively small clientele, and the lukewarm support offered to the Société d'Éducation de Québec, and, perhaps, Lartigue's Montreal École St-Jacques, the hierarchy showed no active interest in the promotion of schooling for the mass of the urban population. The Quebec clergy did initially manifest some openness toward monitorial schooling in relation to the activities of the Société d'Éducation de Québec, which was organized in 1821 under the leadership of the wealthy Quebec prothonotary J.-F. Perrault, and the Protestant printer and politician John Neilson. The curé and future Bishop of Quebec, Joseph Signäy, was initially an enthusiastic supporter of its Lancasterian school. J.-F. Perrault had been promoting Lancaster's methods for some time, and in 1822 translated Lancaster's school manual into French.[49] The Quebec bishop, Msgr. Plessis, presided over the school's first public examination in 1822, a sign of its initial legitimacy as a denominational religious institution. However, Perrault's secular orientation, his association with the Quebec British and Canadian School Society, whose president he became in 1823, and the agitations against him of Bishop Lartigue alienated the Quebec clergy. The Society was advertising a bi-lingual school open to children of all denominations, in which no form of religious dogma would be taught. Perrault, pro-British, liberal, and interested in the spread of Lancasterian schooling first and foremost, was ousted from the Société d'Éducation sometime before May 1825, after Lartigue began an intense campaign against him. As early as October 1823, Lartigue was urging Plessis not to associate himself with the Société d'Éducation "car cet établissement se tourne évidemment en école biblique, c'est-à-dire, en école de protestantisme ou d'impiété." He criticized Plessis for subscribing to Perrault's school manual, and denounced the bastard religious system Perrault was promoting. Perrault resigned from the presidency of the Société d'Éducation and eventually from that of the British and Canadian School as well, using his considerable personal wealth to build and run Lancasterian boys' and girls' schools, which paired monitorial schooling with industrial training. However, he was unable to sustain the schools without financial support from the Assembly and they closed in 1837.[50]

LOWER CANADA THROUGH ENGLISH EYES

In addition to the tactical manoeuvring of religious, secular, and government bodies, Lower Canadians were exposed to the English debate over monitorial schooling directly through the circulation of English books, periodicals, and pamphlets, and through the reproduction of ideas from that literature in the colonial press. Joseph Lancaster published pamphlets and a short-lived periodical, and wrote letters to the colonial newspapers trumpeting his method of education and denouncing those opposed to him. The Catholic clergy joined in this debate as well. Discussion of "systems" of education was especially visible in both the English- and French-language press from 1829, as the Assembly began funding elementary schools, and as editors learned that Joseph Lancaster had received £200 from the legislature to conduct educational "experiments." Partisans of monitorial schooling clashed with proponents of other methods, such as the "intellectual" method of the Belgian Joseph Jacotot, while J.-F. Perrault attempted to promote schools of agriculture on de Fellenberg's model.

One lively exchange took place in the Montreal *Vindicator* newspaper in 1830, in which a correspondent, signing himself only "P," warned against enthusiasm for educational systems. "P" repeated much of the orthodox and romantic Anglican critique of Lancaster's method: "systematizers" were "egregious visionaries" whose "new-fangled notions of Education" would destroy the best memories of youth, sacrificing the pleasures that generations had taken in later life from being able to contemplate their copy-books and sum-books "to the mean economy of Sand writing." Lancaster's pretentious styling of himself as the "Founder" of monitorial schooling was well known to be false; the system had been developed well before him by Andrew Bell, in whom "there is no pomposity."

"P" raised political objections to Lancaster's "system,"since the education of youth was "the cement" that held governments together. It was speculative to break down established differences of "Sect, Rank, Age, Habits, and Dispositions" in the belief that all minds could be instructed in the same manner. Such a proposal was against the natural order of things – "P" invoked explicitly the notion of "the great chain of being" – in which different groups necessarily received different forms of education. Gradation in social relations implied the necessity of gradation in education, with the learner passing carefully through a set of fixed stages of instruction. In the best system of education "there is no harlequinism, no hop-step-and a jump plan, from swaddling clothes, to Coat and Breeches, and then into the Chair of a 'System Professor,'" as was the case with Lancaster.[51]

While the press engaged periodically with the merits and disadvantages of monitorial schooling, and with the prospects of educating members of all social classes, religious and ethnic groups in common, the Lower Canadian Catholic and Anglican clergy faced a final challenge in the wake of the Rebellion of 1837. The Education Commission, chaired by Arthur Buller and appointed by Lord Durham as part of his attempt to sort out colonial governance, advocated the adoption of an Irish-style system of common schooling to be managed locally by elected representatives of rate-payers. Before the anti-liberal reaction of the 1830s, the Irish Bishops had accepted the proposition that there existed a common set of Christian doctrines that could form the basis of a non-sectarian education, with separate religious instruction offered outside school hours. The Catholic and Anglican Bishops sat together on the Irish National Education Commission, although Protestant opposition to schooling in common was intensifying in Ireland as the model was being promoted for Canada.

The Catholic Bishops in Lower Canada worked assiduously to undermine the work of the Education Commission, instructing parish priests not to answer its inquiries with respect to existing educational conditions in the countryside. They refused to engage directly with Arthur Buller's arguments in favour of common Christian education as a way of ensuring social and political harmony in the colony, although they communicated with their Irish counterparts for information about the operations of the Irish system. The Catholic Bishops insisted repeatedly that elementary education was a church prerogative, that only a system of denominational religious school boards was acceptable, and that schooling in common was unnecessary in any case in a colony where the vast majority of the population was Catholic. Leading Protestant clergymen similarly organized to oppose any non-denominational school system.[52]

Monitorial schooling increasingly dropped out of this debate. Its limited and mechanical methods were seen as increasingly ineffective for developing the moral and intellectual capacities of young people in the conditions of an expanding market economy and the growth of a representative system of government. Other methods of "intellectual" education, focussed on the "diffusion of useful knowledge," came to the fore.[53] Moreover, under the School Act of 1841, the Catholic clergy in French Canada effectively used a "dissenting schools" clause to preserve its control of elementary education. This history is beyond my present scope.

CONCLUSION

The Special Collections library at Queen's University at Kingston contains a copy of Robert Southey's *The Origin, Nature, and Object, of the New System of Education,* the definitive Anglican statement on the Bell-Lancaster controversy. The book has been annotated by a Lower Canadian English reader of the early 1830s. Southey claimed that in Ireland, where the experiment was conducted of excluding Anglican doctrines from the school in favour of a common education, the Catholic priests forcefully prevented children from attending such schools. The reader starred this passage heavily and asked with respect to the colonial Assembly, "What do they now? Give grants to the o[ld] d[evil] Lancaster!" And to the claim of Lancaster's partisans that Bell might have invented the monitorial system but that Lancaster was responsible for its spread – a charge Southey was concerned to refute in part – the reader added another marginal star and the footnote "so said Mr Papineau !!!" To this reader, the colonial world seemed to be turned upside down. It was the Catholics who dominated the Assembly, not dissenting Protestants, who were subsidizing Lancaster, undoubtedly knowing that his system would undermine the Established Church. And it was the Patriotes who were mouthing pro-Lancasterian propaganda. Still, as the starred and exclamatory notes indicate, the English anti-Lancasterian discourse allowed this reader to make sense of Lower Canadian educational politics.

The Bell-Lancaster controversy was replayed in Lower Canada in novel ways. Some of the colonial parties were the same, the Established Church in the guise of the National Society and the Royal Institution, the British and Foreign School Society in the guise of the British and Canadian School Society. But the presence of the Catholic Church, the only established Catholic Church in the empire before 1829, the growth of a secular liberal professional class concerned with colonial political reform, and the absence of a developing industrial working class, combined to change the state of play dramatically. Political struggles meant that Lower Canadians got neither the system of Anglican Church-dominated schools that prevailed in England, and that was attempted in the sister colony of Upper Canada, nor the attempts at schooling in common that dominated Irish schooling in the 1820s and 1830s. Ultimately, and despite comparatively lavish expenditure of public monies, rural Lower Canadians got little schooling of any sort.

Instead of projects for the creation of political community framed around abstract Christian morality but centred on concrete common skills of literacy and calculation, the bulk of the rural peasantry remained confined within a narrowly ecclesiastical definition of the ends of learning. The failure of projects for non-sectarian common monitorial schooling in the 1820s and 1830s created some of the conditions for the Catholic Church's effective investment of the education of the people under the School Act of 1841. With its privileges confirmed by the Confederation of 1867, the Church managed to retain elementary and secondary education within a religious framework in parts of Quebec until the passage of a constitutional amendment in 1995.

NOTES

1 Research for this chapter was supported by the Social Science and Humanities Research Council of Canada. I am grateful to Robin Smith and J.-F. Constant for research assistance.

2 Robert Owen, "A New View of Society," in Harold Silver, ed., *Robert Owen on Education* (Cambridge: Cambridge University Press, 1969), 133–7.

3 Robert Southey and Charles Cuthbert Southey, *The Life of the Rev. Andrew Bell* ... 3 vols (London and Edinburgh: John Murray and William Blackwood & Sons, 1845), 3: 21–3.

4 Joseph Lancaster, *Improvements in Education, as it respects the industrious classes* (London: Darton and Harvey, 1805).

5 Parts of the work appear in Andrew Bell, "Experiment in Education" in D. Salmon, ed., *The Practical Parts of Lancaster's Improvements and Bell's Experiment* (Cambridge: Cambridge University Press, 1932 [1808]). Salmon reproduces parts of Bell's fourth edition. One of the issues in the English debate was the changes in content in the various editions of Bell's and Lancaster's work. Bell's early account of the system had been quite short; Lancaster's partisans claimed the much longer fourth edition was swollen with material lifted from Lancaster.

6 Southey and Southey, *The Life of the Rev. Andrew Bell* 2: 116–60.

7 While Bell's partisans denounced Lancaster's cruel and humiliating punishments, his main supporters either treated them as unexceptionable or argued that they were well suited to child nature. The participants were probably aware of reports of the astonishing forms of physical abuse prevalent in the Irish charter schools. On punishment issues more generally, Bruce Curtis, "'My ladie birchely must needes rule': Punishment and the Materialization of Moral Character, from Mulcaster to Lancaster" in N. de Coninck-Smith et al., eds, *Discipline, Moral Regulation and Schooling: A Social History* (New York: Garland Press, 1997): 19–42.

8 Sarah Trimmer, *A Comparative View of the New Plan of Education promulgated by Mr Joseph Lancaster, in his tracts concerning the instruction of the children of the labouring parts of the community; and of The System of Christian Education founded*

by our pious forefathers for The Initiation of the Young Members of the Established Church in the principles of the Reformed Religion (London: R.C. and J. Rivington and J. Hachard, 1805): 51–2.

9 Quoted in Brian Simon, *The Two Nations & the Educational Structure, 1780–1870* (London: Lawrence and Wishart, 1974) 132; Trimmer, *A Comparative View,* also adopted this line, and it was tempered but still present in Herbert Marsh. *A Sermon, preached in the Cathedral Church of St. Paul, London, on Thursday, June 13, 1811. To which is added a Collection of Notes and Illustrations. By Herbert Marsh, D.D. F.R.S. Margaret Professor of Divinity in the University of Cambridge,* 3rd ed. (London: F.C. and J. Rivington, 1811).

10 Henry Lord Brougham, "Education of the Poor," *Edinburgh Review* (17 Nov. 1810): 58–88. Bernard Mandeville, "An Essay on Charity, and Charity-Schools," in Philip Harth, ed., *The Fable of the Bees* (Harmondsworth: Penquin Books, 1970 [1723]), 261–325. Robert Southey, "Bell and Lancaster's Systems of Education," *Quarterly Review* 6, no. 11 (1811): 264–304; for the strategizing around how to deal with this question, which Bell's supporters thought was their weakest point, see Southey to Bell, 6 Oct. 1811, in *Life of Andrew Bell,* 2: 634–5.

11 Simon, *Two Nations,* 133–4.

12 Lancaster, *Improvements,* viii–ix.

13 David Hogan, "The Market Revolution and Disciplinary Power: Joseph Lancaster and the Psychology of the Early Classroom System," *History of Education Quarterly* 29, no. 3 (1989): 389–417.

14 See John Franklin Reigart, *The Lancasterian System of Instruction in the Schools of New York City.* Contributions to Education, No. 81. (New York: Teachers College, Columbia University, 1916), 75–6.

15 James Mill. "On Education," in Terrence Ball, ed., *Political Writings* (Cambridge: Cambridge University Press, 1992), 147, 174, 185.

16 Sydney Smith, "Outlines of a Plan for educating Ten Thousand poor Children, by establishing Schools in Country Towns and Villages; and for uniting Works of Industry with useful Knowledge. By Joseph Lancaster. 8vo. London. 1806," *Edinburgh Review* (Oct. 1807): 61–73.

17 Trimmer, *Comparative View,* 9.

18 Samuel Taylor Coleridge, "Mr Lancaster" [attribution] in David V. Erdman, ed., *Essays on His Times in The Morning Post and The Courier* (London: Routledge & Kegan Paul, 1978) 3: 129.

19 Robert Southey, "Bell and Lancaster's Systems of Education," *Quarterly Review* 6, no. 11 (1811): 264–304, at 289.

20 Brougham, "Education of the Poor"; Smith, "Education of the Poor."

21 "Tracts relative to Bell's and Lancaster's Schools," *Monthly Review Enlarged* 68 (May 1812): 83–95.

22 Trimmer, *Comparative View,* 10.

23 Robert Southey, *The Origin, Nature, and Object, of the New System of Education* (London: John Murray, 1812), 83: "boys should be taught to do their duty because it is their duty – for its own sake, not for what they are to get by doing it." Trimmer, *Comparative View*, 24–5.

24 Southey, "Bell and Lancaster," 289. Southey's rather romantic conservatism shared elements of the socialist critique of monitorial schools. For instance, the use of slates and cards hung on the wall for writing and reading meant that the student could not take pleasure in contemplating or reading over his/her lessons. There would be no book to hand down to the next generation as an item of pride or accomplishment. Southey also favoured the copy book as a place where students could learn decorative writing, in place of the "plain round hand" preferred by utilitarian efficiency.

25 Coleridge, *Essays*, 333.

26 Smith, "Outlines of a Plan for educating Ten Thousand poor Children," 67.

27 Southey, "Bell and Lancaster," 288–9.

28 "First Annual Report of the National Society for promoting the Education of the Poor in the Principles of the Established Church. With an Account of the Proceedings for the Formation of the Society, and an Appendix of Documents; together with a List of Subscribers to the Society in London, and to Societies in the Country, in Union with the National Society. 8vo. pp.198. London. Murray, Albemarle Street. 1812." *Quarterly Review* 7, no. 15 (1812): 1–27.

29 John Bowles, *A Letter addressed to Samuel Whitbread, Esq. M.P., in consequence of the unqualified Approbation expressed by him in the House of Commons of Mr Lancaster's System of Education; the religous Part of which is here shewn to be incompatible with the Safety of the Established Church, and in its Tendency, subversive of Christianity itself. Including also some cursory Observations on the Claims of the Irish Romanists, as they affect the Safety of the Established Church* (London: Hatchard, 1807); reproduced in part in Carl F. Kaestle, ed., *Joseph Lancaster and the Monitorial School Movement. A Documentary History* (New York: Teachers College Press, 1973).

30 Trimmer, *Comparative View*, 58–9; Brougham, "Education of the Poor," 84.

31 Daniel 12:2–3: "And many of them that sleep in the dust of the earth shall awake, some to everlasting life, and some to shame and everlasting contempt. And they that be wise shall shine as the brightness of the firmament; and they that turn many to righteousness as the stars forever."

32 "First Annual Report," 14–5.

33 "Tracts," 95 for the quote; also Smith, "Education of the Poor," 1813.

34 Smith, "Education of the Poor," 1813, 211–13.

35 Musée de la Civilisation, Fonds du Séminaire de Québec, Polygraphie 42, no. 20 H, Rapport du Visiteur d'École pour les Comtés de Bellechasse, L'Ilet, Kamouraska et Rimouski, and addressed to "L'Honorable Chambre d'Assemblée du Bas-Canada, assembleé en Parlement." 21 Aug. 1831.

36 For the spread of the schools, including the early efforts of Thaddeus Osgoode, see George W. Spragge, "Monitorial Schools in the Canadas, 1810–1845" (DPaed, Toronto, 1935).

37 An innovation in British policy with respect to Catholicism; see Philip Lawson, "A perspective on British History and the Treatment of the Conquest of Quebec," *Journal of Historical Sociology* 3, no. 3 (1990): 253–71.

38 Archives de l'archevêchie de Québec [AAQ] registre des lettres, vol. 2, D.M. lettre no.145 Lartigue to Plessis, 27 Jan. 1825.

39 In *Improvements in Education*, 204–5, Lancaster listed Watt's *Hymns for Children; Instructive Hints*; Barbauld's *Hymns*; *Pastoral Lessons*; Trimmer's *Introduction to the Knowledge of the Nature and the Use of the Scriptures*; Martinet's *Catechism of Nature*; Turner's *Arts and Sciences; Scripture Instruction by Question, and Answer*; and Priscilla Wakefield's *Mental Improvement*. Most of these are religious in nature, but they are by Methodists, Anglicans, and Quakers, at the least. The implicit relativization of doctrine is itself secularizing.

40 See Trimmer's *Comparative View* for the Anglican reaction.

41 See the fascinating discussion in Public Record Office of Northern Ireland, ED/10/26/1, "First Report of the Commissioners of Irish Education Enquiry. Presented by His Majesty's Command to both Houses of Parliament." Appendix, No 257. Examination of the Most Reverend Dr Murray, Roman Catholic Archbishop of Dublin; of the Most Reverend Dr Kelly, Roman Catholic Archbishop of Tuam; and of the Right Reverend Dr Doyle, Roman Catholic Bishop of Kildare and Leighlin, on Oath; Thursday, 14th April 1825."

42 Richard Chabot, *Le curé de campagne et la contestation locale au Québec de 1791 aux troubles de 1837–1838* (Montreal: Hurtubise HMH Ltée., 1975). With more space, one could nuance this portrait, because there were a number of highly literate, intellectually inclined priests who actively promoted parish schooling or who encouraged the schools formed by the 1829 Act: L.M.R. Barbier of Berthier, J.-B. Boucher of Laprairie, and the anti-patriote Jacques Paquin of St-Eustache, to name only three.

43 See Bruce Curtis, "State of the Nation or Community of Spirit? Schooling for Civic and Ethnic-Religious Nationalism in Insurrectionary Lower Canada," *History of Education Quarterly* 43, no. 3 (2003): 324–49.

44 McGill University Archives (MUA), Royal Institution for the Advancement of Learning (RI) Accession #447 Folder #9654 187 RG 4, C.48, A. Larue, n.p. Capt St Ignace to secretary R.I., Quebec, 2 Feb. 1829.

45 For examples of these activities, NAC, RG4 B30, School Petition, district 9, Seigneury of Bourg Louis, Portneuf, n.d. 1835; Augustin Gervais, Longueuil, to Gosford, 27 May 1835; MUA, RI, Accession #447 Folder #9663 196 RG 4, C.49, Nairn et al. to Mills, 8 May 1829; Accession #447 Folder #9667 200 RG 4, C.49, Allsop to Mills, 8 May 1829.

46 For the impact of Lancasterian methods on this dominant practice, François
    Furet and Jacques Ozouf, *Lire et écrire. L'alphabétisation des français de Calvin à
    Jules Ferry* (Paris: Les Editions de Minuit, 1977) 1: 155–6; that Lower Cana-
    dian readers still learned first in Latin is suggested by anon., *Rapport d'un
    Québecois sur quelques Écoles Élémentaires du District de Quebec*, CIHM #21452.
    n.p.: n.p., 1834.

47 For more detail, Bruce Curtis, "Joseph Lancaster in Montreal (bis):
    Monitorial Schooling and Politics," *Historical Studies in Education/ Revue
    d'histoire de l'éducation* (2005): in press.

48 Brian Young pointed out the importance of local demand to me; for the case
    described, National Archives of Canada [NAC], RG4 B30 vol.11, 27 Oct. 1835.

49 Joseph-François Perrault, *Cours d'éducation élémentaire à l'usage de l'école
    gratuite, établie dans la cité de Québec en 1821* (Québec: la Nouvelle imprimerie,
    1822).

50 The quotation is from Jolois, *J.-F. Perrault*, 111–12; Lartigue's opposition con-
    tinued to Perrault's later initiatives.

51 *Vindicator*, 27 and 30 Aug. 1830. Notice that "P" is repeating much of the
    standard Anglican critique published in Southey, *The Origin, Nature, and
    Object, of the New System of Education*, and somewhere I have read the
    "hop-step-and a jump" phrase before; I expand on this exchange in "Joseph
    Lancaster in Montreal." This is only one of several ongoing exchanges; see,
    for instance, *La Minerve* in various numbers in the summer and fall of 1829,
    where a French expatriate extols the virtues of Jacotot's method.

52 I deal with these events in Bruce Curtis, "The Buller Education Commission;
    or, The London Statistical Society Comes to Canada, 1838–42" in J.-P, Beaud
    and J.-G. Prévost, eds, *The Age of Numbers/L'ère du chiffre.* (Quebec: PUQ,
    2000), 278–97; "Irish Schools for Canada: Arthur Buller to the Bishop of
    Quebec," *Historical Studies in Education/Revue d'histoire de l'éducation* 13, no. 1
    (2001): 49–58; and "Public Education and the Manufacture of Solidarity:
    Christopher Dunkin's Design for Lower Canada," *Histoire sociale/Social History*
    35, no. 70 (2002): 449–70.

53 For instance, Charles Mondelet,. *Letters on Elementary and Practical Education.
    To which is added a French translation* (Montreal: John James Williams, 1841).

PART THREE

A Laboratory of Modernity

MICHAEL EAMON

Scottish-Trained Medical Practitioners in British North America and Their Participation in a Transatlantic Culture of Enlightenment

Here we find a vast stock of proper Materials for the Art and Ingenuity of Man to work upon. Treasures of immense Worth... The Curious have observ'd, that the Progress of Humane Literature (like the Sun) is from East to West; thus has it travelled thro' Asia and Europe and now is arrived at the Eastern Shore of America ...

– Nathaniel Ames' *Almanack*, 1757[1]

In less than half, MAN'S, Post Deluv'an AGE; / In this SEPTENTRION Clime, there was no STAGE... The MUSES, then, knew not, these frozen Climes; / So sent no Cargo here, of Prose or Rhymes./ But ARTS and TRADE, at length being wafted o'er, / From BRITISH ISLES to this ACAD'AN Shore; / DISCIPLES, then, of the PARNASS'AN TRAIN; /Adventur'd, over, the ATLANTIC Main – Prologue to "Acadius, or Love in a Calm," 1774[2]

every enlightened individual, whether he resides in Paris, at Madrid, or at London, now thinks alike; no variation of climate, no remoteness of place, not even national prejudices, more variable and more remote than either, destroy that unanimity of opinion, which they feel on certain topics essential to human welfare. – *Scots Magazine*, April 1798[3]

From contemporary commentators to present-day scholars, the extent to which the "art," "trade," and "ingenuity of Man" existed in British North America has been the subject of frequent observation and vigorous debate. Did colonial ideas and culture, as British American publisher Nathaniel Ames (1708–64) observed, originate in the East and cross over to the New World? Were ideas and culture like commodities, and how were they consumed? Did colonial Americans accept European ideas and methods in a wholesale fashion, or did they use such ideologies as a foil against which to develop their own unique culture of ideas? Or perhaps, did interconnected networks of exchange exist, leading to what could be seen as a transatlantic "unanimity of opinion," a culture based on the contributions of many regions and sharing "topics essential to human welfare"? The literature on the transference, resonance, and creation of ideas in colonial British North America is vast. This "forbidding range of scholarship,"[4] as has been recently observed, is interdisciplinary in nature, overlapping what has been seen traditionally as social, political, religious, economic, cultural, literary, and intellectual history. Lately, scholars have employed the lens of Enlightenment as one means to focus the several streams of historical analysis that have been used to understand eighteenth-century American thought, ideologies, and culture.

A rich body of historical writings argues that the Thirteen Colonies and, in particular the major centres of New England, constituted the American periphery of Enlightenment. The Enlightenment in America, it has been observed, was an urban phenomenon centred on America's lively seaports and those cities boasting institutions of higher learning and relatively large, literate populations.[5] A lively debate has emerged about whether Enlightenment was derivative in America, or facilitated inherently American aspects of political thought to come to fruition.[6] The idea of Enlightenment in America, reflecting ideas expressed elsewhere by scholars of Enlightenment, soon was used to explain not only specific political ideologies and individuals, but a larger, integrated eighteenth-century culture of ideas, activities, class, and social norms.

This use of Enlightenment in the scholarship has tended to explain select American occurrences, communities, and regions while virtually ignoring others. John Bumsted has particularly observed this inequity in historical interpretation of eighteenth-century Canada. "The question of whether there was an indigenous Enlightenment in English Canada," Bumsted writes, "much less the question of the extent to which external Enlightenment influences touched it – has never been seriously posed, and there is no secondary literature that directly addresses these matters."[7] Indeed, for the breadth of understanding that the scholarship on Enlightenment in America has afforded us, an incomplete picture of colonial British North America – with several avenues of unanswered inquiry – still remains.

Acknowledging the importance of this scholarship on the Thirteen Colonies, and later the United States of America, this paper will expand its purview, focusing on the northern British American colonies in the region that later became known as Canada.[8] A revisiting of the intellectual culture of the North Atlantic world of the mid-eighteenth to early nineteenth centuries is proposed. In particular, it will be argued that the same connections that brought the philosophies and methods of Enlightenment to the southern British American colonies should also be seen to have affected the more northern reaches of British America. Furthermore, it will be suggested that one particularly promising thread traces the actions of Scottish-trained medical professionals during this time. These medical professionals were eclectically trained and their liberal approach exhibited the characteristically Scottish Enlightenment traits of juridical and civic mindedness. Once in the colonies their actions transcended the practice of medicine, branching into such areas as natural philosophy, ethnology, architecture, law, and colonial administration. Along with local military personnel, merchants, clergy, and colonial bureaucrats, these individuals established what could be considered a moderate, colonial *literati* acting as working-level agents of the Scottish Enlightenment in what was to become Canada. Whether in local coffee houses, societies, administrative reports, or personal study, their actions provide tangible examples of the theoretical put into practice as they devised ways to better understand and improve the new society in which they now found themselves.

DEFINING THE SCOTTISH ENLIGHTENMENT

Even before the Scottish physician-turned-author Tobias Smollett (1721–71) wrote that Edinburgh was a "hot-bed of genius" in 1771, contemporary Scottish observers were heralding an unique Caledonian age.[9] During the eighteenth century, it was perceived that a new, innovative spirit of philosophy was flourishing in the writings of Scotia's sons. As the *anonymous* commentator[10] upon David Hume's (1711–76) *A Treatise of Human Nature* observed in 1740, "The philosophical spirit, which has been so much improved all over Europe with these last fourscore years, has been carried to as great a length in this kingdom as in any other. Our writers seem even to have started a new kind of philosophy, which promises more both to the entertainment and advantage of mankind, than any other with which the world has been yet acquainted."[11] Also perceiving an exceptional nature to the era, an author in the *Scots Magazine* boldly asserted in 1763 that, "there is always one period at least to be found, which crowded with men of genius in every art and science ... For my part," the author continued,

"I pour out my heart with the utmost gratitude to Providence for giving me a being in this illustrious period; and I have great reason to congratulate the present generation of my countrymen for enjoying the same blessing."[12]

Elsewhere eighteenth-century writers such as Charles Louis de Secondat Montesquieu (1641–1755), Moses Mendelssohn (1729–86), and Immanuel Kant (1724–1804) were also noticing a unique spirit of the time and defined this era of *Enlightenment* in many ways: as a continuing process of education extending across many generations; as an education in the use of reason; as a philosophical spirit of improvement; as the use of reason, in public, for freeing humanity from prejudice and superstition. These contemporary writers believed that Enlightenment was an ongoing process.[13] Twentieth-century revivalists of the Enlightenment used the term to explain the intellectual legacy of the eighteenth century seen as a finite era of like values and ideas.[14] Originally believed to have flourished solely in the writings of French, German, and British authors, eighteenth-century European Enlightenment – or Enlightenments – has now been seen as a larger Western movement affecting a wide periphery of regions and peoples.[15]

Some scholars have focused specifically on a unique spirit that was perceived to have existed in Scotland. Those who study this specific Scottish Enlightenment have directed their analyses toward the similarities and variations of Enlightenment thought that existed in Scotland and how these ideas were received elsewhere in the eighteenth-century Western world. As in studies of *other* Enlightenments, the meanings, significance, and chronology of this Scottish Enlightenment paradigm are by no means universally accepted, and a large body of work has emerged debating the causes, characteristics, and results of this era.[16] Nonetheless, it has been generally argued that the Scottish Enlightenment was an era pervaded by an ever-present spirit of philosophy and polymathy. As in other regions that experienced the Enlightenment, in Scotland the pursuit of knowledge through experience, the examination of nature, and the improvement of society were paramount.

Across Scotland, as elsewhere in eighteenth-century Europe, coffee houses, taverns, public lectures, and private salons were all forums that fostered Enlightenment ideologies and methods. There, as Richard Sher has observed, a moderate *literati* of educated professionals observed, discussed, and put into practice the popular philosophies of the day.[17] While many characteristics of the Scottish Enlightenment were part-and-parcel of the larger Western Enlightenment, scholars have argued for the existence of unique Scottish elements. These include a critical approach marked by "common sense" and skepticism, a strong sense of civic humanism, a fostering of a "science of man," and an underlying sense of civil jurisprudence.[18] Furthermore, it was the unique grammar school and university system in Scotland – with its characteristic broad base of study, liberalism in pedagogical methods, use of vernacular instruction, and employment of society-based discourse – that became one of the key vehicles for the inculcation of Enlightenment ideals.[19]

This unique combination of liberal and eclectic curriculum, in conjunction with laissez-faire course registration, flexible fee structures, and the use of English as the language of instruction led, as some scholars have observed, to the creation of a popular learning environment for domestic and international students alike. As Richard Drayton writes, Scotland was "directly connected, particularly through Glasgow, with Atlantic and Asian trade and colonies. Its intellectual life," he continues,

> reflected this engagement. Scotland's cultural vitality can in part be explained by local influences, in particular the renaissance in the universities. Edinburgh, Glasgow, and Aberdeen offered instruction in natural philosophy and nurtured scientific research a century before Oxford or Cambridge. Scottish learning was also unashamed in taking a practical concern with material improvement ... Scotland which had been pulled to the centre of the world was capable of cosmopolitan sympathies which it could not have fostered a century before.[20]

Eighteenth-century Scotland, it has been argued, was an intellectual centre for many disciplines, an "Athens of the North" as contemporary Scots observed,[21] from which the diffusion of moral and natural philosophies could be considered part-and-parcel of the establishment of larger, global networks of industry, commerce, and science.

FINDING THE SCOTTISH ENLIGHTENMENT IN EIGHTEENTH-CENTURY AMERICA

The role of Enlightenment, and in particular the Scottish Enlightenment, has figured prominently in the history of ideas in eighteenth-century America. John Clive and Bernard Bailyn were among some of the first scholars to elucidate the striking similarities between eighteenth-century Scotland and America. America, like Scotland, was a "cultural province" of an English-speaking Atlantic world centred on London. However, Clive and Bailyn argued, their provincial status led to affinities which led to the gravitation of the regions to each other.[22]

America drew heavily on the ideas originating from its confrere Scotland, informing not only intellectual culture and educational practice, but also forging a revolutionary ideology. "British North America produced no Hume or Adam Smith," Clive and Bailyn wrote, "but in Edwards and Franklin, Jefferson, Madison, and Adams, Rittenhouse, Rush, Copley, West, Wythe and Hutchinson it boasted men of impressive accomplishment. Its finest fruit, the literature of the American Revolution, has justly been called, 'the most magnificent irruption of the American genius into print.'"[23] Enlightenment, then, was originally seen as a means to better understand Colonial America, to explore America's connection to European thought, and to see the germination of original, or unique ideas informed by the colonial experience.

One long-standing supposition about the American Enlightenment has been that it could only occur in the larger urban centres of the Thirteen Colonies. Carl Bridenbaugh was one of the first to emphasize the link between colonial cities and the rise of Enlightenment in America. For Bridenbaugh the connection was simple; it was in the cities where "the necessary conditions for a vital intellectual life be found: wealth and leisure for patronage, talent for performance, and an audience to enjoy, applaud, and encourage further efforts."[24] In looking for hotbeds of American Enlightenment ideals, scholars have tended to follow Bridenbaugh's lead, turning toward the cities, such as Philadelphia, Boston, and New York, and identifying such notable urban savants as Benjamin Franklin, Thomas Paine, and Benjamin Rush as agents of Enlightenment.[25] In this model, it was only in the larger urban centres where universities, formal literary and philosophical societies, and a sizeable *literati* of scholars, lawyers, clerks, clergy, and merchants could exist and interact. The cities not only fostered a spirit of Enlightenment but forged Enlightenment-inspired, *American* ideologies.

The cities were also the places where Scots, or those who had undergone formal education in Scotland, congregated with other colonists to discuss current events or seek solutions to colonial issues. All manner of intellectual legacies, from the establishment of the American academy and educational system to the creation of the Declaration of Independence and the Constitution, have been attributed to ideas that germinated in eighteenth-century Scotland.[26] Characteristically Scottish critical underlay these events methods – skeptical or didactic in nature, or embracing a "common sense philosophy – "[27] The movement of people and ideas between Scotland and America, it has been argued, provided Americans with a liberal, critical, and even revolutionary way of perceiving their environment. Shared Protestant roots and a brisk tobacco trade, according to Douglas Sloan and Andrew Hook, connected the American colonists with Scotland.[28] With established lines of communication, non-commercial benefits such as the transference of skills and knowledge soon were realized. Sloan observes in particular that new philosophies in education brought by Francis Alison, John Witherspoon, and Samuel Stanhope Smith shaped the early American educational system at all levels. The training of Scottish physicians in particular, epitomized by Benjamin Rush, was instrumental in developing broader academic communities and undertaking professional science while maintaining a particular love of Scottish tradition.[29]

The use of the Scottish Enlightenment to better understand the education, critical thought, and politics of eighteenth-century America has been restricted mainly to the region of the Thirteen Colonies and the nascent United States of America. The fact that other British American colonies have been overlooked can, perhaps, be attributed to their relatively small size and the perception that those areas lacked two of the most important prerequisites for Enlightenment thought: scholarly urban centres and a substantial *literati* class of civic-minded moderates versed in the arts, rhetoric, and *belles lettres*. "The Enlightenment of the eighteenth century nearly passed by the English-speaking colonies of Great Britain to the north of the United States and what is now the Canadian-American border," John Bumsted observes. Rural in nature, with few cities and a small number of well-educated inhabitants, colonial Canada lacked the right environment for Enlightenment thought:

> The diffusion of enlightened ideas required a society that was both urban and urbane, based on educated aristocratic or at least bourgeois classes. It was a movement of the university, the salon, the classroom, the study, the bookshop, the scientific laboratory, and the encyclopedia. British North America had neither cities nor a very well educated population, and the settlers had far more important things to worry about – such as survival in a howling wilderness – than formal book-learning.[30]

Bumsted's observation of colonial Canada as a "howling wilderness" unfit for scholarly pursuits is, perhaps, made tongue-in-cheek. Nonetheless, this idea of the northern British American colonies as rural has had a longstanding influence in shaping both the conscious and unconscious perspectives of the historian.

The focus on the Thirteen Colonies of America may also be attributable to the assumption that the Scottish Enlightenment's civic-minded liberalism and germination of revolutionary ideas could not have found a suitable home in the northern British American colonies. Had not the northern colonies rejected the American Revolution? How could inhabitants who were considered backward, neutral, or uninterested in the liberal ideology of the American Revolution be receptive to other aspects of Enlightenment thought?[31] On the whole, the historiographic approach to Enlightenment and the Scottish Enlightenment in America has naturally focused its analysis on the tangible elements of discontent and reform that formed the roots of the modern American nation. This approach, however, tends to ignore the ideas and culture of those peoples who did not share this point of view, or may have expressed different concerns in different ways. It also reinforces longstanding dichotomies of American exceptionalism between America and England, Whig and Tory, modern and conservative, republican and monarchist ideologies.

Following this pattern, histories of Enlightenment in British North America outside the Thirteen Colonies have seen it as foreign and unwelcome. Works that tell of individuals such as Québec printer Fleury Mesplet, journalist Valentin Jautard, [32] or merchant Pierre Du Calvet fall into this category.[33] These men are almost uniformly portrayed as ahead of their time and misunderstood by an inflexible conservative administration that inevitably censured their actions. In such accounts, the possibility that larger networks of thought, or a general spirit of enlightenment could have existed in a conservative, anti-revolutionary environment is never acknowledged.

On the other hand, many works that do address a particular Scottish influence in the intellectual life of the northern British American colonies have, as W. Stanford Reid observed, exhibited a "filio pietism, a narrow perspective and a dearth of scholarly analysis."[34] This literature clearly observes instances of Scottish intellectual achievement, but does a poor job in explaining how or why such achievement came to be. Too often these histories focus on individual achievement stripped from historical context, or fall prey to vague, overtly nationalistic and Whiggish interpretations of ethnic achievement.[35] Indicative of so many accounts in this latter historiography, one Canadian medical historian argued that Scottish resourcefulness exhibited in many early medical practitioners was rooted squarely in the Caledonian geography. "The source of this genius," it was observed, "is the soil and air of Scotland. Although the one may be rocky and the other keen and harsh their fruits have been rich and given to the world with a generous hand."[36] Observations of this nature do little to improve our historical understanding of Scottish intellectual traditions in the northern British American colonies. Indeed, they unfairly represent the nature of Scottish society by grouping highland and lowland, mainland and island, Protestant and Catholic, and urban and rural Scots together. Furthermore, these generalizations attribute a direct intellectual transference based on an eighteenth-century idea of race. Such vague, race-based interpretations barely scratch the surface of the historical understanding. Their narrow focus does not entertain the possibility that a broader Enlightenment could have informed eighteenth-century colonists with an interconnected system of beliefs and ideas, a system containing elements found throughout the Western world and uniquely in Scotland, and affecting how both Scots and non-Scots perceived, discussed, and solved colonial issues.

The absence of scholarship on the Scottish Enlightenment, or indeed Enlightenment in general, in the northern British American colonies poses several conspicuous questions. Did not towns such as Halifax, Québec, and Montreal share in the transatlantic exchange of ideas, goods, and people experienced by other colonial British North American towns? Were these centres too small to experience the language, habits, and social formations that constituted Enlightenment? Can particular agents or activities be observed in identifying Enlightenment in the northern British American colonies? Or, as has been suggested, did Enlightenment not make any significant inroads in the northern British American colonies that were to become Canada.

REVISITING THE NORTHERN BRITISH AMERICAN COLONIES AND THE PLACE OF THE SCOTTISH ENLIGHTENMENT

The study of the Scottish Enlightenment in British North America offers a starting point for a reinterpretation of Enlightenment on the American periphery. It provides a rich theoretical framework of ideas and methods within a circumscribed timeframe. Considering the multicultural nature of colonial British North America, an argument could be made for the study of other Enlightenment refractions and transferences from France, Germany, England, and elsewhere in British America. In this instance, however, the Scottish Enlightenment can be used to better understand the actions of a large concentration of Scottish-trained medical practitioners in British North America. These colonial physicians and surgeons not only tended to patients and pursued some of the earliest scientific inquiry; many also took on key, non-medical roles as colonial administrators, justices, and community leaders. The achievement of these medical practitioners is occasionally highlighted, but their multiplicity of interests, true diversity of backgrounds, and relationships to larger currents of eighteenth-century thought have rarely been explored.

The idea of medical practitioners as intellectual agents of Enlightenment, and specifically the Scottish Enlightenment, is a common theme
in the scholarship of colonial America and the British Empire. Natural
philosophy and medicine, Charles W.J. Withers observes, were "essential
elements in the intellectual enquiries characteristic of eighteenth-
century Scotland."[37] In regard to the Thirteen Colonies, Scottish-
trained physicians such as William Shippen, Jr., Thomas Cadwalader,
David Hosack, and Benjamin Rush, to name a few, have been credited
with laying the foundations of professional scientific research and
scholarship in the United States.[38] Richard Drayton views migrating
medical professionals as just one part of a larger cadre of "gentlemanly
amateurs" that fanned across the British Empire in the eighteenth century. It was such men whose "observations, information, specimens,
and argument, journeyed from physicians in Edinburgh to absentee
planters in London, parsons in New England, and merchants at Cal-
cutta and Canton."[39]

Enlightenment Scotland offered a unique and flexible learning
environment for Scots and for students of other nationalities who may
have held an affinity with Scottish methods, or may have been disen-
franchised over issues of language, background, or religion. It has
been argued that men such as physician and anatomist Alexander
Monro *secundus*, physician and botanist Francis Home, physician and
chemist William Cullen, and later Cullen's protégé Joseph Black
changed the direction of medical teaching in Edinburgh and raised
the reputation of the school and of Edinburgh medicine throughout
the world.[40] The education was eclectic, mixing physic, chemistry,
moral and natural philosophy. The instruction of medicine offers one
of the many examples of the attraction that a Scottish education had to
a wider transatlantic world.

Medical historians of early Canada have frequently noted a sizeable
contingent of Scottish-trained medical professionals reported in contemporary accounts. Many of these practitioners came to British North
America with the British Army and Royal Navy. Some settled in the
Thirteen Colonies and later migrated north during the American Revolution. Still others were born in British America, travelled to Scotland
for medical instruction, and then returned home to practice surgery
and physic. H.E. MacDermot wrote that early medical practitioners in
Canada were " ... usually military surgeons at first. The majority of
these were Edinburgh-trained, and brought with them the methods of
teaching which that university had adopted from Leyden University."[41]
James Fisher, George Longmore, John Mervin Nooth, Robert Kerr,
William Holmes, James Macaulay, and Adam Mabane are a few more
prominent examples of Scottish-trained medical practitioners who

followed their military service to the northern British American colonies.[42] Historians have also observed the employment of a particular "Scottish method" by these individuals and have underscored the role of Scottish-trained medical practitioners in early medical instruction. Canada's first medical school at McGill was founded by solely Edinburgh-trained physicians.[43]

Determining the exact number of Scottish-trained practitioners who worked in British North America (or indeed anywhere) in the eighteenth and early-nineteenth centuries is, admittedly, difficult. The accounts that exist are at times piecemeal and anecdotal, a situation that has been compounded by poor record keeping and the inherently flexible nature of a Scottish medical education. Further compounding the situation is the peripatetic lives that Scottish-trained medical practitioners led. Nonetheless, Douglas Sloan, for example, observes that at the University of Edinburgh alone between the years 1726 and 1799, 1143 people graduated with the degree MD. Of that total, 237 could be identified as Scots, 254 as English, 280 as Irish, 195 from the West Indies and North America, 26 Europeans, 8 Welsh, 3 Latin Americans and East Indians, and a final 140 were identified as being "British."[44] John Comrie, in his *History of Scottish Medicine*, estimates that in the hundred years following 1765, "no fewer than 650 students coming from the Americas (including the West Indies and Canada) graduated at Edinburgh."[45]

A rough estimate of Scottish-trained medical practitioners specifically in Canada can be obtained through an examination of William Canniff's history of the medical profession from the nineteenth century that summarizes the lives of key medical professionals who lived in Quebec between 1783 and 1791 and in Upper Canada from 1791 to 1850. Of the 268 most complete biographical sketches in this work, 27.6 per cent are noted as being Scottish or having received medical instruction in Scotland. This compares to 18.7 per cent of those listed as being solely trained in the United States of America, 12.7 per cent being solely trained in Canadian medical schools and 12.3 per cent who received their medical education in England. The remaining 30 per cent is made up of practitioners who trained elsewhere, or whose education was unknown. The author also omitted the educational background of any medical practitioners who were trained in the British Army or Navy.[46]

More recently, Allan Marble, in his in-depth analysis of medical practitioners in eighteenth-century Nova Scotia, has traced the lives of 366 physicians, surgeons, and apothecaries between 1749 and 1799. Marble observes that of the 366 medical practitioners, 14 had graduated with MDs, 13 from Scottish universities and one from King's College, New

York.[47] None of the degrees, he points out, were from Edinburgh or Glasgow. Considering the record keeping of the University of Edinburgh and the laissez-faire trend in eighteenth-century Scottish medical education, these proportionally low numbers should not be surprising. The University of Edinburgh only recorded the names of medical students who had graduated MD and published their doctoral theses. Few class lists survive from the eighteenth century and it was not until 1833 that a systematic roll detailing students' names, places of birth, and subjects studied was created. Medical students who opted for a license from the College of Surgeons in Edinburgh, instead of graduating from the university, also do not show up on official rolls.[48] Indeed, a deeper look into Marble's work shows that many of the practitioners – without MDs – had actually spent a considerable amount of time participating in the intellectual milieu of Enlightenment Scotland, and particularly Edinburgh. Men such as Dr John Halliburton, Sr, Dr Alexander Abercrombie, Dr Duncan Clark, and Dr Edward Wyer had all studied in Scotland before settling in Halifax.[49]

The nature of medical instruction, contemporary accounting methods, and other gaps in the historical record make it impossible to construct a definitive record of the education of medical practitioners. Nonetheless, the sources that do exist show that Scottish-trained practitioners account for a sizeable number of those whose education can be ascertained. This training would have familiarized them with philosophical as well as medical methods. It would also have situated them in the dynamic centres of Edinburgh, Glasgow, and Aberdeen, at the height of the Scottish Enlightenment.

In the eighteenth century, medical practitioners, and particularly those who had trained in Scotland, were known to be keen observers of natural and societal phenomena. Contemporary sources often remarked on the propensity of medical professionals to engage in the research and debate of non-medical topics. "It is remarkable that, of all men of letters who attach themselves to any profession, none so willingly quit their occupations to write on other matters as physicians," read an article in the *Scots Magazine*. "Dr Smollett had more frequently his pen," it continued, "than the pulse of a patient, in his hand." Akenside and Armstrong are celebrated for their poetry; and the late Dr Gregory of Edinburgh, has published several pleasing compositions in prose." In conclusion the author pondered, "why [do] physicians write so little on professional subjects? Is a question I know not how to resolve, unless we suppose that, as they are most conversant in the art of medicine, they more clearly perceive its futility."[50]

Present-day scholars have found less cynical explanations for these manifestations of non-medical enquiry. Nicholas Phillipson has argued that the existence of civic morality in the Scottish Enlightenment was a driving force behind eighteenth-century enquiries into a larger "Science of Man." "The Scots had set out to approach what Hume called the 'science of Man,'" Phillipson observes, "in a scientific and secular spirit with the clearly stated intention, sometimes labouriously rehearsed, of helping ordinary men and women to lead happy, useful and virtuous lives in an increasingly complex commercial society."[51] The "Science of Man," Phillipson observes, was an integral part of the Scottish Enlightenment, being the philosophy behind and practice of the rational exploration into the thoughts of the human mind: "Technically, it was founded on a desire to study scientifically what we should call the contents of the mind and what contemporaries called "ideas" or "beliefs." These ideas made intelligible the external world, God and even the self and to understand their origins was the key to understanding the principles of morality, justice, politics and philosophy."[52] A key characteristic of the Scottish Enlightenment, then, was an underlying ideology that the analysis of beliefs and enquiry into knowledge could be broached in a secular, scientific, and altruistic way.[53]

This undercurrent of philosophic exploration and societal improvement, identified by Phillipson and others, can also be found in the eighteenth- and early nineteenth-century writings and actions of Scottish-trained physicians living in the northern British American colonies. James Strachan, Deputy Inspector of Hospitals for British North America – who received his MD at King's College, Aberdeen in 1811 – encouraged his surgeons to use the Army's reporting system as a means, not only to record disease, but to promote scientific investigation.[54] The half-yearly return in particular stood "auspiciously preeminent, not only as indicating to them [the Medical Board] more or less satisfactorily the health of the troops; but as constituting a distinct and permanent record, of the talents – science and diligence of the author."[55] Strachan drew special attention to the "Geology and Botany of the situation" that would provide a source of useful knowledge and amusement.[56]

One such example can be seen in the half-yearly reports of John MacKesy of the 62ND Regiment of Foot when posted as a surgeon in Halifax, Nova Scotia. MacKesy was a seasoned military surgeon, having served campaigns in Egypt, Italy, and the Canadas.[57] Normally, the British Army Medical Corps' bi-annual report followed a standard format that observed key environmental conditions, related any injury or deaths, and gave a brief statement on the condition of the regiment. MacKesy used the bi-annual report as a means to communicate his research and observations of science in the New World back to headquarters and a European audience. In one particular case – identifying himself as a member of both the Medico-Churigical Society of London and the Royal Medical Society of Edinburgh – MacKesy wrote a 155-page treatise on the nature of colonial medical practice and science in the British Army. Not only did MacKesy believe that the pursuits of British army medical officers were advancing science and improving society, he believed that the experience gained from seeing disease in remote stations and testing the theories of the medical schools was also an invaluable service. "The deductions drawn from military and naval practice," he continued,

> extend their utility beyond their immediate circle – the community at large has often partaken of their advantage by the weight of their influence affecting private practice, and correcting, or overthrowing the received dogmas of the schools – there are many improvements now in medicine that first take therein rise from the bold discriminating judgement of some obscure and friendless army or navy surgeon, who had courage enough to despise the generally received dictates of systems, and to think and act for himself while surrounded by a map of harassing & formidable disease.[58]

This thinking corresponds with the writings and lectures of Enlightenment Scotland's premier medical theorist, William Cullen, who wrote in his groundbreaking *First Lines in the Practice of Physic* that, "I apprehend, that, in every branch of science with respect to which facts are daily required, and these consequently giving occasion to new reflections, which correct the principles formerly adopted, it is necessary [from] time to time, to reform and renew the whole system, with all the additions and amendments which it has received and is then capable of."[59] Cullen firmly believed that only first hand experience of nature would lead the observer to the first principles that would furnish a true understanding. His nosology became the most popular system of disease classification and instruction in Britain and was the standard used in the British Army until 1869.[60] Conscious that he had created what could be considered a new dogma, he advocated the continued search for first principles. For medical practitioners like MacKesy, the new world provided a laboratory to investigate nature and question established dogma in the "scientific and laudable spirit of improvement"[61] which pervaded the British Army Medical Corps.

It is clear that several Scottish-trained physicians embraced their lot in the colonies and turned their spare time to the betterment of self through the scientific exploration of their surroundings and improvement of society. However, it could be asked how isolated they were? Were efforts made to communicate their ideas to a greater public? Were there other colonists receptive to their efforts? Considering what has recently been written on the nature of the Atlantic World in the eighteenth and early-nineteenth centuries it is difficult to think that these medical practitioners could not have been connected to their local communities and to larger transatlantic networks.

The study of Atlantic history, as historian Bernard Bailyn has recently observed, is a field of research that has come into its own over the past five decades. "Atlantic history in the broadest sense," he writes, "is the study of the creation of a vast new marchland of European civilization, an ill-defined, irregular outer borderland, thrust into the world of indigenous peoples in the Western Hemisphere and in the outer reaches of the British archipelago."[62] Taking a page from the writings of historical geographer D.W. Meinig, Bailyn has seen Atlantic history as a study of larger Atlantic circuits, "binding together four continents, three races and several cultural systems."[63] In short, Atlantic history has transformed into "the study of a world in motion."[64] Consumption of similar transatlantic goods and ideas provided uniformity to disparate colonists, Atlantic world historians such as T.H. Breen have argued, and this growing consumerism was a hallmark of the British American colonial identity.[65] This idea of the past Atlantic world as a nexus of the movement of people, commodities, and ideas is compelling. In such an environment both *old* and *new* worlds are created and reshaped.

Scholars of eighteenth-century imperial history have also recognized the importance of the interconnected transatlantic world, not only in negotiation and exchange, but in the creation of reciprocities of communication and Enlightenment-inspired knowledge. Ian K. Steele argues that by the mid-eighteenth century the "English Atlantic" became consolidated by expansive communication networks. This consolidation marked the emergence of an overarching transatlantic perspective. In the eighteenth century, "communications changed, and their bias was away from local concerns, favoring perspectives and preoccupations that connected the broader English Atlantic community."[66] Through these lines of communication a spirit of enlightenment, a critical means to see the world, became widely diffused. "The Enlightenment encouraged official Britain," Richard Drayton argues, "to support the study of plants, minerals, and stars around the world. It also contributed a fundamental element to the ideology which sustained the Second British Empire: the faith that Empire might be an instrument of cosmopolitan progress, and could benefit the imperialized as well as the imperializers."[67]

A cursory exploration of contemporary sources such as colonial newspapers and private journals shows that the inhabitants of the northern British American colonies exhibited a desire to consume a vast array of goods similar to their southern neighbours. Advertisements in the *Halifax Gazette*, for example, provide long lists of goods that could be purchased, including fine linens and cloths, stockings, breeches and waistcoats, "Scotch check'd Handkerchiefs ... painting Colours and Oil for painting: ALL SORTS of Paper-hangings for Rooms ... Walnut and Mahogany Tea-chests; Looking Glasses ... fine Green tea; double refin'd loaf Sugar; Brown Sugar; fine eating Oyl in jars ..."[68] As the eighteenth century progressed, advertisements declaring "Just Imported from London," or "Just Arrived" boasted sundries originating in all regions of the British world from East India to the West Indies for those who could afford them.[69]

Books, magazines, newspapers, and pamphlets possessed great value and were also important commodities in the northern British colonies. Estate auction calendars often mentioned the sale of books and some would offer a full inventory of the works available.[70] The deaths of prominent colonial citizens, such as Solicitor General Alexander Gray, Chief Justice William Smith and medical practitioners Dr Adam Mabane and Dr James Bowman led to the publishing of such detailed catalogues.[71] When Quebec merchant Peter Fargues died in 1780, three hundred auction catalogues of his "books and furniture" were published emphasizing, "a choice collection of Books, French and English, by the most reputed authors."[72] Deaths, however, were not the only occasions for large book auctions. The peripatetic colonial lifestyle resulted in frequent moves throughout the Atlantic world. A 1787 auction in Lower Town, Quebec, boasted "a choice and large collection of books being the libraries of several gentlemen who have gone to Europe."[73] When books went "lost," great efforts were also taken to recover them as this notice placed in the *Québec Gazette* for a quintessentially Scottish tome of instruction relates: "MISSING: The second part of the 15th volume of the EDINBURGH ENCYCLOPÆDIA BRITANNICA, supposed to have been lent, or taken by mistake, from the Shop of JAMES AINSLIE, Stationer. Any person who has it will do a favour to the Proprietor by returning it to Mr Neilson."[74]

The inhabitants of the northern British American colonies were participants in larger transatlantic and colonial networks of publishing and print distribution. Published materials of all kinds were available directly from Britain and from printers in cities such as Boston, Philadelphia, and New York. Almanacs, pamphlets, and monographs were first imported and then later printed locally.[75] Early publishers in the northern colonies such as John Bushell,[76] Scotsman William Brown,[77] or later Fleury Mesplet, learned their craft in southern colonial centres such as Philadelphia or Boston and then migrated north. Printed materials, in particular, were held up as a means to bridge both geographic and chronological distances. "By Means of the Press we can sit at Home and acquaint ourselves with what is done in all the distant Parts of the World," the prospectus for the *Quebec Gazette* proclaimed in 1764:

> and find what our Fathers did long ago, in the first Ages of Mankind: By this Means a *Briton* holds Correspondence with his Friend in *America* or *Japan*, and manages his Business: " 'Tis this, which brings the past Ages of Men at once upon the Stage, and makes the most distant Nations and Ages converse together, and grow into Acquaintance." Wherefore, a well regulated Printing Office has always been considered a publick Benefit, insomuch that no Place of Note in the *English* Dominions is at this Day destitute of the Advantages arising therefrom.[78]

Wary of their physical isolation from Britain and other British colonies, inhabitants in the northern British colonies found that an interconnection with the knowledge, as well as the material goods, of the greater world was a principal means to overcome the distance.

It has traditionally been argued, however, that an urban environment marked by universities, intellectual societies, and capable of supporting a moderate *literati* was necessary, along with the interconnected networks of communication for Enlightenment to flourish. In the case of Scotland, Anand Chitnis and Nicholas Phillipson argue that dynamic cities were a prerequisite of the Scottish Enlightenment and that Edinburgh was Scotland's intellectual capital. The Scottish Enlightenment, Chitnis writes, "was an urban movement and its intimacy was prompted, and its progress facilitated, by the forms of social and intellectual expression that towns and urban living encouraged." The fact, he continues, that "the Scottish Enlightenment lay in the universities and the legal and ecclesiastical professions not only emphasises its urban-ness, but also underlines the importance of Edinburgh over the other university towns."[79] Concurring with Chitnis's analysis, Nicholas Phillipson writes that "the key [of the Scottish Enlightenment] lay in the salons, coffee-houses and taverns of modern cities. Here men and women met each other as friends and equals and were able to enjoy the sense of ease that good conversation could bring."[80] This assumption of a requisite "urban-ness," as observed earlier, has also been maintained by authors looking at Enlightenment, and particularly the Scottish Enlightenment, in America.

Recent scholarship on Europe and Australia, however, now questions assumptions of a homogeneous and strictly urban nature of Enlightenment, holding great promise for the study of Enlightenment and its effects in smaller communities. Larger Enlightenment centres have been found to have contained *unenlightened* spaces and *enlightened* areas have been discovered in places traditionally thought too small, or otherwise incapable of supporting Enlightenment. In John Gascoigne and Patricia Curthoys's *The Enlightenment and the Origins of European Australia,* for example, it is argued that the penal colony of Botany Bay, and later the state of New South Wales, was founded and its subsequent development shaped by projected Enlightenment thought. Eighteenth-century Australia was a region boasting no universities, a small population, and even smaller numbers of *literati.* "For though the founding of this remote colony was but a minor event in the larger European scale of things," Gascoigne and Curthoys observe, "it came at a nodal point in European history."[81] The Enlightenment, then, offered Australia's founders key philosophical tools for the colony's development. "Such a mentality," Gascoigne and Curthoys continue, "helped to give the irksome, and even brutal, business of bringing the Australian continent firmly under the sway of British colonial rule something of the character of a civilising mission."[82]

Historical geographer Charles W.J. Withers argues that the growth of intellectual culture in the era of the Enlightenment happened at many levels, or rather in different spaces or geographies. The current scholarship, he observes, is marked by several analyses of particular national and municipal Enlightenment variations. However, a third level – that of institutional and individual geographies – also existed, dividing the municipal spaces into clubs, societies, institutions, and individual interactions of an Enlightenment nature.[83] This type of analysis can also be seen in the works of scholars such as Thomas A. Markus[84] and Chris Philo. Finding an affinity with the theoretical writings of Michel Foucault, Philo in particular explores the existence and use of the spaces of reason and unreason in Enlightenment Edinburgh. As Enlightenment did not occur uniformly across Scotland, Philo finds that *enlightened* places such as salons, libraries, museums, and even hospitals could coexist alongside areas of closed mindedness and intolerance.[85] Through the work of authors such as Withers, Philo, and Gascoigne, the conception of what spaces could experience the spirit of the enlightenment is greatly enlarged. This perspective goes a long way in overcoming the restrictive assumptions of the homogeneous, urban nature of the Enlightenment in America. Were the northern British American colonies too small to harbour Enlightenment ideals? If Botany Bay with its 2000 inhabitants – half the world away from Britain – was influenced by a spirit of enlightenment, could not Halifax, Saint John, Quebec City, or Montreal – perceived as unqualified colonial backwaters – have had *enlightened* areas of reason? The challenge in adapting this method is in finding the enlightened spaces of discussion and activity. Withers suggests that spaces such as coffee houses and the formation of clubs and societies can be associated with the germination of Enlightenment thought. Indeed, the recognition of the importance of these spaces in the intellectual development of the eighteenth and early nineteenth century is not new.[86] Lately, scholars adapting the social theories of Jürgen Habermas have appealed to the idea of interactive space such as print culture, coffee houses, societies, masonic lodges – notably separate from official State and Church manifestations – as an emerging eighteenth-century bourgeois, or Enlightenment, public sphere.[87] Those employing Habermas's ideas have seen the creation of the public, and its role in Enlightenment, as a process with long-standing European origins again manifesting in urban areas with a critical mass of people.[88]

With British colonial expansion across the Atlantic, however, so too stretched a culture of British ideas and institutions. Spaces that contributed to a public sphere, found in large urban areas and reflecting deep-seated origins, started to emerge in smaller areas that lacked the requisite Old World traditions. This proliferation of smaller groups, dispersed widely, created a larger interconnected public that could share traditions and transmit ideas. Jessica Harland-Jacobs examines this phenomenon in regard to the transatlantic expansion of Freemasonry. Freemasonry, she writes, "was one institution that contributed to the development of these intracultural connections in the British Empire. By creating a global network that had both practical functions and ideological dimensions, Freemasonry played a critical role in building, consolidating, and perpetuating the empire."[89] Originally seen as localized, urban manifestations, Enlightenment spheres of public assembly and debate can also be seen to have flourished in smaller areas. In these regions of modest size, new transatlantic publics were formed, connecting thought between small towns and large urban centres and linking colonials with likeminded individuals throughout the English-speaking world. By removing the assumption that only large, urban centres could experience the Enlightenment, a more complex and far-reaching Enlightenment can be conceived. Under such a model, it is the existence of smaller rational, problem- solving groups and these groups' *connectedness* with larger currents of thought that matter in the formation of an eighteenth-century spirit of Enlightenment.

Although modest in comparison to British cities, or the cities of their American neighbours, the inhabitants of the northern British

American colonies did create areas where expanded study, observation, and discussion took place. In spheres of interaction – similar in nature to those found elsewhere in the English-speaking world – groups of individuals formed a small, though active, colonial *literati*. From this initial investigation, it appears that the inhabitants of the northern British American colonies were no different from other British subjects – whether across the Atlantic, or to the south – in the development of intellectual outlets and the pursuit of amusements. [90] The northern British American colonists were voracious consumers not only of mercantile goods, but of cultural attainments such as theatre and books, discussed among lively company in coffee shops, societies, and clubs. It is in this colonial environment that Scottish-educated medical professionals flourished.

A vibrant transatlantic print culture existed in the northern British American colonies. Contemporary newspapers frequently advertised the arrival of new publications from London or Boston. Colonists were encouraged, as in this advertisement from the *Québec Herald*, to avoid disappointment by placing their book orders early:

To the PUBLIC

LADIES and Gentlemen who wish for Magazines, Novels, new Plays, Poems, or Books of any particular sort from England, by the early vessels in Spring, signifying their wants at the *Herald Printing-Office* previous to the first Monday in *January*, they will be accommodated to their satisfaction, on very moderate profit.[91]

For those who could not afford to place orders for books, a cheaper option was to subscribe to a private circulating library,[92] or take out a membership in a public library.[93]

Despite the distance between the colonies and Britain, Scottish surgeon John MacKesy made it quite clear in his writings that he was well-versed in the most recent scientific trends and connected with British intellectual societies. Immediately after identifying himself as a member of medical societies in both London and Edinburgh, MacKesy prefaced his report with a quotation attributed to "Haygarth": "When conclusions are formed from solitary, or even a few cases, the danger of mistake may be clearly understood; but the inference is totally different, when many examples concur to prove the efficacy of a remedy – it is for this reason that medical facts when distinctly discerned become extremely valuable if many of a similar kind are brought into view the conclusions from them by induction afford a high degree of certainty." The quotation in question is the writing of English physician John Haygarth who took classes taught by William Cullen in Edinburgh. Haygarth's later fame came from his expertise in small pox and other contagious diseases and as an advocate for the knowledge that could be obtained from the study of foreign regions.[94] Colonial medical practitioners wanted to maintain a feeling of connect- edness with the greater scholarly community across the Atlantic. In their reports they wanted to prove that they not only understood the greater issues facing society, but could also contribute to that greater society's improvement. Capitalizing on the experience gained in their colonial environment, they used their bureaucratic connection to the larger world to communicate these ideas.

In the northern British American colonies, as elsewhere, an appetite for locally published books, newspapers, and pamphlets also developed. Evidence of such publications shows that colonists consumed and also made efforts to contribute to a larger transatlantic print culture. An advertisement for the new *Royal American Magazine* extolled the virtues of reading for colonists: "LITERATURE being the grand fountain from whence springs, all that is requisite to accomplish rational beings for the enjoyment of social, happiness and fit them for their various employments on this stage of action; it is noble in us to encourage and cultivate every thing tending to promote this great gift of heaven among mankind."[95] The advertisement then encouraged the public not only to subscribe, but to contribute to the publication.[96] In 1788, the publishers of the *Québec Herald* advertised subscriptions to a collection of "original" poems by "various ingenious ladies and gentlemen, who favoured a friend of the Printer with copies; which copies for the benefit of the community, he has favoured the Printer with."[97]

The first known medical publication printed in the northern British American colonies was ordered by Dr James Bowman in 1785.[98] Bowman was sent by Lieutenant-Governor Hamilton to Baie-St-Paul to treat an outbreak of a mysterious and recurring syphilitic illness affecting the regions' French Canadian inhabitants. Understanding that an accessible method was required to inform French-speaking inhabitants of the dangers and treatments of the disease, he requested 2250 copies of Phillipe Louis François Badelard's *Direction pour la guerison du Mal de la Baie St Paul* for distribution to the public.[99] Dr Bowman's work in combating the disease gained attention in British medical publications fascinated by the emergence of a new disease on the periphery of the empire.[100] It is interesting to note that this was not the first time that Dr Bowman had used the services of a colonial printer. The year before he paid to have printed fifty broadsides, not, as could be expected, of a scientific treatise, but of an original poem written upon the death of a certain Miss Willcocks.[101]

Colonial author, painter, and physician Edward Walsh was a keen observer of his surroundings and he produced detailed manuscripts and illustrative watercolours of his travels. In 1800, he wrote and illustrated a four volume account of his travels entitled *A Narrative of the Expedition to Holland* which enjoyed some critical acclaim back in Britain. Born in Ireland, Walsh joined the British Army in the 1780s and took a hiatus from his military career to study in Glasgow where he graduated with an MD in 1791.[102] Walsh's writings show a profound respect of the aboriginal peoples he encountered in British North America. "I soon found myself quite at home," he wrote upon observing a native settlement: "It was surprising to see with what confidence these children of Nature, Man, Women & Child submitted to the operation of vaccination, and that at the very period when the English Peasantry & [?] all the lower classes – obstinately refused – under the most ridiculous Prejudices to receive so great a Boon."[103] Indeed, Walsh's papers include manuscript lexicons and dictionaries of the Osage, Dakota, Cree, Ojibway, Sioux, and Ioway languages as well as observations on many aboriginal religions and traditions.[104]

Walsh's affection for aboriginals is characteristic of the eighteenth-century literature published in Scotland that romanticized the native lifestyle and questioned the classical assumptions about the history and development of man.[105] Also in keeping with contemporary Scottish opinion, his view is in stark contrast to his opinion of rural Britons. Walsh observed that "by far the greater Number of Farmers on the Island [of Prince Edward] are Scottish Highlanders. Ignorant, indolent and Selfish in the extreme who have no ideas of Agriculture, and who are contented to clear away some wood in a slovenly manner, in order to breed cattle from which they derive their sole subsistence."[106] Perhaps reflecting biases gained in his Lowland education, especially in regard to societal and agricultural improvement, Walsh's comments are very much like those of William Cullen in one of his lectures on the practice of physic. "From what we thus know of Indians and Highlanders," Cullen observed, "I think we cannot have a high Opinion of Physic in its natural State."[107] Although Walsh thought that both the aboriginals and the Highlanders lived in primitive states, he believed the former possessed a natural sense that made them amenable to new ideas.

Walsh never published his manuscript on the observations and languages of aboriginal peoples. However, prints of several paintings that he made in his Canadian travels were published and distributed across British North America and in Britain.[108] Walsh, like Bowman, provides another example of a physician who transcended his professional training and endeavoured to communicate both his medical and non-medical experiences and thoughts with a larger public.

Inhabitants of the northern British American colonies did not limit their amusing and investigative pursuits to the reading of and contribution to print culture. Colonists were also very fond of public gatherings in the theatre and local coffee houses where current world and colonial issues could be presented and discussed. The theatre offered welcome entertainment and public interaction to colonists throughout the year.[109] Perhaps a testament to the popularity of this form of entertainment and the expectations of the patrons was the scope of production and sums of money. The *Saint John Gazette* reported that an amateur production in 1789 had "scenes, decorations, and dresses [that] were entirely new and in a very fine style."[110] In 1796, one Halifax production spent over £60 on costumes and sets alone.[111] Lieutenant William Dyott of the 4th Regiment of Foot, treasurer for the Grand Theatre in Halifax, reported that earnings of £400 in the theatre's first year were almost entirely "expended on the house."[112] Dyott declared that he "never saw a play better performed out of London,"[113] after the garrison's production of *School for Scandal,* and after the curtain closed on *The Merchant of Venice* he observed, "it was as complete a thing for the size as I ever saw."[114]

Requisite to most productions was a prologue to set the tone for the evening's performance. These recitations would often be composed and delivered by well-known individuals such as British officers from the local establishment. Ranging from the light-hearted to the overly melodramatic these prologues attempted to emulate contemporary poetic styles with varying degrees of success. Nonetheless, they offer historians valuable insight into the importance of the arts and ideas in the northern British American colonies. The prologues tell of the northern British American colonies as recently transformed wilderness, refined by British civilization, literature and, of course, the performance about to take place. As the prologue to the 1774 comedy "Acadius, or Love in a Calm"[115] observed: "In less than half, MAN'S, Post Deluv'an AGE; / In this SEPTENTRION Clime, there was no STAGE ... The MUSES, then, knew not, these frozen Climes; / So sent no Cargo here, of Prose or Rhymes. / but ARTS and TRADE, at length being wafted o'er, From BRITISH ISLES to this ACAD'AN Shore; / DISCIPLES, then, of the PARNASS'AN TRAIN; / Adventur'd, over, the ATLANTIC Main.[116]

Another prologue, performed in Saint John on 5 January 1795, saw the Bay of Fundy as "a dreary coast" on which the city was raised. However, " 'Twas commerce – commerce smooth'd the rugged strand, / Her streets and buildings overspread the land; / Her piers the mighty

Fundy's tides control, / And navies ride secure within her mole." Despite the benefits that commerce, industry, and security afforded the British colonies, they alone were not enough to sustain the colony: "what are these without the muses' aid! / When swindlers circumvent, or thieves invade: / Or credit staggers with misfortune's stroke ... 'Midst loss, midst profit, still to verse repair; / Verse, which refines the pleasures of success, /Brings hope, and consolation to success."[117]

The existence of amateur theatre, in itself, does not prove the existence of Enlightenment thought. However, the bringing together of the community for an often satirical analysis of current events, performed by the colonists themselves, demonstrates that colonists were connected to larger transatlantic networks. They appreciated and understood contemporary references to characters and stories originating not only in Britain, but throughout the English-speaking world. Furthermore, theatrical prologues further show that colonists did not see their environment as strictly a wilderness. Although distant from Britain and to a lesser extent the southern colonies – later the United States of America – the northern colonists saw their landscape as civilized and able to support their intellectual, industrious, and civil activities.

Coffee houses became one of the informal institutions of colonial life, hosting local theatre as well as many other types of public and semi-public gatherings. From its humble seventeenth-century origins, the coffee house grew into a cultural phenomenon by the eighteenth century, offering a comfortable space for both formal and informal public discussion of ideas in good company. As observed earlier, scholars have argued that coffee house culture was a hallmark of Enlightenment in both Scotland and America. The establishments had a universal appeal that cut across classes[118] and led to the development of societies and clubs that united people of various backgrounds by shared ideas. Coffee houses as spaces of conversation, learning, and business were very popular in the northern British American colonies. Within the first three months of the first edition of the *Halifax Gazette* a new coffee house was advertised "two Doors from the North Gate" where patrons could drink refreshments or be taught dancing or French.[119] A notice, in the same paper, appealed to "Gentlemen in Trade" to meet at the British Coffee House on 26 December 1765, "as Matters of importance would be set before them."[120]

The fascination with coffee houses extended beyond merely attending them locally. Colonial newspapers are replete with articles on coffee house and club life in Britain and the other colonies. Advertisements for *foreign* coffee houses in colonial newspapers provide further evidence of how connected northern British American colonists were with a larger transatlantic world. In 1754, Edward Clarke, the proprietor of the New-England Coffee-House in London, announced in the *Halifax Gazette* that he had just opened an expanded establishment called the "New-York, New-England, Rhode Island and Nova Scotia Coffee-House" in London's Royal Exchange district.[121] Thomas Lever, the new proprietor of the "New-York, New-England, Nova Scotia, Quebec, &c. &c. Coffee-House," in 1761 took out an advertisement in the *Halifax Gazette* relating that his establishment was still open, but had moved to another location "till the Party Walls of the House are rebuilt." As Edward Clark had done before him, Lever invited colonial men of business to frequent his establishment, boasting "the freshest *American*, Foreign and *Liverpool* News Papers."[122] Arguably, the fact that Londoners went to the time and expense to advertise in colonial newspapers shows that colonists were not only seen as key clientele, but were also perceived as well travelled and well connected with the coffee house as a popular eighteenth-century entertainment trend.

British North American coffee houses became key cultural gathering points for individuals and meeting places for local clubs and societies. Merchants Coffee House in Quebec, for example, became known not only for its fine food and drink, but also as a venue of societies, concerts, and theatre.[123] In Halifax, the "Old" Pontac was also a popular place for meetings of Halifax's Freemasons and for more informal literary groups.[124] Scottish-trained medical practitioners played a key role in the coffee-house culture of the colonies. In the convivial environment of the coffee house, medical practitioners discussed literature, science, and current events. In Halifax, it was noted that Drs John Halliburton and Duncan Clark formed a "literary coterie" with local merchants John Bremner, Alexander Brymer, and the Geddesses at the Pontac Tavern to "read papers on social and scientific subjects."[125] The all-night affair, it was observed, was sometimes attended by Prince Edward, Duke of Kent, to whom Clark and Halliburton were Physicians-in-Ordinary.[126]

Coffee houses allowed individuals to gather informally and congregate in organized societies, many of which were formed for the improvement of colonial society. Halifax's North British Society met at the "Old" Pontac and later at the British Coffee House.[127] The North British Society, established in 1768, was a friendly society promoting "commerce and immigration" as the well-being of the Scottish community.[128] Weekly dues went to assisting members when ill, or to pay for funeral costs. Such "friendly" societies were common throughout the British Atlantic world, as were societies that promoted agricultural improvement.

Agricultural improvement was one civic-minded pursuit that became an obsession throughout the English-speaking Atlantic world. Henry

Home, Lord Kames – a central thinker and benefactor of the Scottish Enlightenment – remarked to the president of the Royal Society in his *The Gentleman Farmer being an attempt to improve Agriculture, by subjecting it to the Test of Rational Principles* that "agriculture justly claims to be the chief of arts: it enjoys beside the signal pre-eminence, of combining deep philosophy with useful practice. The members of your Society, cannot employ their talents more profitably for their country, or more honourably for themselves, than in improving and promoting an art, to which Britain is fundamentally indebted for the figure it makes all the world over."[129] The physician William Cullen became one of Scotland's premier researchers, lecturing and publishing in the field of agricultural science. Cullen believed that his research both improved society as a whole, and, of course, had very practical applications in the development of medicines, or "Pharmaceutical Chemistry."[130]

Scottish-trained medical professionals were also instrumental in setting up societies for the promotion of the agricultural sciences in the northern British American colonies.[131] In November 1788, the Society for the Promotion of Agriculture was established in Nova Scotia.[132] The same year, the Agricultural Society of Quebec was founded.[133] The agricultural societies held regular meetings, offered prizes for agricultural research, and published the results of research in the popular press, so that the public would be rapidly informed of any progress.[134] The participation of Scottish-trained medical practitioners in the establishment and operations of colonial agricultural societies shows again the degree to which these individuals were integrated into the life of colonial society and how their contributions exceeded the bounds of their medical vocation.

The nature of the medical profession ensured that practitioners, both military and civilian, interacted with the public, healing the sick and offering medical advice, on a day-to-day basis. John MacKesy believed that his role in the colonies transcended that of surgeon and that he was part of a growing movement where "it must afford the highest gratification to every medical officer of a liberal spirit to perceive the rapid advance in respectability and scientific attainments, which has lately taken place, and now even generally characterize the members of the profession, who are engaged in the public service of the state."[135] Scottish born and educated, Dr John Halliburton provides another example of such a physician, "engaged in the public service of the state." In 1787, he was appointed to the Star Chamber, the executive council for Nova Scotia that advised the Governor. In the same year, he was also elected the moderator of the North British Society of Halifax. The *Annals* of the Society observe that Halliburton was "one of the most popular men who had ever held that office."[136] In the year of Halliburton's election as moderator, the society established a Committee of Charity headed by Halliburton and fellow Scottish-educated physician Dr Duncan Clark.[137] Until Halliburton's election, the society had normally supported the Scottish community in Halifax. However, one of the first actions of Halliburton and Clark's Committee of Charity was to donate £10 to "the negroes at Preston who had suffered greatly during the winter."[138] It is recorded that that act was a watershed for the society that became a regular supporter of various charities throughout the community in the subsequent years.

MacKesy, Halliburton, and Clark are not the only examples of the civic-mindedness of Scottish-trained medical professionals in the eighteenth and early nineteenth centuries. On 4 May 1804, Edward Walsh wrote a letter to Lieutenant-Colonel Green at York, Upper Canada. Walsh talked more about his projects outside his medical practice: a history of the Canadas and its peoples and his designs to improve the look of the Capital. "When I had the pleasure of seeing you at York," he wrote,

I took occasion to mention a Design I had undertaken and which even then was nearly [?] into a resolution – of collection materials for a History of the Canadas, Natural, political and commercial. Ever since I have earnestly embraced every opportunity of adding from all possible sources to my stock of information on the subject. Impressed with sentiments of the vast advantages which must accrue to the British Empire from the improvement of so fine and extensive a Colony. I could not wish the impulse of speculating on the various possibilities of improving and increasing its new Capital ... as it is probable ... [that] the House of Assembly – a new one – will at no remote period be constructed. I have ventured to send a Plan and Elevation for such a Building. It is a first draught it is defective in point of geometrical accuracy – but it is quite sufficient to convey a perfect Idea of the Design and as I understand there is in your employ an ingenious young Architect – it may furnish him with hints on some future occasion.[139]

It is not recorded whether Walsh's plans did indeed influence the creation of the Legislative Buildings in York. However, Walsh's myriad interests in history, art, architecture, design, and linguistics were more than spare time pursuits. He firmly believed in first understanding and then improving the new society in which he now resided.

Scholars such as J.G.A. Pocock have noticed, in addition to the civic humanism, or civic mindedness, exhibited in the Scottish Enlightenment, a powerful sense of civil jurisprudence. This innate Scottish sense of law and justice was a characteristic of eighteenth-century thought that, as Pocock argues, linked Scotland more closely to the thought and traditions of Europe than of England.[140] With only their Scottish medical training, several individuals, John Halliburton among them, took on key administrative and judicial positions and showed a keen sense for legal matters. The life of William Warren Baldwin offers another example. Born in County Cork, Ireland, he graduated MD at Edinburgh in 1797.[141] After emigrating to British North America, he moved to York, Upper Canada in 1802. Finding education lacking in York, Baldwin started a grammar school where he would instruct boys in "writing, reading and classics and arithmetic."[142] In March 1803, the legislature of Upper Canada, noting a critical shortage of legal professionals in the colony, passed an act allowing individuals without an education in law to enter the profession. Baldwin reportedly was the first appointment under the new law.[143] He became the judge of the Surrogate Court for the Home District in 1812 and later became, as some historians argue, an icon of moderate politics and an instigator of the idea of responsible government in Upper Canada.[144]

Adam Mabane is perhaps the most notable example of a Scottish-trained medical practitioner better known for his legal than his medical skills in British North America. Mabane, born in Edinburgh and later educated in medicine there, came to Canada as a surgeon with Sir Jeffery Amherst's forces in 1760. Four years later, without any background in legal studies, Mabane was appointed by the governor, James Murray, to preside over the Court of Common Pleas. Later on he became one of Governor Sir Frederick Haldimand's closest confidants.[145] Mabane acquired a large legal library and educated himself on the finer points of jurisprudence.[146] Historian Hilda Neatby characterized the surgeon-turned-judge as "kind-hearted, hard-working and thoroughly honest."[147] Mabane possessed a great empathy with the plight of French Canadians as marginalized peoples that sparked much controversy throughout his career. Mabane also employed a common-sense approach to the law, which raised the ire of opponents such as William Smith.[148] As Neatby observed, "legal subtleties did not impress him. He was not the man to mistake for the substance what he regarded as merely the shadow."[149] Not only was Mabane an autodidact; he was also a polymath. In addition to his role with the Court of Common Pleas, he was a member of the Legislative Council where he was employed on such various pursuits as educational reform, public library development, and public works. He was a founding member of the Agriculture Society and one of the three justices of the *Cour Suprême*.[150]

The careers of Mabane and Baldwin are admittedly examples on the extreme end of the spectrum. Not every medical practitioner took such a strong interest, or realized such success, in the field of colonial law. Neither should their accomplishments be discounted however. Several lesser-known, Scottish-trained medical practitioners also played key roles in the northern British American colonies as justices of the peace, advocates, and judges.[151] Indeed, British North America did suffer a shortage of trained legal professionals in the late eighteenth and early nineteenth centuries which accounts for the unprecedented opportunity for physicians to practice law. However, as there was no overabundance of formally trained medical practitioners either, what would motivate so many medical practitioners to pursue part- or full-time careers as lawyers, justices of the peace, and judges? Their actions reveal another avenue for further historical investigation in which the possible influence of Scottish Enlightenment education provides an alternative explanation to economic remuneration. As a propensity for civic-minded work marked the lives of Scottish-trained medical professionals, could not a sense of civic duty and the inherent values of jurisprudence inculcated through their Scottish education have also been a factor in the taking on of legal roles?

The revisiting of the role of Scottish-educated medical practitioners in the northern British American colonies offers a fascinating glimpse into a larger historical phenomenon that has yet to be fully explored. Members of this community exhibited a familiarity with the erudition, attitudes, and prejudices of Enlightenment Scotland. Showing a sense of civic mindedness and civil jurisprudence, Scottish-trained medical practitioners headed charitable organizations, worked for agricultural improvement, showed an interest in colonial education, and sometimes involved themselves in extra-professional legislative and judicial roles. During the course of medical practice, and in their spare time pursuits, they fraternized with colonial merchants, military personnel, clergy, and administrators, constituting communities of *literati* in the northern British American colonies. Seeing the work of these medical practitioners in light of recent studies of the Scottish Enlightenment breathes new life into older interpretations and suggests new motivations and philosophies that may have underscored their work.

In turn, seeing these early colonial inhabitants in a new light may enlarge our understanding of the nature of British colonial development in the mid-eighteenth to early nineteenth centuries. Through the cracks of what have previously been believed to be monolithic Tory and authoritarian colonial societies, a complex, informed, and liberal culture of ideas is visible. With further study, the actions of Scottish-trained medical practitioners – along with colonial merchants, clerks, functionaries, and their families – provide what can be seen as an example of liberal, Enlightenment-influenced, civic-minded colonists laying the foundations of civil society in Canada. Fuller study of the Scottish Enlightenment, and indeed the larger Enlightenment, may also be a welcome contribution to the new Canadian historical narrative that has argued a "reconnaissance" of the framework of liberalism.[152] Regardless of what resulted from the actions of these Scottish-trained medical practitioners and their fellow colonists, their study can broaden our understanding of Enlightenment on the periphery of the British Atlantic World. The British Atlantic world in the eighteenth and early nineteenth centuries was one of exchange, negotiation, and movement. Like their colonial neighbours, northern British American colonists aspired to be a part of the commercial, intellectual, and cultural networks of this vibrant world. The time is ripe for a systematic revisiting, or – in many ways – visiting, of the early intellectual life and culture of the northern British American colonies.

NOTES

1 Library and Archives Canada (LAC), Rare Books, AY201B7A44, Nathaniel Ames, "A Thought Upon the Past, Present and Future of NORTH AMERICA," in *An Astronomical DIARY: or an ALMANACK, for the Year of our Lord Christ 1758* (Boston: J. Draper, 1757).
2 *Nova Scotia Gazette and the Weekly Chronicle* (Halifax, 8 Feb. 1774), 4.
3 "ON THE PHRASE *The Enlightened Public*" (Excerpted from *D'Israeli's Miscellanies*) in *Scots Magazine* 65 (Apr. 1798): 875–76.
4 James Raven, *London Booksellers and American Customers: Transatlantic Literary Community and the Charleston Library Society, 1748–1811* (Columbia: University of South Carolina Press, 2002), xviii.
5 For works that argue or acknowledge these circumstances, see Carl Bridenbaugh, *Cities in Revolt: Urban Life in America, 1743–1776* (New York: Alfred A. Knopf, 1955), 422; Henry F. May, *The Enlightenment in America* (New York: Oxford University Press, 1976); and Gary B. Nash, *The Urban Crucible: The Northern Seaports and the Origins of the American Revolution* (Cambridge: Harvard University Press, 1986).
6 Bernard Bailyn could be considered one of the first American scholars to comment on the different uses of Enlightenment in the history of America ideas. See Bernard Bailyn, "Political Experience and Enlightenment Ideas in Eighteenth-Century America," *American Historical Review* 67, no. 2 (1962): 351.
7 John Bumsted, "Canada," in Alan Charles Kors, ed., *Encyclopedia of the Enlightenment,* © 2002, 2005 by Oxford University Press, Inc. *Encyclopedia of the*

Enlightenment: (e-reference edition). Oxford University Press. Accessed through Trent University, 2 Aug. 2006 http://www.oxford-enlightenment.com/ entry?entry=t173.e106.

8 In this paper, "British North America" and "the northern British American colonies" are used to describe what was known in the late eighteenth century as the "British Provinces of North America" being the colonies of Nova Scotia (later Cape Breton, 1784), St John District (later New Brunswick in 1784), St John's Island (later Prince Edward Island in 1799), Quebec (later Upper and Lower Canada in 1791), and Newfoundland under British administration.' "Southern British American colonies" refer specifically to the Thirteen Colonies and related territories that later became the United States of America.

9 Through the words of his character Matthew Bramble, Smollett wrote, "Edinburgh is a hot-bed of genius – I have had the good fortune to be made acquainted with many authors of the first distinction; such as the two Humes, Robertson, Smith, Wallace, Blair, Ferguson, Wilkie, &c. and I have found them all as agreeable in conversation as they are instructive and entertaining in their writings." Tobias Smollett, *The Expedition of Humphry Clinker*, 1771, reprint (New York: Holt, Rinehart & Winston, 1961), 270.

10 It was argued by John Maynard Keynes and P. Sraffa that the anonymous author of this commentary was indeed Hume himself, who could not resist the opportunity to make "an anonymous puff of his work." They observe that some of the arguments made in the Abstract are revisions seen in the second edition of *A Treatise*, and would have been, thus, unknown to anyone except Hume. See *An Abstract of A Treatise of Human Nature, 1740, A Pamphlet hitherto unknown by david hume reprinted with an introduction by J.M. Keynes and P. Sraffa (Hamden: Archon Books*, 1965), xxiii-xxxi.

11 *Ibid.*, 1.

12 *Scots Magazine* 25 (1763), 362–3.

13 See Dorinda Outram, *The Enlightenment* (Cambridge: Cambridge University Press, 1995), 1–3; James Schmidt, *What is Enlightenment?: Eighteenth-Century Answers and Twentieth-Century Questions* (Berkeley: University of California Press, 1996), ix–31.

14 See Ernst Cassirer, *The Philosophy of the Enlightenment*, trans. Fritz C. Koelln and James P. Pettegrove (Princeton: Princeton University Press, 1951); Peter Gay, *The Enlightenment: An Interpretation. The Rise of Modern Paganism* (New York: Alfred A. Knopf, 1966).

15 The idea of separate enlightenments on the fringe of the French Enlightenment grew throughout the 1970s and one of its most succinct scholarly iterations is Roy Porter and Mikuláš Teich, eds, *The Enlightenment in National Context* (Cambridge: Cambridge University Press, 1981). John Gascoigne and Patricia Curthoys's *The Enlightenment and the Origins of European Australia* (Cambridge: Cambridge University Press, 2002) further expands the idea of Enlightenment on the margins to colonial Australia.

16 The historiography on the causes and nature of the Scottish Enlightenment
   is rich and, at times, quite passionate. As Richard Sher observed in the introduction to his *Church and University in the Scottish Enlightenment* (1985), 4:
   "ever since that term [Scottish Enlightenment] was introduced by William
   Robert Scott in 1900 there has been no consensus about its meaning." A case
   in point is the Pandora's box of debate that Hugh Trevor Roper opened in
   arguing that the Union of 1707 was a turning point in the previously barba-
   rous intellectual development of Scotland. Douglas Young, likening Trevor
   Roper to Dr Samuel Johnson for his perceived attacks on Scottish intellect,
   argued a broader seventeenth-century tradition as the origins of the Scottish
   Enlightenment. Other historians such as Anand Chitnis have avoided the
   whole debate over origins in his *The Scottish Enlightenment: A Social History* by
   stating that, 14: "The roots of the Scottish Enlightenment lay deep in the
   nation's history, since the expression of the movement depended on the
   Church, the law, the lawyers and the universities ... The first shoots of the
   Enlightenment began to appear from then, to bud in the 1730s and to
   bloom from about 1750 to the 1780s ... " It is not in the scope of this paper
   to enter into a debate over origins of eighteenth-century Scottish thought,
   but rather to identify the complexity and depth of scholarship that has gone
   into the construction of the Scottish Enlightenment paradigm. See Hugh
   Trevor-Roper, "The Scottish Enlightenment," *Studies on Voltaire and the Eighteenth Century* 58 (1967): 1635–58; Douglas Young, "Scotland and Edinburgh
   in the Eighteenth Century," *Studies on Voltaire and the Eighteenth Century* 58
   (1967): 1967–90; Anand C. Chitnis, *The Scottish Enlightenment: A Social History*
   (London: Croom Helm, 1976); Jane Rendall, *The Origins of the Scottish
   Enlightenment 1707–1776* (New York: St Martin's Press, 1978); R.H. Campbell and Andrew S. Skinner, eds, *The Origins and Nature of the Scottish Enlightenment* (Edinburgh: John Donald Publishers Ltd, 1982); Richard B. Sher,
   *Church and University in the Scottish Enlightenment: The Moderate Literati of Edin-
   burgh* (Edinburgh: Edinburgh University Press, 1985); Alexander Broadie,
   ed., *The Cambridge Companion to the Scottish Enlightenment* (Cambridge:
   Cambridge University Press, 2003).

17 Richard Sher's work popularized the idea of the moderate literati as agents
   of the Scottish Enlightenment. Undeterred by the sometimes controversial
   nature of the definition of the Scottish Enlightenment, he defined it "quite
   simply as the culture of the literati of eighteenth-century Scotland." Sher,
   Church and University in the Scottish Enlightenment, 8.

18 For some writings on the "common sense" and skeptical traditions, see
   E.C. Mossner, *The Life of David Hume* (Oxford: Clarendon Press, 1970);
   Duncan Forbes, "Hume and the Scottish Enlightenment," in S.C. Brown, ed.,
   Philosophers of the Enlightenment (London: Harvester Press, 1979); J.R. Pole,
   "Enlightenment and the Politics of American Nature," in Porter and Teich,
   eds, *The Enlightenment in National Context*; Heiner F. Klemme, "Scepticism and

Common Sense," in Broadie, ed., *The Cambridge Companion to the Scottish Enlightenment*, 117–35. For some of the literature debating civic humanism, the "science of man," and civil jurisprudence, see R.G. Cant, "The Scottish Universities and Scottish Society in the Eighteenth Century," *Studies on Voltaire and the Eighteenth Century* 58 (1967): 1953–66; Nicholas Phillipson, "Towards a Definition of the Scottish Enlightenment," in Paul Fritz and David Williams, eds, *City and Society in the Eighteenth Century* (Toronto: Hakkert, 1973); Campbell and Skinner, eds, *The Origins and Nature of the Scottish Enlightenment*; Nicholas Phillipson, "The Scottish Enlightenment," in Porter and Teich, eds, *The Enlightenment in National Context*, 19–40; J.G.A. Pocock, "Cambridge Paradigms and Scotch Philosophers: A Study of the Relations between the Civic Humanist and the Civil Jurisprudential Interpretation of Eighteenth-Century Social Thought," in Istvan Hont and Michael Ignatieff, eds, *Wealth and Virtue: The Shaping of Political Economy in the Scottish Enlightenment* (Cambridge: Cambridge University Press, 1986); Roger Emerson, "Science and Moral Philosophy in the Scottish Enlightenment," in M.A. Stewart, ed., *Studies in the Philosophy of the Scottish Enlightenment* (Oxford: Oxford University Press, 1990), 11–36.

19 There is a rich literature on the unique nature of the Scottish education system (from grammar school to university) and how it fostered enlightenment thought. R.D. Anderson observed three key elements of primary and secondary education in eighteenth-century Scotland. Rooted in Protestant, egalitarian and civic-minded traditions, a general view existed in favour of a unified education system, with state support (if only as a supporter of the Church's efforts), that would promote social integration (taking its lead from the parish school model). See R. D. Anderson, *Education and the Scottish People, 1750–1918* (Oxford: Oxford University Press, 1995), 24. Roger Emerson has argued that university education in Scotland underwent a monumental change from the end of the late seventeenth century to the end of the late eighteenth century. Emerson observed that Scotland's five universities produced initially clergy and teachers, but after 1730 changed their focus, graduating lawyers, physicians and offering increased instruction in mathematics and natural philosophy. See Roger Emerson, "Scottish Universities in the Eighteenth Century, 1690–1800," in James A. Leith, ed., *Studies on Voltaire and the Eighteenth Century: Facets of Education in the Eighteenth Century* (Oxford: Cheney and Sons, 1977), Volume 167: 453. Other historians, such as J. B. Morrell, have also noted the liberal university model in Scotland and particularly in Edinburgh. Not only were the lecturers highly paid in Edinburgh, as Emerson had observed, but they received direct student fees, and the students had an unprecedented freedom of choice when it came to selecting classes. These aspects added a further market pressure to ensure higher quality teaching, and the instructors, who had total control over curriculum, met these challenges. Morrell called this liberal spirit of choice

the Edinburgh system of *lernfreiheit.* The system encouraged both an eclecti-
cism of formal study and a societal system of informal discussion. See
J. B. Morrell, "Medicine and Science in the Eighteenth Century," in Gordon
Donaldson, ed., *Four Centuries: Edinburgh University Life, 1583–1983* (Edinburgh: Edinburgh University Press, 1983), 41.

20 Richard Drayton, "Knowledge and Empire," in P.J. Marshall, ed., *The Oxford
History of Empire: The Eighteenth Century* (Oxford: Oxford University Press,
1998), 240.

21 A common metaphor with origins in the eighteenth century, some have
attributed it to Dugald Steward's observations that Edinburgh was like Athens. Stewart succeeded Adam Ferguson as professor of moral philosophy at
Edinburgh in 1785.

22 John Clive and Bernard Bailyn, "England's Cultural Provinces: Scotland and
America," *William and Mary Quarterly* 11, no. 2 (1954): 203.

23 Ibid., 202.

24 Bridenbaugh, *Cities in Revolt,* 422.

25 As seen in Adrienne Koch, ed., *The American Enlightenment: The Shaping of the
American Experiment and a Free Society* (New York: G. Braziller, 1965); Andrew
Hook, *Scotland and America: A Study of Cultural Relations, 1750–1835* (Glas-
gow: Blackie, 1975); Eric Foner, *Tom Paine and Revolutionary America* (New
York: Oxford University Press, 1976); Richard B. Sher and Jeffrey Smitten,
eds, *Scotland and America in the Age of Enlightenment* (Edinburgh: University of
Edinburgh Press, 1990); Robert A. Ferguson, *The American Enlightenment,
1750–1820* (Cambridge: Harvard University Press, 1997).

26 Gary Wills, *Inventing America: Jefferson's Declaration of Independence* (New York:
Double Day, 1978); Roy Branson, "James Madison and the Scottish
Enlightenment," *Journal of the History of Ideas* 40 (1979): 235–50; Daniel
Walker Howe, "Why the Scottish Enlightenment was Useful to the Framers
of the American Constitution," *Comparative Studies in Society and History* 31
(1989): 572–87; Sher and Smitten, eds, *Scotland and America in the Age of the
Enlightenment*; Samuel Fleischacker, "The Impact on America: Scottish
Philosophy and the American Founding," in Broadie, ed., *The Cambridge
Companion to the Scottish Enlightenment,* 316–337.

27 See May, *The Enlightenment in America,* 358–61 and Pole, "Enlightenment and
the Politics of American Nature," 192–217.

28 See Douglas Sloan, *The Scottish Enlightenment and the American College Ideal*
(New York: Teachers College Press, Columbia University, 1971); and Hook,
Scotland and America.

29 Sloan, *The Scottish Enlightenment and the American College Ideal,* 228–30.

30 John Bumsted, "Canada," http://www.oxford-enlightenment.com/
entry?entry=t173.e106

31 This large spectrum of explanation for the failure of Revolutionary thought
to take root in the northern British American colonies is a hallmark of the

once active scholarship on Canada and the American Revolution. For examples see Justin H. Smith, *Our Struggle for the Fourteenth Colony: Canada and the American Revolution* (New York: G.P. Putnam and Sons, 1907); J.B. Brebner, *Neutral Yankees of North America: A Marginal Colony During the Revolutionary Years* (New York: Columbia University Press, 1937); Gustave Lanctot, *Canada and the American Revolution, 1774–1783* (Toronto: Clarke, Irwin and Company, 1967); George Rawlyk, *Revolution Rejected, 1775–1776* (Toronto: Prentice Hall Ltd, 1968); and Gordon Stewart and George Rawlyk, *A People Highly Favoured of God* (Toronto: Macmillan, 1972).

32 Mesplet learned the printing trade in London and Philadelphia and later moved to Montreal where he and Jautard published the short lived *Gazette du commerce et littéraire de Montréal*. The liberal tracts of Mesplet and Jautard often endorsed the principles of the American Revolution and were perceived, it has been argued, as too republican for the colonial administration and too liberal for the French clergy of Montréal. Both men were arrested for sedition in 1779. After his imprisonment, Mesplet established *La Gazette de Montréal* in 1785. See Marcel Trudel, *L'influence de Voltaire au Canada* (Montréal: Fides, 1945); Jean-Paul de Lagrave, *Les origines de la presse au Québec (1760–1791)* (Montréal : Éditions de Lagrave, 1975), Denis Monière, *Ideologies in Quebec : The Historical Development*, trans. Richard Howard (Toronto: University of Toronto Press, 1981), Jean-Paul de Lagrave, *L'Époque de Voltaire au Canada: Biographie politique de Fleury Mesplet, Imprimeur* (Montreal: L'Étincelle, 1985), and, more recently, Yvan Lamonde, *Histoire sociale des idées au Québec (1760–1896)*, Vol. 1 (Montreal : Fides, 2000) and Bernard Andrès and Marc André Bernier, eds, *Portrait des arts, des lettres et de l'éloquence au Québec, 1760–1840* (Quebec: Les Presses de l'Université Laval, 2002).

33 Du Calvet was a French Huguenot who arrived in Canada after the British Conquest of Quebec in 1763. A rich merchant who vocally advocated colonial reform, he was also known to have accommodated American rebels during the Revolution. His sympathies were mistrusted by Governor Haldimand who imprisoned him until 1784 after which he fled to England and sued Haldimand for his imprisonment. The issue remained unresolved because he died in a shipwreck two years later. See Andrès and Bernier, eds, *Portrait des arts, des lettres et de l'éloquence au Québec*.

34 W. Stanford Reid, ed., *The Scottish Tradition in Canada* (Toronto: McClelland and Stewart, 1976), vii.

35 For examples that cover this wide spectrum see William Rattray, *The Scot in British North America*, 4 volumes (Toronto: Maclear & Co, 1881); Wilfred Campbell, *The Scotsman in Canada* (London: Sampson Low, Marston & Co. Ltd, 1911); J.M Gibbon, *Scots in Canada* (London: Kegan, Paul, Trench, Trübner Co. Ltd, 1911); James Alexander Roy, *The Scot and Canada* (Toronto: McClelland and Stewart, 1949); Gordon Donaldson, *The Scots Overseas* (London: Hale, 1966). For examples specifically related to the

history of medicine and Scots in Canada, see D.E.H. Cleveland, "Canadian Medicine and Its Debt to Scotland," *Canadian Medical Association Journal* 52 (1945); H.E. Macdermot, *One Hundred Years of Medicine in Canada: 1867–1967* (Toronto: McClelland and Stewart Ltd., 1967).

36 Cleveland, "Canadian Medicine and Its Debt to Scotland," 90.

37 Whithers argues that agricultural improvement was an essential element of the intellectual culture of the Scottish Enlightenment. This culture was one of natural and moral philosophy, earth science, geology, natural history and, as Wither's example of William Cullen's involvement in agricultural improvement shows, medicine. See Charles W.J. Withers, "William Cullen's Agricultural Lectures and Writings and the Development of Agricultural Science in Eighteenth-Century Scotland," *Agricultural History Review* 37, no. 2 (1989): 144–56.

38 For some examples see John D. Comrie, *The History of Scottish Medicine*, Vol. 1 (London: Balliere, Tindall & Co., 1932); Henry Sigerist, *American Medicine* (New York: W. W. Norton, 1934); Sloan, *The Scottish Enlightenment and the American College Ideal*; Hook, *Scotland and America*; W.S. Craig, *History of the College of Physicians of Edinburgh* (Oxford: Blackwell Scientific Publications, 1976); John Duffy, *The Healers: A History of American Medicine* (Urbana: University of Illinois Press, 1979); Roy Porter, *The Greatest Benefit to Mankind: A Medical History of Humanity* (London: W.W. Norton, 1997).

39 Drayton, "Knowledge and Empire," 237.

40 One of the most comprehensive works on the Enlightenment nexus of change in the teaching and practice of medicine is Guenter Risse's *Hospital Life in Enlightenment Scotland: Care and Teaching at the Royal Infirmary of Edinburgh* (Cambridge: Cambridge University Press, 1986). Other works that shed light on this era, or chronicle some of the changes, include Comrie, *History of Scottish Medicine*; Hook, *Scotland and America*; Morrell, "Medicine and Science in the Eighteenth Century"; A.L. Donovan, *Philosophical Chemistry in the Scottish Enlightenment: The Doctrines and Discoveries of William Cullen and Joseph Black* (Edinburgh: University of Edinburgh Press, 1975); Christopher J. Lawrence, *Medicine as Culture: Edinburgh and the Scottish Enlightenment* (PhD thesis, University College, London, 1984).

41 MacDermot, *One Hundred Years of Medicine in Canada*, 111.

42 See Gilles Janson, "James Fisher"; Barbara Tunis, "George Longmore"; Charles G. Roland, "John Mervin Nooth"; Charles G. Roland, "Robert Kerr"; Barbara Tunis, "William Holmes"; Geoffrey Bilson, "James Macaulay"; in *Dictionary of Canadian Biography Online*, «http://www. biographi.ca» (Accessed on 9 Apr. 2006). While all these men were trained in Scotland it is known that Nooth, in particular, had graduated MD from Edinburgh in 1766 and Longmore had degrees from Aberdeen and Edinburgh.

43 Jonathan Meakins, "The Influence of Edinburgh on McGill University and American Medicine," *Edinburgh Medical Journal* 24 (1920): 5–15; Maude

Abbott, *History of Medicine in the Province of Quebec* (Montreal: McGill University, 1931); Cleveland, "Canadian Medicine and Its Debt to Scotland," 90–5; H.E. MacDermot, "The Scottish Influence in Canadian Medicine," *The Practitioner* (1959): 88–92; Yolande Bonenfant, *Trois siècles de médecine québécoise Québec* (Quebec: Société historique de Québec, 1970), 20–1; Barbara Tunis, "Medical Licensing in Lower Canada: The Dispute over Canada's First Medical Degree," in S.E.D. Shortt, ed., *Medicine in Canadian Society: Historical Perspectives* (Montreal: McGill-Queen's University Press, 1981).

44 Sloan, *The Scottish Enlightenment and the American College Ideal*, 27.

45 Comrie, *History of Scottish Medicine*, 1: 340.

46 William Canniff, *The Medical Profession in Upper Canada, 1783–1850* (Toronto: William Briggs, 1894; reprint, Toronto: The Hannah Institute for the History of Medicine, 1980).

47 Allan Everett Marble, *Surgeons, Smallpox and the Poor: A History of Medicine and Social Conditions in Nova Scotia, 1749–1799* (Montréal: McGill-Queen's University Press, 1993), 175–6.

48 See Comrie, *History of Scottish Medicine*, 1: 341 and the Edinburgh University Archives, *Guide 1 —Student Records*, «http://www.lib.ed.ac.uk/resources/collections/specdivision/euaguide1.shtml» (Accessed on 6 Apr. 2006).

49 Marble writes that Abercrombie had attended lectures under Alexander Munro at Edinburgh in 1746–47 (Marble, 244), and that Dr Edward Wyer attended the lectures of William Cullen and William Hunter in 1771–72 (Marble, 285). Local accounts have observed that Dr Halliburton was born and educated in Scotland (*Annals of the North British Society*, 34–6) and Dr Duncan Clark received his MD from Edinburgh (Beamish Murdoch, *A History of Nova Scotia, or Acadie*, [Halifax: J. Barnes, 1867], 3: 263).

50 "Physicians Write Little on Professional Subjects" (Excerpted from *Curiosities of Literature*) *Scots Magazine* 54 (Mar. 1792): 120.

51 Nicholas Phillipson, "The Scottish Enlightenment," 20.

52 Ibid.

53 Pocock has also observed a similar phenomenon in the Scottish Enlightenment, that of an underlying ideology of civic humanism. Historian Roger Emerson has taken to task the interpretations of Pocock and Phillipson as being too reductive, especially in dealing with the origins of the Scottish moral philosophy tradition. Pocock and Phillipson "tend to see the Scottish Enlightenment particularly in terms of its moral philosophy and related disciplines, but they relate these to a republican tradition, classical in origin, but coming to the Scots through Machiavelli, Harrington, and Andrew Fletcher of Saltoun." Emerson does not debate the uniqueness of the Enlightenment of Scotland, but rather argues that it was influenced more by Scottish scientific practices and less derivative of external political traditions. The relationship and interplay between natural and moral philosophy gave the Scottish Enlightenment its uniqueness. Emerson believes that the histori-

ography has understated and misconceived what he observes as "the importance of logic and pneumatics to both fields." See Roger Emerson, "Science and Moral Philosophy in the Scottish Enlightenment," in Stewart, ed., *Studies in the Philosophy of the Scottish Enlightenment*, 32–4.

54 "James Strachan," #1679, in R. Drew, ed., *Commissioned Officers in the Medical Services of the British Army, 1660–1960*, 1: 108.

55 LAC, MG40-F1, Sir James McGrigor Collection, [Wellcome Library, London], Reel A–875, "*Circular No. 7, Medical Department Halifax, 6th Nov. 1819*," by James Strachan, 3.

56 Ibid.

57 "John MacKesy," #2285, in Drew, ed., *Commissioned Officers in the Medical Services of the British Army, 1660–1960*, 1: 151.

58 LAC, MG40-F1, Sir James McGrigor Collection, [Wellcome Library, London], Reel A–875, "*Half-Yearly Remarks and Observations for the Period Ending the 20th December 1819*," by John MacKesy, 6.

59 William Cullen, *First Lines in the Practice of Physic*, 5th ed., (Edinburgh: C. Elliot, 1788), 1: xiii-xiv.

60 Sir Neil Cantlie, *A History of the Army Medical Department* (Edinburgh: Churchill and Livingstone, 1974): 2: 276.

61 "*Half-Yearly Remarks and Observations for the Period Ending the 20th December 1819*," MacKesy, 1.

62 Bernard Bailyn, *Atlantic History: Concept and Contours* (Cambridge: Harvard University Press, 2005), 62–63.

63 Ibid., 55.

64 Ibid., 61.

65 T.H. Breen, "Narrative of Commercial Life: Consumption, Ideology, and Community on the Eve of the American Revolution," *The William and Mary Quarterly* 50 (July 1993): 471–501.

66 Ian K. Steele, *The English Atlantic, 1675–1740: An Exploration of Communication and Community* (New York: Oxford University Press, 1986), 274.

67 Drayton, "Knowledge and Empire," 250.

68 *Halifax Gazette*, 18 Apr. 1752, 1.

69 Such variety did come at a cost as reported by contemporary sources, especially those written by individuals recently arrived from Britain. Young Lieutenant William Dyott was shocked by colonial costs, reporting how officers "were obliged to pay high for messing" and particularly noted the higher prices for essential subaltern staples such as port and sherry. See the entry for 27 July 1787, Halifax, Nova Scotia in Reginald W. Jeffery, ed., *Dyott's Diary, 1781–1845: A Selection from the Journal of William Dyott, Sometime General in the British Army and Aide-de-Camp to His Majesty King George III* (London: Archibald, Constable and Company Ltd., 1907), 1: 30.

70 One calendar published in the *Halifax Gazette* gave the titles of over fifty publications for auction before listing the other household goods such as

furniture, pistols, fishing rods, and quilts. An analysis of the books for auction boasts many current works, including: "CHAMBERS DICTIONARY, 2 Vol. Folio, compleat, of the latest Edition, 3 Vol. of American Magazines. 2 Vol. Gale's Sermons. 2 Vol. Nelson's Justice. Malcom's Book-Keeping. Bailey's Dictionary. Crouch's Customs. Bradbury's Fifth of Nov. Turner's History of Religion. 2 Vol. Cookery. 3 Vol. British Merchant. 4 Vol. Spectacle de la Nature, or Nature delineated. 1 Indian Instructor. 1 Sunday's Entertainment. Dr Watts on Death, &c. Pomfree's Poems 2. Vol. Ovid's Metamorphosis. 1 Song Book, Cupid. Lovel's Herbalist. 4 Vol. viz. 2,3,4,5, of Rabelais. 2 Vols. Of small Pocket Bibles, English, 2 ditto French. Use and Abuse of Matrimony." See Halifax Gazette 16[?] Aug. 1754, 2.

71 See Marie Tremaine,"#789. Mabane, Adam, 1734–1792 and Gray, Alexander, d. 1791," and "#509 Bowman, James, d. 1787," A Bibliography of Canadian Imprints, 1751–1800 (Toronto: University of Toronto Press, 1952), 155; Also, L.F.S. Upton, The Loyal Whig: William Smith of New York and Quebec (Toronto: University of Toronto Press, 1969).

72 Tremaine, "#366. Fargues, Peter, d. 1780, [Catalogue for Sale of Peter Fargues' Books and Furniture, Quebec, 26 Apr. 1780],"A Bibliography of Canadian Imprints, 155.

73 Tremaine, "#526. Phillips & Lane, Auctioneers & Brokers, Quebec [Catalogue of Books]," A Bibliography of Canadian Imprints, 245.

74 Québec Gazette, 9 Nov. 1797, 3.

75 Marie Tremaine (1902–1984), celebrated bibliographer of early Canadiana, argued that a great deal of movement occurred between the northern and southern British colonies in America. Perhaps surprisingly, she observed, much material originally published in the northern British colonies has survived in the United States, unlike in Canada where copies have perished over the years. Of all the eighteenth-century imprints that she could find published in the northern British colonies, a third of the material resides solely in American libraries. See Marie Tremaine, "Canadian-American Relations in Colonial Printing," College and Research Libraries (Jan. 1946): 27–33.

76 Although a printer, Herbert Jefferies, is mentioned as arriving in Halifax with Cornwallis in 1749, no evidence has been found of his actually printing. It is generally thought that the first printer in Canada was Bartholomew Green, Jr. who arrived from Boston and set up shop in Halifax in 1751. Green died soon afterward and it was John Bushell, a former partner, who took over and printed what is acknowledged to be Canada's first newspaper, the Halifax Gazette on 23 March 1752. The first almanac that was recorded as printed in Halifax was the Nova Scotia Calender, or an Almanac for the year of the Christian Æra, 1769, printed by Anthony Henry in 1768. See Tremaine, A Bibliography of Canadian Imprints, 52.

77 William Brown was born in Scotland and later moved to Philadelphia were he worked in the print shop of William Dunlap. In collaboration with

Thomas Gillmore, Brown set up a printing office in Quebec and established the *Québec Gazette* in 1764. Tremaine, *A Bibliography of Canadian Imprints*, 663.

78 "Quebeck : to the public = au public," broadside printed in the printing office of William Dunlap, 1763, University of Toronto, Fisher Library, Canadian Pamphlets and Broadsides Collection, brc f 0072.

79 Chitnis, *The Scottish Enlightenment: A Social History*, 4–5.

80 Nicholas Phillipson, "The Scottish Enlightenment," in Porter and Teich, eds, *The Enlightenment in National Context*, 27.

81 Gascoigne and Curthoys, *The Enlightenment and the Origins of European Australia*, 7.

82 Ibid.

83 Charles W.J. Withers, "Toward a Historical Geography of Enlightenment in Scotland," in Paul Wood, ed., *The Scottish Enlightenment: Essays in Reinterpretation* (Rochester: University of Rochester Press, 2000), 85.

84 For example, see Thomas A. Markus, *Order in Space and Society: Architectural Form and its Context in the Scottish Enlightenment* (Edinburgh: Mainstream, 1982); Thomas A. Markus, "Buildings and the Ordering of Minds and Bodies," in Peter Jones, ed., *Philosophy and Science in the Scottish Enlightenment* (Edinburgh: John Donald Publishers, 1988), 169–224.

85 Chris Philo, "Edinburgh, Enlightenment and the Geographies of Unreason," in David N. Livingstone and Charles W.J. Withers, eds, *Geography and Enlightenment* (Chicago: University of Chicago Press, 1999), 372–398.

86 For some examples, see Robert J. Allen, *The Clubs of Augustan London* (Cambridge: Harvard University Press, 1933; reprint, Hamdon: Archon books, 1967); Aytoun Ellis, *The Penny Universities: A History of the Coffee Houses* (London: Secker and Warburg, 1956); and Lewis A. Cosner, *Men of Ideas: A Sociologist's View* (New York: The Free Press, 1965).

87 The impact of Habermas's ideas has been wide-ranging and considered one of the "most significant historiographical developments" in English-language scholarship since their translation in 1989. For an explanation and critique of the application of Habermas to historical studies see Harold Mah, "Phantasies of the Public Sphere: Rethinking the Habermas of Historians," *Journal of Modern History* 72, no. 1 (2000): 153. Also see James Van Horn Melton, *The Rise of the Public in Enlightenment Europe* (Cambridge: Cambridge University Press, 2001), 1–17.

88 Van Horn Melton, *The Rise of the Public in Enlightenment Europe*, 4–11.

89 Jessica Harland-Jacobs, "'Hands Across the Sea': The Masonic Network, British Imperialism, and the North Atlantic World," *Geographical Review* 89, no. 2 (1999): 239.

90 As historians such as Linda Colley, Catherine Hall, and Kathleen Wilson have observed, British identity in the eighteenth and nineteenth centuries is far from a straightforward matter. The inhabitants of the "northern British colonies" were – as we would observe today – of French, French-Canadian,

German, American, English, Scots, Irish and aboriginal origins, to name a few. This study, however, looks particularly at an English-language intellectual culture and identity that was beginning to be shared throughout Britain and its possessions. Certain elements of this culture could be argued to have Scottish origins. The goal of this study is to add another level of complexity to the multifaceted nature of British and British colonial identity. It is not to argue that this intellectual culture was the only, or prevailing, cultural vector. See Linda Colley, *Britons: Forging the Nation, 1707–1837* (New Haven: Yale University Press, 1992); Catherine Hall, *Civilising Subjects: Metropole and Colony in the English Imagination, 1830–1867* (Chicago: Chicago University Press, 2002); Kathleen, Wilson. *The Island Race: Englishness, Empire and Gender in the Eighteenth Century* (London: Routledge, 2003).

91 *Québec Herald*, 15 Dec. 1788, 3.

92 For example, Thomas Cary's library on St Louis Street in Quebec boasted American and European papers and was open from ten o'clock to three o'clock daily. See Tremaine, "#1037. Cary, Thomas, 1751–1823 [Catalogue of a Circulating Library]," *A Bibliography of Canadian Imprints*, 501.

93 In the winter of 1778–79, the Quebec Library was organized. By 1792, it had over 2400 volumes in English, French, Latin, and Greek. Although it was observed that the "arrangement of Catalogues is an arbitrary matter," the library was "divided into five principal classes, Theology, Jurisprudence, Arts and Sciences, *Belles Lettres* and History, which are again divided and subdivided ... and separate classes have been formed for Poetry, Plays and Novels – History, Biography, Travels – and miscellaneous works." See Tremaine, "#799. Quebec Library. Catalogue / of / English and French / Books / in the / Quebec Library," *A Bibliography of Canadian Imprints*, 371.

94 C.C. Booth, "John Haygarth FRS (1740–1827)," The James Lind Library http://www.jameslindlibrary.org (Accessed 29 Jan. 2005).

95 "The ROYAL American magazine, or UNIVERSAL REPOSITORY [To be published MONTHLY] *To the PUBLIC,*" *Nova Scotia Gazette*, 5 Oct. 1773, 2.

96 Ibid., 2–3.

97 "PROPOSALS FOR PRINTING BY SUBSCRIPTION, *A COLLECTION OF ORIGINAL POEMS,*" *Québec Herald*, 15 Dec. 1788 36.

98 "#454 and #455. Badelard, Phillipe Louis François, 1728–1802, *Direction pour la guérison du Mal de la Baie St Paul*" in Tremaine, *A Bibliography of Canadian Imprints*, 210–11.

99 Ibid., Rénald Lessard, "*Direction pour la guérison du Mal de la Baie St Paul*: La première publication médicale canadienne," *Bulletin canadien d'histoire de la médecine* 12 (1995) : 369–72.

100 For examples, see Franz Swediauer, *Practical observations on venereal complaints. The third edition, corrected and enlarged. To which are added, an account of a new venereal disease ... in Canada* (London/Edinburgh: C. Elliot, T. Kay, and Co., London, 1788); Benjamin Bell, *A treatise on gonorrhœa virulenta, and lues*

venereal, Vol. 2 (Edinburgh: James Watson and G. Mudie, London: J. Murray, 1793).

101 "#444. Wilcocks, Miss," in Tremaine, *A Bibliography of Canadian Imprints,* 206.

102 "Edward Walsh," #1685, Drew, ed., *Medical Officers in the British Army 1660–1960,* 1: 109.

103 LAC, MG19-F10, Edward Walsh Collection, "*Journal of a Voyage from Portsmouth to Quebec,*" 4 Oct. 1803.

104 These detailed manuscripts can be found in LAC, MG19-F10, Edward Walsh Collection.

105 Roger L. Emerson, "American Indians, Frenchmen and Scots Philosophers," in Roseann Runte, ed., *Studies in Eighteenth Century Culture* (Madison: University of Wisconsin Press, 1979), 9: 222–3.

106 LAC, MG19-F10, Edward Walsh Collection, "*Journal of a Voyage from Portsmouth to Quebec,*" 4 Oct. 1803.

107 Emerson, "American Indians, Frenchmen and Scots Philosopher," 231.

108 Over 20 originals and prints of, or after, Walsh's work, as well as several pencil sketches of aboriginal Canadians are held in the collections of Library and Archives Canada, including "View of the Falls of Niagara, 1805," "A View of the City of Montreal and the River St Lawrence from the Mountain, 1811," and "Proposed House of Assembly."

109 The length of the theatre season varied depending on the colony. In late–1780 Nova Scotia, the season followed a similar Fall-Winter pattern as was experienced in London. See Reginald W. Jeffery, ed., *Dyott's Diary,* 1: 62. From an analysis of playbills, it appears that in Quebec the season spanned the year. See Marie Tremaine, "#499. Quebec Theatre [Play Bills], 1786" and "#540. Quebec Theatre [Play Bill], 1787," in *A Bibliography of Canadian Imprints,* 231 and 251.

110 Yashdip Singh Bains, "Painted Scenery and Decorations in Canadian Theatres, 1765–1825," *Theatre History in Canada* 3, no. 2 (1982): 112.

111 Ibid.

112 *Dyott's Diary,* 1: 62.

113 Ibid., 60.

114 Ibid., 61.

115 "Acadius, or Love in a Calm" was a play that satirized life in Nova Scotia, and the cast of characters offers a host of local colonial archetypes. The character Frankport is a local merchant and Acadius is a subaltern with the garrison. Frankport has a "negro servant" named Fortune and the servant's wife is Phebe. One of the love interests is a local girl named Jenny Chowder and the play also has comedic duos such as the two visiting Londoners, Guttle and Guzzle, and Frankport's two creditors, Scentwell and Saveall. The play, perhaps, cut too close to the bone as the anonymous author published a lengthy disclaimer, distancing the characters from actual Haligonians. "THE AUTHOR thinks proper to assure the Public"; a statement in the *Nova Scotia Gazette and*

the Weekly Chronicle read, "that the FABLE of it is, an entire Fiction; and tho' *some* part of the PLACE of *Action* may on a general Construction, *rather* be fixed in this *Province*, than any other part of the Continent of *America*, yet it *cannot* be absolutely so. – The MORAL has a strict *Moral* tendency. The EPISODES and INCIDENTS (he presumes) are *probable, natural* and *diverting*. – And the CHARACTERS, he *insists*, are too *outré* to be *personal* on any Persons *here* or *elsewhere*, within the circle of the Author's acquaintance." *Nova Scotia Gazette and the Weekly Chronicle*, 1 Feb. 1774, 3.

116 Ibid., 4.

117 *Royal Gazette* (Saint John), 20 Jan. 1795.

118 The *Scots Magazine* reprinted an article entitled "Account of the First Introduction of COFFEE into Britain" in 1785, addressing the continued interest in the institution of the coffee house. The article included a poem, written one hundred years earlier, that still reflected the late eighteenth-century perception of coffeehouse clientele: "A Coffee-house, the learned hold / It is a place where Coffee's sold; / This derivation cannot fail us, / For where Ale's vended that's an Alehouse ... Of all some and all conditions, / Even Vintners, Surgeons, and Physicians, / The Blind, the Deaf, and Aged Cripple, / Do here resort and Coffee Tipple." See "Account of the First Introduction of COFFEE into Britain," *Scots Magazine* (May 1785): 248. Smollett's Matthew Bramble also observed the plurality of the coffee house, but was much less charitable, noting a particular superficiality in the self-fashioning individuals who frequented such establishments. "Every clerk, apprentice, and even waiter of tavern or coffeehouse maintains a gelding by himself, or in partnership, and assume the air and apparel of a petit maitre – The gayest places of public entertainment are filled with fashionable figures; which, upon inquiry, will be found to be journeymen, tailors, servingmen, and abigails, disguised like their betters. In short, there is no distinction or subordination left ... " Tobias Smollett, *The Expedition of Humphry Clinker*, 1771, reprint (New York: Holt, Rinehart & Winston, 1961), 100.

119 *Halifax Gazette* Tuesday, 25 Apr. 1752, 2.

120 *Halifax Gazette* Thursday, 26 Dec, 1765, 4.

121 *Halifax Gazette* Saturday, 22 June 1754, 2.

122 *Halifax Gazette* Thursday, 14 May 1761, 2.

123 Merchant's Coffee House enjoyed a broad spectrum of patronage, including hosting the Club of Veterans of 1775–76 (see *Québec Herald*, Dec. 27, 1790, 1), Saint Andrew's Day celebrations (*Québec Herald*, Dec. 8, 1788), public auctions (*Québec Herald*, Dec. 21, 1789, 1) and concerts of vocal and instrumental music (see *Québec Herald*, 18 May 1789, 8.).

124 James S. Macdonald, ed., *Annals of the North British Society of Halifax, Nova Scotia, From Its Foundation in 1768, to its Centenary Celebration March 26th, 1868* (Halifax: "Citizen" Steam Book, Job and General Printing Office, 1868), 45–6.

125 Ibid.

126 Ibid.

127 Ibid., 20–36.

128 These goals are listed in the North British Society's original twenty articles of incorporation. Originally, only Protestant North Britons could seek membership in the society. The charter was changed, however, in 1786 to admit "any man of honour and integrity ... provided he be a North Briton or the son of a North Briton." See *The Annals of the North British Society* (1868), 6–12, 36.

129 Henry Home, *The Gentleman Farmer. Being an Attempt to Improve Agriculture, By subjecting it to the Test of Rational Principles* (Edinburgh: W. Creech, 1776), v. Cited in Withers, "William Cullen's Agricultural Lectures," 146.

130 Withers, "William Cullen's Agricultural Lectures," 152.

131 Complete membership lists for the Agricultural Society of Quebec can be found in various sources such as the *Québec Alamanac* and the *Québec Herald*. Adam Mabane is listed as one of the founding members of the society. A cursory view of the membership shows that among the merchants and clergy, several other medical practitioners from the community such as George Longmore (trained at Aberdeen and Edinburgh), Dr John Mervin Nooth (MD, Edinburgh 1766) were members of the society. See *Almanach de Québec*, 1791; *Québec Herald*, 23 Apr. 1789.

132 Beamish Murdoch, *A History of Nova Scotia, or Acadie* (Halifax: J. Barnes, 1866), 3: 75.

133 *Québec Herald* 13 Apr. 1789, 187.

134 In Apr. 1789, just after the establishment of the Agricultural Society of Quebec, the objectives of the society were published in the *Québec Herald*. "Premiums and honourary rewards, will be offered by the Society with a view to induce the farmers to greater industry, and raise in them a spirit of emulation." *Québec Herald* 13 Apr. 1789, 187. Eight months later the society was already publishing results of research to benefit farmers for the upcoming season. "From the experiments made by Mon. F. Cartier of the Parish of St Antoine on the Chambly River, laid before the Directors of this Branch, it appears that SMUT in wheat, may be effectually prevented by using the following precaution ..." *Québec Herald*, 28 Dec. 1789 44.

135 LAC, MG40-F1, Sir James McGrigor Collection, [Wellcome Library, London], Reel A–875, "*Half-Yearly Remarks and Observations for the Period Ending the 20th December 1819*," by John MacKesy, 1.

136 *Annals of the North British Society* (1868), 38.

137 Duncan Clark was born and trained in Scotland (some reports attribute to him an MD from Edinburgh). He later moved to New York where he was a physician during the American Revolution. He was evacuated with Loyalists to Halifax and worked at the Naval Hospital as well as with having a private civilian practice. He was involved in several societies such as the North British Society (he was twice president) and the Freemasons (he was elected

Grand Master of in 1800). Allan Marble notes reading a version of William Cullen's *First Lines of Physic* with "Duncan Clark" written in the front. See Murdoch, *A History of Nova Scotia, or Acadie,* 3: 263; *Annals of the North British Society* (1868), 45; and Marble, *Surgeons, Smallpox and the Poor,* 221n10.

138 *Annals of the North British Society,* 39.

139 LAC, RG 8, C-Series, Vol. C77 (National Archives, England), Dr Edward Walsh to Lt-Col Green, 10 May 1804, 117–19.

140 Pocock elaborated on his ideas regarding the spirit of Scottish civic humanism arguing the existence of a concurrent philosophy of civil jurisprudence. "The jurisprudential paradigm possesses great strength and attraction," Pocock argued, "and performs services which the civic humanist paradigm does not." Thus, the roots of the Scottish critique of established political structures could also be attributed to these ingrained ideas of law and justice. Pocock further observes that historians had been wary to argue for the co-existence of the two philosophies. Despite this wariness, the great value of this expanded civil jurisprudential view, was clear as it "considers the growth of Scottish social thought in the eighteenth century as an evolution within a tradition of civil jurisprudence which Scotland shared with adjacent Europe rather than with England ... it permits us to study Scottish social thought in the context of a generalized history of western political theory ... " See J.G.A. Pocock, "Cambridge Paradigms and Scotch Philosophers: A Study of the Relations between the Civic Humanist and the Civic Jurisprudential Interpretation of Eighteenth-Century Social Thought," in Hont and Ignatieff, eds, *Wealth and Virtue,* 246–8.

141 Robert L. Fraser, "William Warren Baldwin," *Dictionary of Canadian Biography Online,* "http://www.biographi.ca" (Accessed 9 Apr. 2006).

142 Advertisement in the *Gazette* (York), 18 Dec. 1802, cited in Edith G. Firth, *The Town of York, 1793–1815: A Collection of Documents of Early Toronto* (Toronto: Champlain Society, 1962), 196.

143 Canniff, *The Medical Profession in Upper Canada, 1783–1850,* 234.

144 Edith G. Firth, *The Town of York, 1815–1834: A Further Collection of Documents of Early Toronto* (Toronto: The Champlain Society, 1966), 7.

145 The closeness of Mabane is also reflected in Haldimand's will where he leaves "the sum of Ten thousand Livres Swiss revertible to Mrs Elizabeth Mabane his sister in case she survives him." See LAC, MG23-GII, Vol. 22, "Last Will of Frederick Haldimand," Mar. 1791.

146 Hilda Neatby, "The Political Career of Adam Mabane," *Canadian Historical Review* 16, no. 2 (1935): 137–9.

147 Ibid., 139.

148 Smith, a Loyalist from New York with formal legal training from Yale University, despised Mabane who was anti-American, pro-French, and lacked formal legal training. He writes in his diary, 3 Apr. 1785, "[Sir Guy Carleton] says Genl. Haldimand has recommended Mr Mabane to be Chief Justice of

Canada & that Mabane was a Surgeon's Mate in Canada, that such an Instance ought to be decisive Proof of Mr Haldimand's Inadequacy to rule that Country or represent what is wise respecting it." Later Carleton (Lord Dorchester) returned as Governor and appointed Smith as Chief Justice over Mabane. L.F.S. Upton, ed., *The Diary and Selected Papers of Chief Justice William Smith 1784–1793*, Volume 1, *The Diary January 24, 1784 to October 5, 1785* (Toronto: The Champlain Society, 1963), 212–13.

149 Neatby, "The Political Career of Adam Mabane," 139.

150 See, *Almanach de Québec* (Quebec: Samuel Neilson, 1781 to 1791).

151 A partial list of Scottish-trained medical practitioners who became justices of the peace includes: William Auld, Edinburgh-educated; William Carson, Edinburgh-trained; James Macaulay; William Robertson, Edinburgh-educated; Alexander Thom, Aberdeen-educated; David Mitchell, Edinburgh-trained; Charles-Norbert Perreault, Edinburgh-trained; William "Tiger" Dunlop, Glasgow-trained; Alexander James Christie, Edinburgh-trained. A partial list of judges includes: Robert Kerr; Adam Mabane; William Warren Baldwin; Edinburgh-trained. Source: *Dictionary of Canadian Biography*, Vols 3 to 6.

152 See Ian McKay, "The Liberal Order Framework: A Prospectus for a Reconnaissance of Canadian History," *Canadian Historical Review* 81, no. 4 (2000): 617–45. For a critique and further application of this theory, see R.W. Sandwell, "The Limits of Liberalism: The Liberal Reconnaissance and the History of the Family in Canada," *Canadian Historical Review* 84, no. 3 (2003): 423–50.

JEFFREY L. MCNAIRN

The Malthusian Moment

British Travellers and the Vindication of Economic Liberalism in the Maritime Countryside

British military triumph prompted Thomas Jeffreys, geographer to the Prince of Wales, to publish *The Natural and Civil History of the French Dominions in North and South America* in 1760. The acquisition of new territory and subjects required "more regular, comprehensive and particular" knowledge, including that of a "commonwealth" famed for its "industry, foresight, order and unanimity." Each member "knows what he is to do, and every thing is carried on in the exactest order imaginable." Its "governors" were reportedly chosen to allocate to each "his separate task ... and to punish or banish drones." Those "exiles ... do no manner of work ... they are always lean, the natural consequence of their laziness." More than a century later, John Rowan praised the society in almost identical terms amid his "practical and, it is hoped, useful hints for emigrants and sportsmen" like himself, but added the "permanent and enduring" improvement of the land to its accomplishments and the regulation of "the size of the different households and villages according to the supply" of necessities to the duties of its government.[1] Here, bracketing British victories in the Seven Years War and the union of the British North American colonies, seemed the quintessential imperial fantasy borne of a common view of classical political economy: a well-ordered commonwealth where everyone – or at least every male – laboured industriously or suffered the "natural" consequences.

Such observations comport well with Mary Louise Pratt's view of travellers as a "capitalist vanguard" or the "advanced scouts for capitalist 'improvement'" who identified resources, markets, and trade routes for further exploitation. Expansionist and extractive, they marked colonial lands as "neglected" and their inhabitants as "backward" for failing to "rationalize, specialize, and maximize production."[2] Cultural historians of British North America have focused instead on travellers' role as agents of empire, constructing non-economic identities of the "other," while social and economic historians have emphasized the inaccuracy of their observations.[3] Both unmask largely predictable "racial," gender, and other stereotypes, leaving the impression of travel narratives as little more than a jumble of clichés and prejudices devoid of serious intellectual content. Extending Pratt's insights to the published narratives of British travellers to the Maritime colonies of British North America highlights their unanimous support for economic development and their role in working out the content and implications of particular forms of economic rationality, but fails to place those narratives in the context of the economic ideas and debates within which they were written. Dubbing travellers "advanced scouts" for capitalism implies that capitalism had a singular, uncontested meaning; our only task is then to measure how close they came to articulating and promoting that a priori definition. The phrase "capitalist vanguard" prejudges the very question we need to ask: what was their explicit or implied political economy?

Even when culturally insensitive and ill-informed, the answer is more interesting than invocations of "industry" and "foresight" by Jeffreys and Rowan suggest. The "commonwealth" both lauded in such terms was inhabited by beavers, not humans. The use of American "Indians" as archetypical "primitives" is well known.[4] Instead, this essay focuses on how travellers used transplanted Europeans – the raw material from which prosperous settler societies were to be fashioned – to think about the behaviour and subjectivity required for economic development. Rowan's emphasis on balancing population and resources in an agrarian context gestures toward the broadly Malthusian framework of that use. More than vapid cheerleaders for work and profit, those who visited and wrote about the Maritime colonies in the aftermath of the Napoleonic wars drew with varying degrees of self-consciousness and skill on common ideas while participating in economic debate in ways that might usefully be seen as "Malthusian." This is especially evident in contrast to the political economy of David Ricardo whose work is often taken as indicative of the "classical" tradition as a whole. This was not a matter of influence – tenuous, tortured, and partial at best – but of the tenor and contours of travellers' contribution to a broader transatlantic conversation.[5]

By eavesdropping on that conversation, intellectual historians have discovered a range of voices and paid greater attention to Robert Malthus and other critics of Ricardian "orthodoxy." For instance, once he stopped equating economic thought with stock images of "laissez-faire individualism" and "classical" political economy, Boyd Hilton rediscovered an entire group of "Christian Economists," including John Bird

Sumner, whose *Treatise on the Records of Creation* (1816) popularized Malthus's principle of population as evidence of God's "wisdom and goodness," and Thomas Chalmers, whose *Political Economy in Connexion with the Moral State and Moral Philosophy of Society* (1832) sided with Malthus on nearly every point of his dispute with Ricardo.[6] A line of descent can also be traced from Malthus through Chalmers to Edward Gibbon Wakefield's contention that industrial nations required agricultural colonies to remain prosperous.[7] Claims of concordance rather than consanguinity with a broadly Malthusian framework highlight important elements of travellers' political economy and economic liberalism in their encounter with British North America.

TRAVELLERS AND POLITICAL ECONOMY

Alongside Ireland, colonies posed central questions about how economies develop and why some prosper and others do not. They were important sites of experimentation; laboratories to test "British" economic principles and policies in diverse settings.[8] "The progress of man from a state of nature towards civilization, is always slow, and generally similar" pronounced Christopher Atkinson in the preface to his New Brunswick emigration guide, "but the operation of an enlightened people upon uncultivated nature which was first displayed in the new settlement of America, affords a most interesting subject of contemplation.'[9] Travellers debated the state policies that have preoccupied scholars of economic analysis and empire, but economic psychology – why people produce, consume, and exchange in particular ways – drew more of their attention. Would transplanting "enlightened" Europeans to "America" ensure colonial development or was a new economic subjectivity required as well? What motivates people to work beyond subsistence? Why do some fail to take full advantage of opportunity? How might they be brought to do so? Economic analysis was not, then, confined to formal treatises or policy matters as more disciplinary histories of Canadian economic thought suggest – and in ways that exclude travel narratives and minimize the extent of economic thinking in and about the colonies.[10] If, as Ian McKay argues, twentieth-century tourism and cultural industries sought an antimodern "folk," earlier travellers to the Maritimes were on a quest for modern "homo economicus.'[11]

From the fifth edition of his *Essay on the Principle of Population* (1817) with its more favourable view of emigration and economic development, through his *Principles of Political Economy* (1820), until his death in 1834, Malthus reworked Adam Smith's legacy in light of Britain's economic challenges in the aftermath of the Napoleonic wars: rising national debt and taxes; rapid population growth and urbanization; and increasing reliance on manufacturing and imported food. No nation seemed so advanced economically, but with more able-bodied men on poor relief, food scarcities, and civil unrest, suffering and injustice were all too evident. Early editions of Malthus's *Essay*, first published in 1798, contributed to the anxiety. They dismissed revolutionary hopes that equality and benevolence could replace disparity and self-love, doubted that increased aggregate wealth necessarily improved conditions for the labouring classes, and suggested that there were natural limits to economic growth.[12] Even as economic conditions improved in the 1830s, unease about further growth persisted into the "hungry forties." Economic development stood in need of vindication.[13]

Colonies played an important role in that vindication and thus so did those who visited and wrote about them. A review of one such account in 1832 thought that "of late, innumerable tracts, travels, and pamphlets" on Britain's North American colonies "have engaged the attention of the statesman, the political economist, and the merchant." Indeed, more than twenty narratives were published by visitors to the Maritimes between the end of the Napoleonic wars and 1840 to ascertain, as one put it, "the present state of the inhabitants, and the prospects for new settlers."[14] Assimilating the region to the broader North American settlement frontier, all focused on emigration and agriculture to observe the mass movement of people to an economic environment unlike the one they were leaving in the British Isles; one typified by the relative availability of land, scarcity of both capital and labour, and a preponderance of independent commodity producers.

Earlier, eighteenth-century accounts had been mercantilist, equating Britain's greatness with a favourable balance of trade and growing population. They emphasized the region's natural resources and how they might contribute to imperial defence and Britain's self-sufficiency in the raw materials needed to employ workers "at home." In fact, "it is in the interest of Great Britain ... to discourage, by every possible means, that fatal propensity to emigration." Nova Scotia was to be made "a most valuable Acquisition ... without draining our Mother-Country of its Inhabitants."[15] Later Maritime travel narratives – almost fifty were published between 1840 and 1871 – formed another distinct moment of travel writing. They continued to promote emigration and economic development in ways that will be included here, but they self-consciously partook of "an age of travel."[16] Tourist advice and discussions of non-agricultural production grew in prominence. So did romantic stories that looked back to the region's past rather than ahead to its economic future. Thomas Haliburton's Blue Noses, Henry

Wadsworth Longfellow's Evangeline, and James Fenimore Copper's "Indian" characters made more compelling subjects than emigrant farmers. Almost two-thirds of these accounts, like John Rowan's, centred on big-game hunting, angling, and "wilderness" adventure.[17] The Malthusian moment had passed.

The largest number of those who published accounts between the end of the Napoleonic wars and Confederation were British army and government officers. Most others were of comparable social standing, although one Protestant missionary was an unemployed shoemaker. A young labourer and shiftless blacksmith-turned-poet also published travel accounts. Scots seem overrepresented, but only two were women. Frances Beaven paid particular attention to the role of women in settlement and Isabella Bird found travel liberating, journeying from Shediac to St. John overland rather than by steam as "the ladies and children did ... one of my objects being to see as much of the country as possible." Their judgments, however, differed little from those of their male counterparts.[18] No more than three or four were businessmen. Fewer could claim a literary reputation.

They came to the region to investigate, out of curiosity, on business or official duty, en route to somewhere else, in search of opportunity and adventure, to visit relatives, and to revive their health or fortune. Regardless, their travel narratives were economic in a number of senses: they sought to influence imperial attitudes and policies; to attract immigrants and capital; and to promote trade. Some wrote to further their own economic interests. All reported on how Aboriginal peoples and settlers produced, consumed, and exchanged. Travellers were thereby amateur political economists who selected and framed their observations in light of common economic ideas and assumptions. As the great proselytizer of classical political economy, J.R. McCulloch, wrote, "observations are scarcely ever made or particulars noted for their own sake; it is in the peculiar phraseology of this science, the *effectual demand* of the theorist that regulates the production of the facts or raw materials, which he is afterwards to work into a system."[19] Widely read, travel texts were a principal source of "raw materials" about the Maritimes and added to the general fund of information and opinion from which more systematic accounts of political economy drew. "We have not referred to Captain Moorsom's descriptions of scenery nor to his sketches of society" in *Letters from Nova Scotia*, admitted the *Westminster Review*, for while "they will serve to amuse the reader" it was his "material facts" that warranted attention from statesmen and potential emigrants.[20]

Indeed, Adam Smith gleaned much of the non-British evidence for *The Wealth of Nations* (1776) from travel narratives. His former clerk,

Robert Reid, later wrote to him to describe his New Brunswick farm and journey to Halifax with three "Savages" which had afforded "an opportunity of observing their manners."[21] Perhaps Reid had read *Instructions for Travellers* (1758) in which another political economist had enumerated questions "to enable them to judge the comparative poverty, or Riches of a City, Town, or Country, in passing through it" and thus to improve economic theory "by means of Travelling."[22] According to a conservative periodical, James Johnston's "Liberal" free-trade principles had distorted the conclusions he drew in his *Notes on North America* (1851) from "passing through" New Brunswick. Karl Marx found evidence in the same text to support his theory of rent, concluding that even "quite conservative agricultural chemists" like Johnston were forced to admit that private property was incompatible with fully efficient agriculture.[23] The political economy of Maritime travellers in the post-Napoleonic decades is better described as loosely Malthusian, an association that would have only cemented Marx's antipathy.

POPULATION AND EMIGRATION

Travellers engaged most directly with Malthusian economic thought on questions of population and emigration. Not only were these issues central to debates about the health of the British economy and the value of colonies, but Malthus was most responsible for overturning the mercantilist equation of population growth with prosperity and military might. Instead, Malthus posited a "natural tendency of the human race to increase faster than the possible increase of the means of subsistence." The pressure of population on subsistence increased scarcity and unemployment, lowered wages, and spread poverty until it was arrested by either the positive checks of "vice and misery" that included "epidemics, wars, pestilence, plague, and famine" or the preventive check of moral restraint whereby people delayed marriage. Such new thinking about population growth turned many to colonization as an obvious solution, although Malthus himself judged emigration "a very weak palliative." It might remove part of the "surplus," but natural increase would continue to outpace agricultural improvement and thereby quickly return population to its pre-emigration levels. Emigration was only "a partial and temporary expedient." In 1817, however, Malthus added a long paragraph to his *Essay* conceding that under particular circumstances, "emigration is most useful as a temporary relief; and it is in these circumstances that Great Britain finds herself."[24]

Only Fred De Roos, a naval officer primarily interested in American sea power, echoed Malthus's caution on emigration.[25] Other visitors to the Maritimes were enthusiastic emigration promoters intent on establishing the region as an escape from the Malthusian population trap. Joseph Bouchette, surveyor-general of Lower Canada who had worked in the region, contended that it "seems to be universally admitted" that "there exists, in the mother country, a redundancy of labouring population" and that it was "desirable to throw off the superfluity." A reviewer of Bouchette's volumes rightly insisted that no such unanimity existed, but other travel authors persisted. Joseph Outram, for instance, prefaced his letters on Nova Scotia with a summary of the basic Malthusian principle "that population is increasing in a greater ratio than the production of food." Emigration to Nova Scotia could replace the checks of disease and destitution and transform paupers into "producers of food and consumers of our manufactures." The professional travel writer and lecturer James Silk Buckingham added the costs of charity and poor relief and the "great suffering, from hunger, nakedness, and disease, engendered by want – with great deterioration of morals, in the ignorance and crime unavoidably resulting from such destitution" to the "evils of an increasing population" that cried out for emigration.[26]

Ironically, one of Malthus's most vociferous critics, William Cobbett, had resided in the region for six years (1785–91). Cobbett later denied that England was overpopulated and detested how population theory distracted attention from what he believed to be poverty's real causes. Drawing people away from his beloved English countryside, emigration was a lamentable result of, not a positive solution to, economic distress. It was in opposing emigration that Cobbett referred to Prince Edward Island as "a rascally heap of sand and rock and swamp." The rest of the region was "one great heap of rocks, covered with fir trees." Colonies served only the interests of the idle rich, much like Malthusianism, that "infamous and really diabolical ... mixture of madness and of blasphemy."[27] Yet colonial travel writers were among those convinced that colonies could serve more than the aristocracy and its clients by providing homes for Britain's "surplus" population, agricultural producers to feed Britain's increasing urban population, and consumers to purchase Britain's manufactured goods. Colonization could restore optimism. "Thus," concluded Buckingham, "might we fulfil the first command of the Deity to his creatures, to 'increase and multiply, and replenish the earth.'" Colonization would vindicate economic development; "working out," according to Outram, "the beneficent design of Providence by occupying and subduing the earth."[28]

In framing Britain's postwar problems in terms of overpopulation, if not in their unchecked enthusiasm for emigration, Maritime travellers were Malthusians. Indeed, while discussing emigration from Ireland to Nova Scotia, an anonymous author made the only reference to the political economist by name. "I have read Malthus" he insisted, but criticized the political economist for failing to identify papal doctrine as a cause of overpopulation and contended that his theory failed when tested against the traveller's own observations of Shelburne fishing families who combined poverty with prolificacy.[29] Without invoking his name, other travellers relied on Malthusian ideas to make sense of what they saw. George Head proved the inappropriateness of the "life and habits" of the local Mi'kmaq to his own satisfaction by pointing to their slow population growth despite "the absence of restraints" common to more "advanced" peoples. Conversely, William Scarth Moorsom took the fact that Nova Scotia's non-Native population appeared to double every fourteen years primarily by natural increase as evidence that "the certainty with which a sufficient maintenance can be ensured ... quash[es] all those anxieties respecting the probability of future provision, that act with such preventive force upon the inhabitants of most European states." The principle of population thus "acts as forcible in this province as in any other part of the globe."[30] However it fared against colonial experience, travellers brought the test with them.

Their discussion of population and emigration also reveals travellers' affinities with Malthus's understanding of the methods and scope of political economy. While they might synthesize their observations into concluding chapters to offer more systematic advice to emigrants and intervene more directly in policy debates, several expressed "greatest diffidence and humility, and leave to political economists the elucidation of a subject which involves such difficult and intricate calculations" about what another called "abstract principles of political economy," preferring to limit themselves to a statement of "a few facts."[31] Such disclaimers may have been prompted by a fear of losing readers if their accounts were too controversial or difficult, but they also reflected a preference for observed experience over abstract theory. Thus, in response to "the host of politico-economical queries" from one fictitious correspondent, Moorsom pleaded that there were as yet few statistics and little discussion of "general principles" among Nova Scotians to furnish answers. In the meantime, "I shall merely attempt to sketch the outlines I have observed," relying on "personal impressions produced by casual observation ... and by conversation."[32] Such outlines, however sketchy, still relied on contested economic ideas and assumptions which, in Moorsom's case, included Malthus's principle of population.

By the very nature of how they gathered information and wrote about the colonies, travellers endorsed the inductive method at a time when Ricardian economic analysis sought to construct a deductive model capable of generating clear axioms from "strong cases" derived from advanced economies like Britain's. Most travellers lacked the technical skill to contribute to such a science which, in turn, had little interest in the places they visited or in what appeared from its perspective as the anarchy of their incidental observations. For Malthus, on the other hand, "the science of political economy bears a nearer resemblance to the science of morals and politics than to that of mathematics." He repeatedly appealed to the "test of experience" as "the only just foundation for theory" and insisted on "reasonings from [observable] effects to causes" rather than from theoretical propositions to effects. Such a test was strongest when those effects could be traced in "the different states of society in which man has existed." Travel was transformed into field work. After all, the second edition of his *Essay* (1803) had been much enlarged by information Malthus had recorded in his own travel diaries during a tour of Scandinavia, France, and Switzerland.[33] Travellers to the Maritimes participated in such an inductive and comparative political economy, just as its more systematic accounts informed what they saw there.

LIBERAL PROSPECTS

With the exception of John Mann, a visitor who emigrated to New Brunswick but left discouraged,[34] travel authors stressed the region's economic opportunities, contributing to the flood of print extolling emigration. Into the 1850s, the region was repeatedly described as "young," "new" or in its "infancy," signalling its greater potential for rapid economic growth than "old" countries, not the time lapsed since European settlement.[35] Comparing "new" with "old" shed light on the conditions for prosperity. The first edition of Malthus's *Principles* demonstrated the doctrine of rent "in the early periods of society," but the second edition (1836) argued it was "necessary to direct our attention to the establishment and progressive cultivation of new colonies" instead.[36] Travellers to some of those colonies "anticipate[d] their future greatness" since their resources were "boundless." Everything lay in the future – in "what this unsubdued spot is yet to become."[37] Attuned to the relationship between population and food, what it could become was best measured by the number of inhabitants it could feed. Estimates for New Brunswick ranged from three to nearly five and a half million.[38] Colonies offered unparalleled economic opportunity precisely because they were underpopulated. If, as Julian Gwyn's recent economic history of Nova Scotia concludes, expectations were "excessive," travellers were a major source of the excess. Indeed, claims by James Johnston that New Brunswick could produce enough food for a local population of five and a half million led one

Canadian visitor to caution against opinions "so highly eulogistic, that the candid observer may feel inclined to call in question the veracity of their statements."[39]

Yet, however "eulogistic" about the region's prospects their reports undoubtedly were, travellers cautioned potential emigrants against just such excessive expectations. They insisted that the region was no place for "sanguine *el dorada* expectations." It offered neither a "royal road to wealth and independence" nor an escape "from the fatigues and toils of life" imposed by "the curse of the Almighty" on Adam to labour or starve.[40] On the contrary, emigration was a severe trial; "a hard probation" of physical labour, sacrifice, and privation. "Nature" provided opportunity, but only "industry, perseverance, and *good management*" could transform potential into prosperity.[41] Thus, not everyone prospered, but poverty and failure "appear to be the punishment of indolence and vice; and only tend to prove, that virtuous industry alone will ensure happiness with riches."[42] Travellers insisted repeatedly that "in every instance" people were rewarded with material success for their labour, self-denial, and sound judgment and punished with poverty only for the lack of such virtues.[43] Thus the attempt to prosper *materially* by emigration was a test of *moral* fitness. There could be no firmer repudiation of Bernard Mandeville's infamous paradox that private vice produced public benefit.

Since material results tracked individual effort and moral worth, the test was impartial and inequalities that resulted just. The test was also redemptive. According to Walter Johnstone, an impoverished shoemaker teaching Sunday School and peddling religious tracts across Prince Edward Island, emigrants "are all here placed on a level, and taught one lesson, namely, that *if they wish to eat, they must work*. The unfortunate have here an opportunity, by patient industry and good economy, to attain to comparative comfort and independence. The profligate are urged by their wants to study sobriety and good conduct; and the dishonest have few opportunities to rob and steal." Likewise, Moorsom asked his readers to "take the most accomplished scoundrel from the purlieus of the British metropolis; suppose ... that emigration has fixed him in an American forest-farm" and to then watch the ensuing test result in either his sound moral character or flight. As yet another put it, "industry is the only passport to wealth and honours."[44]

Such insistence implied that the test of economic life was less just in Britain; that there were other passports to success and that individual merit might go unrewarded. Malthus was harshly critical of the "indolence" of Ireland's rural poor. "In defence, however, of the Irish peasant, it may be truly said, that in the state of society in which he has been placed, he has not had a fair trial; he has not been subjected to the ordinary stimulants which produce industrious habits." With every incentive to develop such habits, the Maritimes offered just such a fair trial. "A Late Resident" of Prince Edward Island thought emigration beneficial for "those who have proceeded where an extent of population is such as to prevent the industrious from enjoying the fruits of their labour." Virtue's material rewards were greater and more sure in the Maritimes.[45] Poverty was reserved to chastise or reform. Others emphasized that children became economic assets rather than a liability. Emigrants could look forward to seeing them married, economically secure, and perhaps settled nearby, again in stark contrast to the pressure in Britain to postpone marriage or migrate in search of opportunity.[46] More than providing work for Britain's "redundant" population, the Maritime economy confirmed the tenets of economic liberalism.

But what precisely were the rewards for virtue? Despite disagreement about the mechanics of emigration and resettlement, travellers joined the widespread celebration of "competence and independence" or "comparative comfort and independence."[47] Rather than wealth, this meant property ownership, the social extent of which struck British visitors who, like William Chambers, were more accustomed to seeing tenants than "farming in which each husbandman tills his own land, and has neither factor nor tax-collector to trouble him."[48] In turn, such broad property ownership meant greater family security; the absence of the economic and social dependence that marked subsistence peasants, tenant farmers, and wage-workers; and the absence of the extremes of wealth and poverty visible in Europe.[49] Thus, travellers celebrated the ideal of "competency" that motivated many to emigrate and that continued to guide many North American households. It was the North American equivalent of the widespread endorsement among British political economists of a society with a large middle class that lacked extreme inequalities.[50]

Such a truncated society fostered liberal virtues. Frances Beaven assured her readers that the sons of New Brunswick immigrants "proudly take their place as men, knowing that by their own conduct and talents they may work their way to fortune ... without dread that the might of custom's icy breath can blight their fate for lack of birth or fortune." A Canadian visitor added that "there are no favoured classes – no exclusive privileges – no absurd and depressing monopolies – no checks or hindrances to laudable ambition – no station unattainable by patient industry and honest worth."[51] In a "new" country, the economy functioned as an impartial judge of individual merit, stimulating intellect and worthy ambition, rewarding virtue and exertion, and promoting "manly independence" and loyalty without "servility," among other domestic and social virtues.[52] No wonder Johnston told the "yeomen" of New Brunswick that "there are, at this moment, twenty times the number of your entire population among the slaving labourers and craftsmen of Great Britain who envy your lot."[53]

But how could travellers be so certain of the region's future? Observing its existing population, they recounted stories of individual success or failure as morality tales about the consequences of particular norms and behaviour. Invoking the proverb that "example is better than precept," Harriet Martineau's best-selling *Illustrations of Political Economy* (1832–34) employed fictional narratives to paint a "picture" of the propositions of political economy that would be "more clear and interesting" to general readers. Likewise, Maritime travellers used individual stories to didactic effect, but their "sketches and tales" were purportedly "gleaned from actual observation and experience."[54] Martineau travelled to the United States to test her *Illustrations* against her observations of *Society in America* (1837).[55] Observers of society in the Maritimes grounded their narratives in the observable details of fields, fences, dress, and shelter, but offered them as illustrations or "the visible consequence" of unobservable habits and norms.[56]

BALANCED GROWTH

In a fine example of such morality tales, Frances Beaven compared the fate of two English emigrants to rural New Brunswick. One applied his labour exclusively to farming. Impatient with the slow returns of pioneer agriculture, his neighbour turned to "lumbering." The latter bought provisions on credit from merchants in return for timber delivered the following spring. He was ambitious, enterprising, and laboured hard to extract a colonial staple in response to market demand which enabled him to consume manufactured goods. As a result, he was ruined. The former, relying whenever possible on family labour and the produce of his own farm, surveyed his fine fields from a new house and barn. Years of labour, self-denial, and relative self-reliance "had literally caused the wilderness to blossom as the rose." His neighbour, animated by the profit motive and living by the laws of supply and demand, reaped only failure.[57] How could promoters of economic development disparage market-oriented behaviour? How could such outcomes be just?

Clearly, simply transplanting Britons to the Maritimes to increase their access to productive resources ensured neither their economic well-being nor the region's development. Travellers did not merely moralize about the rewards and punishments of virtue and industry. They contributed to an economic analysis of how such norms could be fostered to reward the worthy and meet the two requirements of growth: the production of a surplus and the use of that surplus to increase productive capacity. How any surplus was used depended on the values and behaviour of those who controlled it.[58] In the Maritimes, dominated by petty commodity producers who relied primarily on family labour, most of any surplus remained in the hands of those who produced it. Thus, their habits determined not only individual economic outcomes, but also the pace of regional economic development. Transplanting economic subjects was insufficient without subject-formation; that is, unless the values conducive to prosperity were internalized.

Just as clearly, Beaven's parable demonstrates that not all economic activities were thought to foster such values. As Graeme Wynn has noted, criticism of the timber trade was widespread and drew on multiple sources. Yet such criticism complicates any view of travellers as seeking only to extract resources, maximize production, and encourage markets. It also resembles Malthus's concerns about Britain's increasing dependence on manufacturing at the expense of agriculture. Sensitive to the social and moral costs of economic change and interested in the conditions for long-term and stable growth, Malthus cautioned against too great a reliance on manufacturing. It increased pauperism; employment and wages were unstable; and workers were at the mercy of fluctuations in demand, changes in fashion, and competition from foreign suppliers. Manufacturing jobs and the larger towns where they were concentrated were also less conducive to workers' health and morality than agricultural labour. A balance between agriculture and manufacturing should be maintained. Even if the latter generated wealth, if it entailed greater risk, insecurity, and cyclical fluctuations harmful to workers' health and morality, "I should have no hesitation in considering such wealth and population as much too dearly purchased. The happiness of society is, after all, the legitimate end even of its wealth, power, and population." Ricardo conceded that agriculture might be more profitable in some circumstances and that it was a necessary prerequisite for manufacturing, but he strove to insulate political economy from such moral and social concerns. Wealth was, after all, the sole object of political economy. If such wealth was best generated by continued industrialization, as Ricardo was convinced it was in Britain, so be it.[59] Maritime travellers, however, shared Malthus's perspective, transposing his concerns about manufacturing to the timber trade. But they insisted that the latter failed to maximize growth precisely because of the habits it promoted. As the fate of the two emigrants in Beaven's parable attested, there was no trade-off between wealth and happiness.

Just as Malthus's concerns about manufacturing moderated over time,[60] so travellers' antipathy toward the timber trade varied and is easy to exaggerate. Most acknowledged that it had paid for imports, built towns, allowed poor emigrants to purchase supplies before their farms became productive, and created local markets for subsequent agricultural surpluses. Even its more determined critics conceded that reorganized on a reduced scale, it could be of long-term benefit to the colonies.[61] Yet the imaginary interlocutor of one traveller declare the timber trade "the ruin of this country."[62] Such hyperbole was especially evident in the aftermath of the commercial crisis of 1826. A number even welcomed the crisis as a harsh lesson to colonial producers on the need to rededicate their efforts to agriculture.[63] Belief in the division of labour was part of the reason. Travellers thought that farming could not be successful if owners of fertile land were distracted, but their concerns centred on those who spent most of their time lumbering. Agriculture taught habits of steady industry, patience, and self-reliance that were not only morally praiseworthy, but also promoted colonial economic development. Lumbering habituated its participants to the opposite norms and so had the opposite effects.

Vulnerable to market fluctuations beyond colonists' control, the timber trade was risky in ways travellers contended agriculture was not. Shifts in British demand or supply from competitors, modifications in British trade policy or even unpredictable weather could ruin individual producers with no regard to their own actions. Several season's worth of labour would then go unrewarded. Agricultural markets, on the other hand, were unlikely to disappear, especially given Britain's increasing reliance on imported food, and even if they did, farming at least provided its producers with food and other necessities. To procure such provisions, lumberers instead went into debt, gambling on an adequate return for their timber the following spring. If their gamble failed, not only did their labour go unrewarded, but their future was blighted by debts that entailed a loss of independence as well as money.[64] Working for others was a form of dependency common in Britain but unnecessary in the Maritimes. Thus, lumbering was "speculative" or even a "lottery."

This uncertainty of a return sapped lumberers' willingness to labour and exercise foresight. If the gamble failed, they were unable to save or otherwise contribute to capital formation for years to come. Even when their labour was well rewarded, "professed lumberers and raftsmen" oscillated seasonally between hard labour in the "wilderness" and idleness in towns where few could resist the temptations of alcohol, extravagant "foreign luxuries," and "expensive entertainments" – a spree of "idleness and enjoyments" – made possible by ready cash from a successful season. The steady industry and delayed gratification of colonial agriculture became repugnant; the food and homespun of colonial farms distasteful.[65] Generating a surplus was not enough if those who controlled it lacked the moral values and habits to forgo unproductive consumption – the heart of most political economists' complaints about large landowners in Britain who had the means but not the desire to save and invest rather than gratify their desire for luxuries.[66]

'Spendthrift habits," the lack of foresight and self-discipline, and the analogy to unproductive elite consumption were most visible in the symbolic realm of dress. Meeting a group of young men on the road, "those who have been lumbering may easily be known among the others," Frances Beaven informed her readers, "by sporting a flashy stock or waistcoat, and by being arrayed in '*boughten*' clothes, procured in town at a most expensive rate in lieu of their *lumber.*" John MacGregor added "flashy" trousers, boots, watch and chain, and umbrella to the picture of cocky youth aping the leisured gentleman. Even "his step," Beaven noted, "is firm and free, as though he trod on marble floor" instead of a precarious structure of debt.[67] The symbolic status accorded to homespun underlined the importance of women's work to household independence. The credit made available by a father's participation in the timber trade raised the expectations and tastes of his daughters. As a result, they "must be dressed in all the elegance of British or French manufacture, and, instead of attending to the duties of domestic economy, their days and nights must be employed in reading novels, butchering tunes upon the pianoforte, and playing cards." Such young women – better flirts than future wives and mothers – contributed as little to their own long-term well-being as to their fathers' farms.[68]

Likewise, male lumberers saved little and worked less on the land, thereby adding nothing to their own or the region's capital. They worked hard, participated in markets, and increased the colony's demand for imported goods, but even the few who succeeded failed to "improve" themselves or the region. For most, the risks of the trade eventually left them in debt, physically impaired, emotionally "dispirited," and without "the inclination and even capacity for consistent and steady industry." Absent the discipline of such steady labour and the prudence imposed by colonial agriculture, lumberers internalized the wrong norms. "Demoralized," they suffered the consequences, but so too did the region's economy.[69]

Mixing transplanted labour with the region's resources, even in a market context, was insufficient. Only when it reflected certain virtues was labour consistently rewarded and growth assured. Travellers contended that the rewards of agricultural labour, while not as immediate, were more certain and permanent because of the virtuous habits such labour fostered (in part, because they were not immediate). They were also an investment, increasing the region's productive capacity and thus improving the returns to future labour.[70] The result was not a few flashy clothes, but the comfort, security, and satisfaction that came from making the "wilderness" blossom to the benefit of family, colony, and empire. Yet were markets and consumption always so problematic? If lumberers failed to use any surplus they generated to improve the region's productive capacity, would colonial farmers, substituting for middle-class capitalists, produce and invest their surplus or would they behave like semi-subsistence peasants who either generated no surplus at all or consumed it? Could individuals be made to alter their behaviour and become habituated to new norms without such catastrophic "lessons" as the commercial collapse of 1826?

EFFECTUAL DEMAND

If the road to prosperity was clearly marked, why did some not take it? Confronted by such people, travellers were forced to grapple with questions of economic motivation. They sought to explain the gap they perceived between the region's economic potential and its actual performance, but it was the gap between supply and demand that, in the same decades, was central to debates about whether Britain's postwar depression reflected a partial or general glut. Ricardo accepted Jean-Baptiste Say's "law of markets" whereby the supply of goods and services generated sufficient income to purchase them. The power to purchase always met the supply, making a general glut of goods and services impossible. A mismatch between supply and demand in particular segments of the market – a partial glut – explained the distress, but would be corrected as rational economic actors responded to the market's price signals by reallocating resources from lost opportunities to new ones. Say's law seemed to promise self-regulating, harmonious, and potentially limitless industrial development. Yet, despite its centrality to Ricardian orthodoxy, doubts about Say's law were widespread.[71]

Malthus certainly thought it failed the test of experience. Whereas, for Ricardo, in modern societies "give men but the means of purchasing and their wants are insatiable," Malthus emphasized the distinction in all societies between the power to purchase and the will to do so. The "will to consume" was as important as the "power to produce" if the productive potential of an area was to be achieved. "The wants and tastes of society" varied. Leisure might be chosen over the work needed to purchase "luxuries." As Malthus wrote to Ricardo, "you constantly say that it is not a question about the motives to produce. Now I have certainly intended to make it almost entirely a question about motives. We see in almost every part of the world vast powers of production which are not put into action, and I explain this phenomenon by saying that ... adequate motives are not furnished to continue production." While there was broad agreement that growth in underdeveloped economies required increased local demand, it was Malthus who was most identified with concerns about aggregate demand, reflecting his belief that markets were not always self-regulating and that while the increased production of food might bring forth the population to consume it, increased industrial production might not bring forth the demand to purchase it.[72]

By rejecting Say's law, Malthus cast a pall over Britain's economic future. Others, most notably Edward Gibbon Wakefield, drew on Malthus and his under-consumptionist critique of Ricardo, but, beginning in 1829, argued that there was still reason for optimism. "Systematically colonized," settler societies might not only absorb Britain's surplus population, but also consume its surplus industrial output and employ its surplus capital profitably. Wakefield proposed settling emigrants in concentrated areas where the price of Crown land would be set high enough to force most of them to sell their labour for wages for a considerable period of time, thereby creating a labour pool for capital and a market for exports. The availability of labour would make larger agricultural enterprises possible, attracting capital that could not be employed as profitably in Britain to aggressively pursue economic surpluses and contribute to local capital formation. Otherwise, Wakefield feared, emigrants would avoid wage dependence and the work discipline it imposed by becoming semi-subsistence farmers who would consume few British manufactures and neither attract capital nor accumulate their own.[73]

Although Wakefield's ideas influenced imperial land policy in the region, the Crown controlled too little land in colonies such as Nova Scotia and Prince Edward Island to conduct a full-scale trial.[74] Travellers also feared the reproduction a semi-subsistence peasantry, and explored an alternative model of development. Whereas Ricardo and his followers drew on recent British experience to argue that capitalists' savings were the principal source of capital accumulation, many travellers to the Maritimes were convinced that enterprising farm families could propel development by improving their land and thus increasing the region's production and productivity. Anticipating John Stuart Mill's famous repudiation of classical orthodoxy on peasant proprietorship, travellers believed that land could be an investment, not just the means of subsistence, even for small-scale owner-occupier households. With security of tenure and in the absence of landlords or a tax-hungry state, such households had the incentive to work harder and invest because the benefits of such frugal behaviour rebounded almost exclusively to themselves.[75] But why would they invest rather than consume or opt for greater leisure? What would provide the necessary work-discipline? Sustaining an important theme from the Scottish Enlightenment, Malthus pointed to the answer. Since he thought that the preference for indolence over goods "seems to be very general in the early periods of society," he found evidence in Alexander Humboldt's observations of South America to suggest that "the greatest of all difficulties in converting uncivilized and thinly peopled countries into civilized and populous ones, is to inspire them with the wants best calculated to excite their exertions in the production of wealth."[76] Wakefield counted on the discipline of capitalist employers, but Malthus, like Maritime travellers, put his stock in "new wants" that would increase agricultural capacity as colonial households strove to satisfy them. If Wakefield proposed a middle-class empire by transplanting both capitalists and labourers, travellers proposed a middle-class empire without such institutionalized inequalities by making as many settlers as possible middle class.

Malthus had turned to South America for evidence, but Moorsom toured rural Nova Scotia to "observe how the wilds of uncultivated nature operate on her adopted children of civilization." He found further evidence for the under-consumption thesis and the economic psychology that underpinned it. Struck, like nearly every traveller, by the "very mixed description" of the population, Moorsom introduced his comparison of Highland and Lowland Scots in Nova Scotia by noting that "great diversity of condition prevails among the settlers, in proportion as their habits have been industrious or indolent."[77] As already emphasized, economic success or failure reflected "habits" or learned group behaviour. During the period of heightened immigration to the region, travellers turned to national or ethnic groups essentialized to express different economic values. The Maritime countryside became a laboratory in which to compare economic types.

Such an approach overshadowed a number of alternative explanations of economic performance, including the quantity or quality of land a group had settled; the circumstances and date of its arrival in the region; and whether it faced discrimination. Since emigrants were not a cross-section of their country of origin, a class element was also obscured. When opining that Scottish emigrants were accustomed to privation, Edward Coke acknowledged he was referring to Scotland's "lower orders."[78] Few others made the clarification. Nonetheless, "nature" had been bountiful and, according to travellers, so too had the British government. Land had been made available, "improved" methods encouraged by agricultural societies and exhibitions, military and naval defence provided, and property and civil rights protected all with little or no direct taxation.[79] Shortfalls in prosperity, then, reflected a failure to internalize the requisite norms.

From his tour of Prince Edward Island, Walter Johnstone of Dumfries-shire, Scotland concluded that "sober and industrious" Lowland Scots made the best emigrants. Their "habits," skills, domestic arrangements, and willingness to endure privations improved their chances of economic success. Highland Scots "and the well-behaved Irish" ranked next, followed by "the English as the most unsuitable of all." Their experience and habits made adapting to colonial agriculture and its sacrifices difficult. For instance, Johnstone thought many English women were unable or unwilling to work in the fields or at domestic manufacturing. Immigrants "in want of steady moral habits" could never be "comfortable," but the habits best suited to the Island were more common in some national groups than others.[80]

Other travellers ranked Highland Scots and especially the Irish lower than did Johnstone. Acadians typically anchored their scale. None talked of "British" settlers. John MacGregor, a former Island merchant and high sheriff, agreed with Johnstone that Lowland Scots made the best immigrant farmers, but placed the English next if they persevered. Highland Scots followed despite their insufficient ambition because the Irish, "more anxious in general to gain a temporary advantage" than undergo the trial of colonial agriculture, worked for wages and fell victim to the temptations of drink. Acadians, despite the remarkable industry of the women, "are not in such easy circumstances as the other inhabitants of the island."[81] The willingness of women to work in the fields was praiseworthy, but reflected badly on their husbands if it was the result of the men's preference for fishing or lumbering over agriculture and reduced their wives to "perfect drudges." Most immigrants, however, came to "consider it '*agin all nature*' for women to work" in the fields for, according to Frances Beaven, "here women's empire is within, not in idleness, for in America, of all countries of the world, prosperity depends on female industry."[82] Here, households were typically seen as a single, though not necessarily equitable or consensual, unit of production and consumption. Here it was also evident that economic habits, including the gender division of labour, varied by national group and correlated with their different degrees of material success. The precise ranking might vary, but the criterion remained the same – the extent to which the group exhibited the habits and virtues travellers deemed essential to colonial economic development and household prosperity. Even as they obscured and minimized the challenges faced by the region's farming households, important precepts of liberal political economy lurked behind otherwise trite expressions of "national character."

Acadians attracted particular attention because, despite their European origins and prolonged residence in the region, they seemed especially unable or unwilling to take full advantage of its opportunities. Some acknowledged differences among Acadian communities or defended them against the more hostile criticisms of their neighbours,[83] but others judged their economic performance harshly. For Joshua Marsden, they were "indolent in the extreme, seldom cultivating more land than is sufficient to supply their present wants," backward in their agricultural methods, and lacking cleanliness and comfort in their "despicable huts." All "this is more culpable" complained another, "as there is no want of a market" to incite improvement.[84] They remained, most concluded, little changed from the seventeenth century,[85] a stationary society amid opportunities for economic advancement.

Relative material poverty proved Acadians lacked the norms necessary for colonial prosperity, but why had they not developed those norms? Why did they not cultivate more land or adopt the latest methods of "improvement?" Repeatedly, the answer was that they were content. They achieved the same level of material success their fathers had and lacked the ambition to achieve more. Their wants were few and easily satisfied. Unaware of or uninterested in "luxuries," Acadians were "therefore independent of them, and live among themselves happy, and comparatively free of cares which accompany the refinements of civilisation." For James Johnston, being satisfied with less was "not so beneficial to the commonwealth" since it limited their economic activity, but "one cannot mix with these people without feeling that this easy contentment may possibly be more productive of positive worldly happiness to them, as individuals, than the restless, discontented striving, burning energy of their Saxon neighbours." Wealth was not synonymous with happiness. Travellers were not accusing Acadians of irrationality for failing to maximize production (although the charge that they clung to agricultural methods that required more effort to produce the same results did). Acadians simply did without economic opportunities they had no need of. As Moorsom put it, "they are satisfied with their condition as it is ... and beyond this they do not care to make any further exertion."[86] Why would they? They pursued non-economic activities they valued more instead of working to obtain material advantages they valued less or not at all.[87] To put it another way, commodities were not worth the labour they cost. Not wanting more, Acadians had no incentive to work more. In the absence of a master, employer, or tax-gatherer, greater industry required the spur of discontent.

Highland Scots were seen through the same interpretative lens. Hardy and able to endure privations, they had yet to learn a better "system of agricultural and domestic management."[88] Again, happiness was the culprit. Without increasing production or productivity, they were able to achieve in the Maritimes as much as their forefathers had in the Highlands before deteriorating conditions had forced their emigration. Upon regaining this level in the colonies, "a spirit of contentment is apt to steal upon them, which becomes a bar to subsequent improvement." Lacking the ambition "for raising themselves and their families to a state of comfort and abundance" they were, said Moorsom, "too easily satisfied" or, as Johnstone put it, "they neither wished nor sought for more."[89] Economic wants and ambition were cultural. Contentment was a bar to prosperity.

If Acadian and Highland farmers were "too easily satisfied," English ones were thought too difficult. To maintain standards of cleanliness and comfort they were supposedly habituated to, many dissipated any capital they brought with them or fell into debt, often abandoning their "wilderness" farms just as their toil was about to reap its rewards.[90] Like ambition, perseverance was central to the region's moral economy. Only Lowland Scots struck the right balance. Having learned "lessons of self-denial" in Scotland, they were more able and willing to make sacrifices, endure hardships, and "supply more of their own wants with their own hands" than the English. Unlike the Acadians and Highlanders, however, they were also ambitious. Willing to forgo luxuries and comforts to acquire and improve property, once their "steady habits" were rewarded, they "at last build respectable homes, and enjoy the fruits of their industry."[91] Opportunities to gratify material wants were delayed in favour of investment, not forgone. Perhaps there was something to a quip repeated by Walter Bagehot that "Adam Smith's economics assumed that there was a Scotchman in every man."[92]

Transplantation to colonies with greater economic opportunities was not enough. By nature, "man" was indolent, not acquisitive and materialistic. The first "spur to industry" was what Malthus called the "goad of necessity." The need for food and shelter, however, was less effective in overcoming idleness and improvidence in the Maritimes because "nature" had been so bountiful that, according to Moorsom, "even indolence can procure" subsistence.[93] Indeed, travellers grumbled that "nature" had been too generous, reducing the pressure on inhabitants to produce. Acadians and Highland Scots showed all too clearly the risk of merely reproducing an old-world peasantry in the "new." The spectre of another Ireland haunted many travellers. The second spur to industry emphasized by Malthus was the pressure of population on subsistence. For those unwilling to lower their standard of living, a period of delayed gratification was required during which habits of industry, economy, and prudence were inculcated,[94] but this stimulant was also weaker in the Maritimes. Young children might increase demands on individual households, but the relative abundance of land and the high cost of labour relative to food meant that there was no need to postpone marriage. Thus, despite their seemingly limited and inefficient production, Acadians were able to marry early and sustain the larger families that resulted.[95]

Resettlement in the region was a partial substitute for population pressure since it too might enforce a period of delayed gratification. One guide was confident that emigrants "will find that the difficulties of settling in a new country will only prove an incitement to labour."[96] Yet the English showed that such difficulties could have other effects. Moreover, for others the test was only temporary. Once resettled might not "that natural indolence which induces a man to rest satisfied if he can '*make out*'" prevail, Moorsom asked.[97] Highland farmers testified to the risk. So did emigrants' sons. Benefiting from their fathers' success and living in a hospitable region, the native-born "did not require to work so hard to obtain" a competency and thus acquired bad habits instead of the virtuous industry emigration had stimulated in their fathers.[98]

What, then, could motivate the effort required to propel economic development beyond "making out?" Several followed Adam Smith in identifying the desire to rise in society and achieve independence as "stimulants to unwearied exertion." Its efficacy was obvious to travellers observing emigrants from England and the Scottish Lowlands, but they joined Malthus in dissenting from Smith's conviction that this desire "comes with us from the womb, and never leaves us till we go into the grave."[99] As observations of Acadian and Highland farmers seemed to demonstrate, the desire to better one's condition was neither natural nor universal. Malthus deemed secondary or artificial wants to be crucial stimulants to industry if economies were not to stagnate from inadequate aggregate demand. With new or more intense wants came new incentives to work, delay gratification, and exercise foresight. "Cultivating a spirit of independence, a decent pride, and a taste for cleanliness and comfort among the poor" was the best means to improve their condition. They would avoid improvident behaviour if it meant "being obliged to forfeit such advantages; and would consequently raise them nearer the middle classes of society."[100]

An anonymous traveller summarized these challenges to regional economic development. Without taxes or rents to pay, a presumably imaginary group of Nova Scotian settlers told him that "'we pocket the whole product of our labours. We have no sufficient stimulus to exertion beyond the obtainment of a competent provision for ourselves and families.'" "'But what,'" the traveller asked, "'is a competent provision?'" "Oh we wish to subsist just as our fathers before us. A small quantity of labour in the summer months gives us all the necessaries of life, and, with respect to luxuries we are wholly ignorant of them."[101] There were too few obstacles to demand greater self-discipline. Without the struggle to overcome them there was no test of moral character and no incentive to "improve." Writing to encourage emigration, travellers did not seriously advocate high taxes, an instant class of landlords to accrue rent,[102] or relocation to a stingier physical environment. The task of development in an underpopulated agrarian colony dominated by owner-occupiers was not to get inhabitants to produce more, but to get them to want to produce more. Despite all their complaints about indolence and slovenly agriculture, travellers' focus, like Malthus's, was ultimately on demand – the motives to consume – rather than the extent or mechanics of production. New wants would create discontent and thus spur the industry by which individuals and societies improved materially and morally. Surveying national groups in the Maritimes, travellers championed a form of what Jan De Vries aptly calls the "industrious revolution." Leisure was to be traded for the more efficient and intense use of family labour directed toward capital accumulation. Once securely underway, household demand would be redirected from domestic production to market goods and the other embellishments of social, aesthetic, and moral life to meet delayed or new aspirations and tastes.[103]

The human instinct to emulate was capable of breaking down old habits and generating those new ambitions and wants. Thus markets served important cultural, as well as economic, functions. Like agricultural exhibitions, they exposed people to "examples" to imitate and compete with and "luxuries" to desire.[104] Accordingly, the tendency of Acadians to live apart and to limit their participation in markets perpetuated a "reverence for the habits of their fathers."[105] John MacGregor offered the best morality tale on this point. "On one occasion," a young Joseph Gallant "ventured to put on an English-made-coat" rather than the homespun costume of his people "and he has never since, even among this relations, been called by his proper name ... which has been supplanted by that of 'Joe Peacock.'" Whereas moralist critics of commerce might see cultural authenticity in the homespun garment and envy and enlarged appetites in the manufactured coat, MacGregor saw opportunities for individual choice and economic growth in the latter. So "religiously tenacious" were Acadians to their ancestral custom that any change in dress was ridiculed, effectively stifling the emulation required to stimulate new wants and the ambition "to rise in the world above the condition in which they have lived since their first settling in America."[106] Likewise, criticism of Highland Scots was generally reserved for those not "mixed" with others "by whose example they might be stimulated to exertion, and from whom they might learn." In the midst of others, the Highland emigrant "ceases to be so easily satisfied, and their pride inspires them with a desire to emulate, and even to excel." Emulation and rivalry created new habits instead of reinforcing old ones. Where the economy was just, these human instincts ensured that the habits acquired were virtuous ones.[107]

Identifying "artificial" wants as a necessary motor of economic development was not inconsistent with criticism of market-based consumption by lumberers, some Irish emigrants, and certain classes of wives and daughters. Repeating a commonplace, MacGregor distinguished a "spirit of enterprise" from "speculative pursuits." The latter were "a source of adventurous rather than profitable enterprise."[108] Lumberers, for example, increased demand by consumption, but their access to cash or credit without the foresight and willingness to delay gratification made them reckless and wasteful. They thereby failed to increase the region's productive assets and remained dependent on the market's demand for their labour and thus vulnerable to its fluctuations. Conversely, farmers' prudence and self-discipline increased the region's productive capacity and made their participation in markets beneficial to themselves and others. They delayed much of that participation until they were independent petty producers who could exchange surpluses from land made increasingly productive by the household labour they continued to invest in it. Such demand, unlike that of lumberers, was sustainable. They did not risk their "independence" and, thus, their ability to invest and consume, on a "gamble." Their demand stimulated additional industry, improved the land, and created conditions favourable to importing manufactured goods and capital from Britain. Virtuous industry ensured that they participated in markets as independent commodity producers; that is, when markets stimulated ambition, offered choice and opportunity, and most closely resembled the liberal ideal of mutually beneficial exchange among equals rather than a threat or loss of control.[109]

Thus, by comparing national groups, travellers confirmed a number of propositions. First, economic opportunity alone did not ensure individual prosperity or economic development. Second, particular moral virtues could be brought to correlate to material success. Third, those virtues and the ambitions and wants that created the conditions by which they could be inculcated were not natural, timeless, or universal traits of some abstract "economic man," but the contingent attributes of particular types of economic subjects in particular settings. Instruction, example, rivalry, and new incentive structures were required to foster the norms and behaviours appropriate to new circumstances, including those that resulted from emigration. Through repetition they too would become habitual or character-forming. For instance, left "unmixed," national groups retained habits that structured their production and consumption in ways that affected their material well-being – a conception of "economic culture" enjoying something of a renaissance as an explanation for persistent failures in international development.[110] Supply and demand did not operate in a cultural vacuum. "Economic man" had to be made, not found in the Maritimes.

It is tempting, then, to see Maritime travellers as amateur ethnographers. Like Malthus, they recognized that accepted minimum standards of living and the value of any commodity relative to its labour costs were matters of social habit or culture, not biological instinct.[111] Yet they lacked a more robust, ethnographic, sense of "culture." Before the 1850s, a few briefly noticed elements of language, costume, music, or dance, but these were not presented as elements of a unique and integrated system of meaning. Travellers of the Malthusian moment were interested in economic habits. Observed differences among national groups were treated as local manifestations of the principles of political economy.

Indeed, comparing Maritime settlers reinforced belief in the universality of those principles: "the peculiarities, distinctive of the natives of all the countries of the world, are the result of local and accidental circumstances" one opined; "the same combination of circumstances effects the same results in the east and the west, the north and the south."[112] Thus, similar judgments shifted easily from British social classes to European settlers and subject "races" in the empire. The Mi'kmaq, for instance, were thought poor from lack of "artificial wants" and the persistence of habits formed by hunting rather than settler agriculture.[113] Likewise, this analysis was applied to occupational groups such as "lumberers" and, in the hands of a visiting agricultural chemist, reflected stages of agricultural development more than nationality.[114] In sum, despite all their attention to national or "racial" groups, ultimately travellers were not interested in the diversity of the region's population, but in what Malthus called "the great causes which render a nation progressive, stationary or declining."[115]

Yet, aware that happiness and wealth were not synonymous, travellers were sensitive to the costs of such progress. Anxieties about those costs were especially evident when travellers reflected on a British economy that precluded most from independence and drove thousands to emigrate or on those residents in the Maritimes who, like the Acadians, were content with less and thereby embodied virtues travellers associated with pre-industrial societies and feared were disappearing in Britain. One especially hostile observer condemned Acadians' Catholicism, ignorance, and stasis, yet conceded that "there is something about them which pleases a stranger." They lived in harmony with each under the paternal care of their priest who settled their few disputes without recourse to the law. Their authentic communities sustained personal, face-to-face relations and distinctive traditions and amusements. Acadians were hospitable to strangers, took exemplary care of the sick, elderly, and orphans, and were paragons of sexual as well as social probity. Honest and innocent, they maintained a "primitive simplicity in dress, manners, and pursuits."[116] Acadians were not happy despite their relative material poverty but because of it. They were untroubled by the insecurities, cares, vanity, and ambitions of competitive neighbours who struggled to work harder to acquire more. Travellers mapped their economic fears as well as their hopes onto the Maritimes.

By the late 1840s, such Acadian villages were represented primarily as tourist attractions – romantic respites from modernity to display "primitive" folk and chaste beauties modelled on Evangeline.[117] The picture painted by travellers of the earlier, Malthusian moment was also tinged with romantic nostalgia for a supposedly simpler, more secure past in the face of post-Napoleonic economic distress. Certainly the sense of a pre-industrial world of community free from the constraints endemic to capitalist development informed later histories of a "moral economy" under threat,[118] but it ultimately revealed why travellers thought the costs of development worth paying. First, Acadians' failure to take full advantage of economic opportunities denied greater benefits to others. As Buckingham insisted, British emigrants could activate colonies' "dormant capacity for wealth" to produce food "far beyond their own power to consume" and thereby relieve Britain of its surplus population and production to the benefit of both emigrants and those who remained behind.[119] The development of colonial resources to complement Britain's industrial economy would offer greater benefits to a greater number of people.

And what if everyone limited production and productivity to satisfy such limited wants? There would be, as Malthus insisted, "no cities, no military or naval force, no arts, no learning, none of the finer manufactures, none of the conveniences and luxuries of foreign countries, and none of that cultivated and polished society, which not only elevates and dignifies individuals, but which extends its beneficial influence through the whole mass of the people."[120] In essence, by choosing custom and contentment over greater economic development, Acadians were selfish. If travellers were nostalgic, they looked less to the supposed "simplicity" of peasant or "savage" life than to an imagined yeoman past in Britain. "I doubt not" one recorded, "that travellers and historians have breathed a romantic colouring over" the "primitive habits" of the region's Aboriginal population. "All of us ... feel delight in the contemplation of a state of society, free from the trammels of artificial life and the conflicts of passions, which would have slumbered peacefully in our bosoms, but for circumstances which may be supposed to have no effect upon the inhabitants the forest," but economic development could not be "supposed" away without supposing away everything it made possible.[121]

Second, it followed that while the Acadian standard of living might satisfy their wants, it was only sufficient "for people in their station"; illiterate and unaware of "the refinements of civilisation." Development brought new cares and constraints, but also unprecedented material comfort and individual opportunity. In response to one traveller's wistful musings about their happiness, his imaginary guide was blunt: "The felicity which they enjoy ... is just that of the dog or the moose."[122] A "higher" form of contentment was possible in the Maritimes by making the right choices instead of blindly following custom.

Finally, however attractive travellers found aspects of Acadian society, it was not a liberal one. To outside observers, it was marked by stifling conformity, priestly paternalism, ignorance, dependence, severely limited opportunities, and stasis. Travellers may have feared that industrialization in Britain threatened social harmony and those virtues they associated with rural and pre-industrial societies, but the widespread propertied independence they sought for the Maritimes would reunite virtue and economic development in a liberal society. By creating new markets and removing the "surplus" population it would help restore economic fairness in Britain as well. Despite the real costs to a way of life, Joe Gallant might well have preferred to keep his British-manufactured coat.

VINDICATION

Had he visited the Maritimes, we can be confident Malthus would have used the opportunity to observe its inhabitants, especially in light of the propositions regarding population, sustainable growth, and aggregate demand he was most identified with. We cannot know what he would have concluded, although "America" often served as his model of the most fortune society.[123] Those who did travel to the Maritimes in the quarter century or so after the Napoleonic wars did so at a particular intellectual and economic moment. In Britain, it was a period of intense interest in political economy, especially as it related to Britain's postwar distress. In turn, those challenges pushed the waves of emigrants to the Maritimes at a time when sufficient land was thought available to reunite most of them with the eventual ownership of sufficient means of production. Travellers were thus prompted to consider the mechanisms of economic development under particular colonial conditions. They selected and framed their observations in light of the common economic ideas and assumptions of their time. Where the ideas and approaches of Malthus and Ricardo diverged, however, travellers' political economy was more akin to the former; emphasizing the economy as a moral trial, but fearing it was an increasingly capricious one in Britain; suspicious that industrialized economies were neither harmonious nor stable; convinced that demand was crucial, but historically and culturally determined; and wedded to an economic psychology that underwrote such an under-consumptionist perspective. Most were, after all, writing at a time when Ricardian political economy was on the defensive.[124]

Travellers may have been the quintessential "improvers," denigrating European and non-European groups as "indolent" or "backward" for failing to take full advantage of economic opportunities they identified, but ideas, not just cultural bromides, were at stake. At a certain level of abstraction, those ideas contributed to the contested "liberal order" emerging in this period.[125] Travellers promoted economic development via the region's further integration into global markets based on formal equality, individualism, and private property. Inequality was a reward for superior industry and virtue and socially useful to the extent that it prompted emulation. Satisfying one's own wants could also foster economic development. Travellers sought to create liberal subjects capable of regulating their economic behaviour within such a pro-development framework. Yet they were not thereby committed to an impoverished view of the self as a relentlessly hedonistic maximizer competing with other atomized subjects in a materialistic world in which morality was reduced to expediency and social relations to the cash nexus. Such a caricature better suited beavers than humans. It misdescribes economic liberalism, substituting a convenient label for the messy intellectual reality in which contemporaries grappled with difficult questions and potentially competing values. It makes it impossible to understand how contemporaries understood the economy and therefore their motives and behaviour. Certainly economic and business historians should be wary of borrowing such an ahistorical conception of "economic man" from mainstream micro-economics.[126]

Such a conception reflects the disdain of liberalism's critics, whether nineteenth-century romantics like Samuel Taylor Coleridge and Thomas Carlyle – who famously dubbed political economy the "dismal science" – or Marx and others on the left. In part because they rejected his principle of population, such critics lumped Malthus together with his friend and contemporary Ricardo although he made an especially poor target for their venom. Like Malthus, travellers did not believe that physical labour, wealth, and markets were always beneficial or that more was always best; they were neither blind to the costs of economic development nor unconcerned with the well-being of local producers. They emphasized the economic agency of households as well as individuals and were more apt to see those individuals as sociable members of groups prone to indolence, temptation, and habit than profit-oriented, selfish atoms. Ambition and wants were historical and cultural, not natural, and while central to prosperity, so too was virtue. Far from materialists intent on endless accumulation, they condemned an excessive regard for profit in the face of other goods such as religion, education, or aesthetics.[127] "Improvement" was as much moral and cultural as economic. There is certainly no need to look beyond liberal political economy for a complex view of human motivation, anxieties about globalization, or an appreciation of issues of gender, cultural difference, and morality.[128]

Indeed, the emphasis on internalizing norms of industriousness and delayed gratification sounds a distinctly Protestant note. Anti-Catholic sentiments about "superstition" were common, although only one traveller linked Catholicism directly to poor economic performance in the region. A Protestant lay missionary actually mocked the "ignorance" of one Highland farmer who held his conversion from Catholicism to Protestantism responsible for new-found prosperity.[129] Yet, while easily translated into secular terms, travellers' political economy was heavily normative. It conceived of humans not as ambitious utility-maximizers, but as the indolent and easily tempted selves of a broadly evangelical sensibility. Narratives of economic life were structured by probationary trial (emigration and resettlement) in which virtue (industriousness, perseverance, and prudence) struggled against vice in the face of temptation (the more immediate rewards of lumbering or wage labour and the "extravagant" consumption they enabled), culminating in a judgment (the commercial crisis of 1826) of reward (prosperity) or punishment (poverty). Redemption through contrition (a change in habits) or the conversion of others was sought.[130] Travellers did not equate wealth with virtue or individual with collective well-being, but that these might cohere reflected the benevolence of "the Author of all good and perfect gifts."[131] Malthus, an Anglican cleric, altered his first writings on population to conform to Protestant. orthodoxy, concluding that "it is the apparent object of the Creator to deter us from vice by the pains which accompany it, and to lead us to virtue by the happiness it produces" – a utilitarianism that owed more to the prominent Protestant thinker William Paley than Jeremy Bentham. The principle of population, for instance, was "a law peculiarly suited to a state of discipline and trial" since, like the requisites for economic development in the Maritimes, it was "constantly directing our attention" to the virtues of prudence, foresight, self-control, industry, and economy.[132] The market economy *was* a moral one.

Thus, economic liberalism was vindicated in the Maritime countryside not because travellers' observations were accurate or culturally astute, but because it was there, they thought, that economic liberalism guaranteed justice and well-being as well as prosperity. While scarcity and injustice might seem inescapable in postwar Britain, the Maritime countryside and other parts of the empire of settlement offered an escape from those limits to a place where the potential for growth was still great and the economic trial fair. Labour and virtue were amply rewarded; indolence and vice punished. Those who were or feared becoming victims of economic development in Britain became its key benefactors in the Maritimes and thus supporters of, rather than a threat to, the emerging liberal order. A new Britain could be fashioned in the colonies on the basis of widespread propertied independence which, in turn, would help alleviate the acute dislocation and suffering evident in parts of the British Isles. By uniting "young" and "old," the imperial economy vindicated belief in the basic principles of economic liberalism.

Indeed, William Paley squared Malthus's dire principle of population with his own belief in a harmonious natural world governed by a benevolent God by arguing that it was "part of the scheme of Providence, that the earth should be inhabited by a shifting, or perhaps circulating population ... When old countries are become exceedingly corrupt, simpler modes of life, purer morals, and better institutions, may rise up in new ones, whilst fresh soils reward the cultivator with more plentiful returns."[133] After touring Nova Scotia, its lieutenant-governor, Lord Dalhousie, concluded that, "Europe, exhausted in strength & failing in vigour. America, British America I mean, is bursting forth with powers of which neither the Government in England or the country here is yet aware. Here are the resources of a great Empire, & we don't yet know how to call them forth; but here they are rapidly expanding."[134] Ultimately, the travel writers who followed Dalhousie thought they knew how to develop those resources to the benefit of both Britain and British America. In their accounts of the region, they became amateur political economists who vindicated economic liberalism.

NOTES

1 Thomas Jeffreys, *Natural and Civil History of the French Dominions in North and South America* (London, 1760), intro., 28–33 and John Rowan, *The Emigrant and Sportsman in Canada. Some Experiences of an Old Country Settler ...* (London: Edward Stanford 1876), preface, 365–6.

2 Mary Louise Pratt, *Imperial Eyes: Travel Writing and Transculturation* (London: Routledge, 1992), 30, 35, 45, 60–2, 146–7, 150–1, 154–5.

3 For the latter usage, see my "Why We Need but Don't Have an Intellectual History of the British North American Economy," in Damien-Claude Bélanger, Michel Ducharme, and Sophie Coupal, eds, *Les idées en mouvement: perspectives en histoire intellecuelle et culturelle du Canada* (Quebec: Laval University Press, 2004), 157–61.

4 Ronald L. Meek, *Social Science and the Ignoble Savage* (Cambridge: Cambridge University Press, 1976).

5 The use of Malthus is, then, partially a heuristic device to emphasize the interpenetration of systematic treatises, travel texts, and colonial circumstances. A comparison of those texts with locally authored emigration literature would be instructive, but while they shared many assumptions, the next section attempts to show that travel literature had a particular relationship to political economy.

6 Boyd Hilton, *The Age of Atonement: The Influence of Evangelicalism on Social and Economic Thought, 1785–1865* (Oxford: Oxford University Press, 1988), vii–viii, 64–5, 77–8, 118 and Donald Winch, *Riches and Poverty: An Intellectual History of Political Economy in Britain, 1750–1834* (Cambridge: Cambridge University Press, 1996), 238, 381. See also A.M.C. Waterman, "The Ideological Alliance of Political Economy and Christian Theology, 1798–1833," *Journal of Ecclesiastical History* 34, no. 2 (Apr. 1983): 231–44. On eavesdropping as a metaphor for intellectual history, see Stefan Collini, "General Introduction," in Collini, Richard Whatmore, and Brian Young, eds, *Economics, Polity, and Society: British Intellectual History, 1750–1950* (Cambridge: Cambridge University Press, 2000), 15.

7 Bernard Semmel, *The Rise of Free Trade Imperialism: Classical Political Economy, the Empire of Free Trade and Imperialism, 1750–1850* (Cambridge: Cambridge University Press, 1970), 11–12, 76–99, 170.

8 Besides ibid., see R.D. Collison Black, *Economic Thought and the Irish Question, 1817–1870* (Cambridge: Cambridge University Press, 1960); Donald Winch, *Classical Political Economy and Colonies* (Cambridge, MA: Harvard University Press, 1965); William J. Barber, *British Economic Thought and India, 1600–1858: A Study in the History of Development Economics* (Oxford: Clarendon Press, 1975); and S. Ambirajan, *Classical Political Economy and British Policy in India* (Cambridge: Cambridge University Press, 1978).

9 Christopher Atkinson, *A Historical and Statistical Account of New-Brunswick, B.N.A. with Advice to Emigrants*, 3rd ed. (Edinburgh: Anderson & Bryce 1844), viii plagiarized from Thomas Haliburton, *Historical and Statistical Account of Nova-Scotia* (Halifax: Joseph Howe, 1829), 1: 2.

10 Both Craufurd D.W. Goodwin, *Canadian Economic Thought: The Political Economy of a Developing Nation, 1814–1914* (Durham: Duke University Press, 1961) and Robert Neill, *A History of Canadian Economic Thought* (London: Routledge Press, 1991) emphasize policy over psychology and the paucity of serious economic analysis. Referring to this paper's sources, the latter declares that "there was no theory and little policy in any of these compendious descriptions" (26).

11 Ian McKay, *The Quest of the Folk: Antimodernism and Cultural Selection in Twentieth-Century Nova Scotia* (Montreal & Kingston: McGill-Queen's University Press, 1994).

12 T.R. Malthus, *An Essay on the Principle of Population ...* , Donald Winch, ed. (Cambridge: Cambridge University Press, 1992), esp. 56–7, 184.

13 Winch, *Riches and Poverty*, 164–5; Hilton, *Age of Atonement*, 5, 21–2, 34–5, 65–6; and Semmel, *Rise of Free Trade Imperialism*, 130, 144.

14 "The British North American Provinces," *Fraser's* 5 (1832): 78–9 and John MacGregor, *Observations on Emigration to British America* (London: Longman, Rees, Orme, Brown and Green 1829), iii.

15 [S. Hollingsworth], *The Present State of Nova Scotia with a Brief Account of Canada, and the British Islands on the Coast of North America* (Edinburgh: William Creech, 1787), 26, 220; and Otis Little, *The State of Trade in the Northern Colonies Considered; with an Account of their Produce, And a Particular Description of Nova Scotia* (London: G. Woodfall, 1748), vi.

16 Andrew Learmont Spedon, *Rambles among the Blue-Noses; or, Reminiscences of a Tour through New Brunswick and Nova Scotia, During the Summer of 1862* (Montreal: John Lovell 1863), 9.

17 For more on shifting preoccupations of travel accounts, see my "Meaning and Markets: Hunting, Economic Development, and British Imperialism in Maritime Travel Narratives to 1870," *Acadiensis* 34, no. 2 (Spring 2005): 3–25.

18 Isabella Lucy Bird, *The Englishwoman in America*, ed. Andrew Hill Clark (Toronto: University of Toronto Press, 1966 [1856]), 54–7, quotation at 67.

19 J.R. McCulloch, *A Discourse on the Rise, Progress, Peculiar Objects, and Importance, of Political Economy* (1824) quoted in Semmel, *Rise of Free Trade Imperialism*, 207–8.

20 *Westminster Review* 13 (1830): 180.

21 Public Archives of New Brunswick, Robert Reid to Adam Smith, 11[?] Sept. 1785. For Smith's use of travel accounts, see Margaret Hunt, "Racism, Imperialism, and the Traveler's Gaze in Eighteenth-Century England," *Journal of British Studies* 32 (Oct. 1993): 352.

22 Josiah Tucker, *Instructions for Travellers* (Dublin: William Watson, 1758), 88.

23 'Recent Travellers in North America," *Quarterly Review* 89 (June 1851): 57 and Marx, *Capital: A Critique of Political Economy*, David Fernbach, trans. (London: Penguin Books, 1981 [1894]), 3: 754n27, 808–9.

24 Malthus, *Essay*, 21–3, 81–5, 370, quotations at 23, 81, 87, 88, 385.

25 Frederick Fitzgerald De Roos, *Personal Narrative of Travels in the United States and Canada in 1826 ...* (London: William Harrison Ainsworth 1827), 174.

26 Joseph Bouchette, *The British Dominions in North America; or a Topographical and Statistical Description of the provinces ... Including Considerations on Land-Granting and Emigration ...* (London: Longman, Rees, Orme, Brown, Green, and Longman, 1832) 2: 233; "British North American Provinces," *Fraser's*, 78; Joseph Outram, *Nova Scotia: Its Condition and Resources in a Series of Six Letters* (Edinburgh: William Blackwood and Sons, 1850), 3–4, 7; and James Silk Buckingham, *Canada, Nova Scotia, New Brunswick, and the other British Provinces in North America, with a Plan of National Colonization* (London: Fisher, Son, & Co, 1843), 434–5, 444. See also Walter Johnstone, *A Series of Letters, Descriptive of Prince Edward Island ...* (Dumfries: J. Swan, 1822), 61. Although French-Canadian, Bouchette might not have objected to being classed a "British" traveller. His nationality seems irrelevant to his view of the Maritimes which relied heavily on the work of John MacGregor.

27 Wallace Brown, "William Cobbett in the Maritimes," *Dalhousie Review* 56, no. 3 (Autumn 1976), quotations at 450, 457; S.D. Scott, "William Cobbett," *Acadiensis* 5 (1905): 209–10, 214–15; and Herman Ausubel, "William Cobbett and Malthusianism," *Journal of the History of Ideas* 13, no. 2 (Apr. 1952), quotation at 252.

28 Buckingham, *Canada*, 458; Outram, *Nova Scotia*, 12; and more generally, Semmel, *Rise of Free Trade Imperialism*.

29 [William Hunter?], *Letters from Nova Scotia and New Brunswick, illustrative of their Moral, Religious, and Physical Circumstances, During the Years 1826, 1827, and 1828* (Edinburgh: Waugh and Innis 1829), 29–31, 102–3.

30 George Head, *Forest Scenes and incidents in the Wilds of North America; Being a Diary of a Winter's Route from Halifax to the Canadas ...* (London: John Murray, 1829), 5–6 and William Scarth Moorsom, *Letters from Nova Scotia: Comprising*

Sketches of a Young Country (London: Henry Colburn and Richard Bentley, 1830), 74–7.

31 De Roos, *Personal Narrative*, 179–80 and A Late Resident of that Colony, *Information to Emigrants: An Account of the Island of Prince Edward* ..., 2nd ed. (London: J.M. Richardson, 1826), 5–6. See also Hugh Murray, *An Historical and Descriptive Account of British America* ... (Edinburgh: Oliver & Boyd, 1839), 3: 98.

32 Moorsom, *Letters*, 42, 44–5, 149.

33 Malthus, *Principles of Political Economy Considered with a View to their Practical Application* (London: John Murray, 1820), 6, 7, 249–51, 257, 314, 342–3, 350, 359, 377, 379, 415, 418, 518, quotations at 2 and 10 and *Essay*, 41, 53, 55, 376, quotations at 15, 50–1, 312. Patricia James, ed., *The Travel Diaries of Thomas Robert Malthus* (Cambridge: Cambridge University Press, 1966) and Brian Dolan, *Exploring European Frontiers: British Travellers in the Age of Enlightenment* (London: Macmillan Press, Ltd, 2000), 47–57. On method, see esp. Stefan Collini, Donald Winch, and John Burrow, "Higher Maxims: Happiness Versus Wealth in Malthus and Ricardo," *That Noble Science of Politics: A Study in Nineteenth-Century Intellectual History* (Cambridge: Cambridge University Press, 1983), 65–89; E.A. Wrigley, "Elegance and Experience: Malthus at the Bar of History," in D. Coleman and R. Schofield, eds, *The State of Population Theory* (Oxford: Blackwell, 1986), 46–64; and S.G. Checkland, "The Propagation of Ricardian Economics in England," *Economica*, New Series 26, no. 61 (Feb. 1949): 45, 51–2.

34 John Mann, *Travels in North America ... from 1816 to 1823* (Glasgow: Andrew Young, 1824), xi, 6, 9–10, 19. Mann returned to New Brunswick later that decade. His subsequent correspondence echoes the pro-emigration arguments of other travellers.

35 Robert Playfair, *Recollections of A Visit to the United States and British Provinces of North America, in the Years 1847, 1848, and 1849* (Edinburgh: Thomas Constable and Co. and London: Adam, and Co, 1856), 266. For "young" see [Hunter], *Letters*, 28; Moorsom, *Letters*, 43; and Campbell Hardy, *Sporting Adventures in the New World; or, Days and Nights of Moose-Hunting in the Pine Forests of Acadia* (London: Jurst and Blackett, 1855), 1: 1–2; for "new" see Atkinson, *Historical and Statistical Account*, 124; and for "infant" or "infancy" see A Gentleman Who has resided many Years in the British Colonies, *A Description of the Island of Cape Breton* ... (London: Sherwood, Neely, and Jones, 1818?), 24; and Charles Joseph Leslie, *Military Journal of Colonel Leslie, K.H. of Balquhain, whilst serving with the 29th Regt. in the Peninsula, and the 60th Rifles in Canada, & c. 1808–1832* (Aberdeen: Aberdeen University Press, 1887), 285.

36 E.A. Wrigley and David Souden, eds, *The Works of Thomas Robert Malthus*, (London: William Pickering, 1986), 5: 120. See also 110 and Salim Rashid, "Malthus's *Principles* and British Economic Thought, 1820–1835," *History of Political Economy* 13, no. 1 (1981): 65–6.

37 MacGregor, *Observations*, viii; [Hunter], *Letters*, 29; and J.F.W. [James Finley Weir] Johnston, *Notes on North America: Agricultural, Economical, and Social* (Edinburgh and London: William Blackwood and Sons, 1851), 2: 138.

38 John MacGregor, *British America* (Edinburgh and London: William Blackwood and T. Cadell, 1832), 2: 222 and J.F.W. Johnston, *Report on the Agricultural Capabilities of New Brunswick* ... (Fredericton: J. Simpson, 1850), 31.

39 Julian Gwyn, *Excessive Expectations: Maritime Commerce and the Economic Development of Nova Scotia, 1740–1870* (Kingston & Montreal: McGill-Queen's University Press, 1998) and Spedon, *Rambles*, 84. [M.C.S. London or M. Shove?], *Adventures in Canada, Being Two Months on the Tobique* ... (London: Smith, Elder, & Co, [1866]), 44 reported "the general opinion [in New Brunswick] to be entirely against" Johnston's report. In fairness, Johnston was estimating a theoretical maximum based on a level of agricultural efficiency not achieved even in England.

40 MacGregor, *Observations*, 18; Atkinson, *Historical and Statistical Account*, xiii; and [Hunter], *Letters*, 178. See also Johnston, *Notes on North America*, 1: 25.

41 Murray, *Historical and Descriptive Account of British America*, 3: 139 and John MacGregor, *Historical and Descriptive Sketches of the Maritime Colonies of British America* (London: Longman, Rees, Orme, Brown, and Green, 1828), iv.

42 A Gentleman, *Description of the Island of Cape Breton*, 44.

43 MacGregor, *Observations*, 17, 43, 51; A Late Resident, *Information for Emigrants*, 6; [Hunter], *Letters*, 28; Christopher Atkinson, *A Guide to New Brunswick, British North America*, 2nd ed. (Edinburgh: Anderson & Bryce, 1843), 3; and Johnston, *Notes on North America*, 1: 64.

44 Johnstone, *Series of Letters*, 52; Moorsom, *Letters*, 143; and [Hunter], *Letters*, 177.

45 Malthus, *Principles*, 396 and A Late Resident, *Information for Emigrants*, 5. See also [Hunter], *Letters*, 29–31, 177–8; Bouchette, *British Dominions*, 2: 140, 217; and Atkinson, *Historical and Statistical Account*, 233–4.

46 MacGregor, *Observations*, 22, 39–40, 43; [Hunter], *Letters*, 81; Moorsom, *Letters*, 77; Bouchette, *British Dominions*, 2: 156–7; Johnston, *Notes on North America*, 1: 88; and Playfair, *Recollections*, 259.

47 A Late Resident, *Information for Emigrants*, 6 and Johnstone, *Series of Letters*, 52.

48 Chambers, *Things as They Are in America* (Philadelphia: Lippincott, Grambo & Co, 1854), 41.

49 Playfair, *Recollections*, 96, 234, 254; [B.W.A.] Sleigh, *Pine Forests and Hacmatack Clearings; or, Travel, Life, and Adventure, in the British North American Provinces* (London: Richard Bentley, 1853), 394; and MacGregor, *Observations*, 42.

50 Daniel Vickers, "Competency and Competition: Economic Culture in Early America," *William and Mary Quarterly*, 3rd series 47, no. 1 (Jan. 1990): 3–29 and on the middle class, see Malthus, *Essay*, 279 and *Principles*, 431.

51 Frances Beavan, *Sketches and Tales Illustrative of Life in the Backwoods of New Brunswick, North America, Gleaned from Actual Observation and Experience During*

a Residence of Seven Years in that Interesting Colony (London: George Routledge, 1845), 3 and Spedon, *Rambles*, 227.

52 Moorsom, *Letters*, 142–3; Bouchette, *British Dominions*, 2: 149; and Beavan, *Sketches and Tales*, 3, 36.

53 Johnston, *Notes on North America*, 2: 212.

54 Beaven, *Sketches and Tales ... Gleaned from Actual Observation and Experience*.

55 Harriet Martineau, *Illustrations of Political Economy* (London: Charles Fox, 1834), 1: xi–xiii, xvi and Caroline Roberts, *The Woman and the Hour: Harriet Martineau and Victorian Ideologies* (Toronto: University of Toronto Press, 2002), 10–25.

56 MacGregor, *Observations*, 43, 49.

57 Beavan, *Sketches and Tales*, 45–50.

58 Barber, *British Economic Thought and India*, 87.

59 Wynn, "'Deplorably Dark and Demoralized Lumberers'? Rhetoric and Reality in Early Nineteenth-Century New Brunswick," *Journal of Forest History* 24, no. 4 (Oct. 1980): 171–6; Malthus, *Essay*, 16, 23, 116, 125, 131, 133, 135, 150, 168, 185, 189 quotation at 174 and *Principles*, 38, 140, 142, 149, 226–39; Collini, Winch, and Borrow, "Higher Maxims," 73–5; and Ambirajan, *Classical Political Economy and British Policy in India*, 216.

60 Geoffrey Gilbert, "Economic growth and the poor in Malthus' *Essay on Population*," *History of Political Economy* 12: no. 1 (1980): 83–96.

61 MacGregor, *Historical and Descriptive Sketches*, 154; MacGregor, *British America*, 2: 295, 303–4, 306–7; Moorsom, *Letters*, 51–2; Bouchette, *British Dominions*, 2: 48, 140, 152–3; and Beavan, *Sketches and Tales*, 46.

62 [Hunter], *Letters*, 33.

63 See ibid., 158; Moorsom, *Letters*, 53; and, on the similar response in Britain, Hilton, *Age of Atonement*, 117–25, 130–6.

64 [Hunter], *Letters*, 35, 37, 126, 154, 156–7; Beavan, *Sketches and Tales*, 46; Moorsom, *Letters*, 52; Bouchette, *British Dominions*, 2: 153; MacGregor, *British America*, 2: 293–7; and Atkinson, *Guide*, 66.

65 [Hunter], *Letters*, 35–6, 127, 155, 159; MacGregor, *Historical and Descriptive Sketches*, 166; and MacGregor, *British America*, 2: 301–3.

66 Barber, *British Economic Thought and India*, 87, 167; and Black, *Economic Thought and the Irish Question*, 135. Malthus famously found such "unproductive" consumption necessary in the specific circumstances of Britain's post-war glut, but such circumstances did not pertain to underdeveloped economies.

67 MacGregor, *British America*, 2: 302 and Beavan, *Sketches and Tales*, 36.

68 [Hunter], *Letters*, 35–6, 12.

69 Ibid., 34; Beavan, *Sketches and Tales*, 47; Bouchette, *British Dominions*, 2: 132–3; and MacGregor, *Historical and Descriptive Sketches*, 167.

70 [Hunter], *Letters*, 158; and Bouchette, *British Dominions*, 2: 146. See also Johnstone, *Series of Letters*, 68–9 and MacGregor, *Observations*, 43.

71 B.J. Gordon, "Say's Law, Effective Demand, and the Contemporary British Periodicals, 1820–1850," *Economica*, New Series 32, no. 128 (Nov. 1965): 438–46.

72 Ricardo's letter is quoted in Christopher Herbert, *Culture and Anomie: Ethnographic Imagination in the Nineteenth Century* (Chicago: University of Chicago Press, 1991), 318n27. For Malthus, see his letter to Ricardo quoted in Walter Eltis, *The Classical Theory of Economic Growth*, 2nd ed. (Houndmills, Bassingstoke: Palgrave, 2000), 150 and *Principles*, 43, 351–75, 379, 497–8, 503, quotations at 9, 119. I am particularly indebted here to Winch, *Riches and Poverty*, 358–61, but see also Semmel, *Rise of Free Trade Imperialism*, 9–10, 208; Black, *Economic Thought and the Irish Question*, 86–7, 137; and Terry Peach, "Ricardo and Malthus on the post-Napoleonic distress: too many producers or a momentary lapse of reason?" in Bernard Corry, ed., *Unemployment and the Economists* (Cheltenham: Edward Elger, 1996), 30–51 which quotes Ricardo writing to Malthus that "Men err in their productions, there is no deficiency of demand" (34).

73 Semmel, *Rise of Free Trade Imperialism*, 110–12, 170, 190 and Winch, *Classical Political Economy and Colonies*, 73–104.

74 See Peter Burroughs, "The Administration of Crown Lands in Nova Scotia, 1827–1848," *Collections of the Nova Scotia Historical Society* (1966) 35: 79–108.

75 J.S. Mill, *Principles of Political Economy* (1847) Vol. 1, chapters 6–7; David E. Martin, "The rehabilitation of the peasant proprietor in nineteenth-century economic thought: a comment," *History of Political Economy* 8, no. 2 (1976): 297–302; Ambirajan, *Classical Political Economy and British Policy in India*, 172–4, 237–40, 242–3; and Semmel, *Rise of Free Trade Imperialism*, 29, 32, 70–1. Thus, leasehold tenure on Prince Edward Island struck several travellers as a disturbing anomaly.

76 Malthus, *Principles*, 470. Sir James Steuart and David Hume had emphasized the importance of "wants" to work in the absence of slavery.

77 Moorsom, *Letters*, 71, 96, 343–4.

78 E.T. [Edward Thomas] Coke, *A Subaltern's Furlough: Descriptive of Scenes in Various Parts of the United States, Upper and Lower Canada, New-Brunswick, and Nova Scotia, During the Summer and Autumn of 1832* (New York: J.&J. Harper 1833) 2: 98. I owe this point to Julia Roberts.

79 Joshua Marsden, *The Narrative of A Mission to Nova Scotia, New Brunswick, and the Somers Islands ...* (Plymouth-Dock: J. Johns, 1816), 26; A Late Resident, *Information for Emigrants*, 12–13, 24; and even the American visitor, Abraham Pryor, *An Interesting Description of British America ...* (Providence: Miller and Huchens, 1819), 14.

80 Johnstone, *Series of Letters*, 55–6. Coke, *Subaltern's Furlough* 2: 98 applies a similar ranking to New Brunswick.

81 MacGregor, *Historical and Descriptive Sketches*, 68–74.

82 Ibid., 69, 74, 117, 181, quotation at 196 and Beaven, *Sketches and Tales*, 26, 79–80, quotation at 29. See also [Hunter], *Letters*, 12; Murray, *Historical and*

Descriptive Account of British America, 2: 212; and Johnston, *Notes on North America*, 1: 81–2.

83　*The Dalhousie Journals*, Marjory Whitelaw, ed. (Ottawa: Oberon Press, 1978), 97; Bouchette, *British Dominions*, 2: 178; Moorsom, *Letters*, 262–3, 334; and Johnston, *Notes on North America*, 1: 70.

84　Marsden, *Narrative of a Mission*, 50 and A Late Resident, *Information for Emigrants*, 23–4. See also MacGregor, *British America*, 2: 247, 274.

85　Eg. [Hunter], *Letters*, 99; MacGregor, *British America*, 2: 108, 247; Moorsom, *Letters*, 259; and Beavan, *Sketches and Tales*, 2.

86　MacGregor, *British America*, 2: 108, 199, quotation at 247; Johnston, *Notes on North America*, 1: 113; 2: 10, quotation at 6; and Moorsom, *Letters*, 259. See also [Hunter], *Letters*, 100.

87　Beavan, *Sketches and Tales*, 2 and A Late Resident, *Information for Emigrants*, 23.

88　MacGregor, *British America*, 1: 408; 2: 183; Johnstone, *Series of Letters*, 44; Moorsom, *Letters*, 344; and Johnston, *Notes on North America*, 2: 61.

89　Murray, *Historical and Descriptive Account of British America*, 2: 210; Moorsom, *Letters*, 344; and Johnstone, *Series of Letters*, 44. See also MacGregor, *British America*, 1: 397, 409; 2: 183.

90　MacGregor, *Historical and Descriptive Sketches*, 68; Johnstone, *Series of Letters*, 55; MacGregor, *British America*, 2: 180–1, 187; and Beavan, *Sketches and Tales*, 35. Note again the elision of class. Presumably not all English emigrants were accustomed to "comfort."

91　[Hunter], *Letters*, 124 and also 190; Johnstone, *Series of Letters*, 55; and MacGregor, *Historical and Descriptive Sketches*, 68–9, quotation at 263. See also MacGregor, *British America*, 2: 181, 183 and Murray, *Historical and Descriptive Account of British America*, 2: 211.

92　Bagehot, *Economic Studies* (London: Longmans, Green, and Co. 1902, [1880]), 125.

93　Malthus, *Essay*, 47 and Moorsom, *Letters*, 344.

94　Malthus, *Essay*, 214.

95　[Hunter], *Letters*, 81; MacGregor, *British America*, 2: 201; and Rowan, *Emigrant and Sportsman*, 231.

96　J.C. Morgan, *The Emigrant's Note Book and Guide; with Recollections of Upper and Lower Canada, During the Late War* (London: Longman, Hurst, Rees, Orme, and Brown 1824), 6.

97　Moorsom, *Letters*, 50.

98　Johnston, *Notes on North America*, 1: 119. See also 2: 175 and MacGregor, *Historical and Descriptive Sketches*, 73, 264.

99　Morgan, *Emigrant's Note Book*, 6 and Adam Smith, *An Inquiry into the Nature and Causes of the Wealth of Nations*, Edwin Cannan, ed. (New York: The Modern Library, 1994 [1776]), 372–3, 581. See Malthus, *Essay*, 47, 105, 198, 314; [Hunter], *Letters*, 81; and Herbert, *Culture and Anomie*, 100.

100 Malthus, *Essay*, 279.

101 [Hunter], *Letters*, 41–3, 50. See also *Dalhousie Journals*, 73.

102 Debates about the feasibility and efficiency of hired versus family labour were more common after mid-century and require closer attention, but even promoters of so-called "commercial" agriculture presented paid agricultural labour as a life-cycle stage rather than a permanent condition – a means to propertied independence rather than an alternative to it.

103 De Vries, "The Industrial Revolution and the Industrious Revolution," *The Journal of Economic History*, 54, no. 2 (June 1994): esp. 255–7.

104 Malthus, *Principles*, 448 and *Essay*, 190. See, for instance, MacGregor, *Historical and Descriptive Sketches*, 59–60; MacGregor, *British America*, 1: 324–5; 2: 314; and [New Brunswick Land Company?] *Practical Information to Emigrants, Including Details, Collected from the Most Authentic Accounts ... of the Province of New Brunswick* (London: John Richardson 1832), 78. E.A. Heaman, *The Inglorious Arts of Peace: Exhibitions in Canada during the Nineteenth Century* (Toronto: University of Toronto Press, 1999) is invaluable here.

105 Moorsom, *Letters*, 259. See also A Late Resident, *Information for Emigrants*, 23; Bouchette, *British Dominions*, 2: 63, 178; and MacGregor, *British America*, 2: 246.

106 MacGregor, *British America*, 2: 199–200; repeated in Murray, *Historical and Descriptive Account of British America*, 2: 212 and Bouchette, *British Dominions*, 2: 178.

107 Murray, *Historical and Descriptive Account of British America*, 2: 211. See also MacGregor, *Historical and Descriptive Sketches*, 70, 263; MacGregor, *British America*, 1: 408; 2: 183; Moorsom, *Letters*, 344; and Herbert, *Culture and Anomie*, 82.

108 MacGregor, *British America*, 2: 131–2, 252. See Boyd Hilton, *Age of Atonement*, 122–3.

109 Winch, *Riches and poverty*, 77–80, 89 and Vickers, "Competency and Competition," 6–7, 10–11, 15.

110 See Lawrence E. Harrison and Samuel P. Hunting, eds, *Culture Matters: How Values Shape Human Progress* (New York: Basic Books, 2000).

111 Herbert, *Culture and Anomie*, 74–149 and E.A. Wrigley, "Elegance and Experience," 55–6.

112 [Hunter], *Letters*, 2, 103. See also, Moorsom, *Letters*, 77 and Johnston, *Notes on North America*, 2: 119.

113 Moorsom, *Letters*, 144–5 and my "Meaning and Markets," 9–15. For the importance of these ideas to missionaries in Jamaica, see Catherine Hall, *Civilizing Subjects: Metropole and Colony in the English Imagination 1830–1867* (Chicago: University of Chicago Press, 2002), 250–1.

114 Johnston, *Notes on North America*, 1: 53–4, 104–5.

115 Malthus, *Essay*, 111.

116 [Hunter], *Letters*, 100 and Bouchette, *British Dominions*, 2: 178 and also 63. See also MacGregor, *British America*, 2: 108–9, 192–5, 198–9, 246–7, 274; Moorsom, *Letters*, 256–9, 334; Murray, *Historical and Descriptive Account of British America*, 2: 168; and Frederic S. Cozzens, *Acadia; or, A Month with the Blue Noses* (New York: Derby & Jackson 1859), 296–8.

117 See esp., Cozzens, *Acadia* and works by Charles Lanman and Charles Hallock.

118 De Vries, "The Industrial and the Industrious Revolution," 258.

119 Buckingham, *Canada*, 451–2.

120 Malthus, *Principles*, 150.

121 [Hunter], *Letters*, 95.

122 MacGregor, *Historical and Descriptive Sketches*, 75; MacGregor, *British America*, 2: 247; and [Hunter], *Letters*, 100. See also Moorsom, *Letters*, 259.

123 Malthus, *Essay*, 16–18, 31–3, 41, 60 and *Principles*, 210, 428.

124 Rashid, "Malthus' *Principles* and British economic thought," 55.

125 Ian McKay, "The Liberal Order Framework: A Prospectus for a Reconnaissance of Canadian History," *Canadian Historical Review* 81, no. 4 (Dec. 2000): 617–45.

126 See my "Why We Need but Don't Have an Intellectual History of the British North American Economy." Conversely, attention to economic thought might suggest new questions to economic historians. On this potential for dialogue, see Donald Winch, "That Disputatious Pair: Economic History and the History of Economics," working paper, Centre for History and Economics, King's College, Cambridge at www.histecon.kings.cam.ac.uk.

127 Eg., [Hunter], *Letters*, 82–3, 189–90, 200–1.

128 Checkland, "The Propagation of Ricardian Economics," 41–2; Winch, *Riches and Poverty*, 5, 289–90, 305; and esp. Winch, "Mr Gradgrind and Jerusalem," in Collini, Whatmore, and Young, eds, *Economics, Polity, and Society*, 243–66.

129 Walter Johnstone, *Travels in Prince Edward Island, ... Undertaken With A Design to Establish Sabbath Schools, And Investigate the Religious State of the Country ...* (Edinburgh: David Brown 1823), 82. The exception was Johnston, *Notes on North America*, 2: 10–11 on the excessive number of Catholic holidays.

130 Compare travellers' language with that of evangelicals in Hilton, *Age of Atonement*, esp. 6, 8, 11, 31–3, 69, 82, 114, 178. See also Waterman, "Ideological Alliance."

131 [Hunter], *Letters*, 80.

132 Malthus, *Essay*, 76 (including the laudatory footnote to J.B. Sumner, *Records of the Creation*,) 208, 217–18, quotations at 224, 385. For Malthus as a public moralist see esp. Winch, *Malthus* (Oxford: Oxford University Press, 1987).

133 Paley, *Natural Theology*, 1802 ed., 513 quoted in Hilton, *Age of Atonement*, 75. For Sumner, see Waterman, "Ideological Alliance," 240–1.

134 *Dalhousie Journals*, 179.

MICHELLE VOSBURGH

"Deserving of Favourable Consideration"

Crown Land Agents, Surveyors, and Access to Crown Lands in Upper Canada

Land, specifically Crown land, was one of the central pivots of Upper Canadian society – a political and economic issue with wide social and cultural implications.[1] The distribution of the Crown lands was one of the most important government activities, and occasioned a great deal of comment from both outside observers and inhabitants who recognized that the activities of settlement were shaping the new society in unmistakable ways.[2] During the colonial period, the method of land distribution went through significant changes, changes that mirrored the conditions, the context, and the vision of the people involved in creating and administering the land policy. By the late 1830s, land sales had replaced grants as the dominant means for the alienation of Crown lands, and the growing competition for a shrinking amount of land highlighted problems within the land distribution system. From 1839 until the closing of the agricultural frontier in Upper Canada in the 1860s, lower level government officials, the Crown land agents and Provincial land surveyors, were on the front lines of land distribution. They worked actively not only to ensure that "deserving" settlers had access to reasonably priced land, but also to keep the land distribution system flexible and responsive to the needs of individual settlers and popular opinion. The local officials had the responsibility of taking the official land policy and making it work.

The context in which that policy operated was a complex one, made even more so because Upper Canada existed within an empire. Subject to the forces controlling that empire, the policy also had to function within a specific and distinct part of the vast British empire. For example, India's large indigenous population meant that the land policies in that region were quite different from those of settlement colonies, including New Zealand, Australia, British North America and, to some extent, South Africa.[3] In the settlement colonies, the British managed, with varying degrees of success, to compel the remnants of indigenous peoples to give up their land claims to vast tracts of land. The climates of the settlement colonies did not lend themselves to the crops grown on the plantations found in the empire's extensive holdings in the more tropical climates. There were efforts to establish large manorial estates, modelled on those created in England and in Ireland with the push for enclosure and improvement. Just as some small farmers managed to survive despite such pressures in Britain and in Ireland, even more of their counterparts in the settlement colonies, not content with the prospect of remaining lifelong tenants, found ways of becoming land owners. They seemed to take the English gentry's desire to possess and improve land and adopt it for themselves in the colonies.[4] The colonists had the added advantage of the availability of large tracts of land that were unsettled and unimproved, waiting, so it seemed, for them to begin to clear and plant.[5] Indeed, many historians point to the sheer amount of land available as a key part of the development of particular attitudes toward land in these settlement colonies.[6] The other key component seems to have been the lawless nature of the frontier.[7] Lacking the resources to enforce official policy, the imperial and, especially, the colonial authorities found it necessary to accede to some degree to local opinion and practice.

Local conditions were important in determining more than just imperial land policy. Robinson and Gallagher have argued that imperial expansion during the mid-nineteenth century can be traced to the policy of free trade. The expansion of trade often required the expansion of the formal, political empire, depending on local circumstances.[8] David Fieldhouse also reasons that official policy in many different areas of the British empire was determined not just by the economic interests of the metropolis, London, but by political concerns that resulted from the conditions and circumstances found on the periphery, in the colonies. Imperialism cannot be explained by one grand theory, but only by examining the dialogue that took place between the metropolis and the colonies, and that involved many factors, including politics and economics.[9] Similarly, John C. Weaver has shown that conditions on the periphery became a key part of the imperial approach to the redistribution of lands on a number of frontiers, particularly within the British empire.[10] Despite directions from London, colonial attitudes greatly affected the distribution of Crown lands. Although it was slow in coming, the Colonial Office began to recognize some of the land distribution methods already in practice in the colonies, and incorporate them into the official policy, but it seems to have been reactive rather than proactive change.[11]

For settlement colonies, local input to land policy was crucial if it was to be acceptable to those for whom the land policy was most important. Peter Burroughs has studied the Crown lands administration in the Australian colonies to understand how London's imperial policies were altered in the local settings, most notably, Edward Gibbon Wakefield's influence on colonial land distribution.[12] Burroughs pointed to the difficulties and constraints of applying imperial policies from London to the distinctive conditions in the Australian colonies. Ultimately, he concluded, the economic and political pressures of a frontier settlement overcame the imperial policies.[13] Raymond Wright went one step further, arguing that high-level civil servants in Victoria reinterpreted directions, thereby altering the official policy created by the colonial government. Notably, Wright looks at how these bureaucrats sought to alter the policy in ways they believed would better suit the local public interest.[14] Likewise, Upper Canada's position meant that the land policy was largely determined by factors that were of specific importance to the colony. It was a matter of practicality to delegate responsibility for and control of land distribution to local authority.[15] Although the actions of Parliament and the Colonial Office did affect the official policy of land distribution in Upper Canada, particularly with the initial practice of land grants to Loyalists and for military service, and then the switch to land sales, it was local circumstances and needs that specifically shaped that policy and the way it was applied. Lillian Gates, in an exhaustive study of the development of the official land policy of the colony, has detailed how local conditions, particularly political and economic, acted to create an official land policy that reflected imperial power and strong elements of American influence, but was a unique product of Upper Canada.[16]

Particularly in the case of Upper Canada and, more generally, British North America, the nearby presence of the United States and the large number of inhabitants from the former Thirteen Colonies meant that the imperial influence on land policy was, if not lessened, certainly altered. The need to compete with the United States for settlers was a significant component in Upper Canada's land policy, but perhaps even more important was the influence of ideas about land that came from the United States. The United States, of course, had initially continued along the path of the land policy of the Thirteen Colonies, particularly the granting of large tracts of land to leading men and families. However, even before the American Revolution it was already becoming evident that the presence of large tracts of "empty" land was having a profound impact on the way in which the colonists, including their leaders, perceived that land.[17] Squatting was already widespread and by the early nineteenth century it was tacitly, if not officially, accepted as a legitimate means to acquiring a piece of land.[18] As with other British colonies, particularly Australia, where squatting became the normal way to acquire land, it was condoned by means of Lockean precepts and by the utilitarian influences felt throughout the English- speaking world. Land was to be used efficiently, without waste, and by means of his labour on the land, to improve it, a man had a clear entitlement to own that land. Claims clubs, organizations of local landowners, existed solely to defend land claims against newcomers.[19]

Along with Lockean rights, historians have also found elements of a moral economy at work in the American context to ensure that land distribution was as wide as possible in the male population. They suggest that the new economies formed on the frontiers were also creating "customs" that were in opposition to the functioning of a free market.[20] Christopher Clark uses a concept he calls "structures of opportunity" to explain how access to property and land ownership was governed in the American northeast. He argues that there was an underlying structure of the rural economy, based not just on economic opportunities for the individual, but also on social, cultural, ideological, and political understandings. Thus, unlike traditional arguments which see the farmers of this region as proto-capitalists, Clark contends that the motivations which drove this society were more complex.[21] "Official" decisions to allow squatters leniency with regard to obtaining the lots on which they had made improvements are one example of the "moral economy" at work. Lenient attitudes toward squatters were largely a result of a belief that improving the land gave the "improver" some rights to the land regardless of their legal relationship to the land. The notion of public lands in the United States gave rise to the perception that the land was there for any member of the public to put into production. Moreover, there was growing popular pressure to make it possible for settlers to acquire their own small piece of land out of the vastness of the American public domain. At the same time it was politically expedient to allow the land to be sold in a free market because of the revenues generated by the sale of public lands.[22] Alan Taylor demonstrates how the struggle for land forced the government to become more conscious of popular viewpoints regarding land and property rights on the frontier in Vermont and the Susquehanna Valley in northern Pennsylvania.[23] The sale of land according to market conditions did not allow for equal opportunity but rather gave those with ready capital an unfair advantage. Yet, the sheer size of the area available made it possible for the government to still make money from the land while allowing those people without much capital the opportunity to buy land. The government was persuaded by popular pressure to extend its role as a developer into one that could maintain a market where most people would have a reasonable chance of participating in the purchase of land, and allow pre-emption rights to squatters and still generate revenue. The belief that every man had a right to be able to acquire a parcel of land was a strong one in the United States; it became a custom, one that was part of the moral economy.[24]

Since these "rights" were an important part of the settlement and distribution of public lands in the United States, the government depended on its local land offices and employees to ensure a fair distribution system, although its equity has been strongly called into question by historians like Paul W. Gates.[25] Gates argues that it is critical to study the documents of the actual distribution of land in order to understand what really happened in that process, in other words, the documents left by the local land agents and officials. Without such research, the picture of the transfer of public lands remains obscure and even inaccurate.[26] In the context of Upper Canada, then, it follows that it is necessary to examine the role of those on the bottom rung of authority, the local Crown land agents and surveyors who oversaw the distribution of land to individuals, to understand the actual process of distribution in the colony. The records left by these men show that they directed the application of the policy, manipulating the regulations to serve their own particular views on what the land policy should be doing. As will be shown, those views clearly reflected ideas about the links between improvement and property, as well as the more populist influences of a moral economy that sought to put land in the hands of as many as possible.

The early vision of the ruling elite as set out by John Graves Simcoe, first Lieutenant-Governor, portrayed Upper Canada as a potential recreation of the best of Britain, and the system of land distribution was to reflect that vision's aims. Simcoe, in many ways, fits the model suggested by C.A. Bayly, when he describes the period of imperial history from 1780 to 1830 as one in which executive authority used land as a reward for service and loyalty, although its goals for the outcomes of that land distribution were hampered by weak control over land use.[27] Simcoe continued with the earlier provision made for refugee Loyalist families to become small land-owning farmers, while also providing for land grants for the children of Loyalists. Recognizing the need for more settlers to spur development of the fledgling colony in order to strengthen its position against the rapidly expanding United States, Simcoe and his advisers made it possible for newcomers who pledged loyalty to Britain to also obtain grants. Military grants to British soldiers and officers would, it was hoped, not only help to secure Upper

Canada as a British possession, but also aid in the development of a British character. Similarly, Simcoe's provisions for the maintenance of the Church of England through the Clergy Reserves were to enhance the Britishness of the colony.

Citing their loyalty and service to the Crown, Simcoe also set the precedent for the allocation of large tracts of land to the ruling class, whose tight familial and class relations inspired the "appellation the 'Family Compact.'" John Clarke's voluminous work examines the amount of lands that passed through the hands of the Family Compact and he has painstakingly traced the complex web of interrelationships of members of the compact and their landholdings.[28] These elite were to become comparable to the British ruling class; they would dispense justice among the tenants and yeoman farmers and lead the government of the new colony. The Family Compact was the colonial equivalent of the aristocracy and country gentry who had benefited from the political economy that had dominated Britain since the end of the English civil war. But its members were also influenced by the factors that created the nineteenth-century "gentlemen capitalists." They were especially desirous of acquiring land for speculation, to raise capital, rather than to establish estates.[29] Only a handful of men, like Thomas Talbot and Archibald McNab, Laird of the Clan McNab, attempted to create large estates with tenant farmers.[30] In practice, the Family Compact members who held large amounts of land were usually speculators striving to maximize their profits while spending as little as possible. As a result they tended to hold their large tracts of unimproved land for future speculative purposes when land prices were higher.

The settlers and emigrants in Upper Canada did not seem inclined to concede to and conform with a vision for Upper Canada like Simcoe's. Most of the Loyalists, although willing to sacrifice their homes and possessions in the new United States to remain under the umbrella of the Crown, were not so amenable to the attempts to recreate Britain's social, political, and economic structures. Their background was steeped in the eighteenth-century British imperial style. As C.A. Bayly put it, the British empire during that period had been loosely controlled, which, inadvertently perhaps, "had encouraged the development of an expansive settler capitalism" predicated on the acquisition of land.[31] Yet, they were now living, because of their loyalty, under a British authority that was trying to reassert control, reacting to the American Revolution. They were Loyalists, but they were also Americans, influenced by cultural and social developments in the Thirteen Colonies, including the principles of freehold tenure and representative government. The American influence was further reinforced by the large influx of American settlers attracted by the promise of free land made by Simcoe in 1791. From the very beginning, Upper Canada was to be influenced by both British and American ideas, a place of exchange and negotiation of those influences.[32] The discussion and evolution of land distribution methods throughout the colonial period reflected Upper Canada's position as a member of the vast British empire and a close neighbour of the United States. Discontent with the conditions in the colony, particularly the methods of land distribution, seemed to grow as the population grew. By the late 1830s, it was clear that frustration with the land distribution system had reached a high point; reform politicians like William Lyon Mackenzie often cited the examples of ownership of large tracts of land by a few, mostly members or associates of the Family Compact, to show how the elite allegedly controlled the colony.[33]

The government and the public had been well aware for some time of the ways in which large tracts of unimproved land hampered settlement through much of the province. Robert Gourlay's *Statistical Account of Upper Canada,* first printed in 1822, showed that this was already the cause of widespread discontent. Gourlay's *Statistical Account* was a rather anti-climatical end to his business in Upper Canada. He was an avid proponent of agrarian reform in his native Scotland, and upon his arrival in Upper Canada soon became involved in the widespread discontent over the imperial refusal to grant lands to prospective American settlers after the War of 1812–14. Although his original address, written to accompany the list of questions to township officials for the purpose of compiling his information on Upper Canada, declared his endeavour to be a scientific one, his later writings on the "alien question" fanned the flames of discontent in the colony. It was within this atmosphere that members of the public discussed and debated possible responses to Gourlay's questions. Only 57 responses to over 700 questionnaires were received. While these responses probably came from communities and individuals who supported Gourlay or sympathized with his stance, they do provide an interesting snapshot of the colony at the time. In particular, probably reflecting their reform sympathies, the responses to the notorious thirty-first question, "What, in your opinion, retards the improvement of your township in particular, or the province in general: and what would most contribute to the same?" led to answers that were remarkably consistent. More often than not they mentioned the presence of the Crown and Clergy Reserves and the large tracts of wild land owned by absentees as major impediments to settlement in the townships and the province as a whole.[34] Absentee landowners often did not pay local taxes, which made the burden on those who did that much greater.

Although Gourlay's own writings on the problems that impeded Upper Canada's development reflected his "most accustomed guise as anti-authoritarian," the responses he received to his address and questionnaire were purportedly printed as Gourlay received them.[35]

Twenty years after Robert Gourlay's career in Canada had come to an end, the issue of land distribution moved closer to the centre of the vision of the imperial powers with the unrest and outbreak of violence in 1837–38. Lord Durham, appointed as governor, came to British North America to investigate the conditions in the two Canadas. Lord Durham and his associates found that the conditions of land distribution that had occasioned protest in Gourlay's *Statistical Account* had not changed. Significant amounts of wild land controlled by absentee proprietors continued to obstruct settlement and impede the construction of roads. Durham's report devoted a great deal of space to the disposal of Crown lands in Upper Canada. The inequities and injustices in the land system, particularly the ability of favoured individuals to receive large grants of land, were examined in detail. These large grants of lands had been the object of hostility from much of the public throughout the province, but the depth of resentment was particularly great in those townships where such grants seriously hampered local development.

Large blocks of wild land, together with the scattered Crown and Clergy Reserves, meant that settlers were isolated, and had to take on the added burden of clearing road allowances on unsettled lots in order to facilitate travel and communications. Durham's comments, largely based on a report by Charles Buller, deplored the disposal of so much land to individuals "greatly beyond the proprietor's means of cultivation and settlement."[36] Durham attributed the violence in Upper Canada largely to the injustices and inefficiencies of the land distribution system.[37] A serious issue in Upper Canada, the problems with poor land distribution methods existed throughout British North America to varying extents and Durham condemned the confusion surrounding land policies, policies which always seemed to be undergoing alterations. He aptly pointed out that the only consistency within the land policies of the British North American colonies was that they managed to alienate more land than individual grantees could ever hope to improve or develop.[38] Durham asserted that the presence of large numbers of squatters in Upper Canada was directly related to the difficulty in obtaining good agricultural land from the Crown through legal channels.[39]

Durham's report, most specifically his recommendations for responsible government, met with a great deal of hostility among the colony's conservatives. However, those conservatives, although in agreement in condemning the idea of responsible government, differed considerably on the issue of administrative reforms. In particular, local officials throughout the province advocated a number of administrative reforms to address the problems identified in Durham's report, particularly those concerning land. Rural conservatives criticized the Toronto elite, with whom they were usually allied, for hampering settlement and the development of the province, just as Gourlay and Durham had.[40] Members of the conservative elite realized that action had to be taken quickly, and appointed the "Royal Commission Set Up to Investigate Business, Conduct & Organization of Various Public Department of Upper Canada" whose report was made public in the 1839–40 *Journal of the House of Assembly*. J.E. Hodgetts has argued that this process of administrative reform, begun immediately after the rebellions, was, in fact, a large part of the practical achievement of responsible government in Canada.[41] The employment of Crown land agents and the hiring of surveyors to conduct inspections and valuations, along with the instructions for their jobs, reflected the civil service reform movement and the desire to make the Crown Lands department more accountable to the government and to the public.

A decade before the rebellions, the government of Upper Canada had shifted land distribution policy in a new direction, away from land grants to land sales, because of the need to augment government revenues. Despite the move to land sales, the presence of large numbers of unfulfilled Loyalist claims (mostly under the provisions for children of Loyalists) and military claims meant that grants, and the redemption of scrip, continued to be a large proportion of the government's activities. By the late 1830s the colonial government began to approach land sales in a much more serious way. This was in part due to the Public Lands Disposal Act of 1837 when the British parliament gave its assent to handing, in essence, complete control of public lands over to the colony's government. This move was reaffirmed with the 1841 Act of Union, even though it went against the recommendations of Lord Durham.[42]

The Land Act of 1837 indirectly set the stage for the creation of a team of regular agents to work on behalf of the Crown Lands department in Upper Canada. This act reflected the influence of Edward Gibbon Wakefield, with its new regulations for land sales. Wakefield's proposals for "systematic colonization" sought to restrict land distribution so as to concentrate agriculture and create a supply of labour. He believed that unrestricted grants of land promoted economic depression and eliminated the labour pool that was necessary to maximize production per unit of land. This inefficiency could be prevented by making it difficult for emigrants to obtain land as soon as they entered

British North America. Instead, they would find it necessary to work for others in the process of developing their farms for a number of years in order to earn the capital necessary to purchase their own land and establish their own farms. Wakefield's plan came too late to be successfully applied in Upper Canada, since so much land had already been alienated and was in the hands of private speculators, both individual and corporate, among them, the Canada Company. Moreover, such a scheme would have occasioned strong public protest. Nonetheless, the principle of active government intervention in the land policy to direct progress remained an important concept in the development and implementation of land policy.[43]

Under the 1837 Land Act, grants of land were no longer allowed, except to those who were entitled to them under existing regulations: United Empire Loyalist and military grants. Land was to be sold: to be offered first at public auction, and lots then remaining unsold could be sold privately. It is important to note here that the act also provided for private sales at a valuation before auction in certain cases with the approval of the Governor and Executive Council. In other words, a window was being left open not only for the acknowledgment of squatters' rights, but also for speculators and others who might use their connections with government.

These provisions in the 1837 act, which was renewed in 1839, added to a growing number of factors that intensified the need for the Crown Lands department to have representatives throughout the province. Crown land agents would arrange public auctions in the vicinity of the lands offered for sale, which, it was hoped, would encourage settlement and development. As settlement moved further away from the centres of power, it became increasingly difficult for intending settlers to communicate with the Crown Lands department. Moreover, it became more expensive and time-consuming for the department to carry out its business, especially in cases where there were difficulties, confusion, or conflicts in determining the details of transactions. Crown land agents became a regular part of the workforce of the Crown Lands department with the official appointment of agents in July 1839. The broad outlines of the land distribution system remained relatively unchanged throughout the rest of the colonial period in Upper Canada. There were periodic investigations and reviews of the land distribution system and the Crown Lands department. In their reports officials bewailed the inefficiencies of the bureaucracy and the seeming inability of the government and bureaucracy to prevent squatting and speculation, but no major lasting changes in the legislation of the land distribution system resulted.[44]

As of 1839, it was Crown land agents, paid on commission, and provincial surveyors responsible for conducting valuations who most often dealt with the individuals who wanted to acquire land in Upper Canada. In using the opportunities afforded by their positions to help "deserving settlers" access land, they were also aiding in the development of Upper Canada according to a vision that was neither fully British nor fully American, but had elements of each.[45] The Crown land agents and surveyors recognized that behind the legislation and regulations of the land distribution system was a belief that settlement and the development of productive farms would create a strong and prosperous Upper Canada. As the agents and surveyors knew, though, there were other factors influencing the distribution of Crown lands, most notably, the need for revenue from the sale of Crown lands to assist a government with heavy financial obligations from projects such as canals, roads, and later railways. The Crown land agents and surveyors often found themselves caught in the middle between these tensions, but their overall commitment to the public interest through the encouragement of settlement remained strong. As J. Alexander, Crown land agent, put it in a letter advocating the retention of the credit system, "the profit or trouble given to the Department should not be taken into account when the settlement of the lands is the object sought in return and now when so many people with small means are looking for home[s] for themselves and their families."[46] The improvements to transportation and communication and the exploitation of resources such as timber alone could not ensure growth and prosperity – settlement had to be encouraged as well.

Among the tasks given to Crown land agents and surveyors was providing the department with information and paperwork required for special cases and disputes. Agents were routinely responsible for conducting inquiries about disputed claims and for assisting claimants in establishing chains of pre-patent sales of rights, a pre-patent assignment search. Where occupants applied to purchase a particular parcel of land, agents were to carry out inspections of the land, note any improvements or degradations thereon, and provide a reasonable valuation for the sale of that land or hire a provincial land surveyor to do so. This was one duty for which the agents received additional compensation. The instructions regarding these duties reflect the careful balance the agents had to maintain: "They are to proceed to this valuation with much attention and caution, avoiding all favor or acception of persons, and avoiding equally too high a valuation which might deter or overcharge purchasers, or too low a one which would diminish the fair proceeds of the public property."[47] In making inspections and valuations, the agents were responsible for finding an equilibrium between conflicting tensions and for providing written justification for their valuation to the department.[48] On the one hand, they were to try to encourage settlement and development of the land, and on the other, there was pressure from the government to maximize the revenue from the sales of Crown land, not to mention their own commission on the sale of land. The inspection role of Crown land agents, in some ways, conflicted with their role as sales agents.[49]

The Crown Lands department and the Commissioner of Crown Lands relied heavily on the local knowledge and judgment of the agents and surveyors as D.B. Papineau, during his term as Commissioner, acknowledged when he wrote to Thomas Baines: "As local Agent, you are better able to form an opinion than the head of a Department living at a distance, who cannot be supposed to know all particulars of a case. This local knowledge in District Agents is one of the chief grounds of the confidence reposed in them by their chief; therefore they must be held responsible for the advice they give."[50] The agents were to "give an opinion as to the merits of the case"[51] and "to offer a suggestion for the consideration of the Department."[52] The Commissioner of Crown Lands routinely adopted most of the resolutions suggested by the agents and surveyors, passing the recommendations on to the Executive Council who were responsible for issuing orders-in-council allowing private sales. Since the Council regularly deferred to the recommendation of the Commissioner of Crown Lands in their decision, the Crown land agents and surveyors were accorded significant influence.

Within the scope of the duties and responsibilities of the Crown land agents was the very important task of dealing with squatters and squatters' claims. Squatters posed an administrative and legal problem for the government, but opinion about the value and contributions of squatters varied widely. Crown land agents and surveyors developed clear criteria by which they judged squatters and their contributions. The agents and surveyors were able to adhere to these criteria because their instructions authorized them to allow "occupants in good faith" or "with improvements" a reasonable opportunity "within a short delay" to purchase the land which they occupied. Interpreting those terms provided the agents and surveyors leeway in dealing with squatters.[53] The colonial government never formally extended pre-emption rights to squatters as had been done in the United States where squatters had the right to be able to purchase the land that they occupied by private sale from the government. Unable, however, to escape the influence of the United States, and the popularity of the idea of pre-emption among many settlers, it became tacitly understood that squatters' rights would receive some recognition from the colonial government. Upper Canada could not ignore land allocation practices in the United States if it wanted to attract and retain settlers on its own public lands.[54] It was made clear, though, that this was a privilege and not a right, and it was dependent upon whether or not a squatter was determined to have a legitimate claim.[55] It was up to the Crown land agents and surveyors to make this decision in most cases, and when the squatters could demonstrate their intentions to become *bona fide* settlers, they found ready allies in the agents and surveyors. Over time, as the agents and surveyors continued to affirm the legitimacy of the claims of legitimate squatters, the strength of the practice of pre-emption was even further reinforced, leaving the government with little choice but to go along because of precedence and popular opinion.

William Belford's disputed claim, as a squatter, to a lot in Belmont township received typical support from the Crown land agent who inspected and valued the lot on the basis of his improvements. In the report, the agent noted that "it would be a hardship to Belford to dispossess him." The other claimant to the lot had little improvement to show and had never paid municipal taxes on the lot, taxes commonly paid by squatters to strengthen their claims. As a result, the agent was unsupportive of the other claim.[56] Surveyor S.W. Hallen outlined the situation of Austin Jacobs, a squatter in East Gwillimbury township, portraying Jacobs in a favourable light to support his claim to the lot. The report noted that Jacobs was a poor man who had occupied the land almost two and half years earlier, during which time he had cleared almost three acres and built a small log house and barn, all of the improvements "effected by his own industry."[57] J. Alexander made more than one request to the department to ask for their decision on the application of Henry Perry to purchase a lot in Mulmur township on the basis of his occupation and improvement of twelve acres.[58] John Carroll made a strong case for occupants in Zorra township to be allowed to purchase a lot that had earlier been assigned to another man named McDermid. Carroll noted that the present occupants were responsible for all the improvements on the lot, which were considerable. Since McDermid had "joined the rebels in 1837 or 8 and left the province and [was] still absent," Carroll reasoned that the present occupants were "the only persons having any claim."[59]

With a lively market in pre-patent land rights, both in squatters' rights and through location and occupation tickets, the Crown land agents and surveyors often found themselves confronted with cases like that of a disputed lot in Bradford Township. Two men, both squatters, claimed the lot – James Summers and John Ross. John Ross had purchased the rights and the improvements of an earlier squatter,

John McDonald. In October 1843, John Alexander, Crown land agent for Simcoe County, justified his advice regarding the dispute: "I am of opinion that John Ross has the best claim to the Lot in dispute, on account of his possession, long settlement in first place, largeness of family and industrious habits."[60] By order-in-council of 21 March 1844, Ross was allowed to purchase the lost the Council concurring with Alexander.[61]

Alexander based his recommendation partly on Ross's "industrious habits." Such character judgments are common throughout the records as an important element in determining the legitimacy of claims. Thomas Steers, agent for Essex, Kent and Lambton counties, carried out an inspection of lots in Adelaide and Warwick townships in 1840. In his report, he made careful note of the character of settlers as part of his recommendations. Typical of a favourable recommendation was his evaluation of the Wiley family: "The Wileys have been [here] since the first settlement ... They are a most industrious hard working family and deserve encouragement and have always been foremost in making roads and assisting newcomers to progress in the Township."[62] Such people were viewed as assets to the community and the province, and agents typically supported their claims even when the official government policy was less encouraging.

In contrast to deserving settlers, others received little support from agents and surveyors. In 1840, the Crown Lands department sent Henry Sullivan to inspect some lots in St Vincent township for which Price Mallory had received a location ticket for a lot containing a mill site. An 1837 order-in-council issued the location ticket on the lot on condition that Mallory build two mills and have them operating within two years of the order. When Sullivan arrived in 1840, the sawmill was not yet in operation and the grist mill was barely able to produce enough flour for the few settlers in the township. Sullivan noted that the location for the mill was poorly chosen, "the stream being scanty even almost dry in some seasons, [and] the dam very leaky and the thing altogether like Mr Mallory himself, of the very worst character." Sullivan went on to say that the mill had begun production long after "the time when by the terms of the agreement a mill should have been in operation." Sullivan's recommendation was that since Mallory had failed to meet the terms of the order-in-council, he deserved no favour from the government.

There are often clear distinctions in the records concerning what constituted a deserving settler in contrast to those whose motives were perceived as self-serving and even exploitative. An example of the latter was found during an inspection of three lots in Wainfleet township in Niagara. It was discovered that nearly all the oak and pine timber on those lots had been removed, which reduced the value of the land by about 50 per cent. The occupants were the sons of the original squatter who had first occupied the land about thirty years before. That man had taken enough squared timber from the lots to supposedly supply the British government with all that was needed to construct "during the late War [of 1812–14] ... the Block houses at Chippewa."[63] The location of the lots, on the upper reaches of the Chippewa River (also known as the Welland River) which empties into the Niagara River above the falls in the village of Chippewa, meant that the timber could easily be floated down the river to Chippewa. The inspector advised that the squatters should not be given any favourable consideration since the money made by selling the Crown its own timber and the use of the lots for three decades were compensation enough for the improvements made on the lots. Good prices and markets meant that plundering of timber was common throughout the colony, as many agents and surveyors found. They were diligent in reporting such activity and routinely condemned it, although they could do little to stop it, short of denying claims. Thomas Steers remarked of a squatters' claim in Maidstone Township: "I think he has none – the lot is badly plundered," implying that the squatter was responsible for the removal of the timber expressly for the purpose of selling it, rather than removing it in order to clear the land for farming.[64]

In contrast, settlers who appeared to be making an effort to clear the land for farming received the support of agents and surveyors. William Webster, a squatter in Zone Township, told the inspector that he was not only "ready to comply with the terms the Department shall deem fit to require" but that he had made considerable improvements. As well as having twelve acres cleared and fenced, along with a log house, Webster had "half the road in front made tolerably good."[65] In a country where roads were an almost constant source of complaint, Webster's work on the road in front of the lot no doubt struck a chord in his favour with the inspector; such effort implied that Webster was there to stay.

The Crown land agents and surveyors often played the role of advocate for people caught in unfortunate circumstances. While compassion may have played a role, perhaps the agents and surveyors also recognized that providing cheap land was a way to supply the poor with the means to support themselves.[66] George Kerr, agent for Lanark county, noted in his memorandum book that he had written to the Crown Land department regarding the improvements that J.L. Sample had made on a lot in Beckwith township. Sample "had been living on the lot twelve years and had all his improvements on it and all he was worth in the world invested in it," and hoped "that he might not be turned out of house and his land given to other parties who had plenty of land besides ... whereas he had no other land in the world and praying he might be allowed to purchase the lot at a valuation."[67] Kerr, sympathetic to Sample's plight, cited Sample's twelve years' residence on the lot as evidence of his legitimacy as a settler. Thomas Baines likewise supported the claim of D. O'Connors to a lot in Pickering township: "he is quite a respectable looking elderly man with a large family, has no other property but this Lot, and no other way of supporting them but from what he raises off it." Baines acknowledged that should his claim be recognized, O'Connors would have a difficult time paying the back rent and hoped that his support as agent, along with a letter from a Dr Herrick on behalf of O'Connors, would convince the department to waive the back rent.[68]

Sympathy went beyond just trying to assist those with little or no capital except for the investment of their time and labour in clearing and farming. Agent John Sharman assisted William Corrigan to retain his possession of fifty acres in Wallace township. Corrigan, after going blind, had found himself deep in debt to a local man, Jesse Jones. Corrigan had agreed to transfer his claim to the south halves of Lots 3 and 4, Concession 13 to Jones, on the understanding that when the debt was discharged, Jones would transfer the land back to Corrigan. However, because of his disability, Corrigan was unable to pay the debt for some time and was compelled to give up his claim to the south half of Lot 3 wholly. Jones transferred the south half of Lot 4 back to Corrigan. Jones had registered the first assignment of both half lots, but had never had the second assignment of Lot 4 back to Corrigan registered. Sharman explained the matter in his report, indicating that he had no reason to disbelieve Corrigan's statements and that Corrigan had fulfilled the settlement duties. The department granted Corrigan permission to purchase the lot.[69] Arrangements to benefit another blind man who was squatting on a lot in Chinguacousy township were proposed by Thomas Baines.[70]

Women, particularly widows, also received support for their claims and petitions from Crown land agents and surveyors. Alexander McNabb wrote to the Commissioner of Crown Lands that Winifred McPherson, widow of James McPherson, had made considerable improvements to the lot in Huron township on which her husband had paid the first instalment. McNabb noted that she was "anxious to pay up the arrears, [and] at same time to be allowed to hold the land in her own name." McNabb supported her request. He wrote that since most of the improvements on the lot had "been made by Mrs McPherson since her husband's death" the sale should be changed from James to Winifred McPherson. So as to further justify the request,

McNabb noted that the fees that Mrs McPherson would have had to pay to the Heir and Devisee Commission "if the purchase was completed under her husband's name" in order to have the title transferred to her as heir, could now be applied to the arrears on the lot, and the money would go directly into the account of the Crown Lands department.[71] F. Ferguson, agent for Victoria and Peterborough counties, requested that the Widow Cornhill be allowed to purchase the land which she occupied at the price set at the time she first occupied the lot. The Commissioner of Crown Lands turned down Ferguson's request, but noted that Cornhill could petition the Governor General in Council for permission to purchase the land at a valuation.[72] Thomas Steers also made note of the six acres improved by a widow and children on a lot they occupied. In support of her claim, he described her as "very industrious and has suffered much privation."[73]

Other disadvantaged individuals in Upper Canadian society also received support from the Crown land agents and surveyors when they met the criteria for deserving settlers despite racial differences. The most important criteria for deciding whether or not a settler was deserving of favourable treatment appears to have been applied to everyone.[74] For example, Alexander Simcoe asked the Commissioner to reduce the amount owing on a lot settled by a black family in his agency: "Sam'l Thomas ... is not able to pay a fair value for the land and should it be exacted would leave him and family without a house or home... May I now beg to enquire if I may carry out the sale ... to Thomas at one shilling per acre, that price being as much as he is able to pay."[75] The inspector, Charles Rankin, spoke well of the efforts of a black man, Williams, who was one of many squatters on the town site of Chatham. Rankin noted that Williams, a butcher, had been living there for several years "and appears to be industrious and is at present supplying the village and neighbourhood with fresh meat." Williams and his family seemed to be faring well in the area and wished to stay, although, as Rankin noted, "the white inhabitants ... describe him as a troublesome character (litigious &c. &c.) and appear very anxious to exclude him from the village." Despite the hostility of Williams's neighbours, Rankin's report of Williams was favourable, and he believed that Williams had the money to purchase the land on which he had several buildings.[76]

The extinguishment of Native American title to the lands of Upper Canada had gone hand in hand with the creation of reserves, where it was hoped the Native peoples could be taught how to live like Europeans. Agricultural pursuits were at the top of the list of the best ways in which they could be assimilated into society.[77] Large blocks of reserved lands were surveyed into regular farm lots, enough of which were retained to accommodate the Natives on the reserve, and the rest were opened to sale to other settlers. The proceeds of the sale of the excess lands went to the Indian Department to administer their work among the Natives. When the Indian lands of the Moravian Reserve were inspected to gauge the progress of settlement, the inspector encountered both white and Native settlers. The inspection of lots occupied by Native Americans was important in highlighting the success or failure of efforts to assimilate the Native peoples. Among the Native American settlers was "Philip Jacob, the Chief, [who] lives on this lot, has a good House and 17 acres good tillage."[78] Jacob was a deserving and legitimate settler because he had a house and considerable land in production.[79] The inspector was applying the same criteria (perhaps even more stringently) to Jacob's efforts as to any other settler but the receipt of title to the lot because of effort was especially important in this instance because of Jacob's position as chief. Jacob was a model for other Native Americans. In contrast, the inspector noted that although "John Huff Indian has 40 acres of tillage some good, some has been allowed to run wild." The inspector was not as encouraged by Huff's efforts because of the indications that Huff was not as diligent a settler as he might be, and as with any other settler found in similar conditions, the report was not as favourable.[80]

These attempts by Crown land agents to act as advocates for people whom they saw as deserving settlers reveal elements of a moral economy at work. This moral economy, quite simply, sought to provide access to a reasonably sized, reasonably priced parcel of land for all those deemed to be deserving. In the same way, Crown land agents and surveyors often acted to ensure that legitimate settlers had access to land at a reasonable price, often in response to pressures from speculators and the government to limit supply and increase prices. In a petition to the Governor General in 1850, residents of Wellesley township protested that the land prices set by the government were too high. The matter was referred to the Commissioner of Crown Lands who asked Andrew Geddes to report on the situation. Geddes' report supported the petitioners' argument and the department later informed Geddes that "the reduction in the prices of lands both in that Township and in the Township of Mornington as suggested by you has been sanctioned."[81] A reduction in land prices in Geddes' agency meant a reduction in the amount of commission he would receive from their sale; yet that was his recommendation.

George Kerr, agent for Lanark county, was actively engaged on behalf of squatters who wanted to purchase land. Kerr's appointment in 1859 came during a time when the government was trying once again to discourage future squatters and convince those already squatting to purchase the land where they resided. One of the tactics employed was to charge squatters rent for the time that they had been in illegal possession of the lot. Those who had become squatters because they lacked the capital to purchase land found themselves considerably indebted to the government because of the rent charges. George Kerr often made appeals for a reduction in rent charges so that squatters could afford to purchase the lots. For example, he wrote to the department on behalf of Mr Ahern, a squatter: "if the lot is burdened with the rent with which it is chargeable ... he ... would not be able to purchase, neither is the land worth it. He is willing to pay the valuation price and 10 years rent in addition which I think is as much as it is worth."[82] Kerr advocated reductions of the amount of rent payable because of the inability of the purchaser to afford the full amount, or because the additional money would put the price far beyond the real value of the land. By doing so, he was intervening to enforce the principles of a moral economy: the opportunity for people to be able to obtain land at fair and affordable prices.

Agents like Kerr played a crucial role in mitigating some of the effects of attempts to change land policy that came with political changes. The government's oscillations in enforcing these aspects of the land policy made it difficult for agents to find a balance when dealing with squatters and occupants. Public opinion vied with the determination of some governments and officials to force squatters to purchase the lots on which they were living and to enforce settlement duties and the collection of arrears. The circulars sent out by the department to the agents demonstrate the underlying conflict over the direction of the land policy and the relative importance of encouraging settlement in comparison to revenue from land sales. For example, in December 1842, a circular sent out to the agents informed them that they were to entertain pre-emption claims on Clergy Reserves only when occupants made payment within a period fixed by the agent.[83] In an effort to eliminate the squatting problem on Clergy Reserves several years later, another circular, dated 14 March 1846, informed agents that pre-emption privileges would expire on the 1 January 1847. Squatters not making application to purchase and paying all rents owing since the date of occupation by 1 January 1847 would not be considered to have any special claim to those lots.[84] The deadline provoked protest from occupants unable to raise the money necessary to comply with the order, and another circular, dated 23 December 1846, informed agents that "a further delay is granted to parties so circumstanced."[85] Similarly, when the government began an earnest attempt to close out the sales of remaining Crown lands in the settled townships in 1859 by forcing squatters to purchase the land they occupied or else forfeit their improvements, it again backed down from initial deadlines.[86] The government's lack of clear direction left the agents to try to find a workable balance between the benefits that squatters often brought to the community and the illegalities of their occupation. It became the self-appointed task of many agents to persuade the Crown Lands department and the government to work with settlers and to make the process of acquiring land more flexible and responsive to the needs of the people who would settle the land and build farms.

Flexibility in payment schedules and interest relief were two of the areas in which agents and surveyors worked on behalf of individual settlers and whole communities. With economic fluctuations, changing political situations, and the uncertainty of agricultural production from year to year, those who purchased Crown lands often found themselves in arrears. Crown land agents often cited circumstances such as poor soil conditions, poor crops, a lack of transportation to markets, and the sheer difficulty of clearing the land for agricultural purposes as reasons for extending the time allowed to pay for Crown land purchases.[87] The Commissioner of Crown Lands requested that Alexander McNabb comment on the destitution and suffering of many settlers in his agency after the Commissioner received a letter from D.S. Macpherson, a Member of the Legislative Council, on the subject. McNabb concurred with Macpherson that the high local taxes and the relative newness of the settlement, plus several years of bad crops, were placing a heavy burden on the settlers who also owed payments on their lands. McNabb suggested that the settlers should be granted an additional five years to make up their arrears to the department even though his commission on those payments would also be deferred.[88] William Stewart of West Gwillimbury township, who signed himself "your undutiful servant," wrote to J. Alexander, Crown land agent for Simcoe County, asking for additional time to make his payment. "If you will please to bear a little longer with me with the help of God I think I shall be able to pay you in the course of 2 weeks I do expect this week if spared to have my wheatt thrashed and butcher my hogs and next week go to the city with a load."[89] Stewart's request was not the first that Alexander had received. Earlier, in 1844, Alexander evidently had felt that a significant number of settlers in his agency would need such allowances. He wrote to the Commissioner of Crown Lands asking if the department would allow him to extend additional time for payment to those squatters who had legitimate claims without having to refer each individual case to the department.[90] Individual settlers, if their situation was desperate, often received the support of the Crown land agents in asking for extensions for making payments. In December 1859, Crown land agent Alexander McNabb asked that an extension be granted for Mr Day who was "one of the best settlers in the Township of Greenock and as he has complied as regards improvement with the Conditions of Sale ... I beg leave to recommend that he be allowed until the first of January 1861 with the understanding that all arrears be then paid up."[91] If the Crown land agents trusted in the integrity of the settlers and believed them to be good settlers, then the agents acted as advocates in this way for them, despite the fact that extensions would defer the payment of the agents' commission.

In 1859, in a letter accompanying a report of inspection, J.B. Askin systematically laid out a list of reasons why a particular group of settlers, lacking capital, ought to be allowed ten years to pay for their lots on a former Indian reserve. His first reason was very simple. The settlers had only what they could make from the labour they applied to the land to pay for the lots; moreover, they did not have adequate collateral to obtain loans at reasonable interest rates. Second, the local assessment for school and municipal taxes was so high that settlers found it difficult to raise enough cash to pay both the taxes and the current required instalments. Next, Askin spoke of the deterrent to settlement that the current high prices for land created. His fourth point remarked on the extension of government credit: "the improvements and the Buildings erected are a sufficient guarantee to the Government that the money due with the interest will be fully paid in time." His last two points most clearly indicate his opinion regarding the necessity of government assistance for settlers: "5[thly] If they are not relieved from pressure to meet the demands due the Gov't (by giving time) they must sacrifice and abandon their best labour and time and go to the States where better terms are offered to the Settler, who is there considered as a valuable acquisition to the State and whose labour and energies is considered as deserving of encouragement. 6[thly] I consider every good Settler whose residence in the Country is permanent to be worth to the Province £100 and when he leaves this Province with his family to settle elsewhere the Country loses that sum if not more."[92] Askin believed in the doctrine of improvement and the need for settlers to further the development of the colony and urged the government to give settlers more time to pay for their lands. The short-term costs and difficulties accrued by the government would, Askin argued, be offset by the settlers' efforts in improving the land and putting it into production. Other Crown land agents and surveyor-inspectors made similar arguments in favour of extending credit through an instalment plan for purchasing Crown lands, indicating a concern that settlers without much capital be given opportunities to purchase lands directly from the Crown instead of from speculators who would charge crippling interest rates. Askin's report also raised a critical issue in the development and administration of land policy in Upper Canada: the public lands of the United States. It was important to make the Crown lands attractive with low prices and easy terms in comparison to the United States, yet also prevent the familiar abuses like speculation and squatting that plagued that land distribution system.

As the amount of land available for settlement shrank, it seemed that the tensions regarding land policy grew, especially during periods when demand for land was high. In 1854, during a period of rapid land acquisition and settlement, the role of the Crown land agents and surveyors became even more crucial. The situation in which many found themselves highlighted the difficulties and problems they had to work through. The account of one of the Crown land auctions held in the fall of 1854, and the subsequent fallout from that auction, demonstrates the role of the Crown land agent and the expectations placed on them by the government, the Crown Lands department, the settlers, the public, and even themselves.

On Monday, 11 September 1854, the village of Elora was witness to the arrival of hundreds of people. They were there because Andrew Geddes, the Crown land agent for Wellington county, was ordered to auction off the land of the township of Minto in the northwest corner of the county. Several months before, an official notice of the auction appeared in newspapers throughout the province. The fine print outlined the terms of sale and conditions. Geddes estimated that over 600 men had assembled in the street in front of the agency office by the time the auction began. Given earlier reports of what was happening in Minto township and the dire predictions for the outcome of the auction, Geddes and his assistants must have been anxious about what might transpire during the auction. Just days before the auction, the Toronto *Leader* noted that in Minto "there is such contention, wrangling, and even fighting amongst the would-be squatters, that respectable parties are almost afraid to go into the township." The article predicted, correctly as it turned out, the likelihood of violence at that auction where Geddes "will find himself beset with a herd of savages hooting, yelling, swearing, fighting."[93] It is no surprise then that Geddes had made arrangements to have, in addition to the auctioneer and several clerks, a bailiff and several prominent local gentlemen to oversee the auction.

The crowds that appeared the next day as the auction continued, were even larger. On Tuesday, as Geddes described, "in the afternoon the fellows had a regular fight, some 40 or 60 of them more or less, and next day when they came to pay their faces were patched in all directions. I have no doubt but some of them thought me very cross, as I told them plainly, that they should have *fair-play*, but if they made any noise and were refractory, I would at once *close the sale* [emphasis in original]." Andrew Geddes' weariness is evident in his letter of 16 September 1854: "Here I am sitting all alone, after a week of hard work, selling the Lands in the Township of Minto. I commenced on Monday Morning at 10 o'clock and went on till five in the afternoon. After Tea [I] took payment from a few, whose Lots were not disputed. On Tuesday Morning [I] commenced at 8 A.M. & took payments till within a quarter of ten AM. At 10 [I] opened the Sale again and by 12 Noon, had gone over the whole 18 Con. [I] Commenced at once taking payments and continued steady till 4 o'clock this afternoon, that is from Tuesday at one P.M. till Saturday at 4 P.M. say from 9 in the morning till 5 in the afternoon." [94]

Both squatters and speculators were present at the auction in Elora. The conditions of sale for the lands of Minto included the rule that no individual could purchase more than 200 acres of land. The speculators, under the guise of acting as agents for absentee purchasers, obtained a great deal of land at that auction, outbidding would-be settlers. The speculators at the Minto auction and at other auctions throughout the province paid the first instalments on those purchases but largely ignored the other conditions of sale that required actual settlement and improvements. Crown land agents would later support the claims of legitimate squatters on lots held by absentee owners.

After the auction, the sales of many of the lots could not be completed because of disputes over claims. Although Minto Township was technically opened for sale and settlement on 11 September 1854, in reality, settlement had begun long before. Andrew Geddes was probably not far from the truth when he estimated that three-quarters of the lots in Minto were occupied before the auction.[95] Squatting, although often ignored or downplayed in the literature on land policy and settlement in Ontario, was widespread. The government, even though it tried to discourage squatting, was never very successful at it since public outcry and protest resulted in extensions to deadlines or failures to enforce the edicts. The effect of this was to merely give squatters every confidence that their residence and improvements would give them a superior claim to purchasing that land. This is what happened at the auction of the lots of Minto township. Geddes' records indicate that nearly 300 of the lots had disputed claims, most because squatters or people who had purchased squatters' improvements had prior claims. As with all Crown land agents, Geddes had been instructed to give squatters first chance at purchasing the land if their claims were legitimate. This task reached enormous proportions at large auctions like the one at Elora, not only because of the number of lots sold but because of the amount of squatting.

Although the auction only lasted a day and half, Geddes spent the rest of that week and some of the next hearing the claims of the squatters and making decisions about their legitimacy. In many cases, the claims were tenuous, the only evidence being the word of the claimants. Other claimants had made only token improvements, putting up a shanty, or slashing a small amount of timber, in order to be able to sell their "claim" for cash to intending purchasers. Other cases were more complicated because claimants had made significant improvements on the lots. In such instances, neighbours might be called upon to give affidavits outlining how long a squatter had resided on a lot and the extent of their improvements. It was not just the presence of squatters that made Geddes' task so difficult, but the market in land claims. Rights in lands were being actively traded before legal ownership was ever obtained from the Crown and it was the Crown land agent who routinely encountered such transactions and the resulting claims. In Minto, anticipation of demand for the lots led many to squat in order to establish a claim. Some squatted because they wanted to become purchasers and settle in the township, but others were only looking to profit from their squatting, selling their "improvements" or claim to the lot to those who wished to purchase the lot from the Crown. Distinguishing between the legitimate settlers and the so-called "professional squatters" was difficult in places like Minto township where even some of the legitimate settlers had only been able to make small improvements, or had only had the opportunity to purchase "rights" based on questionable improvements. Responsibility for sorting all this out fell on the shoulders of the agents.

Along with aiding legitimate settlers and discouraging others, agents sought to curb the efforts of speculators. Although Andrew Geddes himself was under considerable suspicion in the late 1850s regarding speculation, he acted on behalf of legitimate settlers who ran into difficulties with speculators. In August 1865, Geddes wrote to the Commissioner on behalf of Samuel Halliday who wished to purchase a lot in Peel. Halliday made an application to purchase even though one instalment had already been paid on the land by Benjamin Sutherland in 1847, eighteen years earlier. Geddes supported Halliday's request, since the land was unoccupied and unimproved. The sale to Sutherland, so Geddes recommended, should be cancelled on the basis of the non-fulfillment of the conditions of sale that required actual settlement and improvement. Geddes made note of evidence that indicated Sutherland was likely a speculator whose speculative holdings were impeding settlement. Sutherland, he stated, "is a man of wealth and has lately purchased an additional farm. He also holds a Lot in Maryborough I am told on which no settlement has been made and only the first instalment paid."[96] The securing of land by paying the first instalment was a favourite tactic of speculators, who counted on the laxness of the government in enforcing the conditions of sale that required actual settlement and improvements, and in enforcing regular annual payments. Geddes' successor as Wellington county's agent, James Ross, made a similar recommendation for a squatter who was residing on land evidently purchased for speculative purposes at the 1854 Minto auction. In 1867, Ross reported to the commissioner that Samuel Whitman, who petitioned to be able to buy the lot on account of improvements made thereon, ought to be allowed to buy the lot. "This Lot was purchased in September 1854 by David Morrison, at that time an assistant editor in the *Leader* office who has since left the country. As it is to be inferred that David Morrison has abandoned his claim from never attempting to carry out the conditions of sale, nor having paid any thing in addition to the first instalment, I can see no objection to allowing Whitman to purchase."[97]

Although the Crown land agents and surveyors worked on behalf of deserving people in order to facilitate the process of becoming land owners, many were not doing so just on a moral principle. Records from the Crown Lands department show that at least some speculated in Crown lands themselves. It was a common practice for a number of years for the government to pay surveyors in land, which gave them a decided interest in land prices. Some Crown land agents, in defiance of the regulations that governed their appointments, also speculated to varying extents, or else they had close ties to speculators. Many of the agents had other businesses. It was openly acknowledged in a report on the Crown Lands department that most agents did not make enough from their commissions as Crown land agents to be able to make a living, and it was expected that they had other sources of income.[98] These speculative activities and other business ventures were not completely at odds with their efforts on behalf of legitimate settlers, though. It was widely accepted that the faster the land was cleared and put into production the greater the economic growth and strength of the colony both on a provincial and local scale. For example, Kingston lumber merchant and Crown land agent Allan MacPherson would have benefited from the development of the agricultural hinterland through settlement both by means of the availability of the raw materials needed for his mills and the sale of his lumber products to the surrounding community.[99] Similarly, speculators who held wild land would also directly benefit from higher prices for their land if the lands around were settled and cleared and the beginnings of roads already in place. It thus made sense, for a number of reasons, to encourage "deserving" settlers to acquire Crown lands.

Early in Upper Canada's existence, the presence of large tracts of land had been the major source of tension in the land distribution practices in the colony. There was more to the debate, however, than just the physical presence of large tracts of land, and once the shift to land sales was made, a number of other problems became more apparent. Settlement was to be encouraged, in order to further the development of the province, even if that meant extending goodwill to squatters, yet there was also pressure from speculators who saw the opportunities for capital development through speculation. For a government that always seemed to be strapped for cash for large public projects such as canals and later railways, Crown lands could be an important source of revenue. Yet raising the prices for Crown lands only discouraged would-be legitimate settlers and encouraged squatting or emigration to the United States where land was cheaper. These tensions are clearly reflected in the records of the period. Placed in a situation where they worked for the Crown and served the settlers, the Crown land agents and surveyors found themselves at the juncture where policy met reality. The implementation of government policy was largely in their hands, and they acted according to their view of the public interest in their handling of land distribution. That public interest, influenced by notions of improvement and the moral economy of providing access to land ownership for everyone, involved giving willing individuals and families the opportunity to acquire a reasonable amount of land on which to build a farm at a reasonable price. Consistently, the local officials worked to even further reduce the barriers to land acquisition for those whom they considered "deserving of favourable consideration." Crown land agents and surveyors were powerful allies and advocates for those people who showed themselves ready and willing to become *bona fide* settlers and thus contribute to the development and future prosperity of the colony. The agents had a self-appointed function: that of active mediation between the government, speculators, squatters, and settlers in order to ensure that deserving settlers had access to land that they could transform into productive farms.

NOTES

1 Upper Canada will be used throughout this paper to describe that area and political jurisdiction which is now southern Ontario. Politically, Upper Canada was created in 1791 when Quebec was divided into Upper and Lower Canada.

Although Upper Canada officially became Canada West in 1841 with the creation of the Province of Canada, the name Upper Canada remained in popular use until it was renamed Ontario at Confederation in 1867.

2 John C. Weaver, *The Great Land Rush and the Making of the Modern World,* *1650–1900*, (Montreal & Kingston: McGill-Queen's University Press, 2003), 24; G.M. Craig, "British Travellers in Upper Canada, 1815–1837," *Ontario History* 43 (1951): 180.

3 Eric Stokes, *The English Utilitarians and India* (Oxford: Clarendon Press), 81–139.

4 Weaver, *Great Land Rush,* 24

5 G.E. Mingay, *A Social History of the English Countryside* (London: Routledge, 1990), 51; Michelle Vosburgh, "The Crown Lands Department, the Government, and the Settlers of McNab Township, Canada West," conference paper, Canadian Historical Association, May 2005.

6 Weaver, *Great Land Rush,* 21. Much of the American historiography on this issue can be traced back to the impact of Frederick Jackson Turner and his frontier thesis which placed responsibility for a strong independence and democratic culture in the United States on the frontier experience. Patricia Nelson Limerick, "Turnerians All: Dreams of a Helpful History in an Intelligible World," *American Historical Review* 100 (June, 1995): 697–716.

7 Weaver, *Great Land Rush,* 73.

8 John Gallagher and Ronald Robinson, "The Imperialism of Free Trade [1953]," reprinted in William Roger Louis, ed., *Imperialism: The Robinson and Gallagher Controversy* (New York: New Viewpoints, 1976), 59.

9 D.K. Fieldhouse, *Economics and Empire, 1830–1914* (Ithaca: Cornell University Press, 1973), 86, 464,

10 Weaver, *Great Land Rush,* 19.

11 Ibid., 21.

12 Peter Burroughs, *Britain and Australia 1831–1855; A Study in Imperial Relations and Crown Lands Administration* (Oxford: Clarendon Press, 1967), 12–34.

13 Ibid., 10–11.

14 R. Wright, *The Bureaucrats' Domain; Space and the Public Interest in Victoria,* *1836–1884* (Melbourne: Oxford University Press, 1989).

15 Peter Burroughs, "Imperial Institutions and the Government of Empire," in Andrew Porter, ed., *The Oxford History of the British Empire: The Nineteenth Century* (Oxford: Oxford University Press, 1999), 3: 170–1.

16 Lillian F. Gates, *Land Policies of Upper Canada* (Toronto: University of Toronto Press, 1968).

17 See, for example, Weaver's discussion of the land speculation activities of prominent Virginians, *Great Land Rush,* 96–109.

18 Paul W. Gates, *Landlords and Tenants on the Prairie Frontier* (Ithaca: Cornell University Press, 1973), 47.

19 Allan G. Bogue, "The Iowa Claims Clubs: Symbol and Substance," *Mississippi Valley Historical Review* 45 (1958): 231–53.

20 See, for example, Craig T. Friend, "Merchants and Markethouses: Reflections on Moral Economy in Early Kentucky," *Journal of the Early Republic* 17 (1997): 553–74; Ben Maddison, "From 'Moral Economy' to 'Political Economy' in New South Wales, 1870–1900," *Labour History (Australia)* 75 (1998): 81–107; David H. Unser, Jr., *Indians, Settlers and Slaves in a Frontier Exchange Economy: The Lower Mississippi Valley before 1783* (Chapel Hill: University of North Carolina Press, 1992).

21 Christopher Clark, "Economics and Culture: Opening up the Rural History of the Early American NorthEast," *American Quarterly* 43 (1991): 286.

22 See, for example, the discussions in Daniel Feller, *The Public Lands in Jacksonian Politics* (Madison: University of Wisconsin Press, 1984) and Roy M. Robbins, *Our Landed Heritage: The Public Domain, 1776–1936* (Princeton: Princeton University Press, 1942).

23 Alan Taylor, " 'To Man Their Rights' The Frontier Revolution," in R. Hoffman and P.J. Albert, eds., *The Transforming Hand of Revolution; Reconsidering the American Revolution as a Social Movement* (Charlottesville: University Press of Virginia, 1995), 255.

24 Ruth Bogin, "Petitioning and the New Moral Economy of Post-Revolutionary America," *William and Mary Quarterly* 45 (1988): 391–425; Allan G. Bogue, "The Iowa Claims Clubs: Symbol and Substance," 231–53; Sean Cadigan, "The Moral Economy of the Commons: Ecology and Equity in the Newfoundland Cod Fishery, 1815–1855," *Labour/ Le Travail* 43 (1999): 9–42; Craig T. Friend, "Merchants and Markethouses" 553–74; Peter C. Mancall, "The Moral Economy of the Eighteenth-Century Backcountry," *Reviews in American History* 20 (1992): 453–8 and Alan Taylor, *Liberty Men and Great Proprietors: The Revolutionary Settlement on the Maine Frontier, 1760–1820* (Chapel Hill, NC: Institute of Early American History and Culture, 1990).

25 Gates, *Landlords and Tenants*, 9–12.

26 Ibid., 1–2.

27 C.A. Bayly, *Imperial Meridian: The British Empire and the World, 1780–1830* (London: Longman, 1989), 8.

28 John Clarke, *Land, Power, and Economics on the Frontier of Upper Canada* (Montreal & Kingston: McGill-Queen's University Press, 2001), 481–512; John Clarke, "Aspects of Land Acquisition in Essex County, Ontario, 1790–1900," *Social History/ Histoire Sociale* 11 (1978): 98–119; John Clarke, "The Role of Political Position and Family and Economic Linkage in Land Speculation in the Western District of Upper Canada, 1788–1815," *Canadian Geographer* 19 (1975): 18–34; Leo A. Johnson, "The Settlement of Western District 1749–1850," in F.H. Armstrong et al., eds, *Aspects of Nineteenth-Century Ontario* (Toronto: University of Toronto Press, 1974), 23; Leo A. Johnson, "Land Policy, Population Growth and Social Structure in the Home District,

1793–1851," *Ontario History* 63 (1971): 41; J.K. Johnson, *Becoming Prominent; Regional Leadership in Upper Canada, 1791–1841* (Montreal & Kingston: McGill-Queen's University Press, 1989), 52.

29 P.J. Cain and A.G. Hopkins, *British Imperialism, 1688–2000*, 2nd ed. (Harlow, England: Longman, 2002), 647–9.

30 There was some tenant farming practised in Upper Canada. Catherine Anne Wilson, *A New Lease on Life; Landlords, Tenants, and Immigrants in Ireland and Canada* (Montreal & Kingston: McGill-Queen's University Press, 1994).

31 Bayly, *Imperial Meridian*, 76.

32 Jane Errington, *The Lion, the Eagle and Upper Canada* (Montreal & Kingston: McGill-Queen's University Press, 1987), 33–5.

33 Colin Read, "The Duncombe Rising, Its Aftermath, Anti-Americanism, and Sectarianism," *Social History/Histoire sociale* 9 (1976): 47–69; Colin Read and Ronald J. Stagg, eds, *The Rebellion of 1837 in Upper Canada: A Collection of Documents* (Toronto: The Champlain Society and Carleton University Press, 1985).

34 Robert Gourlay, *Statistical Account of Upper Canada*. 2 vols (reprinted Yorkshire, England: S.R. Publishers, 1996). The first volume contains the township reports. At the end of that volume, Gourlay created an index to the opinions expressed in the reports (623–5). The second volume contains, among other things, Gourlay's review of much of the material included in the volumes.

35 S.F. Wise, "Robert Fleming Gourlay," *Dictionary of Canadian Biography*, 9: 332.

36 *Lord Durham's Report*, 222–4.

37 *Lord Durham's Report*, 218.

38 *Lord Durham's Report*, 210.

39 *Lord Durham's Report*, footnote 2, 210–1.

40 Carol Wilton-Siegel, "Administrative Reform: A Conservative Alternative to Responsible Government," *Ontario History* 78 (1986): 105–6.

41 J.E. Hodgetts, *Pioneer Public Service: An Administrative History of the United Canadas, 1841–1867* (Toronto: University of Toronto Press, 1955), 270–3.

42 Gates, *Land Policies of Upper Canada*, 256.

43 Donald Winch, *Classical Political Economy and Colonies* (Cambridge, MA: Harvard University Press, 1965) 93–4, 118–29.

44 Michelle Vosburgh, "Agents of Progress: The Role of Crown Land Agents and Surveyors in the Distribution of Crown Lands in Upper Canada, 1837–1870" (PhD thesis, McMaster University, 2004) 64–68.

45 "General Instructions to the District or Resident Agents of the Department of Crown Lands," Nov. 1845, Crown land agents' records for Simcoe County, RG 1–499–0–9, Archives of Ontario (AO).

46 J. Alexander to Commissioner of Crown Lands, 12 Feb. 1866, Crown land agents' records for Simcoe County, RG 1–499–0–13, AO.

47 "Agents' Duties," 5: 1, "General Instructions to the District or Resident
Agents of the Department of Crown Lands," Nov. 1845, Crown land agents'
records for Simcoe County, RG 1–499–0–9, AO.

48 Commissioner of Crown Lands to William Jackson, 13 Sept. 1861, 172, Commissioner of Crown Lands' outgoing correspondence to land agents, RG
1–6–3–9, AO.

49 Bruce Curtis examines the role of school inspectors in the administration of
rule in "Representation and State Formation in the Canadas, 1790–1850,"
Studies in Political Economy 28 (1989): 63; "Class Culture and Administration:
Educational Inspection in Canada West," in Allan Greer and Ian Radforth,
eds, *Colonial Leviathan: State Formation in Mid-Nineteenth-Century Canada*
(Toronto: University of Toronto Press, 1992), 103–6. In some ways, this role
parallels part of the duties of Crown land agents and surveyor-inspectors, but
it also presented a dilemma to employees whose first duty was, purportedly,
to *sell* land.

50 Commissioner of Crown Lands to Thomas Baines, 19 Dec. 1845, 647, Commissioner of Crown Lands' outgoing correspondence to land agents, RG
1–6–3–3, AO.

51 Commissioner of Crown Lands to E.P. Smith, 27 May 1847, 578, Commissioner of Crown Lands' outgoing correspondence to land agents, RG
1–6–3–4, AO.

52 Commissioner of Crown Lands to P. McMullen, 27 May 1847, 577, Commissioner of Crown Lands' outgoing correspondence to land agents, RG
1–6–3–4, AO. See also Commissioner of Crown Lands to James Stevenson, 18
Aug. 1847, 667, and 4 Sept. 1847, 687, Commissioner of Crown Lands' outgoing correspondence to land agents, RG 1–6–3–4, AO.

53 "Sales of Crown Lands," 13: 2, "General Instructions to the District or Resident Agents of the Department of Crown Lands," Nov. 1845, Crown land
agents' records for Simcoe County, RG 1–499–0–9, AO.

54 Document compilation volume, Crown Lands department, RG 1–65–0–1, AO.
Included in this volume are several items from the United States, demonstrating Canadian interest in the policies and laws of the United States regarding
public lands: "Pre-Emption Circulars to Registers and Receives of the United
States Land Offices" (Washington: A.O.P. Nicholson, Public Printer, 1857)
and "Circular from the General Land Office, showing the manner of proceeding to obtaining title to public lands, by purchase, by location with warrants or
agricultural college scrip, by pre-emption and homestead," 17 Sept. 1867
(Washington: Government Printing Office, 1867). Information about the
American system of public lands disposal was also sought during at least one of
the investigations into Crown lands management in Upper Canada, Testimony
of Jonathan White, and response of A.N. Morin to Select Committee, 5 Apr.
1855, Select Committee on the Present System of Management of Public
Lands – Report, *Journals of the Legislative Assembly*, 1854–55, Appendix M.M.

55 Gates, *Land Policies of Upper Canada*, 264.

56 Inspection report, Belmont Township, Lot 13, Conc. 9, 29 June 1861, 122–3, Inspection and valuation returns on land for various districts, RG 1–95–19–3, AO.

57 S.W. Hallen, Inspection of lots in York County, Lot 114, Conc. 1, East Gwillimbury township, 112, Inspection and valuation returns on land for various districts, RG 1–95–19–3, AO.

58 J. Alexander to Commissioner of Crown Lands, 17 Feb. 1854, Crown land agents' records for Simcoe County, 1835–58, RG 1–499–0–12, AO.

59 John Carroll to Commissioner of Crown Lands, Zorra, 31 Oct. 1845, Crown land agents' records, Brock District, Oxford Co., 1840–61, RG 1–494–0–4, AO.

60 J. Alexander to Commissioner of Crown Lands, 11 Oct. 1843, Crown land agents' records for Simcoe County, 1835–58, RG 1–499–0–12, AO.

61 J. Alexander to Commissioner of Crown Lands, 13 June 1844, Crown land agents' records for Simcoe County, 1835–58, RG 1–499–0–12, AO.

62 Return of Inspection of Lands assigned to the Indigent Settlers in the Townships of Adelaide and Warwick by Thos. Steers, Agent, 1840, RG 1–95–14–9, AO.

63 Lots 58, 59, 60, Concession 7, Wainfleet, Return of inspection of Crown lands in Niagara, 1839, RG 1–95–12–1, AO. The problem of squatters being in occupation only to strip the timber from lots was a common one. See for example, 25 Jan. 1868 to Commissioner of Crown Lands, Crown land agents' records for Midland district, RG 1–576–0–9, AO.; Peter Carroll, Lot 9, Conc. 3 Township of Oxford West, Return of Inspection of Clergy Reserves in London District, 1828–33, RG 1–95–14–1, AO.; Thomas Steers, Lot 4, Conc. 5 Township of Oxford, Inspection Reports Western District Clergy Reserves, 1840–41, RG 1–95–15–14, AO.; Elias Moore to John S. Buchanan, Commissioner of Crown Lands, 10 Sept. 1844; General Remarks for Townships of Bayham, Malahide, Dunwich, Return of Clergy Reserves, London and Huron Districts, 1844–45, RG 1–95–14–11, AO.

64 Thomas Steers, Inspection of Clergy Reserves, Townships of Sandwich, Maidstone, Rochester, West Tilbury, 1842–43, RG 1–95–15–6, AO. See also A.S. Cadenhead to Commissioner of Crown Lands, 24 Nov. 1870, Crown land agents' records, Wellington County, RG 1–495–0–31, AO.

65 Abraham Steers, Report on the Inspection and Valuation of the Indian Reserve in the Township of Zone, 1844, RG 1–95–15–9, AO.

66 For a discussion of the influence of evangelicalism and Malthusian ideas on concern for the poor and poor relief in Britain during this period see Boyd Hilton, *The Age of Atonement: The Influence of Evangelicalism on Social and Economic Thought, 1785–1865* (Oxford: Clarendon Press, 1988), 73–114.

67 Memorandum Book, 18 Apr. 1859, 12, Crown land agents' records for Lanark County, RG 1–578–0–2, AO.

68 Thomas Baines to Commissioner of Crown Lands, 8 Dec. 1845, Crown land agents' records, Home District, 1839–57, RG 1–569–0–7, AO.
69 Corrigan's name also appears as Carigan in the file documents. South ½ Lots 3 & 4, Concession 13, Wallace Township, File No. 2494/65, Numeric land files, RG 1–246–3, Box F–128, AO.
70 Thomas Baines to Commissioner of Crown Lands, 21 Nov. 1845, Crown land agents' records, Home District, 1839–57, RG 1–569–0–7, AO.
71 Alexander McNabb to Commissioner of Crown Lands, 29 Oct. 1861, Crown land agents' records for Bruce County, RG 1–491–0–1, AO.
72 Commissioner of Crown Lands to F. Ferguson, 13 Aug. 1845, 474–5, Commissioner of Crown Lands' outgoing correspondence to land agents, RG 1–6–3–3, AO.
73 Thomas Steers, Return of Inspection of Lands assigned to the Indigent Settlers in the Townships of Adelaide and Warwick, 1840, RG 1–95–14–9, AO.
74 As yet, there is no clear understanding of patterns of race and ethnicity in the distribution of lands in the colonial period. It may be that other outside influences, such as social pressure for segregation, and the establishment of particular areas for the settlement of particular groups, precluded the need for Crown land agents and inspectors to cite such information. Or, it may be that economic considerations prevailed; if settlers were seen to be worthy then they deserved assistance. Perhaps being "worthy" for these groups included the consideration that they were living in socially acceptable areas.
75 J. Alexander to Commissioner of Crown Lands, 11 Jan. 1849, Crown land agents' records for Simcoe County, RG 1–499–0–12, AO.
76 Charles Rankin, "Report – Squatters in Chatham," 31 Dec. 1834, 226, Surveyor-General's incoming correspondence, RG 1–2–1, Vol. 45, AO.
77 For example, Inspection Report, General Remarks, 21, Indian Affairs, Series A, Indian Land Records, RG 10, Vol. 731, National Archives of Canada (NAC).
78 Canada West, Inspection Report, Orford and Zone Townships, Moravian Reserve, 1857, 77–8, Indian Affairs, Series A, Indian Land Records, RG 10, Vol. 1038, NAC.
79 Jacob was also a good example of what the British and Canadian governments were trying to achieve in "civilizing" native Americans. For an introductory discussion of this, see John L. Tobias, "Protection, Civilization, Assimilation: An Outline History of Canada's Indian Policy," *Sweet Promises: A Reader on Indian-White Relations in Canada* (Toronto: University of Toronto Press, 1991), 129–30.
80 Canada West, Inspection Report, Orford and Zone Townships, Moravian Reserve, 1857, 79–80, Indian Affairs, Series A, Indian Land Records, RG 10, Vol. 1038, NAC.
81 23 May 1850, Crown land agents' records for Wellington County, RG 1–495–0–26, AO.

82 Memorandum Book, 22 Nov. 1859, 42, Crown land agents' records for Lanark County, RG 1–578–0–2, AO.

83 Circular from Commissioner of Crown Lands, Dec. 1842, Crown Lands department Orders and Regulations, RG 1–67–0–1, AO.

84 Circular to agents from Commissioner of Crown Lands, 14 Mar. 1846, 6119, Crown Land Administration Files, Regulations and Orders, RG 1–9 Vol.11 Env. 6, AO.

85 Circular from Commissioner of Crown Lands, 23 Dec. 1846, 412, Commissioner of Crown Lands' outgoing correspondence to land agents, RG 1–6–3–4, AO.

86 Circulars, 22 July 1859, 499; 19 Jan. 1860, 580, Commissioner of Crown Lands' outgoing correspondence to land agents, RG 1–6–3–8, AO. "Crown Lands," Chatham *Weekly Planet,* 22 Dec. 1859, 29 Dec. 1859; Gates, *Land Policies,* 31.

87 J. Alexander to Commissioner of Crown Lands, 27 Jan. 1866, Crown land agents' records for Simcoe County, RG 1–499–0–13, AO.; Thomas Baines to Commissioner of Crown Lands, 19 Jan. 1843, Crown land agents' records for the Home District, RG 1–569–0–5, AO.

88 Commissioner of Crown Lands to William Jackson and Alexander McNabb, 12 May 1865, Commissioner of Crown Lands' outgoing correspondence to land agents, RG 1–6–3, AO.; Alexander McNabb to Commissioner of Crown Lands, 24 July 1865, Crown land agents' records for Bruce County, RG 1–491–0–1, AO.

89 William Stewart to J. Alexander, 3 Jan. 1853, Crown land agents' records for Simcoe County, RG 1–499–0–2, AO.

90 J. Alexander to Commissioner of Crown Lands, 5 Nov. 1866, Crown land agents' records for Simcoe County, RG 1–499–0–12, AO

91 Alexander McNabb to Commissioner of Crown Lands, 6 Dec. 1859, Crown land agents' records for Bruce County, RG 1–491–0–1, AO.

92 J.B. Askin to Commissioner of Crown Lands, 25 Feb. 1859, 336–7, Inspection Reports &c Indian Affairs, Series A, Indian Land Records, RG 10, Vol. 733, NAC.

93 "Crown Lands – The Right of Pre-emption," Toronto *Leader,* 8 Sept. 1854.

94 Andrew Geddes to J.C. Tarbutt, 16 Sept. 1854, Crown land agents' records for Wellington County, 216–18, RG 1–495–0–28, AO.

95 Andrew Geddes to Charles Chalmers, 25 Sept. 1854, Crown land agents' records for Wellington County, 220–1, RG 1–495–0–28, AO.

96 11 Aug. 1865, 24, Crown land agents' records for Wellington County, RG 1–495–0–29, AO.

97 1 Aug, 1867, 229, Crown land agents' records for Wellington County, RG 1–495–0–29, AO.

98 Joseph Cauchon, Commissioner of Crown Lands, addresses this issue in several places in his "Annual Report of the Commissioner of Crown Lands for 1856," *Journals of the Legislative Assembly*, 1857, Appendix 25.

99 Allan MacPherson to Col A.J. Derottenburgh, 24 Dec. 1855, letter book, Allan F. MacPherson fonds, F 575, AO.

BRYAN PALMER

Popular Radicalism and the Theatrics of Rebellion

The Hybrid Discourse of Dissent in Upper Canada in the 1830s

> I could repeat a thousand stories,
>   About the Radicals and Tories,
> The Banks, the Merchants and Mechanicks,
>   The Church Reserves and Ceaseless Panicks
> That all of you must know as well,
>   Or better far, than I can tell.
> But what's the use of telling o'er
>   A string of news you've heard before.[1]

The current historiography of Upper Canada is curiously unconcerned with what was once a major preoccupation: the character of
radicalism in a period that saw a pronounced politics of dissent, culminating in a rare rebellious uprising.[2] Whereas older writings exhibited
obvious partisanship, there is no denying that scholarship on Upper
Canada in the 1830s, prior to the 1990s, was insistent on seeing the
period in political terms and staking out interpretive ground attentive
to the primacy of questions associated with the meaning and significance of the radical edge of the age.[3] To be sure, the liberal,[4] conservative,[5] or Marxist[6] writing on the 1830s has not aged particularly well.
There were serious shortcomings within all schools of thought. But
what is striking in reading the major relevant studies of the last decade
is how far they are outside older readings of Upper Canada in the
1830s. Like much historical writing in our time, there is a tendency to
sidestep engagement with conventional preoccupations. In the resulting displacement, claims made on behalf of the sophistications of
newer approaches – be they theoretical or analytic – are often oddly
complacent in their inattention to past scholarship, perhaps even to
aspects of the past itself that bear on their concerns and arguments.[7]

My approach in this paper is to try to resituate the politics of Upper Canadian dissent in the 1830s at a particular interface. The popular radicalism of the 1830s[8] was a hybrid of transplanted practices, thoughts, assumptions, and sensibilities. In the material circumstances of a new and emerging society, these translated into an ensemble of arguments about rights that was simultaneously British and American, rooted in readings of Enlightenment thought and Age of Revolution ideology that were not so much articulated in the texts of politics as in the theatrics of discontent that both animated the highly politicized atmosphere of everyday life and lent elections, tavern debates, even domestic relations new meanings. I draw not so much on concerns with constitutional issues, the diversity of constituencies of reform and localized elite governance, or the substantive scrutiny of key tenets of various ideologies, be they liberal or conservative. Rather I try to place the meanings of popular radicalism more on the surface of everyday life in the period, as they were lived, articulated in languages that were often extreme and symbolism that was consciously used to strike chords of sympathy in particular quarters. These meanings were in formation, rather than settled, and that has confused many interpretive forays into this period, but a fresh look at the rituals, rhetoric, and refusals of the era, especially in the representational realm of political theatre, will perhaps take us back to some old scholarly concerns at the same time as it follows more contemporary routes of analysis.[9] If I return to what an older scholarship often accented, the *oppositions* that ran through the politics of the period, I also acknowledge certain shared, and influential, reciprocities, exploring these through the lens of representation that figures so forcefully within a range of contemporary academic preoccupations.

JOSEPH GOULD, THE BLACK ROD, AND COMPACT RULE

Let me begin with Joseph Gould, whose father had migrated from the United States to take up farming in the Uxbridge area. Gould joined the ranks of political dissidents in the late 1820s and 1830s, a moderate reformer driven to rebellion in 1837 by a combination of Tory obstinacy, Sir Francis Bond Head's patronizing paternalism, the cajoling of William Lyon Mackenzie, and charges of cowardice from the ranks of those pushing armed insurrection. Gould's life was summarized in 1887 by W.H. Higgins, and like countless accounts of the settlement of Upper Canada, his placed the accent on the rough egalitarianism of the popular classes and their penchant for politics. When Gould came to York in 1830 he was bewildered by the inhabitants, who were "all politicians," spending their time "talking politics and walking the streets." The backwoods farmer was at first taken aback by the contentiousness of this agitated political scene: "excitement ran so high that quarrels between neighbours were of frequent occurrence." Knowing "little or nothing of the constitution of the country," Gould read the newspapers and soon gravitated to Mackenzie and the Reformers. His prose was peppered with the discourse of dissent: he railed against "despotic tyranny" and a "grasping oligarchy," protesting "the open corruption and bribery everywhere prevailing," losing political patience with governors whom he described as "superannuated old military officers, or tenth-rate Poor Law Commissioners who knew nothing about the principles of popular government, and had no sympathy with the people over whom they were sent to rule." Against Francis Bond Head he nurtured particular resentments, as much directed against the haughty demeanor of the British figurehead as against his policies.[10]

Indeed, Gould's sense of political grievance was nothing if not intensified by the ritualized articulation of political inequality visible in the structured pomp and ceremony of what he came to see as the imagery of despotism:

First to be seen was the Lieutenant Governor, a mere figurehead, surrounded by six placemen, called Executive Councilors, who held the Governor as a mere puppet in their hands to do their will. These were appointed by the Crown during pleasure, and were not responsible to any other body. They received large pay and salaries for their services, and had sinecures that made them quite independent of the popular will. Their duty was to advise the Governor on all matters pertaining to the Government, and to recommend candidates to office. Below them sat an assembly – mostly of old men – some lame, some halt, some nearly blind, some quite deaf. These men had a chairman, or speaker, to preside over them – mounted on a high chair, called a throne, with a table in front of him. A clerk sat at the high table to record the proceedings, and before him on the table was laid the mace, representing a brass crown, and at the other end of the room stood a little black-haired, black-eyed man in black coat and black knee-britches, and black silk stockings and pumps. The duty of the latter was to carry the brass crown before the speaker when he left the chair, and to summon the chamber below when required by the Governor. On these latter occasions he carried a little black rod in his hand to rap at the door of the Chamber and this was called the "Black Rod." The men composing this chamber were called the Legislative Council. They were appointed by the Crown for life and were not responsible to any man or set of men for anything they should do ... .They had the power of supervision over all legislation.[11]

Gould was eventually pressured to take up arms against this oligarchic rule, and for his troubles was arrested and, ironically, incarcerated in the Legislative Council chambers. After a month's confinement, he was paraded before five figures of august Family Compact authority, Messrs. Jamieson, Jones, Gurnett, Sullivan, and Robinson. When asked what he did for a living, Gould answered that he had a sawmill and a small farm. "What more do you want that you should rebel?" thundered an obviously irate Jamieson. "I want my political rights," responded Gould with coolness. "Why you have got them now – quite enough for so young a man as you," replied the patriarchal Jamieson. Gould shot back with a list of grievances, drawn from the well of Reform resentment. Having had enough of this, Jamieson turned on his heels and huffed: "You are a dangerous fellow and you ought to be hung for believing and spreading your damned treason."[12]

JOHN PRINCE AND THE RECIPROCITIES OF TERROR: THE SUBTERRANEAN TERRAIN OF POPULAR RADICALISM

Gould did not go to the gallows. He even managed to narrowly escape transportation to Van Dieman's Land.[13] That the Black Rod did not come down on him with its full force is part of the overlapping social constructions of a liberal/conservative historiography that accents the lenience of Upper Canadian authority in the suppression of the Rebellion (which is seen as "reasonably" handled by moderate interpreters and as the folly of a "lunatic fringe"[14] by more extreme commentators). But what Jamieson wanted was on occasion enacted by his counterparts in the suppression of the uprising. Thus, John Prince ordered five prisoners captured in the December 1837 Patriot invasion of Windsor summarily executed. Prince's extra-legal executions were done in ways that were consciously meant to enhance the impact of what Fred Landon, one of the most sensitive of the early radical-liberal historians of the Upper Canadian rebellion, once referred to as a "veritable reign of terror."[15] Carried out by Prince's quartermaster, Charles Anderson, the killings were staged with bloodthirsty glee, at widely separated points, for the benefit of the greatest number of onlookers. This was done in the face of officer protests to deal with the prisoners according to the laws of the land, and the refusal of a First Nations man, involved in the capture of the Patriots, to participate in the butchery. "No we are Christians," said the Native, "we will not murder them – we will deliver them unto our officers to be treated as they think proper." When Prince was entreated "not to let a white man murder what an Indian has spared," this humanitarian, if racist, plea, fell on deaf ears. "Damn the rascal, shoot him," was Prince's curt condemnation.[16]

Tory judges had long counselled the use of "terrible examples" to prove that "justice does array herself in terrors when it is deemed necessary."[17] The period 1837–39 was one such moment when justice could be seen to be dripping in blood, at least by some of its victims. "Where there was one patriot last fall there are now ten," wrote a correspondent to *Mackenzie's Gazette* in August 1838, explaining this as a "consequence of the abominable conduct of the government agents and volunteers, who have plundered, pillaged, ravished, and committed all sorts of excesses throughout the winter."[18] The climate was conditioned by a flood of correspondence from across the colony, warning of dire consequences if authority did not act to suppress the drift to revolt. John Black, a recently arrived British emigrant, wrote in a panic to Francis Bond Head from Chippewa in November 1838, pleading to be granted a hearing with the Queen and demanding that his safety be guaranteed, for "the enemy is powerful." Begging Bond Head to "send a speedy dispatch to England," Black warned, "Let the Empire awake. Let it not run itself for a few Treacherous speculators ... all is Speculation, Craft, Policy, Perjury, and Trachery. I cannot trust even you. All being bribery." Black's admonitions to trust in the information he could provide perhaps faltered on his request to be paid £20 for information on rebellious doings in his locale, but other reports were no less fearful. From Brockville came the claim that the loyal supporters of the Crown were "surrounded by a great number of disaffected persons who would at once join the standard of rebellion were it raised in the Province." An Ingersoll correspondent narrowed his complaint to identifying a singular threat: "A Yankee rascal of the name of N.P. Hoague ... has threatened that if any rising took place that the whole of Ingersoll's buildings and property should be burned; this fellow is a wagon-maker – has no stake in the country, but is a perfect firebrand." Oaths of allegiance were refused in Belleville, where dangerous societies were forming, harbouring sympathies for rebellion, while in Delaware, Scots farmers were rumoured to have been lured toward the Rebel camp by claims that the government was about to introduce tithes to pay for the Church of England. The era was often depicted as one of "party spleen and commotions," a Perth writer reporting bluntly, "Revolutionary party are organizing themselves to disturb the peace of this province."[19] Jeremiah Smith and Joseph Walker wrote to Sir Francis Bond Head on the goings on in the nursery of radicalism, Lloydtown, immediately after the suppression of the Mackenzie uprising: a marauding band of twenty rebels brutalized loyalists in the street and, in defiance of all deference, pulled off "their hats twirling them in the air and hurraing for Mackenzie stating that they were to be at the same nefarious business again." Begging His Excellency "to devise a plan in this sad emergency to better our wretched and defenceless condition," Smith and Walker pleaded for the suppression of "these wretched Men ... prowling about with feelings malignant and revengeful."[20]

For all the claims of a liberal/conservative historiography that authority reacted with lenience and moderation to the movement of organized sedition, there was, of course, a counter-revolutionary terror unleashed. One Lockport, New York exile claimed that thousands had fled Upper Canada in the aftermath of the Rebellion, "driven from their farms, their shops, their professions, their families, and their homes by the lawless violence of an excited and unprincipled soldiery."[21] Even allowing for exaggeration, it is apparent that a terror was unleashed in the late 1830s and very early 1840s that was the last gasp of an old order forced to respond to the demands of dissidence with violence. In April 1839 came a Tory plea for restraint, occasioned by fear that loyalist shootings on American steamers on the St Lawrence and other acts of retribution were having an adverse effect on calming a discontented populace: "I should point out to your Excellency the painful anxiety which I am constantly exposed to from an unnatural state of things which compels this Government to be as much on its guard against the acts of its ultra friends as those of its enemies, and to apprehend almost as much mischief from the loyal as from the disaffected inhabitants of the country."[22]

This, and copious other evidence, nevertheless distracts us from seeing and hearing the activities and resonances of popular radicalism. For the thunder of Tory terror was the loud clap of only one hand in the reciprocities of a political culture that, by the late 1830s, had come to be ordered by irreconcilable antagonisms. The terror of oligarchic officialdom had long been opposed by a counter-terror of those ground down by oppression and slights large and small. Dr John Newburn of Stamford had his barn burned in June 1839. Newburn was a backer of the Family Compact who had made statements about rebel cowardice. Threatened with a tar and feathering, confronted by a musket-toting blacksmith who informed him impolitely that bullets were a cure for the Queen's Evil, Newburn was warned by a radical innkeeper on the eve of the Rebellion that he and his family were targeted to be butchered. He rode out the storm but later saw one of his outbuildings go up in flames. As he turned to the courts to secure redress, the loyalist gentleman was denounced throughout the district and, according to

Newburn, "The Magistrate, who had dared to perform his duty, was styled, *in the language of the People*, A Tyrant and Oppressor."[23]

Newburn's complaint, worded as it was in a hostility to The People and their politics of dissent, echoed across the colony. In 1840 two men from Norwich wrote to the Lieutenant-Governor to report that a man had come into their workplace to tell them that they and "all British subjects are to be murdered. He said they are bound by oath (as soon as the first stroke to be struck) to turn out at Night, and surround each house and set Fire to it, and burn all men, women, and children – we thought we would let your Excellency know for we can't rest easy in our beds – surely there ought to be a force stationed here for it is a bad place."[24] There were similar reports from Newmarket, and in the London District spies claimed that Hunters from Detroit had been dispatched to burn the government buildings in Toronto and elsewhere, to destroy Colonel Prince and his property, and to execute Sir Allan MacNab.[25] In Kingston a militia colonel found his dog shot and a note left on his gate: "God damn Colonel Hill and all his crew shall die so God help me, if I have the strength to kill the old bugger let the curse of God await him. He had better have stayed home." The Chief Magistrate of the same locale was promised "death and destruction" if he dared pass judgment on Patriot invaders and captured Rebels.[26]

As rumours spread that the insurrectionists had taken Toronto, resentments long buried surfaced in condemnations of local Tory figureheads. A postmaster-coroner unleashed a political tirade of grievance and retribution: "You d——d Tory your Dye is Cast your doom is sealed Your person and property is Consigned to a Conflagration and I shall rejoice to see it. You may escape one week and the longest two weeks and then you will come as a supplicant to me, and what judgment will I meet out to you; then we will have the Laws of Liberty established here, we will not be ruled by Tryanny and oppression any longer."[27] A Toronto official was the recipient of a typical 1838 or 1839 threatening, anonymous letter: "you damned crab your officiousness last winter against the cause of liberty shall meet its just reward ... death shall be your work nothing can save you I think I see the case quiver your limbs shall give."[28] From upstate New York, letters were posted to the "chief magistrate of Kingston upper canady," promising revenge if any Patriot invaders were banished or put to death: "I can rais in a fornit a army of 10000 affective men that neather fears death nor hell they are redy and willing when they are calde upon if you put them or cos them to be put to death nothing but death shall hinder you & your executors from sharing the same fate."[29]

With subterranean streams of rebelliousness unblocked in the Upper Canada of the 1830s, the world seemed, to some, turned upside down. Those who had for so long dispensed fear, found themselves on the receiving end. In Sandwich the following paid announcement was printed:

> Having received certain threatening letters against my life and Property, I hereby give notice that from this day, on every evening at sundown, I shall cause 12 spring guns with wires and strings complete and each loaded with 30 buck shot, to be set about my house and farm buildings, also 2 man traps. All persons are hereby warned not to come within the grounds on which my premises are built between *sun rise and sun-set*.[30]

It was signed John Prince.

Notices such as these appeared as Tory mobs assailed post-Rebellion bands of reformers gathered at "Durham Meetings," the defeated "Liberals" ironically emboldened by a representative of Empire (known as "Radical Jack") sent to the colony to address the shaken foundations of order:[31]

> O the "Family Compact" is made of a set
> Of most ignorant ninnies, who office do get,
> . By lying and cheating, for with poison they fill
> All our Governors' ears: but my hearties, keep still;
>   For Durham is coming
>   To give them a drumming
> That he surely shall do with a hearty good will.
>
> Then the two hundred couples of brothers and cousins,
> Will all to the right about turn them by dozens,
> And the John O'Groats Bishop and rattlesnake tail
> Of the "Compact" uprooted will be by the gale,
>   Which swiftly is coming ·
>   To give them a drumming
> And the plans of Lord Durham shall ever prevail.[32]

At one such example of "Lynch Law at Cobourg," the clash of forces resulted in torn flags, torched podium scaffolding, and head wounds, a Reform newspaper declaring, "This is Tory government and Canadian freedom ... Such conduct will rouse the spirit of the people by making them know and feel that they are very slaves and deserve to be so if they do not maintain their rights in the face of every opposition."[33] Prior to the public clash of forces, a Reformer's livestock had been cruelly "altered" in the dead of night; the cattle-maiming involved a Durham bull.[34]

The *Niagara Chronicle* fanned the flames of discontent by reporting on Radical political charivaris and nightly effigy burnings in Buffalo, where the protections of Republican indifference to such transgressions gave free rein to Patriot anti-Toryism:

> The "Sovereigns" of Buffalo had a glorious carnival of three days duration Last week – they had a regular auto-de-fe of effigies. On the first night Captain Drew was brought to the stake under the "Liberty Pole." Sir Allan Napier MacNab was the victim the second night, and on the third, Sir George Arthur, Chief Justice Robinson, and some other bloody Britisher, whose name we have not learned, suffered martyrdom. All the cracked fifes, fiddles, and bugles in the modern Gomorrah were screeching Hail Columbia and the Rogues March – the latter was played in character. Tar and feathers are now at a premium in the City of Sympathy, as no more of these exhibitions can take place without a fresh supply ... A great deal of readable enough English has recently been expended in the discussion of the question: Is There to be War?[35]

As late as 1841, political meetings in support of the government were challenged and disrupted. In Ingersoll, a blacksmith designated a "traitor" threatened riot against supporters of the state, and faced down a Justice of the Peace with the statement that he lacked the strength to arrest him, adding for good measure, "there are too many Jack knives among us."[36] This, then, was a theatre of popular politics animated by clear enough popular understandings of antagonisms, one that rocked the old, paternalist order of Upper Canadian governance to its very foundations.

THOMAS TALBOT: PATRIARCH PATERNALIST AND THE DEMISE OF OLD AUTHORITY

One measure of this change was the socio-political transformation of a bastion of older, localized, compact rule, the Talbot District, centred in St Thomas.[37] Compact authority, as a longstanding historiography has made abundantly clear, was loosely consolidated on an interlocking grid of compacts, many of which were only tangentially structured into the official York-Kingston axis of Family Compact governance.[38] Southwestern Ontario's Thomas Talbot was perhaps the leading example of a crusty, militarily designated patriarchal authority, the personification of what Graeme Patterson has called a "courtier compact." In 1817 the settlers in the St Thomas area convened to honour their leader and benefactor with the proverbial address to paternal authority:

> Sir, Having assembled to commemorate the institution of this highly favored Settlement we beg leave to present you with the tribute of that high respect, which we collectively express, but which we individually feel. From the earliest Commencement of this happy patriarchy, we date all the blessings we now enjoy: And regarding you as its founder, its patron, and its friend, we most respectfully beg leave to associate your name with our infant institution. To your first arrival at Port Talbot, we refer as the auspicious hour which gave birth to the happiness and independence we all enjoy, and this day commemorate. In grateful remembrance of your unexampled hospitality, and disinterested zeal in our behalf, and contemplating with interested feelings under your friendly patronage and patriarchal care, we have unanimously appointed the 21st of May for the Talbot Anniversary. And this public expression of the happiness among ourselves, and of our gratitude to you, we transmit through our children to our latest posterity.[39]

A pristine statement of paternalism's successes and compact governance's victorious incarceration of its subject population in the categories and identifications of its making, this homage identified the social, economic, and political glue that held a nascent social order together, suggesting how patriarchy proved a powerful rationale for elite rule, a gender-based diffusion of the metaphor of family authority into the realm of civil society.

By 1832, however, the paternalist capacity to bond together elements of the social formation was weakening, and the Father's power was shaken. Talbot was forced to issue his own address, prefaced by a revealing acknowledgment:

> Notice: Having seen the proceedings of different Meetings held in the Talbot Settlement on the subject of imagined grievances, and of finding that it is now necessary to ascertain the real sentiments of the inhabitants, so as to at once put down the fever (by a few only) manifested, to encourage disaffection to the British Government, I give this notice, recommending a general meeting of my Settlers on St George's Day, the 23rd of April, next, the King's Arms at St Thomas, at noon, when I shall attend.
>
> Thomas Talbot
Father of the Talbot Settlement[40]

Talbot, jocularly known as Thomas Tough, a "jolly plethoric rubicund aristocratic steward" whose "Despotic Self" was excused by his "kind and benevolent heart" and his zealous protection of his settlement from "Yankee organizations" offensive to the local "Ripstavers and Gallbursters," sensed his paternalist power and patriarchal authority waning in the 1830s, under assault from political reformers and land-hungry Scots quick to refuse the mantle of deference he demanded.[41] John Howison described the Talbot settlers as a "lawless, unprincipled rabble consisting of the refuse of mankind, recently emancipated from the subordination that exists in an advanced state of society ... a democracy of the most revolting kind ... addressed by the titles, *sir, master,* or *gentleman.*"[42] This kind of identification occurred only in the later 1820s and took on new force in the 1830s. Indeed, as late as 1824, Mackenzie noted in the *Colonial Advocate* that he had seen Talbot, enjoyed his company, and hoped his "children, for so he may call all the settlers in Middlesex, will teach their little ones to revere him as Peter Patriae, founder of his country."[43]

When Talbot appeared before his charges in 1832, however, he needed to shore up his sagging political authority with more than the reverence the young feel for the old. British flags flew in abundance, banners of scarlet were emblazoned with crowns and the words "Sir John Colborne and the Constitution," 300 footmen, accompanied by fife and drum, bellowed out "Rule Britannia," and Talbot was escorted to the assembly by 200 horsemen, with a bugler at their head. Mounting the podium at the King's Arms Hotel, Talbot regaled the crowd, pausing for good effect to take some snuff. He decried the presence in his settlement of what he referred to as a few "black sheep," and then went straight to the heart of the matter of sedition:

> it was not until recently that these intruders openly declared them-
> selves. It was not until they formed a damned cold water society
> here, at which they met night after night in secret enclave to con-
> coct measures for the subversion of our institutions, that I was
> aware of the prevalence of such principles. This well organized
> band first commenced the study of their tactics at Ealahide where
> they have the greatest strength and where they had the advantage
> of the military skill of a Yankee deserter for a drill seargeant, aided
> by a tall stripling, the son of a former UE Loyalist, whom they trans-
> formed into a flagstaff ... They next tried their strength in
> Yarmouth, where aided by a few Hickory Quakers they succeeded
> in organizing a committee of vigilance whose duty I suppose was to
> sound the conch shell of sedition in every valley and on every hill,
> where aided by certain characters who making a cloak of religion

to cover their seditious purposes and who secretly lent them the
light of their countenances they prospered to the present time.[44]

From other quarters, too, came denunciations of "peddlers and
strolers," and attributions of dissent to "runaway negroes and people
who have neither habitation nor property in the country." At the end
of the Talbot meeting, it was claimed that only one man hurrahed for
Mackenzie, described as a "stout looking Tennessee Negro." Merchants, likely Americans, who harboured reform sympathies, were
assailed as grasping Jews, and Colonel Talbot was quick to point the
finger of faction at "Ryersonain strolling priests." Clearly any counter
to paternalist authority – temperance society or dissident religion
(both of which smacked too much of a feminized challenge to the
rough masculinity of the frontier), economic alternative or race
(which ran headlong into the culture and content of conventional
power) – was grist for Talbot's theatrical pronouncements from the
platform of the King's Arms.[45] For his part, the curmudgeonly Colonel
thought he had done rather well, writing complacently to Sir John
Colborne, "I had a splendid turn-out on St George's Day, when the
rebels were all silent and quiet, and I gave my children some wholesome advice. The disaffected are but few, considering all the noise that
has been made."[46]

THE THEATRE OF DENIGRATION

What we are seeing here is a beleaguered, albeit complexly differentiated, patriarchal paternalist authority challenged by a diverse set of
economic, political, and cultural transformations. All were associated
with the consolidation of a market society and the consequent hetero-
geneity of a population no longer capable of being subsumed under
the rule of older compacts. Given that Upper Canada's governance
had so long been defined by paternalists of whom Talbot was arguably
one of the more obstinate and extreme, rather than through any narrowly conceived Constitutionalist practice, and that the relations of
subordination were lived in particular locales far distant from the
Black Rod of the York Executive Council, it is not surprising that the
politics of dissent in Upper Canada unfolded less within the formal
structures of institutional politics than in a confrontational theatre
and counter-theatre in which rhetoric and symbolic representation figured forcefully. This was a public sphere as much of performance,
however, as it was of logical debate and articulate speech and it easily
slipped into postures of extremism, in which both language and
symbolic activity could veer toward the violent.

Consider, for instance, the Tory-Orange denunciation of the Reform candidacy of Mathew Howard in the Johnstown District in eastern Ontario in 1830. Said to be supported by Methodists and social levelers, one Howard meeting drew this sarcastic response from the conservative press:

> a great noise was heard at the doors of the Committee, when lo in walked Mathew Mushroom Howard, Esquire, carrying a Millstone round his neck and supported on the right and the left by the most reverend fathers William Hallock and James Cameron his tail and other habillments upheld by an innumerable host of 'Saddle Boys.' Cameron introduced Howard: Gentlemen, slaves, Mr M.M. Mulberry Mushroom Howard is a Miller, a grist Miller, a Farmer, a Trader, a straw hat Maker, a pumpkin pie maker, an onion sauce stewer and ... a mighty clever man and what more do you want for the good of the country.[47]

There is in this account a denigration of the popular classes, a virtual repudiation of the rights of producers, broadly defined, to partake of political action. The message of Howard is ridiculed in its egalitarianism, and the appeal to the rights of all citizens is scoffed at in the duality, "Gentlemen, slaves." The usual linking of dissident religion, race, and plebeian status is evident as an entrenched Tory paternalism in the 1830s finds the Reform challenge difficult to take seriously. After a Howard victory, however, the response of reaction accelerated to an uglier physical intervention. In an 1833 electoral gathering outside of what is now Athens in Leeds County, reformers placed one David Fairbairn in the Chair, only to find that this action of constituting authority in the hands of a mere painter drew the ire of assembled Tory Orangemen. A mob dragged the mechanic from the podium, and in a craft equivalent of tarring and feathering, varnished him with red paint, also taking the time to pull Howard and other well-known Reformers away from the meeting and dump them in the snow. Leeds elections would be punctuated with tumultuous riots for the next three years.[48]

THE ENIGMA OF CLASS IN THE 1830S

This reaction introduces into the realm of power, bounded by compact rule, oligarchy, paternalism, and patriarchy, the element of class.[49] It is a shadowy presence in the Upper Canada of the 1830s, for the social formation in this period of nascent capitalist development is by no means demarcated clearly by obvious material polarizations. Yet what is striking is the extent to which aspects of the theatre of popular politics are infused with trade and craft symbolism and a rhetoric of occupation. The link between labour and politics was recognized intuitively by an antagonistic paternalism, just as it was lived out by those producers of town and country who had assimilated a populistic grasp of the labour theory of value. At a Radical London District gathering in 1837, the *Liberal* claimed that the 1,000-strong throng was the largest political assembly in the history of the Middlesex townships, adding its description of those who came together: "It is true there were none of the Squirearchy there, none of the Office-holders, none of the half-pay, half-witted Aristocrats, but the cultivators and OWNERS of the land were there, the WORKINGMEN were there – the people and intelligence of the country were there."[50] Paternalism, with its accent on the master side of the master/man relation, choked audibly on the kind of producer ideology that was beginning to be voiced in the 1830s:[51]

> Ye merry mechanics, come join in my song,
> And let the brisk chorus go bounding along:
> Tho some may be poor and some rich may be,
> Yet all should contented be and happy and free.
>
> Ye tailors of ancient and noble renown,
> Who clothe all the people in country and town,
> Remember that Adam, your father and head,
> Though lord of the world was a tailor by trade.
>
> Ye Masons who work with stone, mortar and brick,
> And lay the foundation in deep, solid, and thick,
> Though hard be your labour, yet lasting your fame,
> Both Egypt and China your wonders proclaim.
>
> Ye smiths who forge tools for all trades here below,
> You have nothing to fear while you smite and you blow.
> All things may you conquer, so happy your lot,
> If you're careful to strike while the iron is hot.

Then follow stanzas on stevedores, cabinetmakers, hatters, carders and spinners, coopers, printers, coachmakers, and shipbuilders.[52] The constituency of popular radicalism, as the list of those 885 individuals confined on charges of insurrection and treason in the aftermath of the Rebellion indicated, was the broad array of producers.[53] In those regions, such as the Home District, where capitalist development was more advanced, the shock troops of rebellion were most definitely the dispossessed labourers of town and country. Fully 300 of the roughly 400 arrested there were labourers.[54]

By 1836 Orange figurehead and aspiring Tory political wire-puller Ogle Gowan could write to Charles Jones of the Reform threat in language that merged perceived dangers in the political arena with the discourse of class: "The radicals here in Bastard and Crosby are getting up a union! ... How superlatively absurd are the Radicals when their craft is likely to be endangered."[55] Tories such as Christopher Hagerman and John Beverley Robinson understood well the necessity to placate the mechanics in the emerging political crisis, although in the case of Robinson he deplored the resulting intrusions of class into the techniques of governance. "Everybody knows everything," he wrote in despair to Sir John Colborne, "and all the shoemakers and tailors in town are discussing ... the 'Cabinet pudding.'"[56] After the routing of the Reform cause in the 1836 election, Bond Head was quick to compare the newly constituted Tory assembly with that of its predecessors. His language was as unmistakably condescending as was his penchant for class dichotomizations. Convinced that the people of Upper Canada "detest democracy, ... revere their Constitutional Charter, and are consequently staunch in their allegiance to the King," Bond Head reveled in the 1836 election "returning" to rightful authority men of a certain station: "In place of blacksmiths and carpenters reeling from daily labour with no farther knowledge than that which appertained to their calling, and with obstinacy and perverseness proportionate to their ignorance and vulgarity, we have for the most part GENTLEMEN of an intelligence, information, and talent, capable of discussing the measures which they are called upon to deliberate and decide."[57] Three years later, a trio of carpenters said to possess "no property, principles, or influence," would erect a mock gallows on the banks of the Humber, hanging effigies of John Beverly Robinson, Christopher Hagerman, and Bond Head, suspending signs from their dangling bodies: "I will condemn right or wrong; we must have a rebellion; and I will prosecute unto death."[58] To the west, in St Catharines, there were reportedly Chartist meetings called. As Upper Canadian political unions, Lower Canadian Sons of Liberty, and British working-class radicalism seemed to fuse, English textile workers siding with the struggle for "Canadian liberty" and the London-based Workingmen's Association offering an Address to the Central and Permanent Committee of the Patriots of the County of Montreal, beleaguered Tories pounced on the threatening class character of political mobilization. "Canadian Chartists," declared the Cobourg Star, were a "contemptible collection of chiefly liberated traitors, notorious rebels, and men without either character, property or education."[59]

Small wonder that an anonymous "Observer" concluded, in 1842, that the politics of an incipient class experience lay at the root of Upper Canada's recent unsettledness. He thought the province "infested with a vile crew of incendiaries," declaring that, "The very chips of democracy are those Mechanicks that pour in upon us from the States – Even at home they are discontented; and ever thriving for mastery and from their envious hearts and evil dispositions they are driven about, from place, to place, and like Cain become wanderers and vagabonds on the face of the Earth, with their hands against every one and every ones hands against them except the members of their own felon community." Convinced that upon their arrival in Canada, such miscreants enlisted "in the Corps of the rebellious," and that they sustained "the faction of which Mackenzie, Ryerson, and Bidwell are the heads" with their discord and disaffection, "Observer" suggested that mechanics and labourers from the British Isles be encouraged to emigrate to Canada. Their numbers, he suggested, would "reduce the wages at once," thereby materially undercutting the "hateful presence," "upsetting impudence," and "envious malignity" of a pernicious class. Driving such mechanics either out of the province or into economic submission would nip the germ of "future rebellion" in the bud, laying a foundation on which the constitution and laws protective of life and property could survive. "Intense and unremitting perseverance" was required to thwart the "felon cheats slanderers and Democrats of the States," who were infinitely worse than "the Wolves and Bears of the Wilderness," but "the industry of Old England, of Canada, and the human race demand it." "Observer" called on the nascent Upper Canadian state to wage a class war of retaliation against the masterless men of the emerging capitalist labour market, a "proletarian imaginary" that some clearly both loathed and feared deeply.[60]

This is not, of course, to argue that Upper Canada in the 1830s was a fully formed class society, with a mature process of class formation and the institutions, perspectives, and struggles of a workers' movement close at hand. That would not come for forty or fifty years, and then only incompletely. It is to argue that we have something, to borrow E.P. Thompson's metaphor, of a field of force operative in which the theatre of politics moves within the oscillations of a class formation clearly in motion and a class society obviously in the making. Pulled to one magnet pole or another of class formation, sometimes suspended in a highly unstable, even erratic state, the actors within the theatre of politics in the 1830s are not dressed in the unmistakable fashion of class, nor do they speak lines easily scripted with the accent of a proletariat. But neither is the period devoid of the demarcations of nascent class formation.[61]

In the words of William Lyon Mackenzie's Toronto paper, *The Constitution*, "Labour is the true source of all wealth," and good governance was premised on this maxim:

> What is bad government, thou slave
> Whom robbers represent
> What is bad government thou knave
> Who lov'st bad government
> It is the deadly will that takes
> What labour ought to keep
> It is the deadly Power that makes
> Bread dear and labour cheap.[62]

For Mackenzie to make even this kind of elementary stand for the producing classes, linking political reform to the cause of labour, broadly defined, was sufficient to draw the wrath of constituted authority which, yet again, found its resentments most effectively voiced in the verse of vernacular denunciation:

> Sermon or song for a boodle he spins ya
> Pulpit or dungill, its all the same to Mackenzie
>
> Speer ye who holds the Reformers in prate
> Yelpin like curs at the Kirk and the State
>
> Crazed with religio-politico frenzy
> Sheep-stealin, maggot-eye seein Mackenzie
>
> Who day a think on a mission was sent
> The breedin of Johnny's bulldogs to prevent
> Because they made havoc on Janathan's hens see
> Who but the white liver't mawkin Mackenzie
> Midden-bred, filthy-jakes scourin Mackenzie
>
> Ken ya know who truly hae need o Reform
> Who but the unlicket cubs of the storm
> Got on mischance by the father of sin see
> Ryerson, Radcliffe, an roarin" Mackenzie
> O what an orthodox trio, Mackenzie
> Methdoy Yankees and Pagan Mackenzie[63]

This kind of diatribe, so easily aimed at the contentious Mackenzie, slipped over into the generalized theatre and counter-theatre of politics in the 1830s. From Bytown came this 1836 "Recipe to Make an Ultra Radical":

> Take the herbs of Hyprocisy and the root of pride each of them two hands full. Two ounces of Ambition and Vain Glory, bruise them in mortar of faction and boil them in a quart of dissembling tears. Set them over the fire of sedition, till you perceive the scum of Falsehood arise on the top, then strain in the rough cloth of Rebellion, put it in the bottle of envy, then stop it down with the cork of Malice, let it stand and settle and make it into pills ... called Conspiracy. Take two over night and three the next morning and then you will know how to cozen and cheat, and curse the church, pull down bishops, behead kings, let knaves rule over the nation, and cut the throats of all honest men.[64]

Mackenzie, of course, gave as good as he got:

> Ye false Canadians! Tories! Pensioners! Placemen! Profligates! Orangemen! Churchmen! Spies! Informers! Brokers! Gamblers! Parasites and knaves of every description, let me congratulate you! Never was a vagabond race more prosperous. Never did successful villainy rejoice in brighter visions of the future than you may indulge. Ye may plunder and rob with impunity – your feet is on the people's necks, they are transformed into tame, crouching slaves, ready to be trampled on.

Ever willing to personalize his attack, Mackenzie named the McNabs, Robinsons, Gowans, Hagermans, Boultons, Princes, Strachans, Merrits and other Compact figures as "refuse and scum of God's creation ... besoms of heaven's wealth against poor sinners, let loose from below ... to curse a portion of mankind ... mocking the idle hopes of those who believe that you would do ought for a suffering and ruined population."[65]

THE HYBRID DISCOURSE OF DISSENT

To work toward a conclusion, it is useful to pause to provide an analytic note. The popular radicalism of Upper Canada in the 1830s was a hybrid, one in which the crossings of a transplanted, transatlantic world were evident in a plebeian attachment to the rough egalitarianism of a nascent capitalist order still governed by an *ancien régime*. Precisely because that old order was itself transplanted, it lacked a measure of longstanding legitimation, and the winds of change blew through it with gusto in the 1830s. But the hybridity of this contested terrain was not only the complex amalgam of British, American, and Canadian that took root in the soil of productive and cultural life in the new world of muddy York and in the clearings and the bush described by Susanna Moodie.[66] To understand the popular politics and power relations of the 1830s it is necessary to treat seriously the meaning of patriarchy, paternalism, and class in this new world order, and in doing so the failures of the Rebellion of 1837 can be seen in new ways.

First, patriarchy. This was the unquestioned, often unarticulated foundation of the social and cultural assumptions of the age. It linked domestic life and political rule, spilling over necessarily into the economic realm, it being no accident that the metaphorical term of derision aimed directly at power was that of the Family Compact. Patriarchy was the foundation of Upper Canada's social formation in the pre–1840 years, its institutionalization a pervasive presence in all spheres of activity, and one that dominated the relations of private life, in which an unquestioned subordination of women and children to male authority prevailed. The family as the basic unit of social life was headed by a ruling patriarch, whose powers of governance were widely understood to be far-reaching. Women and children were, of course, never totally powerless, but the boundaries within which they could operate were always understood to be limited by male prerogative. In the sphere of popular politics patriarchy was of such significance precisely because Upper Canadian society early established the family as the model, not only for the private realm, but of public life: civil society was an extension of the domestic relations of governance and subordination.[67]

Thus in Upper Canada, patriarchy was identified by reformers, with Tory figureheads referred to explicitly as white-haired patriarchs, and it was assumed by ruling authority itself, as when Talbot referred to himself as the Father of His Settlement, or when Jamieson chastised Gould, commenting that he had quite enough political rights for a man of his young years. The dominance of the father in the family became the rationale for the absolute dominance of father-like figures in the various communities that linked Colonel John Prince's western outpost of the Windsor region to the Bytown gentry. Mackenzie's actual *naming* of elite rule as *the* Family Compact was never merely metaphorical: the connections of family were, of course, embedded in powerful posts, dispensed through patronage, but more to the point, authority itself was conceived as familial, justified as an ideology *and* practised as a set of entitlements that existed (in the eyes of the powerful) prior to any responsibilities or obligations. It was the generalized

symbolism of this congealing of governance as a political phenomenon associated with compact practices, and authority as familial, so
widespread as to be universally understood, that secured Mackenzie's
labelling a powerful presence in the 1830s and beyond.[68]

Second, paternalism. This was intricately related to patriarchy, yet
distinct from it. Paternalism was the set of practices through which
patriarchal and class authority was lived and experienced, from both
above and below, and there were varieties of paternalism, as scholars as
different as Graeme Patterson and Sean Cadigan have shown.[69] They
turned on the reciprocities and mediations of the superior and the
subordinate, the texture of everyday life in which the dominated submitted to the power of ruling authority because of governance's
acknowledgment that its right to rule was balanced by its need to provide, and not only materially, but in a host of other ways as well. Paternalism was thus never a one-way street, but a constantly negotiated
exchange relation. If it was backed up with an immense coercive
capacity, it was also held in place by the powerful subordinating apparatus of moral, religious, economic, and political identifications that
bound layers of society into a seemingly common kinship.

Opposition to Mackenzie, for instance, was early voiced in a language challenging his right to consider himself worthy of patriarchal,
paternal respect. In 1830 the *Brockville Gazette* assailed the York agitator for mistreatment of his son, his mother, and his journeymen printers. Claiming that Mackenzie had beaten his son John with "Turkish
barbarity," these "unnatural cruelties" forcing "the poor youth ... to fly
from thee," the paper asked derisively, "What thinkst thou of the
parental character?" When Mackenzie's mother supposedly protested,
the reformer ostensibly ridiculed "thy mother before thy servant [mak-
ing] a laughing stock of her." Mackenzie's "filial character" was thus
also found wanting. And to close the paternal circle, the editor's relations with his workmen were queried: "Hast thou never played the
tyrant among thy workmen? Never exacted untimely hours of attendance? Didst thou never subject men, of inferior capacity and conduct
for low wages? and didst thou never defraud them of even these
wages?" Mackenzie simply did not measure up to a standard of manliness, his accuser closing "with disgust at these glances at thy domestic
character, as a parent, a son, and a master." He who could not rule his
family and his business dealings with proper decorum was, necessarily,
unfit to rule society.[70]

In the transplanted world of Upper Canada, there is abundant evidence of cracks in the wall of this paternalism, but there are equally
clear-cut indications that the constant arm-twisting in the paternal
arena consolidated elite governance and secured the hegemony of

compact rule. When the cracks widened, the fissures flowing most emphatically out of the diversification of economic life and the making of market society, one measure of which were the incomplete intrusions of class, they would reconfigure the body of paternalist and patriarchal power, most especially as they were visualized and acquiesced to from below, to the extent that this once robust mechanism of hegemony carried less and less of its majesties and terrors. Both the challenges and counter-thrusts of authority were nowhere more clearly played out than in the theatre of popular politics, which saw the rise of radical dissent throughout the 1830s.

In all of this the language and identification of paternalism was a constant, surfacing in Bond Head's charges to the electors in 1836, and structuring the tone and meaning of loyalist resolutions such as this, passed in St Catharines in 1838 by American residents:

That the Leaders of the Revolutionary Party have endeavored to excite the sympathy and secure the support of the Inhabitants of the United States, to their desperate enterprise, by comparing the situation in this province to that under the older colonies which sought a separation from the British Empire, and have pretended to draw a parallel, which this meeting is enabled to declare fallacious, as well from a knowledge of the political circumstances of the two countries, derived, in the one case, from the page of history, and in the other from a conviction that the British Government entertains toward us feelings the most mild and paternal.

The fusion of patriarchal and paternal authority was evident in pardon proclamations of the same year, where the responsibilities of lesser patriarchs were ordered hierarchically, due obeisance demanded to God, Sovereign, Country, and Family:

Let me take this affecting and impressive occasion to entreat you for the future to remember your duty to your Sovereign, your wives, and to your children, to all of whom you have been restored, by the Mercy of the Government you assisted in attempting to overthrow. To your Queen; you not only owe obedience and submission on all lawful occasions, but also your strength in arms and your lives if necessary, in defence of her Crown. To your wives, you owe manly protection, attachment to your homes and firesides, peaceable and respectable demeanor and, for their sake, if for no other, you should be foremost with all of your power to save your Country from the miseries of war in which your conduct so nearly involved it. To your children you owe a

religious moral and loyal education. The man who teaches your
child insubordination and Treason is more your enemy than he
who attempts to take your life and property. The Almighty has left
the maintenance and comfort of your children dependent upon
your bodily exertions; upon your immortal interests he has cast
the responsibility of training their tender minds in the path of
religion, and loyalty and obedience.[71]

How could such a powerful concoction of hegemonic responsibilities be challenged? It is, third, when class is brought into the argument
that some explanatory possibilities of note emerge with respect to the
politics of the 1830s. The discourse of popular radicalism was a hybrid,
in part, because class lacked even the elementary clarity that a more
developed capitalist formation would have provided. The ambiguities
and even contradictions of this period in Canadian history dictated
that class alignments were in the making, rather than in any sense
made or overmade, as they would be in future moments of class
upheaval and challenge, from 1886, through 1919 and 1946, to the
present.[72] This ensured that they were posed ambivalently. The popular radicalism of Upper Canada *was* class ordered, but it often took on
the symbols, the rhetoric, the defiant posturing of struggles other than
those of class – Irish and American republicanism, for instance, or religion or race – where class meaning lay buried in demands to overthrow the entrenched age-old rule of monarchs, a demand that, once
unleashed, led toward calls for democracy and the marshalling of plebeian forces that threatened an assault on the longstanding edifice of
elitist class power.

Within the rhetoric of Reform journalism in 1836 and at the mon-
ster rallies of Radical Reformers in 1837, for instance, there was reference to erecting huge liberty poles. The American eagle figured
prominently on banners, and the slogans "Liberty or Death," "Daniel
O'Connell," "Bidwell, and the Glorious Minority," and "1837, Victoria
and a good beginning" were carried proudly. Pikes, muskets, swords,
trumpets, and cannon were often depicted on placards and flags.
Loaves of bread smothered in butter were hoisted on sticks, or made
the object of target practice, a Radical statement on what many
regarded as Bond Head's insultingly "homely phrase" that "to dispute
with me, and live on bad terms with the Mother Country, you will ...
only quarrel with your bread and butter."[73] There was reference to
Revolution:

Take this piece of advice from an ignorant elf
Let each ipso facto reform one himself

And then my dear Roger, you'll see in conclusion,
A glorious, a grand, a great, Revolution.

A young boy paraded with a sign of a girl over which was pencilled the
phrase,

Of Monarchs tender, Monarchs tough,
We thank our stars we've had enough.[74]

This, then, was a conflicted socio-political environment, in which the
emerging tensions of class formation were evident, even if they were
not moved by a pristine class consciousness and the presence of
mature, formal working-class institutions. This has led the most sophisticated conservative historian of the era to conclude, "Considerations
of economic interest, as is so often the case in the Canadas, seemed to
be outweighing ideological commitment. Considerations of 'class'
seemed to be outweighing those of 'nation.'"[75]

This kind of perspective takes us in new directions of understanding
with respect to the failure of the rebellious uprising. Little has been
made of the enigma of class in the turbulence of the 1830s. Too much
has been made in past historical writings of the ineptness of Mackenzie
as a leader, of the military confusions of the eleventh hour that debili-
tated rebel ranks. An older conservative historiography constructed
the Rebellion of 1837–38 as a tragicomedy of fated failure, depicting
the popular radicalism of the age as something of a nonentity: Loyalism, rather than Rebellion, was the hallmark of nineteenth-century
Canada. This view was later countered by a radical liberal/Marxist
historiography, but this writing never really swept aside the condescending view of the challenge posed in the 1830s. A conservative presentation of Mackenzie and the insurrection as one of those historical
"deviants" easily marginalized in the linear march of Progress and
Nationhood has been too easily assimilated in contemporary historical
writing, which generally pays inadequate attention to Upper Canada as
the site of a spirited, if limited, opposition to inequality, oppression,
and exploitation.

PATRIARCHAL POWER AND THE FAILURE OF POPULAR RADICALISM IN THE 1830S

In explaining the failure of the Upper Canadian Rebellion, and in
understanding the popular radicalism that helped to shape it, the analytic possibilities are indeed more interesting and expansive than conventional wisdoms would suggest. I would like to bring into relief the

pervasive continuity of patriarchal authority and the ways in which it obscured already blurred class lines within the Reform ranks. At exactly the same moment that the Family Compact was being assailed by Mackenzie and others, patriarchy survived and remained unchallenged in the domestic and socio-economic realm. This is evident in a reading of the newspapers of the decade, which are full of notices of runaway wives and, less commonly, absconding apprentices. Such "advertised" escapes warned that no one should treat with these dependants economically and that in the future the patriarchal and paternalist masters would not be responsible for the debts and actions of their charges. They appeared under the same illustration that often graced notices of runaway slaves in the United States' south, and sometimes offered rewards for the return of these subjects, albeit modest ones, ranging from a penny to a few pence. Francis Collins of the *Canadian Freeman*, in jail for his political ideas at the time 'his' apprentice left his employment, offered this curt reminder that Radicals, too, were capable of insisting that patriarchal authority be recognized: "As this boy has always received good treatment, and has thus basely taken advantage of my confinement under a political persecution, to abscond, it is hoped that no person will harbor or employ him." Patriarchy thus lived in the social, economic, and domestic realms, as it was being subjected to increasingly harsh condemnation in the political sphere.[76]

It remains questionable, then, how resolute the Radicals were in their opposition to patriarchy and paternalism, as distinct from their antagonism to how these forms were practised by an odious oligarchy. A warning to "Runaways, Horsethieves, and all other long legged, long nosed, long eared, long mouthed, and long winded inmates of the Devil's Kitchen" from Cobourg's Tom Tough, indicated the class limitations bred in the bone of acceptance of patriarchal authority. Advocating a colony-wide society of tradesmen to keep an eye on apprentices about to take to the roadways, Tough snorted,

> You Scoundrels: We have been tormented long enough with you, and so long as you are allowed to escape from the hands of justice with impunity, so long as we are aware we shall be cursed with your prowling, marauding, swindling and thieving practices. More than one hundred of you have made your escape from this and the two adjoining towns within a very few weeks, and if it was not that you are constantly replaced with a more hungry set, we would say amen to it all.[77]

Patriarchal, paternalist assumptions about class place and, also, gendered power, underlie such statements and explain Mackenzie's oscillating relations with his printers. They toasted him and he them in the 1830s only to find that, within a few years, they found themselves locked in a nasty strike. This complexity, rather than any blunt depiction of Mackenzie as simply a grasping, exploitative capitalist deserving of nothing but radical condemnation is what marks the age.[78]

And that complexity is what situates the promise and the tragedy of insurrection in the 1830s, marking the decade as a fulcrum on which socio-economic transformation and the making of modern capitalist society, with its freedoms and its constraints, perched precariously. The popular radicalism of the period was, in Fredric Jameson's words, something of a "political unconscious," an articulation of an alternative that spoke to new and largely uncharted depths of change, in which the very substance of the relationships of rule were poised as if staring into an abyss.[79] The boundaries of political possibility were being redrawn, not only in the tangible relations of land and labour, but in the materialized subjectivity of mind and style as well.

POPULAR RADICALISM AND THE END OF THE OLD ORDER: CRISIS AND THE SCAR OF PATRIARCHY

This was no secret at the time. It did not take John Beverly Robinson long to conclude that, in the aftermath of the Rebellion, oligarchic authority now rested on a fragile and increasingly unstable foundation. He bemoaned the fact that the scruples and first principles of his beloved gentrified order seemed to have vanished in the conduct of public affairs. The old values and loyalties, indeed the British connection to Empire and its stabilities of governance, seemed to count for less and less among what remained of the Compact layer of patriarchal rulers. If Robinson would indeed oppose the drift of the times, he often privately despaired about the seeming inevitability of the displacement of a way of life, a style of paternal rule that demanded what could no longer be secured, acquiescence and unquestioning loyalty. In the face of Lord Durham's report, which he judged "highly injurious" to "the state of public feeling in Upper Canada," he worried about the fate of "men of judgment and right feeling." The theatrical politicization of life in Upper Canada, culminating in the drama of reform and reaction in the 1830s, helped write *finis* to the undisputed right to rule of Robinson and those for whom he harboured a regard that, in its convictions and honour, could not be reproduced cavalierly. A way of political being, constituted in a particular kind of economy and lived in the vise-grip of patriarchal expanse *and* limitation, ended forever with the 1830s. The John Beverley Robinsons of Upper Canada knew it.[80]

Allan Napier MacNab, staunch Tory defender of King & Country in 1837, provides an ironic comment on this passing of the *ancien régime*, one in which loyalty and honour figured forcefully, at the very moment that its time had both been successfully defended and historically defeated. Awarded with a Knighthood in recognition of his gallant defence of Her Majesty's colonial interests, MacNab appeared, in the aftermath of 1837–38, to have reached the paternal pinnacle of influence and reverence. When his militia men paid him homage, presenting MacNab with a sword valued at 100 guineas, the old commander responded politely with patriarchal gratitude: "While living I shall cherish this Gift, among the richest prizes of my life – and dying, shall bequeath it, as the most venerated heir loom which a father could transmit to his Children." But behind the public façade of familial grace lay the private recognition of the new realities, put to popular doggerel by Charley Corncobb, "poet laureate of reform":

Toryism's sun is set
Tis down, tis gone forever
Some say that it will start up yet,
But will it? Nonsense, never.

As MacNab was feted by the Upper Canadian Assembly, he scrawled on the back of its printed testimonial the terse comment, "Not worth a fart."[81]

The ways in which that harsh judgment were lived by those who saw patriarchal authority undermined to the point of inevitable defeat have not really registered with historians, but the wounds were deep, and they cut across lines of class in ways that complicated the politics of alternative in Upper Canada in the 1830s. There is perhaps no more dramatic an indication of this than Robert Baldwin. Moderate and judicious in his politics, he recoiled from much of the popular theatre of antagonism to authority, just as he rebelled against the aribitrariness of oligarchy and compact rule. His was, ironically, one of the voices that would be heard loudest in the emergence of modern political institutions and the procedures of civil society, Baldwin's name linked unmistakably with Responsible Government and the respectable reform of political life that flowed out of the defeat of the Rebellion, channeled in reasoned constitutionalist direction. Yet Baldwin, too, lived within the bounds of a disintegrating patriarchy, albeit of an extreme, personalized sort. By 1851 he had come to question where all the agitation of the 1830s had led. He complained bitterly of the "reckless disregard of first principles" that he judged to be running rampant in the seismic political shifts of his time. He was apprehensive about "widespread social disorganization with all of its fearful consequences." "If the sober mind of the country is not prepared to protect our institutions," he reflected, there was little hope for the future. As he made his exit from the political stage, a Reformer from the district of Sharon, represented in the legislature by Baldwin, wrote to the chastened Radical, William Lyon Mackenzie, offering a prescription for success in the changed political times of the 1850s: "The watchword is to be no lawyers, more farmers and machinists." It would not quite work out that way – barristers would remain commonplace in politics – but that the matter could be articulated in such a counterposed language of class spoke tellingly about the accelerating pace of socioeconomic change.[82]

Baldwin stood astride the class divisions of the epoch, and their uncertain outcome troubled him greatly. One critical institution – patriarchy – was obviously centrally placed in Baldwin's appreciation. It cut deeply into the political and social relations of Upper Canada, and while it affected women, the young, and those incarcerated in the dependencies of class most adversely, it registered elsewhere as well. Baldwin was predeceased by his wife, who was also his cousin, and throughout the last years of his life he carried a written memorandum in his waistcoat pocket. It stated that should he be carried away suddenly, he was not to be buried before an incision was made into the cavity of his abdomen. It was Robert "Responsible Government" Baldwin's last wish that he should go to his grave, his God, and eternity bearing the same surgical wound as his wife, the scar of a Caesarian section.[83]

The power of patriarchy left its mark, then, on the bodies of those who lived within its defining authority, in the terror of loyalist repression as well as in the theatrics of dissent. It scarred the politics of popular radicalism, which never quite shed its indebtedness to the politics of a civil authority rooted in understandings of familial duty. In the hybrid, transplanted world of Upper Canadian politics in the 1830s this meant that the aspirations of those who so often staged a counter-theatre of insurrection and rebellion were destined in the short run to be thwarted. But in the longer unfolding of Canadian political culture, the blows against patriarchy and paternalism, first struck on the ambiguous anvil of class, did indeed sound the death knell of the *ancien régime*. Popular radicalism made history in the 1830s, if not in ways that it either entirely understood or proved able to articulate with political precision.[84]

NOTES

1 "New Year's Address," *St Catharines Journal,* 3 Jan. 1839.
2 Consider, for instance, the unfortunately neglected Edwin C. Guillet, *The Lives and Times of the Patriots: An Account of the Rebellion in Upper Canada, 1837–1838 and of the Patriot Agitation in the United States, 1837–1842* (Toronto: Thomas Nelson and Sons, 1938), and the still extremely useful S.D. Clark, *Movements of Political Protest in Canada, 1640–1840* (Toronto: University of Toronto Press, 1959), 255–508.
3 Fred Landon, "The Common Man in the Era of the Rebellion in Upper Canada," in F.H. Armstrong et al., eds, *Aspects of Nineteenth-Century Ontario: Essays Presented to James J. Tallman* (Toronto: University of Toronto Press, 1974), 154–70.
4 Categorizations of liberal historiography are by necessity rather elastic. Especially significant are contrasting assessments of the leading figure in the Upper Canadian Rebellion, William Lyon Mackenzie. Nevertheless, a long line of basically liberal commentary on the Rebellion draws its interpretive meaning from considerations of the importance of the event, the justification of grievance, and the role of the uprising in consolidating a new, and improved, social order. I consider the following to be representative: Charles Lindsey, *The Life and Times of William Lyon Mackenzie, with an Account of the Rebellion of 1837–1838 and the Subsequent Frontier Disturbances, Chiefly from Unpublished Documents,* 2 Vols. (Toronto: P.R. Randall, 1862); John Charles Dent, *The Story of the Upper Canadian Rebellion,* 2 Vols. (Toronto: Blackett Robinson, 1885); Dent, *The Last Forty Years: Canada Since the Union of 1841,* 2 Vols. (Toronto: George Virture, 1881); Fred Landon, ed., *An Exile from Canada to Van Diemen's Land: Being the story of Elijah Woodman transported overseas for participation in the Upper Canadian troubles of 1837–1838* (Toronto: Longmans, Green, 1960); Landon, "The Duncombe Uprising and Some of Its Consequences," *Proceedings and Transactions of the Royal Society of Canada* 25 (1931): Section 2, 83–98; Benjamin Wait, *The Wait Letters,* introduction by Mary Brown and afterword by Michael Cross (Erin, ON: Press Porcepic, 1976).
5 The conservatism of older works such as D.B. Read, *The Canadian Rebellion of 1837* (Toronto: Blackett Robinson, 1896) and Robina and Kathleen M. Lizars, *Humours of '37: Grave, Gay, and Grim – Rebellion Times in the Canadas* (Toronto: William Briggs, 1897) continued into the late twentieth century with Frederick H. Armstrong's defence of oligarchy. See Armstrong, ed., Henry Scadding, *Toronto of Old* (Toronto: Oxford University Press, 1966), esp. xx for a conservative statement defending oligarchy; Armstrong, "The Oligarchy of the Western District of Upper Canada, 1788–1841," in J.K. Johnson and Bruce G. Wilson, eds, *Historical Essays on Upper Canada: New Perspectives* (Ottawa: Carleton University Press, 1989), 513–36; and for a distilled statement of animosity to William Lyon Mackenzie, Armstrong,

"William Lyon Mackenzie: Persistent Hero," *Journal of Canadian Studies* 6 (Aug. 1971), 21–35. While a more middle-of-the-road scholarship tended to blur lines of differentiation between liberal and conservative accounts, the historiographic trend was toward a more subtle conservatism. See Aileen Dunham, *Political Unrest in Upper Canada, 1815–1836* (London: Longmans, Green, 1927); Gerald M. Craig, *Upper Canada: The Formative Years, 1784–1841* (Toronto: McClelland and Stewart, 1963); Colin Read, *The Rising in Western Upper Canada, 1837–1838: The Duncombe Revolt and After* (Toronto: University of Toronto Press, 1982); Colin Read and Ronald J. Stagg, eds, *The Rebellion of 1837 in Upper Canada: A Collection of Documents* (Ottawa: Champlain Society and Carleton University Press, 1985). This latter group of writing might well be appreciated as crossover scholarship bridging interpretation and sustaining a liberal/conservative historiography.

6 See, as rare examples, Stanley B. Ryerson, *1837: The Birth of Canadian Democracy* (Toronto: Francis White, 1937); Ryerson, *Unequal Union: Confederation and the Roots of Conflict in the Canadas, 1815–1873* (Toronto: Progress Books, 1968); Margaret Fairley, *The Spirit of Canadian Democracy: A Collection of Canadian Writings from the Beginnings to the Present Day* (Toronto: Progress Books, 1946); Fairley, *Selected Writings of William Lyon Mackenzie* (Toronto: Oxford University Press, 1960); Catherine Vance, "1837: Labour and the Democratic Tradition," *Marxist Quarterly* 12 (Winter 1965): 29–42; Andrew Bonthius, "The Patriot War of 1837–1838: Locofocoism with a Gun?" *Labour/Le Travail* 52 (Autumn 2003): 9–44.

7 Consider, for instance, how little informed by an older body of writing on the Rebellion are some current texts: Allan Greer and Ian Radforth, eds, *Colonial Leviathan: State Formation in Mid-Nineteenth-Century Canada* (Toronto: University of Toronto Press, 1992); Cecilia Morgan, *Public Men and Virtuous Women: The Gendered Languages of Religion and Politics in Upper Canada, 1791–1850* (Toronto: University of Toronto Press, 1996); Jeffrey L. McNairn, *The Capacity to Judge: Public Opinion and Deliberative Democracy in Upper Canada, 1791–1854* (Toronto: University of Toronto Press, 2000).

8 For one recent account which takes this popular politics of radicalism seriously and scrutinizes it usefully through an examination of petitions and other mobilizations see Carol Wilton, *Popular Politics and Political Culture in Upper Canada, 1800–1850* (Montreal & Kingston: McGill-Queen's University Press, 2000).

9 Consider, for instance the direction of James Epstein, *Radical Expression: Political Language, Ritual, and Symbol in England, 1790–1850* (New York: Oxford University Press, 1994); E.P. Thompson, "Hunting the Jacobin Fox," *Past & Present* 142 (Feb. 1994): 94–140; and John Brewer, *Party Ideology and Popular Politics at the Accession of George III* (London: Cambridge University Press, 1976), which differ from the accent on ideology evident in studies of Upper Canada such as Jane Errington, *The Lion, the Eagle, and Upper Canada: A Devel-*

oping Canadian Ideology (Kingston & Montreal: McGill-Queen's University Press, 1987); David Mills, *The Idea of Loyalty in Upper Canada, 1784–1850* (Kingston & Montreal: McGill-Queen's University Press, 1988). That the historiography of the Upper Canadian Rebellion, *the* central event in the 1830s, needs an infusion of ideas and creative thinking is evident in the presentation in Allan Greer, "1837–1838: Rebellion Reconsidered," *Canadian Historical Review* 76 (Mar. 1995): 1–18.

10 W.H. Higgins, *The Life and Times of Joseph Gould: Reminiscences of Sixty Years of Active Political and Municipal Life* (Toronto: C. Blackett Robinson, 1887), esp. 54–9, 100–3.

11 Ibid., 55–6.

12 Ibid., 109.

13 See Benjamin Wait, *Letters from Van Dieman's Land written during Four Years Imprisonment for Political Offences committed in Upper Canada* (Buffalo: A.W. Wilgus, 1843).

14 Sydney Jackman, *Galloping Head: The Life of the Right Honourable Sir Francis Bond Head, Bart., P.C., 1793–1875, Late Lieutenant-Governor of Upper Canada* (London: Phoenix House, 1958), 90.

15 Fred Landon, *Western Ontario and the American Frontier* (Toronto: McClelland and Stewart, 1941), 166.

16 R. Alan Douglas, *John Prince: A Collection of Documents* (Toronto: Champlain Society, 1980), xxvi-xxvii, 28–31.

17 John Beattie, *Attitudes Towards Crime and Punishment in Upper Canada, 1830–1850: A Documentary Study* (Toronto: University of Toronto Centre of Criminology, 1977).

18 Quoted in Clark, *Movements of Political Protest,* 404.

19 Provincial Secretary's Correspondence, Public Archives of Canada (PAC), RG 5 C1, John Black to F.B. Head, Chippewa, 18 Nov. 1838, Vol. 8, #1085; Jas Morris et al., to J. Joseph, Brockville, 1 Dec. 1837, Vol. 9, #1142; John Haycock to J. Joseph, Ingersoll, 11 Dec. 1837, Vol. 9, #1172; C. Murray to J. Joseph, Belleville, 12 Dec. 1837, Vol. 9, #1178; Wilson Mills to A.B. Hawke, Delaware, 31 Oct. 1838, Vol. 13, #1665; Joseph Daily to F.B. Head, Picton, 2 Aug. 1837, Vol. 7, #820; G.H. Read to Head, Perth, 6 Nov. 1837, Vol. 8, #1077.

20 Charles R. Sanderson, ed., *The Arthur Papers; being the Canadian Papers Mainly Confidential, Private, and Demi-Official of Sir George Arthur, K.C.H. Last Lieutenant-Governor of Upper Canada* (Toronto: University of Toronto Press, 1957), 52–3.

21 Civil Secretary's Correspondence, Upper Canada Sundries, PAC, RG 5 A1, Petition of John Van Orman to S.G. Arthur, Lockeport, New York, 22 Mar. 1838, Vol. 189, pp. 105267–8.

22 Provincial Secretary's Correspondence, PAC, RG 5 C1, George Arthur to His Excelency, H.S. Fox, Government House, Toronto, 24 Apr. 1839, Vol. 16, #1992.

23 Provincial Secretary's Correspondence, PAC, RG 5 C1, Dr John Newburn to
    Harrison, Stamford, 8 June 1839, Vol. 18, #2168; P. Delatre to J.B. Harrison,
    Drummondville, 11 Apr. 1840, Vol. 26, #700.

24 Provincial Secretary's Correspondence, PAC, RG 5 C1, Francis Davis and
    Joseph Ayan to George Arthur, Norwich, 21 Apr. 1840, Vol. 27, #887.
    Norwich had been described, in 1837, as "a regular nest of Radicals." J.P.
    Askin to J. Joseph, London, 12 Nov. 1837, Vol. 8, #1088. See also Read, *The
    Rising in Western Upper Canada*, which contains much on Norwich.

25 Provincial Secretary's Correspondence, PAC, RG 5 C1, Statement of Artemus
    W. Cushman, London District, 1 July 1840, Vol. 32, #1378, p. 14792.

26 Provincial Secretary's Correspondence, PAC, RG 5 C1, J. Hill to J. Macaulay,
    Kingston, 15 June 1839, Vol. 14, #1795.

27 Civil Secretary's Correspondence, Upper Canada Sundries, PAC, RG 5 A1,
    John Davis to C. Hagerman, St John's. 19 Jan. 1838, Vol. 85, pp. 103263–4.

28 Civil Secretary's Correspondence, Upper Canada Sundries, PAC, RG 5 A1,
    Anonymous Letter sent to George Munroe, Toronto, no date [1838–39?].
    On anonymous threatening letters see E. P. Thompson, "The Crime of Ano-
    nymity," in Douglas Hay et al., *Albion's Fatal Tree: Crime and Society in Eigh-
    teenth-Century England* (New York: Pantheon, 1975), 255–344.

29 Quoted in *Bathurst Courier and Ottawa Gazette*, 14 Dec. 1838.

30 *Western Herald*, 6 June 1839.

31 Provincial Secretary's Correspondence, PAC, RG 5 C1, Adam Meyers to J.
    Macaulay, River Trent, 7 June 1839, Vol. 18, #2165. On Durham see Leon-
    ard Cooper, *Radical Jack: The Life of John George Lambton* (London: Cresset
    Press, 1959), and on the Durham meetings in Upper Canada, Wilton, *Popu-
    lar Politics*, 194–220.

32 *Upper Canada Herald*, 23 July 1839.

33 *Upper Canada Herald*, 16 July 1839.

34 *St Catharines Journal*, 11 July 1839.

35 Reprinted in *Bathurst Courier and Ottawa Gazette*, 1 Feb. 1839.

36 Provincial Secretary's Correspondence, PAC, RG 5 C1, P. Graham to S.B. Har-
    rison, Woodstock, 9 Feb. 1841, Vol. 51, #3044.

37 See C.O. Ermatinger, *The Talbot Regime, or, the First Half Century of the Talbot
    Settlement* (St Thomas: Municipal World, 1904); James H. Coyne, ed., *The Tal-
    bot Paper* (Ottawa: Transactions of the Royal Society of Canada, 1909); Fred
    Coyne Hamil, *Lake Erie Baron: The Story of Colonel Thomas Talbot* (Toronto:
    Macmillan, 1955).

38 For a sense of the historiography of Compact rule and the diffusion of Tory
    factionalism see Robert E. Saunders, "What Was the Family Compact?",
    Hugh G. J. Aitken, "The Family Compact and the Welland Canal Company,"
    and Terry Cook, "John Beverley Robinson and the Conservative Blueprint for
    the Upper Canadian Community," all in Johnson and Wilson, ed., *Historical
    Essays on Upper Canada* (Toronto: McClelland and Stewart, 1975), 122–39,

153–70, 338–60; S.F. Wise, "Tory Factionalism: Kingston Elections and Upper Canadian Politics, 1830–1836," and "Upper Canada and the Conservative Tradition," in Wise, *God's Peculiar Peoples: Essays on Political Culture in Nineteenth Century Canada* (Ottawa: Carleton University Press, 1993), 91–114, 169–84; Graeme Patterson, "An Enduring Canadian Myth: Government and Family Compact," in Johnson and Wilson, eds, *Historical Essays on Upper Canada*, 485–512; H.V. Nelles, "Loyalism and Local Power: The District of Niagara, 1797–1837," *Ontario History* 58 (June 1966): 99–114; Frederick H. Armstrong, "The Carfrae Family: A Study in Early Toronto Toryism," *Ontario History* 54 (Sept. 1962), 161–81. For the best discussion see Graeme H. Patterson, "Studies in Elections and Public Opinion in Upper Canada," (PhD thesis, University of Toronto, 1970).

39 Ermatinger, *Talbot Regime*, 110, 117–18, with quote on 352–53; Nicholas Flood Davin, *The Irishman in Canada* (Toronto: Maclear and Company, 1877), 113.

40 Hamil, *Lake Erie Baron*, 189.

41 See, especially, "Historical Sketches of the Stewardship of Thomas Tough," *St Thomas Journal*, 13 Dec. 1832, reprinted in Coyne, *Talbot Papers*, Part 2, 146–47; Hamil, *Lake Erie Baron*, 188–210.

42 John Howison, *Sketches of Upper Canada: Domestic, Local, and Characteristic* (Edinburgh: Oliver and Boyd, 1821), 172–6.

43 *Colonial Advocate*, 2 Sept. 1824.

44 Hamil, *Lake Erie Baron*, 188.

45 Patterson, "Studies in Elections and Public Opinion," 94–102. Race was used by both advocates of Compact rule and their opponent reformers. Thus a riotous procession of anti-Reform Orange elements assailed Liberal voters in London in 1836. Heading the noisy parade was "a Negro with a national standard ... shouting five pounds for any Liberal heads." As Tories in London mounted mobilizations of intimidation directed at the outerlying Middlesex County Radical meetings of 1837, they marshalled support of the Wilberforce community of Ohio blacks who had settled north of London. The response of the Reform press was to chastise the composition of these Tory political crowds as composed of "squalid Orangemen and NEGROES!" or to deride the local Compact's inability to galvanize the "Niggers" of Wilberforce. See Landon, "Common Man," 166; Landon, *Exile to Van Diemen's Land*, 41–2; Read, *Rising in Western Upper Canada*, 71, 73.

46 Landon, *Exile to Van Diemen's Land*, 63.

47 Quoted in Patterson, "Studies in Elections and Public Opinion," 220.

48 *Cobourg Star*, 20 Mar. 1833; Civil Secretary's Correspondence, Upper Canada Sundries, PAC, RG 5 A1, George Crawford et al., to J. Joseph, Brockville, 20 June 1937, Vol. 176, p. 97247. For a broader discussion note Donald H. Akenson, *The Irish in Ontario: A Study in Rural History* (Kingston & Montreal: McGill-Queen's University Press, 1984).

49 What follows draws on an argument first elaborated in Bryan D. Palmer,
    Working-Class Experience: The Rise and Reconstitution of Canadian Labour,
    1800–1980 (Toronto: Butterworth's, 1983), 45–59.

50 Quoted in Read, *Rising in Western Upper Canada,* 72.

51 An empiricist mainstream Canadian historiography has steadfastly refused to
    see nascent class formation in the Upper Canada of the 1830s as significant,
    but historians of trade unions, labour law, and class conflict have identified
    the decade as one of beginnings, however hesitant and complicated. See,
    among a number of sources that could be cited, Eric Tucker, "'That Indefi-
    nite Area of Toleration': Criminal Conspiracy and Trade Unions in Ontario,
    1837–1877," *Labour/Le Travail* 27 (Spring 1991): 15–54; Bryan D. Palmer,
    "Kingston Mechanics and the Rise of the Penitentiary, 1833–1836," *Histoire*
    Sociale/Social History 13 (1980): 7–32; Palmer, "Labour Protest and Organiza-
    tion in Nineteenth-Century Canada," *Labour/Le Travail* 20 (Fall 1987):
    61–84. One recent treatment of political culture in the period acknowledges
    that most historians of Upper Canada have tended to see class eclipsed as an
    explanatory variable with respect to political commitments by such indices of
    identity as religion and nationality, at the same time that it suggests the
    salience of differentiations that turned on the material structures of early
    class formation. See Wilton, *Popular Politics and Political Culture,* esp. 229. This
    resonates with interpretations of early timber work and canal labour in the
    1830s, where the accent is placed on both the development of class distinc-
    tions and their mediation by power and paternalism. Consider, for instance,
    Michael S. Cross, "The Shiners' War: Social Violence in the Ottawa Valley in
    the 1830s," *Canadian Historical Review* 54 (1973): 1–26; H.C. Pentland,
    Labour and Capital in Canada, 1650–1860 (Toronto: Lorimer, 1981). There
    is too little treatment of the 1830s in the essays in Paul Craven, ed., *Labouring*
    Lives: Work & Workers in Nineteenth-Century Ontario (Toronto: University of
    Toronto Press, 1995). The 1840s and 1850s would see increasing class agita-
    tion, the former decade associated with canal labour upheavals, the latter
    with what the contemporary press dubbed "an insurrection of labour," the
    centrepiece of which was a rash of strikes by craftsmen in 1853–54. See Ruth
    Bleasdale, "Class Conflict and the Canals of Upper Canada in the 1840s,"
    Labour/Le Travailleur 7 (Spring 1981): 9–40; Peter Way, *Common Labour:*
    Workers and the Digging of North American Canals, 1780–1860 (New York: Cam-
    bridge University Press, 1993); and the excellent unpublished account in
    Paul Campbell Appleton, "The Sunshine and the Shade: Labour Activism in
    Central Canada, 1850–1860," (MA thesis, University of Calgary, 1974). Evi-
    dence of working-class activism in the 1830s, 1840s, and 1850s is also pre-
    sented in the appendices on strikes and riots in Palmer, *Working-Class*
    Experience, 299–320, data dropped from the second edition of this book for
    space considerations.

52 Palmer, *Working-Class Experience*, 31–3; Eugene Forsey, *Trade Unions in Canada, 1812–1902* (Toronto: University of Toronto Press, 1982), 9–13. The verse appears in a newspaper that opposed the Reform cause, although such doggerel was also appearing in more radical circles, where the producer ideology was gaining credence. *Brockville Gazette*, 30 Aug. 1830; 7 Dec. 1830. I am grateful to Sean Cadigan for first providing me with the reference.

53 See Lindsey, *Life and Times of Mackenzie*, Vol. 2, Appendix I, 373–400.

54 See Leo A. Johnson, "Land Policy, Population Growth and Social Structure in the Home District, 1793–1851," in J.K. Johnson, ed., *Historical Essays on Upper Canada*, 32–57; Leo A. Johnson, *History of the County of Ontario, 1615–1875* (Whitby: Corporation of the County of Ontario, 1973), 95–127.

55 Quoted in Patterson, "Studies in Elections and Public Opinion," 278.

56 Civil Secretary's Correspondence, Upper Canada Sundries, PAC, RG 5 A1, Macaulay to Arthur Monohan, Kingston, 11 June 1936, Vol. 167, pp. 91314–16: "Hagerman has made all right here with the Mechanics and is sure of his election." For context see Palmer, "Kingston Mechanics and the Rise of the Penitentiary," 7–32. Robinson is quoted in McNairn, *Capacity to Judge*, 197.

57 Read and Stagg, eds, *Rebellion of 1837*, 10; Francis Bond Head, *A Narrative* (London: John Murray, 1839); Dunham, *Political Unrest in Upper Canada*, 164–76; Dent, *The Story of the Upper Canadian Rebellion*, 329–43; Landon, "The Common Man," 166. Bond Head quote from Palmer, *Working-Class Experience*, 51.

58 Civil Secretary's Correspondence, Upper Canada Sundries, PAC, RG 5 A1, Thomas Fisher to the Lieutenant-Governor, no date [1839], Vol. 219, pp. 121052–54.

59 *Cobourg Star*, 3 July 1839; 10 July 1839; 11 Sept. 1839; Charles Lipton, *The Trade Union Movement of Canada, 1827–1959* (Montreal: Canadian Social Publications, 1968), 12–13; Ryerson, *1837*, 72–3, 132–6; Ryerson, *Unequal Union*, 64–5; "The Permanent and Central Committee of the County of Montreal to the Workingmen's Association of London," *Montreal Gazette*, 20 Jan. 1838.

60 Civil Secretary's Correspondence, Upper Canada Sundries, PAC, RG 5 A1, An Observer to McMahon, York, Feb. 1842, Vol. 257, pp. 140295–8. Sir John Colborne noted as early as 1832 that Mackenzie drew on the support of "Mechanics who lived some time in the States before they settled in the Province." See Clark, *Movements of Political Protest in Canada*, 415.

61 E.P. Thompson, "Eighteenth-Century English Society: Class Struggle Without Class?" *Social History* 3 (May 1978): 133–65.

62 William Kilbourn, *The Firebrand: William Lyon Mackenzie and the Rebellion in Upper Canada* (Toronto: Clarke, Irwin, 1977), 147; "What Is Bad Government?" *The Constitution*, 9 Nov. 1836.

63 Quoted in Palmer, *Working-Class Experience*, 50.

64 *Bytown Gazette*, 9 June 1836.

65 *The Constitution*, 12 July 1837.

66 Chris Raible, *Muddy York: Scandal and Scurrility in Upper Canada* (Creemore, ON: Curiosity House, 1992); Susanna Moodie, *Roughing It in the Bush, or, Forest Life in Canada* (Toronto: Bell and Cockburn, 1913), esp. 245–50. Still worth consideration is the presentation in Leo A. Johnson, *History of the County of Ontario*, 65–127.

67 My accent on patriarchy and its *political* significance is thus different from the current concern with gender regulation. See Morgan, *Public Men and Virtuous Women*; Lykke de la Cour, Cecilia Morgan, and Mariana Valverde, "Gender Regulation and State Formation in Nineteenth-Century Canada," in Greer and Radforth, eds, *Colonial Leviathan*, 163–91. See for other useful statements Katherine McKenna, *A Life of Propriety: Anne Murray Powell and Her Family, 1755–1849* (Kingston & Montreal: McGill-Queen's University Press, 1994); Elizabeth Jane Errington, *Wives and Mothers, School Mistresses and Scullery Maids: Working Women in Upper Canada, 1790–1840* (Kingston & Montreal: McGill-Queen's University Press, 1995); Janice Potter, "Patriarchy and Paternalism: The Case of the Eastern Ontario Loyalist Women," *Ontario History* 81 (March 1989): 3–24.

68 I am here adapting something of the argument in Graeme Patterson, "An Enduring Canadian Myth," but reading it somewhat against its analytic grain.

69 Patterson, "Studies in Elections and Public Opinion"; Sean T. Cadigan, "Paternalism and Politics: Sir Francis Bond Head, the Orange Order, and the Election of 1836," *Canadian Historical Review* 72 (Sept. 1991): 319–47; Cadigan, "Paternalism in Upper Canada, 1800–1841," (MA thesis, Queen's University, 1987).

70 *Brockville Gazette*, 18 Sept. 1830, quoted in Cadigan, "Paternalism and Politics," 341.

71 Civil Secretary's Correspondence, Upper Canada Sundries, PAC, RG 5 A1, Vol. 251, pp. 136654–7.

72 For a broad overview see Bryan D. Palmer, "What's Law Got To Do With It? Historical Considerations on Class Struggle, Boundaries of Constraint, and Capitalist Authority," *Osgoode Hall Law Journal* 41 (Summer/Fall 2003): 465–90.

73 See, for instance, *The Constitution*, 27 July 1837; 17 Aug. 1836; 7 Sept. 1836; 2 Aug. 1837; 9 Aug. 1837; Ryerson, *Unequal Union*, 120; Jackman, *Galloping Head*, 90, 107.

74 *The Constitution*, 2 Aug. 1837.

75 Patterson, "Studies in Elections and Public Opinion," 120.

76 For one discussion of runaway wives see Errington, *Wives and Mothers*, 44–8. For the Collins statement, see *Gore Gazette*, 24 May 1829. Cadigan has an extensive discussion of runaway apprentices and paternalism in "Paternalism in Upper Canada," chapter 6.

77 *Cobourg Star*, 13 Feb. 1833.

78 It is obviously entirely the point of this paper that the contradiction in Mackenzie's espousing a populist labour theory of wealth, even lauding 'his' printers organizing their own union, and then, at the point of class conflict, lashing out at the journeymen for their "interested" spirit and "arbitrary means" was not an individual "failing." Rather it was a determined, structured relation centred in the paternalism of the 1830s workplace. Thus, the argument in F.H. Armstrong, "Reformer as Capitalist: William Lyon Mackenzie and the Printers' Strike of 1836," *Ontario History* 59 (Sept. 1967): 187–96, misstates the complexity of the interpretive issues. See, as well, James McCarthur Conner, "Trade Unions in Toronto," in Jesse Edgar Middleton, *The Municipality of Toronto: A History* (Toronto: Dominion Publishing, 1923), 1: 555–7. The writing on Mackenzie is of course voluminous, but Lillian F. Gates, "The Decided Policy of William Lyon Mackenzie," *Canadian Historical Review* 40 (Sept. 1959): 185–208 and F. K. Donnelly, "The British Background of William Lyon Mackenzie," *British Journal of Canadian Studies* 2 (June 1987): 61–73 continue to repay reading.

79 Fredric Jameson, *The Political Unconscious: Narrative as a Socially Symbolic Act* (Ithaca, NY: Cornell University Press, 1981).

80 Patrick Bode, *Sir John Beverley Robinson: Bone and Sinew of the Compact* (Toronto: University of Toronto Press, 1984); Robinson's letters, scattered throughout Sanderson, *The Arthur Papers*, Vol. 2; John Beverley Robinson, "A Defence on Constitutional Grounds," in David W. Earl, *The Family Compact: Aristocracy or Oligarchy?* (Toronto: Copp Clark, 1957), 119–28.

81 Donald R. Beer, *Sir Allan Napier MacNab* (Hamilton: Dictionary of Hamilton Biography, 1984), 146–7; Charley Corncob quoted in Palmer, *Working-Class Experience*, 58.

82 On the persistence of lawyers in politics see Donald Swainson, "The Personnel of Politics: A Study of the Ontario Members of the Second Federal Parliament" (PhD thesis, University of Toronto, 1968). For a statement that overemphasizes continuity among the personnel of governance, to the detriment of an appreciation of what had altered with the passing of the *ancien régime* see J.K. Johnson, *Becoming Prominent: Regional Leadership in Upper Canada, 1791–1841* (Kingston & Montreal: McGill-Queen's University Press, 1989).

83 The above paragraphs on Baldwin draw on Michael S. Cross and Robert L. Fraser, "'The Waste that Lies before Me': The Public and Private Worlds of Robert Baldwin," Canadian Historical Association, *Historical Papers* (1983), 164–83; Cross and Fraser, "Robert Baldwin," in Frances G. Halpenny and Jean Hamelin, eds, *Dictionary of Canadian Biography*, Vol. 18 (1851–60) (Toronto: University of Toronto Press, 1985).

84 See Karl Marx, "The Eighteenth Brumaire of Louis Bonaparte," in Marx and Engels, *Selected Works* (Moscow: Progress Publishers, 1968), 97.

DARREN FERRY

"The Original Idea Has Been Considerably Amplified"

Culture, Authority, and the Emergence of a Liberal Social Order in the Central Canadian Mechanics' Institute Movement, 1828–60

In November of 1848, a young journeyman printer named Alexander Archibald Riddell asked the lecture committee of the Toronto Mechanics' Institute for permission to present a lecture to the Institute entitled "The Rights of Labour." Highlighting the plight of the skilled working classes in Canada, Riddell attempted to enlighten his fellow journeymen and other members of the Toronto Mechanics' Institute about the advantages, virtues, natural rights and even the temptations and frailties of skilled workers in colonial society. While remaining optimistic as to the material recompense of "artisans and labourers" in mid-century Canada, Riddell offered the following counsel to his fellow mechanics:

> For a working man to think of promotion – that is, to think of getting advanced in the world without any effort on his part, is a great mistake; and, though some few now and then rise in the world without any apparent industry on their part, still, you may depend on it, there are none of those who form the truly independent portion of the higher orders, who are so happy, so contented, so vigorous, so healthy and so charitable, as those who have grown from the grain of a mustard seed into a great tree. Nothing can produce a prouder feeling in the heart of man, than the knowledge of having *pushed* his way through the world, till he has become independent of the world. Man can enjoy nothing which will cause that pleasantness of feeling and that nutritious taste, which the *fruits of industry* will produce.[1]

Although the board of management of the Toronto Mechanics' Institute ultimately rejected Riddell and his lecture on the natural rights and liberties of the workingman, his views are significant in understanding the evolution of social relations from the early nineteenth to the mid-nineteenth century in the central Canadian Mechanics' Institute movement.

On one level, the language of Riddell's lecture mirrors the discourse of typical nineteenth-century advocates of "industry and improvement," a discussion focusing on the political economy of liberalism, individual improvement, and the promotion of a hardy work ethic. Accomplishing an agenda of cultural consensus required the endorsement of a broad liberal mandate in Mechanics' Institutes, to include all the diverse political, social, economic, and religious forces in the colonies in the pursuit of burgeoning commercial progress. Within the fluid and fluctuating social structure of the British American colonies, the professional, commercial, and mercantile "middling sorts" of the mid-Victorian period relied on an ideology of liberal governance to maintain cultural and social authority.[2] Similarly, Riddell's apparent approval of the principles of honest industry, economic independence, and emulation allows the historical observer to conclude that Riddell endorsed the sentiments preached by adherents of this "liberal" social order. Safeguarding the doctrines of the early producer alliance – a socio-economic coalition comprising artisans, mercantile and manufacturing elites, and other "liberally" like-minded individuals – Riddell and the directors of Mechanics' Institutes in the mid-Victorian period employed the discourse of economic liberalism to solidify their vision of commercial prosperity. Although more recent historiography challenges the unifying possibilities of the producer alliance, the cross-class cultural appeal of organizations such as Mechanics' Institutes at mid-century reveals a measure of appreciation for liberal ideology among all classes and interests.[3]

However, Riddell's lecture on "The Rights of Labour" also illustrates a subtle critique of the ruling elites, particularly the mercantile and professional "patricians" of soon-to-be outmoded Family Compacts and *Château Cliques*. While lauding the truly "independent" individuals, who came to their fortune through the fruits of their own industry, the emerging manufacturing and commercial classes, Riddell condemns the formerly privileged mercantile and professional elites and others of the "idle rich" throughout his lecture. Riddell's address also demonstrates that tolerance for the liberal social order not only required constant mediation and negotiation between various class interests, it also harboured conflicts between more conservative and elitist patricians and an emerging and opposing plebeian culture.

While this binary societal vision of early nineteenth-century Canada is more in evidence given its structural fluidity and rather tenuous class formations, Riddell's socio-political criticism of cultural authority illustrates that "class struggles without class" did in fact occur in Mechanics' Institutes before mid-century.[4] And yet, Riddell's address also foreshadowed the more blatant socio-economic conflicts in Canadian society a decade later as industrial capitalism began to take root in urban areas. By distinguishing the "truly independent" individuals in the higher orders who "pushed their way through the world" from those with inherited wealth, Riddell recognized a developing power in the Toronto Mechanics' Institute, the emerging manufacturing and commercial middling classes. By the later decades of the nineteenth century, Riddell's prognostications would prove to be accurate; clerks, merchants, and the manufacturing middle classes in the Toronto Mechanics' Institute and in other urban Institutes overwhelmed the skilled working classes in terms of membership and support.[5] Therefore, the duality of accommodating and/or masking the liberal social order before mid-century and the burgeoning socio-economic discord inherent in the emergence of industrial capitalism by the 1860s demonstrates a fundamental evolution of social relations in the Canadian Mechanics' Institute movement.

Promoters of adult education and the Mechanics' Institute movement in the colonies did in fact attempt to establish cultural consensus through trying to meet the needs of all classes, rather than simply concentrating on the educational requirements of the skilled working classes, as the movement tended to do in Great Britain. What is so distinctive about the Canadian Mechanics' Institute movement as opposed to the Institutes in Great Britain is the flexibility exhibited by these educational voluntary associations in their rapid acclimatization to the colonial experience. Even as the directors of urban Mechanics' Institutes endeavoured to adapt their institution to the particular needs of a liberal social order in the early decades of the nineteenth century as well as to the commercial middling classes in mid-century central Canada, in rural areas the Institutes were used as a means of safeguarding a small-town cultural authority based on the primacy of agriculture. Class relationships in the countryside were far more fluid and complex, given the interaction of the agricultural community with other classes. This rural class diversity produced an even greater enthusiasm among directors of Institutes in small villages and towns to create an atmosphere of cultural inclusiveness. Mechanics' Institutes in the early to mid-nineteenth century, therefore, proved adept at modifying the ideology, practices, and functions of their organizations depending on the varying circumstances of colonial society, as they appealed to a considerable rural population and the embryonic urban centres in central Canada.

The Mechanics' Institute movement in Great Britain began in early nineteenth-century Glasgow, as education pioneer George Birkbeck established the Institutes for the diffusion of scientific knowledge in the industrial arts among the artisan classes. In 1824 a Mechanics' Institute was founded in London under the patronage of Henry Brougham, who introduced lectures, a library, and night classes to the artisan community. Placing an emphasis on mutual instruction among workers, Brougham introduced a small fee to keep the workers independent, although he also requested liberal financial support from the commercial middling classes to aid the London Mechanics' Institute.[6] Since the Mechanics' Institute movement in Britain quickly lost momentum by mid-century, many scholars have debated both the purpose and effectiveness of the Institutes as an instrument for educating the industrial classes. Centring on the middle-class promoters' domination of the ideology and function of the Institutes, British historians disagree about the motivations behind bourgeois ascendancy over the movement. With the rise of industrialization, Mechanics' Institutes became a focal point for the spread of such middle-class values as utility, morality, and thrift, and consequently some historians conclude that middle-class tradesmen and professionals enforced a strict social control over the operation of the Institutes to preserve the burgeoning industrial social order. Conversely, labour historians of the working class argue that radical artisans ignored Mechanics' Institutes when their offices were usurped by the middle classes. As a result, skilled workers interested in the "pursuit of knowledge under difficulties" managed to preserve both their independence and the advocacy of working-class radicalism while using the Mechanics' Institutes to further their own educational needs.[7]

Mechanics' Institutes also gave both middle-class and artisan radicals access to new scientific theories, which elite scientists attempted to monopolize through the development of professional science associations such as the Royal Society of London and the British Association for the Advancement of Science. Therefore, "marginal men" in the Institutes could participate in the technological revolution, while at the same time rebelling against the traditional scientific method of more aristocratic practitioners of science. The popularization of science in the mid-century Mechanics' Institute movement in Great Britain permitted both the industrial and the commercial middle classes – as well as the working classes – to carve out a cultural niche within an Old World society caught in a state of social flux. Still other historians contend that Mechanics' Institutes were simply a consequence of the

Industrial Revolution, where the deepening formation of the middle classes occurred through the ascendancy of a new industrial social order. Along with with literary societies, temperance organizations, the reformation of aristocratic scientific associations, and mutual improvement societies, Mechanics' Institutes became centres of cultural activity for middle-class citizens in Great Britain.[8]

Canadian historiography regarding Mechanics' Institutes closely mirrors the scholarly work in Britain, concluding that Mechanics' Institutes reflected the entrenchment of middle-class hegemony in central Canadian society. Although there is some recognition that the working classes retained agency in choosing whether or not to become members, historians view the supremacy of the middling sort in mid-century Mechanics' Institutes as a social control impulse, while more recent scholarship focuses on the Institutes as a vehicle for both middle-class and nascent state formation.[9] Canadian scholars also have a tendency to scrutinize the Institute movement by degrees, rather than examining the movement as a whole. Much of the literature on Mechanics' Institutes in Canada has analyzed the Institutes either as pioneers in adult education, or as the precursors of the public library movement. These historians are also united in their dismissal of the Mechanics' Institute as a constructive force, presenting the failure of the Institutes to provide access to education for the working classes as a conundrum of high educational expectations coupled with the reality of limited resources and competing agendas.[10] However, nineteenth-century Mechanics' Institutes in developing urban areas in the colonies did in fact endeavour to imitate their counterparts in Great Britain through offering educational benefits to the skilled working classes.

The earliest Mechanics' Institutes in Canada were established in Lower Canada, with the creation of the Montreal Institute in 1828, and the founding of the Quebec Mechanics' Institute in 1831. The Quebec Mechanics' Institute stated that their main object was the improvement of the operative class, as "the instruction of Mechanics, at a cheap rate, in the principles of the Arts which they practice, as well as in all other branches of useful knowledge, is a measure calculated to improve extensively their condition and habits, and to add largely to the resources and prosperity of the Country."[11] The Montreal Mechanics' Institute incorporated this sentiment into their initial rules of association, legislating that skilled workers were to form at least two-thirds of the committee of management. Chief Justice Thomas Aylwin explained the reasoning behind the glorification of the mechanic in his inaugural address before an audience in the newly built Mechanics' Hall in 1854. Aylwin noted, "the mechanic is alike useful and necessary; he is the backbone of society, and its best interests are linked with him and his prosperity ... whatever tends, then, to improve and elevate mechanics as a class, directly contributes to our best interests, and urges on all the other classes to make similar efforts towards progress and advancement." This appeal from one of the leading members of Montreal society not only underscores the concerns of the middling sort over working-class violence and discontent in the city of Montreal, but also the need to incorporate the artisan into the liberal social order.[12] A similar ideology emerged in London, a "rising industrial town" that desperately required educated artisans and mechanics. In their request for a Mechanics' Institute, the London executive claimed that the mechanics and artisans in their locale were "highly respectable, and ... assist in a large degree by their industry, character and contributions to make up the aggregate of our public and common weal." As a result, the constitution of the London Institute likewise stipulated that two-thirds of its management was to come from the skilled working classes.[13]

Despite these efforts to promote education among the operative population, skilled workers in urban areas often recognized that the day-to-day operation of Mechanics' Institutes rested in the hands of directors and executives from the middling classes. Mechanics and other skilled workers would express their dissatisfaction with Institute boards of management through angry letters to city newspapers and riotous board meetings. Periodicals in Toronto, Hamilton, and London all received letters from "A Mechanic" bemoaning the state of their respective Institutes, as shady election procedures, the poor state of the various libraries, and other abuses were summarily exposed as bourgeois perfidy. The London Mechanics' Institute executive realized after their first year that both radical artisans *and* the conservative merchant classes could halt the progress of the Institute, as "fears were doubtless entertained by the overcautious, and prejudices by the doubtful; apathy by the lukewarm and indifference or animosity by foes."[14] Institute executives from the middling classes could also articulate their frustrations with the apathy and the dearth of education to be found among the working classes. The promoters of the Kingston Mechanics' Institute lambasted the leading mechanics of the city for their lack of interest, as they had "ample opportunity" to form their own society before the "younger tradesmen" took the reins. An essay contest celebrating the erection of the Montreal Mechanics' Hall in 1854 also illustrated the disdain of middling-class directors for their working-class patrons. In judging the fifth place entrant – an essay entitled *Labour Directed by Industry, the Source of all Wealth and Prosperity* – the judges noted that it was "apparently the unostentatious effort of an uneducated mechanic, who, had he possessed the advantages of the other Essayists, might have produced something worthy of a higher place in the report of the Committee."[15]

Despite these early manifestations of class discord, the membership figures of central Canadian Mechanics' Institutes at mid-century suggest that the Institutes were highly successful in recruiting the skilled working-class element and suffusing the Institutes with a liberal worldview of progressive commercial progress. The membership figures reveal a solid and active skilled working-class constituency. In the Montreal Mechanics' Institute, skilled workers made up from 44 to 68 per cent of the ordinary membership of the Institute from the years 1856 to 1864. Similarly, when the London Mechanics' Institute received its charter of incorporation in 1852, nearly a third of its ordinary membership came from the skilled working classes.[16] The membership figures of the Toronto Mechanics' Institute reflect a similar pattern, as the working classes actively participated in the activities of the Institute. Membership books document that a full 34 per cent of the ordinary membership of the Toronto Mechanics' Institute at mid-century came from the operative classes of the community. However, a further examination of membership records also illustrates that while a healthy proportion of members came from the skilled working classes, more than half the members joining the Toronto Mechanics' Institute came from the middling sort.[17] Evidently, securing the co-operation of various occupational groups in the educational and cultural activities of central Canadian Mechanics' Institutes entailed the construction of a liberal ideology appealing to all segments within the community, while engineering consent to a rising commercial social order.

In contrast with Mechanics' Institutes in Great Britain – organizations whose sole original aim was the establishment of educational opportunities for the working classes – Institute promoters in urban central Canada recognized from the outset that Mechanics' Institutes should benefit the community at large. Even though the directors of the Quebec Mechanics' Institute were very clear that the Institute was to improve the lot of the skilled worker, it would also extend its educational advantages to the entire community. The Institute would bring together "in one association men of different pursuits and acquirements" for the purposes of mutual improvement, enlarging the minds of each member, and tending "to the advancement of the interests of society generally, and this province in particular." The directors of the York Mechanics' Institute understood that interclass co-operation would expand the influence of the Institute, with "the combination of all classes in a great object of public good, which cannot fail, in the end, to enhance the power of the nation, and add to the happiness of individuals composing it."[18] The management of the Ottawa Mechanics' Institute likewise saluted the fact that while the origins of the Institute rested with the skilled working classes, it was now "extensively patronized by all classes, the wealthiest as well as the poorest." Extolling the virtues of their open library, the Institute's directors boasted that any member of the public could walk through its doors and acquire the specific volume needed to assist in the various labours of its burgeoning commercial population.[19]

However, early manifestations of this ethos of classlessness camouflaged a cultural middling-class outlook, as directors from the commercial/professional middling classes in urban Mechanics' Institutes jockeyed for position with their skilled working-class constituency. In the fifth annual report of the York Mechanics' Institute in 1836, the executive planned to emulate Institutes in Britain by offering premiums to the mechanics of the city, to demonstrate their skills and labour to the general populace. However, the directors of the York Institute also noted that such a display would benefit the liberal social order, by opening up new avenues of profitable industry, promoting education, lessening crime, and elevating the character of the people. Of course, while the directors of the Hamilton Mechanics' Institute welcomed the membership of both young men and the "liberal and wealthy," they lamented the fact that the labours of the Institute always depended "on the exertions of the few."[20] In a lecture to the York Mechanics' Institute in 1832, William (Tiger) Dunlop lauded the Mechanics' Institute as an institution that housed "the combination of all classes in a great object of public good." Dunlop was even more forthright in his defence of the liberal social order, as he described how the "middle classes" formed a communicating link between the propertied orders and the working classes, disseminating harmony throughout society. In a material sense, as a superintendent and land agent with the Canada Company, Dunlop envisioned himself as part of this middling sort, as he was neither a propertied landholder nor a skilled worker. And yet his description of the "middling classes" was also a highly discursive liberal construction, as Dunlop noted that while only a minor portion of society could be men of "rank and influence," the middling classes reinforced a liberal sense of emulation and ambition. This liberal philosophy ensured that "every man sees that the door is open to him to possess these distinctions, and every man feels anxious to promote the good of the community."[21]

By mid-century, the directors of the Toronto Mechanics' Institute stilll preached the values of class inclusion, despite the increasing presence of manufacturing and commercial elites. And yet Richard Lewis, the future president of the Toronto Mechanics' Institute, continued to view society through traditional binary lenses when he noted that the Institute would only progress if "a noble fraternity of all classes, high and low, aristocratic and plebeian" worked together in harmony. The opening of the Mechanics' Hall in 1854 was therefore an event of great significance to the whole liberal community, providing for the education and refinement of the entire populace, and inciting every branch of industry into "laudable amelioration" and "generous emulation."[22] Although the directors of the Ottawa Mechanics' Institute cherished their working-class roots, they congratulated themselves on the fact that they were extending the benefits of the Institute to all members of the community, particularly the manufacturing and commercial classes. Indeed, the executive noted that some of the "best educated men" in Ottawa took a great interest in the progress of the Institute, and thus called on others of wealth and influence – the professional men, merchants, manufacturers, and master mechanics – to loosen their purse strings and donate books and other financial assistance. Obviously these men responded, as it was noted in 1857 that the Institute was "not *merely* a Mechanics' Institute, but is also devoted to the higher branches of art and science, and numbers among its members and supporters professional men of distinguished ability and the first mercantile men of this section of the Province."[23]

The 1861 annual report of the Hamilton Mechanics' Institute is an apt illustration of the shifting liberal values of Mechanics' Institutes from the "middling sort" to the mercantile and commercial middle *classes,* a shift which accompanied the development of industrial capitalism by the 1860s and 1870s. Although the executive of the Hamilton Mechanics' Institute promoted an inclusive ideology, appealing for harmony between the classes in a co-operative venture of self-improvement, the 1861 annual report exposed the middle-class directors of the Institute as agents of the emerging industrial order. Committed to offering public lectures, adult education classes, and the amenities of their public library to all interested parties in Hamilton, the executive boasted that while "the professed object, as the name implies, is the improvement of our artisans and working classes of every grade, there is reason to fear that this design has in many instances been lost sight of, or perhaps we should say, *the original idea has been considerably amplified,* as other classes of the community rather than operatives constitute not unfrequently the majority of subscribers and attendants." While on the surface this pronouncement acknowledged the problems of the Hamilton Mechanics' Institute movement in bringing education to the working classes, in reality the directors of the Institute exulted in its appeal to the burgeoning industrial and commercial elites. Not only were the Institute promoters in Hamilton more concerned with self-education as a means of keeping the working classes from committing crime and participating in trade unionism, a scant nine years after the incorporation of the Institute, the directors attempted to change the name of the Mechanics' Institute to the more middle-class appellation of the "Gore Literary and Scientific Institution."[24]

While urban Mechanics' Institutes in mid-century central Canada responded to the needs of the emerging liberal social order, Institutes in the rural countryside attempted to solidify an alliance between local agricultural interests and a rural commercial class. Rural Mechanics' Institutes in the colonies were, therefore, far more successful than their counterparts in Britain, where small-town and village Institutes did not offer formalized educational training, but rather informal tutoring and the unsystematic formation of mutual improvement societies.[25] However, initial efforts to provide educational opportunities to the skilled working classes in rural areas appeared to mirror the disorganized British experience. Both the Mitchell and Paris Mechanics' Institutes lacked sufficient funds to appoint a qualified instructor and, therefore, relied on classes of loosely organized mutual instruction rather than formalized tutoring. In 1858, the Elora Mechanics' Institute opened a mutual instruction class whereby members could present papers and essays to their colleagues, and then discuss the subject brought forward. This would be more effective than a mere debating society and "likely to enlist more in the cause of mutual improvement than the class system." However, some Institutes, like the Institut des Artisans in the town of Laprairie just outside Montreal, ran highly successful education classes for its operative population. The annual report of the Institut in 1854 readily explains the accomplishments of these night classes, as the membership figures tallied thirty mechanics out of a total membership of sixty-five. As the qualifications to receive government grants for Institut des Artisans in Canada East required functioning night classes, the Laprairie Institut's focus on educational endeavours is entirely understandable.[26]

Although the experience of rural Mechanics' Institutes with adult education and night classes accomplished mixed results, in other respects Institutes in small towns and villages functioned as well as their urban equivalent. However, given the rather limited overtures to the education of the operative classes, the directors of Mechanics' Institutes in the countryside identified their constituents by categories, and the vast majority were not skilled workers. The economy of nineteenth-century Canada was still highly agrarian, with pockets of manufacturing concentrated in relatively few urban centres. A settled and stable class of independent farmers largely represented the middling sort in early to mid-nineteenth century rural areas, while in small towns, self-employed tradespeople formed the backbone of the local economy.[27] Mid-nineteenth-century Mechanics' Institutes thrived in rural areas because of a reliance on the ideology of liberal inclusiveness shared with the urban Institutes. In advertising the library of the Niagara Mechanics' Institute, the executive claimed that the townspeople could discover a goodly number of volumes "complete with instruction and information for all classes." The Paris Mechanics' Institute went even further, declaring that the lectures and library of the Institute were for the benefit of all classes and interests in the community. While the library contained limited volumes, the executive of the Paris Institute believed that no one would go "empty away from this Emporium of Knowledge providing they are not over hard to please."[28]

Unlike members of urban Mechanics' Institutes, where budding participation in commercial ventures allowed Institute directors to consider the needs of the nation as a whole, many rural associations viewed class inclusion as a liberal ideology confined to their locality. Appeals to the goodwill of the community could also prove to be points of contention for the directors of rural Mechanics' Institutes, particularly if townspeople failed to make use of the amenities of the institution. The plainly frustrated directors of the Paris Mechanics' Institute could not understand why such a valuable institution of knowledge was so sparingly attended. In the fourth annual report of the Paris Institute, the executive noted that they were "exceedingly sorry to have the painful duty of recording the seeming indifference that prevails toward so useful an Institution." Summoning the last vestiges of civic pride from the village, the executive boldly claimed that "all the eyes are upon Paris, when they see or hear Paris people carry off the palm of victory from their neighbours at curling, cricketing and music, they actually think that seeing we excel so well at these, that the field of the mind will not be left a moral waste, overrun with the rank weeds of ignorance."[29]

From the beginning of the rural Mechanics' Institute movement, directors of small-town Institutes recognized that appealing solely to skilled workers would be a grave mistake, and made significant overtures to agricultural inhabitants. In accordance with this sensibility, the Guelph, Streetsville, and Fergus Institutes were all given the designation "Mechanics' and Farmers' Institutes" by their directors in order to unite the disparate members of the rural community. The Fergus Farmers' and Mechanics' Institute went so far as to request that two-thirds of the management of the Institute to be either working mechanics or farmers, while the Guelph Farmers' and Mechanics' Institute trumpeted the fact that its library held volumes for the education and the benefit of both the "Artizan and the Agriculturalist."[30] Despite these expressions of interclass benevolence, by mid-century the socio-economic interaction of the various occupations also produced strong class tensions within small-town and village Institutes. Class frustrations simmered in the Guelph Farmers' and Mechanics' Institute, where the directors often berated the agricultural portion of the community for not appreciating the efforts of the town Institute. Three years after the formation of the Institute in 1849, the directors lamented the fact that "so few of the agricultural population of the vicinity have yet availed themselves at mutual improvement to be derived at a very trifling share." In 1859, the directors removed the appellation "Farmers" from the official name of the Guelph Mechanics' Institute, as a result of the apathy displayed by the farmers of the town.[31]

Both urban and rural Mechanics' Institutes in Canada embraced the participation of women in furthering the development of the Institute movement in the community and in this respect differed from the Institutes and mutual improvement societies in Great Britain. Mechanics' Institutes in the Old World were particularly restrictive in their early manifestations, although by mid-century the regulated contribution of women was grudgingly accepted.[32] In the vision of Mechanics' Institutes in early to mid-nineteenth-century central Canada, women were strongly encouraged to become members and indirectly participate in their activities, despite the continual preaching of the doctrine of domesticity in both rural and urban Mechanics' Halls. However, the endorsement of women as members of these organizations resulted in limited participation as they served solely as figureheads and spectators. This dichotomy would later prove to be problematical for colonial Mechanics' Institute promoters as they attempted to broaden women's participation along strict gendered lines.[33]

As early as 1843, women were permitted to be members in the Montreal Mechanics' Institute, where the directors placed female members in the same category as apprentices and sons of members. Women were also given free admission to lectures in the Toronto Mechanics' Institute as early as 1835, and by 1845 there was at least one female on the roll of ordinary members – the confectioner Elisabeth Dunlop – indicating that there were no restrictions on membership based on gender. Similarly, in the London Mechanics' Institute, women were permitted to join as full members and at a reduced initiation fee in 1851. Unfortunately it appears that only one female member took advantage of this offer, a Mrs J. Monsarrat, according the membership list compiled in 1852.[34] The Ottawa Mechanics' Institute lauded the efforts of the women in the community to present a highly successful bazaar in 1854, as the proceeds added significantly to the coffers of the Institute:

> In fact the present flourishing state of the Institute is chiefly due – and acknowledged with pleasure by the committee to be due – to the cordial and generous co-operation and assistance of those Ladies who, on this occasion, as on all others, have been the foremost in lending the most active and successful aid in promoting the best interests of the community ... To these Ladies the Committee cannot adequately express the grateful sense which it entertains of their noble exertions and the magnificent result of these exertions for the Institute.

While the women of Ottawa greatly reduced the debt of the local Mechanics' Institute, their achievement did not garner them any privileges other than free admission to the winter course of lectures.[35]

While women were encouraged to attend these "public" lectures, those who actually did heard a reinforcement of the domestic ideology. When Thomas Keefer gave his lecture on manufacturing to the members of the Montreal Mechanics' Institute, he condescendingly noted that the prosperity of Montreal did concern women, as it was "the annual balance sheet which determines the concerts and pianos, the summer jaunt and the seaside baths, the furs and the velvets, the silks and the satins, the parasols and the scent bottles, and all the innumerable and comprehensive elements which form a material basis for what is called domestic bliss." Likewise, during the course of lectures in 1855, the members of the Ottawa Mechanics' Institute heard lectures on the "Rights of Women" and "Domestic Affections" describing an identical domestic ideology.[36] Walter Eales, in his lecture to the Toronto Mechanics' Institute, described women as a "valuable class of the community," yet the only efforts to specifically recruit women members was the inclusion of vocal music in the program of the Institute; they were excluded from the more functional portion of the Institute's work. However, their presence was crucial for the extension of the Institute into the community, for "without their courtesy and cheerful countenances at our Soirees, Tea Meetings, Pleasure Excursions and Lectures, we would be out of our element."[37]

Given the limited number of male participants in small villages and towns, women were made particularly welcome in the reading rooms of rural Mechanics' Institutes. A sizeable portion of the recent literature regarding women and rural life concludes that social events held in towns and villages offered opportunities for women to become more prominent in the public sphere, as the shared nature of agricultural work led to more mutual social activities.[38] From the beginning of the rural Mechanics' Institute movement, invitations to lectures, concerts, and festivals were extended to the women of the community, illustrating the seriousness of Institute directors' intention to incorporate women into Institute functions. Both the Orillia Mechanics' Institute and the Laprairie Institut des Artisans encouraged women to attend any public meeting of the Institute, often free of charge. The initial inclination of the management of the Paris Mechanics' Institute' was to allow women to join the reading room for free, but strained financial circumstances compelled them to charge the ladies five shillings per year as members.[39] Policies such as this allowed women in small towns and in the countryside to take the initiative and join rural Institutes in respectable numbers. The Niagara Mechanics' Institute welcomed its first female member in 1852, while recording the fact that 20 per cent of new members in 1856 were women. Similarly, out of ninety-four members tallied in the Mitchell Institute in 1866, three local women were prominently featured. And yet, mirroring the experience of women in urban Mechanics' Institutes, early participation of women in rural Institutes was limited to indirect involvement, rather than complete and active membership.[40]

Another fundamental approach in ensuring harmonious relations in Mechanics' Institutes was the elimination of sectarianism and political partyism. This was not a unique colonial practice as Mechanics' Institutes in Great Britain also desired the removal of sectarian and political turmoil. The triumph of British Mechanics' Institutes over the twin demons of sectarianism and partyism was mixed, for while radical Chartists condemned the Institutes as instruments of the rising industrial bourgeoisie, Institutes in Britain did in fact create a measure of cultural consensus.[41] In mid-nineteenth century Canada, the eradication of these conflicts not only ensured the triumph of the liberal social order, it was also an attempt to construct an inclusive liberal citizenship that transcended apparent socio-political divisions which had marred social relations in the pre-rebellion colonies. In this sense, Mechanics' Institutes reflected the desire for political "normalization" so prevalent in political, social, and educational discourse after the Rebellions. Even though colonial Mechanics' Institutes proved to be adept at purging sectarian and political discord from their operations, conflicts between political and religious opponents did frequently arise in various Institutes. The suppression of these sentiments, potentially damaging to the community, often determined the success or failure of central Canadian Mechanics' Institutes in the mid-nineteenth century.[42]

In the case of the first Montreal Mechanics' Institute the elimination of sectarianism and political partyism became highly problematical. Its early history, from 1828, reflected a great deal of sectarian conflict between the members of the Church of Scotland and Anglicans, as well as between Reformer and Tory. When the Institute was reorganized in 1840, the elimination of such quarrels was paramount in the thinking of Institute administrators and lecturers. Political and religious questions in and of themselves were not detrimental to harmonious relationships, as William Bristow asserted in his 1850 lecture to the Montreal Mechanics' Institute. The spirit of party politics and a liberal public spirit were easily distinguishable. The party spirit sought to further private or individual advancement and an ascendancy of one part of the population over the remainder, while a "liberal" and publicly minded individual promoted the general welfare.[43] To avoid similar sectarian conflict, the directors of the London Mechanics' Institute not only outlawed religious discussions in the Institute, they also decreed that no religious denomination be allowed to congregate in the new Mechanics' Hall. However, sectarian disagreements did arise when the Reverend William Bettridge lectured to the London Institute in 1853. During his lecture, Bettridge denounced as a "dangerous influence the religious opinions of a certain class of the community ... " The Institute board, concerned that many members of the Institute were members of this unnamed religious body, stated that the lecture introduced "Religious Animosities among us, and that therefore this Institute disclaims being identified with the promulgation of any such sentiments as destructive to its best interest and general advancement." Despite this breach of protocol, Bettridge was only mildly reprimanded by the board of directors, as he clearly was unaware of the Institute's policy on such matters.[44]

The Toronto Mechanics' Institute implemented the guiding principle of no political or religious discussions in their assemblies, despite the participation of members from every political faction. The first membership list of the Institute reflects the diversity of political opinion, as prominent Tories W.B. Jarvis, George Denison, John Strachan, and John Macaulay met side by side with Reformers – and some future rebels – such as Charles Duncombe, John Rolph, William Dunlop, William Baldwin, and James Lesslie. The patron of the Toronto Mechanics' Institute, Lord Sydenham, stated firmly in 1840 that the contentions of party politics had no place in a liberal institution of self-improvement. Demonstrating his love for the philosophy of utilitarianism, Sydenham noted that Mechanics' Institutes were indispensable to the liberal political process, as they refined minds, elevated characters, and made better citizens. Walter Eales, a painter by occupation, echoed this sentiment in claiming that knowledge purified the political process while simultaneously supporting principles of Christianity.[45] Religious toleration was also essential; the Toronto Institute Library Committee in 1852 ordered several books on religious subjects. Requesting books by Episcopalians, non-conformists, and authors of other denominations, the committee charged the purchasers with the simple caveat to "guard against works of a sectarian or polemical character." Another function of the Library Committee was to root out *irreligion* in the Mechanics' Institute and to protect the Christian faith. A member subsequently wrote to the Library Committee requesting the removal of a book on Christ that offered only "half-praise" and denied the divinity of scripture. The complainant asked for the work to be excluded from the library in order to protect members from the influence of pernicious "freethinking" material.[46]

Despite assurances that the Toronto Mechanics' Institute would keep political and religious discussions at bay, the simmering political undercurrents in the Institute surfaced in 1848 in the case of the non-delivered lecture of A.A. Riddell, noted earlier. In November, Riddell requested permission to give his lecture on "The Rights of Labour." The general board of the Institute procrastinated for two weeks, allowing the Lecture Committee itself to cast the determining vote. The Committee resolved to allow Riddell to give his lecture if he agreed to alter certain parts that were considered objectionable. It is assumed that Riddell refused, as the lecture was never given. In refusing to alter his text and "negotiate" certain standards, Riddell no doubt cemented the opinion of some Board members on the argumentative nature of the working classes.[47] Even though Riddell believed that the elevation of the artisan did not mean the degradation of the other members of the community, he acknowledged that the notion of Labour and its rights was entirely a political question, and therefore addressed the subject of labour in a more political fashion rather than one focused solely on the discourse of "class." Recognizing the potential dangers of political dissonance inherent in his lecture, Riddell offered an introduction that he hoped would defuse possible objections to his address:

> The subject I have chosen being considered by some persons a political one, and political observations being wisely excluded from this Institute, lest during and subsequent to the reading of any lecture bearing upon politics the passions of some get aroused and the prejudices of others become excited ... I have been constrained to confine my discourse within much narrower limits than I should

have felt inclined to do had this been originally intended for anywhere else in order that I might not, in the slightest degree, violate
the well determined regulations of the Institute – a place where
men of all opinions have united together for the attainment of
laudable objects, and where men of all creeds have met, and still
continue to meet – in harmony and in love.[48]

On the surface, Riddell's lecture simply disturbed the codes of conduct inherent in the lecture system, while on a deeper level the lecture
managed to question the entire "liberal" social and political order.
Despite his protestations, Riddell's lecture was heavily political, stud-
ded with references to natural rights, liberty, and the discourse of popular politics used by mid-century Upper Canadian radical reformers. It
is also apparent that Riddell himself realized that some portions of the
lecture would not escape the committee censor's scrutiny. A reference
to the famous reform agitator William Cobbett showed Riddell's true
colours, as did his unwillingness to completely remove his radical
political references when he noted in the margin, "I'd have seen them
d_d before I'd left this out." Riddell's radical politics of confrontation
conflicted with the ideal of harmony and brotherhood, forcing the
committee's hand in preventing the lecture from being presented.
However, the highly political undercurrents in Upper Canada led conservatives, reformers, and Tories alike on the Board of the Institute to
censure Riddell's lecture.[49]

In the context of small villages and towns where dependence on
neighbourly benevolence was paramount, disagreements between reli-
gionists and political opponents could ruin the progress of a local
Mechanics' Institute. To this end, the bylaws of many rural Mechanics'
Institutes reflected the need to keep partyism and "polemical divinity"
from the conversations of Institute members. The Paris Mechanics'
Institute levied a fine of sixpence for introducing political or religious
subjects in any debates occurring in the Institute. If the offending
member dared to attempt further discussions of this nature, expulsion
was the final punishment affixed. The Paris Institute also went to the
extreme of creating a censorship committee for the library, and in
1858 the committee removed two issues of the *Westminster Review* for
articles leaning to infidelity.[50] Although the Guelph Mechanics' Institute banned religious and political controversies from their meetings,
they also ordered that "all the instructions delivered, whether by lectures or classes, under its sanction, shall be based on the direct recognition of the authority of Divine Revelation." John Ardagh, a local
physician, taught this liberal principle of religious and political
toleration before the Barrie Mechanics' Institute:

Our very constitution prohibits the introduction and discussion of
those subjects which most speedily enlist the passions and disturb
the harmony of mutual intercourse. To my mind it constitutes no
small recommendation that we here possess a neutral ground, on
which men of all parties may contend without rancour and bear
away palms which do not cost their opponents one embittered or
unhallowed feeling. We have common subjects on which all may
agree, without being taxed with any interested compromise of
opinion, and concerning which they may differ, without alteration
in mutual feelings, or diminution of mutual esteem. A bond of fel-
lowship is thus frequently formed between those whom circumstances would otherwise have kept for ever asunder; and if men
come at all into collision, they are actuated by feelings of generous
rivalry, not so closely interwoven with the absorbing interests of life
as to arouse the meaner passions of jealousy.[51]

The experience of both the Laprairie and Drummond county
Institut des Artisans in Canada East are perfect examples of the need
to incorporate all political and religious views of the community into
the local Mechanics' Institute. An ideology of co-operation and harmony was critical to the success of the Instituts, as they comprised both
English and French members of these towns. While the Laprairie
Institut insisted that political subjects were "defendu dans les salles de
cette société," the directors insisted that all lectures, debates, and
transactions occur in the French language. And yet this condition was
tempered by the fact that the majority of members were in fact
Canadiens, and that English members were heartily welcomed.[52] Even
though the origins of the Drummond County Institut des Artisans
were to be found among the English community, steps were taken by
the directors to ensure the continued participation of French members. When a prominent French member – the physician Dr Vallée –
spoke in the French language, an English member objected and stated
that a member of the Institut ought not to address meetings in both
languages. President J.B. Eric Dorion, the noted Rouge supporter,
decided "there was nothing to prevent the same speaker from speaking in two, or more, languages on the same question," sustaining the
decision of the council with a vote of seven to five. This set the tone for
future meetings of the Institut, as often there were four English and
four French members on the executive committee. Correspondingly,
the minutes alternated between French and English depending on the
mother tongue of the secretary, and provisions were made to purchase
fifty English and fifty French books to establish the Institut library. By
1861, the conduct of a culturally sensitive directorate ensured a great

deal of success among the French population, as members of French origin reached a high of 60 per cent in the Institut.[53]

Although the Institut des Artisans in Drummond County instituted cultural unanimity in the function of its operations, clearly the Rouge/ Reformer background of many of its members influenced the political tone of the debates. Thus, the Institut in Drummond County is a fascinating example of how Canadiens adopted and adapted associations of English origin for their own use. Even though French Canadians would assist in the creation of unique Lower Canadian organizations that were far different from Mechanics' Institutes in Upper Canada, channelling the socio-political experiences of Canadiens by way of British institutions was not unique to the Institut des Artisans of Drummond County.[54] Many of the topics deliberated in the Institut in Drummond County reflected the liberal Rouge political position, particularly when the votes were tallied in the debates. Overwhelmingly preferring republican government, representation by population, secret balloting, annexation, non-sectarian schools, and the removal of property qualifications for the vote, their true colours were revealed when members voted unanimously that L.J. Papineau was the greatest statesman in his time. In many respects, the Institut des Artisans in Drummond County closely imitated the Institut Canadien in Montreal and in Quebec, both in political ideology and in debating methodology.[55]

However, while the tone of the debates favoured a more adversarial Rouge political outlook, many of the topics for debate focused on local politics and institutional reform, signifying deference for the liberal social order in the countryside. Favouring such local political positions as the establishment of a common school, a levied tax for the erection of the town hall and a building for the Institut as well as local enforcement for prohibition, members of the Drummond County Institut des Artisans evidently supported local governance and the apparatus of nascent state formation. And yet members also critiqued local political processes, as they debated the merits of the entire municipal system, the difficulties of the local credit foncier, and even squashed a motion to establish a volunteer company in the district. Members of the Institut also protested specific actions of the Durham city council which they considered improper or erroneous. These debates indicate that local communities and local organizations did in fact interact with the state in establishing new public institutions, and did participate in liberal governance at the local level.[56]

A similar reverence for the respectability of the liberal social order was evident in the mid-century workings of the Barrie Debating Society, the forerunner of the Barrie Mechanics' Institute. Even though the directors often proscribed politically charged topics for debate ranging from the merits of capital punishment, the justification of the 1837 rebellion, and the best means to achieve Canadian independence, maintaining decorum and order was obviously paramount to the executive. Enshrined in the bylaws of the society were directives aimed at the debates, noting that it was imperative that there be "no improper or obscene language used, no swearing or other offensive conduct and no personal offensive remarks made."[57] As with the Rouge element in the Drummond County Institut des Artisans, obviously the members of the Barrie Debating Society were either Reformers or political radicals, since they favoured universal suffrage, the secret ballot, and the secularization of the Clergy Reserves. However, problems developed when the Society held a series of mock parliaments, as the debates focused squarely on Canadian party politics. In September of 1854, the Speaker in the mock parliament rose and offered, "That this House disapproves of the course taken by the ministry in regard to the measures to be introduced as stated in the eighth paragraph of the speech, vis. the bill relating to the Rebellion of '37 and the one on the Rebellion Losses Bill. These topics are in all cases to be avoided as likely to be productive of ill-feeling among members of this club and therefore the House would severely censure the course taken by the ministry in bringing them in." Even in November as the new Speaker rejoiced in the fact that he now had the power to "end the chaos in our meetings," his joy was short-lived, as the Debating society disbanded and a new Mechanics' Institute was chartered one month later.[58]

New world politico-religious controversies would also invade Mechanics' Institutes, as the Carleton Place Mechanics' Institute discovered in 1849. The president of the Carleton Place Institute, John Gemmill, a stonemason from Glasgow, also operated a small family farm in nearby Lanark County. However, the roots of artisan self-improvement were difficult to break in Gemmill, as he attempted to form a committee to petition the government in Canada West to "place Mechanics' Institutes on the same footing as agricultural societies."[59] Even more disturbing to the members of the Carleton Place Mechanics' Institute was Gemmill's reaction to Governor-General Lord Elgin's favourable response to the invitation to become the patron of the Institute. Gemmill's radical politics were exposed when he wrote the Civil Secretary to dismiss the "appointment" of Elgin as patron of the Institute, stating "as President of the Carleton Place Library Association and Mechanics' Institute, I have the honour to enclose your favour of 30 November and beg that you will inform His Excellency that a society of Scotchmen can exist without patronage." Appalled that one of their directors, "so-called loyal members of the

Crown," would be so insulting, the other members of the executive expelled Gemmill without delay, noting that "by such improper conduct [he] has made himself wholly unworthy of remaining a member of this society constituted for the express purpose of improving the intellectual and moral condition of the community." This sectarian episode clearly affected the members of the Institute, for a few months later the Carleton Place Mechanics' Institute disbanded.[60]

Another approach to increase harmony and co-operation among the various interests in early nineteenth-century Mechanics' Institutes was the advocacy of a liberal philosophy of honest industry and the political economy of hard work. Like Mechanics' Institutes in Great Britain, urban Institutes in mid-century Canada ensured the promotion of a producer *ideology* of an emerging liberal social order. Thus Mechanics' Institutes would not only support the mid-century producer alliance of independent yeomen, artisans, and manufacturers, they would also create a cultural identity for an emerging liberal order in need of consent. However, as with British Mechanics' Institutes, the endorsement of the producer ideology inherent in the liberal social order was not automatic, as radical members of the working classes and their allies could contest "accepted" notions of liberal political economy.[61] And yet the flexibility of this particular philosophy in the colonial context ensured that Mechanics' Institutes in small towns and villages could also participate in the ideological construction of the liberal social order. The doctrine of honest industry preached in Mechanics' Institutes was also adaptable to the agricultural sector in rural areas, although once again some divergence of opinion emerged between various classes on how to accomplish this task.

At mid-century, leading commercial men such as Thomas Keefer and William Bristow gave prominent addresses on economic science to the Montreal Mechanics' Institute. According to these lecturers, the source of wealth in a community was personal hard work on the part of every member of society, since it was by "honesty, by industry, by prudence, by frugality, and by perseverance that individuals thrive ... the aggregate of these qualities in a people, joined to public spirit, form the basis of national prosperity."[62] Despite the fact that there was agreement on the means to achieve national greatness, members of urban Mechanics' Institutes were free to select the economic *policy* they believed would best facilitate this process. William Bristow claimed that only free trade and reciprocity with the United States would increase productiveness, for free trade would allow individual enterprise to thrive as "the good to the community is effected solely through self-interest, the most powerful stimulus that can be employed to excite the industry, and sharpen the intellect and ingenuity of man."

Thomas Keefer stated that neither unencumbered free trade nor pro-
tectionism without modification was desirable, as both policies partook of the character of class legislation. While Keefer remained
rather vague on how economic prosperity was to be accomplished,
clearly the alliance of the producing classes as well as the co-operation
of capital and labour was essential in overcoming animosities and furthering the economic advancement of the nation.[63] The prominent
politician Robert Baldwin Sullivan gave two influential lectures
between 1847 and 1848, one in the Hamilton and the other in the
Toronto Mechanics' Institute, which dwelled emphatically on the values of "earnestness, energy and industry." Unlike his commercial
counterparts in Montreal, Sullivan believed that the correct approach
to accomplish these objectives was the creation of home markets and
the protection of the manufacturing sector.[64]

Skilled workers also revealed a vested interest in the perpetuation of
these ideas, as noted in the non-lecture "The Rights of Labour" by the
printer A.A. Riddell to the Toronto Mechanics' Institute in 1848. The
necessity of honest industry and labour was a recurrent theme in his
address, as Riddell claimed that labour itself was not degrading, but
"enobling to those engaged in it, of great advantage to society, and
highly acceptable to God, and requires no strainings on the many fac-
ulties of common men." Using a rather liberal rhetoric of self-help,
Riddell insisted that the operative classes needed to elevate themselves
and acquire independence by being attentive to business and sober at
all times, and "to read and to think; to be upright and candid; to be at
home when not at work, and last, but not least, to enrol his name
among the members of the Toronto Mechanics' Institute." The artisan
must likewise obey the principles of political economy outlined by
Adam Smith and others:

> The manufacturer, workman or labourer, is far from being a recipi-
> ent of charity when he receives his wages ... it is nothing more than
> an *exchange* between two parties, calculated to be for the benefit of
> both. The labourer receives, in the place of the actual produce of
> his labour, its value in money or some other exchangeable article –
> the improvement in value of the master's material being his recom-
> pense for the outlay in wages. From this, it may be inferred, that
> both should be *equally independent of each other*, for both are *depend-
> ent* upon one another. No man can subsist without labour.[65]

Walter Eales, a painter by occupation, expressed similar views on political economy in his lecture to the Toronto Mechanics' Institute. Recognizing that those rising to opulence and wealth did so through

"perseverance and industry," Eales claimed that through knowledge and hard work, the future progress of the working man "depends upon himself, and any degree of proficiency is within his reach." Echoing the sentiments of Riddell, Eales stated categorically that Mechanics' Institutes would elevate the intellect, cultivate a sense of domestic affection, foster domestic piety, and promote moral culture among the skilled working classes.[66]

Of course, the noteworthy difference between the lectures of Walter Eales and A.A. Riddell is that the Toronto Mechanics' Institute permitted Eales to deliver his discourse, and denied that privilege to Riddell. Riddell's insistence on the liberal gospel of honest industry only faintly concealed his political radicalism. The radical notions inherent in the "Rights of Labour" appeared at the beginning of Riddell's discourse, where he asserted that those who labour "are justly entitled to comfortable dwellings, substantial food, protection in their persons, their property and their religion, the right of private judgment sufficient for their support when sick or out of employment, and hours for recreation and improvement." While this statement by itself was innocuous, the lecture committee's censors crossed out a particular sentence regarding the elevation of the mechanic, which claimed that they should "partake plentifully of the fruits which their hands had earned." While Riddell recognized that the rights of the working man included respect and esteem from the other classes, his true colours were subsequently revealed when he wrote in the marginalia, "Respect and esteem do not fill the belly, even in Canada."[67] Riddell's lecture also harboured a nascent populist outlook, a philosophy that not only called for greater representation on behalf of "the people," but also distinguished those individuals deemed non-producers – lawyers, doctors, and other professionals – from the producing classes. In his appeals for working-class rights and privileges, Riddell equated the apprenticeship of artisans with the studies of the professional classes, claiming with thinly veiled hostility that while "artizan cheerfully assists the professionalist in the upholding of his rights, he is far from acquiescing in the arrogant pretensions this class seems anxious to assume."[68]

The value of honest industry was a theme that also recurred in lectures and debates in small-town Mechanics' Institutes, as rural Institute members frequently deliberated principles of political economy among themselves. Even though Mechanics' Institutes in rural areas were often a far distance from the hub of manufacturing, there was a strong correlation between industry and the need to boost the economic advantages of the village or town. In a lecture to the Hemmingford Institute, the High Anglican Churchman Francis Fulford counselled the members of the Institute that honest labour occurred through individual effort, adding to the achievements of the community as a whole:

> But with regard to labour, what I want to point out to you is, that every man's labour belongs to the community, because as the community is befitted by the general wealth, they have by the same rule an equal interest in that which produces the wealth, viz., labour. So by the same showing society are losers when labour is misapplied ... But there is one great fact which should be ever present in our minds, that in whatever way we may apply our labour, unless we are actuated by a strict principle of honour and integrity, we can never hope to see our operation successful. And as with the wealth so with the character of nations, it of necessity takes its tone from individuals.[69]

Reliance on this type of resilient work ethic would not only lead to economic wealth, it would also lead to a liberal and moral community dependent on one another.

Lecturers addressing small-town and village Mechanics' Institutes outlined the importance of the commercial, manufacturing, and agricultural sectors working together in the producer alliance for the prosperity of the community at large. William Merritt, in his lecture to the St Catherines Mechanics' Institute bluntly stated that it was the petty jealousies and rivalries existing between Quebec, Montreal, and Toronto that ruined trade. To this Reformer and successful commercial agent, if the competing commercial interests in Canada would unite in one common effort they would surpass the United States in prosperity. This united endeavour would benefit every class in society; the farmer and manufacturer would enjoy cheaper transport rates, and the merchant would be able to seek a larger market for his goods. In spite of the restrictions placed on political discussion in the Institute, clearly such a proponent of free trade as Merritt could not resist stating that reciprocity would place the industrial sector in the same flourishing condition as their American rivals. On the other hand, Francis Fulford in his lecture to the Hemmingford Mechanics' Institute, recognized his particular constituency when he asserted that all classes of society should be focused on the improvement of agriculture. For Fulford, "the interests of the manufacturer and the farmer are not conflicting, but ... they are mutually interested in developing their respective trades; for it is only by bringing about a higher state of farming that we can hope to see machinery more generally used in cultivation."[70]

Patterned after institutions of mutual improvement and adult education in Great Britain, Mechanics' Institutes in early to mid-nineteenth century central Canada proved to be adept at acclimatizing to colonial society. Not only did Mechanics' Institutes provide adult education, subscription libraries, and mutual instruction for their constituencies, they also promoted an inclusive ideology that opened their institution to the wider community. Promoting a "liberal" cultural consensus in burgeoning urban areas and in rural towns and villages, Mechanics' Institutes accommodated all interests, classes, and occupations in the first few decades of the nineteenth century. However, by mid-century, Mechanics' Institutes were critical in assisting both the rural agrarian and the emerging liberal social order to realize some measure of cultural cohesion. The educational legacy of Mechanics' Institutes is also highly ambiguous, given its class and gender conflicts, and more particularly the political and religious discord that took place within hallowed Mechanics' Halls. For some skilled workers and their radical allies, the exposure of the Janus face of Mechanics' Institutes as organizations pandering to the needs of the middling sort caused major rifts in both the urban and rural Institute settings. While in some respects the discord prevalent in many Canadian Mechanics' Institutes reflected Old World attitudes and problems, in reality both the successes and the failures of the Institute movement were grounded in the colonial experience.

NOTES

1 See A.A. Riddell, "The Rights of Labour," Baldwin Room, Metropolitan Toronto Reference Library (hereafter MTL), unpublished lecture, 1848, 30.

2 On the theory of liberal governance, see the work of Bruce Curtis, "'Littery Meritt,' Useful Knowledge, and the Organization of Township Libraries in Canada West, 1840–60," *Ontario History* 78, no. 4 (Dec. 1986): 285–311 and his masterful *Building the Educational State: Canada West, 1836–1871* (London, ON: Althouse Press, 1988); Jean-Marie Fecteau, *Un nouvel ordre des choses: La pauvreté, le crime, l'Etat au Québec, de la fin du XVIIIe siècle à 1840* (Montreal: VLB, 1989) and also his article, "État et associationnisme au XIXe siècle québecois: éléments pour une problématique des Rapports État/société dans la transition au capitalisme," in Allan Greer and Ian Radforth, eds, *Colonial Leviathan: State Formation in Mid-Nineteenth Century Canada* (Toronto: University of Toronto Press, 1992), 134–62. See also the work of Jeffrey McNairn, *The Capacity to Judge: Public Opinion and Deliberative Democracy in Upper Canada, 1791–1854* (Toronto: University of Toronto Press, 2000), 63–115 and 261–90 as well as his contribution, "The Malthu-

sian Moment" in this volume, and particularly Ian McKay, "The Liberal
Order Framework: A Prospectus for a Reconnaissance of Canadian History,"
Canadian Historical Review 81, no. 4 (December, 2000): 617–45.

3 For the first stirrings of the producer alliance, see L.R. MacDonald, "Merchants against Industry: An Idea and its Origins," *Canadian Historical Review*
56 (1975): 266–80 and particularly the work of T.W. Acheson, *Saint John: The
Making of a Colonial Urban Community* (Toronto: University of Toronto Press,
1985). Challenges to Acheson's vision of the producer alliance generating
unifying liberal doctrines can be found in Martin Hewitt, "Science, Popular
Culture and the Producer Alliance in Saint John, N.B.," in Paul A Bogaard,
ed, *Profiles of Science and Society in the Maritimes Prior to 1914* (Fredericton, NB:
Acadiensis Press, 1990), 243–75 and Daniel Samson, "Industry and Improvement: State and Class Formation in Nova Scotia's Coal Mining Countryside,
1790–1864," PhD Thesis, Queen's University, 1998.

4 For a structural model of "patrician" and "plebeian" in British society, see
the essays in E.P. Thompson, *Customs in Common: Studies in Traditional Popular
Culture* (New York: The New Press, 1991) and particularly Dror Wharman,
*Imagining the Middle Class: The Political Representation of Class in Britain, c.
1780–1840* (Cambridge: Cambridge University Press, 1994). For Canada's
"moral economy," see Bryan Palmer, *Working-Class Experience: Rethinking the
History of Canadian Labour, 1800–1991*, 2nd ed. (Toronto: McLelland and
Stewart, 1992), 42–9 and his contribution, "Popular Radicalism and the
Theatrics of Rebellion" in this volume; Sean Cadigan, "Planters, Households
and Merchant Capitalism: Northeast-Coast Newfoundland, 1800–1855," in
Daniel Samson, ed., *Contested Countryside: Rural Workers and Modern Society in
Atlantic Canada, 1800–1950* (Fredericton, NB: Acadiensis Press, 1994),
150–61. On the application of the binary model of society in Upper
Canada, see Nancy Christie's contribution in this volume, "The Plague of
Servants."

5 On socio-economic change and Mechanics' Institutes after mid-century in
Britain, see J.P Hemming, "The Mechanics' Institutes in Lancashire and
Yorkshire Textile Districts from 1850," *Journal of Educational Administration
and History* 9, no. 1 (Jan. 1977): 18–31 and John Laurent, "Science, Society
and Politics in Late Nineteenth-Century England: A Further Look at
Mechanics' Institutes," *Social Studies of Science* 14, no. 4 (Nov. 1984):
585–619. For Canada, see Bryan Palmer, *A Culture in Conflict: Skilled Workers
and Industrial Capitalism in Hamilton, Ontario, 1860–1914* (Montreal &
Kingston: McGill-Queen's University Press, 1979), 49–52 and Ellen Ramsay,
"Art and Industrial Society: The Role of the Toronto Mechanics' Institute in
the Promotion of Art, 1831–1883," *Labour/Le Travail* 43 (Spring 1999):
71–103. For an increasingly middle-class presence in late Victorian
small-town Institutes see Andrew Holman, *A Sense of Their Duty: Middle-Class*

Formation in Victorian Ontario Towns (Montreal & Kingston: McGill-Queen's University Press, 2000), 105–29.

6 See Mabel Tylecote, *The Mechanics' Institutes of Lancashire and Yorkshire Before 1851* (Manchester: Manchester University Press, 1957), particularly chapters one and two; see also Edward Royle, "Mechanics' Institutes and the Working Class," *Historical Journal* 14, no. 2 (1971): 305–21.

7 See Steven Shapin and Barry Barnes, "Science, Nature and Control: Interpreting Mechanics' Institutes," *Studies in Social Science* 7 (1977): 31–74 and A.D. Garner and E.W. Jenkins, "The English Mechanics' Institutes: The Case of Leeds, 1824–1842," *History of Education* 13, no. 2 (Apr. 1984): 139–52. See also E.P. Thompson, *The Making of the English Working Class* (Harmondsworth: Penguin, 1968), 817–20; Richard Johnson, "'Really Useful Knowledge': Radical Education and Working Class Culture, 1790–1848," in J. Clarke, C. Critcher and A Johnson, eds, *Working Class Culture: Studies in History and Theory* (New York: St Martin's Press, 1979), 75–102 and particularly Jonathan Rose, *The Intellectual Life of the British Working Classes* (New Haven and London: Yale University Press, 2001), 58–91.

8 Ian Inkster pioneered the work in this field; see Inkster, "Aspects of the History of Science and Culture in Britain, 1780–1850 and Beyond," in Ian Inkster and Jack Morrell, eds, *Metropolis and Province: Science in British Culture, 1780–1850* (London: Hutchinson, 1983), 3–14 and particularly the edited collection of his own articles on British Mechanics' Institutes in *Scientific Culture and Urbanisation in Industrializing Britain* (Aldershot: Ashgate, 1997). See also Roger Cooter, *The Cultural Meaning of Popular Science: Phrenology and the Organization of Consent in Nineteenth Century Britain* (Cambridge: Cambridge University Press, 1984); Howard Wach, "Culture and the Middle Classes: Popular Knowledge in Industrial Manchester," *Journal of British Studies* 27, no. 4 (Oct. 1988), 375–404; R. J. Morris, *Class, Sect and Party: Leeds 1820–1850* (Manchester and New York: University of Manchester Press, 1990), 161–203 and Alison Winter, *Mesmerized: Powers of Mind in Victorian Britain* (Chicago: University of Chicago Press, 1998).

9 For the social control thesis, see Patrick Keane, "A Study in Early Problems and Policies in Early Adult Education: The Halifax Mechanics' Institute," *Social History/Histoire Sociale* 8, no. 16 (Nov. 1975): 255–74 and also Nora Robins, "Useful Education for the Workingman: The Montreal Mechanics' Institute, 1828–1870," in Michael Welton, ed., *Knowledge for the People: The Struggle for Adult Learning in English Speaking Canada, 1828–1973* (Toronto: Ontario Institute for Studies in Education, 1987), 20–34. Mechanics' Institutes as a vehicle for middle-class hegemony and state formation is covered in Martin Hewitt, "Science as Spectacle: Popular Scientific Culture in Saint John, New Brunswick, 1830–1850," *Acadiensis*, 18, no. 1 (Autumn 1988): 91–119; Elsbeth Heaman, *The Inglorious Arts of Peace: Exhibitions in Canadian*

Society During the Nineteenth Century (Toronto: University of Toronto Press, 1999), 3–20 and Ramsay, "Art and Industrial Society," 71–103.

10 On the adult education side, see the work of Patrick Keane, "Priorities and Resources in Adult Education: The Montreal Mechanics' Institute 1828–1843," *McGill Journal of Education* 23, no. 2 (Spring 1988): 171–87. For Mechanics' Institutes as the first public libraries, see James Eadie, "The Napanee Mechanics' Institute: The Nineteenth Century Mechanics' Institute Movement in Microcosm," *Ontario History* 68, no. 4 (Dec. 1976): 209–21; Jim Blanchard, "Anatomy of Failure: Ontario Mechanics' Institutes, 1835–95," *Canadian Library Journal* 38, no. 6 (Dec. 1981): 393–8; Curtis, "'Littery Meritt'," and Lorne Bruce, *Free Books for All: The Public Library Movement in Ontario, 1850–1930* (Toronto: Dundurn Press, 1994), 3–70. The following presentation emulates the work done on Mechanics' Institutes in the parallel colonial experience of Australia; see Philip Candy, "The Light of Heaven Itself: Contributions of Mechanics' Institutes to Australian Cultural History" and Marc Askew, "Conflict, Consensus and Culture: The Geelong Mechanics' Institute to 1900" in Philip Candy and John Laurent, eds, *Pioneering Culture: Mechanics' Institutes and Schools of Arts in Australia* (Adelaide: Auslib Press, 1994), 1–28 and 102–25.

11 See the *Rules of the Quebec Mechanics' Institute* (Quebec, 1832), 3–4 and 28 as well as the *Catalogue and Rules of the Library and Reading Room of the Quebec Mechanics' Institute* (Quebec, 1841), 1–2.

12 Thomas Aylwin, *Inaugural Address Delivered on Occasion of the Opening of the New Mechanics' Hall* (Montreal, 1855), 6–11; *Report of the General Committee of the Mechanics' Institute of Montreal* (Montreal, 1855) and *Constitution and Laws of the Montreal Mechanics' Institution* (Montreal, 1833), 3–7. Aylwin most likely wanted to avoid expressions of Irish worker discontent such as the Lachine Canal strike a decade earlier; see Raymond Boily, *Les Irlandais et le canal de Lachine: la grève de 1843* (Montreal: Leméac, 1980).

13 See William Judd, ed., *Minutes of the London Mechanics' Institute 1841–95,* occasional paper #23 (London, 1976), 96 and the London Mechanics' Institute records, London Public Library, Vol. 1, minute book, 1841–50, Constitution and bylaws, as well as the meeting of 8 Mar. 1842. See also the records of the Toronto Mechanics' Institute, Archives of Ontario (hereafter AO), MU 2020, Vol. 1, minute book, 1831–36, 5 Mar. 1832 and 19 Feb. 1836 as well as Vol. 8, 1848 and 1851 annual reports and the Toronto Mechanics' Institute fonds, MTL, L1, series B, Vol. 1, board meeting minute book, 1840–48, 13 Nov. 1848.

14 Judd, *Minutes of the London Mechanics' Institute,* 104 and the London Mechanics' Institute records, London Public Library, Vol. 1, minute book, 1841–50, first annual meeting, 3 Jan. 1842. For nascent class discontent in the Toronto and Hamilton Mechanics' Institute, see McNairn, *The Capacity to Judge,* 96–9 and Palmer, *A Culture in Conflict,* 51. Similar sentiments emerged

in Maritime urban areas; see Hewitt, "Science, Popular Culture and the Producer Alliance."

15 See Aylwin, *Inaugural Address*, 14–15 and the *British Whig* (Kingston), 11 Mar. 1834. See particularly James Reilly, "The Political, Social and Economic Impacts on the Emergence of the Kingston Mechanics' Institute in the Pre-Confederation Period," MA Thesis, Queen's University, 1994.

16 For the membership figures of the Montreal Institute, see Harry Kuntz, "The Educational Work of the Two Montreal Mechanics' Institutes," MA Thesis, Concordia University, 1993, 222–9 and Robins, "Useful Education for the Workingman," 31–4. For London, see Judd, *Minutes of the London Mechanics' Institute*, 62–4.

17 For the membership figures in the Toronto Mechanics' Institute, see the Toronto Mechanics' Institute fonds, MTL, L1, series E, Vol. 2, membership lists, 1855–66.

18 See the Toronto Mechanics' Institute fonds, MTL, L1, series M, folder n.d.–1851, unbound papers, annual report, 4 Jan. 1833; see also the *Rules of the Quebec Mechanics' Institute*, 3–4 and the *Catalogue of the Quebec Mechanics' Institute*, 1–2.

19 See the Ottawa Mechanics' Institute and Athenaeum fonds, National Archives of Canada (hereafter NAC), MG 28 I 1, Vol. 2, meetings of trustees and members, reorganization meeting, Jan. 1853, and annual reports, 19 Mar. 1861. See also the records of the London Mechanics' Institute, London Public Library, Vol. 1, minute book, 1841–50, annual report of 1841 and Vol. 2, minute book, 1851–65, library committee minutes, 13 Jan. 1851 and annual report of 1857.

20 See the records of the Hamilton Mechanics' Institute, Hamilton Public Library, Special Collections, minute book, 1839–51, 24 Feb. 1840 and 28 Feb. 1844, as well as the Toronto Mechanics' Institute fonds, AO, MU 2020, Vol. 1, minute book 1831–36, 5 Mar. 1832 and 19 Feb. 1836.

21 See William Dunlop, *An Address Delivered to the York Mechanics' Institution* (Toronto, 1832), 6–7 and 14–15. These beliefs were similar to those of the rising manufacturing interests; see Hewitt, "Science, Popular Culture and the Producer Alliance"; Heaman, *The Inglorious Arts of Peace*, 3–28 and Ramsay, "Art and Industrial Society." Dunlop's politically discursive vision of the "middling sort" echoes the arguments found in Wharman, *Imagining the Middle Classes*.

22 Toronto Mechanics Institute fonds, MTL, L1, series M, unbound papers, 1852–63, letter of H. Rogers to the Institute, 20 Nov. 1852 and the report on the laying of the cornerstone of the Mechanics' Hall, 17 Apr. 1854. See also Richard Lewis, "Lecture on Education," in the *Journal of the Board of Arts and Manufacturers of Upper Canada* 2 (Nov. 1862): 338–9; the *Annual Report of the Toronto Mechanics' Institute for 1855* (Toronto, 1855), 7–8, 11 and the *Annual Report for 1860* (Toronto, 1860), 10–11.

23 See the Ottawa Mechanics' Institute and Athenaeum fonds, NAC, MG 28 I 1,
    Vol. 2, meetings of trustees and members, Jan. 1853 and 27 Mar. 1857.
24 See the report of the Hamilton Mechanics' Institute, *Journal of the Board of
    Arts and Manufacturers of Upper Canada* 1 (Apr. 1861), 106–7; see also the
    records of the Hamilton Mechanics' Institute, Hamilton Public Library,
    Special Collections, minute book, 1839–51, 24 Feb. 1840; 28 Feb. 1844; 28
    Feb. 1845; 5 Apr. 1848 and annual meeting, 22 Feb. 1850. On education as
    a vehicle for the middling classes to control working-class propensities to
    crime, see Alison Prentice, *The School Promoters: Education and Social Class in
    Mid-Nineteenth Century Upper Canada* (Toronto: McLelland and Stewart,
    1977). For a discussion of the middle-class nature of the Hamilton
    Mechanics' Institute, see Palmer, *A Culture in Conflict*, 49–52.
25 There is scant literature on Mechanics' Institutes in the British countryside;
    see C.J. Radcliffe, "Mutual Improvement Societies in the West Riding of
    Yorkshire, 1835–1900," *Journal of Educational Administration and History* 18,
    no. 2 (July 1986); Michael Watson, "The Origins of Mechanics' Institutes of
    North Yorkshire," *Journal of Educational Administration and History* 19, no. 2
    (July 1987): 12–25 and Rose, *Intellectual Life of the British Working Classes*,
    61–72. See also Mike White, "Respectable and Useful: The Institute Move-
    ment in West Australia" and Askew, "Conflict, Consensus and Culture," in
    Candy and Laurent, eds., *Pioneering Culture*, 102–25 and 126–35 as well as
    Donald Akenson's study of the Gananoque Mechanics' Institute in *The Irish
    in Ontario: A Study in Rural History* (Montreal & Kingston: McGill-Queen's
    University Press, 1984), 218–22.
26 See the records of the *Société Litteraire de Laprairie*, Eliseé Choquet fonds,
    Archives Nationales de Quebec à Montreal (hereafter ANQ), P60, box 1, file 4.174
    and file 4.180, the annual report of 1858. See also the Elora Mechanics'
    Institute fonds, Wellington County Archives (hereafter WCA), MU 60, minute
    book, 1857–70, 21 and 30 Apr. 1858; the Mitchell Mechanics' Institute
    fonds, Stratford-Perth Archives, minute book, 1854–70, 11 Mar. 1854 and
    the records of the Paris Mechanics' Institute, AO, MS 359, reel 2, minute
    book, 1843–62, 9 Jan. 1846 and 6 Dec. 1847.
27 Douglas McCalla argued that economic development in rural Ontario was
    fuelled by the complex nature of markets in rural areas, while Gordon
    Darroch maintained that middle-class formation should not be viewed solely
    as an urban phenomenon founded on non-manual work, since in rural areas
    independent yeomen formed the middle class. See McCalla, *Planting the
    Province: The Economic History of Upper Canada, 1784–1870* (Toronto: Univer-
    sity of Toronto Press, 1993) and Darroch, "Scanty Fortunes and Rural Mid-
    dle Class Formation in Nineteenth-Century Rural Ontario," *Canadian
    Historical Review* 79, no. 4 (Dec. 1998): 621–59. See also David Burley, *A
    Particular Condition in Life: Self-Employment and Social Mobility in Mid-Victorian
    Brantford, Ontario* (Montreal & Kingston: McGill-Queen's University Press,

1994). For the importance of rural markets in Quebec, see the work of Serge Courville, "Un monde rural en mutation: le Bas-Canada dans la première moitée du xixe siècle," *Social History/Histoire Sociale* 20, no. 40 (Nov. 1987): 237–58.

28 See the Paris Mechanics' Institute fonds, AO, MS 359, reel 2, minute book, 1843–62, second annual meeting, 2 Apr. 1842 and fifth annual report, 7 Apr. 1846. See also the Niagara Mechanics' Institute fonds, AO, MU 2022, MS 566, Vol. 1, minute book, 1848–62, 11 Nov. 1857, 14 Nov. 1857.

29 See the Paris Mechanics' Institute fonds, AO, MS 359, reel 2, minute book, 1843–62, fourth annual meeting, 2 Apr. 1844, 7 Apr. 1846, 7 Jan. 1857; James Dallas, *A Lecture on the Aims and Usefulness of Mechanics' Institutes* (Barrie, 1865), 3–7 and J. Travers Lewis, *Lecture Delivered before the Brockville Library Association and Mechanics' Institute* (Brockville, 1855), 3–5, 16–17. Rural Mechanics' Institutes also followed the "familialist" model of other organizations like church congregations and temperance societies; see Nancy Christie's introduction, "Family, Community and the Rise of Liberal Society," in her edited collection *Households of Faith: Family, Gender and Community in Canada, 1760–1969* (Montreal & Kingston: McGill-Queen's University Press, 2002), 3–20.

30 See the Fergus Public Library fonds, WCA, A993.36, MU 281, series 2, subseries 2, minute book, 1857–96, meeting of 21 Aug. 1857 and the Guelph Public Library fonds, Guelph Public Library, Farmers' and Mechanics' Institute minute book, 1850–72, 28 Jan. 1856.

31 See the Guelph Public Library fonds, Guelph Public Library, Mechanics' Institute minute book, 1850–72, 14 Jan. 1852, 17 Jan. 1854 and 11 Jan. 1859, as well as the Mitchell Mechanics' Institute fonds, Stratford-Perth Archives, minute book, 1854–70, 21 Jan. 1861.

32 See Tylecote, *The Mechanics' Institutes of Lancashire and Yorkshire*, 17–25; Radcliffe, "Mutual Improvement Societies in the West Riding of Yorkshire," 2–8; Jane Purvis, *Hard Lessons: Lives and Education of Working Class Women in Nineteenth-Century England* (Minneapolis: University of Minnesota Press, 1989) and Janet Cunliffe Jones, "A Rare Phenomenon: A Woman's Contribution to Nineteenth-Century Adult Education," *Journal of Educational Administration and History* 24, no. 1 (Jan. 1992): 1–17.

33 For this paradoxical view of women in voluntary societies such as temperance associations, the exhibition movement, and other voluntary organizations see Janet Noel, *Canada Dry: Temperance Crusades before Confederation* (Toronto: University of Toronto Press, 1995), 89–102; Cecilia Morgan, *Public Men and Virtuous Women: The Gendered Languages of Religion and Politics in Upper Canada, 1791–1850* (Toronto: University of Toronto Press, 1996), 208–18; E.A. Heaman, "Taking the World by Show: Canadian Women as Exhibitors to 1900," *Canadian Historical Review* 78, no. 4 (Dec. 1997): 599–631 and especially Ramsay, "Art and Industrial Society," 87–9.

34 See the records of the London Mechanics' Institute, London Public Library, Vol. 2, minute book, 1851–70, 27 Jan. 1851 and Judd, *Minutes of the London Mechanics' Institute,* 64. See also the Toronto Mechanics' Institute fonds, MTL, L1, series E, Vol. 1, membership list, 1833–48 and Kuntz, "Educational Work," 229–30, 447–8.

35 See the Ottawa Mechanics' Institute and Athenaeum fonds, NAC, MG 28 I 1, Vol. 2, minutes of meetings of trustees and members, 6 Dec. 1854 and 28 Feb. 1855.

36 See Thomas Keefer, *Montreal and the Ottawa: Two Lectures Delivered Before the Mechanics' Institute of Montreal* (Montreal, 1854), 3 and also the records of the Ottawa Mechanics' Institute, NAC, MG 28 I 1, Vol. 3, managing committee minutes, 23 Nov. 1855.

37 Walter Eales, *The Benefits to be Derived from Mechanics' Institutes* (Toronto, 1851), 9–12, 15–16. Such activities no doubt reinforced the emerging hegemony of the industrial patriarchy; see Catherine Hall and Leonore Davidoff, *Family Fortunes: Men and Women of the English Middle Class, 1780–1850* (Chicago: University of Chicago Press, 1987).

38 See Nancy Osterud, *Bonds of Community: The Lives of Farm Women in Nineteenth Century New York* (Ithaca and London: Cornell University Press, 1991), 247–74 and Karen Hansen, *A Very Social Time: Crafting Community in Antebellum New England* (Berkeley and Los Angeles: University of California Press, 1994). For the Canadian context, see Marguerite Van Die, "The Marks of Genuine Revival: Religion, Social Change, Gender and Community in mid-Victorian Brantford, Ontario," *Canadian Historical Review* 79, no. 3 (Sept. 1998): 524–63 and in particular, Catherine Wilson, "Reciprocal Work Bees and the Meaning of Neighbourhood," *Canadian Historical Review* 82, no. 3 (Sept. 2001): 431–64. Of course, just permitting women to join Mechanics' Institutes did not overly disturb the rural social order.

39 See the Paris Mechanics' Institute fonds, AO, MS 359, reel 2, minute book, 19 Jan. 1856, 14 Feb. 1856; J.E. Curran papers, NAC, MG 30 C85, Vol. 4, Orillia Mechanics' Institute minute book, 1864–72, bylaws of 1864 and the records of the *Société Littéraire de Laprairie,* Elisée Choquet fonds, ANQ, P60, box 1, file 4.180, the annual report of 1858.

40 See the Niagara Mechanics' Institute fonds, AO, MU 2022, MS 566, Vol.1, 19 Nov. 1852, 20 Nov. 1856 and the Mitchell Mechanics' Institute records, Stratford-Perth Archives, minute book, 1854–70, 15 Oct. 1866.

41 For the dismissal of the Institute movement by radical workers and "intellectual Chartism" in Britain see Tylecote, *The Mechanics' Institutes of Lancashire and Yorkshire,* 34–56; Royle, "Mechanics' Institutes and the Working Class"; Johnson, "Really Useful Knowledge"; and Wach, "Culture and the Middle Classes." For Institutes as a hegemonic project, see Morris, *Class, Sect and Party,* 182–7; Martin Hewitt, *The Emergence of Stability in the Industrial City: Manchester 1832–1867* (Aldershot: Ashgate, 1996), 105–18 and Brian Lewis,

The Middlemost and the Milltowns: Bourgeois Culture and Politics in Early Industrial England (Stanford: Stanford University Press, 2001), 248–86.

42 Education and expressions of state formation are often viewed as agents of middle-class hegemony and harmonization; see many of the essays in Radforth and Greer, *Colonial Leviathan*; Alison Prentice and Susan Houston, *Schooling and Scholars in Nineteenth Century Ontario* (Toronto: University of Toronto Press, 1988); Curtis, *Building the Educational State;* and Heaman, *The Inglorious Arts of Peace.* And yet some Institutes could be immersed in politico-religious conflicts; see Keane, "A Study in Early Problems and Policies in Early Adult Education"; Palmer, *A Culture in Conflict,* 49–52; Hewitt, "Science, Popular Culture and the Producer Alliance"; and Ramsay, "Art in Industrial Society."

43 See William Bristow, *The Commercial Prospects of Canada: A Lecture Delivered Before the Montreal Mechanics' Institute* (Montreal, 1850), 24–5; James Bovell, *A Lecture on the Future of Canada* (Montreal, 1849), 1–2; and Keefer, *Montreal and the Ottawa,* 23, 31–2. The sectarian disagreements of the early Montreal Institute are mapped out in Kuntz, "Educational Work," 79–90; see also the *Constitution of the Montreal Mechanics' Institution,* 12.

44 The Rev. Bettridge picked an unusual location to lecture against voluntarism, although accusations like this were typical of the sectarian battles of the time; see Curtis Fahey, *In His Name: The Anglican Experience in Upper Canada, 1791–1854* (Ottawa: Carleton University Press, 1991), 202–5. See also the record of the London Mechanics' Institute, London Public Library, Vol. 1, minute book, 1841–50, 4 Mar. 1843 and the 1850 annual meeting, as well as Vol. 2, minute book, 1851–70, 24 Jan. 1853.

45 Walter Eales, *The Benefits to be Derived from Mechanics' Institutes* (Toronto, 1851), 12–13; Toronto Mechanics' Institute fonds, MTL, L1, Board minutes, 1840–48, series B, Vol. 1, 10 Sept. 1841 and Special meetings, 1854–83, series B, Vol. 7, 4 Oct. 1854 as well as the records of the Toronto Mechanics' Institute, AO, MU 2020, Vol. 1, minute book 1831–36, membership lists. See also the article by Ian Radforth, "Sydenham and Utilitarian Reform," in Radforth and Greer, eds, *Colonial Leviathan,* 64–102.

46 Toronto Mechanics' Institute fonds, MTL, L1, Board meetings, 1848–54, series B, Vol. 2, report of the Library Committee, 9 Feb. 1852 and series M, folder 1864–77, letter of W.T. Withrow to the Institute, 1864.

47 See Heaman, *Inglorious Arts of Peace,* 20, 330. For the details of this episode see the Toronto Mechanics' Institute fonds, MTL, L1, series B, Vol. 1, Board minutes1840–48, 15 Nov., 21 Nov. and 5 Dec. 1848; series M, folder n.d.–1851, letter of A.A. Riddell, 13 Nov. 1848.

48 A. A. Riddell, "The Rights of Labour," in the MTL, unpublished lecture, 1848, 1–6, 16–18.

49 Riddell was a staunch friend of noted radical Charles Clarke, who shared these philosophies; see Ken Dewar, "Charles Clarke's *Reformator:* Early Victo-

rian Radicalism in Upper Canada," *Ontario History* 78, no. 3 (Sept. 1986): 233–52. Prentice and Houston discovered that Riddell followed in the artisan tradition of self-improvement, becoming first a school inspector and then a doctor after his printing days were over; see Prentice and Houston, *Schooling and Scholars,* 231 and Riddell, "The Rights of Labour," 4–8, 18.

50 See the Paris Mechanics' Institute fonds, AO, MS 359, reel 2, minute book, 1843–62, bylaws, 15 May 1858 and the Niagara Mechanics' Institute fonds, AO, MU 2022, MS 566, Vol. 1, 18 Dec. 1855; the *Bylaws of the Owen Sound Mechanics' Institute,* 14 and the Mitchell Mechanics' Institute fonds, Stratford-Perth archives, minute book, 1854–70, 9 Jan. 1854.

51 See John Ardagh, *An Address Delivered Before the County of Simcoe Mechanics' Institute* (Barrie, 1858), 19–20. See also the *Constitution, Rules and Regulations of the Guelph Farmers' and Mechanics' Institute* (Guelph, 1855), 4.

52 See the records of the *Société Litteraire de Laprairie,* Eliseé Choquet fonds, ANQ, P60, box 20, file 4.173, constitution et règles, 1853.

53 See Johanne Menard, "L'Institut des Artisans Du Comté du Drummond 1856–90," *Recherches Sociographiques* 16, no. 2 (1975): 207–18 and the Drummond County *Institut des Artisans* fonds, NAC, MG 28 I 142, Vol. 1, minute book, 1856–58, 26 Dec. 1856, 10 Sept. 1857 and 3 Dec. 1857.

54 Donald Fyson's work on the Canadiens' use of the British court system in Lower Canada is invaluable in this regard; see his contribution "The Canadiens and British Institutions in Quebec, from the Conquest to the Rebellions" in this volume. For more on Rouge political beliefs, see J.P. Bernard, *Les rouges: libéralisme, nationalisme et anticléricalisme au milieu du XIXe siècle* (Montreal: Presses de l'Université de Québec, 1971).

55 See the Drummond County *Institut des Artisans* fonds, NAC, MG 28 I 142, Vol. 1, minute book, 1856–58, 26 Dec. 1856; 8 Jan. 1857; 12 Feb. 1857 and 14 Jan. 1858 as well as Vol. 2, minute book, 1858–90, 3 June 1858 and 9 Jan. 1862.

56 See the Drummond County *Institut des Artisans* fonds, NAC, MG 28 I 142, Vol. 1, minute book, 1856–58, 15 Jan. 1857; 26 Mar. 1857; 27 May 1857; 15 Oct. 1857 and 7 Jan. 1858 as well as Vol. 2, minute book, 1858–1900, 27 Jan. 1859 and 6 Dec. 1860. For similar responses to institutional reform in the Eastern Townships, see J.I. Little, *State and Society in Transition: The Politics of Institutional Reform in the Eastern Townships, 1838–1852* (Montreal & Kingston: McGill-Queen's University Press, 1997).

57 See the Barrie Debating Club and Mechanics' Institute fonds, Simcoe County Archives (hereafter SCA), minute book, 1854–56, bylaws of the debating club, and the debates of 23 Jan. 1854; 27 Feb. 1854 and 14 July 1854.

58 See the Barrie Debating Club and Mechanics' Institute fonds, SCA, minute book, 1854–56, bylaws of the debating club, 27 Feb. 1854; 9 Aug. 1854 and 27 Sept. 1854; on 7 Dec. 1854 the first meeting of the Barrie Mechanics' Institute took place. On Reformer and/or radical political ideology, see Dewar, "Charles Clarke's *Reformator*."

59 The Carleton Place Mechanics' Institute fonds, NAC, MG 9, D8/4, minute book, 1846–49, 10 Mar. 1849. For the ideological roots of artisan self-improvement in rural Ontario, see particularly Gerald Killian, *David Boyle: From Artisan to Archaeologist* (Toronto: University of Toronto Press, 1983), 2–39. I am indebted to Jane Errington for information about John Gemmill's occupation and activities in Lanark County.

60 It seems that President Gemmill was caught up in the radical political and religious controversies in the Church of Scotland; see Michael Gauvreau, "Covenanter Democracy: Scottish Popular Religion, Ethnicity, and the Varieties of Politico-Religious Dissent in Upper Canada, 1815–1841," *Histoire Sociale/Social History* 36, no. 71 (May 2003): 55–83. See also the Carleton Place Mechanics' Institute fonds, NAC, MG 9, D8/4, minute book, 1846–49, 7 May 1849, 32 and 12 May 1849, 33.

61 On the promotion of an industrial agenda in British Mechanics' Institutes, see the edited collection of Ian Inkster, *The Steam Intellect Societies: Essays on Culture, Education and Industry, 1820–1914* (Nottingham: University of Nottingham Press, 1985). On the ideology of the producer alliance in the Canadian context, see MacDonald, "Merchants against Industry" and Hewitt, "Science, Popular Culture and the Producer Alliance," 243–75. The notion of a producer *ideology* arising just after mid-century is explored in Gregory Kealey, *Toronto Workers Respond to Industrial Capitalism, 1867–1892* (Toronto: University of Toronto Press, 1980), 124–50; Bryan Palmer, *A Culture in Conflict*, 97–122; Ramsay, "Art and Industrial Society," 74–95 and Heaman, *Inglorious Arts of Peace*, 21–27.

62 See Bristow, *Commercial Prospects of Canada*, 10–11 and 25; Brown Chamberlain, *Our Country and our Duty to It* (Montreal, 1854), 13–14 and Keefer, *Montreal and Ottawa*, 5–6. Industrialists in Ottawa likewise viewed their city as a commercial power, and thus lectures were often presented on economic subjects in the Ottawa Mechanics' Institute. See Edward Van Cortlandt, *An Epitome of a Lecture on Ottawa Productions* (Ottawa, 1853) and George Perry, *The Staple Trade of Canada* (Ottawa, 1862).

63 See Bristow, *Commercial Prospects of Canada*, 5–9; Keefer, *Montreal and Ottawa*, 6–8, 23–32; Bovell, *A Lecture on the Future of Canada*, 1–4; Reverend John Cook's lecture in the Quebec Institute, *The Advantages of Life Assurance to the Working Classes* (Montreal, 1848), 3–6 and also Hugh Baker's lecture to the Hamilton Mechanics' Institute, *A Lecture on Life Assurance* (Hamilton, 1848).

64 See Robert Baldwin Sullivan, *Address on Emigration and Colonization, Delivered in the Mechanics' Institute Hall* (Toronto, 1847), 3–8 and Sullivan, *The Connection between Agriculture and Manufactures of Canada* (Hamilton, 1848), 4–12, 32–6. See also the lecture of Rev. Adam Lillie, *Canada, Its Growth and Prospects* (Brockville, 1852), 12–16, 37–9 and Walter Arnold, *Money and Banking: A Lecture Delivered to the Mechanics' Institute, Toronto* (Toronto, 1862), 1–4, 30–4, 45–8.

65 See Riddell, "The Rights of Labour," 5–8, 19–22.

66 See Eales, *The Benefits to be Derived from Mechanics' Institutes*, 4–7, 16–18. These arguments also appeared among skilled workers in the Maritimes; see Hewitt, "Science, Popular Culture and the Producer Alliance," 243–75.

67 As noted, this philosophy borrowed heavily from Canadian forms of mid-Victorian radicalism; so despite his adherence to the producer ideology, Riddell's lecture was rejected. See Riddell, "The Rights of Labour," 10–16, 18–23 and 35–6; Prentice and Houston, *Schooling and Scholars*, 231 and Dewar, "Charles Clarke's *Reformator*," 243–52.

68 See Riddell, "The Rights of Labour," 10–12. Populism did not only emerge in the class turbulence of the 1890s, its tenets emerged throughout Ontario's earlier history as well; see Ramsay Cook, "Tillers and Toilers: The Rise and Fall of Populism in Canada in the 1890s," CHA *Historical Papers* (Guelph, 1984), 5–20 and especially Sid Noel, "Early Populist Tendencies in Ontario Political Culture," *Ontario History* 90, no. 2 (Sept. 1998), 173–87.

69 Francis Drummond Fulford, *The Misapplication of Labour* (Montreal, 1859), 8, 25–6. See also Dallas, *Lecture on Aims*, 3–7; Ardagh, *An Address Delivered before the County of Simcoe*, 2–6 and Lewis, *Lecture Delivered before the Brockville Library Association*, 3–5.

70 See Fulford, *Misapplication of Labour*, iii–iv and also William Merritt, *A Lecture Delivered by the Hon. William Hamilton Merritt before the Mechanics' Institute of St. Catherines* (St Catherines, 1857), 11–12, 17–18.

Contributors

Nancy Christie teaches in the Department of History, Trent University, and is the author of two prize-winning monographs, *A Full-Orbed Christianity: The Protestant Churches and Social Welfare in Canada* and *Engendering the State: Family, Work and Welfare*. She has also edited several volumes relating to questions of gender and family, including *Households of Faith* and *Mapping the Margins*. She is currently completing research on the history of family letter-writing in Canada.

Bruce Curtis teaches in the Department of Sociology and Anthropology at Carleton University. His current research project, "Governing Lower Canada through Education," is intended to produce a detailed historical sociology of schooling, literacy, and politics over the period 1790–1840.

Michael Eamon has worked as a historian and archivist for several federal government agencies, most recently Library and Archives Canada. He holds an MA in history from Queen's University, Kingston, and an MPhil in the history and philosophy of science from the University of Cambridge. He is currently writing a PhD dissertation on the Enlightenment in eighteenth-century British North America.

Darren Ferry has taught Canadian History at McMaster University. His book *Uniting in Measures of Common Good: Voluntary Associations and the Construction of Collective Liberal Identities in Central Canada, 1830–1900* will be published by McGill-Queen's University Press in 2008. He is currently researching aspects of popular liberalism in nineteenth-century central Canada.

Donald Fyson, professor at the Département d'histoire of Université Laval, is a specialist in eighteenth-, nineteenth- and twentieth-century Quebec history. His particular interest is the relationship between state, law, and society, which is explored in his prizewinning book *Magistrates, Police and People: Everyday Criminal Justice in Quebec and Lower Canada, 1764–1837* (Toronto: Osgoode Society / University of Toronto Press, 2006). His current research projects include violence between men in Quebec and Lower Canada, 1764–1850, and the nature of penal justice in Quebec City, 1856–1965. He is a member of the Centre interuniversitaire des études québécoises (CIEQ).

Michael Gauvreau teaches history at McMaster University. He is the author of *The Evangelical Century: College and Creed in English Canada, A Full-Orbed Christianity: The Protestant Churches and Social Welfare in Canada,* and *The Catholic Origins of Quebec's Quiet Revolution.* He is currently exploring the connections between Catholicism, liberalism, and federalism in postwar Quebec.

Jeffrey L. McNairn is a member of the Department of History, Queen's University, Kingston, with particular interests in state-civil society relations and intellectual history. He is currently working on a project entitled "Insolvent, Imprisoned, Bankrupt: Failure and the Law in Common-Law British North America, 1752–1869."

Bryan D. Palmer, the Canada Research Chair in Canadian Studies at Trent University, is the editor of *Labour\Le Travail* and the author of ten books, a number of which have been translated into Greek, Korean, Portuguese, and Spanish. His most recent publication is *James P. Canon and the Origins of the American Revolutionary Left, 1890–1928* (Urbana and Chicago: University of Illinois Press, 2007).

J.G.A. Pocock is Harry C. Black emeritus professor of history at Johns Hopkins University. His work has focused on the history of political and historical thought in the British Kingdom and the west of Europe: *The Ancient Constitution and the Feudal Law* (1967 and 1987), *The Machiavellian Moment* (1975 and 2003), and *Barbarism and Religion* (four volumes to date, 1999–2005). He has enlarged this work into a study of British history, pluralized and extended in archipelagic, Atlantic, and global directions, in which his New Zealand origins have played a significant part: *The Discovery of Islands: Essays in British History* (2005). He welcomes the opportunity to explore early Canadian history in the settings thus provided.

Michelle Vosburgh obtained her PhD in history from McMaster University in 2004 and now teaches part-time in the History Department at Brock University. Current and forthcoming publications include articles on land policy and land distribution in pre-Confederation Ontario and the effects of globalization on land tenure practices in the developing world. She is currently completing a manuscript about the role of Crown land agents and deputy provincial surveyors in the administration of government land policy in pre-Confederation Ontario.

Todd Webb is assistant professor of history at Laurentian University, Sudbury, Ontario. He is currently working on a thematic biography of the Upper Canadian politician Robert Baldwin, provisionally entitled "Robert Baldwin's World: A Nineteenth-Century Politician in Context." He is also in the process of transforming his doctoral dissertation into a book, under the title "The Religious Atlantic: British Wesleyanism and the Formation of an Evangelical Culture in Nineteenth-Century Ontario and Quebec."

Brian Young teaches Quebec history at McGill University. He is particularly interested in the history and culture of the nineteenth-century bourgeoisie.